THE CHRIST IN THE BIBLE COMMENTARY
Volume Five

THE
CHRIST IN THE BIBLE
COMMENTARY

Volume Five

Romans
First Corinthians
Second Corinthians
Galatians
Ephesians
Philippians
Colossians

Dr. Albert B. Simpson

CHRISTIAN PUBLICATIONS
CAMP HILL, PENNSYLVANIA

Christian Publications
3825 Hartzdale Drive, Camp Hill, PA 17011

The mark of ✟ *vibrant faith*

ISBN: 0-87509-502-X
LOC Catalog Card Number: 92-70937
© 1994 by Christian Publications
All rights reserved
Printed in the United States of America

94 95 96 97 98 5 4 3 2 1

Cover Design: Step One Design

Unless otherwise indicated, Scripture taken from the HOLY BIBLE:
NEW INTERNATIONAL VERSION. Copyright © 1973, 1978, 1984
by the International Bible Society. Used by permission
of Zondervan Bible Publishers.

CONTENTS

Romans

Introduction 1

1. The Power of the Gospel 7
2. God's Picture of Sin.. 17
3. The Sin of the Jew.. 27
4. The Righteousness of God... 33
5. The Law of Faith 43
6. The Blessings That Flow from Justification 53
7. Sanctification through Death and Resurrection 63
8. Sanctification by the Grace of God 71
9. Sanctification through the Spirit.. 79
10. Divine Providence 89
11. God's Purpose Regarding Israel and the World.................. 99
12. Consecration and Service... 107
13. Consecration in Relation to Our Civil and Social Duties.. 117
14. Consecration in Relation to Our Duty to the Weak
    and Erring... 125
15. Practical Consecration in Relation to the Evangelization
    of the World 133
16. Object Lessons of Christian Service 141

First Corinthians

1. The Unity of the Church.. 151
2. The Teaching of the Church 159
3. The Ministry of the Church 167
4. The Purity of the Church 175
5. The Church and the Christian in Relation to the World .. 183
6. The Christian Ministry: Its Authority and Support.......... 191
7. Living in the End of the Age... 199

8. The Ordinances of the Church 207
9. The Supernatural Gifts and the Ministries
   of the Church 215
10. Love, the Crowning Grace of the Church
   and the Christian 223
11. The Worship and Fellowship of the Church 231
12. The Hope of the Church 239
13. The Lord's Day 247
14. The Support of the Church: The Principle
   of True Spiritual Giving 255

Second Corinthians

1. Victorious Suffering 265
2. The Dependableness of God 273
3. Victory 281
4. Paul's Testimony about His Ministry 289
5. Paul's Testimony Concerning Supernatural Life
   for the Body 297
6. Paul's Testimony about Salvation 303
7. Paul's Testimony about Holiness 311
8. Two Kinds of Sorrow 319
9. Our Spiritual Warfare 325
10. The Grace of Giving 331
11. The Things Paul Gloried In 339

Galatians

1. Free Grace, or Christ in Galatians 349
2. Free Grace in Our Sanctification 357
3. Burden Bearing 365

Ephesians

1. Chosen in Him 375
2. Redemption through His Blood 385
3. Saved and Sealed 393
4. The Spirit of Illumination and Revelation 401

5. Resurrected and Seated in the Heavenlies 409
6. Brought Near 419
7. The Mystery of the New Life: the Indwelling Christ........ 427
8. The Church in the Heavenlies 435
9. The Spiritual and Practical.. 443
10. The Conflict in the Heavenlies 451

Philippians

Introduction 463
1. The Christian Temper as Exemplified and Illustrated
   in Paul 465
2. The Christian Temper as Exemplified in Christ.............. 471
3. The Christian Temper as Illustrated in the Friends
   of Paul 479
4. The Christian Temper, Supernatural and Divine............. 485
5. The Christian Temper, Aggressive and Progressive 493
6. A Spirit of Love, Joy and Peace................................. 501
7. Whatever Is Lovely 509
8. The Great Secret.. 517
9. The Boundless Sufficiency 525

Colossians

1. Christ in Colossians.. 535
2. The Christian in Colossians.................................... 543
3. The Christian Worker in Colossians 551

ROMANS

INTRODUCTION

The epistle to the Romans is the greatest of Paul's epistles. It is the most compact system of theology in existence. Its great theme is the gospel of Christ, of which the apostle declares, in introducing this epistle, that he is not ashamed, and of which the whole epistle is a beautiful, logical and deeply spiritual unfolding.

It may also be called a treatise on the life of faith in its successive stages—as he himself expresses it, "by faith from first to last" (Romans 1:17).

ITS THEMES

It has five great themes.

1. Sin

The first is the unfolding of the doctrine of sin. In the first three chapters he turns the searchlight upon the heart of man, and draws a picture of human wickedness in both Jew and Gentile, a picture whose truthfulness is made evident by the fact that even heathen people recognize it as an accurate photograph today of their own hearts.

2. Salvation

The next theme is salvation, and he unfolds it in the third, fourth and fifth chapters in all its great principles and conditions, summing up his theme with a sublime contrast between Adam and Christ—the two great heads of humanity—and between the ruin wrought by one and the glorious redemption accomplished by the other.

3. Sanctification

His third theme is sanctification, which he presents with great fullness and variety in the sixth, seventh and eighth chapters. He shows that the principle of sanctification is death to self and sin through the cross of Christ and life through His resurrection delivering us from the bondage of the law and our struggles under its power as unfolded in the seventh chapter. He then intro-

1

duces us in the beautiful eighth chapter to the liberty, power and glory into which we come through the Holy Spirit and a life of abiding communion with the Lord Jesus Christ.

4. The Coming of the Lord

Then he pauses for three chapters more and discusses the great theme of God's purpose for man as it respects the Jew and the Gentile, and the glorious plan which is to reach its fuller consummation at the coming of the Lord Jesus Christ.

5. Consecration

Having settled these profound questions in theology, he comes back, (chapter 12) to the practical questions of Christian life, and closes the epistle with the last great theme, namely, practical consecration and service in the power of the Spirit, and he unfolds this with reference to all the phases and relationships of our Christian life. It is indeed a sublime synopsis of the gospel in all its fullness, and stands unequalled among all the writings of the New Testament for logical clearness, profound thought, powerful argument, deep insight into the Scriptures and the human heart, comprehensive breadth of view, compactness of matter, force of statement, sublimity of conception, deep spirituality and practical application to the needs, obligations and relationships of human life. It is Paul's paragon epistle, and the Holy Spirit's most complete compendium of Christian theology.

It is scarcely necessary that we should give more than the briefest outline of the history and circumstances which led to the writing of this epistle. These and other matters of a similar character will be found much more fully set forth in such works as Conybeare and Howson's *Life and Epistles of St. Paul.*

PAUL AND ROME

It is enough to say that he had not yet visited Rome when he wrote this epistle, but it is obvious from the terms of it that he had many friends there, and had met with many members of the Roman church in other places. It seems quite probable that it had been founded through the influence of Aquila and Priscilla, his most intimate friends, and that, in some sense, through them and others, it was the outcome of his own spiritual life.

He had greatly desired to visit them, as he tells them in the 13th verse of the first chapter: "I do not want you to be unaware, brothers, that I planned many times to come to you (but have been prevented from doing so until now)."

When he writes this epistle he is still praying "that now at last by God's will the way may be opened for me to come to you" (1:10b). "I long to see you," he adds, "so that I may impart to you some spiritual gift to make you strong—that is, that you and I may be mutually encouraged by each other's faith" (1:11–12).

In the following chapters, which are expository rather than exegetical, the great themes of the epistle will be found unfolded in their logical order and their spiritual bearings. It is only necessary here to refer briefly to the introductory passages in the first 16 verses of the epistle.

PERSONAL ALLUSIONS

1. We have some very beautiful references to Paul himself in this introduction.

a. He begins by calling himself "a servant of Christ Jesus" (1:1).

We need scarcely say that the word "servant" means slave. Paul loved to call himself the bondslave of Jesus Christ. He was so entirely given up to the will of his Master that he counted all his life no longer his own but the absolute property of his Master. He desired no will of his own, and lived only to please and glorify Christ.

This is a very beautiful conception of Christian life and character, and it is the foundation of all true service.

b. He calls himself "an apostle" of Jesus Christ (1:1). The word "apostle" means "one sent," and in Paul's case it doubtless means the special apostleship unto which he was called as one of the witnesses of the resurrection of Christ, one of the tokens and conditions of which was, that he had seen the Lord Jesus in His risen life.

c. He says he had been "set apart for the gospel of God" (1:1). That is, he had been set apart to this special ministry and consecrated to it, by the separating and sanctifying grace of the Holy Spirit. Separation from sin, from the world, from self, from others, separated unto Christ and unto Christ's work, is essential to true apostleship and service.

d. He had received grace and apostleship: "Through him and for his name's sake, we received grace and apostleship to call people from among all the Gentiles to the obedience that comes from faith" (1:5). Grace is essential to apostleship.

e. He tells them in the most solemn manner, of his service: "God, whom I serve with my whole heart in preaching the gospel of his Son, is my witness" (1:9).

His service was a spiritual service. It was not mere natural activity, but it sprang from a heart full of the Holy Spirit, and wholly given to the Master's work.

f. He tells them of his affectionate remembrance of the Roman Christians: ". . . how constantly I remember you" (1:9b). What a beautiful example of love, love that knows how most effectually to bless! This is the true ministry of human affection and fellowship and it is the highest ministry even of Paul.

g. He tells them of his strong desire to visit them, and his earnest prayer to God to give a prosperous journey by the will of God to come to them: "in my prayers at all times; and I pray that now at last by God's will the way may be opened for me to come to you" (1:10).

He recognizes God in all his plans and movements, and counts his very traveling arrangements a matter of special providential arrangement.

h. He gives his reasons for wishing to visit them, that he might enrich them by the communication of "some spiritual gift" (1:11) and that he might be equally benefited by some spiritual blessing from them.

In this we see a fine touch of modesty. His chief reason for visiting them was to bless them. But he did not presume to think that he alone could communicate blessing, but expected to receive as much as he imparted: "that is, that you and I may be mutually encouraged by each other's faith" (1:12).

i. He tells them of his previous efforts to visit them, and of the hindrances which had prevented, recognizing those hindrances as perhaps from the adversary, as he very plainly tells us in another place that Satan hindered him from going to the churches and carrying out the purposes that he had formed: "I do not want you to be unaware, brothers, that I planned many times to come to you (but have been prevented from doing so until now)" (1:13).

j. He expresses in very emphatic language, his obligations to the whole world to give the gospel especially to the Gentiles: "I am obligated both to Greeks and non-Greeks, both to the wise and the foolish" (1:14).

It was not, to him, an act of special generosity and extreme consecration, that he should devote his life so assiduously and so self-sacrificingly. He was simply a trustee, and he felt that he had no right to hold the gospel for himself alone, but that he was bound to communicate the blessings that had been given to him to the whole human family, especially to the Gentile nations, to whom God had made him an apostle.

How much obligation also rests upon us! Some people think it is a mark of peculiar consecration to become a missionary and carry the gospel to the heathen. Paul regarded it as simply an obligation, from which he could not be excused without staining his soul with the blood of others.

k. He expresses his confidence in the gospel as the power of God unto the salvation of men. He is not ashamed of it, but believes that it is the only agency that can truly save men, and that it will prove efficient to their salvation whenever properly proclaimed and truly received: "I am not ashamed of the gospel, because it is the power of God for the salvation of everyone who believes: first for the Jew, then for the Gentile" (1:16).

l. Finally, he expresses the whole principle and secret of his life when he says: "That is why I am so eager to preach the gospel also to you who are at Rome" (1:15).

This was the spirit of Paul, and this is the spirit of every true disciple and missionary of Christ—ready to the utmost of our power: "That is why I am so eager to preach." How much this means would fill some of us with wonder and humiliation, if we would only let God show us how much it requires of us.

LOCAL REFERENCES

2. He tells us in this introduction, something of his friends, the Christians at Rome. We have a little picture of the church of whom he was writing, as well as of Paul.

a. He says they are the called of Jesus Christ: "And you also are among those who are called to belong to Jesus Christ" (1:6). It is a great thing to be called of Jesus Christ, to have been noticed, chosen and marked out as the objects of His grace and His salvation, while others have been left in sin and blindness.

b. He calls them beloved of God: "To all in Rome who are loved by God and called to be saints" (1:7). This is a high and precious distinction, and it is true of all who love the Lord Jesus Christ. They are the beloved of God, and "he hath made us accepted in the beloved" (Ephesians 1:6, KJV) and loved even as He.

c. They are "called to be saints" (Romans 1:7b). The word "saint" means sanctified, holy, consecrated, filled with the Holy Spirit, living wholly to God and pleasing Him by lives of sacred faithfulness and holy obedience. Every Christian is called to be a saint, and God has made provision for the carrying out of this high calling.

d. He commends them for their faith, which is spoken of throughout the whole world (1:8). This is a very high commendation, and one which all Christians might well emulate and imitate.

e. And finally, he speaks of them as so filled with the Holy Spirit that they could even impart to him some comfort and blessing; for there may and should be this communication between the teacher and the taught, that he "who receives instruction in the word must share all good things with his instructor" (Galatians 6:6): "I long to see you so that I may impart to you some spiritual gift to make you strong—that is, that you and I may be mutually encouraged by each other's faith" (Romans 1:11–12).

LESSONS ABOUT CHRIST

3. He tells us something about Christ:
a. He is "a descendant of David" (1:3).
b. He is the Son of God according to the Spirit: "who through the Spirit

of holiness was declared with power to be the Son of God by his resurrection from the dead: Jesus Christ our Lord" (1:4).

This expression, "the Spirit of holiness" (1:4), may mean the Holy Spirit, who bore witness to Christ's deity by the resurrection from the dead, or it may mean Christ's own spiritual and divine nature.

c. He tells us that Jesus is the Author of our grace and the Object of our service: "Through him . . . we received grace and apostleship" (1:5).

d. Jesus is the One who calls us to His service and kingdom: "Among those who are called to belong to Jesus Christ" (1:6).

LESSONS ABOUT THE GOSPEL

4. This introduction tells us something about the gospel. Paul was "set apart for the gospel of God" (1:1b).

a. It is the gospel of God, that is, God's ministry of good tidings to the world.

b. It is "the gospel he promised beforehand through his prophets in the Holy Scriptures" (1:2).

c. It is called "the gospel of his Son": "God, whom I serve with my whole heart in preaching the gospel of his Son, is my witness" (1:9). It is good news of Jesus Christ. Christ is the theme of the gospel, and Christ is also the Author of it.

d. It is the power of God unto salvation: "I am not ashamed of the gospel, because it is the power of God for the salvation of everyone who believes: first for the Jew, then for the Gentile" (1:16).

e. It is a trust for all the world. It is given for all nations, and we are bound to give it to all men: "Through him and for his name's sake, we received grace and apostleship to call people from among all the Gentiles to the obedience that comes from faith. . . . I am obligated both to Greeks and non-Greeks, both to the wise and the foolish. That is why I am so eager to preach the gospel also to you who are at Rome" (1:5, 14–15).

f. It is a revelation of the deeper fullness of Christ, as we are able to receive it through the exercise of a higher and stronger faith: "For in the gospel a righteousness from God is revealed, a righteousness that is by faith from first to last [from faith to faith, KJV], just as it is written: 'The righteous will live by faith' " (1:17).

This is really the keynote of this great epistle. It is an unfolding of the successive stages and degrees of faith, on the part of the believer, which introduce him to the higher experience of God's grace and righteousness as he advances step by step from the faith that saves to the faith that sanctifies, the faith that heals, and the faith that consecrates him to a life of holy service and fruitfulness. So may He lead us on, as He conducts us through the pages of this inspired volume of Christian theology and experience!

CHAPTER 1

THE POWER OF THE GOSPEL

I am not ashamed of the gospel, because it is the power of God for the salvation of everyone who believes: first for the Jew, then for the Gentile. For in the gospel a righteousness from God is revealed, a righteousness that is by faith from first to last, just as it is written: "The righteous will live by faith." (Romans 1:16–17)

This passage forms a sort of text for the whole epistle of Paul to the Romans.

The object of this profound and comprehensive treatise is to unfold the fullness and power of the gospel as the revelation of the righteousness of God to be received by us through faith, and as he expresses it here, "by faith from first to last" (1:17). That is, through the various stages of our faith as it rises step by step from the first experiences of salvation to all the fullness of our sanctification and service for God.

SECTION I—*The Power of the Gospel*

Paul was going to Rome, and if ever anything on earth was the embodiment and expression of power, it was old Rome. Greece represented the culture of the world; Babylon, its luxury and pride; Israel, the ethical idea and the development of moral truth; but Rome was the embodiment of force and strength, as no other nation of the past.

The material culture of Roman life was directed to the development of the highest form of physical perfection. The military power of Rome was unrivaled, and that great imperial colossus crushed beneath its iron heel the last vestige of independence from the surrounding nations and peoples, until, in the visions of Daniel and John, it became a great monster, stamping beneath its cruel feet the liberties of the world and the hapless victims of its despotic power.

Yet Paul was going to Rome to defy this proud colossus and to attack its citadel of heathenism in the name of Jesus of Nazareth.

His only weapon was a humble sword, forged by no human wisdom and claiming no earthly prestige. And yet he was not ashamed of that humble weapon, but he waved it even in the face of the palace of the Caesars and with unfaltering boldness, he cried: "I am not ashamed of the gospel, because it is the power of God for the salvation of everyone who believes: first for the Jew, then for the Gentile" (1:16).

And before two centuries had elapsed, the pride and power of Rome had fallen before that weapon and the city of the Caesars had acknowledged the gospel of Christ as the religion of the Roman Empire and the world. And as the ages have rolled on since then, the only power that has been found equal to the demands and needs of a lost world is the gospel of Jesus Christ; and the only pity is, that its friends have sometimes been ashamed of it and tried to substitute some of the carnal weapons of culture for the old, rugged sword which has won so many battles and has lost none of its ancient power, if only wielded by the Spirit of God, in the hands of believing men who are not ashamed of its simplicity and its fullness.

The other day, a remarkable testimony was given by one of the best known writers of modern fiction, the author of sensational literature of a low character and one who has most firmly believed in the principle of positivism.

In speaking of these things, he has recently said, in substance: "I have been a positivist for 30 years, but I must confess that it has failed as a remedy for the evils of human society, and as I look around me for some hope for the world, the only thing that I can find that promises to meet the need is a true religious belief; but alas! Where shall I find it in its purity and power, even among its friends?"

Alas! The complaint is but too true. The friends of truth and Christianity have almost grown ashamed of its ancient simplicity and power, and they have substituted so many things for it and handicapped it with so many fetters and weights that it has scarcely had a chance to prove its divinity and omnipotence.

It is quite wonderful what Christianity is accomplishing today, when we think of what it has to contend with among its own advocates and followers. And yet, everywhere it goes, it is proving its divine character and its mighty efficiency.

One of the most distinguished of modern travelers, who went over all the East with a prejudice against evangelical missions, has become their devoted friend through the results she has witnessed in Japan and other countries.

What is the power of the gospel of Christ?

POWER TO CHANGE OR DESTROY

1. It is an authoritative message from the throne of the universe and it carries with it issues and influences that are fitted to change eternal destinies.

There are some words that have no special authority or power. I read the morning newspaper simply as a discussion of public questions. I read the books in my library, simply as collections of human opinions and thoughts on various subjects. I may believe them or not, as I please. They interest me, perhaps they instruct me, they entertain me, but they come to me with no authority.

But in a very different sense do I receive a summons from the court, a verdict from the jury, or a decree from the judge upon the bench. These are words that settle things. They are actual forces. They determine destinies. They change the course of lives. They are words that must be met and answered and acted upon. They come with power and authority.

This is the character of the gospel. It is the voice of God to a revolted world and a subject-race. It is a message from the throne to men and women who are accountable to the Sovereign Ruler who sends it. It contains the sentence of condemnation which has been passed upon all the race and from which they cannot escape but by the remedy which God has appointed.

It contains, also, the announcement of that remedy and the authoritative assurance that all who accept it will be forgiven and received into the love and confidence of their offended Sovereign and treated as His friends and His children.

It brings to every man who receives it the opportunity of life eternal, and it adds to every one who rejects it the awful guilt of an aggravated and sinful disobedience to the command of infinite love.

We speak it to men, not as a matter of counsel or advice, not as a matter for discussion of opinion, but as a direct message from God, invested with His supreme sanction: "He who listens to you listens to me; he who rejects you rejects me" (Luke 10:16).

The bearer of such a message as this goes forth among men with the dignity of a divine ambassador and is able to speak with the authority of his Master and with a sense of power which no human message could ever give; and the man who hears this gospel may know that if he will accept it, it has power to instantly reverse his eternal destiny, to close the gates of hell, to cancel the curse of doom, to lift him out of the kingdom of darkness and to open to him the blessed and glorious prospect of a pure and happy life below and a glorious immortality above.

The gospel, the moment it is received, changes his entire career and lifts him from sin to salvation, from hell to heaven. But it must be believed or we cannot come into touch with its power.

Over on the street corner, 30 years ago, you might have seen an Italian fruit-seller, bearing the marks of noble birth and better days. Suppose you were sent to him with a message from the Italian government, telling him that he might return in safety to his native land and resume his old patrimonial estate, for the political decree that had been standing against him had been annulled, his exile cancelled and amnesty declared for him and all his political associates.

Now if that man believed your message, he would accept the amnesty and return to his native land, and a few weeks afterward you might have found him in his splendid villa, or among the courtiers and nobles of the land and all because he had believed your message and it had raised him from obscurity and exile to honor and blessing.

If however, he should fail to believe your message and should say, "This is only a trick to betray me to my enemies," he would refuse the kind offer you had brought him, he would remain at his wretched little fruit stand and years and years later, you would see him going deeper and deeper down, until at last his life would end in an ignominious grave—and all because he failed to believe your simple message.

Precisely such are the effects that follow the unbelief of the sinner. God sends you a message of amnesty, reconciliation and salvation. If you will believe it, you will receive His forgiveness, you will become His child, you will enter into His friendship, you will rise to the dignity of a Christian, you will be regenerated, purified and possessed by the Holy Spirit, you will be exalted by the glorious hopes and the sacred employments of your new life, you will rise from grace to grace and from glory to glory, until some time you will "shine like the sun in the kingdom of [your] Father" (Matthew 13:43).

But if you refuse to believe it, if you will remain unpardoned and unsaved, borne down by inward sin and outward temptation, you shall sink deeper and deeper into corruption and discouragement, and at last be lost in the depths of eternal ruin and despair—all because you refused to believe in the tidings of God's grace and love. It is only for "everyone who believes" (Romans 1:16) that the gospel is the power of God unto salvation.

THE POWER OF THE HOLY SPIRIT

2. The gospel is the power of God because it is accompanied with a divine and supernatural energy through the Holy Spirit, which makes it a living force in the hearts and lives of all who receive it.

This gospel is much more than a piece of information, or even an authoritative message. When rightly preached in the power of the Holy Spirit, it is accompanied by an actual, supernatural presence and power which enables it to produce effects far beyond what the truths themselves might seem fitted to effect. Not only is the power of the Holy Spirit promised to the true preacher of the gospel, but it is also promised to accompany the hearing of it in the hearts of the people. Both are necessary to the true effect of the gospel. No man has a right to preach it without the anointing of the Holy Spirit. This was the way Paul preached, in the demonstration of the Spirit and of power.

Even the Lord Jesus Christ Himself did not attempt His public ministry until He had received the Holy Spirit at His baptism; and if the Son of God did not attempt to preach and perform His ministry without the Spirit, it is rank presumption and impertinence for any man to dare to do so. It does not make any difference how much a preacher knows, or how many letters of the alphabet he is entitled to affix to his name; he has no right to stand up and preach the gospel, even in the smallest pulpit, or to the humblest people in the land, unless he knows that he has been divinely ordained and is God's ambassador to men.

If the preacher has this divine anointing, he may be quite sure that besides the unction which will come with his own word and the tact, tenderness and force with which he shall be enabled to speak, there will also be an accompanying power in the heart of the hearer. A secret Witness will stand in every pew and whisper in every heart, "You are the man!" (2 Samuel 12:7); a mysterious and solemn echo will repeat the message in the sinner's ear and even Felix will tremble as Paul reasons "on righteousness, self-control and the judgment to come" (Acts 24:25). "When he comes, he will convict the world of guilt in regard to sin and righteousness and judgment" (John 16:8).

This is the power that makes men realize that they are sinners. This is the light that reveals Jesus as the eternal Savior and makes it easy to trust Him. This is the hand that breaks the fetters of "the world, the flesh and the devil" and sets the spirit free for holy love and serving.

This was the glory of Paul's great commission and the commission of every true ambassador, "to open their eyes and turn them from darkness to light, and from the power of Satan to God, so that they may receive forgiveness of sins and a place among those who are sanctified by faith in me" (Acts 26:18). And whenever God's word is spoken in power, then there is a power present sufficient to enable every honest heart to believe it, to receive it and to experience its blessed effects.

God commands no man to do anything without giving him the power to do it. And so, if He is now commanding any man to repent, believe and obey, that very command contains in itself the power to enable you to do it, as much as when He said of old to the man with the withered hand, "Stretch out your hand," (Matthew 12:13), or to the sleeping corpse of Nain, "Young man, I say to you, get up!" (Luke 7:14).

INHERENT POWER

3. The gospel contains, in the nature of things, a message full of power.

The truths which it unfolds are fitted, when understood and believed, to influence the heart and life with intense force.

It literally means, "glad tidings." Now, there is great power in either ill or good tidings. I have seen a person faint under bad news and I have seen the face shine as with the light of heaven and the life renewed and restored by good news.

The gospel is the best news a sad and sinful world ever heard.

Deliverance

First, it is good news of deliverance. It tells of escape from danger and doom, from the curse of sin, the power of Satan and the dark shadow of the eternal future. Surely there is power in such tidings as these.

Is there inspiration and cheer in the glad message to the shipwrecked crew, that rescue is at hand? Is there joy and hope in the tidings of pardon to the long-imprisoned convict? Does it quicken the pulse and flush the cheek with the glow of glad encouragement, to know that the crisis of disease is over and that the sufferer at last is convalescent? Oh, how much better the tidings that guilt is canceled, God is reconciled and heaven is won, that death is robbed of its sting and sorrow turned into everlasting joy, through His salvation!

Some men are sinking through discouragement and despair. If they would only believe the good news, their hearts would rise with enthusiasm to a nobler and a better life.

It is said that once a skilled artisan in the employ of an Oriental king had become almost useless in his daily tasks; his hand had lost its cunning and his work was marred by constant failure. The king sent for him and asked him what had caused the surprising change. "Ah!" said he, "it is my heart that makes my hand unsteady. I am under an awful cloud of calamity and discouragement. I am hopelessly in debt and my family is to be sold as slaves. I can think of nothing else from morning to night and as I try to polish the jewels and cut the facets in the diamonds, my hand trembles and my fingers forget their wonted skill."

The king smiled and said: "Is that all? Your debt shall be paid, your family saved and your cares dispelled. You may take the word of your king and go to work again with a free and fearless heart." That was enough and never was work so skillfully done, never were such exquisite carvings and cunning devices in precious gems as the hand of this happy artisan devised when set at liberty from his fears and burdens.

This is the way we can come into true service of God. We must first be saved and set at liberty and then our work must be the glad and grateful return of ransomed souls.

The gospel brings the glad news that all this has been done for us, and the moment we believe it we are saved and the very consciousness of our deliverance has the power to lift us to a love, a purity and a devotion, that nothing else could have accomplished.

Love

Again, the gospel is the good news of love.

There is a strange power in the consciousness of being loved. It will bring sunshine to the face of a child, or cover it with clouds and gloom, to know or doubt a mother's love.

It is said that one of the most distinguished statesmen of the times of the American Revolution was once a hopeless drunkard. He had been engaged to a beautiful girl, but his dissipation had compelled her to break the engagement and sever herself from his influence, which was dragging her down. She had not ceased to love him, or to pray for him. One day she was passing along a suburban road. She saw him lying intoxicated by the sidewalk, his face exposed to the broiling, blistering sun and swollen with drink and exposure. Her tender heart was deeply moved, and as she passed by she took her handkerchief and gently spread it over his stupid, sleeping face.

An hour or two later he awoke and saw the handkerchief and her name upon the corner of it. He sprang to his feet and a glad thrill of hope and courage came to his heart. "She loves me still," he said, "all is not yet lost. For her sake I will redeem my life." And he did. The love of that woman saved him. There was power in that single name and the glad message which it expressed, to rescue that lofty intellect and that gifted man from the depths of a drunkard's grave.

Oh, how much more power is there in the love of Christ to save lost men from despair, if they can only believe that He loves them! And how can any doubt it, who will look at the story of His birth and His cross, and think for a moment how He has followed you through all your sinful career and your worthless life, longing to save you, ready at any moment to rescue you and undertake the infinite burden of your future existence?

Yes, if you can only believe that He loves you and will love you forever, it will lift you out of anything. Paul says of that love, that it made him beside himself and constrained him, like a great torrent shut up between restricting shores, until it swept with resistless current over all its banks in tides of power and fullness.

This was the secret of Paul's mighty life, the consciousness of the love of Christ and a sublime and heroic devotion to His person and His service. And it is the strongest force that can come to any human life. It may be yours, if you will believe the glad tidings of the gospel.

Help

The gospel is also the glad tidings of help.

When the garrison at Lucknow was beleaguered in that awful enclosure, with famine threatening them within and the Sepoys waiting without for carnage and outrage, the last hope of the garrison was the coming of Havelock and Sir Colin Campbell with reinforcements. And yet they came not. As the days and the weeks went by, the supplies diminished, the heat increased, the cannonade grew fiercer and the rebels more defiant, until at last it seemed that they must surrender.

One morning, a Scotch lassie listening with her well-trained ear, thought she heard in the distance the sound of the Highland pipes. She cried out: "They're coming! They're coming! Dinna ye hear it? It's the pibroch and the slogan!"

Nobody else could hear it, but her ear was not mistaken and ere long they knew that the Highlanders were marching on Lucknow and that help at last had come.

It was a thrilling sight to look at those old residency walls a few years ago and read once more the story of those heroic days and think how that message of help had power to save the beautiful city of Lucknow and the lives of those women and children from horrors worse than death.

But there is a better message of help for sinking souls. Over the waste of life's wreck-strewn sea, over the years that have been lost and cursed, there comes the sweet-voiced message not only of forgiveness for the past, but of power to save to the uttermost and to keep from sin and Satan, the most crushed and hopeless lives.

Like the music of heaven, like the memory of cradle songs and childhood hymns, can't you hear it saying "He is able to save completely" (Hebrews 7:25)? "And I will put my Spirit in you and move you to follow my decrees and be careful to keep my laws" (Ezekiel 36:27). He "is able to keep you from falling and to present you before his glorious presence without fault and with great joy" (Jude 1:24). It is glad tidings for helpless hearts, for ruined lives, for wills that have lost their strength and lives that have been bound by the chains of habit in the bondage of Satan and despair.

Yes, even if your body be wrecked with disease and sin, the power that saved Augustine from the effects of a dissolute youth and gave him both holiness and health, with 60 years of glorious service, can rescue you, restore you and enable you to recover all the years that the locusts have eaten.

Hope

Once more, the gospel is good news of hope.

There is immense power in a well-founded hope. Ambition is the inspiration of millions of lives and even a false ambition has often lifted an ignoble life into something like grandeur. The gospel gives us a sure hope and a hope as glorious as it is certain and it is fitted to elevate and inspire us to the noblest of heroisms. Believe it and rise to meet it and let its power draw you with holy magnetism from selfishness and earthiness to the high and holy capacities of a consecrated life.

SECTION II—*The Progressive Steps of Faith*

This passage tells us not only of the power of the gospel, but also of the progressions of faith. "For in the gospel a righteousness from God is revealed, a righteousness that is by faith from first to last [from faith to faith, KJV], just as it is written: 'The righteous will live by faith' " (Romans 1:17).

The Epistle to the Romans is really the unfolding of three successive stages of faith. First, there is the faith that saves us, in the third, fourth and fifth chapters. Next, there is the faith that sanctifies us, in the sixth, seventh and eighth. Then we have the faith that consecrates us to the service of God, in the closing chapters of this precious epistle.

It reveals to us the successive stages "from faith to faith." The same faith that saves you, when rightly applied, will sanctify you and also bring you the power of the Holy Spirit, with all the fullness of a consecrated life.

It is a little lever which God puts into your hand, which you can apply to every situation of need and which will lift you up above all that harms and hinders into all the fullness of His great salvation.

God's purpose in all His dealings with us is to make us grow into something higher. The greatest calamity that can come to a soul is to be satisfied with its present condition.

Someone asked me the other day about a friend—"Is he happy?" I said, "Yes, as happy as he can be, but that is not much." I thought of an oyster out there in the bay that is fattening on the nutritious water of the little pool where it is fed and fitted for the metropolitan markets. That oyster is just as happy as it can be. It has all it wants and it is filled to repletion. So some people are just about as happy as an oyster.

Go a little higher and take up that little pet kitten that sits on your lap, or plays at your feet. It has a soft carpet, a warm room, a kind mistress, dinner and supper, and a kind hand to rub it down in its playful or affectionate moods. That is all it wants. It looks no higher, wants no higher heaven than to sit and purr on the cushion and the warm hearth rug.

And so we have known people who were just as happy in their way as an oyster or a kitten. I remember a woman who once told me that she had no need of God. She was satisfied with her husband's love and her baby's fond embraces. Her heart was filled with these pleasures. She was supremely happy.

There are people who eat and sleep and live an animal existence to the full. They are not bad people. They are earthly souls. They are as happy as they can be, but they have no capacity for the highest happiness and the noblest satisfactions. God save us from such content and give us those hungerings and thirstings and longings and outreachings, which cannot rest short of God's highest things!

These are the vessels He makes that He may fill them with Himself. These are the capacities for higher living and holier aspiration and endeavor. These are the promptings of a loftier faith and a more divine life. These are the golden steps in the ladder of eternal progression that lead us "from faith to faith" unto all the maturity of spiritual manhood and all the heights of grace and glory.

CHAPTER 2

GOD'S PICTURE OF SIN

Romans 1:18–32

Back of the rainbow is the storm cloud. The story of redemption comes out of the dark tragedy of sin.

There are two revelations in this chapter. One is "a righteousness from God is revealed . . . that is by faith from first to last" (1:17), as we have seen in the previous chapter.

The other is "The wrath of God is being revealed from heaven against all the godlessness and wickedness of men" (1:18). This is a lurid flame from heaven, like a thunderbolt out of the midnight sky, revealing in its fiery blaze a most frightful picture of ghastliness and horror. It is God's picture of sin.

THE JUDGMENT OF GOD RESPECTING SIN

"The wrath of God is being revealed from heaven against all the godlessness and wickedness of men" (1:18). This is God's standpoint against sin. It is not a matter of sentiment at all. It is not a misfortune, a disease, a peculiar development of the cranium, but it is a matter of law, right and principle.

Sin is the transgression of God's eternal law, a deviation from that which is and ever must be right and an act and state which God is bound to condemn and punish by every attribute of His being and every interest of the universe which He governs.

It is as necessary for God to hate sin as it is for Him to love righteousness. God can forgive *sins,* but He never can forgive or tolerate *sin.* There is but one thing for Him to do with it and that is to destroy it.

This is a matter that is already settled, and must be forever settled, by the very nature of God. The wrath of God is already revealed from heaven, the judgment is passed, and the sinner is condemned already.

The word "wrath" expresses much more than a mere judicial sentence. It denotes the intense personal hatred of God's whole being against sin. God not only condemns it and deals with it as a Judge, but He abhors it with all His holy attributes, and must as certainly strike it wherever it comes in contact with Him, as the flame consumes the tinder, or as the lightning smites the interposing obstacle.

God can love the person of the sinner, even while He hates unutterably the sin He perceives in him. But if we are not separated from sin, we must be the objects of His eternal wrath; for evil cannot dwell in His sight, and iniquity cannot be tolerated by His holiness.

GOD'S TWOFOLD INDICTMENT AGAINST SINFUL MEN

"All the godlessness and wickedness of men" (1:18). Sin is here classified into two departments. Godlessness represents the sin which has reference to God and wickedness that which relates to our fellow man.

There are two directions in which God's measuring line sweeps. One is horizontal and takes in the circle of this world, the other is vertical and takes in the sweep of the heavens.

The horizontal line is a short one. The whole diameter of our globe is but 8,000 miles, and at no spot can our circle reach more than 4,000 miles from where we stand. But if we sweep the line up to the perpendicular and reach up to the heavens, you can go millions and billions of miles before you reach the farthest dimensions of creation; and how far you must go to reach the utmost dimensions of God, no human thought can span. Ah! That is the higher measurement of right and wrong.

The duty we owe to God is like the vertical dimension, infinitely vaster than all we owe to our fellow man. You may be a loving father, a gentle mother, an honest businessman, a loyal citizen, an upright neighbor, a devoted friend. There may be no flaw in your human record, there may be no criticism upon your character and relationship to your fellow man. But God? How do you stand with Him? Have you filled up all that mighty circle that spans the heavens? Have you loved "the LORD your God with all your heart and with all your soul and with all your strength" (Deuteronomy 6:5), with everything that is within you? Is even the love of wife and child part of the greater love of God? Or has your life been one of mere morality and practical godlessness?

The great majority of men are utterly separated from God. Our normal life is entire dependence upon God; but man has become detached from his center and is living a self-centered life, in which God is not in all his thoughts and has nothing whatever to do with his motives, aims and principles.

It is this practical neglect of God which constitutes godlessness, and makes man a god unto himself, and an impious rebel against the authority of heaven.

Under these two classifications all forms of sin are included, and under this twofold indictment all the world stands guilty before God.

THE AGGRAVATIONS OF SIN

The apostle next points out the deeper, darker shadows of sin as they are aggravated by a number of considerations.

1. The Abuse of Light

The first aggravation mentioned is that they "suppress the truth by their wickedness" (Romans 1:18b). It is far worse to sin against light than in ignorance, and God here charges all men with having sufficient light to aggravate their guilt, for He adds, "since what may be known about God is plain to them, because God has made it plain to them. For since the creation of the world God's invisible qualities—his eternal power and divine nature—have been clearly seen, being understood from what has been made, so that men are without excuse" (1:19–20).

That is to say, even those who do not have the Bible and know nothing of divine revelation, have sufficient light from reason and natural conscience to render them responsible. God's eternal power and Godhead are manifested by the things which are made of the material creation. "How do you know there is a God?" was asked of an Arab on the desert. "Because I have seen His footprints. How do I know that a camel passed my tent last night? Because I have seen his footprints in the sand, and I can tell you which way he went, and his size, and even the color of his hair, by the hairs that have dropped along the way.

"How do I know there is a God? I see His footprints in the skies, the desert sand and the desert oasis, in every flower, and tree, and in my own body and soul. I know Him by His footprints."

God has written on every human conscience and consciousness enough of His mighty name to make them accountable at His judgment seat, and given sufficient conception of right and wrong to make them guilty when they disobey the instincts of conscience. And they have disobeyed. The testimony of missionaries in all lands is that they have never found a human soul without this instinct of a guilty conscience, and a sense of wrong, and without some idea of worship, some conception of God and some method of propitiating the invisible powers for conscious will.

This light, while it might have been a guide to the truth, is an aggravation of their sin. How much more the clearer light and the higher truth of God's Word have been given to those who have received the divine revelation!

This was the greater sin of the Jew. This is the still higher responsibility of the Christian, and this will be the knell of uttermost despair in the prisons of the lost: "Ye knew your duty, but ye did it not."

2. The Conceit of Human Wisdom

"For although they knew God, they neither glorified him as God nor gave thanks to him, but their thinking became futile and their foolish hearts were darkened. Although they claimed to be wise, they became fools" (1:21–22).

It is an awful fact that the ages of highest culture have always been the times of deepest moral degradation in the history of the world.

When Greece and Rome were at their best in art and literature, every form of vice and crime demoralized society, and the shameful records are still seen in the uncovered frescoes of Pompeii and the unholy art and literature of classic times.

Dr. Dollinger has stated that, until the time of Christ, ancient literature does not once condemn the unnatural crimes which are mentioned in this chapter of Romans and which were prevalent in those lands and ages.

The same is true of the golden age of Italian art, and among Oriental countries today. Japan, while the most advanced in civilization, is deeply steeped in immorality and shameless wickedness. Mere culture, without Christ, only increases man's power for evil and his independence of God, and when man tries to be wise without God, God always makes him a fool; for God's purpose is that no man shall be independent of Him, or able to be wise or strong, apart from Jesus Christ whom He has given to be wisdom and strength for man. God's plan for man is dependence upon Himself, and man's independence is practical atheism.

Today, men are trying to discard the Bible. But French infidelity led to the French Revolution; and the modern school of Pantheism, Positivism, Christian Science and the occult arts of Satan will bring a repetition of the story of Sodom and Gomorrah, the worship of Venus and Astarte, the licentiousness of the Borgias and the court of Louis of France.

3. Idolatry

The next step is the degrading of God into an image of man by idolatry: "and exchanged the glory of the immortal God for images made to look like mortal man and birds and animals and reptiles" (1:23).

Here we see the downward progression. The first step is "images made to look like mortal man," and ancient statuary was always made to represent God in the form of human types with all the lusts and passions of "mortal man." But it did not stop there.

"The Descent of Man" is a good deal deeper than Darwin has developed the process. The whole animal creation next comes in order in the downward progression of idolatry.

First, the higher forms of bird life are called into requisition as types of deity, as we see in the sculptures of ancient Egypt and the superstitious auguries of Rome, through the flight of birds.

Next, the images sink to the grosser forms of "four-footed beasts" (1:23, KJV)—the sacred bull, the holy cow and almost all the forms of animal life are reproduced in the idolatrous symbols of almost all false religions, especially those of Egypt, Assyria and India. But it soon reaches the lowest depths; and the dragon, the serpent and all the countless forms of creeping things and noisome reptiles become the representatives of the glorious deity, until finally, the extreme is reached, and the worship of God becomes simply the worship of the devil. Almost all Oriental religions develop into demon-worship in the end.

The creature, instead of becoming the steppingstone to the Creator, becomes a substitute for Him: "They exchanged the truth of God for a lie, and worshiped and served created things rather than the Creator—who is forever praised. Amen" (1:25).

It is impossible to give to anyone who has not seen it an adequate conception of the degradation of idolatry. The first impression which one receives is the utter lack of interest and attractiveness about it. Everything looks so poor, so cheap, so depressing, so common and so utterly lacking in interest. The mummeries of paganism will go on with the laughing and chattering of women and children, and all sorts of tricks and contrivances to even cheat their gods. Many of their rites are filthy and disgusting, and the finest temples in Benares are but stables for cows and cages for monkeys, and the sacred brutes walk about in their uncleanness and are worshiped, while all around them are the most obscene objects consecrated to religious worship.

If ever God made anything advertise its own folly, it is heathenism. It bears upon its very face the stamp of its devilishness and stupidity, and if any man or woman wants to read "The Light of Asia," with the most thorough appreciation of its absurdity, let them go to Benares, where this system had its birth, and read the extravagant pictures of Mr. Arnold amid the filth and obscenity of this foulest city of the world, and see what Buddhism has done for the world and what it is able to promise for the future.

4. Immorality

Then there is the degradation of their own bodies and the lusts of uncleanness and unnatural vices (1:24, 26–27).

They begin by degrading God, and they end by degrading themselves: "Therefore God gave them over in the sinful desires of their hearts to sexual impurity for the degrading of their bodies with one another. . . . Because of this, God gave them over to shameful lusts. . . ." (1:24, 26), etc. The instincts of modesty require us to veil the whole of this hideous picture, but the demands of truth compel us to emphasize it, especially in the days in which we live.

How true it was of ancient heathenism, let their own literature tell, and let the unveiled paintings that have been brought forth from the excavations of Pompeii confirm the hideous record! But it was not in ancient Greece and Rome only that these things existed. Mrs. Bishop has told us something of the awful degradation of morals in Eastern lands; and every authority in India will confirm the statement that unnatural vice is almost universal, and the scenes of Sodom and Gomorrah are the rule, rather than the exception.

But even in our own civilized land, these things, we are sorry to say, are not unknown. Thoughtful men are dismayed at the condition of many of our schools, and the seeming impossibility of allowing any children, even of the same sex, to associate too intimately together.

It would seem as if natural vice had become too tame for the heated passions of our time, and that Satan had to flavor his foul dishes with the spice of unnatural lust, and even beastly degradation, in order to satisfy the prurient and hideous tastes of our polluted age.

Wickedness ripens in our day in a very few months, and boys and girls have lived through the whole category of Sodom and Pompeii, before they have reached maturity.

Nay, we have known of even grosser crimes and more bestial depths, even in the light of our own New York City, until it has not seemed that it would be strange if some of our cities should disappear in a blaze of flame or be engulfed in a yawning earthquake in a moment.

The effect of this is soon apparent. "Men . . . received in themselves the due penalty for their perversion" (1:27). This is the sad story of the wrecked constitution, the ruined manhood, the blighted womanhood, the great proportion, perhaps, of the cases of insanity which strew the shores of human life on every side, and whose sad story eternity alone will fully reveal.

5. Atheism

Next there is the rejection of God altogether by willful unbelief and atheism (1:28).

When men love sin, they soon find that it is an extremely awkward thing to retain their faith in God. They must either give Him up or put Him into their own likeness. And so the logical effect of wickedness is infidelity: "they did not think it worthwhile to retain the knowledge of God" (1:28a). God was too holy to sanction their crimes, and so they dispensed with Him. Infidelity does not spring from lack of light, usually, but from a bad heart and a bad life.

If you are a skeptic it is because the wish is father to the thought, and you desire to be free from the restraint of His sovereign will and holy authority.

When the prodigal wanted to have his own way, he got as far from his father as possible. If you are an infidel, depend upon it, it is because in heart you are a bad man. Of course you will not believe this, but you will find it out before you get through.

The Psalmist has given us a picture of the atheist. "The fool says in his heart,/ 'There is no God' " (Psalm 14:1a). He said it in his heart first, and then he tried to learn it in his head. But wait a moment. Listen!

"They are corrupt, their deeds are vile;/ there is no one who does good. . . . All have turned aside,/ they have together become corrupt;/ there is no one who does good,/ not even one" (14:1b, 3).

There is no alternative. How could such a man believe in God? It would be a logical inconsistency, and for his own peace of mind, he bursts away from the restraints and fetters of a religious conscience and a divine law.

But there is an awful retribution for this.

6. Judicial Blindness

The next step is terrible: "he gave them over to a depraved mind, to do what ought not to be done" (Romans 1:28b). They chose the devil, and God gave them all the devil they wanted. They desired sin, and God let them have their fill of sin, and so they became baptized with the spirit of Satan, possessed with the love of vileness, and absolute incarnations of evil spirits.

There is such a thing as being possessed of the devil, and there is such a thing as being possessed of God. Men can get so under the influence of Satanic passion that it will control them like an irresistible law, and they may even think that it is good and divine. He has thrown this evil spell over men and women in all ages. They thought they loved the unholy when they were simply worshiping Satan in all the orgies of a devilish sensualism.

Men can become so controlled by Satanic influence, that they cannot resist profanity, blasphemy and every sin.

This is what was meant by the hardening of Pharaoh's heart (Exodus 10:1). God did not do it until he had refused to be guided by God; but when he made his choice, God let him have it to the full. This is the awful threatening that we find about the last days—"For this reason God sends them a powerful delusion so that they will believe the lie" (2 Thessalonians 2:11). Oh, let us beware how we reject the light, because the penalty of refusing it is told in the vision of the darkness in which we stumble, and know not why we stumble!

This is perhaps the most terrible of all God's retributions—the blighting of the soul's life and vision, and the giving of men over in their minds and hearts to the power of evil.

7. Wickedness

Now comes the fruition of wickedness in their daily life (Romans 1:29–31). We have four classifications:

1. The sins of the heart: covetousness, maliciousness, envy, malignity, hatred of God, spite, pride, ingenuity in inventing evil, ignorance, implacability and merciless cruelty.

2. The sins of the home: disobedience to parents, without natural affection.

3. The sins of the tongue: whisperers, backbiters and boasters.

4. The sins of the life: unrighteousness, fornication, murder, deceit and covenant-breakers.

Oh, what a harvest of wickedness, and how easy to find its prolific weeds on every wayside, and in almost every garden!

Finally, the last and darkest touch in the picture is the deliberate willfulness with which men will proceed in this, when they know its wickedness and the final judgment of God upon it. The climax of this awful revelation of sin is in the closing verse: "Although they know God's righteous decree that those who do such things deserve death, they not only continue to do these very things but also approve of those who practice them" (1:32).

This, too, is true. Men reach such a depth of evil, that even if they knew the next breath would be their last, they would use it to curse the Holy Spirit.

They even think it brave to hold to their lips the drink that will paralyze their life and put them in a drunkard's grave, and they will not hesitate to drink it. Yes, they delight in evil, they have chosen their course, and, like Judas, they shall go to their own place (Acts 1:25).

Their wickedness has become intentional, their character has become stereotyped, their course is deliberate and final, and there remains nothing but "a fearful expectation of judgment" (Hebrews 10:27) and the fullness of the hell which has already begun.

Beloved, let us take heed of the beginnings of sin. Let us be careful how we reject the light and turn aside from its faintest ray. Let our eyes be open and our hearts alert to the perils of our age, and let us send the gospel to the world which is floating in the darkness of sin, and for which there is no remedy but the grace of God.

Let us likewise in the spirit of His love, go forth to live and die with lost and dying men, and prove that the gospel is the power of God unto salvation, even to the most degraded of men.

And if there be a soul to whom this picture brings the consciousness that it is true of you, oh, remember that the consciousness of your lost condition is not enough to save you! A purpose to reform is not sufficient to rescue you. You need a stronger hand, you need a mightier strength, you need the righteousness of God, the blood of Jesus, the power of the Holy Spirit.

When the steamer "Atlantic" went down in Long Island Sound, her bell remained for days in a portion of the wreck, ringing out a sad and solemn remained for days in a portion of the wreck, ringing out a sad and solemn dirge, which seemed like a call to the sleepers in those slimy depths to awake, but they did not awake, and at last it sank, itself, beneath those dark waters.

So, there are lives floating about on the dark sea of sin that have not life enough to realize their situation. A voice has been ringing out a wild alarm, but it is not strong enough to awaken them, and they are going down to sink into the lake of fire, unless a mightier helper is found. But there is help even for them.

The love of God is a help strong enough to stand against all the un-righteousness of men, but we must fully recognize the sin, the sentence, and the judgment.

There is help revealed from heaven. The righteousness of God and the gospel of Jesus Christ are "the power of God for the salvation of everyone who believes" (Romans 1:16). Let us open our hearts to this blessed revelation. Let us take it for ourselves, let mercy triumph over judgment (James 2:13) and let the God that delights in mercy see, in the salvation of men, "of the travail of his soul, and be satisfied" (Isaiah 53:11, KJV).

CHAPTER 3

THE SIN OF THE JEW

So when you, a mere man, pass judgment on them and yet do the same things, do you think you will escape God's judgment? (Romans 2:3)

In the former chapter we have looked at God's picture of the sin of the Gentile world. But now the apostle turns to the circumcision, the children of light and privilege and high profession, and he charges upon their conscience the guilt of yet more aggravated sin, and finally sums up God's great indictment against both Jew and Gentile, and pronounces the verdict of guilty upon both, and leaves them silenced and helpless under the judgment of God.

DIFFERENT STANDARDS OF JUDGMENT

1. He unfolds the principle of God's judgment respecting both Jew and Gentile.

All will be judged by the same divine tribunal, but all will not be judged by the same standard. As many as have sinned without law shall be judged without law. The heathen who have not the law of divine revelation will be judged by the law of conscience and the sense of right and wrong which God has implanted in every human breast; but this affords no hope for their ultimate salvation, for it will be found that they have not kept this law, and that they will stand convicted of their own conscience and the judgment of God, confessing, "we knew our duty, but we did it not."

The great need of the world is not so much the knowledge of right and wrong as the power to choose to do right.

The Jew will be judged by the law and the measure of light that he has received through the Old Testament, and he, too, will be found condemned even by the verdict of his own Scriptures and conscience.

The hearers of the gospel will be judged according to the gospel, and their condemnation will be, not because they have broken the law or sinned against their own conscience, but preeminently because they have rejected the Lord Jesus Christ; for "whoever does not believe stands condemned already because he has not believed in the name of God's one and only Son" (John 3:18b).

THE CHARACTER OF GOD'S JUDGMENT

2. Next we have the character of God's judgment.

a. It will be most merciful and gentle. God is long-suffering and slow to pronounce or execute judgment, and when He does it, it will be with the greatest gentleness, and with allowance for excuse or palliation. While judgment lingers now, it is the long-suffering of God that would lead us to repentance, and yet men "show contempt for the riches of his kindness, tolerance and patience, not realizing that God's kindness leads you toward repentance" (Romans 2:4).

This very tenderness of God will only make His final judgment more terribly severe. The displeasure of a friend is far more serious than the capricious anger of a hasty and passionate foe. When one who has always loved us turns against us there is little hope left, and when the Savior who died, the Father who waited long, and the Holy Spirit who pleaded for our salvation, withdraw their mercy, and hand us over to judgment, then, indeed, will begin the long night of everlasting despair.

b. God's judgment is just:

> God "will give to each person according to what he has done." To those who by persistence in doing good seek glory, honor and immortality, he will give eternal life. But for those who are self-seeking and who reject the truth and follow evil, there will be wrath and anger. There will be trouble and distress for every human being who does evil: first for the Jew, then for the Gentile; but glory, honor and peace for everyone who does good: first for the Jew, then for the Gentile. For God does not show favoritism. (2:6–11)

In that judgment all will be inexorably dealt with according to their actual deserving. Every secret thing will be brought to light: every motive, thought and feeling, every consequence and issue of our acts and lives.

Every allowance will be made, but every aggravation will be weighed, and the judgment will be impartial, strict and irreversible.

If we take the place of condemned sinners, and throw ourselves on the mercy of God, He has made provision through the gospel of Christ for the exercise of His mercy in the most glorious and generous manner. But in order to receive it, we must lie at the feet of Christ in utter helplessness and self-condemnation.

There is a fine phrase in the Epistle to the Hebrews where the apostle, in speaking of the all-searching light of God, uses the words, "Everything is uncovered and laid bare before the eyes of him to whom we must give account" (Hebrews 4:13b). The literal translation of this phrase is: "All things are stripped and stunned." This is the force of the Greek words. The figure is that of an athlete in the Coliseum who has fought his best in the arena, and has at length fallen at the feet of his adversary, disarmed and broken down in helplessness. There he lies, unable to strike a blow or lift his arm. He is stripped and stunned, disarmed and disabled, and there is nothing left for him but to lie at the feet of his adversary and throw up his arms for mercy.

c. The sin of the Jew and of those who, like him, have sinned against light, will be found to be greatly aggravated by his higher professions.

The more we claim to be, the more will be exacted from us.

The Jews were very fond of passing judgment upon others, and thinking of themselves as occupying the higher places. "If you are convinced that you are a guide for the blind, a light for those who are in the dark, an instructor of the foolish, a teacher of infants, because you have in the law the embodiment of knowledge and truth—you, then, who teach others, do you not teach yourself?" (Romans 2:19–21a).

But this only made their conduct the more glaring when they committed the very sins which they reproved in others. We who have a very large gospel should have a very consistent life. The eyes of the world, and of the religious world especially, are keenly fixed on those who teach the gospel of Christ's fullness and claim a Savior who saves to the uttermost. As someone has said, we are either libels or Bibles, and we ought to be epistles as well as apostles of the truth.

The sin of the Jew was aggravated yet more by his privileges, opportunities and higher teaching. It was to him a great advantage every way, to have the oracles of God, and to know His will and His covenant, and yet, notwithstanding all this, his life was worse than that of the Gentile which made the very name of God to be blasphemed among the heathen.

SUMMARY OF CHARGES

3. The apostle sums up the charges against both the Jew and the Gentile, and brings the testimony of God's Word out of their own Scriptures, to confirm the verdict.

In 3:10–17 he especially quotes the 14th and 53rd Psalms as God's fearful charge against the wickedness of men. This passage contains a fourfold classification of man's sin. First, negatively, the things that are lacking; second, positively, the sins of the heart; third, the sins of the tongue; and, fourth, the sins of the life.

Under these four categories the world has been found utterly and irretrievably guilty and lost. Every way you look at man, he is fallen and under the judgment of God.

In the New Testament, the words used to denote sin are very varied and suggestive. The most common of these terms means "to miss the mark." Another very common expression means to overstep the mark; a third, to fall when we should have stood; a fourth, to be ignorant when we should have known; a fifth, to diminish what should have been rendered in full measure; a sixth, to disobey a voice; and a seventh, to disregard the law, and to be willfully careless.

In every way that God can look at man, he is wrong and ruined, and the whole race lies condemned at the footstool of judgment.

LOST AND HELPLESS

4. Finally, man is not only condemned, but utterly helpless ever to justify himself, or rise again into the favor of God: "Therefore no one will be declared righteous in his sight by observing the law; rather, through the law we become conscious of sin" (3:20).

Not only are we lost, but we can do nothing to save ourselves, and we are left absolutely at the mercy of God. God is very merciful in thus destroying our last hope of self-justification; just as the prisoner at the bar, if he cannot disprove the charges against him, is far wiser to plead guilty and throw himself on the mercy of the court. Now, this is the only way that God can ever interpose for the sinner. We have no rights by law, and if we claim any, we shall lose everything.

Now, this is the position that God wants to bring us to, where we shall cease our struggles and our attempts at self-defense or self-improvement, and throw ourselves helplessly upon the mercy of God. This is the sinner's only hope, and when he thus lies at the feet of mercy, Jesus is ready to lift him up and give him that free salvation which is waiting for all who are helpless enough to be willing to receive it.

This, too, is the greatest need of the Christian seeking a deeper and higher life, to come to a full realization of his nothingness and helplessness, and to lie down, stripped and stunned, at the feet of Jesus, as the apostle does in the seventh chapter: "What a wretched man I am! Who will rescue me from this body of death?" (7:24). Then shall he be able to answer in the joyful cry of the next verse, "Thanks be to God—through Jesus Christ our Lord!" (7:25a). And the Savior's sanctifying power will come in all the fullness of the blessed chapter that follows.

The greatest hindrance to our salvation and our sanctification is ourselves, and God has to get us out of His way before He can work.

In that old Roman arena as the gladiator lay helpless and ready to die, it was the custom to allow the spectators in the gallery to determine his fate, and as his antagonist looked up to those tiers of cruel spectators, he watched their verdict. We all know how it was given. The inverted thumb was the signal of death, and the uplifted thumb the command to spare his helpless life, and as those fingers were pointed upward in all those tiers of seats, he sprang to his feet, a saved man, through the mercy of the multitude.

Ah! that brutal company was but a feeble figure of Christ's mercy. The moment we lift up our eyes and hands to heaven, we know that His bleeding hands are raised to His Father's throne, and His tender voice is pleading for us, and we know we may rise to our feet and claim His great forgiveness and His almighty help and grace. Guilty, condemned, wretched, helpless, deserving only doom, we can rise in His name and say in the face of earth and heaven and hell: "Who is he that condemns? Christ Jesus, who died— more than that, who was raised to life—is at the right hand of God and is also interceding for us" (8:34).

God's great object in all His dealing with men is to bring them to realize their utter need of Him and the salvation that He has provided through the Lord Jesus Christ. His controversy with man is not so much on account of their other sins as the one sin of rejecting His only Son and the great redemption which He has provided at such a cost. If men will but see their guilt and helplessness, He is always ready to forgive and save, to uplift the crushed and sinking soul and make the very worst of men the brightest trophies of His grace and power.

It is not the transgression of the moral law that ruins souls, but the rejection of the Lord and Savior Jesus Christ.

Many years ago I knew a man of fine culture and superior family who was addicted to the habit of intemperance and steadily sinking under its awful power. I prayed with this man for years and at last the way was opened to reach him with the gospel. He allowed himself to come under its influence to some extent, but it only deepened his intense pride, self-righteousness and antagonism to Christ, until finally he said to me one day, "I want to be a better man, I mean to give up my evil habits and I am able to do so if I choose. I believe in morality, but I do not want your Christ and your religion. I am able to save myself."

My heart strangely sank, and from that hour my prayers for that man seemed to have lost their spring. I went away from that city where he lived and did not return for some time; but on my return for a few days some years later, I was shocked to read in the morning paper that this wretched man had been found dead in a barroom the day before and had gone into eternity in the midst of his sins, with a hardened and unbelieving heart that refused Christ because he would not believe in his own helplessness and throw himself, as a sinner, upon the mercy of God.

This is the secret of salvation, of sanctification and of every spiritual blessing: "Blessed are the poor in spirit, for theirs is the kingdom of heaven" (Matthew 5:3).

The law can show us our sins, but it cannot deliver us from them, any more than we can wash our face in the looking glass when we see there the picture of our uncleanness. "For what the law was powerless to do in that it was weakened by the sinful nature, God did by sending his own Son in the likeness of sinful man to be a sin offering. And so he condemned sin in sinful man, in order that the righteous requirements of the law might be fully met in us, who do not live according to the sinful nature but according to the Spirit" (Romans 8:3–4).

CHAPTER 4

THE RIGHTEOUSNESS OF GOD

But now a righteousness from God, apart from law, has been made known, to which the Law and the Prophets testify. This righteousness from God comes through faith in Jesus Christ to all who believe. There is no difference, for all have sinned and fall short of the glory of God, and are justified freely by his grace through the redemption that came by Christ Jesus. God presented him as a sacrifice of atonement, through faith in his blood. He did this to demonstrate his justice, because in his forbearance he had left the sins committed beforehand unpunished—he did it to demonstrate his justice at the present time, so as to be just and the one who justifies those who have faith in Jesus. (Romans 3:21–26)

There is such a thing in human courts as condemning a man to save him. A wise lawyer, when he perceives that his client cannot prove his innocence, will always advise him to plead guilty and then throw himself upon the clemency of the court. Mercy cannot be exercised until guilt is confessed.

And so God has to prove man guilty in order to save him. The two first chapters of Romans are God's fearful indictment against the Gentile and the Jew, and He finally sums up the whole case by pronouncing both Jew and Gentile under sin, and laying them prostrate and guilty before God, with every mouth stopped and every excuse silenced.

Then He begins to reveal the plan of salvation through the atonement and righteousness of Jesus Christ.

Once in a French prison a Russian prince, through the prerogative of Napoleon, was permitted to pardon a convict. So he proceeded to question the different men he met, with a view to finding someone worthy of his clemency. But every man professed to be entirely innocent and, indeed, greatly wronged and unjustly punished.

At last he found one man who was qualified to receive forgiveness—the only guilty man in all the prison—and he had nothing to plead for himself, but frankly confessed his unworthiness and acknowledged that he deserved all the punishment he had received.

The prince was deeply touched by his humility and penitence and he said to him: "I have brought your forgiveness, and in the name of your emperor I pronounce you a free man. You are the only man I have found in all this place ready to acknowledge his guilt and take the place where mercy could be extended to you."

This is the place that God is bringing men to, and when He gets them there He loves to lift them up to His bosom and pronounce upon them, not the sentence of condemnation, but of acquittal and forgiveness.

In the beautiful allegory of Mansoul [in the book *Holy War*], written by John Bunyan, we have an account of the surrender of the garrison to King Immanuel. They resisted as long as they could, but beleaguered and starving, they were finally compelled to give up the conflict and yield themselves to the mercy of their conqueror.

His answer was that every one of them must come forth into his presence with chains upon their necks and crying, "We are guilty and worthy of death." And so, in great humility and fear, they marched forth from the city gates and threw themselves at his feet. They expected the severest punishment, for they had resisted to the bitter end and knew that they deserved nothing but death.

But as soon as they had echoed their humble confession, King Immanuel ordered the trumpet of the herald to proclaim in the hearing of all his camp, that they were freely pardoned through his mercy and restored to his favor, that their city should be rebuilt, should become his own royal capital and be treated with peculiar favor, and that they should be adopted as the children of the king.

They were overwhelmed with astonishment and burst out into tears of gratitude and shouts of praise.

Yes, this is the glorious paradox of divine mercy. "For God has bound all men over to disobedience so that he may have mercy on them all" (11:32).

The passage before us unfolds with extraordinary force and clearness the principles of the divine salvation.

IT IS CALLED THE RIGHTEOUSNESS OF GOD

1. We are so accustomed to think of redemption as an expedient for the relief of man that we quite forget its greater and diviner aspect as the revelation of the righteousness of God.

The purpose of Christ's work was not merely to relieve man from a dangerous situation, but much more to reveal God in the highest attitude and aspect of justice, wisdom and love, not only for His own glory, but also for the highest dignity and security of redeemed man. God has made the plan of salvation more a matter of justice and righteousness than even of grace and mercy, so that all through this Epistle to the Romans, the term "righteousness" predominates in describing the plan of salvation.

This is the difference between Christianity and all human religions. They try to bring God down to the level of man's sinfulness, and adjust the moral scale to the low standard of man's actual condition.

God's plan of salvation is the opposite of this and aims to bring man's condition up to the level of divine law. Not one principle of justice is compromised, not one jot or tittle of the law is modified or evaded. Every requirement of justice is met, and when man is saved, he is enabled to stand without a blush of shame, and claim his acquittal from the very decree of eternal justice, as much as from the gentle bosom of forgiving mercy.

I remember a noble friend of 20 years ago, a businessman of high standing among his fellows. I often used to mark his manly bearing, the high and noble dignity of his face and his walk, and the profound respect in which he was held by all his acquaintances. One day I learned the secret.

He had failed in business long years before, and was offered a settlement by his creditors involving a compromise of his debts. This he would not accept, but asked only for time and opportunity to pay every dollar, with interest; and he went back again to the struggle of life to do this, and never ceased from his high purpose until he had redeemed his pledge and met the claims of every man to the last cent. Then he walked the streets of that city with a majesty of a king among men. He was not forgiven, he was justified.

This is what God aims to do in the plan of salvation. He does not want to pass over the transgressions of the sinner by a mere act of kindness. He wants us to know that every sin has been actually dealt with, punished and ended, and that we are in just the same position with the law of God as if we had never sinned; nay, better still, as if we had kept every command of the law blamelessly. Through our great Substitute, sin has not only been met and punished, but through His atonement, we are made blameless and the same as if we had suffered ourselves.

The term justify means to declare righteous. It does not necessarily imply that the one declared righteous *is* righteous. In fact, it is assumed in the case of the sinner that he is *not* righteous. It is the ungodly that God justifies, but he is recognized not in himself but in the person of his Substitute, the Lord Jesus Christ; His righteousness is regarded as ours and for His sake we are treated even as He.

The life which He laid down is accepted for our forfeited life and the obedience which He rendered is accounted as our obedience. "God made him who had no sin to be sin for us, so that in him we might become the righteousness of God" (2 Corinthians 5:21). So the sinner can look in the face of even the Holy Spirit and say, "Therefore, there is now no condemnation for those who are in Christ Jesus" (Romans 8:1). He can face the great Accuser and cry, "Who is he that condemns? Christ Jesus, who died . . . is also interceding for us" (8:34). He may look even in the face of his conscience and at the victims of his very crimes, and with a heart breaking with humble contrition, he can still cry, "Who will bring any charge against those whom God has chosen? It is God who justifies" (8:33).

THE GROUND OF THIS RIGHTEOUSNESS

2. This is set forth by three terms that are very significant. The first is *redemption*. "The redemption that came by Christ Jesus" (3:24b).

This denotes a definite transaction through which we are purchased back from a condition of liability to punishment through a price or ransom definitely paid.

The salvation of man is based upon a very definite transaction between the Father and the Son—the covenant of redemption entered into in the ages past and actually fulfilled by the Lord Jesus Christ when He came incarnate on earth and died on Calvary. The Father stipulated in this covenant that, for certain conditions, He would give to His Son the eternal salvation of His people. These conditions involved the offering up of His life on the cross, His perfect obedience and all the mediatorial acts which our Saviour is now fulfilling.

These conditions have been absolutely fulfilled and now it is a matter of redemption right for God to forgive the believer and save the penitent and trusting soul. Therefore, we read that "If we confess our sins, he is faithful and just and will forgive us our sins and purify us from all unrighteousness" (1 John 1:9). It is a matter of righteousness for Him to do so. So, again, we are told "In him we have redemption through his blood, the forgiveness of sins, in accordance with the riches of God's grace" (Ephesians 1:7).

The second of these terms is *propitiation*. This word literally means *covering*. It is also used as a corresponding word in the Old Testament to signify cleansing. The literal idea, however, is that of covering. It suggests the mercy seat in the tabernacle. The position of the mercy seat was strikingly significant of its spiritual reference. It was the covering of the ark. Underneath it and within the ark lay the tablets of the law which man had broken and which witnessed against his sin.

Over it hovered the Shekinah, symbolic of God's all-seeing eye. That eye was looking down upon the ark. Had it seen only that broken law and the sin against which it testified, it could only have flashed its holy fires against the transgressors, and could not have rested in covenant love upon the worshipers in that sacred place.

But it did not see the sin at all, for between the ark and the Shekinah was the mercy seat, the covering lid of pure gold always sprinkled with the blood of atonement. God saw only the blood, and it covered the sin. So we read such words as these: "Blessed is he/ whose transgressions are forgiven,/ whose sins are covered" (Psalm 32:1). "He hath not beheld iniquity in Jacob, neither hath he seen perverseness in Israel" (Numbers 23:21a, KJV). "He is the atoning sacrifice for our sins, and not only for ours but also for the sins of the whole world" (1 John 2:2).

The third term used is *His blood.* Of course this refers to His death. The blood is the life, and the offering of Christ's blood always expresses His vicarious sacrifice for sin. The ransom was His life, the propitiation is His blood. He has stood between us and the just consequences of our guilt, and "The LORD has laid on him the iniquity of us all" (Isaiah 53:6b). "He himself bore our sins in his body on the tree, so that we might die to sins and live for righteousness; by his wounds you have been healed" (1 Peter 2:24).

This is the core of Christianity. This is the essence of the gospel. This is the ground of our justification. God has set forth Jesus Christ so emphatically that His great atonement cannot be misunderstood or evaded by any honest mind, and He is the propitiation through His blood, by whom God can "demonstrate his justice, because in his forbearance he had left the sins committed beforehand unpunished . . . so as to be just and the one who justifies those who have faith in Jesus" (Romans 3:25b, 26b).

THE EFFICACY OF HIS ATONEMENT

3. "Because in his forbearance he had left the sins committed beforehand unpunished . . ." (3:25b).

The language here is very expressive, and it intimates that in the past and up to the time of Christ's death, God was forbearing with sin, but it was not settled for.

There are two Greek words used, expressive of the two thoughts that stand forth here in bold relief. One is *paresis*, and the other *aphesis*. *Paresis* means to pass by, *aphesis* to put away. Under the Old Testament, it was *paresis*; under the New it is *aphesis*. Then, it was forbearance. Now, it is remission. Then, God overlooked sin, not lightly nor capriciously, but in view of the settlement that was to be made by Christ on Calvary and which was recognized as already accomplished through "the Lamb that was slain from the creation of the world" (Revelation 13:8). But the ransom was not literally paid, and so God dealt with men in forbearance and in anticipation of the coming atonement.

Christ had, as it were, given His promissory note for the payment of the ransom and God accepted it and dealt with believers under the old covenant, under the assumption that it would be paid. Christ redeemed it on Calvary and thus it was taken out of the way, nailed to His cross and the full efficacy of His atonement became real. Sin was now put away, canceled, annihilated.

He had come to finish transgression, to make an end of sin, to bring in everlasting righteousness; and now we who accept the Lord Jesus are not only taken on probation and dealt with as objects of forbearance, but we are wholly justified, we are eternally saved and received into the fellowship and communion of God, even as His own beloved Son, in whom we are accepted.

"I tell you the truth, whoever hears my word and believes him who sent me," Jesus said, "has eternal life and will not be condemned; he has crossed over from death to life" (John 5:24). "My sheep listen to my voice; I know them, and they follow me. I give them eternal life, and they shall never perish; no one can snatch them out of my hand" (10:27–28).

The work of Jesus Christ is complete, final, eternal: "Because by one sacrifice he has made perfect forever those who are being made holy" (Hebrews 10:14). "But now he has appeared once for all at the end of the ages to do away with sin by the sacrifice of himself. . . . He will appear a second time, not to bear sin, but to bring salvation to those who are waiting for him" (9:26b, 28b).

Is not this a glorious redemption, a divine foundation, a strong consolation, a Rock of Ages? Is not this a better resting place for your confidence and hope than all your transitory feelings and variable experiences? Is not this a blessed place to rest when the brain gets clouded and the heart gets sad and cold, and the adversary hurls his fiery darts into the self-accusing conscience?

Well do I remember a dear old saint who had brought scores of souls to Christ in a long and useful Christian life. But as her sun began to go down, clouds gathered around her horizon, her brain grew weak, her faith became dimmed and she thought she was no longer useful to Jesus Christ and He no longer wanted her. Blessed soul! How sweet it was to tell her that her salvation rested upon the immutable Word of God and that she was safe in Jesus Christ, the Rock of Ages, that nothing could ever shake!

Oh, beloved, let us be sure that we are fast anchored to this eternal Rock—the redemption of our Lord Jesus Christ.

THE TERMS OF THIS DIVINE RIGHTEOUSNESS

4. "And are justified freely by his grace" (Romans 3:24). This is almost a redundancy, for freely and grace mean the same. But the design of the writer is to express the idea with all possible emphasis. This salvation, all the way through, is the gift of God. We cannot earn it, deserve it nor work it out ourselves. We must receive it, from beginning to end, directly from our Father's hands, on equal terms of mercy and personal worthlessness. Our

works, experiences and usefulness have nothing whatever to do in securing our salvation.

I have no more right to my salvation because I have been serving Jesus 35 years than that poor man who last night received Jesus in the Cremorne Mission and has just stepped out of a life of reeking uncleanness. When I stand in the presence of my Lord my only plea must be:

Saved by grace alone,
This is all my plea—
Jesus died for all mankind
And Jesus died for me.

There is no difference in the standing of all men at the gateway of life. "For all have sinned and fall short of the glory of God, and are justified freely by his grace" (3:23–24a). And whatever else we have along with this—whatever of holiness or usefulness God has permitted any of us to enjoy—this also is through the riches of His grace. "What do you have that you did not receive?" (1 Corinthians 4:7a). Even Paul had to say, in speaking of his salvation, "I was shown mercy" (1 Timothy 1:13b) and then he added of his subsequent career, "The grace of our Lord was poured out on me abundantly, along with the faith and love that are in Christ Jesus" (1:14).

It is true there is a great difference at the end, but there is none at the beginning. On equal terms we enter the gates of mercy, all alike condemned; and then we are permitted, in the great goodness of God, to strive for the crown of recompense and press toward the goal in the race for victory.

It is just the same as if, in some great public school, free admission should be given to all who applied, irrespective of their personal circumstances and merits, but after they are admitted freely to the school there are prizes given to the boys according to their diligence and proficiency in the various studies.

So God takes us all in as helpless, worthless sinners, but after we enter the school of Christ as the beneficiaries of His grace, we are invited and permitted to press forward to the higher rewards which He offers to the diligent and faithful.

But even the power to gain the reward and strive for the mastery is still the gift of grace, through the purchase of Christ's precious blood, and the gift of the Father's sovereign love.

THE MEANS BY WHICH THIS GIFT IS RECEIVED

5. It is received by faith in the Lord Jesus Christ: "This righteousness from God comes through faith in Jesus Christ to all who believe. There is no difference" (Romans 3:22).

Again, in the 27th verse (KJV), "the law of faith" is spoken of. This is the principle underlying the whole gospel system. Every blessing must be received by faith. This is the only way in which a gift can be received. There is no merit in an act of faith. It is simply taking what God gives with thanks and trust.

It is certainly a very blessed act, because when the heart receives the love and grace of God it exercises a most blessed influence on our life and character, but in itself it is not a work of merit, but simply the means by which we receive what God has to give.

It is the law of faith. It is the principle on which God is acting with men. "And without faith it is impossible to please God" (Hebrews 11:6a). This faith is more fully unfolded in the following chapter, as we shall see. But meanwhile, let us realize its essential importance in our own lives and accept it as the principle and law of our life, as it is the law of God's administration for sinful men.

God has the boundless riches of His grace for the most lost and sinful, if they will only accept the gift and receive it by simple trust; but we shall be lost by unbelief much more certainly than by the darkest crime of which human nature is capable.

It is said that once an English landlord, in order to teach his peasantry the lesson of trusting God, offered on a certain day to pay the debts of all his tenantry if they would bring him a statement of all their debts and accept as a gift his generous bounty.

The morning came and he waited in his office until the hour of noon, according to the announcement which he had widely published. The people gathered in curious knots around the street and wondered what it all meant. They could not understand such liberal generosity and they waited for someone to go in and prove that he really meant it and then they would all go in for their share. But the day wore on and none of them seemed willing to go in.

At last an aged couple came along and, tottering up the steps, approached the door. The people outside crowded around them and said eagerly, "Now be sure to hurry through and tell us all about it."

The old couple went in, and the landlord received them very kindly, looked over their statement, paid the debts gladly and then asked them if there was anything more he could do for their comfort. He said that he had a certain sum of money that he intended to spend in this way, but none of the people seemed to want it. So he gave the old couple enough to buy a little cottage and provided for all the needs of their closing days. They poured out their thanks with tears of joy.

When they arose to go, he detained them a few moments, chatting pleasantly with them, until the clock struck 12; then he arose, opened the door for them to pass out and said: "The time that I appointed in the announcement has now expired and other engagements call me away." He bade them goodbye and as they tottered feebly down the steps the crowd eagerly pressed about them, asking, "Did he really pay your debts? Did he mean it?" The old people looked at them with astonishment in their faces and said, "Why, of course he did."

The people now hastened to the door, anxious to enter, but before they reached it he had passed out, and with a polite bow hurried away, saying, "Good morning, neighbors; I am sorry you were so late, but another engagement calls me away. The time has expired, the opportunity has passed." Oh, how sorry they were that they had not trusted his word!

The next Sabbath, as he talked with them in his mission hall about the promises of Jesus and what they mean, many hearts realized, as they had never done before, the folly and wickedness of unbelief and the blessedness of trusting God and of remembering, "He means just what He says."

CHAPTER 5

THE LAW OF FAITH

Where, then, is boasting? It is excluded. On what principle? On that of observing the law? No, but on that of faith. (Romans 3:27)

There are natural laws and there are spiritual laws, and the natural are often types of the spiritual. The whole material universe is governed by one great principle which holds everything in harmony—the law of gravitation. Through the operation of this law, the stars and planets fulfill their orbits, and the particles of matter are kept from flying to pieces and are held in cohesion—in the mountain, the atmosphere and even the human body.

God needs no elaborate machinery to operate His mighty universe, but with infinite wisdom and power He has just breathed this great force into nature, and the wheels revolve and the planets roll in obedience to this mighty law.

Again, in the social world, God has arranged a corresponding law, as simple yet as far-reaching and effectual. We might call it the law of social gravitation. It is the principle of mutual confidence. Stand in some great thoroughfare and look at the multitudes as they ceaselessly hurry by and you often wonder where they all live and how the world holds so many people without their getting into confusion and anarchy. And yet these multitudes, like the bees in yonder busy hive, all go to their own place. They are bound together by social ties, business ties and political ties that keep them in perfect adjustment.

God has put into the heart of that mother the instinct that makes her take care of her children, into the hearts of those businessmen the common interests that bind them together, into the hearts of the multitude the instincts of patriotism that unite them in states and countries; and so, all of earth's mighty millions are governed by one great vow between man and man, as perfect as the law that governs the movements of the spheres. It is the law of faith.

Now in the spiritual world God rules by the same great principle. He is the natural Center and Sun of the whole moral and spiritual system. It is His will that all beings should be bound to Him, as the planets to their suns, by the law of confidence, trust and love that will make them true to Him and righteous toward each other. This is the law of faith. As long as His creatures trust Him and obey Him, they are happy and holy; but when this bond is broken, they break away into disorder and destruction, just as surely as our earth would become a wandering star if she drifted from the sun, and would be wrecked amid the wastes of immensity.

The fall of man in Eden came through the breaking of this law of spiritual gravitation. The wily tempter succeeded in destroying man's trust, and two things immediately followed. First, man began to hide from God; then next, he began to accuse his fellow. Adam lost his love for God and his love for Eve at the same moment, and since that day the human family has been continually getting farther from God and more separated from one another.

Therefore when Jesus came the first thing He did was to reestablish the law of faith. For this reason the very condition of eternal life is to believe God. The very first thing men are called to do is to learn to trust, and the condition of blessing under the gospel is faith in God, so that the very law of Christianity is faith.

In the previous paragraph, in the third chapter of Romans, the apostle has unfolded the plan of redemption and the ground of God's righteousness for sinful men. He then takes up the means by which His righteousness is to become available. This is faith. "This righteousness from God comes through faith in Jesus Christ to all who believe. There is no difference" (3:22).

This is the one condition through which we receive the divine righteousness and the salvation of Jesus Christ. But a condition so important requires to be made very plain, and therefore the entire fourth chapter is devoted to the exposition of faith and the illustration of this important law.

He shows them that it has always been the condition of God's blessing, even under the Old Testament; and in order to prove this, he cites the examples of Abraham and David, the two most prominent saints of the old dispensation.

Abraham represented the patriarchal and David the kingly period, and both of these, he shows, were saved and dealt with by the Lord under the law of faith.

Abraham was the Columbus of faith, the great discoverer of this promised land; and David was the Joshua of faith, the great conqueror of this new world of holy possibilities.

Abraham, however, was justified by faith: "Abraham believed God, and it was credited to him as righteousness" (4:3). David also expressed the same truth when he said in Psalm 32:1-2, "Blessed is he/ whose transgressions are forgiven,/ whose sins are covered,/ Blessed is the man/ whose sin the LORD does not count against him/ and in whose spirit is no deceit."

This is evidently the righteousness which is not intrinsic, but comes to the person receiving it by a divine reckoning, and not by a personal right.

Then he unfolds four great features of this principle of faith, as illustrated especially in the story of Abraham.

IT IS FAITH WITHOUT WORKS

> If, in fact, Abraham was justified by works, he had something to boast about—but not before God. What does the Scripture say? "Abraham believed God, and it was credited to him as righteousness."
>
> Now when a man works, his wages are not credited to him as a gift, but as an obligation. However, to the man who does not work but trusts God who justifies the wicked, his faith is credited as righteousness. David says the same thing when he speaks of the blessedness of the man to whom God credits righteousness apart from works:
>
> "Blessed are they
>   whose transgressions are forgiven,
>   whose sins are covered.
> Blessed is the man
>   whose sin the Lord will never count against him."
>   (Romans 4:2–8)

It was not in any sense connected with Abraham's own personal acts of righteousness, but was an act of God's free grace bestowed upon Abraham just as it is now bestowed upon any sinful man.

The peculiarity of faith is that it gives up our works, and takes God's works instead. The man who works for a thing expects to do it himself; the man who believes for a thing expects God to do it. "Now we who have believed enter that rest . . . for anyone who enters God's rest also rests from his own work, just as God did from his" (Hebrews 4:3a, 10).

IT IS FAITH WITHOUT DISTINCTION

> Is this blessedness only for the circumcised, or also for the un-circumcised? We have been saying that Abraham's faith was credited to him as righteousness. Under what circumstances was it credited? Was it after he was circumcised, or before? It was not

after, but before! And he received the sign of circumcision, a seal
of the righteousness that he had by faith while he was still uncircumcised. So then, he is the father of all who believe but have
not been circumcised, in order that righteousness might be
credited to them. And he is also the father of the circumcised
who not only are circumcised but who also walk in the footsteps
of the faith that our father Abraham had before he was circumcised.

It was not through law that Abraham and his offspring
received the promise that he would be heir of the world, but
through the righteousness that comes by faith. (Romans 4:9–13)

It does not rest upon the fact that Abraham belonged to the privileged
class, because Abraham was justified before he was circumcised, and thus
recognized as a Jew.

In fact, it was because he was already justified by faith that he was circumcised. He had the reality first, and then he was entitled to the outward sign
and seal.

So Abraham represents the Gentile world and the provision of the gospel
for them as fully as for the Jew, and teaches us that believers of every age inherit the promises, whether they be Jew or Gentile.

The gospel of faith is not the birthright of the few, but the inheritance of a
sinful world, on the simple condition of believing God and accepting the
promises through Jesus Christ.

IT IS FAITH WITHOUT SIGHT

As it is written: "I have made you a father of many nations." He
is our father in the sight of God, in whom he believed—the God
who gives life to the dead and calls things that are not as though
they were.

Against all hope, Abraham in hope believed and so became the
father of many nations, just as it had been said to him, "So shall
your offspring be." (4:17–18)

This is a very wonderful passage. It lays the deep foundations of faith, and
unfolds its profound principles in such a manner as to distinguish it forever
from all its counterfeits.

It teaches us that Abram believed God, to the extent of counting the
things that are not as though they were. This is illustrated in his life, in the
fact that he accepted the promise of Isaac as a certainty long before it occurred and so fully counted upon it that he even took the new name,

Abraham, which was the outward confession of this faith.

Before a criticizing and scorning world he calls himself the father of a multitude of nations, when the one from whom they were to come was as yet unborn and, according to all natural possibilities, never could be born—as *his* child, at least.

In the account of God's covenant with Abraham in the 17th chapter of Genesis we have a very wonderful unfolding of the principle of faith, in counting the things that are not as though they were.

God comes to Abraham as *El Shaddai*, the Almighty God, revealing Himself in the form that seemed to challenge Abraham's highest trust, and He then proceeds to give him His covenant in three very wonderful revelations. The first of these is in the future tense—the promise, "I *will* confirm my covenant between me and you and *will* greatly increase your numbers" (Genesis 17:2, italics added).

Abraham accepts this as faith ever does in its first stages, in the future tense, and believed that God would do as He had said.

But now he comes nearer and gets upon his face before God, and God begins to talk with him more intimately, giving him a second message. But this is in the present tense. God never repeats Himself. When He speaks to us He has always something more to say. So now it is: "As for me, this *is* my covenant with you" (17:4a, italics added). The thing has now become a present fact, and so Abraham receives it and takes a step further, from the future into the present. This is the faith that takes God's gift and counts it real.

But this is not all. Once more God speaks, and now it is another step further on. He moves from the present into the perfect tense, and His next word is, "No longer will you be called Abram; your name will be Abraham, for I *have* made you a father of many nations" (17:5, italics added).

Henceforth it must be thought of, spoken of, acknowledged as something completed and past. In the eyes of men it is not yet a fact, nor even a probability; but in the sight of God it is done, and faith counts the things that are not as though they were.

Now in all this Abraham was just imitating God. The true reading of this passage (Romans 4:17) is, "Like Him whom he believed, even God, who quickeneth the dead, and calleth those things which be not as though they were."

In acting in this way, Abraham simply acted like God. This is the way God acts. He speaks of "the Lamb that was slain from the creation of the world" (Revelation 13:8). Now, Christ was not slain actually before the creation of the world, but in the purpose of God. He was to be offered on Calvary, and God acted as if this were really done. It was so certain that God counted it as if it were already accomplished, and on the ground of this He saved the Old

Testament saints and acted toward them on the understanding that the price was already paid and the redemption already consummated.

So we find God acting continually in His dealings with His people. God came to Gideon and said, as He met him on his threshing floor where he was hiding from the Midianites, "The LORD is with you, mighty warrior" (Judges 6:12). Now, Gideon was anything but a mighty warrior; indeed, he was as frightened as he could be, and at that very time was hiding from his enemies. The message must have astonished him. But God immediately added, "Go in the strength you have and save Israel" (6:14).

But the strength was not Gideon's, but God's. God constituted that strength, and from that moment Gideon could count it as though it was, and so he went and delivered Israel. The things that were not, he counted as though they were. The power of God became his power, and the unseen crystallized into the real.

So Jesus said to the man that lay at His feet helpless, "Son, your sins are forgiven" (Mark 2:5b). That word made the forgiveness real, and as the man accepted it and rose up to meet it, it was actually fulfilled in him.

In this same way the sinner is saved. Tonight, some poor, reeking drunkard in yonder mission may kneel at the altar of penitence, and a voice will say to him, "Son, your sins are forgiven," and that which an instant before was not true, will become true by his claiming it. Abraham's faith will again be fulfilled, and that man will go forth into a new life and a happy future by counting the things that are not as though they were.

So Jesus said to His disciples, speaking of the future, "You are already clean because of the word I have spoken to you" (John 15:3). A moment before they were not clean, but they became clean the moment they accepted it and counted it real.

And so we must take our sanctification by faith, counting it real before it is real. Just as simply speaking the marriage vow constitutes that girl a wife, puts out of existence her former single life and puts before her a new future, so that simple act of faith constitutes a new life in Christ, and brings us into union with Him as our Sanctifier and Keeper.

So, again, that simple word of healing constituted that which it proclaimed. "You may go. Your son will live" (4:50a) brought about a state of things which did not exist a moment before. God called the thing that was not as though it were, which answering to the word, came to pass as He had spoken.

So, again, in the promise He has given in connection with prayer, when we ask, we must believe that we do receive the things that we ask, and we shall have them.

The very element of faith is the unseen. It is not correct to say, I have seen, therefore I believe. The true formula is "Blessed are those who have not seen and yet have believed" (20:29b). For the faith that brings us into contact with the gospel is "being sure of what we hope for and certain of what we do not see" (Hebrews 11:1). It not only believes in the thing that does not exist, but it acknowledges it, proclaims it, steps out upon it, puts its weight upon it, and acts as if it were really so.

This was true of Abraham. When the promise of Isaac came to him, it seemed impossible that he could have a son through Sarah, his own wife, for she was aged and infirm. For a while Abraham, like other people, went to work to try to help God in the difficulty. With the consent of Sarah, he took unto himself a handmaiden, and Hagar became the mother of Ishmael, through no purpose of evil, or no gross or earthly motive, but simply from an honest desire to bring about God's promise. The only effect of this expedient was to bring sorrow to all concerned, most of all to Sarah and Abraham themselves.

And when they got through trying, God asked Abram to believe that this thing would come to pass through Sarah; and He not only made him believe but confess it to all his neighbors before it happened by taking the name Abraham; and it is probable that he had to explain why he took it, so as to make it very clear and explicit.

When they got through criticizing him God began to act, and before long the thing was fulfilled. Isaac was born, and the thing that seemed impossible came to pass. God quickened the dead; He supernaturally revived the power of Sarah and the child was born as one out of the grave.

This is the way God always loves to work. He can do a great deal more with a dead man than with a living man. In fact,

> God chose the foolish things of the world to shame the wise; God chose the weak things of the world to shame the strong. He chose the lowly things of the world and the despised things—and the things that are not—to nullify the things that are, so that no one may boast before him. (1 Corinthians 1:27–29)

IT IS FAITH WITHOUT DOUBT

> Without weakening in his faith, he faced the fact that his body was as good as dead—since he was about a hundred years old—and that Sarah's womb was also dead. Yet he did not waver through unbelief regarding the promise of God, but was strengthened in his faith and gave glory to God, being fully persuaded that God had power to do what he had promised. (Romans 4:19–21)

This is the last phase of Abraham's faith. "He staggered not," (Romans 4:20, KJV)—literally, he *wavered* not. There is a great difference between staggering and wavering. To stagger indicates that one is about to fall, but wavering implies a much milder form of weakness. Abraham did not even manifest the flutter of a doubt; not a fiber of his being shrank; not for a moment did he hesitate. When the command came to sacrifice his son, "early the next morning Abraham got up" (Genesis 22:3a) and instantly obeyed.

It is not great doubts that hurt us, but little ones. Moths are mightier foes than fierce conflagrations and midnight robbers. The man that never wavers will never be tempted to stagger. The time to meet the doubt is at its beginning, in the faintest form of questioning. The only safe place for faith is in absolute, unfaltering confidence, every moment, in the love of God. If we once begin to question, we are inevitably lost. If we believe God we must believe Him utterly. The closer our relationship to people is, the more perfectly will be our confidence.

A man must have absolute trust in the one that lies nearest his heart. The faintest question or doubt is fatal to happiness or peace. If we believe God, we must believe Him entirely. Wavering always springs from unbelief. We may call it by all the gentle names we like, but it literally means I do not quite believe my God.

Again, we are told that he did not look at the obstacles. "He considered not his own body" (Romans 4:19a, KJV). If we look at outward things we will never have unfaltering faith. If we trust because we feel happy, we will soon cease to feel happy, or trust either. If we feel confidence in our healing because we see improvement, we will soon cease to improve. If we believe God is answering our prayers because we see something happening, we will soon cease to see anything.

The revised version of this passage, however, is better. He did look at the difficulties without being discouraged by them. "He considered his own body without being weakened in faith." It is a great thing to be able to look at the adverse side without being weakened in faith, to take in the full situation, to let Satan make out his inventory completely, to admit all his resources, and then to say, "Yes, this is all true—*but God*—God is equal to it, notwithstanding all."

"Who shall separate us from the love of Christ?" (8:35a). Then he names them all, one by one: tribulation, distress, persecution, famine, nakedness, peril, or sword; and rising above them all, he cries:

> No, in all these things we are more than conquerors through him who loved us. For I am convinced that neither death nor life, neither angels nor demons, neither the present nor the future, nor any powers, neither height nor depth, nor anything else in all

creation, will be able to separate us from the love of God that is in Christ Jesus our Lord. (8:37–39)

Again, it is added, "Being fully persuaded that God had power [was able, KJV] to do what he had promised" (4:21). The word "able" here is literally "mighty." It means that God is not only able to do it, but that it is easy for Him to do it; it required no struggle, effort or sacrifice. All Abraham wanted to know was that God said it—then it would surely come to pass. No matter about the source from which it was to come. God had infinite resources, and it was nothing for Him to accomplish His purpose or fulfill His mightiest word.

We see here the very essence of faith. It is not merely an intellectual process. Abraham's faith reposed on God Himself. He knew the God he was dealing with. It was a personal confidence in One whom he could utterly trust. The real secret of Abraham's whole life was that he was the friend of God, and knew God to be his great, good and faithful Friend, and, taking Him at His word, he had stepped out from all that he knew and loved and gone forth upon an unknown pathway with none but God; and all the way along he leaned upon Him as upon a true and trusted Friend.

Beloved, are we trusting not only in the Word of God, but have we learned to lean our whole weight upon Himself, the God of infinite love and power, our covenant God and everlasting Friend?

Now we are told that Abraham glorified God by this life of faith. The true way to glorify God is to let the world see what He is and what He can do. God does not want us so much to do things as to let people see what He can do. God is not looking for extraordinary characters as His instruments, of whom people will say, "Why yes, it is nothing for him to do it," but He is looking for humble instruments through whom He can be honored throughout the ages; and the man who trusts his God is really doing higher service than the greatest workers and the most brilliant men whose lives may be but a reflection of their own radiance and a monument to their own glory.

The apostle closes this chapter by telling us that God expects substantially the same faith from us under the gospel, and we shall inherit the same blessings as Abraham if we follow in the footsteps of his faith, for

The words "it was credited to him" were written not for him alone, but also for us, to whom God will credit righteousness— for us who believe in him who raised Jesus our Lord from the dead. He was delivered over to death for our sins and was raised to life for our justification. (4:23–25)

Surely if Abraham, in the dawn of revelation with but a few scattered rays of heavenly light, could so fully trust in God, how much more should we, after centuries of gospel light and in the full meridian blaze of the Holy Spirit's inspiration, be able to trust Him too, with a strength and steadfastness that even Abraham never knew.

"Therefore, since we are surrounded by such a great cloud of witnesses, let us throw off everything that hinders and the sin that so easily entangles, and let us run with perseverance the race marked out for us" (Hebrews 12:1). "God had planned something better for us so that only together with us would they be made perfect" (11:40).

CHAPTER 6

THE BLESSINGS THAT FLOW
FROM JUSTIFICATION

Therefore, since we have been justified through faith, we have peace with God through our Lord Jesus Christ, through whom we have gained access by faith into this grace in which we now stand. And we rejoice in the hope of the glory of God. (Romans 5:1–2)

This chapter is an inventory of the treasures in the house of faith and the blessings that flow from justification by faith. In the preceding chapters the apostle had unfolded the principles of God's righteousness and the conditions through which it is received; and now, before he closes this second chapter on the divine salvation, he proceeds to enumerate and sum up the special blessings of this great salvation. In so doing he anticipates a little the subject of sanctification, which is to come in the next chapter; and so we find some things in this enumeration which properly belong to the sanctified life. We must not think this strange or illogical, because while in the nature of things justification and sanctification are distinct and are very distinctly treated in this epistle, yet in the mind of God they are associated very closely, and in the experiences of the believer they ought not to be as widely separated as they usually are.

Indeed, it seems to be the thought of God that they should immediately succeed each other. When God's people left Egypt, He meant them to go immediately into the land of Canaan, and if they allowed an interval of 40 years to intervene, it was not because God wanted it.

And so, in the Pentecostal experience of the Apostolic Church, it would seem as if all who accepted Jesus were at once taken into His fullness and received the baptism of the Holy Spirit, the same as the apostles—passing at once into the sanctified life, living in entire consecration—so that it could be said, "No one claimed that any of his possessions was his own . . . and much grace was upon them all" (Acts 4:32b, 33b).

Through the lowering of the Christian standard, there has come about a kind of Christianity which has no spiritual warrant; a condition in which people are justified and yet do not expect to live a holy life—and do not live it, until through truer teaching and the preparation of God's Spirit they are awakened to realize the true life of holiness to which God has called them, and after years of wandering they at length come into the experience of sanctification which they should have known from the first.

While the summary of blessings which the apostle unfolds in this chapter has reference chiefly to the fruits of justification, yet it reaches out into all the fullness of the believer's sanctified life and takes in, by anticipation, some of the things which are to be more explicitly unfolded in the chapters that follow.

"PEACE WITH GOD"

"Therefore, since we have been justified through faith, we have peace with God" (5:1). The revised and correct reading is, "Let us have peace with God." Dr. Marvin R. Vincent, in his critical notes on this verse, says: "This is undoubtedly the true reading, but the commentators have been perplexed to understand why it should be put in this way rather than in the simple indicative mood—we have peace. Why should he say, 'let us have peace,' when we have it already? For the peace spoken of here is not a feeling of peace, but it is the condition of heaven, a reconciliation with God through the redemption of the Lord Jesus Christ."

We are brought out of a condition of alienation and separation into one of acceptance and peace. The controversy is ended. There is no condemnation. We are regarded and treated as friends and received into His family as children and joint heirs with Christ. Now why should it be said, "let us have peace," when we have it already?

Well, there is doubtless a very profound reason for it, and perhaps it will appear if we were to put the emphasis on the word *have*. Let us *have* peace. God has made it, now let us take it. Many persons are trying to make peace, but peace is already made through Jesus Christ, and all that God asks of us is to take the reconciliation that He offers and have the peace that He has arranged. Many persons are acting toward God as if He were at war with them, as if everything were against them and God was their worst enemy. The truth is, "God was reconciling the world to himself in Christ" (2 Corinthians 5:19a), and the death of Jesus was the outflow of His own personal and sovereign love; and when we see this and know it, we are ready to lay down our arms and become His friends.

After the Old French War, it is said that a French frigate was seen fleeing from an English warship in the Southern Seas. The British cruiser pursued the fugitive and, after a hard chase, overtook her. The Frenchman hauled up the white flag and surrendered, and as he presented his sword to his conqueror, the Englishman laughed at him and asked him what he meant by surrendering.

"Why," he said, "didn't you know the war was over, and peace has been made for months?" "Why, no," said the Frenchman. "I thought we were still at war and I tried to escape. When I could not, the only thing left for me was to surrender. But I have been so long away from civilized ports and the news of the world that I did not even hear that peace was made." The men cordially shook hands, the sword was given back to the Frenchman and they sat down together as comrades. The war was over and they said, "Let us have peace," because peace was at headquarters.

This is what God means. Peace is made for every man who will take it through Jesus Christ, turn from his sins and accept the Savior as his Redeemer and Lord. Don't try to please God by your own works, and earn His favor, but frankly accept His forgiveness, turn from your rebellion and disobedience and accept the peace which has been sealed through the precious blood of Christ.

Perhaps the verse might be explained in another connection. Let us hold fast to the peace which we have with God. Let us live in it, recognize it and never doubt it. It is not a truce but a permanent peace. It is not an armistice but an absolute amnesty, a great treaty of peace, signed and ratified forevermore.

A poor woman in one of Mr. Whittle's meetings in Glasgow was brought into light by a little verse in the fifth chapter of John: "I tell you the truth, whoever hears my word and believes him who sent me has eternal life and will not be condemned; he has crossed over from death to life" (5:24).

The evangelist gave her the verse, written on a little card, and sent her home rejoicing with her little son. They both went to bed that night, happy as angels. But in the morning she came down to breakfast as gloomy as ever, her face all clouded and her heart utterly discouraged. She had had a night of conflicts, doubts and fears, and when her little boy asked her what was the matter, she could only burst into tears and say, "Oh, it is all gone. I thought I was saved, but I feel just as bad as ever."

The little fellow looked bewildered and said, "Why, mother, has your verse changed? I will go and see." He ran to the table and got her Bible with the little card in it, and turned it up and read, "I tell you the truth, whoever hears my word and believes him who sent me has eternal life and will not be condemned; he has crossed over from death to life."

"Why, mother," he said, "it is not changed a bit. It is just the same as it was last night; it is all right." And the mother looked with a smile at the little preacher, whose simple trust was used of God to save her; and taking him in her arms, she thanked God that her precious verse was still the same and her peace as unchanged as the everlasting Word of God. Is that what the apostle means? We are justified, now let us have and hold fast to the peace. It is not merely forgiveness, but it is an everlasting decree. Let us walk in the strength of it and never allow the shadow of a doubt or fear to cross the sunlit sky of our heaven.

"ACCESS BY FAITH INTO THIS GRACE IN WHICH WE NOW STAND"

There is also grace to keep us as well as to save us, and to keep us not falling but standing, and standing fast in holy obedience and steadfast victory.

The word "access" means right, liberty, unbounded freedom and power, a throne of grace to which we can always come and obtain mercy and find grace to help in time of need.

A kind lady once sent to Rowland Hill a sum of money to give to some poor curate. Rowland Hill, with his shrewd English sense, did not give it all at once, but sent enough to pay the man's debts and give him a start, and then added at the bottom of the letter, "More to follow." Every week or two there came another letter with the same mysterious words—"More to follow"—until the poor curate got used to it, and the little message grew into one of our sweetest hymns.

When Jesus Christ forgives a man's sins and accepts him as a child, He undertakes a good deal more than human love would be equal to. Nothing but infinite grace bought on Calvary would induce Him to take all the follies, provocation, disobedience and failures which all of us have laid upon our blessed Lord, and for which He has so graciously provided until the very word makes us ashamed, while at the same time it makes us trust Him more. The Apostle Paul, speaking of his salvation, said that he obtained mercy; and then he adds of his later experience, "The grace of our Lord was poured out on me abundantly, along with the faith and love that are in Christ Jesus" (1 Timothy 1:14). The very faith and love were but gifts of divine grace. Every step of the way is dependent upon Him. Apart from Him we can do nothing (John 15:5). "From the fullness of his grace we have all received one blessing after another" (1:16).

Now, all this grace and all this fullness come to us by Him. The person of Jesus Christ is the channel through whom our life is maintained as well as created. Every moment we are held to Him personally by utter dependence, as a baby to its mother, as a tree to its root.

JOY IN THE PROSPECT AND HOPE OF THE GLORY OF GOD

This means the joy of salvation, the joy that springs from knowing that we are accepted and looking forward to our final and full salvation in the glory of the Lord.

This is a different joy from that meant in the 11th verse. This is the first "joy of the soul in its earliest love." It is founded upon the fact of its salvation and the hope of heaven.

It is a wonderful thing to find that we have escaped the wrath of God, the judgment due to our sins and the dreadful prospects of a lost soul, and been translated at once into all the privileges and hopes of the kingdom of God. No wonder that the newborn soul springs at once into an ecstasy and gladness which often becomes—alas!—but a memory of "the blessedness we knew when first we saw the Lord." This is all right. It is a wonderful and glorious thing to be saved and to have the hope of the glory of God. Don't clip the wings of the little bird, don't cut back the free growth of the springing vine, don't sober down that happy child—the devil will do that soon enough. They need all the spring and the sweetness, all the triumphant gladness of this hour. The settling will come in God's time and way, and all the better if there is a good deal to settle.

THE DISCIPLINE OF TRIAL

"We glory in tribulations, also" (Romans 5:3, KJV). It is rather remarkable that the two words employed in this expression are both extreme words, one denoting the highest triumph, and the other the profoundest suffering. Sorrow is spoken of not by an ordinary term, but by a word denoting the hardest kind of sorrow. *Tribulation* is literally derived from a root signifying a flail, and it means a kind of suffering that leaves us bruised and beaten, as the wheat that has been threshed on the summer floor.

On the other hand, the word *glory* expresses the very highest kind of joy and triumph. It is not mere enduring, patience or even long-suffering, but it is triumphant, and even ecstatic, joy. It suggests the idea that while ordinary joy may carry us through ordinary trials, when we come to the deepest afflictions and the hardest places we must have the very highest experiences of divine joy and rise even to the spirit of glorying in the Lord.

But there is also a sober side to trial: the quiet, steady schoolroom of patience and proving which must follow the long strain that so often comes after the first victorious conflict.

"Tribulation worketh patience; patience (not experience, but), proving; and proving, hope, a hope that maketh not ashamed" (5:3b–5a, author's translation). This is the deep, settled establishing that comes through patient suffering and the joy of the Lord. We want the joy to inspire us for the long-continued test, and then, when faith is proved, and patience has its perfect work (James 1:4), there comes a holy confidence which "maketh not ashamed," and a sense of the divine love which has been proved in the severest ordeal which can come to human hearts and lives.

This is the glory of our great salvation, that it sustains the human heart in the trying hour. Other things will do with prosperity, health and highest happiness, but Christ has this supreme glory, that His grace shines most conspicuously when everything else fails, and that the Christian's brightest hours are often those that are overshadowed by earth's heaviest trials.

THE ASSURANCE OF GOD'S LOVE

> God has poured out his love into our hearts by the Holy Spirit, whom he has given us. . . .
> Since we have now been justified by his blood, how much more shall we be saved from God's wrath through him! For if, when we were God's enemies, we were reconciled to him through the death of his Son, how much more, having been reconciled, shall we be saved through his life! (Romans 5:5b, 9–10)

There is a revelation of the love of God in the moment of conversion through the grace of Jesus Christ and the promise of salvation. But there is a deeper experience of the divine love which comes to the soul after it has been proved and tried and brought into the intimacy of His fellowship. This comes from the Holy Spirit pouring out the love of God into the heart.

There are atmospheres in Christian life that greatly differ. Some of God's children live in a cellar all their days, where the light is dim and the air damp; others live in shaded rooms and dim light, where the sun seldom shines; but others dwell in the very sunlight of God's perfect love. The element of their being is not duty, conscience, doctrine, intellectual conviction or even Christian work, but divine love—the sweet, mellow, warm air of the Father's house and the Father's heart, the love of God poured out into the heart like the warm sunshine by the Holy Spirit abiding in the heart, and dwelling ever on God's glorious gift and everlasting pledge of His perfect love, His own beloved Son.

Others talk about their love, "But God demonstrates his own love for us in this: While we were still sinners, Christ died for us" (5:8).

THE LIFE OF CHRIST IN US

"How much more shall we be saved from God's wrath through him!" (5:9b). The grace of Christ is the starting point of Christian life and the ground of our justification, but the life of Christ, our risen Lord, is the source of our spiritual life. His intercession for us at God's right hand and His indwelling life in our hearts bring to us the strength and grace that keep us day by day and carry us victoriously through all our pressures and trials.

Faith in a crucified Savior alone may give earnestness and depth to our

Christian life, but it is only the revelation of a living Christ that can elevate us to the heights of grace and inspire us with the strength we need for victorious living.

We are saved by His faith in a very real and precious sense, but in a yet more glorious manner we are saved by His life.

JOY IN GOD

Then the climax of all these blessings is reached in the 11th verse when he says, "But we also rejoice in God through our Lord Jesus Christ, through whom we have now received reconciliation [atonement, KJV]." This is a different joy from that meant in the third verse. There the joy is based upon a thing, here it is drawn from a person. There it is the joy that springs from the hope of our coming glory, here it is joy in God Himself, through our reconciliation to Him and our fellowship with Him.

This word *atonement* means literally "at-one-ment." It denotes not only our reconciliation to God but, we believe, denotes also our being brought into perfect harmony with God in all His will and introduced to such perfect fellowship that we have His very own joy in our heart and life.

This is the joy that is not subject to vicissitudes, nor influenced by circumstances. It springs from the very heart of God Himself, and is as eternal as His own blessedness.

Now these are the blessings of the justified, and with such a catalog of glorious things the apostle finally sums up the chapter by a magnificent contrast between Adam and Christ, and the fall of man through the former, and his redemption through the second Adam, the Lord Jesus.

He gives us the points in which they agree. In both cases the consequences came through a single individual. Our ruin comes from Adam, our redemption comes through Christ.

Again, in both cases, the consequences spring from a single act. By one act of disobedience Adam ruined his posterity, by one act of atonement Christ redeemed His.

Again, in both cases, the acts of the individual descend to his posterity. Adam wrecked his whole race by disobedience, Christ saved His spiritual seed by His atonement, and so the verse is true, "For as in Adam all die, so in Christ all will be made alive" (1 Corinthians 15:22).

There are two generations in the world, the Adam race and the Christ race, and we all belong either to one or the other. We have received our natural life from Adam; but if we are born from above, we are the seed of Christ, and are partakers of His obedience and His life.

Then he contrasts these two heads of humanity:

a. One has brought a heritage of sin, the other has brought a divine righteousness. "For just as through the disobedience of the one man the many were made sinners, so also through the obedience of the one man the many will be made righteous" (Romans 5:19).

b. One has brought us condemnation, the other has brought us justification. "Consequently, just as the result of one trespass was condemnation for all men, so also the result of one act of righteousness was justification that brings life for all men" (5:18).

c. One has brought us death, the other, life. So we read that, "For if by the trespass of the one man, death reigned through that one man, how much more will those who receive God's abundant provision of grace and of the gift of righteousness reign in life through the one man, Jesus Christ" (5:17).

d. The consequences of Christ's redemption are greater than the consequences of Adam's sin and fall, for "where sin increased, grace increased all the more, so that, just as sin reigned in death, so also grace might reign through righteousness to bring eternal life through Jesus Christ our Lord" (5:20b–21).

This is true in the fact that the redemption of Christ elevated humanity to a much higher place than Adam could ever have inherited for most of his posterity.

Christ has not come to restore the saved to Adamic purity or an Eden paradise. The holiness that Jesus gives is far higher than the holiness that Adam knew. It is that we should be partakers of the divine nature, and the glory to which He raises us is transcendently greater than paradise restored.

A single redeemed man in the glory of the ages to come will be higher than the whole human race could have been in the Adamic life, and the number of the redeemed will be vaster, no doubt, than all that ever have been or ever shall be lost. The day is doubtless coming when the myriads of planets that sweep across the immensities of space shall be colonized—yes, ruled by ransomed man—and all the universe shall be a monument to the grandeur of Christ's redemption.

In a more individual sense it is also true that grace superabounds over sin in every life that fully yields itself to Christ. God loves to take the most lost of men and make them the most magnificent memorials of His redeeming love and power. He loves to take the victims of Satan's hate, and the lives that have been the most fearful examples of his power to destroy, and use them to illustrate and illuminate the possibilities of divine mercy and the new creations of the Holy Spirit.

He loves to take the things in our own lives that have been the worst, the hardest and the most hostile to God, and transform them so that we shall be the opposites of our former selves.

The sweetest spirits are made out of the most stormy and self-willed; the mightiest faith is created out of a wilderness of doubts and fears; and the most divine love is transformed out of some heart of hate and selfishness.

Boanerges becomes John, Jacob becomes Israel, Simon the son of Jonas becomes the lowly and glorious apostle, crucified with downward head.

The grace of God is equal to the most uncongenial temperaments, to the most unfavorable circumstances; and its glory is to transform a curse into a blessing and show to men and angels of ages yet to come that "where sin increased, grace increased all the more" (5:20b).

CHAPTER 7

SANCTIFICATION THROUGH DEATH AND RESURRECTION

In the same way, count yourselves dead to sin but alive to God in Christ Jesus. Therefore do not let sin reign in your mortal body so that you obey its evil desires. (Romans 6:11–13)

In this chapter, the apostle begins the third section of his epistle. In the first section he gave us the picture of sin; in the second, of salvation through the righteousness of God and the atonement of Christ, received by faith, and brings us into a state of justification. In the third section, he deals with sanctification.

He begins by asking: "Shall we go on sinning so that grace may increase?" (Romans 6:1). And he answers the question at the very outset by a tremendous "By no means!" (6:2).

We will notice that from this time he uses the singular number in speaking about sin. In the earlier picture he spoke of our *sins*—our acts of sin. "For all have sinned and come short of the glory of God" (3:23). But now he speaks of sin, the state and character of evil from which all our acts spring, as the miasma exhales from a fetid marsh, as the water flows from an unclean fountain.

Justification deals with our *sins*, but sanctification deals with our *sin*. God can forgive *sins*, but *sin* He can never forgive nor tolerate. It must be destroyed and removed, and the very idea of continuing in sin is met at the threshold by the solemn "By no means!" (6:2), which requires from every follower of Christ that "holiness [without which] no one will see the Lord" (Hebrews 12:14).

But how is this deliverance from sin to be brought about? The answer involves three points, which the apostle unfolds in these three chapters.

1. We are sanctified, not by the improvement of the old nature, but by its death and the resurrection life of the Lord Jesus Christ, instead.

2. We are sanctified, not by our old master, the law, or by any efforts or struggles of our own, but by the free gift and grace of the Lord Jesus Christ, and through union with Christ alone.

3. We are sanctified by the indwelling life and power of the Holy Spirit in us and filling our spirit, soul and body with the life of Jesus Christ.

It is on the first of these points that we shall dwell at present, as it is unfolded in the first portion of the sixth chapter of Romans. In developing this thought, the apostle presents a number of points with great logical force and clearness.

BAPTISM

1. The principle of death and resurrection is set forth in the symbol of Christian baptism. "Or don't you know that all of us who were baptized into Christ Jesus were baptized into his death?" (6:3).

This, then, is the true meaning of baptism. It is the appropriate symbol of death and resurrection, and not only of death, but of a death so definite and final that it is followed by burial, so that the old life is out of sight forever, and we are detached from it as thoroughly as the soul is separated from the body that lies in the grave.

NATURE

2. The same principle is again set forth in the symbol of planting. "If we have been united with him like this in his death, we will certainly also be united with him in his resurrection" (6:5).

This is Christ's own chosen figure to represent His own resurrection. "Unless a kernel of wheat falls to the ground and dies, it remains only a single seed. But if it dies, it produces many seeds" (John 12:24).

Nature is full of this principle of death and resurrection. Every springtime reiterates it, every harvest springs from it, every flower and tree proclaims it. The little seed must disappear, corrupt and die, and out of its bosom come the germs of life and fruitfulness. That is God's parable of true spiritual life.

THE CROSS

3. The death of Jesus Christ on the cross laid the foundation of our death and resurrection. When He was offered up on Calvary, it was not only for our sins, but for our sinfulness. In Him we were recognized by God as hanging on that cross with Him, and dying when He died, so that His death represents our death, and when we recognize it, appropriate it and identify ourselves with it, it becomes the same as if we had been crucified and our old life had gone out with His. "For we know that our old self was crucified with him so that the body of sin might be done away with, that we should

no longer be slaves to sin—because anyone who has died has been freed from sin" (Romans 6:6–7).

APPROPRIATING FAITH

4. There must be, on our part, a definite appropriation of Christ's death for our sanctification, and a committal of ourselves to Him in death and resurrection.

While the death of Christ is available for all who will claim it, it is effectual only to those who do claim it. It is necessary, therefore, that we make this an actual fact in our experience and yield ourselves unto death with Christ; then it becomes a fact in our life and the Holy Spirit makes that which we have reckoned, real in our own experience.

There must be a definite planting of the seed in the ground. There must be an actual yielding of the life to be crucified with Christ. There is a moment when we consent to die and pronounce sentence of death upon ourselves, and then God executes it and reckons it to us when we have claimed it for ourselves. Now it is assumed by the apostle that we do this in our baptism. This is the real meaning of baptism in its deepest significance, and it is taken for granted that all who are baptized enter into this experience.

The fact is, however, that many do not take in baptism all that it really means and it becomes to them only an acknowledgment of salvation and a confession of Christ for the forgiveness of sins.

In the divine plan, sanctification is closely connected with justification and assumed as immediately following it. The fact is that in the Christian life of many persons it comes at a later period. But this is not God's intention and, therefore, the New Testament assumes that sanctification is to accompany or immediately follow the first action of faith. This is what really did occur with the first disciples on the day of Pentecost. As soon as they had received Jesus, they also received the Holy Spirit, and this should be the experience of all Christians. But with many persons this is not their experience. They are baptized into Christ for the forgiveness of their sins and at a later period they come to receive the Holy Spirit as their Deliverer from indwelling sin.

In this chapter, however, it is spoken of as something immediately connected with their baptism and to which that act committed them. In any case, it is a definite act and must have a clearly marked point of time in the experience of every sanctified soul.

Beloved, have we thus passed sentence of death upon ourselves? Have we committed ourselves to death with Christ? Have we made that definite and complete surrender which brings to us the power of His death and separates us from our former self?

DEAD TO SIN

5. Through this definite act of committal and the effect of Christ's death, which it appropriates, we become dead to sin.

Now let us understand exactly this Scriptural expression. It is not said that sin is dead—by no means. Sin is very far from dead. It surrounds us on every side like the dark and murky atmosphere, like an overflowing flood. But we are dead to sin.

What is dead? Is it a part of us? Is it one of our natures that is dead? Is it some principle in us that is dead? Is it the evil in us that is dead? No, *you* are dead, the whole of you. The old man as an individual—the person—is as if he were not the same person any more, but had passed out of existence and another person had been born from above and dropped right out of heaven to earth instead. "I have been crucified with Christ" (Galatians 2:20a)—not my sin or my sinful nature, but "I," the old man, the former individual. Both good and bad have died alike, my strength and my weakness, my sin and my self-sufficiency, my good qualities and my bad; and "I no longer live, but Christ lives in me" (2:20b).

RECKONING

6. The act of self-surrender must be followed by the attitude of reckoning. Having taken this position, we must adjust ourselves to it and henceforth abide in it. We must not be everlastingly getting crucified over again and going through a continual reconsecration and recrucifixion, but we must count it once for all done and finished, and we must steadily reckon that it is so, in spite of how it might seem.

Here is the very crucial point and secret of its power. It is in the reckoning that the secret of our strength will always be found. And so we read:

> For we know that since Christ was raised from the dead, he cannot die again; death no longer has mastery over him. The death he died, he died to sin once for all; but the life he lives, he lives to God.
> In the same way, count yourselves dead to sin but alive to God in Christ Jesus. (Romans 6:9–11)

Here it is very plain that the apostle recognized our crucifixion as being as definite and complete as Christ's, and accepted once for all; that we are not to be always getting crucified, that there is a fatal power in the doubting to bring back the old man to life.

Now we are touching here an important and extraordinary principle, both in nature and in grace. We become what we count ourselves. Let even a child begin to consider itself base and wicked and it will soon grow reckless and bad.

There is a strange story in modern fiction of a man who lived two lives, one mean and horrible and the other noble and lofty. At certain times a spell was thrown over him and he considered himself another man, and while that consciousness was upon him he acted like this man in every way, and was just as base, sordid and vile as his ideal. He feared this awful influence, and when it came upon him he was filled with horror and dismay and tried in vain to resist it. At other times he counted himself the other man; then he was noble, just the opposite of his former self.

"For as [a man] thinketh in his heart so is he" (Proverbs 23:7, KJV). The consciousness of guilt degrades a man. The fear of evil paralyzes the soul. The sense of innocency elevates the purpose.

Let that woman feel that she is a true wife, and all her womanhood is exalted. But let the thought come into her mind that she is degraded and in a wrong relationship; let her find that she is not a wife, and immediately the consciousness of wrong defiles her and fills her with shame and every temptation of sin.

Therefore God has fortified us in our new life by the spirit of faith against the power of evil. He allows us to take a stand in Christ, and then the Holy Spirit makes it an actual experience, and gives us faith to hold fast to it, and abide in the consciousness of it, that it may cleanse and elevate our whole being.

"But," you say, "how can I reckon myself dead, when I find myself continually filled with the old thoughts, suggestions and incitements to sin?" Ah, beloved, it is just here the power of reckoning comes in. When the old self seems to return, refuse to recognize it as yourself, and that attitude will destroy it. When the corpse insists on rising from the grave and thrusting itself upon your consciousness, let the wand of faith wave over it and bid it back to its grave, and it will return to its place in the cemetery of the soul.

We know that in modern spiritualism the faces of the dead sometimes seem to return and speak to their friends in living tones, and thousands of the dupes of spiritualism believe that these faces are really alive and represent the fathers, mothers and friends who have died. But we know this is not true. The man who died a year ago is still in his grave, and were you to go out to yonder cemetery you would find his dust. This is a delusion painted by the devil on the mind. Treat it as an illusion and it will vanish; but talk to it, believe it, and it will stay and have the same influence upon you as if the dead man were really before you.

So when your old self comes back, if you listen to it, fear it and believe it, it will have the same influence upon you as if it were not dead; it will control you and destroy you. But if you will ignore it and say, "You are not I, but Satan trying to make me believe that the old self is not dead. I refuse you, I treat you as a demon power outside of me, I detach myself from you!" If you treat it as a wife would her divorced husband, saying: "You are nothing to me; you have no power over me. I have renounced you; in the name of Jesus I bid you hence"—lo! the evil things will disappear, the shadow will vanish, the wand of faith will lay the troubled spirit and send it back to the abyss, and you will find that Christ is there instead, with His risen life to back up your confidence and seal your victory.

Satan can stand anything better than neglect. If you ignore him he gets disgusted and disappears. Jesus used to turn His back upon him and say, "Get behind me, Satan!" (Matthew 16:23). So let us refuse him, and we shall find that he will be compelled to act according to our faith.

In the early annals of the Church, Mr. Jamieson tells us, there was a beautiful Christian girl in Antioch whom a wicked man sought to seduce. For this purpose he employed a magician and sent him to practice upon her mind his devilish arts and throw over her the spell of unholy thoughts and passions. This wicked man himself became enamoured of the fair Christian maiden and, proving false to his employer, tried to win her for himself; and by some diabolical dealing he succeeded in injecting into her mind thoughts, feelings and imaginations to which she was an utter stranger.

She found, to her horror, that she was entertaining thoughts and feelings from which her pure inner spirit recoiled but was utterly unable to cast out. Gradually she became discouraged and wondered if her own heart was growing impure under this hideous influence which almost mastered her and made her reckless.

At last she went in her distress to her pastor, the good Bishop of Antioch, and told her story. Then he told her this was not her sin at all and explained to her that it was simply a temptation of the evil one; that these feelings were not her own but entirely foreign to her, and that if she so treated them they would have no power over her. He instructed her to refuse them and treat them as the thoughts of Satan or of some other mind, and stand against them in the consciousness of her own purity and innocence. As she did so she found the visions vanished; the Holy Spirit filled her and she rose to a strength she had not known before.

Soon the man who had been exercising his vile arts upon her was quite broken down and came to her and confessed his sin and told her that from the moment when she took her new stand that he felt that his power was broken and that a mightier power was crushing him.

Beloved, "this is the victory that has overcome the world, even our faith" (1 John 5:4b). Let us abide in our reckoning and God will make it real.

THE LIFE SIDE

7. But we must not be always dealing with death. Sanctification is not

merely the death of the old but the resurrection life of the new. And so we read also, "If we have been united with him like this in his death, we will certainly also be united with him in his resurrection" (Romans 6:5). "Just as Christ was raised from the dead through the glory of the Father, we too may live a new life" (6:4). "In the same way, count yourselves dead to sin but alive to God in Christ Jesus" (6:11). The death is for a moment, but the life is forevermore. The death is one act, the life is a perpetual succession of acts and experiences.

Some people are always living in the atmosphere of the cemetery, and carrying about with them the smell of the mold. God would have us get through with the death, as Jesus did, and dwell in the life forevermore, "For we know that since Christ was raised from the dead, he cannot die again; death no longer has mastery over him" (6:9).

Just as we have to yield ourselves to the death by a definite act and follow it up by a constant attitude of reckoning, so we must take Christ as our life by a definite appropriation and must retain Him by continual recognition.

It is not that we feel ourselves living, because the life is not in our feelings. "For you died, and your life is now hidden with Christ in God" (Colossians 3:3). We do not always feel it or say it. We just have it laid up in Him and transferred to us, and we are continually counting upon it and claiming it, going forth in dependence upon it, reckoning upon it as we would draw upon our bank and expect the draft to be honored; and as we do so, we find that the life is supplied to us through Him, and we are enabled to overcome in all the situations of our life.

YIELD

8. There is yet one more step in this beautiful progression, and that is the habitual yielding of ourselves to God in the new attitude of dependence and obedience. "Offer yourseves to God, as those who have been brought from death to life; and offer the parts of your body to him as instruments [or, weapons] of righteousness" (Romans 6:13b).

Now the yielding spoken of here is not at all the act of surrender by which we consecrate ourselves to God to be sanctified. That is all presupposed as over and past. We have now come into the attitude of death and resurrection. The yielding is subsequent to this and its true consequence. We have become united to Christ in His death and resurrection, and we should now simply act accordingly in all the details of life as they come to us from day to day. As a wife who has been married to her husband now takes a new attitude and yields herself to him in obedience and affection, so we, now standing to Christ in a new relation, habitually, constantly, moment by moment, yield ourselves to Him for each member in detail to be used for His will, service and glory.

Now this is not yielding ourselves that we may be crucified, that we may be purified, that we may be chastened, that we may accept the sword which cuts deep into our being; but it is yielding ourselves as those that are already dead—and now alive from the dead—for self-forgetting service and holy obedience.

It is a very different thing to yield yourself that you may die, and to yield yourself as one that is alive from the dead. The one is yielding yourself to the surgeon's knife for the operation, the other is volunteering as a soldier for service and duty.

God wants us in the attitude of service, and out of the attitude of self-consciousness. There is nothing more distressing than to be continually watching your sanctification and nursing your spiritual state, or superintending your growth and living in the hospital of an invalid experience. And there is nothing so wholesome as leaving yourself with Christ, pressing on in self-forgetting service to glorify God and save others.

The very expression used here, "weapons," implies the opposite of a subjective state. Our attitude is an aggressive one. We have taken the sword of God into our own believing and consecrated hands, and yielded ourselves unto Him to possess us, fill us and make the best of us. We are going forth at His command, in His will, for His glory, and the very unselfishness of the whole situation has in it the most sanctifying and elevating power.

Beloved, so let us die, so let us live, so let us reckon, so let us yield, so let us prove all the fullness of this wonderful divine method of sanctification through death and resurrection by Jesus Christ our Lord.

CHAPTER 8

SANCTIFICATION BY THE GRACE OF GOD

For sin shall not be your master, because you are not under law, but under grace. (Romans 6:14)

So, my brothers, you also died to the law through the body of Christ, that you might belong to another, to him who was raised from the dead, in order that we might bear fruit to God. (7:4)

These passages express the great truth underlying the seventh chapter of Romans and constituting the second section of Paul's treatise on sanctification. His first principle was that it is to be death and resurrection, not through the old man—man's improvement—but through a new life received through the resurrection of Jesus Christ. His second principle is that it is not through the old master—the law—or any of our struggles and efforts, but through our union with the Lord Jesus Christ as our new husband, and the life directly imparted by Him bringing forth fruit unto us, unto holiness and God.

SECTION I—*Our Death to the Old Husband, the Law*

He first gives us a picture of our marriage to the law, personated here as a husband, just but severe. "The sinful passions aroused by the law were at work in our bodies, so that we bore fruit for death" (Romans 7:5b). This is a very vivid metaphor based on the marriage relation, and expressing the strong workings of sinful passions awakened in us by the law, and yielding the offspring of wickedness and sin. This was through no fault of the law; our old husband is described not as unjust or cruel, but as wholly just and good. But we were unholy, and everything awakened in us partook of our evil nature and developed our sin. The more the law reproved our evil desires, the more they increased, so that even that which was good was made

71

evil unto us. This old husband, while good and just, was obliged to be severe by his very justice. Had we been always right, he would have been always kind, and rewarded us with his smile and favors; but by his very nature he was bound to condemn our sin and punish us with inexorable severity. There was nothing of mercy, and he makes no allowance whatever for failure; the slightest deviation from the law will bring inevitable punishment.

There is no more pathetic illustration of the rigor of the law than the story of Moses himself, the founder of the law. Once only, in his beautiful and almost blameless life, he broke his own law, and the result was that he lost the promised land. There could be no exception made; he must himself be an example of its inexorable righteousness, and so for that one disobedience he was excluded from the inheritance for which he had suffered so much to lead his people.

And so in this picture we see the law sternly condemning the sin from which it could not save. Our old husband could tell us of the right and punish us for the wrong, but he had no power to forever cleanse the evil from our nature, or give us the power to keep his own commandment; and when we disobeyed, he could do nothing but strike us down and at last slay us with the sword of his righteous judgment. This was the most merciful thing he could do, and when he killed us at the last we were at length free from his dreadful bondage. Therefore the apostle says in another place, "For through the law I died to the law so that I might live for God" (Galatians 2:19).

"For example, by law a married woman is bound to her husband as long as he is alive, but if her husband dies, she is released from the law of marriage. . . . So, my brothers, you also died to the law through the body of Christ, that you might belong to another, to him who was raised from the dead, in order that we might bear fruit to God" (Romans 7:2, 4).

In two ways we have become dead to the law; first, by the law itself telling us, and secondly, by the death of Christ for us on the cross. Jesus died on Calvary through the stroke of law, and we are recognized as having died in Him, so that we are now free from our old husband, and our obligations are entirely to another, even the Lord Jesus. Therefore we should not seek to be sanctified by the law, or look for spiritual improvement apart from Jesus Christ, our true Husband, and the only source of our true light.

The law represents not only the Ten Commandments, but everything that is based on our own efforts and our own strength. The law represents what man can do, and grace what God can do. Sanctification is wholly the gift of God's grace as much as justification, and we shall never know the first half of our text, "For sin shall not be your master," until we know the second part, "Because you are not under the law but under grace" (6:14).

Our higher Christian life is not an attainment but an obtainment, granted as freely as the forgiveness of our sins through the blood and righteousness of Jesus Christ. It must be forever true of the garments of the bride of the Lamb, " 'Fine linen, bright and clean,/ was given her to wear.'/ (Fine linen stands for the righteous acts of the saints.)" (Revelation 19:8).

SECTION II—*Our New Husband*

The picture is a beautiful one; in Ezekiel 16 we are represented as a woman, lying in her blood at the feet of her former husband, who has bruised and beaten her for her falsity and crimes, and at last has taken her very life. There she lies, a poor, hopeless, lifeless thing. But as she lies in her blood, lo! a glorious Being passes by. It is the Son of God, the Prince of Life. He beholds her in her lifelessness and shame. He looks upon her with intense compassion. Speaking Himself of the same scene, He says: "Then I passed by and saw you kicking about in your blood, . . . Later I passed by, . . . and saw that you were old enough for love" (Ezekiel 16:6a, 8a).

His heart goes out to her in intense and almighty mercy; He touches her with His hand. He lifts her into new life. He raises her from the dead. He washes her from her blood and stains. He clothes her in His own white raiment. He adorns her with His own loveliness. He makes her beautiful through His comeliness, and then He gives her His love. He makes her His wife. He marries her to Himself, and He imparts to her all that He is and all that He has and makes her the joint heir of His glory and His kingdom. This is the beautiful figure of this passage, and this is the sublime vision that runs through the whole story of the Bible from Paradise to Patmos, from the bridal of Eve to the marriage of the Lamb.

Now, the application of this sublime figure to the subject of sanctification is very clear and intensely important. Just as sin was the fruit of our marriage with the law, so holiness is the fruit of our union with Jesus. All the duties and graces of the Christian life are personated as the daughters of a marriage, born of the love of Jesus working in our hearts, and the vital union and communion of our spirits with His bringing forth the fruit of the Spirit, which is "love, joy, peace, patience, kindness, goodness, faithfulness, gentleness and self-control" (Galatians 5:22–23). These are the children of the heavenly marriage, the daughters of the divine Bridegroom, through us His bride, by virtue of the Holy Spirit working in us and bringing us into living union with Him. This is the great mystery of the inner life. There is something here which mere intellect cannot understand and coarse materialism could only misunderstand and abuse. Back of every earthly love, back of your marriage to your husband or your wife, back of the tender affection of those two young hearts that do not even understand themselves, there is a great eternal mystery of which these things are the imperfect earthly shadows and types.

God gave you a father's love that you might understand the eternal Father; a mother's tenderness, that you might comprehend the Motherhood of the Holy Spirit; a brother's affection, that you might appreciate the Friend who sticks closer than a brother; a child's filial love, that you might know what it is to say "Abba, Father" (Romans 8:15b) to your heavenly Parent.

And so He has given to most of us some touch of the tender fondness, for which all other loves give way, the exclusive affection of two hearts for each other alone in order that through it, as by a parable and a picture, we might rise to the conception of that mightiest of all loves and most magnificent of all marriages, the eternal union between the Lord Jesus Christ and the hearts that come into His perfect fellowship and learn to call Him *Ishi*, my Husband (Hosea 2:16).

Nor can I explain, perhaps, to your satisfaction, how it is that I can feel to my Redeemer the exquisite and holy throb of love that corresponds to the marriage relation, and that enables me to look in His face and lean on His breast and pour out my heart into His and drink His Spirit into mine, as no earthly relationship can express. Yet it is so. Nor can I exactly explain how it is that once He was to me only a Savior, a Teacher and a Master, but there was a time when He became to me also a Friend and a Husband, and wakened in my heart longings, responses and delights which I had not known before. Yet it is so. And many of you know it in your deepest spirit though you could not make it plain to one that has never felt it.

Now it is this blessed and heavenly fellowship with our divine Husband which brings forth the fruit of holiness in the sanctified life. If you do not know Christ in this way you cannot know all the holiness of His sanctified grace. If you are a stranger to this experience you have yet to enter into the summerland of love. You are living in the frigid, or at best in the north temperate zone, and there are fruits and flowers that will not bloom and brighten in these northern latitudes. You must move down to the tropics, or you shall never know the sweet fragrance and rich luxuriance of the highest and deepest spiritual life.

And if you would know these things in all their fullness, the secret is not in straining and struggling, but in receiving more richly of this fullness and living more intimately in His fellowship and Bridegroom love.

> "In that day," declares the LORD,
>   "you will call me 'my husband' [*Ishi*, KJV];
>   you will no longer call me 'my master' [*Baali*, KJV]. . . .
> I will betroth you to me forever;
>   I will betroth you in righteousness and justice,
>   in love and compassion.
> I will betroth you in faithfulness,

and you will acknowledge the LORD." (2:16, 19–20)

There I will give her back her vineyards,
　　and will make the Valley of Achor a door of hope. (2:15)

It is from the place of betrothal that the vineyards come. How beautifully He says to His restored bride in the Prophet Hosea,

I will heal their waywardness and love them freely, . . .
I will be like the dew to Israel;
　　he will blossom like a lily.
Like a cedar of Lebanon he will send down his roots;
　　his young shoots will grow.
His splendor will be like an olive tree,
　　his fragrance like a cedar of Lebanon.
Men will dwell again in his shade.
　　He will flourish like the grain.
He will blossom like a vine, . . . (14:4–7a)

And then God adds, "Your fruitfulness comes from me" (14:8).

SECTION III—*The Transition*

We have one more picture in this section, viz.: the struggle of the old life under the old husband and the climax reached at last in deliverance through the revelation of Jesus Christ as our Sanctifier and Lord.

This occupies the last part of the seventh chapter of Romans. There is no portion of the Scriptures that has been such a battleground for the theology of sanctification as this. One thing, at least, is very certain about it. It is not a picture of Christian life as it ought to be, for the apostle has already decided the question in the first verse of the sixth chapter—that the life of captivity to sin, here described, is not the life the Christian ought to live. "Shall we go on sinning so that grace may increase?" (6:1) is his explicit question, and the answer is without evasion or compromise: "By no means!" (6:2).

That means God forbids a disciple of Christ to continue in sin, or be content with the life described in this chapter, and certainly Paul did not stay there even if he was there at one stage of his experience. Undoubtedly, it is a dramatic picture of a real struggle which he passed through, and through which most sanctified souls pass, in passing out of the old life into the new.

First, we have the effect of the law in revealing him himself, and convicting him of sin. He says, "Indeed I would not have known what sin was except through the law. For I would not have known what coveting really was if the law had not said, 'Do not covet.' But sin, seizing the opportunity afforded by the commandment, produced in me every kind of covetous desire. For apart from law, sin is dead" (7:7b–8). Then he goes on to tell us how the consciousness of sin was developed. "Once I was alive apart from the law" (7:9a). That is, I felt happy and right, and free from condemnation, and even from the workings of sin. But there came a change, the commandment came forbidding him to do the things that he was doing; and then, like a torrent checked or a wild beast at bay, all the strength of his evil nature asserted itself. Then he adds, "Sin sprang to life and I died" (7:9b), that is, he became conscious of all the force of evil in his heart and gave up his hope and comfort in despair.

Is not this the experience usually of the young disciple? His early experience is cloudless and delightful. He has not yet seen the depths of his own evil heart and thinks, perhaps, that there are no such depths of sin in him. But suddenly, some great sacrifice is demanded, some cherished thing is to be cut out of the life, some difficult obedience it to be performed, some secret sin is revealed; and then the whole strength of the will concentrates upon that issue and the battle is a sharp and decisive one.

The first result often is deep discouragement and he is almost ready to give up in despair and say, "I do not think I ever was a Christian." The commandment comes, sin springs to life and he dies. Then along with this revelation of sin comes the distinct recognition of an opposite principle: the new life in him through the regenerated heart which is undoubtedly there, notwithstanding the surrounding corruptions.

And so we read, "For in my inner being I delight in God's law" (7:22). This inward man which delights in the law of God is undoubtedly the new man, the regenerated soul, born from above. Notwithstanding our corruptions and struggles, let us never give up the confidence of our salvation. We are the Lord's children, although we are full of fault and blame. The nugget is genuine gold, although it is mixed with much rough rock and native ore. In due time the great Refiner will cleanse it from the dross; but be careful and do not throw it away because it still has some dross.

Next, we see the honest struggle between these two natures. The new and heaven-born heart is opposed by the old natural heart, and a terrible struggle ensues in which the good is often defeated by the evil, yet never yields its consent. "But I see another law at work in the members of my body, waging war against the law of my mind and making me a prisoner of the law of sin at work within my members" (7:23). Now, this is the struggle in which so many Christian lives spend all their earthly existence. It is an honest and earnest conflict, and God gives full credit for the intent, but looks with sorrow upon the failure which is so needless and vain.

What is the struggling soul to do? To continue the fight forever? What did Paul do? Listen: "What a wretched man I am! Who will rescue me from this body of death?" (7:24). When we can do nothing else we can at least give a good cry. When it came to the worst Paul just lifted up his voice and called for help. With his little ship sinking in the rough waters he shouted for aid. and such a cry is never heard in vain. God heard him, and a moment later, lo! the vision beyond the surf was of the white sails of the lifeboat coming to his aid with Jesus in the prow, waving His hand in encouragement and victory, while Paul answers back with a shout of triumph, "Thanks be to God—through Jesus Christ our Lord!" (7:25). And now the lifeboat is quickly attached to the sinking ship and quickly bears it across the rough waters into the open sea of peace and grace and glory into which we pass in the following chapter.

The seventh chapter of Romans is the hopeless struggle of the new heart with the old heart in a saved man. The eighth chapter of Romans is the victory of the same man over his old enemy and all others, when something is added to his life, viz.: the indwelling presence and power of Jesus Christ, and the Holy Spirit to fill him and keep him in triumph over all his foes. The closing verse of the seventh of Romans gives us the key to the whole chapter in the words, "I myself"; it is the story of what I, myself, can do, it is the best that the good self is able to accomplish, while the eighth is the best that Christ in us is able to accomplish, and the key to the eighth chapter is, "In Christ," and "Christ in [us]" (Romans 8:1, Colossians 1:27).

I, myself, can choose the right and struggle for it, but cannot fully accomplish it. With the mind I can serve the law of God, but with the flesh I will still often serve the law of sin. But when I come into the higher place of union with Christ, then "through Christ Jesus the law of the Spirit of life set me free from the law of sin and death" (Romans 8:2).

In the fifth chapter of Galatians the same conflict is described: "For the sinful nature desires what is contrary to the Spirit, and the Spirit what is contrary to the sinful nature" (5:17). Usually we spell the word "spirit" with a small "s" and that keeps us in the seventh chapter of Romans—our spirit struggling against our flesh. The true way to spell it is with a capital "S" and this takes us into the eighth chapter of Romans, and makes the struggle no longer between our spirit and our flesh, but rather between the divine Spirit and our evil nature. The battle is not ours but God's, and the victory is sure and complete; and so the apostle says in Galatians, "So I say, live by the Spirit, and you will not gratify the desires of the sinful nature" (Galatians 5:16).

In conclusion, let us sum up the whole subject. First, have we seen our need of sanctification and been convicted for the deeper work of the Holy Spirit in our hearts? Secondly, if so, let us not seek it in the wrong way—

through the works of the law and the struggles of our own will. But thirdly, let us get married to Christ and receive His life as the principle and spring of the holy desires, aspirations and attainments that we never can work out by ourselves.

A dear friend gives this rather comical but very expressive illustration of what we have been trying to explain. Two factory girls met the other day on the street and the one accosted the other with the question, "Say, Lizzie, where are you working now?" Lizzie looked at the questioner with an indescribable expression of lofty contempt and replied, "Working! Why, I am not working, I am married." She had given up working and had gotten married, and had somebody now to support her.

Well, the story has a real point: let us give up working and get married to Christ; let us cease from our struggles and receive His overflowing life and love; and then spontaneously will spring from our happy hearts and lives the fruits of holiness and the heaven-born graces of love and joy, of righteousness and service, of patience and long-suffering, which all our efforts can never attain, but which through His grace shall spring from Him and then return to Him and flow out to others in glory and blessedness.

CHAPTER 9

SANCTIFICATION THROUGH THE SPIRIT

Those controlled by the sinful nature cannot please God.
You, however, are controlled not by the sinful nature but by the Spirit, if the Spirit of God lives in you. And if anyone does not have the Spirit of Christ, he does not belong to Christ. (Romans 8:8–9)

We now come to the third section of the apostle's treatise on sanctification, in which he shows that sanctification is not through the flesh, but through the Spirit. These verses which we have just quoted contrast the two lives—the flesh and the Spirit—and declare their irreconcilable and eternal antagonism.

THE FLESH

It is very important at the outset that we understand exactly what is meant by the terms flesh and Spirit. The flesh just means our whole natural life. It is not our body, nor even our carnal nature, but the whole old man, including all that was born of Adam, spirit, soul and body. "Flesh gives birth to flesh, but the Spirit gives birth to spirit" (John 3:6). Everything born of the flesh is flesh.

Some teachers seem to leave the impression that only the material part and the soulish part of our nature are essentially wrong, and that the spiritual part is somehow higher and better; and so men have been trying to get rid of matter and soul, and get into spirit. But this is all a mistake. The natural spirit of man is just as evil as his soul, and needs just as much to be crucified and superseded by the Spirit of God. The whole of our Adam life is fleshly and must be laid down, and brought, through the death of Christ, into the resurrection life—not only the evil things in us, but those which we have accounted good. "The grass withers and the flowers fall;/ because the breath of the LORD blows on them" (Isaiah 40:7).

Not only must the corrupt flesh of Noah's time be destroyed by the flood, but even the natural affection of Abraham for his Isaac must be crucified, and then come forth, after the scene on Mount Moriah, as a resurrection love, by a new affection that had passed through the fire, and henceforth loved its object not for its own sake, or even for the sake of the object, but in and for God alone.

THE SPIRIT

What is meant by the Spirit? It means not our human spirit, but the Holy Spirit. It should be spelled with a capital "S" all through. The meaning is made very plain by the words, "You, however, are controlled not by the sinful nature [the flesh, KJV] but by the Spirit, if the Spirit of God lives in you" (Romans 8:9).

A spiritual man, then, is a man who has the Holy Spirit. There is a great difference between this and our own converted spirit. There must come a distinct epoch in every sanctified life when the converted spirit becomes the abode of the divine Spirit, and the Holy Spirit comes to reside and abide as the source of all our life and strength.

There are two sides to this abiding. In one sense the Spirit is in us, in another we are in the Spirit. It is like a great ocean into which we plunge until it is all around us and becomes the very element in which we live, but as we come into the ocean, the ocean comes into us, and fills us and overflows until it encompasses us on every side, and becomes the very element of our being.

Now, we note in this passage a very remarkable variety in the terms in which the Holy Spirit is spoken of. First, He is spoken of as the Spirit of God, then as the Spirit of Christ, and then as Christ. This is all most suggestive. The Spirit of God represents His true deity as He was revealed in the Old Testament. The Spirit of Christ represents the New Testament revelation of the Holy Spirit, as we see Him in the person of Jesus, and His deity is softened, humanized and brought nearer to us by His residence in Jesus Christ.

THE SPIRIT OF CHRIST

He is the Spirit who lived in Him, and by whom all His works were done. Jesus did not go forth to His ministry until He received the Holy Spirit, nor are we better able to go forth to any service for God without His enduing wisdom, power and love. It is delightful to know that when we receive Him, we receive the One who inspired the whole ministry of our blessed Lord, and He comes to us with a tenderness and almost a humanness which the Old Testament revelation could never bring.

But more than this: He is not only the Spirit of Christ, but He is called Christ Himself. He comes to reveal Christ and to bring His personal presence into our heart and life.

Like a divine painter He stands in the background and draws upon the canvas the face of another, even the face of Christ, and we do not see the hand that draws the picture, but only the face that He reveals.

Like a perfect telescope, He brings to us the revelation of the heavenly worlds, and as we look through the reflector, or the tube, we do not see the instrument, but only the object which it brings to us.

Therefore the indwelling of the Holy Spirit in us is practically the indwelling of Christ, and the most direct consciousness of the heart in which the Spirit dwells is of the person of Jesus rather than of the person of the Holy Spirit, although both are known to us, and it is right to commune with either or with both. It is a life in the Spirit, and it is at the same time a life in Christ. It is abiding in the fellowship of the Holy Spirit, and yet Christ speaks of it as abiding in Him.

Now these two lives are very vividly contrasted in this chapter:

SECTION I—*The Life of the Flesh*

1. Weak

It is weak: "For what the law was powerless to do in that it was weakened by the sinful nature" (8:3a). Our natural life is weak in all spiritual and natural directions. It has many high aspirations, but it is unable to accomplish them.

The poetry, philosophy and even the fine art of past ages are full of high ideals, but men have never been able to realize them. Seneca, Cicero and Marcus Aurelius could tell us of deep longings for "the true, the beautiful and the good"; Plato and Zeno could unfold many of the principles of higher ethics, but they could not reach these patterns themselves.

The marble statue, the painted canvas, the poetic dream, could idealize virtue, but the marble statues were better than the men who molded them, their poems were higher than their authors, their philosophy was purer than their lives; and they fell back from the momentary dream into the slimy depths of corruption and shame.

The worst of men often have better thoughts and resolve to break their chains, but like the Laocoon in ancient story, they sink at last, crushed in the folds of the hideous serpent that they resist in vain. "The flesh is weak" (Matthew 26:41, KJV).

2. Wicked

But it is not only weak, it is wicked. "The sinful mind is hostile [enmity, KJV] to God" (Romans 8:7a). It is not merely an enemy of God, but it is embodied, intense, unmitigated enmity. Everything in it and about it is hostile to God. It hates His law, His will, His ways, and even His plan of salvation and mercy through Jesus Christ. "It is evil, and only evil," and there is nothing really good about it.

It may have much benevolence and apparent virtue, but when it comes to direct relations with God, it always shows its malignity and its utter depravity.

3. Hateful

The flesh is not only at enmity with God, but it is hateful to God. "Those controlled by the sinful nature [the flesh, KJV] cannot please God" (8:8). God takes no pleasure in any part of the natural man. The whole Adam race, as well as the Adamic earth, is under a curse. Cain may bring his brightest offerings, the fairest flowers and the richest fruits, to the altar of Jehovah, but they will be rejected with the worshiper. They are fleshly things, born of the sin-cursed earth, and with Cain they must be rejected.

The flesh may be as beautiful as the daughter of Jairus, as she lay in her loveliness a moment after death, or as hideous as the body of Lazarus, corrupting in the grave. It matters not whether it presents itself in robes of fashion in the heated ballroom or in the ecclesiastical millinery of the ritualistic altar. It matters not whether it comes to the march of the music of the carnival of revelry and the lewd songs of the drunkard and debauched, or in the splendid choruses of the opera, oratorio or religious quartette. It is equally displeasing to God.

Its beautiful music, its eloquent sermons, its elaborate good works, its costly benevolence, as well as its filthy excesses and brutal lusts, are alike offensive and accursed in the holy eyes of Him who has sworn, "I am going to put an end to all people" (Genesis 6:13).

4. Incurably Bad

The flesh is incurably bad. "It does not submit to God's law, nor can it do so" (Romans 8:7b). It never can be any better. It is no use trying to improve the flesh. You may educate it all you please. You may train it by the most approved methods, you may set before it the brightest examples, you may pipe to it or mourn to it, treat it with encouragement or severity; its nature will always be incorrigibly the same.

Like the wild hawk which the little child captures in its infancy and tries to train in the habits of the dove, before you are aware, it will fasten its cruel beak upon the gentle fingers that would caress it, and show the old wild spirit of fear and ferocity. It is a hawk by nature, and it can never be made a dove. "The sinful mind is hostile to God. It does not submit to God's law, nor can it do so" (8:7).

The only remedy for human nature is to destroy it, and receive instead the divine nature. God does not improve man. He crucifies the natural life with Christ, and then He imparts the resurrection life of Christ and educates the new man into all the maturity of the life divine.

The strongest argument I know for eternal punishment is—eternal sin. When a lost soul gets out into the liberty of eternal sin, it will reach possibilities of wickedness that we can scarcely conceive today, and will sin enough in a single hour to condemn it for a million years.

No, if the hallowed influences of Christianity and the Holy Spirit do not bring men to God, the atmosphere of perdition will certainly accomplish less. The wretched soul will grow more miserable and more malignant through the everlasting ages, and "evil men and impostors will go from bad to worse, deceiving and being deceived" (2 Timothy 3:13).

SECTION II—*The Life of the Spirit*

In contrast with the flesh, this chapter unfolds the fruits of the indwelling Spirit in the believer's life.

1. No Condemnation

There is no condemnation: "Therefore, there is now no condemnation for those who are in Christ Jesus" (Romans 8:1). This is essential to progress in holiness. We must keep in the light of God's love and the full assurance of His acceptance if we would grow in grace; but it is not until we receive the Holy Spirit and come into this deeper union with Christ, expressed by the phrase "unto Christ," that we pass out of condemnation and begin to live in the perpetual light of His countenance. The unsanctified soul is always getting into condemnation; it is ever sinning and repenting and trying to come out from under the shadow of God's displeasure.

But when we receive the indwelling Spirit, the first effect is to lift us into a life of perpetual peace and the unbroken consciousness of God's acceptance, approval and love. Henceforth it is true of us, "The sun will no more be your light by day,/ nor will the brightness of the moon shine on you,/ for the LORD will be your everlasting light,/ and your God will be your glory" (Isaiah 60:19). "So now I have sworn not to be angry with you,/ never to rebuke you again" (54:9).

2. Deliverance

There is deliverance from the power of indwelling sin: "Because through Christ Jesus the law of the Spirit of life set me free from the law of sin and death" (Romans 8:2).

Two laws are mentioned here. The first is the law of sin and death. It is that principle in our fallen nature which operates with the power and uniformity of a law and leads us to sin and death. We are unable to resist this law through the mere force of our human will. But we put the natural law under its opposite, viz.: the spiritual life in Christ Jesus. That is the life of Jesus Christ brought into our heart by the Holy Spirit and operating there as a new law of divine strength and vitality, and counteracting, overcoming and lifting us above the old law of sin and death.

Let me illustrate these two laws by a simple comparison. Sitting at my desk by the law of gravitation my hand naturally falls upon the desk, attracted downward by the natural law which makes heavy bodies fall to the earth.

But there is a stronger law than the law of gravitation—my own life and will. So through the operation of this higher law—the law of my vitality—I defy the law of gravitation, and lift my hand and hold it above its former resting place and move it at my will. The law of vitality has made me free from the law of gravitation.

Precisely so the indwelling life of Christ Jesus, operating with the power of the law, lifts me above and counteracts the power of sin in my fallen nature.

This is the secret of sanctification. It is not so much the expulsion of sin, as the incoming of the Holy Spirit, which has broken the control which sin formerly exercised, lifting me into an entirely new sphere of holy life and victory.

3. Practical Righteousness

There is practical righteousness: "in order that the righteous requirements of the law might be fully met in us, who do not live according to the sinful nature but according to the Spirit" (8:4). Sanctification is not a mere sentiment or interior experience, but it leads to practical righteousness, or fulfillment of the law in our heart and life, so that we walk according to the Spirit and fulfill the righteousness of the law.

The difference between this and the Old Testament morality is that the righteousness of the law is fulfilled *in* us first, and then *by* us in practical obedience.

4. Habitual Obedience

There is habitual obedience: "Those who live in accordance with the Spirit have their minds set on [do mind, KJV] what the Spirit desires" (8:5b). We can all remember the time when our mother used to say to us, "Now, mind what I say. Mind your work, mind my words and orders." That meant, of course, that we were to set our mind upon it, to give diligent heed to it, and carefully to obey her wishes in everything.

So in our spiritual life we are to mind the Holy Spirit, our true mother—and to hearken and obey in all things.

5. Life and Peace

This indwelling life of the Spirit brings us life and peace: "The mind of sinful man is death, but the mind controlled by the Spirit is life and peace" (8:6).

This literally means, "the minding of the Spirit is life and peace." This life in the Holy Spirit brings us divine peace and an overflowing life, full of the deep consciousness of God's approval, presence and blessing. It is, indeed, a sweet and happy life, where we "come in and go out, and find pasture" (John 10:9), and our Shepherd makes us lie down in green pastures and leads us beside the waters of rest, anointing our head with oil and making our cup overflow (Psalm 23:2, 5).

6. Physical Healing

It brings us physical healing and quickening: "And if the Spirit of him who raised Jesus from the dead is living in you, he who raised Christ from the dead will also give life to [quicken, KJV] your mortal bodies through his Spirit, who lives in you" (Romans 8:11).

There is no doubt that this passage refers to the life of the Spirit in our body. It is the mortal body that is here spoken of and it means the present body, liable to death, and cannot mean the dead body at the time of the resurrection. It is the Spirit who now dwells in us that quickens us while He dwells, and the quickening here described is not the raising from the dead of the lifeless corpse; the word literally means the exhilarating and reviving of the life that is not extinct, but exhausted and waning. It is applied to Abraham in the fourth chapter, referring to the quickening of his exhausted energy, in order that Isaac might be begotten when he himself was past age.

Now, this divine quickening of our mortal frame is one of the privileges of our life in the Spirit. It is only for those in whom the Spirit dwells, not as an occasional visitor, but as an abiding Guest.

There may be many a poor home that you often visit, but when you come to live in a house and make it your home, you are very likely to repair what needs repairing to make it clean and comfortable, renewing the broken windows and leaking roof, and regarding it as your healthful and happy home.

Now while the Holy Spirit only visits you at times, He will not undertake to alter the dwelling, but if you give Him the keys and make it His home, He will make it a home worthy of Himself and of you. He will make it a blessed home, and bring His retinue of heavenly beings to make it a little picture of heaven.

7. Mortification

It brings the mortifying of our members: "If by the Spirit you put to death the misdeeds of the body, you will live" (8:13b). The Holy Spirit is the only One who can kill us and keep us dead. Many Christians try to do this disagreeable work themselves, and are going through a continual crucifixion, but they can never accomplish the work permanently. This is the work of the Holy Spirit, and when you really yield yourself to the death, it is delightful to find how sweetly He can slay you.

Some modern legislatures have adopted electricity as the mode of capital punishment, and by the touch of the dynamic spark, they tell us, life is extinguished almost without a quiver of pain. But however this may be in natural things, we know the Holy Spirit can touch with celestial fire the surrendered thing and slay it in a moment, after it is really yielded up to the sentence of death. That is our business, and it is God's business to execute that sentence and to keep it constantly operative.

Let us not live in the ways of perpetual and ineffectual suicide, but reckoning ourselves dead indeed, let us leave ourselves in the hands of the blessed Holy Spirit, and He will slay whatever rises in opposition to His will, and keep us true to our heavenly reckoning and filled with His resurrection life.

8. Divine Guidance

Divine guidance is the next privilege of our life in the Spirit: "Because those who are led by the Spirit of God are sons of God" (8:14). He guides us, counsels us, points out our way and sweetly leads us in it.

9. Sonship

Another privilege is the witness of our sonship. "For you did not receive a spirit that makes you a slave again to fear, but you received the Spirit of sonship. And by him we cry, 'Abba, Father' " (8:15).

The Holy Spirit brings us into a more intimate and childlike consciousness of our sonship. The word "Abba, Father" is the same as our "Papa," and expresses a very tender filial affection.

The indwelling life of the Holy Spirit brings us out of the distance and the dread of our old life into the very bosom of the Father, and enables us to cry instinctively, with the simplicity of a child, "Abba, Father!"

Many Christians are living as servants, rather than as sons, and in the Old Testament, rather than the New; but it is the mission of the Holy Spirit so to unite us to Jesus and bring Him into our hearts that we become identical with Him in His sonship and look up to the Father with the same love and trust that He feels—His Father and our Father, His God and our God.

10. Spirit of Hope

The next effect of the Holy Spirit is, to awaken in us the Spirit of hope:

> I consider that our present sufferings are not worth comparing with the glory that will be revealed in us. The creation waits in eager expectation for the sons of God to be revealed. For the creation was subjected to frustration, not by its own choice, but by the will of the one who subjected it, in hope that the creation itself will be liberated from its bondage to decay and brought into the glorious freedom of the children of God.
> We know that the whole creation has been groaning as in the pains of childbirth right up to the present time. Not only so, but we ourselves, who have the firstfruits of the Spirit, groan inwardly as we wait eagerly for our adoption as sons, the redemption of our bodies. For in this hope we were saved. But hope that is seen is no hope at all. Who hopes for what he already has? But if we hope for what we do not yet have, we wait for it patiently. (8:18–25)

This splendid passage unfolds the attitude which we, along with the "whole creation," sustain toward the coming of our Lord. We "wait in eager expectation" and a mighty hope, and with groanings and travailings of Spirit, for the redemption of our body and of the whole creation from the bondage of corruption, into the glorious liberty of the children of God. And this mighty hope enables us not only to endure "our present sufferings" but to triumph over them, and regard them as "not worth comparing with the glory that will be revealed in us."

Such a hope must be born of the Holy Spirit, and when He comes in His fullness into the consecrated heart, this is one of His most blessed operations.

Then it becomes not a theory, not a doctrine of the Lord's coming, but a personal hope of unspeakable sweetness and power, influencing and controlling all our life, and lifting us above our trials and our fears.

11. Firstfruits

The Holy Spirit prepares us for the coming of the Lord and to be among "the firstfruits" at His appearing. There is a remarkable expression here which has a deeper meaning than appears on the surface: "We ourselves, who have the firstfruits of the Spirit" (8:23).

It means that the Holy Spirit is preparing a first company of holy and consecrated hearts for the coming of the Lord and the gathering of His saints, and that these will be followed later by the larger company of all the saved.

There is a first resurrection, in which the blessed and holy shall have part, and for this He is preparing all who are willing to receive Him in His fullness. This is the happy privilege of those who receive the fullness of the Holy Spirit, that they are called and qualified for the marriage of the Lamb, and trained to form part of His Bride. Transcendent honor! Unspeakable privilege! May God enable us to have a part in this blessed hope!

12. Ministry of Prayer

The Holy Spirit helps us in the ministry of prayer: "In the same way, the Spirit helps us in our weakness. We do not know what we ought to pray for, but the Spirit himself intercedes for us with groans that words cannot express. And he who searches our hearts knows the mind of the Spirit, because the Spirit intercedes for the saints in accordance with God's will" (8:26–27).

The Holy Spirit becomes to the consecrated heart the Spirit of intercession. We have two advocates. We have an Advocate with the Father, who prays for us at God's right hand; but the Holy Spirit is the Advocate within, who prays in us, inspiring our petitions and presenting them, through Christ, to God.

We need this Advocate. We know not what to pray for, and we know not how to pray as we ought, but He breathes in the holy heart the desires that we may not always understand and the groanings which we could not ourselves utter nor comprehend.

But God understands, and He, with a loving Father's heart, is always searching our hearts to find the Spirit's prayer, and to answer it in blessing. He does not wait until the prayer is formally presented, but He searches the heart and finds many a prayer there that we have not discovered, and answers many a cry that we never understood. And when we reach our home and read the records of life, we shall better know and appreciate the infinite love of that divine Friend, who has watched within as the Spirit of prayer, and breathed out our every need to the heart of God, and of that Heavenly Father who, waiting to be gracious, has so often fulfilled His own great promise, "Before they call I will answer;/ while they are still speaking I will hear" (Isaiah 65:24).

Such are some of the steps in the life we may live in the Holy Spirit. It is indeed a glorious life, and it is the privilege of all who will cease from themselves and receive the Holy Spirit and the blessed Christ He brings to abide in them and live out His own blessed life in their mortal bodies.

Let us receive the Holy Spirit. Let us mind Him. Let us obey Him. Let us be led by Him, and let us follow on in all His perfect will until we reach the fullness of our spiritual maturity and are prepared for the coming dispensation, with its larger developments and grander prospects and possibilities.

CHAPTER 10

DIVINE PROVIDENCE

And we know that in all things God works for the good of those who love him, who have been called according to his purpose. (Romans 8:28)

This passage begins the fourth section of the Epistle to the Romans. The theme of this section is the providence of God, first, respecting the individual Christian, and then, as it has reference to nations and communities, especially the Hebrew nation. This larger view of the subject is discussed in the ninth, 10th and 11th chapters of this great epistle. The last 12 verses of the eighth chapter are devoted to the unfolding of God's special providence respecting His own children.

FOR HIS SAINTS

1. The standpoint from which we are to regard the providence of God is first presented with great clearness, and it is a point of much significance and solemnity. God's providence is not the same to every person, and it is not promiscuously true that all things work together for good; but it is only to "those who love him, who have been called according to his purpose" (8:28).

It is very much like looking at an immense army, splendidly uniformed, equipped, mounted and armed, and led by a masterly general. The feelings with which we could look at such an army would depend very much upon which side we were on. If they were our friends we would look at them with pride and confidence; but if we were on the opposing side their very strength and splendor could only fill us with dismay.

We are to look in this connection at the majestic armies of God's providence, which move through all the earth in constant obedience to His will and pursuance of His plans; but they will either be a terror or a joy, according as we are on God's side or against Him.

There is no more cruel delusion than to preach to people indiscriminately that everything is all right anyhow, and is going to come out right at last. There is nothing more really unkind than to stand by the bed of sickness or the bier of death and speak honeyed and idle words of consolation when God is speaking in terrible tones of warning and reproof. Our sympathies cannot really heal the hurt of hearts that are wrong, or hold back the inevitable wheels of retribution that are moving in obedience to the solemn principles of God's government which no man can turn aside. "Tell the righteous it will be well with them,/ for they will enjoy the fruit of their deeds./ Woe to the wicked! Disaster is upon them!/ They will be paid back for what their hands have done" (Isaiah 3:10–11).

There is no promise in the Bible more comforting than this beautiful verse, but there is none whose comfort must be claimed so absolutely in connection with its setting in the context and with the conditions which are here annexed to it. It follows the unfolding of our life in the Spirit in the previous verse, and in Christian experience it necessarily comes after the things of which the writer has just been speaking. It is for those who have received the Spirit of Christ and who are walking therein in all the blessed fullness which this precious chapter unfolds; it is for them that all things work together for good. Or, to use the very language of the text itself, it is for "those who love him, who have been called according to his purpose" (Romans 8:28).

This is no superficial and light expression. It is very easy to say that we love God and not mean anything by it. I remember once talking with a man who had just come out of a drunken brawl, and I tried to convict him of his sin and lead him to see his need of Christ; but I could not make the least impression on his conscience. He seemed to think he was all right, and when I finally asked him if he had ever fulfilled the great commandment, "Love the Lord your God with all your heart and with all your soul and with all your mind and with all your strength" (Mark 12:30), he said "Why, yes, I always loved God; I never had anything against Him." That is about the extent of most people's love to God; but that is not the love that a bride will accept from her husband or a child from its mother, nor will God accept it in fulfillment of His greatest command.

The people that love God are more fully described in this verse by another expression—"those . . . who have been called according to His purpose." What is His purpose? It is defined in the next verse. "For those God foreknew he also predestined to be conformed to the likeness [image, KJV] of his Son" (Romans 8:29).

This is God's purpose, to conform us to the image of His Son. People, therefore, who love God and for whom all things work together for good, are those that have yielded themselves to God's purpose and are allowing Him to conform them to the image of His Son; that is, to make them like

Jesus Christ—to sanctify them, separate them, and bring them into their Master's will and their Master's likeness.

Thus it will appear by a logical necessity that if we are to have the providence of God on our side, we must be ourselves on God's side. As Abraham Lincoln once said when somebody was urging the importance of praying that we might have God on our side: "It seems to me," said the wise statesman, "much more important we should be on God's side, and then we shall have no trouble of having God on our side." Let us get into the will of God and make it the supreme purpose of our life, and then every force and agency in earth and heaven and hell are bound to work together for our good.

The sanctified man is the man who has come into the purpose and will of God, and such a man, in renouncing his own will, has gained immeasurably more than he has lost. True, he has lost himself and his own selfish will, but he has found his God, and all things are his, and even God is for him in every attribute of His being and every form of His providence.

IN CHRIST

2. The condition of God's providence is also clearly stated in this passage. Verse 32 says, "He who did not spare his own Son, but gave him up for us all—how will he not also, along with him, graciously give us all things?" Here we see again the same "all things" as were mentioned in verse 28, but now they are connected with the person: "with Him." They all hang upon Christ, and we can only have them by having Him first.

It is much the same as when the Master said during His earthly life, "But seek his kingdom, and these things will be given to you as well" (Luke 12:31). We cannot get the gifts of God until we first accept the greatest gift, with whom they all come, the Lord Jesus Christ. It is no use to go to God and ask Him for temporal blessings and minor requests, while we have neglected His own greatest requirement of us, that we should believe on His Son, Jesus Christ, and accept Him as our personal Savior.

In fact, it is an impertinence to ask God for anything while we are neglecting His great salvation and refusing to submit ourselves to Jesus; but when we accept Him, all other things are counted in. It is much the same as marrying the heir of a millionaire. It is a small thing for us to get his fortune when we get his child. God's providential gifts are all guaranteed to us by His great redemption gift, and He has bound everything else up so with Christ that having Him we must have all else.

It is said that once a great Egyptian king was about to rear a splendid obelisk in the public square, and fearing that the engineers might be careless and let it fall, he took his only son, the heir to the throne, and he tied him to the top of the obelisk, and said, "The life of my son is bound up with the safety of this obelisk; if it falls, he perishes." It is needless to say that that obelisk was reared with tenderest care and safely placed at last upon its pedestal.

And so God has linked the life of His only Son, the Lord Jesus Christ, with the safety of every Christian. He has bound our lives, as it were, with the person of Jesus Christ, and if He can fall, so can we. But if aught of ill would come to us, it would come just the same to Him. Therefore, when Paul was persecuting the early Christians, the Lord Jesus spoke to him from heaven, and said, "Why do you persecute me?" (Acts 9:4). Wondrous mystery of eternal love, wondrous gift of God!

> Behold the best, the greatest gift
> Of everlasting love!
> Behold the pledge of peace below
> And perfect bliss above!

ALL THINGS

3. The all-embracing comprehensiveness of God's providence is very strongly expressed in this promise. It touches all things, and it weaves them all together in a perfect chain of cooperation and divine overruling, so that if one thing may work against us, the next thing will cooperate with it to make it work for us. And while in their separateness many things seem unfavorable, yet as God binds them up and weaves them together, they form a perfect plan of blessing. We must, therefore, wait His time to see the outcome of things which we do not now understand.

Like a blocked map made in sections, we may try to put three or four of the sections together and see nothing but confusion, but when all the pieces are furnished and each drops into its place in the general plan, then all is perfect symmetry and not a single one could have been spared. Now God wants us to claim His providential working in our lives, just as much as His spiritual working in our hearts.

Temporal Things

Men may depreciate what they call temporal blessing, and talk about the higher sacredness of the spiritual realm; but the fact is that God has always loved to glorify Himself by working in temporal things and showing that they are subordinate to and controlled by His spiritual workings.

There are two expressions in the third chapter of Ephesians which are very striking in their connection. "Now to him who is able to do immeasurably more than all we ask or imagine" (Ephesians 3:20a). This describes God's out-working, the things that He is able and willing to do for us; but this is entirely dependent upon His in-working within our hearts, as the next clause expresses it: "according to his power that is at work within us" (3:20b). If God is only working in you mightily, there will be no trouble about His working out for you the events which your eyes can see and your senses can discern.

Jacob

The whole story of the Bible is full of God's out-working and in-working, as they keep pace one with the other. Look at Jacob in the great hour of his peril yonder at Peniel. He is in extreme distress, all his contriving and working have failed at last. His cruel and angry brother with a fierce army is coming to meet him, and before tomorrow's sun shall set it seems almost certain that the blood of his wives and children will be poured out on the desert sands. What can he do? Nothing more. God must do it now if anything is to be done.

But where does God begin? Outside? No. He first works in Jacob's heart. "So Jacob was left alone, and a man wrestled with him till daybreak" (Genesis 32:24). Ah! that night of prayer was God's in-working, and when the morning dawned Jacob was a new man spiritually. He had touched God, and henceforth had power with God and with men. And before the noontide of the next day the out-working had also come. He met his brother and all his fierce followers, but there was no hostility and there was no harm; they fell on each other's neck in the embrace of forgiving love and perfect reconciliation. God had wrought the external miracle because Jacob had already entered into a greater miracle in his own soul.

Daniel

Look again—yonder in Babylon a solitary man is standing for righteousness and God in the face of the two great empires of Babylon and Persia. His name is Daniel. His character is a miracle of goodness. Man can find nothing against him except it be concerning the laws of his God. Lions cannot terrify him, kings and palaces cannot tempt him aside. He has stood firm against all the splendid bribes of the grandest of earth's empires, and God has found a man he can depend upon even in Babylon. That is God's inworking.

Look at him on his face before God for 21 days in fasting and prayer until the very angels come from heaven and bear the answers to his petitions! Can such a life ever be vain? It is impossible. At the touch of those believing prayers all the wheels of providence were set in motion, and even upon his very throne, proud Cyrus, flushed with the conquest of the world and ruling the proudest empire of the past, is compelled in answer to Daniel's prayers to publish to the world the most extraordinary proclamation that ever came from the lips of a heathen king:

> The LORD moved the heart of Cyrus king of Persia to make a
> proclamation throughout his realm and to put it in writing:
>
> "This is what Cyrus king of Persia says:
> 'The LORD, the God of heaven, has given me all the
> kingdoms of the earth and he has appointed me to build a
> temple for him at Jerusalem in Judah. Anyone of his people
> among you—may the LORD his God be with him, and let
> him go up.' " (2 Chronicles 36:22b–23)

And in response to that proclamation, the long train of returning captives
went back to Zion, and Israel's national life was restored once more, in order
that Christ might be born among his own people in Bethlehem of Judea.

Pentecost

Look at another picture: The coming of the Holy Spirit on the day of Pentecost was the greatest spiritual blessing of the New Testament age; but this was accompanied by just as wonderful providential events. Was there ever anything more wonderful than the gathering together on the day of Pentecost of that strange company that came from all countries, tribes and tongues, and met in that upper room to receive together the baptism of the Holy Spirit, and speak for God as the Spirit gave them utterance in every human language, and then go back to all their peoples and tribes and repeat the story which they had heard and learned? But that was exactly what happened through the marvelous providence of God on the day of Pentecost.

All through the book of Acts we see the same wonderful manifestations of the Holy Spirit's power to work externally in keeping with His internal working.

Philip

Look at Philip of Samaria: In the height of his wonderful work there, a command comes to him, "Go down to the desert," and he immediately obeys (Acts 8:26). It would be very much the same as if in the midst of a great revival God should suddenly call some public man to leave his work and go off to some lone spot, where every opportunity of usefulness seemed precluded. This was just what Philip was told to do, and he immediately obeyed and went down to Gaza.

As he walked across the barren wastes, wondering what it all meant, suddenly a cloud of dust appears on the horizon, and the signs of an approaching cavalcade. It is a caravan traveling to Africa. A great prince of Ethiopia is returning to his home with a sad and disappointed heart. He has been seeking for the truth and has not found it. The priests of Jerusalem have not been able to answer his heart's cry. Philip immediately obeys the impulse to join him, and sitting in his chariot, in a few moments he has preached to him the gospel of Jesus and led him to accept Him as his Savior.

And before that day is ended, the prince is on his way to his distant home, an ambassador of Christ, to publish the gospel among his people, and probably to lead multitudes to the Savior and be one of the founders of Christianity in that great continent, where through the first five centuries the Church of Jesus had its greatest strongholds. This was God's out-work through Philip, who had consented to receive His in-working.

Peter

Look at one more picture only: It is Peter, the great apostle to the Jews. A rigid sectarian, almost a bigot; a high-churchman we could call him today. The thought had not even entered his head that the Gentiles could ever be received to an equal share in the blessings of the gospel. But God designed to make all this different, and so He took Peter apart and began to teach him. Upon the housetop in Joppa one day Peter was waiting in prayer before God, when suddenly a vision appeared, and God showed him that he must think of nothing henceforth as common or unclean; but that he must look upon the Gentiles as equally dear to God with the Jew, and be willing to give the gospel alike to all, and recognize all nations equally in the one household of faith.

Just as Peter has learned his lesson, there is a knock at the door. A number of messengers have come. They are waiting for him, have just come all the way from Caesarea with a request from Cornelius, the Roman commander at the capital, that he will come and preach the gospel to him and tell him about Jesus.

It is again the out-working hand of God ever keeping step with the in-working Spirit, and as Peter obeys and hastens to Caesarea, he finds a whole household waiting for the message; the Holy Spirit comes down in power upon them, and a new dispensation is inaugurated, even the gospel for the Gentiles, through which even we ourselves have come into the privileges of salvation.

These are but some samples of the way God loves to work for the heart that is truly united to Him, and if we will but let Him have the throne of our inner being, He will love to make all things bend to our interests, and work together for our good. And it will indeed be true, "If God is for us, who can be against us?" (Romans 8:31).

We have nothing more important in these days of practical men and real events than that God Himself is more practical and more real than any of the things with which we come in contact. Indeed, the whole framework of human affairs is just God's own providential machinery, through which He wants to work, and use the commonplace things of life to manifest His glory and build up His kingdom. The affairs of nations, the business of commerce, the occupations of every day are God's own links of providence which the Holy Spirit is able to bind into a chain of holy power, fastened to the throne and bringing this revolted world into union with Himself.

God has no other way of showing Himself to some men except through the things which they can see and touch, and He wants us in these last days to be the instruments through whom He can reveal Himself to an unbelieving world. And so in the past days God has been overruling the affairs of nations, and working in the operations of missionaries for the spreading of His gospel and the hastening of His coming. And the miracles of His providence in the healing of men's bodies, in the supplying of financial resources to carry on His work, in the removing of obstacles, the opening of doors, and the overruling of what seemed hostile circumstances for the furtherance of His kingdom, have been not less wonderful than the story of the Acts of the Apostles.

Let us trust Him more in the needs of our own lives; let us commit our difficulties and our temporal needs and necessities to His loving care.

> Leave to His sovereign sway
> To rule and to command;
> With wonder filled thou soon shalt own
> How wise, how strong, His hand.
>
> He everywhere hath sway
> And all things serve His might,
> His every act pure blessing is,
> His path unsullied light.

OUR FINAL SALVATION

4. The purpose of God is back of His promise and His providence. "And those he predestined, he also called; those he called, he also justified; those he justified, he also glorified" (8:30).

This is the endless chain of God's eternal purpose, and the guarantee of our security and blessing if we are within that purpose. God's purpose is not spoken of here as an absolute degree of salvation for a certain number of persons, irrespective of all conditions on their part, and making it certain that they must be saved no matter what they do. It is a purpose to conform them to the image of His Son.

God elects men not to be saved but to be holy, and if they are made holy it is inevitable that they must be saved. The purpose of God is always recognized in the New Testament as centered in Jesus Christ. We were chosen in Him before the foundation of the world, and when we become united to Him we come into the divine purpose; and when we wholly yield ourselves to that purpose in entire consecration it guarantees our full salvation, and like an endless chain binds us to the throne and the glory everlasting.

You have seen the great cable in one of our cities which runs the cable cars. You will notice that this is an endless chain, moving on without interruption and able to carry very much more than the weight that is attached to it. Now when the car is attached to this cable it moves with it and comes into contact with all the strength of the cable, so that it is just as easy to go up as down the steep declivities. It is carried by a power beyond itself, and all it needs is to keep the attachment.

God's purpose for us is just a great cable fastened to the throne and encircling eternity. When we yield ourselves to Christ and to all His perfect will we come into touch with a power and a purpose as mighty as God Himself, and our weak will and feeble efforts are backed up by a strength that is immutable, eternal and divine; so that the divine purpose and the glorious doctrine of God's election is full of comfort to the heart that is wholly yielded to the purpose, and we know that in spite of earth and hell—yes, and even in spite of ourselves—He is able to save us to the uttermost (Hebrews 7:25, KJV) and keep that which we have committed to Him against that day (2 Timothy 1:12, KJV).

PROTECTION

5. Divine protection from every enemy is guaranteed by this promise and providence. "If God is for us, who can be against us?" (Romans 8:31b).

VINDICATION

6. Vindication against every accuser is also guaranteed by this promise and providence. "Who will bring any charge against those whom God has chosen? It is God who justifies. Who is he that condemns? Christ Jesus, who died—more than that, who was raised to life—is at the right hand of God and is also interceding for us" (8:33–34).

PROVISION

7. Divine provision for our every need is also guaranteed. "How will he not also, along with him, graciously give us all things?" (8:32b). Every necessity is but a draft on the bank of His divine resources, and we may take it to Him as a claim upon His promised fullness. "And my God will meet all your needs according to his glorious riches in Christ Jesus" (Philippians 4:19).

SECURITY

8. Our eternal security is pledged by God's providence and promise. "Who shall separate us from the love of Christ?" (Romans 8:35a). And then comes the triumphant answer, after all the possible obstacles and enemies have been mentioned one by one, "No, in all these things we are more than conquerors through him who loved us" (8:37). Our trials will be turned to helps; our enemies will be taken prisoners and made to fight our battles. Like the weights on a clock, which keep it going, our very difficulties will prove incentives to faith and prayer and occasions for God becoming more real to us.

Not only will we escape from those who attack us, but their very attack will become an unspeakable benefit by making us stronger for the discipline and leaving them weaker for the defeat. We shall get out of our troubles not only deliverance but triumph, and in all these things be even more than conquerors through Him that loved us.

Our security depends not upon our unchanging love, but on the love of God in Christ Jesus toward us. It is not the clinging arms of the babe on the mother's breast that keeps it from falling, but the stronger arms of the mother about it which will never let it go. He has loved us with an everlasting love, and although all else may change, yet He will never leave us nor forsake us.

Have you ever seen a ploughman make a straight furrow? He does it by two stakes, the nearer and the farther, and as he keeps them both in line he is able to keep his line absolutely straight. It is the farther stake that keeps him from swerving. We, too, are ploughmen in a heavenly husbandry. Let us keep our eye not only on the nearer, but on the farther stake of His blessed coming and our eternal hope beyond these skies of cloud and change; for His eternal covenant covers all the future as well as all the past, and "neither death nor life, neither angels nor demons, neither the present nor the future, nor any powers, neither height nor depth, nor anything else in all creation, will be able to separate us from the love of God that is in Christ Jesus our Lord" (8:38–39).

CHAPTER 11

GOD'S PURPOSE REGARDING ISRAEL AND THE WORLD

> *I speak the truth in Christ—I am not lying, my conscience confirms it in the Holy Spirit—I have great sorrow and unceasing anguish in my heart. For I could wish that I myself were cursed and cut off from Christ for the sake of my brothers, those of my own race, the people of Israel. Theirs is the adoption as sons; theirs the divine glory, the covenants, the receiving of the law, the temple worship and the promises. Theirs are the patriarchs, and from them is traced the human ancestry of Christ, who is God over all, forever praised! Amen. (Romans 9:1–5)*

In the last section we traced the providence of God with respect to God's saved and sanctified people. In the present section the apostle unfolds the principles of God's providence as respects the larger field of the world, and more particularly the Jewish nation, God's covenant people.

The apostle had already established in earlier chapters, the great principle that the gospel applies to all men alike as sinners, irrespective of race and class. So far as salvation is concerned, "there is no difference between Jew and Gentile—the same Lord is Lord of all and richly blesses all who call on him" (Romans 10:12).

But, lest it might be supposed from this that all God's promises to Israel are thereby turned aside and transferred to the Gentiles, he now takes up the question of God's purpose for Israel and His special providence with respect to His chosen people.

Was God's ancient covenant set aside by some afterthought and rendered of none effect by Israel's disobedience, or has there been an immutable purpose running through all the centuries like a golden thread, and reaching out to its final fulfillment in the coming ages?

The discussion of this great question occupies the next three chapters, and forms the profoundest and clearest treatise in the Scriptures on Israel's place in connection with the Gentiles, the gospel, the Christian dispensation and the coming of the Lord.

PAUL'S LOVE TO ISRAEL

1. The apostle's own interest in the subject is obvious. It was very near and dear to his heart—so dear that he could truly say, "Brothers, my heart's desire and prayer to God for the Israelites is that they may be saved" (10:1), and that he could almost wish himself accursed from Christ, if by this awful sacrifice his countrymen could be saved (9:3).

Every heart that is in true sympathy with Christ feels in this way respecting Israel. We cannot truly understand our Master's Spirit if we do not sympathize with His "kinsmen according to the flesh" (9:3b, KJV), and long and labor to save them and bring them into His covenant and will.

All who are interested in the fulfillment of prophecy and the coming of the Lord will ever cherish an intelligent and earnest interest in the seed of Abraham, and will be found laboring and praying for "the peace of Jerusalem" (Psalm 122:6a).

GOD'S COVENANT

2. Paul reviews Israel's calling and God's covenant with them. The apostle recognizes and magnifies the importance of Israel's place in God's purpose and covenants. ". . . the people of Israel. Theirs is the adoption as sons; theirs the divine glory, the covenants, the receiving of the law, the temple worship and the promises. Theirs are the patriarchs, and from them is traced the human ancestry of Christ, who is God over all, forever praised! Amen" (9:4–5). Separated from the nations, that they might be kept a pure and peculiar people, God made them the repositories of His oracles, the witnesses of His truth and the representatives of His name on earth, admitted them to the most sacred covenant with Himself, made them the teachers of the world and, above all else, kept them as an ancestral line through whom His own Son at length came, in the flesh.

He has given to them promises extending through a thousand generations, which have only begun to be fulfilled. It is doubtless true that there is a spiritual Israel, and that they are not all Israel which are of Israel, and that, in a sense, the promises to Israel are fulfilled to the New Testament Church; yet the promise is still true to the literal Israel, and while Japheth is entitled to share the tent with Shem (Genesis 9:27), he has no right to steal the tent and turn Shem out, robbed of his promises and his inheritance.

The apostle most distinctly recognizes the permanency of God's covenant with Israel as God's chosen people through God's ancient election and His unchanging plan, and so he adds,

> And so all Israel will be saved; as it is written,

> "The deliverer will come from Zion;
>   he will turn godlessness away from Jacob.
> And this is my covenant with them
>   when I take away their sins."

> As far as the gospel is concerned, they are enemies on your account; but as far as election is concerned, they are loved on account of the patriarchs, for God's gifts and his call are irrevocable. (Romans 11:26–29)

THEIR FAILURE

3. Paul establishes Israel's failure to fulfill God's purpose concerning them and their temporary rejection on account thereof. They disbelieved and disobeyed God, and in consequence they were broken off from their own olive tree, and God had to say to them, "All day long I have held out my hands to a disobedient and obstinate people" (10:21).

Through every age of Israel's national history they failed, notwithstanding all God's goodness and grace. The patriarchal age ended in the sin of Israel's sons and their going down to Egypt. The deliverance from Egypt was followed by the wanderings in the wilderness, and the conquest of Canaan terminated in 400 years of declension. The kingdom of David and Solomon ended in Solomon's mournful backsliding and the division into two kingdoms of Israel and Judah. The 10 tribes went out into captivity and apparent extinction. The kingdom of Judah was carried away to Babylon, and even when God restored His captive people and sent His own Son to them as their Prophet, Priest and King, "He came to that which was his own, but his own did not receive him" (John 1:11). He was rejected and crucified, His apostles and disciples were persecuted, and God had to give up Israel for ages of darkness and sorrow unspeakable and unparalleled.

Not only has God permitted the Gentiles to trample them down, but He Himself has visited them with the most dreadful of His judgments—the spirit of slumber and judicial blindness, and the veil still hides the Savior from their eyes, so that the dreadful words of their own prophetic Scriptures have been fulfilled to them:

As it is written:

"God gave them a spirit of stupor,
   eyes so that they could not see,
   and ears so that they could not hear,
to this very day."

And David says:

"May their table become a snare and a trap,
   a stumbling block and a retribution for them.
May their eyes be darkened so they cannot see,
   and their backs be bent forever." (Romans 11:8–10)

God told them that all this would happen to them if they disobeyed Him and broke His covenant. In the 26th chapter of Leviticus He announced to them that if they were unfaithful He would bring upon them seven times (or ages) of affliction and judgment (26:18), and for 2,500 years these seven ages have been slowly and terribly fulfilled, until at length the years have almost run out, the "times of the Gentiles are nearly fulfilled, and Israel's times are coming into view once more."

THE GENTILES

4. The calling of the Gentiles to take Israel's place is revealed:

As he says in Hosea:

"I will call them 'my people' who are not my people;
   and I will call her 'my loved one' who is not my loved one,"

and,

"It will happen that in the very place where it was said to them,
   'You are not my people,'
they will be called 'sons of the living God.' "(Romans 9:25–26)

Again I ask: Did Israel not understand? First, Moses says,

"I will make you envious by those who are not a nation;
   I will make you angry by a nation that has no understanding."

And Isaiah boldly says,

"I was found by those who did not seek me;

I revealed myself to those who did not ask for me." (10:19–20)

Again I ask: Did they stumble so as to fall beyond recovery? Not at all! Rather, because of their transgression, salvation has come to the Gentiles to make Israel envious. But if their transgression means riches for the world, and their loss means riches for the Gentiles, how much greater riches will their fullness bring! (11:11–12)

If some of the branches have been broken off, and you, though a wild olive shoot, have been grafted in among the others and now share in the nourishing sap from the olive root, do not boast over those branches. If you do, consider this: You do not support the root, but the root supports you. (11:17–18)

I do not want you to be ignorant of this mystery, brothers, so that you may not be conceited [wise in your own conceits, KJV]: Israel has experienced a hardening in part until the full number of the Gentiles has come in. (11:25)

We Gentiles have been in danger of becoming "wise in our own conceits," and imagining that the gospel was given especially for us. We must not forget that our place is purely a parenthesis, and that we have come in through Israel's failure, and have simply been grafted in as branches into a tree that was there before ever we were born. We were outcasts and strangers, and have simply been invited in to share the shelter of Israel's tent, but we must take heed lest we despise the original owners of the tent, and seclude them from their own prerogatives.

Israel had her time of probation and we have ours. It is almost run out. Let us make the best of it, profit by their example, and take heed lest we repeat their sin and share their judgments.

Israel's fall is the riches of the world! Israel's casting away, the reconciliation of the world. But let us "not be arrogant, but be afraid. For if God did not spare the natural branches, he will not spare you either" (11:20b–21).

ISRAEL'S REMNANT

5. Meanwhile, even during Israel's suspension as a nation, there is a remnant of Israel, all through the ages, who are saved. "Isaiah cries out concerning Israel: 'Though the number of the Israelites be like the sand by the sea,/ only the remnant will be saved' " (9:27).

God did not reject his people, whom he foreknew. Don't you know what the Scripture says in the passage about Elijah—how he appealed to God against Israel: "Lord, they have killed your prophets and torn down your altars; I am the only one left, and they are trying to kill me" ? And what was God's answer to him? "I have reserved for myself seven thousand who have not bowed the knee to Baal." (11:2–4)

There has probably never been a period in the history of Israel when there have not been some to represent the true spiritual seed of Abraham. The number of those who have turned to Christ from among the Hebrews at the present day is large and constantly increasing.

Such names as Delitzch, Edersheim, Saphir and Rabbinowitch, represent the fruit that God is gathering from the fig tree of Israel, even in the present generation.

The extraordinary movement that has circulated the New Testament in Hebrew in less than five years among a half million Jews, or rather to the extent of half a million copies, is the most remarkable sign of our times, and shows that the heart of Israel is beginning to turn to their true Messiah.

It has been stated that there are more than 50,000 converted Jews in the world today. At least we know that as there were 7,000 in Israel, even in the time of Ahab and Jezebel, God has His remnant yet, even amid all the pride and unbelief of this unbelieving nation. Let us thank God for the increasing number of Hebrew Christians, and labor and pray for the ingathering of the first fruits of these people, as well as from the Gentiles.

ISRAEL'S RESTORATION

6. Israel as a nation will yet be restored to their land and their national independence, and will be brought to accept Christ as their Messiah, and to turn from unbelief to God, and when they do thus return to God and accept the Savior their restoration will bring wonderful blessing to the whole world.

Again I ask: Did they stumble so as to fall beyond recovery? Not at all! Rather, because of their transgression, salvation has come to the Gentiles to make Israel envious. But if their transgression means riches for the world, and their loss means riches for the Gentiles, how much greater riches will their fullness bring! (11:11–12)

For if their rejection is the reconciliation of the world, what will their acceptance be but life from the dead? (11:15)

And if they do not persist in unbelief, they will be grafted in, for God is able to graft them in again. (11:23)

And so all Israel will be saved, as it is written:
"The deliverer will come from Zion;
  he will turn godlessness away from Jacob.
And this is my covenant with them
  when I take away their sins."

As far as the gospel is concerned, they are enemies on your account; but as far as election is concerned, they are loved on account of the patriarchs, for God's gifts and his call are irrevocable. Just as you who were at one time disobedient to God have now received mercy as a result of their disobedience, so they too have now become disobedient in order that they too may now receive mercy as a result of God's mercy to you. (11:26–31)

There is a great and glorious field of prophecy and promise in these passages. They make it very certain that God's covenant shall be literally fulfilled to His ancient people, and that this will include not only national restoration, but salvation through their conversion to Christ. This is to come about through the coming of the Lord Jesus Christ. "The deliverer will come from Zion;/ he will turn godlessness away from Jacob" (11:26b).

It is probable that Israel will return to their own land in unbelief. There is every indication at the present time of the accomplishment of this fact within a very short time. A very decided movement toward Palestine has begun among the Hebrew people.

Within the past few years the movement known as Zionism has been thoroughly organized in all the Hebrew communities in various parts of the world, and its chief object is to take measures for the colonization of Palestine by the Jews.

After the nation shall have been reestablished in Palestine, the Lord Jesus, at His coming for His saints, shall show Himself to Israel as He did to Paul on the way to Damascus, and they shall be converted by the vision of their Lord. "They will look on the one they have pierced" (John 19:37). Then shall follow a time of great tribulation, but at the end Christ shall return for His saints in glory and establish His millennial reign on earth, and then Israel shall become the queen of nations and her people the great evangelizers of the world.

THE WORLD'S BLESSING

7. Their restoration shall be to the rest of the Gentile world as life from the dead.

In the 15th chapter of Acts the apostle has given us the perspective very clearly. First the Lord visits the Gentiles to take out of them a people for His name. This is the work that is now going on through the great missionary movement among the Gentile nations, and its object is to gather a company of firstfruits from the people of every tribe and tongue unto the Bride of the Lamb, to meet Him at His coming. "After this," the Lord says, "I will return/ and rebuild David's fallen tent" (Acts 15:16a). This is the restoration of Israel and the coming of the Lord.

Then comes the third stage, "That the remnant of men may seek the Lord,/ and all the Gentiles who bear my name,/ says the Lord, who does these things" (15:17). This is to bring about the salvation of the race, and all the Gentiles.

Such, then, is Israel's place in the purpose of God, and such is our high calling in the closing days of the times of the Gentiles. May God help us to become true "men of Issachar, who understood the times and knew what Israel should do" (1 Chronicles 12:32a), and to work in cooperation with our great Leader in speedily gathering the firstfruits of the Gentiles, and the preparation of Israel for the coming of the Lord!

CHAPTER 12

CONSECRATION AND SERVICE

Therefore, I urge you, brothers, in view of God's mercy, to offer your bodies as living sacrifices, holy and pleasing to God—this is your spiritual act of worship. (Romans 12:1)

We have now been led in the course of this wonderful treatise through the revelation of sin, salvation, sanctification and God's providence and purpose respecting His people and the world, up to the coming of our Lord.

He now proceeds to the practical part of the epistle, and by all these blessings that have been received and all these mercies that have been unfolded, he calls us to consecrate ourselves to God for the service which should be the outcome of all these blessings.

GOD'S ORDER

It is most important to notice the place of consecration with reference to sanctification. A mistake in theology or terminology will not hinder God's blessing. God's grace is so full and free that He will give it by any door through which the poor sinful soul may come in the name of Jesus, yet there is a clear and definitely revealed order of spiritual blessing which it is better for us to know and follow, and which the apostle most definitely unfolds in this epistle.

According to that order, salvation comes in the third, fourth and fifth chapters, sanctification in the sixth, seventh and eighth, and now in the 12th chapter consecration follows in its true place, as an entire offering up of our saved and sanctified life to be used for the service and the glory of God.

THE HEBREW OFFERINGS

These two steps will be apparent if we remember the two great offerings of the Hebrew tabernacle. The first was the sin offering. It was the type not only of consecration for service, but of surrender, of sanctification and cleansing. It was the seventh chapter of Romans in type.

The sinful man, conscious of the evil within him and powerless to remove it, comes before the altar of his God, bringing as his substitute a spotless lamb. He lays his hand upon its head and confesses his sin, and it passes over into the lamb, which immediately becomes a mass of sin and uncleanness. It is not sacrificed. It would be sacrilege to consecrate it; it would defile the altar. There is only one thing to do with it: take it out beyond the camp, cut it open and lay it, with all its ghastliness, upon the consuming fire which ever burns, as a type of God's hatred of sin.

It teaches us that the sinful heart cannot be offered to God in consecration. It must be laid at the feet of Jesus for cleansing, and as of old we still may lay our hands upon the Lamb of sacrifice and transfer our sin to Him. Then our sin passes out to Him and His righteousness and Spirit pass into us and we are sanctified by His life and indwelling.

But there was another offering, quite different. It was the burnt offering. After the sinner was cleansed through the sin offering, he brought his burnt offering—a lamb, too. Laying his hand upon it to identify himself with it, it was accepted and cut into a thousand pieces to indicate that every part of it was precious, and then it was burned in the holy fire on the altar as a sweet-smelling savor unto the Lord.

This is the type of consecration as taught in this beautiful picture of Romans. Sanctified now through the death and life of Christ, we bring our offering and lay it before God's altar, and it is accepted with approval and delight: "as living sacrifices, holy and pleasing to God" (12:1).

This is consecration in its true spiritual sense, and this is the beautiful picture in the 12th chapter of Romans.

It will be noticed in this verse that the offering is presented "holy and pleasing to God" (12:1).

SERVICE

Now the great object of sanctification or consecration is service. God wants to use us, and He cannot use us until He gets us purified through His own indwelling Spirit.

The popular idea of holiness is that it is to prepare us for heaven. But we find that old Zechariah had light enough to know that God's great purpose of grace for His people was "to rescue us from the hand of our enemies,/ and to enable us to serve him without fear/ in holiness and righteousness before him all our days" (Luke 1:74–75).

Let us now look first at some of the characteristics, and then at some of the consequences that true consecration has unfolded in this picture.

SECTION I—*Its Characteristics*

1. It is voluntary. "Therefore, I urge you, brothers, . . . to offer your bodies . . ." (Romans 12:1a).

The first condition of the ancient burnt offering was, "He must present it at the entrance to the Tent of Meeting, so that it will be acceptable to the LORD" (Leviticus 1:3). You are already the Lord's, by right of purchase, creation and new creation, but now you recognize that right, and with your own free consent give yourself to Him to live as one that is henceforth the bondslave of love and the property of God.

2. It is hearty. "Therefore, I urge you, brothers, in view of God's mercy, to offer your bodies . . ." (Romans 12:1a). It is drawn forth, not by the fear of punishment, but by the remembrance of mercies and the glad response of a living, believing heart.

You cannot consecrate yourself to God fully until you know, love and trust Him. You cannot put yourself into the hands of a dreaded foe, or even an uncertain force. You want to know that He is your Friend. Therefore, all this revelation of God's grace has preceded, and it is in view of all this that we now come, drawn by the mercies of God, allowing every one of them to become a cord of love to bind the sacrifice to the horns of the altar.

It is infinitely good of Him to be willing to take us at all. We count it an unspeakable privilege to be able to come, and we fly to His arms as a child to its mother, as a bride to her husband, as the steel to the magnet that attracts it.

The word "urge" here is literally *paraclete*. "I *paraclete* you," and *Paraclete* is the name of the Holy Spirit. It means that the Holy Spirit is pleading with us to give ourselves to God. But He will not press us beyond our will, nor will He accept the sacrifice if given with reluctance and fear. Let us, therefore, present ourselves with wholehearted gladness.

3. It is a very definite consecration. "Offer your bodies . . ." (12:1). It is not merely some emotional sense of spiritual ecstasy, but a real, practical contract for service, quite as much as when a laborer gives his time and labor to his employer, to belong to him during the hours of labor.

It means to give your eyes to see for Him, your ears to hear only what He is pleased to have you hear, your tongue to speak always at His bidding, your hands to be employed for Him, your feet to walk for Him, your physical senses to be possessed by Him, controlled by Him, and in everything subject to His will.

4. It is not only a physical, but a spiritual consecration, "your spiritual act of worship [reasonable service, KJV]" (12:1b).

It is not a dead body you bring to Him, like the old Jewish sacrifice, but your living body, the life you are to live, or, as the Revised Version has it, "your pleasing service."

You are not only to give your outward members, but your inward powers, faculties and capacities, your whole surrendered self. Your brain is His to think for Him. Your reading is for Him. Your very intellectual and aesthetic tastes are His, to be used for His glory and not for your own gratification.

The other day I noticed in the last issue of one of our leading religious weeklies, on the first page—the principal editorial of the week—an article headed "What Is the Best Reading?" A whole page was given to the discussion of the monthly magazines and the question of their decadence or their improvement. This was the reading for God's children, and their best reading! We could not wonder that such food gave poor Christians something worse than spiritual dyspepsia.

Our affections, our friendships and our friends are to be His—used for Him and controlled by His perfect will. Our whole inner being is to be one constant outflowing of the incense of prayer and praise, trust and love, as a sweet-smelling savor unto God.

> Like a golden censer glowing,
> Filled with burning incense rare,
> All my heart is upward flowing,
> In a cloud of ceaseless prayer.

5. This offering is "holy and pleasing [acceptable, KJV] to God" (12:1).

It has been made holy by the grace of Christ revealed in the previous chapters, and the fact of its being offered to God makes it doubly holy, and the altar sanctifies the gift.

It is accepted. God is pleased to accept the gift, and we may know the moment the gift is presented with a sincere, loving heart, the seal of heaven falls upon it, the fire consumes the sacrifice, and God again says: "This is my Son, whom I love; with him I am well pleased" (Matthew 17:5).

SECTION II—*The Effects of Consecration*

1. Separation

It separates us. "Do not conform any longer to the pattern of this world, but be transformed by the renewing of your mind" (Romans 12:2a).

This separation is twofold. It is negative and positive. It separates us from the world by taking us out of it. "Do not conform" (12:2a). But it separates us from the world in a much better way by taking the world out of us. "Be transformed by the renewing of your mind" (12:2a). This is the true separation. This was the way Christ was separated from the world. He had no affinity for it. Like the sea fowl which plunges into the miry water, and yet rises without a drop adhering to its shining wings, like the pure gold that can go through the flame untouched, so Jesus passed through all scenes and associations with sin without any response in His holy heart.

Man's way is to shut himself up in a monastery and so keep out of the world. God's way is to put Christ into the heart, and so keep the world out of us. Man's way is to give up the dance and the theater. God's way is to get the dance and the theater out of us. The desires of the consecrated girl gravitate heavenward, and the pleasures of the ballroom have no charm for such a heart. This is so much easier than the other way, and then it becomes second nature.

2. Brings Us into the Will of God

The next result of consecration is to bring us into the will of God. "Then you will be able to test and approve what God's will is—his good, pleasing and perfect will" (12:2b).

The consecrated spirit is wholly united to the divine will. It chooses it, delights in it and wants to meet it in all its fullness.

There are three stages here in the description of the divine will: the positive, comparative and superlative. There are some who only aim to reach the good will of God. There are others who press on to the pleasing will of God, to a life which pleases God and has the testimony constantly of His acceptance. But there is a perfect will of God into which we may enter and realize all for which He has called us and saved us.

3. Leads to Self-renunciation

True consecration leads to self-renunciation. "For by the grace given me I say to every one of you: Do not think of yourself more highly than you ought, but rather think of yourself with sober judgment, in accordance with the measure of faith God has given you" (12:3b).

The highest spiritual life is always the lowliest.

It does not minister to spiritual egotism, but destroys it. It does not lead us to recognize our own sanctification, faith or spiritual powers, but rather to see our nothingness and helplessness and entire dependence upon Christ. Its language—with Paul—is, "Not that we are competent in ourselves to claim anything for ourselves" (2 Corinthians 3:5); "I am less than the least of all God's people" (Ephesians 3:8); "I have been crucified with Christ and I no longer live, but Christ lives in me." (Galatians 2:20a). Its spirit is that of deep humility and self-forgetting lowliness.

4. Receives Strength and Sufficiency

True consecration recognizes and receives the strength and sufficiency of Christ and draws its health and life from Him with holy boldness. "In accordance with the measure of faith God has given you" (Romans 12:3). The power of the consecrated life is the grace of the indwelling Spirit of the Holy Christ.

5. Leads to True Individuality

True consecration leads to true individuality. "Just as each of us has one body with many members, and these members do not all have the same function, so in Christ we who are many form one body, and each member belongs to all the others. We have different gifts, according to the grace given us" (12:4–6a).

If the spiritual body were composed of one or two features it would be a monstrosity. If you were made a finger, don't try to be a foot. If you were called to be a fragrant rose, don't continually fret because you are not a sunflower or an orange tree. Be yourself, with Christ shining through you and living in you, and you will fit into your niche and accomplish your high calling.

The most agreeable wood finishing of a building is the natural wood showing all the simple fiber and grain of the tree shining through the translucent varnish. A common pine board, when genuine and natural, is far prettier than the most elaborate daubs of paint. God wants each of us to be true to the natural grain, and then varnished with the crystalline glow of the Holy Spirit.

6. Adjustable to Others

The truly consecrated spirit is adjustable to others, and easily fits into its place in the body of Christ. "We are all members of one body" (Ephesians 4:25b).

The more fully we receive the Holy Spirit, the more perfect will be our fellowship with the people of God and the more simple our adjustment with all other Christians. One who has but a limited measure of grace is apt to be angular, impracticable, determined and hard. But one who is really filled with God can easily see good in others, as well as his own leadings, and work in harmony and fellowship even amid great varieties of temperament and taste.

The secret of true fellowship and cooperation is to see God in one another, and not adhere to the human, but to the divine. Thus, as each of us fits into God's place for us, we will all together make a perfect whole, and nourished by that which every joint supplies, the whole body will grow up to the full stature of Christ.

7. Leads to Definite Ministry

True consecration will lead to definite ministry in the body of Christ.

> We have different gifts, according to the grace given us. If a man's gift is prophesying, let him use it in proportion to his faith. If it is serving, let him serve; if it is teaching, let him teach; if it is encouraging, let him encourage; if it is contributing to the needs of others, let him give generously; if it is leadership, let him govern diligently; if it is showing mercy, let him do it cheerfully. (Romans 12:6–8)

Each of these ministries is equally important in its place. One is called to be a public teacher, another to be a soul-winner, another to be the executive head in some department of Christian work, another a successful merchant and a generous giver, and by his means supply the resources necessary to advance the work of Christ.

Let each be true to his calling, and let everyone have a calling and a definite work for God. There is no place for drones. There is no single member of the body that can be excused from some special ministry, and yet there is no one whose ministry can be regarded as more important than another's. As each is called and fitted, let him be true to his calling and his trust in the power of the Holy Spirit. No one, or two, or 10 should monopolize the work of any church, but all together, in holy, harmonious fellowship, should cooperate in consecrated service. This is the model church. This was the apostolic church, and this is true consecration.

8. Shows Itself in Practical Ways

True consecration especially shows itself in the social and practical duties of life.

> Love must be sincere. Hate what is evil; cling to what is good. Be devoted to one another in brotherly love. Honor one another above yourselves. Never be lacking in zeal, but keep your spiritual fervor, serving the Lord. Be joyful in hope, patient in affliction, faithful in prayer. Share with God's people who are in need. Practice hospitality.
>
> Bless those who persecute you; bless and do not curse. Rejoice with those who rejoice; mourn with those who mourn. Live in harmony with one another. Do not be proud, but be willing to associate with people of low position. Do not be conceited. (12:9–16).

The apostle now brings down the spirit of consecration to the entire range of our social and religious life and presents a very beautiful picture of the consecrated man in the home, the social circle, the business office, the hour of sorrow and the time of gladness.

It will make us affectionate, sincere and tender in all the relationships of life. We will not be hard and cold, but "be devoted to one another in brotherly love" (12:10a).

It will make us very sincere in our expressions of regard, and sanctify us from all the sham phrases of society and the empty compliments with which the world deceives its friends. "Love must be sincere" (12:9a).

It will make us frank in our expressions of disapproval of that which is evil, and intent in our devotion to that which is good. It will make us energetic and enterprising in our business, and yet devout in the midst of the world's bustle and constant in our devotion to the service of God, for His glory.

It will make us bright and beautiful Christians, "joyful in hope" (12:12a), but at the same time it will balance our characters and steady our wing, by making us "patient in affliction" (12:12b) and keeping us "faithful in prayer" (12:12c), and held in holy confidence, calmness and inward recollection by the consciousness of God's overshadowing presence.

It will make us sensitive to the joys and sorrows of others, simple-hearted in sharing their happiness and quick to feel their pain, as we "rejoice with those who rejoice, and mourn with those who mourn" (12:15).

It will make us very tender in our consideration of the poor and the homeless, and lead us to "share with God's people who are in need" (12:13a) and to share our hospitality with the household of faith.

It will give a beautiful modesty to our bearing and make us not "conceited" (12:16b), but considerate and condescending even to those of lower rank and social standing.

The condescension here spoken of, however, is not to people, but to things. The Revised Version renders it "condescend to things that are lowly." To the high and consecrated nature nothing is mean. Even the most menial labor is honorable if done by an honorable and noble hand.

Above all things, the consecrated spirit will make us upright and honest in all relations to our fellow men. "Be careful to do what is right in the eyes of everybody. If it is possible, as far as it depends on you, live at peace with everyone" (12:17b–18).

It will keep us out of wrangles, quarrels, controversies and difficulties, and make us careful to avoid all debt, injustice and dishonorable transactions of every kind, so that we can look in the face of every human being without shame, and be blameless, harmless, "children of God without fault in a crooked and depraved generation, in which you shine like stars in the universe" (Philippians 2:15).

9. Shows Itself in Times of Trial

The truly consecrated heart shows itself most truly in the time of trial, and under the pressure of unkindness and wrong.

> Bless those who persecute you, bless and do not curse. Rejoice
> with those who rejoice; mourn with those who mourn. Live in
> harmony with one another. Do not be proud, but be willing to
> associate with people of low position. Do not be conceited.
>   Do not repay anyone evil for evil. Be careful to do what is right
> in the eyes of everybody. (Romans 12:14–17)

The truly consecrated soul will leave its case in the hands of God, and He
will avenge its wrong. As the Revised Version has it, "I will recompense"
(12:19). If we are truly consecrated, we will desire His mercy and blessing
for those who have wronged us.

Our business is to "bless and do not curse" (12:14) and heap upon the
heads of our enemies the fiery coals of our love and benediction.

Many a life that has triumphed amid prosperity and praise breaks down
under misunderstanding, misrepresentation and cruel wrong.

Nothing but the Spirit of Him who, "when they hurled their insults at
him, he did not retaliate" (1 Peter 2:23), when He was pierced, mocked and
crucified, gave prayers and blessings in return—nothing but His grace can
enable us to stand triumphantly in the hard places that come sooner or later
to every life that is truly given to God. This is the crowning glory of patience
and love.

10. Overcomes Evil with Good

The great principle of a life of victory and consecration is: "Do not be
overcome by evil, but overcome evil with good" (Romans 12:21). This gives
us the true secret of the life of faith. It is not by resisting evil directly that we
overcome it so much as by receiving the life and power of Christ, and letting
Him purify us by the expulsive power of a higher principle and a more
divine life.

It is the bringing in of the light that drives out the darkness. It is the
presence of the alkali that destroys the acid.

The indwelling Spirit of Christ brings the exclusion of sin and the world.
When the presence of God came into the ancient tabernacle there was no
room for Moses, and when the Holy Spirit comes into the soul, He will dis-
possess the power of evil.

A gardener had tried to straighten a willow that insisted on growing distorted and lopsided. All his pruning and his trimming were ineffectual to
make the branches grow on the other side of the tree.

He was about to give up in despair, when it occurred to him to investigate
the subterranean sources of its life. He took his spade and dug down, and

found a little stream on the side where the branches were growing, and the reason was obvious. The tree grew on the side where the stream was. He dug a little channel on the other side of the tree, and lo! the next year the tree straightened itself, the branches grew from the other direction, and the willow became symmetrical and beautiful. It could not be compressed or forced into symmetry, but it was gently turned into it by the attraction of a new and spontaneous life.

This is God's remedy for evil: "Overcome evil with good" (12:21b). There is none good but God; fill the heart with Him and His life and love, and we shall be lifted above the region of evil, and as the trees and plants of righteousness fill all the garden of the Lord, the weeds of the wilderness will disappear, and "the favor of the Lord our God [will] rest upon us" (Psalm 90:17a).

CHAPTER 13

CONSECRATION IN RELATION TO OUR CIVIL AND SOCIAL DUTIES

Romans 13

The New Testament always recognizes the existing conditions of human society, and among them the fact and right of civil government. Christ never encouraged His followers to take any position of antagonism to the political institutions of their time, but on the contrary instructed them to submit themselves to every ordinance of man for the Lord's sake, whether it be to the king, as supreme, or to them who are appointed by him for the administration of government.

If there ever was a time when the gospel had abundant cause to protest against the governments of the day it was in the time of Paul, when the cruel Nero sat upon the throne and the other heads of government used their power to oppress the followers of Jesus. But notwithstanding all this, we have the very strongest teaching in this passage that "the powers that be" (Romans 13:1, KJV) are to be recognized as God's appointed ordinances for the administration of justice, and that the true Christian will be a patriot and faithful citizen and do his duty in every relationship of life, thus commending the gospel of Christ even to the governments of the world and letting them see that Christ's kingdom is not of this world, nor in antagonism to any human authority.

CIVIL DUTIES

Therefore, he goes on to say, "Give everyone what you owe him: If you owe taxes [tribute, KJV], pay taxes; if revenue [custom, KJV], then revenue; if respect [fear, KJV], then respect; if honor, then honor" (13:7). Even the very tax collector is recognized as God's minister, and we are to pay our tribute without complaint, "Not trying to please men but God" (1 Thessalonians 2:4b).

Jesus thus acknowledged His own obligation to earthly governments and His own liability for tribute (see Matthew 17:24–26). And so, when we meet the same claims, it is delightful to realize that we are doing it for Him, as well as for ourselves and He will accept the gift and supply the means. Therefore we are to meet cheerfully and honestly every requirement of civil duty, giving tribute to whom tribute, custom to whom custom is due.

"Tribute" might well cover all requirements for taxes, and "custom" has reference rather to duties imposed on goods, and the same expression is still used in our commercial phraseology. All attempts, therefore, to defraud the authorities by smuggling, whether on a large or small scale, are prohibited by this and are unworthy of a disciple of Christ.

SOCIAL DUTIES

Not only so, but the smaller courtesies that are due to every social rank are here required from God's obedient children. "Fear," or reverence, and honor are to be given to all according to their stations. There is no true independence shown by rude disregard to the amenities of social life; there is no real dignity in refusing to acknowledge the higher station of another. Christ was never so noble as when He knelt with girdle and towel to wash the disciples' feet; or when He stood before Pontius Pilate in the judgment hall and recognized even him as His judge. Paul stood before Felix and Festus, none the less influential in his magnificent appeal because he fully recognized their dignity and authority.

The greatest curse of the land and our exaggerated democracy is the loss of reverence for age and authority, and the spirit of coarse, rude impudence, independence and lawlessness, which is destroying the true spirit of the youth of America and training them for the times of Antichrist and the lawlessness of the last days.

SECULAR DUTIES

"Let no debt remain outstanding [owe no man any thing, KJV], except the continuing debt to love one another, for he who loves his fellowman has fulfilled the law" (Romans 13:8). This short sentence covers the whole field of our mutual duties as man to man. True consecration reaches not only upward to God, but outward to the whole human family, and makes us righteous and blameless in our relation to every human being.

Undoubtedly the passage is to be taken literally, as well as in its more comprehensive reference. It forbids debt under all circumstances where it could involve anyone else in loss or injury. This is a very practical question and one which touches every line of human and social life. It is well that we should understand exactly what it means. Does it forbid literally and utterly our going into debt and contracting an account in business matters which remains unpaid for a longer or shorter time? Does it forbid the borrowing of money, the giving of promissory notes and the ordinary methods of human business transactions? If so, it would become an almost impossible prohibition according to the present methods of commercial procedure. We do not believe that this is its meaning, but that it really forbids our incurring any debt which we are not able to pay, and which we do not, at the time, know that we are able to pay.

I may be the owner of a house and owe half its value to the man from whom I have bought it, or the man who has advanced a loan upon it, and yet feel that I am conscientiously within the limits of the Word of God, provided that my house is of sufficient value to secure my creditor in his loan; but were I to go and borrow this money without security and in such a way as to involve him in any risk of losing it, I should be disobeying this prohibition. I have no right under this verse to go to a store, and purchase goods on account unless I know I have the means or the security to protect the party from whom I borrow from the possibility of loss. All reckless speculation, all loose and careless running into debt are forbidden by this wise and righteous enactment of the law of love.

MORAL OBLIGATIONS

In the verses that follow, the apostle also distinctly recognizes our obligation to the moral law in the sixth, seventh, eighth, ninth and 10th commandments. And while a Christian ought to be above this law in the sense that he does not require it to hold him from sin, because he is admitted into the higher plane of life which carries along with it all these things, yet he is never at liberty to transgress these commandments. He may rise above the law, but he is not at liberty to break the law.

I do not keep from murder because I fear the laws of the State of New York, but because my moral and religious principles lift me above the laws regarding murder; and yet that does not leave me at liberty to commit murder. In like manner I do not keep from stealing and slander because the Ten Commandments forbid it, but rather because the divine nature in me renders this thing unnatural and repulsive. I am thus lifted above the law, and yet, were I to stoop to commit these crimes, I would again come under the law by becoming a transgressor. For the law is not made for righteous persons, but for transgressors; as long as you obey it you are free; but the moment you disobey, you come beneath its ban.

True consecration, at the very least, ought to produce the highest morality, for even Jesus has said, "Unless your righteousness surpasses that of the Pharisees and teachers of the law, you will certainly not enter the kingdom of heaven" (Matthew 5:20).

THE LAW OF LOVE

The great principle of social righteousness and practical consecration is the law of love. "Love does no harm to its neighbor. Therefore love is the fulfillment of the law" (Romans 13:10), "and whatever other commandment there may be, are summed up in this one rule: 'Love your neighbor as yourself' " (13:9b). It is always better to have a principle than a manual. God's way is to touch things at the center, and let the extremities take care of themselves. Instead of sending a man to pick off all the old leaves from the forest trees, He lets the new sap and the new leafage come, and the new life throws off the old. Instead of sending an army of men with spades and shovels to clear away the ice and snow, He sends the spring sunshine, and in a few days the rivers are flowing and the winter is passed.

I have seen in a country village in the wintertime the roofs covered with drifting snow, in some cases many feet deep. Now one way of clearing off the drifts would be to send the inhabitants to the tops of their houses to shovel off the snowbanks into the street. But I have noticed the little spiral wreaths of smoke curling up from every cottage chimney as the morning fires were kindled, and lo! before an hour had passed, the heat of the house within had melted the snow upon the roof, and it was pouring down through every gutter and pipe without the touch of human hands. This is God's way.

How beautifully it works in the natural world and in the instincts of human affection! He does not put that mother under orders to nurse and feed her children, to work for her husband, to toil late and early for her little household in the nursery and kitchen until they have grown up and taken their places in life. No; He simply puts a little touch of wifely and motherly love in that true heart, and for love's dear sake she will toil and patiently endure what no earthly compensation could ever purchase from her. God just lights the fire of her heart, and lo! It moves the machinery of life.

And so in the higher spiritual world, God gives us His own love, and He bids us work, not according to slavish rules and minute exactions, but He just says, "Love does no harm to its neighbor" (13:10a). "Now live it out in holy freedom, and when I come again, your life shall be measured by the standard of love." And so we find in the last judgment that lives are weighed in the scale of human love. "For I was hungry and you gave me something to eat, I was thirsty and you gave me something to drink, I was a stranger and you invited me in, I needed clothes and you clothed me, I was sick and you looked after me, I was in prison and you came to visit me" (Matthew 25:35–36).

We will find this principle of very wide and constant application. For example, a prominent Christian lady wrote the other day, in one of our religious monthlies, these words:

God has been bringing to me lately, with great pointedness, some of His words; among others this has been applied to my conscience, "Speak evil of no man" [Titus 3:2a, KJV]. Now, I used to think that it was right to obey this when I was in public or in social circles, but that it was no harm to speak freely to my husband about these things; but God has been showing me that His Word is of constant application, and that I have no freedom to disobey it even in the privacy of my own home and with my heart's dearest friend.

It will subtract half of our talk from the story of life; it will simplify a thousand questions of social duty; it will bring many a little self-denial, and many a little loving service that we have not thought of before, simply to live in this great law. "Love does no harm to its neighbor" (Romans 13:10a). "Love your neighbor as yourself," (13:9b) and yet higher still, "Love each other as I have loved you" (John 15:12b).

This great principle of love is the true interpreter of the law. The seventh commandment is not fulfilled by a mere outward abstinence from immorality, but by a spirit of loving consideration for the purity, welfare and happiness of all with whom we sustain human relations. Therefore, the question of murder is merely a question of love to our brother. Therefore, the question of stealing involves every act that would injure our brother's prosperity. Therefore, the command forbidding false witness against our neighbor is violated whenever we speak any word which is calculated to injure a brother in his reputation and influence. Therefore, the 10th commandment, "You shall not covet" (Deuteronomy 5:21a) prohibits all selfish desires which could even wish evil to another, or covet anything which would deprive him of his rights.

At the same time the law of love puts its own limitations on its own acts as the dearest and highest love. It is not love merely for the one individual with due regard to all the complicated interest involved. For this reason the sixth commandment does not require us to promote our brother's prosperity by that which would injure others. The ninth commandment does not forbid us bearing witness against our neighbor when it is necessary for us to protect an individual from the unworthy influence of another; only we must be very sure that the statement made is absolutely true, and that the protection is absolutely necessary, and that in giving it we are not doing a greater injury to the one against whom we are bearing our testimony, for love can always protect the interests of both and act for the good of both, even the most unworthy.

THE SUPREME MOTIVE

The great incentive to practical consecration is the near coming of our Lord:

And do this, understanding the present time. The hour has come for you to wake up from your slumber, because our salvation is nearer now than when we first believed. The night is nearly over; the day is almost here. So let us put aside the deeds of darkness and put on the armor of light. Let us behave decently, as in the daytime, not in orgies and drunkenness, not in sexual immorality and debauchery, not in dissension and jealousy. Rather, clothe yourselves with the Lord Jesus Christ, and do not think about how to gratify the desires of the sinful nature. (Romans 13:11–14)

This passage brings the sublimest of hopes into direct touch with the most practical of duties. It lets the very glory of the coming kingdom shine into our kitchens, and shops, and homes, and everyday life, as a great searchlight and a divine inspiration. It takes the vision of the transfiguration (Matthew 17:2) down from the mountaintop to the plain, and enables us to live every moment under the powers of the world to come.

1. It tells us that the night is nearly gone, and that the day is just at hand. If this were true in Paul's day, how much more must it be true today? Already the Morning Star of hope has arisen in many a heart and the first gleams of the sunrise can be seen.

2. It bids us, "wake up from your slumber" (Romans 13:11). Sleep is a condition in which real things seem unreal and unreal things seem real. To the dreamer the land of dreams appears to be a world of actual persons and things, yet the realities of life all around him are quite unrealized. The flames may be bursting into his chamber; the robber may be stealing away his treasures; the dearest interest of life may be at stake, and yet he is unconcerned, while about some imaginary trouble his whole mind is stirred into agony and suspense as he dreams of some fancied peril or grasps some imaginary joy. So many are sleeping in the spiritual realms, incessantly occupied about imaginary things and utterly insensible to the actual concerns of their highest being. Let us wake out of sleep; let us be alert; let us be alive to the great necessities that really concern us.

3. Let us put off the garments of the night and the indulgences of the night—the loose robes of pleasure and flowing garments of repose. The festal pleasures of the hours of darkness are not for the children of the day. Let us cast off the works of darkness.

4. Let us arm ourselves for the day. Before we put on our clothes let us put on our weapons, for we are stepping out into a land of enemies and a world of dangers; let us put on the helmet of salvation, the breastplate of faith and love, and the shield of faith, and stand armed and vigilant as the dangers of the last days gather around us.

5. Let us put on the Lord Jesus Christ. This is our robe of day. Not our

own works or righteousness, but the person and righteousness of the Lord Jesus Christ, who gave us His very life and becomes to us our all-sufficiency.

6. Let us walk as the children of the day. "Not in orgies and drunkenness; not in sexual immorality and debauchery, not in dissension and jealousy" (13:13b). These are the things of the night and are not even to be thought of by the children of the day.

The spirit of strife and envying is just as defiling as the spirit of licentiousness and lasciviousness; all belong to the darkness. But the children of the day are to walk in righteousness and live circumspectly, soberly and godly, "while we wait for the blessed hope—the glorious appearing of our great God and Savior, Jesus Christ" (Titus 2:13).

7. Let us say "no" to the flesh, the world and the love of self, and learn that holy self-denial in which consists so much of the life of obedience. "Make no provision for the flesh" (Romans 13:14b, KJV); give no recognition to our lower life. Say "no" to everything earthly and selfish. How very much of the life of faith consists in simply denying ourselves! We begin with one great "yes" to God, and then we conclude with an eternal "no" to ourselves, the world, the flesh and the devil.

If you look at the Ten Commandments of the Decalogue, you will find that nearly every one of them is a "You shall not." In the 13th chapter of First Corinthians, with its beautiful picture of love, you will find that most of the characteristics of love are in the negative, what love "does not, thinks not, says not, is not." And so you will find the largest part of the life of consecration is really saying "no."

The dress of an Oriental woman is all fastened on her person by one little knot. Yards and yards of cloth drop in a most elegant fashion, and are all suspended from one little fastening. And so, our spiritual garments are all fastened on one little "not," and if that gives way our garments fall, and we are left naked and ashamed.

In the last chapter, we saw the great principle of overcoming evil with good. Here, just as emphatically, we have the corresponding principle of keeping the good by denying the evil.

Let us learn the divine power of this little weapon, "no." When Satan tempts us, let us learn to say "no"; when the flesh clamors for its rights, let us learn to say "no"; when the world allures with its brightness and its fascinations, let us learn to say "no"; when subtle self would insinuate its claims above all else, say "no," and thus let life become one everlasting "yes" to God, and one uncompromising "no" to self and sin. Thus shall we walk as the children of the day, and be ready for the breaking of the everlasting morning.

CHAPTER 14

CONSECRATION IN RELATION TO OUR DUTY TO THE WEAK AND ERRING

> We who are strong ought to bear with the failings of the weak and not to please ourselves. Each of us should please his neighbor for his good, to build him up. For even Christ did not please himself but, as it is written: "The insults of those who insult you have fallen on me." For everything that was written in the past was written to teach us, so that through endurance and the encouragement of the Scriptures we might have hope.
> May the God who gives endurance and encouragement give you a spirit of unity among yourselves as you follow Christ Jesus. (Romans 15:1–5)

The glory of practical Christianity is that while it deals with the highest and most sublime principles of truth, yet it applies them to the most practical and commonplace things of human life and holds a perfect balance between the highest and the lowest things, the loftiest devotion and the commonest duty.

The natural religions of the world all fail in this respect. Buddhism is purely speculative. Confucianism is purely moral. Christianity combines both, and teaches us at once to "never be lacking in zeal, but keep your spiritual fervor, serving the Lord" (12:11).

The earlier chapters of this epistle are devoted to the theory of sanctification, but in these closing chapters it is applied in the most practical way to every possible relationship of life.

It has already been presented to us in relation to our social and civil duties, but in these chapters a more delicate phase of practical consecration is worked out with infinite wisdom and heart-searching power, and many of the most difficult questions of duty are settled by great principles which carry a self-evidencing power in their very enunciation.

There is no class of persons more difficult for an earnest Christian to deal with than those with whom one is often thrown in contact, who are described in this passage as "weak." It is much easier to have to deal directly with open enemies and the people of the world than with those who really belong to Christ, but seem to be inconsistent and unworthy of the name.

It very often happens that the most earnest souls are thrown into contact with these very uncongenial associates. They are often met with in the same family, in the same Christian work, in the same church, in the same secular calling—compelled to be in constant contact and yet utterly unlike in their character.

These are little diamonds, or little bits of diamond dust, genuine, indeed, but of no further use than to polish the larger diamonds. It is often very difficult to see why the strong, the bold, the uncompromising follower of Christ should be hampered and hindered by such associations; but they will be found at last to be God's most valuable purifying agencies, and we shall find them our greatest blessings.

The apostle tells us how we are to deal with them.

FELLOWSHIP

1. We are to receive them. We are not to reject them and try to get away from them. God has a place for them in His Church. We are not to try to get up an *elite* company of congenial, pleasant Christian associates, in every way desirable; but we are to accept all the conditions which God has mingled in this world, and to receive them in His name, and count it the highest proof of His confidence in us, that He entrusts them to our spiritual care and fellowship.

The most profitable church in which one's lot can be cast, and the very best school in which our character can be developed, is just such a combination of various elements, and even trying surroundings.

The Master's highest test of Peter's love was not feeding the lambs or the sheep, but the feeble sheep, and nothing but God's highest love can qualify and fit us for this trust.

SCHISM

2. We are to receive them without controversy. "Accept him whose faith is weak, without passing judgment on disputable matters" (14:1). There is nothing that so rends the body of Christ and destroys all unity in Christian life as religious controversy, especially about nonessential matters.

For half a century the churches of Scotland were divided up into half a score of Presbyterian bodies, on a lot of microscopic points, and nearly a hundred Christian sects testify to the baneful effects of ecclesiastical strife.

There is room for an infinite variety of opinion on minor points, but there is no need to flaunt our opinions in the face of our brethren, and provoke them to criticism and controversy. Things which, if allowed to rest, would never be serious difficulties, when agitated grow into an exaggerated importance, and Christian love becomes suspended on a lot of side issues and separated from its true center.

There are, it is true, great essential principles that we cannot compromise, respecting the person and work of Christ, the simplicity of the great salvation, the fullness of redemption and the future life; but the platform is broad enough to hold the great body of evangelical Christians and bridge over the hundred little differences that need never have been publicly emphasized.

There is a strong power in words to injure and separate. A thought is comparatively harmless, but when you clothe it and express it and send it out for public recognition, it becomes not only a thorn of contention, but a thistle seed to bring a thousand contentions wherever it alights.

LIBERTY

3. Liberty of conscience on the part of every man to act according to his own convictions is one of the strongest principles of all true unity in the body of Christ.

"Each one should be fully convinced in his own mind" (14:5). "I am fully convinced that no food is unclean in itself. But if anyone regards something as unclean, then for him it is unclean" (14:14).

These simple words carry with them a principle of extreme importance. We need scarcely say that this passage does not refer to the question of moral right or wrong, because there are some things that are essentially and eternally right and wrong. The word "unclean" here is a ceremonial term, the same word used in the vision of Peter (Acts 10:9–16), where he was taught to regard nothing as common or unclean, and the passage refers entirely to things outside the pale of morals. Stealing, slander, lust and murder are essentially wrong, but there are a thousand things outside the pale of right and wrong that are not essential or important. Keeping certain days, matters of dress, eating and drinking—these are the things which he says are not wrong in themselves, but are to be entirely regulated by the instincts of conscience.

If you think it wrong to drink tea and coffee, and yet do so, you are committing a sin; if you think it wrong to wear a colored dress, and do so against your conscience, you are committing a sin; if you esteem it wrong to work on Christmas or Good Friday, and go against your conscience, you are committing a sin. If, however, you have no conscience on these subjects, you are free. There is nothing more sacred in the universe than the voice of conscience. Even the heathen devotee, bowing at the shrine of his idol, is entitled to our respect. He may be misguided, but he is obeying what is to him the voice of God.

When a man looks me in the face, after I have said all I can say to convince him of some truth, and says he is honestly walking according to the law of God as he understands it, I must accept it and I dare not sit in judgment on him and compel him to accept my conscience instead of his own. But he is bound just as much to accept my conscientious convictions as I am to accept his, and both of us are most solemnly bound to be sure that our conscience is right, and that we have consecrated it in the light of God's Holy Word and will; for in the day of final judgment, a misguided conscience, even if honestly obeyed, will not save us from the consequences of error.

At the same time it is the only rule by which man can act, but God will go deeper and judge man by eternal and immutable truth. But we must judge man according to the law of conscience, except in those matters where God already by His own law has determined the right and the wrong.

This principle, then, of respecting the conscience of our brethren in things nonessential, is the true secret of toleration and Christian unity.

JUDGE NOT

4. Judging one another in matters of conscience is forbidden:

> The man who eats everything must not look down on him who does not, and the man who does not eat everything must not condemn the man who does, for God has accepted him. Who are you to judge someone else's servant? To his own master he stand or falls. And he will stand, for the Lord is able to make him stand. . . .
>
> You, then, why do you judge your brother? Or why do you look down on your brother? For we will all stand before God's judgment seat. . . .
>
> Therefore let us stop passing judgment on one another. Instead, make up your mind not to put any stumbling block or obstacle in your brother's way. (Romans 14:3–4, 10, 13)

We are not to judge our weak brother in obeying his conscience in something which we cannot see; but our weak brother is not to judge us in acting with liberty in a matter which to him seems so important. The toleration is to be mutual, and each is to leave the other to the judgment of God.

It is even implied that when we sit in judgment upon another, we provoke God to reverse our judgment, and even do more for one on whom we pronounce the judgment than He would otherwise have done. "And he will stand, for the Lord is able to make him stand" (14:4b).

God is jealous of His own prerogative of judgment. There is a wonderful law of retribution which invariably brings back upon our own heads the judgment we pass upon others. "Therefore let us stop passing judgment on one another. Instead, make up your mind not to put any stumbling block or obstacle in your brother's way" (14:13).

THE TEST OF FAITH

5. The principle of faith with reference to all our own acts is emphasized, and is most important in respect to the whole range of things referred to in this chapter.

"So whatever you believe about these things keep between yourself and God. Blessed is the man who does not condemn himself by what he approves. But the man who has doubts is condemned if he eats, because his eating is not from faith; and everything that does not come from faith is sin" (14:22–23).

It is a safe rule never to do anything about which we have the slightest doubt, and always to delay our decisions and actions until we are absolutely sure. Then shall we have the happiness of having our conscience on our own side and of carrying with us our own approval. But a shadow of doubt is enough to make us miserable and to involve us in the consciousness of sin and wrong.

Next to the approval of God, there is nothing so sublime as the consciousness in your deepest being of meeting your own sense of right and acting according to your highest convictions. Let us, therefore, always take time to make sure of our action, and then act in certainty and "full assurance of faith" (Hebrews 10:22).

But along with this is the yet higher principle of love, in sacrificing our own preferences and refraining from what our own conscience would fully approve for ourselves for the sake of another, lest by our act another's conscience might be wounded and another's steps might be stumbled.

This is one of the finest principles in Christian ethics, and one of the most lofty and beautiful lines of Christian self-denial possible for the disciple of Christ. "Everything is permissible," said Paul, "but not everything is constructive" (1 Corinthians 10:23b).

I may be perfectly free myself to do many things, the doing of which might hurt my brother and wound his conscience, and love will gladly surrender the little indulgence so that she may save her brother from temptation. There are many questions which are easily settled by this principle. For example, the use of stimulants, which in the judgment of some is forbidden by Scripture, yet to other intelligent Christians seems to be an open question, and they argue that the Bible does not prohibit the use of wine.

Supposing that this were even so (which we only admit for the sake of argument), still the higher law of love would lead them to abandon the use of stimulants because of the harm they do, and the inability of thousands to withstand the temptation.

So there are many forms of recreation which in themselves might be harmless and, under certain circumstances, unobjectionable; but they have become associated with worldliness and godlessness and have proved snares and temptations to many a young heart in life; and therefore, the law of love would lead you to avoid them, discountenance them and in no way give encouragement to others to participate in them.

It is just in these things that are not required of us by absolute rules, but are the impulses of a thoughtful love, that the highest qualities of Christian character show themselves and the most delicate shades of Christian love are manifested.

You are not compelled to do it, but your doing it for Jesus' sake will add to your crown many a jewel of indescribable glory when the Master shall weigh all acts and recompense all works.

REPRESENTING CHRIST

6. The great principle that must regulate all such questions is given us in the opening verses of the 15th chapter, and may be summed up in one sentence—act to every one, and in everything, as if you were the Lord Jesus.

"Accept one another, then, just as Christ accepted you, in order to bring praise to God" (Romans 15:7). This is a sublime principle, and it will give sublimity to life. It is stated elsewhere in similar language—"And whatever you do, whether in word or deed, do it all in the name of the Lord Jesus" (Colossians 3:17a).

This is our high calling: to represent Christ; to act in His behalf and in His character and Spirit, under all circumstances and toward all men. "What would Jesus do?" is a simple question which will settle every difficulty, and always settle it on the side of love.

But we cannot answer this question rightly without having Jesus Himself in our hearts. We cannot *act* Christ. This is too grave a matter for acting. We must *have* Christ, and simply be natural and true to the life within us, and that life will act itself out.

Oh, how easy it is to love everyone and see nothing but loveliness when our own heart is filled with Christ; and how every difficulty melts away and everyone we meet seems clothed with the Spirit within us when we are filled with the Holy Spirit!

I remember a beautiful sunset, the last time I left my father's house. As we drove along in the evening hour, the western sky became a mass of amber and gold, and the banks of clouds were piled like myriads of many-colored gems. I watched it until my eyes were almost dazed with the sunset glory;

and I turned and looked at the people beside me, and they were all amber and gold. I looked at the fields in every direction, and they were all amber and gold. I looked away to the distant horizon, and everything was amber and gold. Everything was colored by the sunset glory.

Yes, I thought, *and when our eyes are fixed upon Him, everything is God-touched and glorified, and the commonest things of life become divine, the hardest things easy, and the most repulsive things beautiful and attractive.*

This is the secret of love, of joy, of victory: to be filled with Him, to be one with Him, to abide in Him and to minister Him in the world in which we are called to represent Him. It is the old prayer:

> Help me to live like Thee,
> Help me to live like Thee,
>   By Thy wonderful power,
>   By Thy grace every hour,
> Help me to live like Thee.

Only it is transformed and lifted to a higher meaning:

> Live Thou, Thy life in me,
> Live Thou, Thyself in me;
>   By Thy wonderful power
>   By Thy grace every hour,
> Live Thou, Thyself in me.

CHAPTER 15

PRACTICAL CONSECRATION IN RELATION TO THE EVANGELIZATION OF THE WORLD

To be a minister of Christ Jesus to the Gentiles with the priestly duty of proclaiming the gospel of God, so that the Gentiles might become an offering acceptable to God, sanctified by the Holy Spirit.

Therefore I glory in Christ Jesus in my service to God. I will not venture to speak of anything except what Christ has accomplished through me in leading the Gentiles to obey God by what I have said and done—by the power of signs and miracles, through the power of the Spirit. So from Jerusalem all the way around to Illyricum, I have fully proclaimed the gospel of Christ. It has always been my ambition to preach the gospel where Christ was not known, so that I would not be building on someone else's foundation. Rather, as it is written:

"Those who were not told about him will see,
and those who have not heard will understand."
(Romans 15:16–21)

We have seen the relation of a consecrated life to our social and civil duties, and to our mutual obligations in the body of Christ. But now, in the closing portion of this epistle, the great apostle reaches the climax of this thought and theme, and leads us up to the influence of a consecrated life in connection with the evangelization of the world and the great work to which he devoted the largest portion of his own life—the preaching of the gospel to the Gentiles.

It would seem very strange if the Apostle Paul had got through a treatise on Christian life and doctrine without touching this great theme. Indeed, it is the true outcome of all divine life and real consecration.

In the very first paragraph of his epistle, we find him referring to this theme in the strongest terms.

> I am obligated both to Greeks and non-Greeks, both to the wise and the foolish. That is why I am so eager to preach the gospel also to you who are at Rome.
> I am not ashamed of the gospel, because it is the power of God for the salvation of everyone who believes: first for the Jew, then for the Gentile. (1:14–16)

And in the last chapter of the epistle, and the last verse but one, he closes with the same sublime thought:

> . . . the mystery hidden for long ages past, but now revealed and made known through the prophetic writings by the command of the eternal God, so that all nations might believe and obey him—to the only wise God be glory forever through Jesus Christ! Amen. (16:25b–27)

Here in the closing section of the body of the epistle, he more fully unfolds some of the principles that lie back of the great work of evangelization, and he illustrates them by his own testimony and experience.

He tells us that Jesus Christ is the minister of God not only for the Jews, but also for the Gentiles:

> So that the Gentiles may glorify God for his mercy, as it is written:
>
> "Therefore I will praise you among the Gentiles;
>   I will sing hymns to your name."

Again, it says,

> "Rejoice, O Gentiles, with his people."

And again,

> "Praise the Lord, all you Gentiles,
>   and sing praises to him, all you peoples."
>   (15:9–11)

God's great gift of His Son was not for any one class or race. "For God so loved the world that he gave his one and only Son, that whoever believes in him shall not perish but have eternal life" (John 3:16).

We have no right to accept His salvation for ourselves, and leave a billion of our brethren, whose souls are just as precious as ours and for whom Christ died, without even the knowledge of His great salvation.

It is not a matter of beneficence to give the gospel to the nations, it is simply a matter of obligation. We are "obligated both to Greeks and non-Greeks," both to the Jew and the Gentile, "both to the wise and the foolish" (Romans 1:14).

We are simply guilty of breach of trust and spiritual dishonesty and crime, if we withhold the gospel from any of our fellow beings whom it is within our power to reach.

The evangelization of the world, therefore, is the highest obligation of the true Christian, and neglect of it will leave the guilt of souls upon the Church of Jesus Christ.

> O Church of Christ! what wilt thou say
> When, in the dreadful Judgment Day,
> They charge thee with their doom?

PAUL'S MINISTRY TO THE GENTILES

Paul says that he was specially called "to be a minister of Christ Jesus to the Gentiles with the priestly duty of proclaiming the gospel of God" (15:16a). The word "minister" here used is a peculiar term in the original. It is the same word used in Romans 13:4a, respecting civil rulers: "For he is God's servant [minister, KJV] to do you good."

Paul recognizes his call to preach the gospel to the Gentiles as having just as much authority and importance as the office of an emperor or king. He calls himself specifically the ambassador of Jesus Christ, and recognizes himself as called to represent the King of kings and Lord of lords among princes, and in the face of rulers and kingdoms; and that there is One that stands behind him saying, "All authority in heaven and on earth has been given to me. Therefore go and make disciples" (Matthew 28:18b–19a).

It is this that gives courage to the ambassador of Christ in dangerous and difficult fields. It was this that enabled an Arnot to face the perils of Central Africa, and a Paton to stand undaunted before the savages of Tanna, because he knew that he represented the Mighty One who had created the savage beasts of the jungle and the yet more savage men who could not touch his life until the Lord Himself should give permission or command.

But Paul used another term for minister here, that is quite suggestive: "proclaiming [ministering, KJV] the gospel of God, so that the Gentiles might become an offering acceptable to God, sanctified by the Holy Spirit" (Romans 15:16b). The word "minister" here is the word used to denote the office of the priest, as the former denotes the coming of the ambassador.

We are priestly ministers, as well as royal ambassadors. Our ministry is not only to be armed by omnipotence and inspired by courage from on high, but it is to be in the lamb-like spirit of gentleness, tenderness and prayer. It is a loving sacrifice for God, and its work is a priestly offering laid upon the altar of God and acceptable to God through Jesus Christ.

This is a very beautiful and practical conception of missionary work. There is a great difference in being consecrated to our work and consecrated to our God. We may be consecrated and fitted to do missionary work, and utterly fail if He should call us to do something different. But when we are consecrated to Him, we shall be ready for anything He may require of us, and be as well qualified to serve Him by the sickbed of a brother, or even in the secular duties of home, as in standing in the pulpit or leading a soul to Christ.

Paul's conception is holy work, or a special sacrifice, and directly unto Christ, and Christ alone; and he stood as one should stand at the altar of incense, lifting up with holy hands the Gentile nations unto God, and laying all his work like fragrant incense before the throne, pleased only with what would please his Master and stand the test of His inspection and the seal of His approval in that glorious day.

This is the spirit of true service. This is the highest, noblest missionary work.

THE HOLY SPIRIT AND MISSIONS

Paul's glory was that God had set His seal upon his mission work by giving the power of the Holy Spirit to witness to it through signs and wonders and by the power of the Spirit of God, "in leading the Gentiles to obey God by what I have said and done" (15:18b).

This was all that he cared to remember in connection with his work. He says nothing of the numbers gathered in, or the apparent results, as we would estimate them today, but his glory is that God has wrought through him, and that the work has been divine.

How different modern and ancient missionary work! Nowadays, the record usually includes a delightful farewell meeting, the clasp of multitudes of hands in blessing, an ample outfit, a secure support, a pleasant ocean voyage, a welcome on the foreign shore, a home support, a field made ready, perhaps a chapel in which to preach, and a thousand encouragements and comforts from loving hearts and hands.

Now look at the ancient picture. A stormy passage across the Aegean Sea, perhaps on the wave-washed deck of an ancient sailing vessel, landing at

Philippi among utter strangers, a walk about the city in search of employment, a humble job in some tent factory, a few days' toil at a loom, and then comes the Sabbath. Of one thing we may be very sure, that Paul and Silas did not work on this day. Perhaps they lost their job, but they kept their conscience clear.

The Sabbath morning finds them walking along the riverside until at last they reach a little company of women meeting for prayer. Before the day is over, the first European convert has accepted the gospel and the evening finds them lodging in the house of Lydia and beginning their ministry in the marketplace.

But before the week is ended they are lying in the inmost dungeon of a Roman prison, bound and bleeding, and their work seeming to have come to a disastrous close.

Some missionaries might have said, "We have made a mistake; the field is not open; the difficulties are too great." But Paul and Silas had taken God with them in their great missionary journey. They saw only an occasion for Him to work; and so, ere long, their prayers turned to praises and their prison was ringing with their songs of holy trust and gladness, until the answer came from heaven, the prison doors were burst open and the cruel jailer cried out, "What must I do to be saved?" (Acts 16:30b).

It was God's way of putting His seal on the work; and so, as surely as we go into any work for God and ask Him to put His stamp upon it, He will bring up some tremendous crisis in which none but He can bring us through, and so signalize it by His glorious deliverance.

This is the way that God shows His power, and difficulty is but a challenge for His divine interposition. And so again and again in Paul's missionary work God put His hand upon the work by delivering him out of the most trying situations. Look at him at Derbe and Lystra—beaten by the mob, dragged beyond the city gates and left for dead. He simply rose upon his feet as the disciples gathered around him and, taking strength from the Living One, went forth to his work as if nothing had happened (14:19–20).

Look at him again, on his way to Rome to fulfill the promise made in this very epistle, standing on the rocking deck of the little ship as it toiled in the Euroclydon (27:14, KJV), and bravely triumphed over the angry storm and the terror of the captain and the crew, leading them by his triumphant faith to the shore. Or, again, on the shores of Malta, flinging from his hand the viper that threatened his life (28:3–5), and turning the very hate of Satan into God's most protecting love; and then going forth throughout the island, to pour into other hearts the blessing which he himself had received.

This was the way that Paul did his mission work, and turned every curse into a blessing and every assault into a victory.

This is the very way God still wants to send forth His workers and seal their labors with His mighty hand. But you must first know His power in your own life, and then it will be easy to claim it for the lives of others, and as the seal of your work. There is nothing that God will not do for you if you will first let Him do it in you.

This is the greatest need of foreign work today, both at home and abroad, a mighty baptism of the Holy Spirit. This will produce missionary enthusiasm, the consecration of means, the calling of true workers, the preparation of the power that you most need, and this will open the hearts of the heathen, will break the barriers and bars of brass asunder, and will give the triumphs of the gospel in the face of idolatry and opposition.

One of the most delightful features of our missionary work in the past few years has been the remarkable outpouring of the Holy Spirit in foreign lands and the beginning of the signs and wonders that have been promised in connection with the last days and the coming of the Lord.

This has been manifested not only in the lives of such men as Paton, MacKay, and many others of our own generation, but it has been still more manifest in the wonderful ingathering of thousands of souls in India, Burma, and the [Pacific] Islands.

It is still more marked in the past few years in the deepening of spiritual life on the part both of the missionaries and the national churches, and it is beginning to be manifest in the power of God in answer to the faith of His children, in the healing of diseases and the manifestations of the supernatural power of God, as in apostolic days, even in the midst of heathen darkness.

This mighty work of the world's evangelization is too vast for us. It must be the work of the Holy Spirit and the omnipotence of God. Let this be the special prayer for our missionaries in foreign lands, that God will own them, and will, through them, illustrate the wonders of His ancient power! And let it be the ambition of every true minister of Christ to be an instrument of God, and to have the seal of heaven upon all his work!

Paul said he would not dare to speak of anything except what Christ had wrought by him. All else was to him worthless and transitory, and only that shall remain in our eternal record, and only that will be worth remembering which God has done through us, and sealed with the stamp of His mighty hand.

THE SCOPE OF PAUL'S MISSIONARY WORK

There is no more sublime spectacle in the records of Christianity than this lone man, in an age when the methods of travel and transportation were so restricted—steamships, railroads and modern civilization unknown—in a single lifetime, almost half of which was spent in prison, traversing the whole world, and preaching the gospel of Christ in regions which were then more remote than China or Siberia are to us today.

He says that "from Jerusalem all the way around to Illyricum, I have fully proclaimed the gospel of Christ" (Romans 15:19) and that he is now about to go to Spain, because he has "no more place for me to work in these regions" (15:23). He has so fully accomplished his work that he is at liberty to undertake a still wider range of evangelization and is already on his way to distant Spain to preach the gospel there.

Where was Illyricum? It included the present provinces of Servia [now Serbia] and Dalmatia [the coastal area of Croatia], and a large part of European Turkey, regions where even now the gospel is but imperfectly proclaimed; and Spain was as the vast confines of Europe. And yet, yonder brave pioneer was even now turning his footsteps to tell to the people of Tarshish the wonderful story of divine love. With a score of such men, the whole world could be evangelized in less than a generation.

The glory of his ministry was this, that he preached the gospel in "the regions beyond" (2 Corinthians 10:16).

THE REGIONS BEYOND

"It has always been my ambition," he says, "to preach the gospel where Christ was not known, so that I would not be building on someone else's foundation. Rather, as it is written: 'Those who were not told about him will see,/ and those who have not heard will understand' " (Romans 15:20–21).

The churches at home are crowding 100,000 into one little circle which we call "the home field" and giving one Christian worker to every 60 of our population, while China has one missionary to every 200,000–300,000; and the ambition of a young minister is often to succeed some distinguished name or to follow into some place made ready for his hand. What an ignoble aim compared with the apostle's glorious purpose—that he might be used of God to carry the gospel for the first time to myriads who have never heard it, that he might have a work all his own and in the last great day might be permitted to present to God races and tongues as his crown of righteousness!

God is putting this ambition in some noble hearts today, but the time will not be long when it will be possible. Soon, very soon, the message will have been proclaimed to every creature and it will never be possible again to sow the seed in the virgin soil, or be the first to tell of the love of Jesus to the human soul.

> Let us go to the regions beyond,
> 　Where the story has never been told;
> To the millions that never of Jesus have heard,
> 　Let us take the sweet story of old.

There is also a "region beyond" even in Christian work at home. There are many things that we can do: there are neglected souls which the multitudes pass by; there are neglected pathways which the workers do not tread; there are cellars and garrets and lonely cottages where the routine worker never thinks of turning aside to enter; there are unattractive missions and uncongenial services, unloved and uninteresting talks and toils, which the Master will recognize and recompense and say, "whatever you did for one of the least of these brothers of mine, you did for me" (Matthew 25:40b).

The poor widow of Constantinople could not build the splendid temple, or even pay for one stone in its magnificent walls, but she could gather the long grass from the wayside and spread it along the road over which the stones were to be carried, to save them from being scratched and torn as they went by. It was a little service to smooth the passage for the workers, but when the temple was dedicated, it is said the angels wrote on it, "This church the widow Eudoxia built for God."

The other day there was a service to be done for a certain work of God, which would be the last thing that many would have thought of doing. It was not the sending out of a missionary; it was not the planting of a new mission; it was not the giving to some object which would bear good fruit. But it was the meeting of an old debt which was keeping back a young worker from the field; it was putting money into what some would call a hole, where little fruit would be seen from the investment, so far at least, as that particular sum was concerned, and yet would set a worker free to go to the uttermost parts of the earth.

But God had a faithful servant to whom He whispered in the night season His gentle command, and the heart was more than ready to obey the vision; and before the week was ended that little that had been laid aside for Jesus, too sacred to touch for any personal need, was laid at the Master's feet for this unusual claim. The obligation was met, the obstacle was removed, and the worker was left free to go forth with the seal of God upon his life and ministry.

Ah, these are the things that the Holy Spirit loves and that the Master will signalize at His coming! There are such "regions beyond" for all of us. May God give each of us the glory of having our own work and not another's!

Paul says he made it a point to do this. The word used is very emphatic. "It has always been my ambition [I have strived, KJV] to preach the gospel where Christ was not known" (Romans 15:20a). The word "strive" literally means a point of honor with God; it might be made more—a point of honor to the workers themselves. Then shall the world soon know the joyful sound, and the herald proclaim, "Look, he is coming!" (Revelation 1:7a).

CHAPTER 16

OBJECT LESSONS OF CHRISTIAN SERVICE

Romans 16

*A scroll of remembrance was written in his presence concerning those
who feared the LORD and honored his name.*
*"They will be mine," says the LORD Almighty, "in the day when I
make up my treasured possession." (Malachi 3:16b–17a)*

This chapter is a page from the book of life, and it gives us an idea of
how the records of our lives will appear when the books shall be opened.

The long genealogical tables which we sometimes pass over in reading our
Bibles are by no means dry and uninteresting. To the divinely taught mind
they are chapters from the book of remembrance, and some day others may
read our names, as we are reading theirs.

They tell us how God appreciates and remembers the lives and services of
His children, and discriminates, with loving fidelity, between the better and
the best.

This chapter forms the climax to the principles which have just been unfolded in the previous pages, and we see them here in action and practice.

THE MINISTRY OF WOMEN

1. We have a glimpse of women in the Apostolic Church. The majority of
the Christians here named and noted are women, and they receive the
highest rank and recognition.

Surely if, in that day, when the restrictions of social life and the public
opinion of society made woman's public services so difficult, she had attained so high a place, how much more should she accomplish in this day of
freedom and equality, when the gospel has freed her from every fetter and
given her the place of honor and preeminence she now enjoys.

There is no doubt that the apostle limits woman's sphere in the Church of God; but only within the restraints required by her nature and her distinct place in the social economy.

Like a great river which when it flows within its channels is a blessing, but when it overflows its banks it becomes a desolation, so woman can only reach her highest mission when she moves in her true sphere.

In the First Epistle to the Corinthians (chapter 12), Paul gives her the right to prophesy, and he tells us that prophesying means to "speak . . . for . . . strengthening, encouragement and comfort" (1 Corinthians 14:3). This includes about all that any Christian woman ever wants to say. The only limitation there required is, that she shall have her head covered, which is a symbol of modesty.

The woman, therefore, who will keep in the modest place that both nature and the Bible require, may speak about anything that is unto "strengthening, encouragement and comfort."

Later he seems to limit this by requiring the women to "remain silent in the churches" (14:34). In another passage he adds, "I do not permit a woman to teach or to have authority over a man; . . . For Adam was formed first, then Eve" (1 Timothy 2:12–13).

It is quite certain that the apostle placed women under certain limitations. We believe that these had only to do with the exercise of authority in the churches. God did not mean woman to rule, but to love, suffer, and help. Her heart, and not her head, should be put in the ascendant. Her yieldedness is strength; her gentleness is her scepter. She is not called to exercise ecclesiastical authority, or take her place in the ordained ministry and government of the church; but in the ministry of testimony and teaching, both in public and in private, and in every office of holy love consistent with the principles of Christianity, she has boundless right and freedom.

There was one special ecclesiastical office given to women in the early church, and it is beginning to be revived in our own time. It is the office of deaconess. This was the position of Phoebe, first mentioned in this passage (Romans 16:1). The word "servant" here means, literally, deaconess.

The office of deaconess was very much the same as that of our city and foreign missionary. It was to teach, testify, and especially to minister to the sick and suffering in the primitive churches. It was recognized then as distinctively as the office of deacon, elder, or bishop; and while it gave woman no ecclesiastical authority, yet it recognized her proper ministry in an official way, and opened the widest doors of usefulness.

In our own day, the ministry of woman has been greatly honored of God, and while few women are called to leadership and it is doubtful if they are adapted to it, yet their ministry of help has been most blessed, and our missionary boards are more and more indebted to them than to any other source for the resources that have enabled them to extend their operations in all lands.

Indeed, it is sometimes said with reference to the bequests of men and the living offerings of consecrated women, that the missionary operations of some societies have been largely sustained by dead men and live women! May God more and more extend, honor and bless the ministry of women!

THE CHURCH IN THE HOUSE

2. We have next a glimpse of "the church in [the] house" (16:5, KJV).

We read of several "churches in the house" in the New Testament, the most prominent of which was the church in the house of Aquila and Priscilla. Indeed, for the first two or three centuries there were no ecclesiastical buildings as we understand them now. All their meetings were in private houses or upper rooms.

The first churches used for the preaching of the gospel and the worship of Christians were heathen temples transformed into Christian assembly rooms. It is probable that the Church was much more pure before it had church buildings than it has ever been since. It has been by no means certain that the addition of ecclesiastical buildings increased the purity and power of the Church.

When the apostle speaks of the Church he does not mean the church building, but the ecclesiastical society. When he asks women to keep silent in the churches he does not mean the building, but the assembly of the *Ecclesia*.

There is no doubt that the assembling of God's people in private houses and upper rooms had very much to do with the sweet and simple spirit of primitive Christianity. It was not only the church in the house, but it was also the house in the church. It would be well if our modern ecclesiasticism had more of this simple fellowship.

There is no sweeter picture in apostolic Christianity than good Aquila and Priscilla, the simple pair who entertained and helped Paul so kindly, and who were used of God to bring Apollos, the greatest intellect of the early Church, to know the fullness of Jesus and the power of the Holy Spirit.

In the single instance we see the power of the Christian home. Aquila and Priscilla could not preach like Apollos, but they could very lovingly bring Apollos to see the truth as it was in Jesus, and to become a great instrument in God's hands for preaching the gospel with power from on high.

Beloved, how is it with your house? Has it the church in the house? Beloved, how is it with your church? Is it the house of the church, filled with the spirit of unity, love and devotion to the common interest?

THE MINISTRY OF HELPERS

3. This chapter gives us a beautiful picture of helpers in Christ.

All the names mentioned in this chapter were simply helpers. There were no leaders, but again and again we read such expressions as these: "my fellow workers [helpers, KJV] in Christ Jesus" (16:3b), "who worked very hard for you" (16:6), etc.

The Church of God is overrun with captains. She is in great need of a few more privates. A few rivers run into the sea, but a far larger number run into other rivers. We cannot all be pioneers, but we can all be helpers, and no man is fitted to go in the front until he has learned well how to go second.

A spirit of self-importance is fatal to all work for Christ. The biggest enemy of true spiritual power is spiritual self-consciousness. Joshua must die before Jericho can fall.

God often has to test His chosen servants by putting them in a subordinate place before He can bring them to the front. Joseph must learn to serve in the kitchen and suffer in prison before he can rise to the throne, and as soon as Joseph is ready for the throne, the throne is always waiting for Joseph. God has more palaces than accepted candidates. Let us not be afraid to go into the training class, and even take the lowest place, for we shall soon go up, if we really deserve to.

A PAGE FROM THE BOOK OF LIFE

4. We have a very touching picture here of the lowly members in the church of Rome.

A great many of those named in this chapter are slaves. In the records of the catacombs almost all these names have been found registered as slaves belonging to some Roman family. But here we find them side by side with the most distinguished names. The chamberlain [director of public works] of Corinth and Quartus, the brother—who was doubtless a slave—send their greetings in the same sentence.

The various households here mentioned are all remembered by Paul with a recognition as kindly as their masters are remembered.

It may have often seemed strange to us that the New Testament did not condemn slavery. Of course, the whole spirit of its teaching is fatal to the cruel institution of serfdom, but Christ and His apostles uttered no definite and explicit denunciation of the system of human slavery—and yet the world was full of it and every important Roman family had its bondmen, and still the Bible is silent about it. Why?

The answer brings out a most beautiful fact, viz.: that the spirit and power of the gospel, when it reached the slave in his fetters, lifted him above his bondage and made him a free man in Christ and the brother of his master in the heavenly family.

This toleration of existing social conditions made the miracle of grace more marked and brought out some of the most beautiful features of primitive Christian love.

There is no more touching picture than that of Philemon and Onesimus, his slave, and the fine points of Christian consideration which the Apostle Paul was able to emphasize in his letter to his friend.

The gospel does not come to declare against the rich or force the poor into a higher social position apart from the natural conditions of human life, but it comes to so exalt the spirit of the lowly and give them such new power in their personal life and character that they will rise above their social restrictions and disadvantages and claim an equal place in the brotherhood of Christianity and the family of God.

No one is too lowly to be remembered in the Book of Life, or too lowly to be used of God and filled with the power of the Holy Spirit.

THE MINISTRY OF SUFFERING

5. The ministry of suffering is beautifully recognized in this chapter. Paul speaks of his "relatives who have been in prison with me" (16:7).

This is one way we have of winning a crown and working for our Master. We can suffer with Him, and if need be, we can suffer with His suffering ones. Paul often speaks of those who are "not ashamed of my chains" (2 Timothy 1:16b). There is a very beautiful passage in Hebrews, where the Christians are asked to "remember those earlier days . . . when you stood your ground in a great contest in the face of suffering. Sometimes you were publicly exposed to insult and persecution; at other times you stood side by side with those who were so treated" (Hebrews 10:32–33).

In a work like this it is very certain that, as we stand for God and for present truths, we shall be often misunderstood and perhaps even persecuted; and God recognizes with great tenderness and love the loyal devotion which stands true to the principles and leaders of such a movement until the day of probation is over and the hour of triumph comes—as it always comes to the truth and the right.

If you can do nothing else, my brother, you can at least be true, and there is nothing more dishonorable and sad than to prove a traitor to the trust committed to you and to the brethren with whom God has called you to stand and serve.

None of us are anything in ourselves, nor should we wish to draw persons to ourselves. But if God has permitted us to represent these great truths, principles and aims which the Spirit of God has inspired, which the full development of Christian life requires, and which a perishing world needs in this crisis age, then he is an enemy of God and must become his own enemy who opposes or weakens such a movement; and he who can do nothing more than simply stand true and give his loyal love, sympathy and prayers, is a partner in the work, a comrade in the great campaign, and shall share the recompense in the day when God shall remember our works and give us our crowns.

THE MINISTRY OF LETTER WRITING

6. We see in this chapter the ministry of correspondence. It is a remarkable fact that Paul had so many friends in Rome, and had so many personal greetings to send to them all, although he had never even visited this city. How did he get acquainted with them? Chiefly by correspondence. True, he had met some of them in other places; but most of them were friends to whom he had written, and who had written to him.

What are you doing with your pen? Is your private correspondence dedicated to God—or to idle gossip?

GOD REMEMBERS

7. This chapter reminds us of God's personal remembrance of each of His children, and the recompense He has in store for them in the final day.

It will not always be the day of toil and trial. Some day we will hear our names announced before the universe and the record read of things that we have long forgotten. How our hearts will thrill and our heads will bow as we hear our own names called, and then the Master recounts the triumph and the services which we had ourselves forgotten! And perhaps from the ranks of the saved He will call forward the souls that we have won for Christ and the souls that they in turn had won, and as we see the issue of things that have perhaps seemed but trifling at the time, we will fall before the throne and say, "Not to us, O LORD, not to us/ but to your name be the glory!" (Psalm 115:1a).

There was once an English preacher on his way to a little country church to fulfill an engagement to preach, and as he stopped and tied his pony at a little country inn on the way, he went in and lay down to rest. He was much discouraged. He was a target for abuse and misrepresentation. He was unpopular and the gospel that he preached was despised.

As he lay down he felt so weary that he wished his work was ended. He fell asleep and dreamed that he had been going to a little village church to preach and had stopped at a little inn to rest; and had lain down upon a couch in his chamber, wishing that he might die—and that he did die.

In his dream he was borne up by the angels in the air to the land of glory, and as they lifted him up he was ushered in and seated in a waiting room resplendent like a palace, where he was told to wait a few moments until the Master Himself should come to meet him.

As he waited there for his Lord to appear, he began to look around the temple upon the tapestries that so richly hung upon the walls, and as he gazed upon them he thought he recognized in the beautiful surroundings a picture of his own life.

He could see his birth, his infancy, his childhood, his early manhood, his conversion, his fallings and restorations, his toils and services for Christ, the souls he had won, the sermons he had preached, all the places he had visited and all the wonderful outcomings of these things, reaching away into issues that he had never dreamed of. And as the meaning of his life opened out in all this glorious blessing, his heart was thrilled with wonder, until at last he came to the close, and he saw the chamber, the little pony by the door, the dead man lying on the couch and the congregation waiting in the little village church for the preacher; and then the great unfinished work and the wonderful possibilities that might have been.

Then his heart became filled with sorrow and he wished that he had not died, and he longed to be back again on the little pony, on the way to the little country church; and as he wept, he suddenly awoke. And lo! He was lying on the little sofa and the pony was standing at the door. He got down on his knees and thanked God that he was still alive. He went on to labor and to wait, with new courage and hope, until the work was all finished and the hour at last came when he, the blessed Richard Baxter, entered into "the saints' everlasting rest" of which he had so often spoken.

Beloved, the pages are going up every day for the record of our life. We are setting the type ourselves by every moment's action. Hands unseen are stereotyping the plates, and soon the record will be registered and read before the audience of the universe and amid the issues of eternity.

FIRST CORINTHIANS

CHAPTER 1

THE UNITY OF THE CHURCH

What I mean is this: One of you says, "I follow Paul"; another, "I follow Apollos"; another, "I follow Cephas"; still another, "I follow Christ."

Is Christ divided? Was Paul crucified for you? Were you baptized into the name of Paul? . . . So then, no more boasting about men! All things are yours, whether Paul or Apollos or Cephas or the world or life or death or the present or the future—all are yours, and you are of Christ, and Christ is of God. (1 Corinthians 1:12–13; 3:21–23)

The first epistle to the Corinthians deals largely with the principles and life of the Church of Christ. It is a picture at once of Christ's ideal for His Church and the Church's failure to meet it. But the very faults of this particular church were overruled in God's providence as occasions for the profound teachings of the Holy Spirit respecting the true character, government and work of the Church. We have, therefore, in this epistle an outline for an apostolic Christian Church in its unity, purity, discipline, government, life, work, worship and glorious destiny.

The church in Corinth had a most providential and even romantic inception. Sent by a special divine commission to Greece, the apostle had preached the gospel in Philippi, Thessalonica, Berea and Athens amid much persecution, and finally arrived at Corinth, the great metropolis of commerce and culture.

His work at first was greatly hindered by the opposition of the Jews, and he seems to have written to his friends in Thessalonica to pray for him that the Word of God might have free course and be glorified in this difficult field (2 Thessalonians 3:1). The prayer was answered in a most signal way.

First, the Jews bitterly opposed him, so that he withdrew from them and turned to the Gentiles, beginning his work in the house of Justus, adjoining the Jewish synagogue. This was followed by a great outpouring of the Spirit of God, so that Crispus, the chief ruler of the synagogue, believed, and many of the Corinthians also believed and were baptized.

Then God spoke to Paul in a special vision saying, "Do not be afraid; keep on speaking, do not be silent. For I am with you, and no one is going to attack and harm you, because I have many people in this city" (Acts 18:9–10).

All this was wonderfully fulfilled in the apostle's immediate experience, and for a year and a half he continued teaching the Word of God among them.

Then the Jews made another frantic effort to destroy his work when Gallio, the new Roman governor, came into office. They brought charges against Paul, hoping to take advantage of the governor's ignorance or weakness. But with true Roman indifference Gallio refused to entertain their petty theological strifes, and before Paul needed to answer a single charge the complaint was dismissed and his accusers were driven from the judgment seat. Then the mob turned upon the defeated Jews, and beat their ruler, Sosthenes, unmercifully.

It would almost seem from a little coincidence that Sosthenes may have been compelled to appeal to Paul's friends for protection. At least we know what treatment he would have received if he had done so. At any rate, either this or some other Sosthenes was converted to Christ at Corinth; and when Paul wrote the letter to the Corinthian church, he associated Sosthenes with himself in the greetings of the epistle. It would indeed be a fine touch of divine irony and a glorious revenge for the apostle if Sosthenes had been truly converted from an enemy to a friend, from the man that sought to destroy them into the associate of Paul himself in the oversight of the little church at Corinth.

From the apostle's letter to this church we are able to form a very good idea of its condition. Living as they did in a city of extraordinary wealth and culture, they were remarkable for their intelligence and for the extent and variety of the gifts of the Spirit which they exemplified, but we do not find the same recognition or commendation of the graces of the Spirit. It seems probable that their intellectual culture was far in advance of their spiritual culture, and the result was a condition of sectarian strife and division which drew from the apostle the most earnest and affectionate admonitions and appeals, and which became at length the occasion for the most sublime picture of the supremacy of love which the Holy Scriptures contain.

Let us notice at this time some interesting and instructive points connected with the membership and gifts of the Corinthian church, and more especially the unity of that church.

SECTION I—*The Membership of the Church*

SANCTIFIED IN CHRIST

They are described first as those "sanctified in Christ Jesus" (1 Corinthians 1:2). This refers no doubt to our standing with Jesus Christ as those who are set apart as belonging to Him, and who are recognized by God as saved and sanctified through the purchase of His redemption and by virtue of their standing in Him. Every believer who has become truly united to Christ is recognized by the Father as one with Christ in all the fullness of His grace. When we take Him by the initial act of faith, we take Him in all His fullness, and we are accepted in Him and recognized as one with Him, even in the things which have not yet been realized in our experience. Therefore we are recognized by God as not only crucified with Christ, but risen with Him, and even sitting with Him in heavenly realms.

All this has not yet come into our actual experience, but all this belongs to us by right of our redemption and union with our glorious Head. We are therefore spoken of as "sanctified in Christ Jesus" (1:2).

CALLED TO BE HOLY

But, secondly, they are next described as those that are "called to be holy" (1:2). We are to enter in personally and experientially to all which belongs to us by right. We are to be saints in our hearts and lives, and live up to the high standing which we have in Christ Jesus.

There is a miner who has found a piece of ore richly veined with gold, but still mingled with coarse rock and sand. He takes it to some wealthy assayer or dealer in the precious mineral and offers it for sale. The man examines it and knows its mixed condition; but knowing also its inherent value, he purchases it perhaps for several hundred dollars and it becomes his property. Then he puts it through the processes of the mill, crushing it, washing it, melting it and refining it until at last it flows out a stream of unalloyed gold worth five times what he paid for it, without a particle of mingled rock or sand. It is much cleaner now than when he purchased it, but it is not any more his own now than it was then. It belonged to him in its mingled state; it belongs to him still, but it has been cleansed, separated and prepared for its true use.

This describes the two processes of salvation and sanctification, our standing and our state, our acceptance in the Beloved first, and then our conformity to His image later. Just because we are accepted in Him, we are to press forward into all to which He has called us. This is our high calling: "called to be holy" (1:2).

NO NARROW SECTARIANISM

But, in the third place, there is still another clause which must be included in the circle of fellowship to whom the apostle addresses his letter: "together with all those everywhere who call on the name of our Lord Jesus Christ— their Lord and ours" (1:2). There must be no narrow sectarianism about the church in Corinth or anywhere else. It includes all who belong to Christ, and He belongs to them as much as He does to us. There is no place in the apostle's mind for denominationalism or bigotry of any kind. Christian fellowship must in the very nature of things be as large as the whole household of faith; for the body is one, and if you restrict it you narrow yourself and cut off your own very life.

SECTION II—*The Gifts and Graces of the Church*

The apostle was able to speak in very high terms of the endowments of this church at Corinth. He attributed all to the grace of Jesus Christ, but he could honestly say of them that they had received an unusual supply of the gifts of His grace. "For in him you have been enriched in every way—in all your speaking and in all your knowledge. . . . You do not lack any spiritual gift" (1:5, 7). Their meetings were full of bright, deeply spiritual testimonies. Their views of the truth were clear and fresh and strong. The gifts of tongues and of utterance and even of miracles were widely prevalent and strongly marked in their history as a church, and they were prominent among the apostolic churches for the abundance and the power of their spiritual enduements.

Then their attitude about the Lord's coming was all right. They had not settled down in worldly self-complacency, but they were waiting for the coming of the Lord Jesus Christ, and the apostle felt sure that God would confirm them unto the end that they should be blameless in the day of the Lord Jesus Christ. This is very high testimony. Had you or I visited this Corinthian church we would no doubt have been much impressed with its prosperity, its intelligence, its power and its brilliancy in teaching, testimony and Christian work.

SECTION III—*Its Lack of Unity*

Notwithstanding all this, there was one grave defect and cause of reproof and blame which filled the apostle's heart with deep concern and sorrow. The unity of the Church is essentially part of her constitution as the body of Christ. Just as the human body cannot be divided without death, so schism and separation are fatal to the life of the body of the Lord Jesus Christ. The system of denominationalism is essentially human, and contrary to the highest will of our glorious Head. No single doctrinal principle is important enough to displace the Lord Jesus Christ Himself as the one name that alone should dominate His Church. The fact that God has overruled and used a divided Church is no sort of reason for supposing that He approves of it. But there are far worse evils than denominationalism. Within the same denomination and congregation there are frequently greater dissensions and divisions than among the various churches and sects. It is not union but unity that God wants, and that is a matter of life and love.

The true unity of the Church is broken not only by open schisms, but by social and secret strifes, strains, envyings, jealousies and grievances among the Lord's people. As sins against love, which is the supreme grace of Christianity, these are carnal signs and grievous wrongs against the body of the Lord.

One of their chief causes is the lack of sanctification. They are the evidence of a carnal state. They all spring from the old sinful nature, whereof the apostle says: "For since there is jealousy and quarreling among you, are you not worldly (carnal, KJV)? Are you not acting like mere men?" (3:3). By another figure he describes them as a result of immaturity and an infantile condition: "Brothers, I could not address you as spiritual but as worldly— mere infants in Christ" (3:1).

Again, another cause of these divisions is the undue attachment to men as men; human leadership with earthly hero worship is the source of this great evil which has weakened and divided the body of the Lord Jesus Christ. It is altogether wrong.

THE EFFECTS OF DIVISION

The effects of division in the body of Christ are very sad.

First, they hurt the Head. Just as the scratch or wound in the feeblest member of the body at once communicates itself to the senses of the brain, so Christ is hurt by all our strains and strifes, and often He has to repeat the cry to His thoughtless children, "Why do you persecute me?" (Acts 9:4).

Full of profoundest truth as well as tenderness, was the answer of the old Scottish martyr mother as she saw little Margaret Wilson, the maiden martyr of Perth, struggling and choking to death at the hands of her cruel foes in the sands of the Solway. "It is Christ," she said, "in one of His members, wrestling there."

When we wound the brethren, we wound the Lord Jesus; and when the body is torn asunder, the Head is caused to suffer in sympathetic pain.

Secondly, we hurt ourselves. The body is so one that the pain we inflict upon another member reflects itself upon us. There is a settled law of retribution that brings back upon the author of unkindness the reflex action of his own conduct. There is many a body that is suffering with sickness, and many a spiritual life that is dwarfed and stunted in consequence of injustice and wrong which ought long ago to have been confessed and righted.

Thirdly, we hurt the whole body of Christ. It is not the individual only that we injure, but the cause of which we are a part. Spiritual deadness of the Church of Christ is largely due to her divisions. The lack of apostolic power has come in consequence of the severed life of spiritual organism.

Fourthly, not only do we hurt the body, but we hinder the testimony of Christ's Word before the world. The unity of the Church was designed by Him to be His most powerful witness to the unbelieving world, and the absence of this unity is the most powerful obstacle to unbelieving men in the way of their acceptance of the gospel of Christ. Even the infidel Gibbon was forced to acknowledge that the unity of the primitive Church was a testimony to the world which they could not gainsay. But, alas! it can no longer be said today, "See how these Christians love one another," but rather the admonition must needs be emphasized, "If you keep on biting and devouring each other, watch out or you will be destroyed by each other" (Galatians 5:15).

DEVELOPING THE SPIRIT OF UNITY

How will we cherish the spirit of unity and overcome the divisions and strifes of the children of God?

1. *The supreme secret must ever be to cling closer to the Head.* The nearer we come to Him the more closely will we touch each other. As the spokes of the wheel near the center, they grow closer to each other. As the little birdlings press up to the mother's breast, they press more closely to one another.

2. *We must be filled with the Spirit.* The little pools along the seashore are united when a great tidal wave sweeps along the shore, and so the baptism of the Holy Spirit alone can unite the sects and parties of divided Christendom in the full tides of the common element of their life. The absence of unity is an evidence always of a low spiritual condition, and the remedy for division is the quickening of spiritual life and the filling of the Spirit.

3. *We are to recognize our brethren as ours.* The apostle has given us a blessed remedy for the strifes and strains of Christians. "So then," he says, "no more boasting about men! All things are yours, whether Paul or Apollos or Cephas or the world or life or death or the present or the future—all are yours" (1 Corinthians 3:21–22). We are to make common cause with them, and so take them in that we shall feel ourselves responsible even for their very faults. Then there will be no place for rivalry, jealousy or separated interests. You know if your child does wrong and even greatly tires you; you feel it is your child and almost as if it were your own disgrace and failure, and instead of condemning mercilessly and throwing off the erring one, you

take the fault to yourself and lovingly seek to help and to save. If another's child did the same thing you would condemn and blame and feel no such responsibility. The whole question is whose child it is. Make it yours and love immediately comes into play.

Now this is what the apostle means by recognizing not only all things as ours, but all people as ours, yea, our brethren. When therefore we see good in them we rejoice as if it were our own. When we see evil we mourn, pity, forgive and forbear and help and deal just as we would with ourselves.

It was thus that Daniel took upon himself the sins and faults of his own people and confessed them as if they were his own transgressions, and in this he was but imitating Christ, for "God made him who had no sin to be sin for us" (2 Corinthians 5:21).

4. *But finally the real secret of union is for each of us to be fully saved from the spirit of self and strife and sin, and filled with the disposition and temper of the Lord Jesus Christ.* There could be no strife if every believer were a Christ-filled man or woman, baptized with the gentleness and love of the Lord Jesus. While the carnal nature is allowed to sway us, we can never have real unity with one another. It is a painful confession, but it is probably one that would be reechoed by almost all those who have had intimate dealings with a large variety of professing Christians, that there is no single line of failure and sin on the part of the children of God, especially those who confess to know something of the deeper life of the Spirit, than the infirmity of temper. The spirit of irritation, depression or sensitiveness—you may call it what you please, by the finely drawn phrase of being tired, or the more honest name of ill nature—it is the one place where the great majority of most earnest Christians are conscious of not really living the life of the Lord Jesus Christ. It is better to recognize it and call it by its right name, and then with an utter surrender and unreserved confession, a single purpose and an uncompromising faith, take the grace of God, the power of the Spirit and the indwelling life of Christ against it, and enter into an eternal covenant never again to willingly sin against love.

CHAPTER 2

THE TEACHING OF THE CHURCH

Christ . . . the wisdom of God. (1 Corinthians 1:24)

It is because of him that you are in Christ Jesus, who has become for us wisdom from God—that is, our righteousness, holiness and redemption. (1:30)

We do, however, speak a message of wisdom among the mature. (2:6)

The city of Corinth was a center of Greek culture and philosophy. It is to this the apostle alludes when he speaks of the Greeks as seeking after wisdom. The word for wisdom is *sophia,* which is the base of our word philosophy. They were very proud of their *sophia.* The apostle comes to them with a new doctrine. He has a *sophia* too, but it is not like theirs. It is contrary to all human ideas and conceptions, but it is as high above the wisdom of man as the heavens are high above the earth. He unfolds it in the first and second chapters of this epistle.

SECTION I—*It Is a Paradox and a Contradiction*

It is contrary to all human ideas and notions. Just as the wisdom of men is foolishness with God so the wisdom of God is foolishness with men. They cannot understand it nor appreciate it that God has no interest in their finely spun webs of philosophical speculation. How little God cares for things that man most highly esteems appears from the apostle's statement that God has not called the wise men after the flesh, the mighty and noble, but He has gone out of His way to choose "the foolish things of the world to shame the wise; God chose the weak things of the world to shame the strong. He chose the lowly things of this world and the despised things—and the things that are not—to nullify the things that are, so that no one may boast before him" (1:27–29).

It is not merely that the wise and the mighty have not chosen Him, but He has not chosen them. He has passed them by intentionally, and has taken the instruments that man despises and acted contrary to all human probabilities and modes of judging.

SECTION II—*It Is Personal*

It is not a mere connection of philosophical principles and abstract ideas, but it is the revelation of a Person. Christ is the wisdom of God. It is not a chart of the way He gives us, but it is a guide to lead us all the way. It is not a volume of ethics, but it is a true and living Friend. It is not even a new experience in our own hearts, but a real living and indwelling Christ, who comes to be to us all that we cannot be and do for us all that we are unable to do. "It is because of him that you are in Christ Jesus, who has become for us wisdom from God—that is, our righteousness, holiness and redemption" (1:30). It is not that we are made wise, but Christ is made our wisdom. It is not that we are made righteous, but Christ is made our righteousness. It is not that we possess a self-contained sanctity, but Christ is made unto us sanctification. It is not that we are enabled to deliver ourselves from our circumstances and disabilities, but Christ is made unto us redemption.

Suppose that I were carrying on a business under financial difficulties and with insufficient capital. I go to a friend who is wealthy and ask him to help me by advancing $1,000. My friend listens to me and gives me his check for the amount. But after a year I return to him, and am compelled to tell him that I am still as much embarrassed as before, and that I am under the painful necessity of asking him to help me again, and I struggle on as before. At last I am compelled once more to seek help, and ashamed and embarrassed I promise him that I will never ask for help again if he will once more relieve me. He looks me frankly in the face and says, "I will not help you, for my help is useless. You will again fail as you have already done." Then he gives me a kind, encouraging look and adds, "but I will tell you what I will do: I will come into your business, and I will put my brains, my experience, my credit and my boundless capital into it, and I will carry it on myself for you. And all that you will have to do will be to give me the control and then share the profits." I would be a very foolish man if I declined this generous offer. And so I hand my business over to my friend, and take him and all he has instead of his help.

That is what Christ does for us. It is not His blessing He gives us, but Himself. The gospel is the revelation of Jesus. The good news that God has sent us is that God Himself has come in the person of His dear Son to be our All in All.

SECTION III—*It Is Practical*

It teaches us not idle theories, but real needs, and makes complete provision for all the most important conditions of our life.

The philosophy of Plato, the loftiest of the Grecian thinkers, had in it three great elements: namely, the true, the beautiful and the good. But of what use are these things to the human heart in the struggle with sin, sorrow and the grave? What good will it do the guilty, dying man to paint for him the vision of the true, the beautiful and the good when he is sinking in despair? He wants somebody that can comfort, forgive and save him. What use is it to that poor passion-driven soul struggling against the demon within, to hold out to him your finespun theories of sentiment and poetry? He wants the power that can overcome the power of sin and lead him into righteousness and peace. What use is it to a life involved in sorrow, failure and adverse circumstances to sing your golden dreams and talk in the air about the true, the beautiful and the good? He wants some mind to help, some way of escape, some power that is stronger than himself and stronger than death. Here is where the supremacy of the divine *sophia* comes in.

A Chinese man has told us the testimony of his conversion and his acceptance of Christianity. "I was in a deep pit," he said, "sinking in the mire and helpless to deliver myself. Looking up I saw a shadow at the top, and soon a venerable face looked over the brink and said, 'My son, I am Confucius, the father of your country. If you had obeyed my teachings you would never have been here.' And then he passed on with a significant movement of his finger and a cheerless farewell, adding, 'If ever you get out of this, remember to obey my teachings.' But, alas, that did not save me and I sank deeper in the mire.

"Then Buddha came along, and looking over the edge of the pit he cried, 'My son, just count it all as nothing. Enter into rest. Fold your arms and retire within yourself and you will find nirvana, the peace to which we all are tending.' I cried, 'Father Buddha, if you will only help me to get out I will be glad to do so. I could follow your instructions easily if I were where you are, but how can I rest in this awful place?' Buddha passed on and left me in my despair.

"Then another face appeared. It was the face of a man beaming with kindness and bearing marks of sorrow. He did not linger a moment, but leaped down by my side, threw His arms around me, lifted me out of the mire and brought me to the solid ground above. And even then did not bid me farewell, but took off my filthy garments, put new robes upon me and bade me follow Him, saying, 'I will never leave you nor forsake you.' That is why I became a Christian. It was because Jesus Christ did not come to me with theories and speculations, but practical help in time of need."

And so this divine *sophia* is a complete supply for all our needs. "Christ . . . who has become for us wisdom from God—that is, our righteousness, holiness and redemption" (1:30). The Greek construction allows us to translate the first "and" after wisdom by the word "even" or "that is." It is like a bracket containing a number of particulars under a general head. Wisdom is a generic term including all the others, and under it the three great elements of this wisdom are righteousness, sanctification and redemption. Just as the Platonic philosophy had three things in it—the true, the beautiful and the good—so the Christ *sophia* has in it three things—namely, justification, sanctification and complete deliverance.

RIGHTEOUSNESS

1. It brings us righteousness. This has reference to our relations with God and our standing under His law. We are guilty and condemned, and we need to be right with Him.

Now, Christ has provided for this by taking the place of the guilty, bearing the penalty of his or her sin, obeying for his or her broken law and giving to us the benefit of His standing and making us "accepted in the beloved" (Ephesians 1:6, KJV). In Him we are counted as if we had already died for our sins, and His righteousness and merits are imputed to us that we stand before our Judge not only forgiven, but accepted, justified and blameless even as He.

There is something in His atonement which not only satisfies God, but satisfies our conscience, and the guilty soul knows that it is right with heaven, and looking in the face of inexorable justice it can say, "Therefore, there is now no condemnation for those who are in Christ Jesus" (Romans 8:1).

SANCTIFICATION

2. The next need of our life is sanctification—that is, to be right in our own hearts and lives, to be delivered from the inherent power of sin and enabled to overcome temptation and walk in harmony with the will of God.

This, Christ also becomes to us. He who died for us lives in us. He who bestowed upon us the gift of righteousness, as against our past transgressions, bestows as freely the gift of rightness for our personal life. He is made unto us sanctification, filling us with His Holy Spirit, living in us with His own pure and perfect life. He imparts to us what He had already imputed to us. His purity, His peace, His love, His patience, His long–suffering, His gentleness, His courage, His strength, His very faith, are inbreathed through our being and continually supplied as we abide in Him. Therefore we can say, "I no longer live, but Christ lives in me. The life I live in the body, I live by faith in the Son of God, who loved me and gave himself for me" (Galatians 2:20).

REDEMPTION

3. But we need also redemption. This word means deliverance, and especially deliverance through a ransom. It covers all the other needs of life: deliverance from disease, deliverance from Satan's power, deliverance from circumstances, deliverance from this present evil world, deliverance at last from death itself to the full realization of the glorious resurrection.

This also comes to us in Christ. This also is included in our redemption rights, and this also is realized as we more and more fully enter into His life and receive Him into ours. By and by it will be fully consummated when death's last shackle shall be severed, and we shall rise to the glory into which He has already entered as our prototype and forerunner.

Is not this a practical message to bring to suffering, dying men? Is not this better than the dreams of philosophy and the visions of poetry? Is not this a practical and present help for wrecked humanity, and does it not seem passing strange that men will still dream on and waste their strength in the wretched sophistries which have been long ago exploded, and which have no more power to remedy the wrongs of humanity than a butterfly has strength to lift a mountain to the skies?

SECTION IV—*It Is Progressive*

This divine *sophia*, this glorious message which God has given to His Church, is too vast to be received in a moment, but it leads on into the depths and heights of God and all the possibilities of Christian growth and maturity. And so in the second chapter of First Corinthians the apostle leads us into the deeper development of the Christian doctrine and experience. He says there are fundamental truths which are intended for beginners, but there are deeper teachings for the maturer minds. Just as the ancient philosophy had its simpler and profounder teachings, the one for the public and the other for the initiated, so Christianity has the simple gospel for the world, and to them we are to know nothing but "Christ and him crucified" (1 Corinthians 2:2). But "we do . . . speak a message of wisdom among the mature" (2:6). There are deeper truths for those who are able to understand and receive them, but, as he expresses it later, we must adapt these to the capabilities of our hearers. The secular mind cannot understand them at all. The babes in Christ can only be fed with milk, and it is to the mature disciple alone that we can give the deeper truths of God's complete revelation, presenting "spiritual truths to spiritual men" (2:13, margin).

There are three classes of minds spoken of in this passage.

THE NATURAL MAN

First, there is the natural man, which literally might be rendered the "psychical man," or "soul man." This is the man of merely intellectual development, but he has no spiritual life. This man cannot perceive or receive the things of the Spirit of God; indeed, they are foolishness unto him. He has not the capacity to apprehend them. He would need a divine mind in order to grasp them. This is the reason why men of genius and the highest culture are often unable to apprehend the more spiritual truths of Christianity and are strangers to many of its deeper experiences.

BABES IN CHRIST

Next, there is an infant or child stage of Christian experience—babes in Christ—with much of the worldly mind in them. These, he tells us, cannot grasp the deeper things of God, but they must be fed with a spoon and nourished on the milk of the Word: the simplest principles of the gospel, Christ the Savior, the doctrine of forgiveness of sins, the primary truths of Christianity.

THE SPIRITUAL MIND

But, thirdly, there is the spiritual mind. This is a mind to think His thoughts and see with His eyes. He calls it in another part of the passage "the Spirit who is from God" (2:12). "We have . . . received . . . the Spirit who is from God, that we may understand what God has freely given us. . . . The Spirit searches all things, even the deep things of God" (2:12, 10).

To the heart that has received the Holy Spirit, divine truth is made clear and vivid by new spiritual apprehensions. We have not only a divine revelation, but we have a divine illumination. We have not only heavenly light, but we have heavenly sight with which to behold it. We have not only the written Word, but we have the living Word to re-echo it in the secret chambers of our being and to make it to us spirit and life.

Now, the apostle is calling upon these Corinthians to press forward into all the depths and heights of this divine progression, and to be no longer babes but men in Christ Jesus. It is the same lesson that he afterwards gave to the Hebrew Christians, "Therefore let us leave the elementary teachings about Christ and go on to maturity" (6:1).

A babe is a very beautiful thing in its time and place, but a very ridiculous thing when dressed in an old man's clothes, and rendered preposterous and absurd by an old man's years. It is one thing to be a babe. It is another thing to be a dwarf. The Church is full of dwarfed Christians today, and the result is childish infirmities, childish follies, the disposition to fight or the disposition to play, and the lack of suitable earnestness and power.

Now, the wise teacher or preacher will adjust himself to the conditions of his hearers. To one class he will know nothing but Jesus Christ and Him crucified, to another he will give the unsearchable riches of Christ, feeding milk to babes, and presenting spiritual things to spiritual minds.

SECTION V—*Conclusion*

Finally, the doctrine of Christ's Church is not only a supernatural revelation, but it requires a supernatural vision to behold it. We cannot even understand it rightly without the Holy Spirit, therefore the world cannot accept the gospel without the touch of His illuminating grace. Our wisdom and our genius, and even our most earnest struggling, cannot bring us into the thoughts and things of God. We need to take the open Bible to the open windows of heaven. We need not the gift of inspiration to write another Bible, but the gift of illumination to understand the Bible that the Holy Spirit has already given. Often have these great words, "No eye has seen,/ no ear has heard,/ no mind has conceived/ what God has prepared for those who love him" (1 Corinthians 2:9), been referred to some future experience in the heavenly life. On the contrary, they describe an experience into which we should enter now, for he adds, "God has revealed it to us by his Spirit" (2:10). These are the things we ought to need now, and unto which we may enter here by the teaching and the leading of our Divine Interpreter—the Holy Spirit. He is waiting to lead us into all the fullness of the thoughts of God and the mind of Christ. One secret is an open ear, the other is an obedient life. He will speak to the soul that loves to listen. He will speak again to the life that hastens to obey. Let us hearken. Let us obey and let us launch out into the deep, and explore the boundless continents of truth, the countless worlds of light, the vast and glorious expanses of heavenly vision which are waiting to open before the souls that dwell on high, for their "eyes will see the king in his beauty/ and view a land that stretches afar" (Isaiah 33:17).

CHAPTER 3

THE MINISTRY OF THE CHURCH

So then, men ought to regard us as servants of Christ and as those entrusted with the secret things of God. (1 Corinthians 4:1)

I planted the seed, Apollos watered it, but God made it grow. (3:6)

For we are God's fellow workers; you are God's field, God's building.
By the grace God has given me, I laid a foundation as an expert builder, and someone else is building on it. (3:9–10)

God has put us apostles on display at the end of the procession, like men condemned to die in the arena. We have been made a spectacle to the whole universe, to angels as well as to men. (4:9)

Even though you have ten thousand guardians in Christ, you do not have many fathers, for in Christ Jesus I became your father through the gospel. (4:15)

His work will be shown for what it is, because the Day will bring it to light. It will be revealed with fire, and the fire will test the quality of each man's work. (3:13)

These various passages convey to us under a great variety of imageries a most complete and vivid picture of the Christian ministry. Speaking of the ministry we do not refer exclusively to the ordained ministry or the technical ecclesiastical office. God makes His ministers, and then the Church recognizes them and sets them apart; but man cannot make a preacher any more than he can make a convert.

The Christian ministry, while it has divinely appointed varieties and offices, yet is open to every earnest soul who will receive the grace and gifts of the Holy Spirit and use them in humility for the glory of God and the good of man. And as we use these gifts we reach a higher degree of efficiency, and a larger and more divinely equipped ministry.

In what we shall say therefore we include all classes and degrees of Christian workers and witnesses for Christ, with special reference, of course, to those who are more fully set apart as ambassadors of Christ to men. They are described here by six striking figures:

MINISTERS

1. The first figure is "ministers." "Let a man so account of us, as of the ministers (servants, NIV) of Christ" (4:1, KJV). Literally, the word might be translated the "sub-ministers." There is a touch of humility about it that is beautifully in keeping with the spirit of Paul himself and of his great and lowly Master. The very name of Paul was adopted because it means "the little," and his humility deepened in the ratio of his spiritual blessing. He wished to take the lowest place in the Christian ministry even as his blessed Master, who girt Himself with the towel of a servant and said to His disciples, "The Son of Man did not come to be served, but to serve, and to give his life as a ransom for many" (Matthew 20:28). Once, indeed, He struck a deeper chord when He said: "Whoever wants to become great among you must be your servant" (20:26).

The spirit of pride is bad enough in a private Christian. It is worst of all in a Christian minister. The very apostasy of the early Church came about through the competing claims of the rival bishops, patriarchs and popes, and the sectarianism of today is largely due to the partisanship which exalts men or leads men to exalt themselves to the dishonor of Jesus Christ. The minister who would be honored by his Lord must lie low at His feet, even as the bending stalks of the autumn grain tell of their rich and ladened ears of corn.

STEWARDS

2. Next, Paul speaks of stewards of the mystery of God. The efficient steward is the housekeeper. To him were committed the treasures of his master, his wardrobe, his supplies and the management of his domestic affairs and often of his business. He was a trusted chief servant whose business was to take care of his lord's estate and to dispense his hospitality to his guest and family.

Such a steward was Eliezer, Abraham's servant who took his master's treasures and went forth to win for his son a bride. He attracted her confidence and love toward his noble master, first showing her and then bestowing upon her the rich treasures which he had brought.

The ministry of Christ is appointed to dispense the richest treasures of

God's grace. To us are committed the mysteries of the kingdom of heaven. Paul tells us what some of these mysteries are. One of them was the glorious secret of Christ's indwelling through the Holy Spirit. This was the mystery that had been hid from ages and generations, and was at last made manifest to the saints, which is Christ in you, the hope of glory. This glorious mystery the apostle longed to communicate to all the world, to tell them of the power and of a Presence that could be a substitute for all their weakness, failure and sorrow; that could sustain them amid all emergencies, distresses, temptations and conditions, giving them a charmed life and a talisman of power and victory, no matter what might come.

Another was the mystery of the Church, the body of Christ, the wonderful fellowship, not of cultured society, political alliance or even family and kindred ties, but of a common life in Christ and a common love to one glorious Head, and all the glory to be revealed in that heavenly body and blessed bride. This was one of the glorious mysteries that he loved to proclaim.

Another was the mystery of the kingdom, the coming of the Lord, the plan of the ages, the meaning of the times, the purpose of the dispensation, the secret of the last times, which so many have missed and which is so blessed to understand.

Oh, that the ministry of today might better know and more faithfully impart to the household of faith the mystery of the kingdom and the treasures of the Father's house. Then would we cease to sorrow over the wretched degeneracy of the modern pulpit and a large part of the modern Church. Then would men lose their taste for the silly sensation, the empty trivialities, the lengthy recreations which bear so often the very name of religion, and invade so frequently the sanctity of the pulpit and the very sanctuary of God.

A day or two ago we had a report in one of the daily papers of the sermon of one of our greatest preachers, a sermon that probably has been circulated among hundreds of thousands of readers, and it was all about this much misused text, "Oh, wheel" (Ezekiel 10:13, KJV). He began at the spinning wheel, the factory wheel, the locomotive wheel, he wound up with the modern bicycle, and sent his people away extolling the glories of modern civilization and worshiping the wheel and the man that rode it.

What a sad travesty of the Christian ministry! Happier is he who, like the wise expert builder, brings out of his treasures things both new and old, and, like the faithful and wise steward, waits on his Master's household and gives them a portion of meat in due season, feeding them on living bread, and knowing and displaying the treasures on which angels gaze with longing wonder.

EXAMPLES

3. Next, Paul points out that we are patterns and examples. "We have been made a spectacle," he says, "to the whole universe, to angels as well as to men" (1 Corinthians 4:9). We stand, as it were, in an arena, and the galleries are filled with invisible beings. The world is looking at us, the angels are looking at us, the demons are watching us, the Lord Jesus Himself is surveying us and expecting us to do our duty. In every thought we think, every action we perform, every battle we lose or win, Christ is honored or dishonored. There is a devilish leer on the devil's face and a shadow upon the face of Jesus when we do ill, but when a shout of victory comes from angel watchers, then the call, "Well done," comes from our loving Lord.

Perhaps this is the greatest work we do: to be gazed at, to be living examples of what we teach and preach. Paul recognized it, and how nobly, patiently and humbly he lived his life! He tells us modestly in this passage, he fought with others not to have the best place, but to be the greatest sufferer and the lowliest and most self-sacrificing of all. This is the silent testimony that every life is either recording or missing. This is the book that men will read whether they read our tracts or not; and this is the illustration of our teachings and testimonies, which adds 10 thousandfold to their force and effectiveness.

SPIRITUAL FATHERS

4. Those in the ministry are spiritual fathers. So deeply sympathetic, intense and personal was the apostle's ministry that he even imparted, as it were, his own very life to his children in the Lord. "In Christ Jesus," he says, "I became your father through the gospel" (4:15). What he meant was "I am more than your teacher, I am more than your example, I am more than the servant who waits upon you and the steward who feeds you. I am the very progenitor and medium through whom your life has been derived."

True ministry will not stop short of giving its very self, and God will give to us the power through the Holy Spirit to love and win and draw to Jesus the lost to whom He sends us with a soul-begetting power. If the Church is the Bride of the Lamb, her children are the fruit of this divine union, and when our hearts are filled with Christ's great love we will find an outstretching longing and affection for sinful men which will really communicate to them the very life of God. Then they shall be to us even as our own life, and like Paul we shall bear them upon our hearts, suffering for their temptations, trials and even sins, and nourish and cherish them as we would our very children. The true minister is a real father. Falsely has the name been appropriated by a false ecclesiastical system, but nonetheless ought it to be true because the caricature and counterfeit has misused it.

HUSBANDMEN

5. Next Paul declares that we are husbandmen. The fine figure of the spiritual husbandry supplies many lessons for the true ministers of Christ. Of course, the soil must be prepared. No wise worker will throw the seed upon the barren rocks, but will seek, by watching and by prayer, the breaking up of the sods, the softening of the ground and the opportune season for casting in the precious seed.

Then, of course, the seed is essential. All our plowing and harrowing and watering and culturing will be useless without the living truth. We cannot deceive or coax people into the religion of Jesus. We cannot mesmerize them into being Christians. There must be the real grain of truth. The wise worker will always give them the gospel, the clear statement of saving truth through Christ's blood and righteousness and by simple faith in Him.

Then there is watering as well as planting. The seed may not immediately germinate. It may require much prayer and care and many a tear before we will see it spring.

The true husbandman will not forget the necessity of transplanting. Out in China and Japan it is beautiful to see the rice fields when they are first sown broadcast, and the plants spring up a perfect sea of green on the soft and watered plain. But that will never make a ripe harvest. Each of those plants must be separated and replanted quite a distance apart in regular rows, with room to develop. Then they grow into fruit-bearing rice plants. So our souls must be led on to the next stage, to the deeper life, to the second experience, to the full surrender and the baptism of the Holy Spirit. All Christian work that stops short of this will end in bitter disappointment. The apostle always expected his disciples to receive the baptism of the Holy Spirit, to be sealed and stamped with the touch of God Himself, and thus armed against failing.

Then every true minister will want his fruit to bear fruit in its turn, to go on unto reproduction and multiply his seed, sown again and again. Our fruit would be like ourselves. If we are soul-winners the souls we lead to Christ will be soul-winners, too. If we are easy and self-complacent they will be the same. It is glorious to propagate our work and multiply it a thousandfold in the lives of others.

Once in a Scottish parish a criticizing elder had made the remark to his pastor at the close of a communion service, "Only one addition to the church, and he is only a boy." The elder was disappointed and the pastor was deeply humiliated. That had been the whole result of three months' work, apparently. That Sabbath night he was deeply affected, and pleaded with his people for a revival among them, and asked those who were interested and wished to talk with him to remain. When the meeting closed the congregation went out, including the elder, and when he stepped down from the platform to take the after-meeting there was only a boy waiting. It was the new member. The pastor prayed and then he talked with this boy. He found that he was a young Scottish lad who desired to be a missionary. This cheered him greatly, and gave him a kind of an outlook of something better. He encouraged him, and after a while the lad went to college and in due time was appointed a missionary to Africa.

Very many years passed, but one day a distinguished and venerable missionary was being talked about all through the land. He was preaching in the most influential pulpits. He was speaking in great assemblies. He was dining at the tables of nobles and princes. He was consulting with the British potentate. He had been instrumental in adding half a continent to the British empire, and opening up South Africa to civilization and the gospel. It was Robert Moffat, the prince of missionaries. Before that season was over he had hastened to the Scottish parish, and clasped the hand of the minister who had wept one day because of the fact that there was just one new member and he was only a boy. The handful of grain upon the top of the mountain had grown to be a mighty forest that shook like Lebanon. God make us such spiritual husbandmen and give us such glorious harvests.

BUILDERS

6. Finally, Paul mentions that we are builders. He calls himself a wise masterbuilder (KJV). It is no small thing to be a wise builder. The wise builder will look well to the excavation. The first thing is not a stately house, but an ugly hole. Death must come before life, going down before going up. A true worker will not be afraid of thorough work and deep conviction.

Then he will be careful about good foundations, great, solid, eternal truths, and deep and strong convictions. Not so much mere emotion as thorough purpose and will, full set and unreservedly decisive for God and righteousness and Jesus Christ in His atoning blood, His perfect righteousness and His finished work, the basis of faith and hope. Conversion that is founded on mere emotional excitement will be followed by backslidings as numerous and quick. It is the truth about Christ that saves. "Other foundation can no man lay than that which is lying there," as the words literally mean, "which is Jesus Christ" (3:11, author's translation).

It is not, however, the truth about Christ merely—it is the personal Christ, the receiving of Christ, the union of the soul with Christ, which is the real foundation and the living stone.

Again, the wise masterbuilder will look out for his materials. He wants real transformations, souls radically regenerated, lives divinely transformed. Not the flesh but the spirit. Not the old nature pleased and coaxed into the Church by modern attractions, but hearts that have really felt the touch of

God and belong to the spiritual kingdom. Not wood, hay and straw, but gold, silver and costly stones.

Then the wise builder will be sure to see that the building is erected according to the drawings and the pattern shown. Alas, how much Christian work is not according to God's plan! Men are building up a partisan cause trying to please the luxurious and selfish class, trying to fit into the tendencies and conceits of the people, trying to get the world converted, or, as a good many are doing now, believing it is not so badly wrong anyhow, and just swimming with the tide. God's plan is very clearly laid down: to preach the gospel as a witness to all the nations, to gather out from the many the Bride of the Lamb, to haste and meet our coming Lord.

But the builder's work will be thoroughly tested. Our church reports and our lists of membership will soon pass away. Only that will remain which can stand the fire of testing day: "revealed with fire" (3:13). There are six kinds of work that shall be tried. Three are good. The gold represents that which is divine and comes from the Holy Spirit. The silver also represents that which is precious, and connected with redemption and the gospel. Precious stones probably represent the adornments of the Christian character, the beautiful graces of the Christian life, the qualities that will shine in the day when He makes up His jewels. All that we have done to build those materials into the Church of the living God will remain for our joy and eternal recompense.

But, on the other hand, there is the wood, the best of the perishable materials; useful for much, but only temporary. It represents the transient work of the humanitarian or educational or social improvements which cannot pass into the eternal and spiritual. The hay represents a lower class. Hay is good to feed horses, and may represent that which is indirectly used to help God's agencies, but is not an integral part of these great spiritual forces. There are many who help with God's work without being a part of it and really in it. They are of some use here, and those that count upon them will get something from them; but they will drift away in the ashes of the last great hurricane.

The stubble seems to represent the worn out, exhausted, withered wreckage of things that are dead and worthless. All these things will dissolve in the conflagration of His coming, and woe to him who will suffer the loss of all his lifework and who is to be saved as by fire. But happy is he who will not only stand the test himself but will have the souls that he has loved and led for his joy and crown of rejoicing in the presence of Christ at His coming.

Many years ago a bold adventurer entered into a contract to build a lighthouse at the extreme point of England's storm-swept coast. When it was finished he dared the howling tempests to do their worst, and entering the lighthouse on the eve of a frightful storm he cried, "Blow, ye winds; rage, ye waves, and try my work." When the morning dawned eager watchers from the shore looked out in vain for even a vestige of that work. The cruel waves were breaking over the wreck of his life and his labor, and all was lost.

Long afterward a wise and humbler builder erected the Eddystone light-house. Fencing out the waves and digging deep down to the living rock, he anchored his foundations to the bedrock, and slowly and steadily built the dome, where he placed as the motto of his work this mightiest inscription, "Praise to God." Many a storm has tested it, but it has stood them all, the monument of his genius as well as his humility.

God grant that when the last storm shall sweep and the ashes of a dissolving world shall drift upon the hurricane of that tremendous day, watchers from yonder heavenly heights, as they look out upon the testing of our work, shall say, "Thank God, it stands!"

CHAPTER 4

THE PURITY OF THE CHURCH

If anyone destroys God's temple, God will destroy him; for God's temple is sacred, and you are that temple. (1 Corinthians 3:17)

Do you not know that your body is a temple of the Holy Spirit, who is in you, whom you have received from God? You are not your own; you were bought at a price. Therefore honor God with your body. (6:19–20)

Corinth, we have already seen, was at the center of both the world's culture and moral and social corruption. The very name Corinth became the synonym of social dishonor. It was inevitable, therefore, that the Church of Christ should be in danger of contamination from the prevailing influences; and it is not surprising to find that, at a very early stage, gross and grievous instances of unholy practices reached the apostle's ear. Among them was a common report of an incestuous marriage among members of the church, and, what was much more serious, the toleration of this abuse by the public sentiment of the church itself. Therefore he proceeds in the early chapters of this epistle to deal with this question in no compromising way.

First, he reasserts in most emphatic language the absolute necessity of personal holiness on the part of all disciples of Christ, and the high standard of discipline in the fellowship of believers as a whole. He makes special provision for the extreme case which had risen among them. He gives explicit directions that the offending members be solemnly and publicly excommunicated from the Church of Christ, and handed over in the name of the Lord Jesus to the judgment of God, through Satanic power, even to the extent of the death of the offender, if necessary, in order that he may be brought to repentance even at the last moment, and his spirit saved in the day of the Lord Jesus Christ.

Church discipline is here recognized as a very solemn thing, and something which is sure to bring, if properly exercised with due regard to the authority and will of God, the interposing hand of God Himself and the judgment from which no excuse or evasion can protect the false and daring offender.

How salutary it would be if this simple apostolic precedent should be more commonly followed and more divinely efficient than it is in the lax religions of this compromising age.

Still further in the same chapter, this apostle directs that they are to withdraw their fellowship at the Lord's table and in the communion of the saints from every brother who is licentious, covetous, idolatrous, a railer, a drunkard or an extortioner. It is not possible to separate ourselves from business correspondence or worldly association with ungodly men, but in the fellowship of the Church of Christ the atmosphere of His sacred sanctuary must be kept unsullied and heavenly (1 Corinthians 5:1–6, 11–12).

Having thus provided for the public discipline of obdurate and inconsistent members of the church, Paul proceeds to emphasize the necessity of personal holiness on the part of individual members by a series of vivid illustrations and impressive appeals.

THE FEAST OF THE PASSOVER

1. He shows the importance of holiness on the part of the people of God by a forcible illustration, the Feast of the Passover, and its typical significance. He asks,

> Don't you know that a little yeast works through the whole batch of dough? Get rid of the old yeast that you may be a new batch without yeast—as you really are. For Christ, our Passover lamb, has been sacrificed. Therefore let us keep the Festival, not with the old yeast, the yeast of malice and wickedness, but with bread without yeast, the bread of sincerity and truth. (5:6–8)

The Paschal feast was the first of the annual ceremonial rites of the Jews, and was especially suggestive of the fellowship of Christ's redeemed people in all future ages. One of the most marked features of that great rite was the inexorable exclusion of all leaven from the feast and the household. Prior to the celebration of the Passover it was customary for the father, with lighted candle, to pass through the house, inspecting every chamber, even looking under every bed, chair, sofa and article of furniture, and then solemnly declaring that there was no leaven in any portion of the house or member of the household. Leaven has, therefore, always stood in the Word of God as the symbol of corruption. In our Lord's great parable in the 13th chapter of Matthew, it represents the introduction of impurity into the Church of

Christ, until the whole house became saturated with the unholy elements of fleshly corruption.

One of the very first questions of the apostle in his great treatise on salvation is, "Shall we go on sinning so that grace may increase?" And his unqualified answer is, "By no means!" (Romans 6:1–2). "Everyone who confesses the name of the Lord must turn away from wickedness" (2 Timothy 2:19), is the very inscription we read stamped upon the cornerstone of the Church of Jesus Christ. He can save the sinner, but the sin must be utterly renounced and laid over upon the Lord Jesus Christ for crucifixion and eternal separation. Purge out the old leaven, the flesh, the carnal life, the whole of the old creation, and reckon yourself dead indeed unto sin, but alive unto God through Jesus Christ, our Lord. We are to be a new lump and God recognizes us as unleavened.

Then we are to carefully watch against the introduction of the new leaven, the leaven of malice and wickedness, every form of evil and sin, and to present to God the unleavened bread of sincerity and truth—truth representing God's revealed truth without alloy, and sincerity representing our honest, upright heart holding the truth in righteousness, and obeying it in singleness of purpose.

THE SANCTUARY AND TEMPLE

2. His next illustration and incentive to holiness is drawn from the ancient sanctuary and temple of God. "You yourselves are God's temple" (1 Corinthians 3:16), he says, holy, sacred, and therefore we must keep it pure, for "If anyone destroys God's temple, God will destroy him" (3:17). With the utmost sacredness God has always guarded the holy sanctuary of His manifested Presence. When He came down on Sinai, the mountain was fenced and isolated from any unhallowed touch. Into His ancient shrine no man could pass till he had offered his sacrifice on the altar, and washed his hands and feet in the laver of cleansing. Into the innermost sanctuary of His presence but one could pass, and he only once a year, with spotless garments and sprinkled blood. When Uzzah presumed with reckless hands to touch the sacred symbol of God's sanctuary he was smitten with instant death (see 2 Samuel 6:6–7). When the rash Uzzah tried to offer sacrifices unauthorized, he felt the instant touch of leprosy upon his brow, and hastened out to hide himself from the awful token of his judgment and his shame (see 2 Chronicles 26:16–20).

Not less sacred is the presence of the Holy One even amid the larger mercy of the New Testament age. Well may the apostle ask if

anyone who rejected the law of Moses died without mercy. . . . How much more severely do you think a man deserves to be

punished who has trampled the Son of God under foot, who has
treated as an unholy thing the blood of the covenant that
sanctified him, and who has insulted the Spirit of grace?
(Hebrews 10:28–29)

In the mind of God, and in the judgment of the Holy Scriptures, the heart
of the believer is a more sacred shrine than the ark or the sanctuary of old.
God would have us look upon ourselves as His temples with the same sacredness, and guard our inmost thought and being from the profaning touch or
the faintest shadow of evil, either in imagination or word or deed. We should
walk softly through the world as though we were sons of Levi bearing the ark
of God, and having enthroned within us His majestic Presence, before whom
angels veil their faces with their wings, and cry, "Holy, holy, holy" (Revelation 4:8). This divine self-respect, this holy consciousness of God, will lift us
above the approach of temptation and toleration of sin.

PAST EXPERIENCE

3. He next appeals to their past experience and their escape from evil
through their conversion and consecration to God. "And," he says, "that is
what some of you were. But you were washed, you were sanctified, you were
justified in the name of the Lord Jesus Christ and by the Spirit of our God"
(1 Corinthians 6:11). Is it not enough that you have once escaped this
slough of sin? Can you bear to think of again being involved in the slime? Is
not the very memory hideous enough to fill your soul with horror? Can you
ever look upon it again with toleration or indulgence?

And yet, alas, how many, even after their salvation as brands from the
burning, and their sanctification from the power of corruption, have allowed
themselves, like Lot's wife, to look back to Sodom until they have gradually
become accustomed to the vision of sin, and the picture has insensibly lost
its terrors and the old sin begins to reassert its power. Before long it is true of
them, as the apostle expresses it so sadly, they have forgotten that they were
purged from their old sins; and, it is still more sadly true, they return like the
dog to his nauseating feast and the swine to her wallowing in the mire, and
their last state is worse than the first.

MEMBERS OF HIS BODY

4. He next appeals to them by their union with the Lord Jesus Christ as
members of His body, and bound by every tie of love and loyalty, to be
separated unto Him, and true to the sacred bond of that heavenly marriage
with which He has honored His Bride. The apostle uses very strong figurative language in this passage, and describes our union with Christ under the
image of the perfect oneness of the marriage bond.

> The body is not meant for sexual immorality, but for the Lord,
> and the Lord for the body. . . . Do you not know that your
> bodies are members of Christ himself? . . . He who unites himself
> with the Lord is one with him in spirit. (6:13, 15, 17)

It is not only in the public and collective capacity of the Church that we are thus wedded to our heavenly Bridegroom, but individually we are here thus represented as personally united to Him. And our very body is in some sense specially constituted to be the recipient of His life, while His body is constituted also to be the Head and Fountain of our life physically as well as spiritually.

This holy mystery the divine Spirit alone can teach. It is hardly necessary to say that it must be guarded from every possible touch of materialism and coarseness. It is as unutterably pure as the heaven of heavens, and high above the faintest suggestion of earthly passion or sentimental love, but it is none the less vital, real and unspeakably sacred. This should keep us pure even as the wife is kept pure, not by the restraints of law, not by confinement or force, but by the choice of an exclusive affection, that by its very nature shuts out others from her heart and makes her the property of one alone. By this holy sanction He bids us keep our purity unspotted for the day of His glorious coming and the consummation of our perfect union. "Listen, O daughter, consider and give ear," He says to His Bride; "Forget your people and your father's house./ The king is enthralled by your beauty;/ honor him, for he is your lord" (Psalm 45:10–11). By and by the message will follow, "In embroidered garments she is led to the king" (45:14).

REDEMPTION AND DIVINE OWNERSHIP

5. Our redemption and divine ownership are urged as the ground of a watchful and wholehearted sanctity and consecration. "You are not your own; you were bought at a price. Therefore honor God with your body" (1 Corinthians 6:19b–20). Not only are we united to our Lord by this intimate and exquisite bond, but we are owned by Him by virtue of His redeeming purchase and precious blood. He has bought us, and we have no right to let another control us, or even hold ourselves for ourselves apart from Him.

In the old slave times there were two mulatto slaves who had grown up on the same plantation, the one a beautiful quadroon girl, and the other a young man of bright and handsome person. Both had become fondly attached through their frequent association. This young fellow had labored long and hard with the double object of purchasing, at once, her liberty and his, and then making her his wife. But hard times came upon their old master, and he was obliged to sell his slaves. The occasion was announced, and on that terrible block stood this beautiful trembling girl. In the foreground was a coarse, brutal planter from the Mississippi, who had determined to buy her for the basest of reasons. In the background stood the young mulatto watching the sale, because he had determined to buy her, if he could, and set her free. Up went the figures while his heart beat fast as they rose very near his limited sum of $1,000. Then, at last, with a gulp in his throat, he made his bid of $1,000, while everybody wondered. The planter looked at him with a leer for a moment, and then he bid $50 more. The poor mulatto sank back. The hammer fell, and the girl was sold to her brutal owner. With heart nearly broken the young man hastened to his master, and asked him if he would take a thousand and let him buy himself. The kind master consented and the young slave was free. Then he went to this Mississippi planter and asked him to look at him and examine him. Said he, "Would you be willing to exchange me for the girl you bought yesterday? I am free, but will sell myself to you as a slave if you will set her free and take me as her substitute." There was a brief conflict between the base passions of this selfish man, but finally greed prevailed. He knew the man was worth much more than the woman and he consented, hoping, doubtless, to be able after a little to get them both. Papers were made out, and the joyful slave went to tell his loved one that she was free by the cost of his own liberty and life, and then he added, with touching simplicity, "Be good, for my sake, and always remember that you belong to me." And so they parted, but the vessel in which he sailed was burned and he lost his life. Then this brutal man came back and tried to force her to give herself up, as he had lost her substitute. But she held firmly to her rights and papers of liberty, and the law sustained her. Then he tried to cajole her and bribe her, but her noble and simple answer was, as temptations came again and again, "He bought me, I belong to him." Oh, that this divine incentive might bind our hearts to Him, and make the watchword against temptation and the pledge of sacrifice and service, "I belong to Him!"

THE SACREDNESS OF THE BODY

6. Finally, the sacredness of the body is the last incentive to which the apostle appeals for our purity of life. This material form is as sacred and as holy as the spirit which dwells within it. God has honored it by giving it in some sense a likeness to Himself and making it the incarnation of His own blessed and glorious Son. Some day it will sit upon the throne of the universe, and be the most glorious object in the eternal ages. Oh, let us keep it pure. Let us consecrate it to its highest possible employ, and let Him fill it now with His holiness, His health and all the enduements and possibilities of His Holy Spirit, and fit it for the highest usefulness below and the noblest destiny above.

The old version has wrongly read this passage. It exclusively applies to the body. The true reading is, "Honor God with your body" (6:20). So let us present our bodies a living sacrifice, a reasonable service, holy and acceptable unto God.

CHAPTER 5

THE CHURCH AND THE CHRISTIAN
IN RELATION TO THE WORLD

*Brothers, each man, as responsible to God, should remain in the
situation God called him to. (1 Corinthians 7:24)*

*What I mean, brothers, is that the time is short. From now on
those who have wives should live as if they had none; those who
mourn, as if they did not; those who are happy, as if they were not;
those who buy something, as if it were not theirs to keep; those who
use the things of the world, as if not engrossed in them. For this
world in its present form is passing away.*

I would like you to be free from concern. (7:29–32)

The relation of the Church of Christ and the individual Christian to the
secular and social world is a subject of deep practical importance, and the
apostle has discussed it with great fullness of detail in this important epistle.
We shall take up at this time the relation of the Christian to secular business, to the home and to society.

SECTION I—*The Christian in Relation to Business*

Our secular callings are part of God's divine order and province for each of
our lives. There is nothing necessarily wrong in secular business, and there is
nothing essentially more holy in withdrawing from the occupations of life
and giving one's self exclusively to what might be called the work of the
ministry. Our Lord Jesus Christ Himself lent His sanction both to business
and the home, by spending the first 30 years of His life in a carpenter's shop
at Nazareth, and performing His first miracle at a wedding. Yet, Christians
are very apt to get the idea that they can serve God better by withdrawing
from business and from worldly occupations and giving their time exclusive-

ly to Christian work. This is by no means the teaching of the Holy Scriptures. God needs His best men in the place where men most congregate. And the most useful ministries of life may be proclaimed in the kitchen, the factory and the counting room where we come in contact with men who will not come to listen to our preaching, but who cannot help seeing the lives we live and reading the epistles which are written in the living characters of daily duty and faithfulness. It is much harder to find a thoroughly consecrated businessman than a score of preachers. If God has cast our lot, therefore, in the sphere of secular life, let us abide in the calling wherein we are called, with God, and adorn the doctrine of God, our Savior, in all things.

But let us be sure that we abide therein with God. Let our business be wholly consecrated to Him. Let Him be the Senior Partner in every firm and the Proprietor in every interest. Then shall our business speak for Christ with practical and mighty emphasis; then shall we be able to count upon the counsel and help of a Friend whose constant love and ceaseless providences will bind us to Him by a thousand cords of grateful remembrance.

In the previous chapter the apostle takes up an extremely practical question in connection with the secular business, and severely censures the Corinthian Christians for going to law with their brethren in the civil courts of unbelievers. This he regards as a shameful abuse, and one that greatly dishonors Christ in the presence of His enemies. He very plainly intimates that while God's children may resort to the powers that are ordained of God under certain circumstances for their protection against the world, it is very different with respect to their own brethren. Some other means of settling differences and disputes among the children of God should be resorted to rather than the decisions of the ungodly, and the tribunals where wicked men strive for unjust advantage and ignore the name of Christ and the authority of the divine Lawgiver.

Are there not some who read these lines who stand reproved before the tribunal of conscience and God's Word for unscriptural methods of business? Yea, he adds, not only does brother go to law with brother, but brother defrauds brother, and provokes to ungodly litigation by injustice, dishonesty and wrong. May God help us so to live that our very business shall become not merely an avenue of selfish gain, but a pulpit of far-reaching influence and a testimony of righteousness and godliness before an unbelieving world.

SECTION II—*The Christian in Relation to the Home*

He next takes up the subject of marriage and family life in the same practical way, and his teachings strike home with searching reproof to the compromising lives of many of God's children in these degenerate days.

A DIVINE INSTITUTION

1. First of all he recognizes marriage as a divine institution for human society, and in every way honorable and right if properly consummated. There is no special sanctity attached to the unmarried state, and there is no reflection of a lower degree of holiness as in any way connected with Christian marriage. The Holy Scriptures give no countenance whatever to the monkish notion that married life is in itself gross or unholy. The Bible's first picture of humanity is a happy, hallowed home. And Christ's first manifestation of His love and power for sinful men was made at Cana; and the closing vision of the book of Revelation opens upon a marriage scene and a glorified Bride sitting by the side of her ascended and regnant Lord and King.

MUST MEET GOD'S CONDITIONS

2. But marriage must meet God's conditions if it is to have His approval. The very first condition is that it will be only "in the Lord" (1 Corinthians 7:39, KJV). The Scriptures utterly discountenance the marriage of a Christian woman to an ungodly man, or the opposite, and no faithful minister of the gospel ought ever to celebrate such a ceremony and have a part in such a sacrilege.

You may excuse your disobedience under many a pretext; you may talk with plausible earnestness of your purpose to influence and save the erring one, but you will find that one drop of ink will go farther than a whole fountain of crystal water, and that God will not lend Himself to your well-meaning attempts which have been in daring defiance of His own wise and loving prohibition. Obedience is much better than sacrifice, and the far-too-costly sacrifice in this case often means a life of misery, a lost crown, and perhaps a heritage of woe bequeathed to innocent children who should never have been born.

A DISJOINTED MARRIAGE

3. Assuming, however, that marriage is disjointed and that this inequality is found to exist perhaps through the fact that both were unconverted at the time of marriage, or many other possible causes, what is the teaching of the Scriptures in regard to such a marriage already consummated? Are we justified in breaking it because the parties are not united in their faith? Certainly not. You cannot put away your wife because you have been lifted up to consecrated life and she is still a stranger to it; you cannot justly neglect your home and leave your family unprovided for while you go to do missionary work. You are bound by every obligation of piety to stand by your unsaved

partner. God will make the offspring even of this union hallowed, and for the sake of the Christian member of the household will give the special privileges of His grace to those who are unsaved so far as they are willing to receive them. "For the unbelieving husband has been sanctified through his wife, and the unbelieving wife has been sanctified through her believing husband" (7:14), that is, is made hallowed by the marriage relation. "Otherwise your children would be unclean, but as it is, they are holy" (7:14), that is, in the ceremonial and legal sense.

But while this is fully recognized, yet there is a gentle provision in the New Testament allowed for the class of cases which may arise where the unbelieving one is not willing to remain with the believing partner, and the husband or wife discards the Christian companion. What are we to do in this case? Very clearly the apostle says, with delicate wisdom, a brother or sister is not in bondage in such a case. "If the unbeliever leaves, let him do so" (7:15). An amicable separation in such case is entirely scriptural, and often best for the harmony of the household and the true interests of both parties. However, this is not a divorce and this does not justify either party in remarrying. One would think they had enough of it already, and that the dictates of experience as well as delicacy would be sufficient to prevent the outrageous abuse of the marriage law which is demoralizing our modern society.

It seems wise and necessary to state with great clearness the Bible law respecting divorce for the protection of innocent lives that are constantly in danger of making grave mistakes through the laxity of public opinion on this subject. It is the judgment of the great body of evangelical churches in Christian lands, and it is fully borne out by the sound and strong teachings of the Holy Scriptures, that there is but one course that can justify divorce, and that is actual unfaithfulness to the marriage bond by one of the parties. Where that has occurred, the innocent party has the right to divorce the guilty one and having so done has always the right to remarry; but the divorced person has not the right to remarry.

Cases are constantly seeking the counsel of Christian ministers where some innocent and thoughtless woman has been drawn into an engagement of marriage with a divorced man. It may be he has allowed himself to be divorced simply by default because he was quite willing to let an uncongenial partner break the bond by legal proceedings, but by so doing he has involved his good name under a serious cloud, and he has no right to involve any innocent woman with him in the compromise. Such marriages might be recognized in all sections of the country, but according to the accepted standard of ecclesiastical law and according to the public opinion of most Christian lands it would be entirely discredited, and it certainly is not in harmony with the lofty standards of the Holy Scriptures.

RISE TO HIGHER GROUND

4. But the apostle rises to higher ground. While marriage is constituted as scriptural and honorable, and while, when once formed, it is to be guarded from reckless attempts at dissolution and invested with every holy sanction and safeguard, yet there are many instances when even marriage is most undesirable, and when life's highest usefulness may be far better secured by a single life and free from the embarrassments and complications of domestic bonds. The old-fashioned notion that matrimony is the natural destiny of every woman is an insult to the capacity and independence of a true woman. God has made her by His grace and assistance abundantly equal to all the necessities of life and the highest possibilities of existence, and there are innumerable cases in which it is just as true as ever, "He who marries the virgin does right, but he who does not marry her does even better" (7:38).

There are many forms of Christian service where we would be turned aside from the highest efficiency and the freedom necessary for entire obedience to the call of God, by becoming entangled with the restraints of another life and obliged to regulate our duty by the circumstances and preferences of another. Where God has called you forth to be His messenger in some difficult field and some high and holy enterprise for Him, be very sure that you do not let the preference of selfish affection hinder your liberty or disqualify you from the most efficient service. Be very sure that you do not merely restrict your own liberty, but involve another life in the perils and privations for which that life may be unequal, and thus two lives may be crippled or limited in their usefulness by an affection as shortsighted and selfish as it was sincere.

Those of us that are called to engage in public service and deal with lives that are consecrated to missionary work are constantly coming in contact with most excellent young people who, after having received from God the distinct call to high and holy service, usually in the mission field, have become engaged without a due regard to God's claim upon their lives. We know some lives which today are blighted and disappointed in consequence of a fatal error in this direction. They have lost their high calling to the field of honor; and, alas, it usually happens that the union for the sake of which they made the sacrifice has turned out to be a bitter disappointment and sometimes a final separation.

Let us be careful how we steal from the altar of heaven the sacrifice which we have placed there; in taking it to our nest, a coal of fire may cling to it which will set aflame our home and leave our life a heap of smoldering ruins.

A SELFISH END

5. One other point is worthy of important emphasis, and that is that those who are married, and married in the Lord, be very careful that they do not make their happiness and affection a selfish end, or a restraint upon the freedom of the other in the Master's work. It is in this connection the apostle says, with much practical solemnity, "You were bought at a price; do not become slaves of men" (7:23). Many a woman has brought upon herself spiritual leanness and even bitter sorrow by trying to hold her husband for her own gratification and encompassing his Christian work with so many strains, entanglements and jealousies as to prove a hindrance instead of a helpmate, and a stumbling block in both their paths. And many a man has made a tremendous mistake in thinking his wife existed for his own pleasure, and that he had the right to control her conscience, her religious freedom, her time and her life, and absorb her as part of his own gross and earthly life.

That which we thus cling to, we are sure to lose, and what we trustfully and lovingly give to God we shall doubly gain in the end. Marriage should not be a weight and restraint upon either life, but a blessed addition of strength and an impulse toward high and heavenly things.

Dr. Arnot has compared these unhappy unions to two ships at sea chained together about 20 feet apart, and dashing into each other's sides with every rolling wave, until they rasp and tear each other to pieces and go down to the bottom together. If they were close enough to be one they would sail the billows together, or if they were miles apart they would surmount the waves alone; but they are just near enough and far enough to be a mutual curse and a source of destruction. God help us to hold our friends, affections and our social ties as sacred trusts for Him, and as avenues of unselfish blessing to and through each other.

SECTION III—*The Christian in Relation to Society*

The apostle speaks in the same series of paragraphs about the attitude of Christians to the social gatherings of life with special reference to the heathen feasts and social entertainments. He lays down a number of principles in connection with this subject which have still a very practicable application to our present-day life. It is true we are not concerned with the question of meat sacrificed to idols, but we are concerned with the principle on which that particular matter was to be regulated and that applies to all questions of our social life.

One of these principles is, " 'Everything is permissible'—but not everything is constructive" (10:23). That will settle a great many questions. Is it for the good of others? Is it for the glory of God? Is it the most practical use of my time, that I should engage in this thing?

The next principle is, " 'Everything is permissible for me'—but I will not be mastered by anything" (6:12). This applies to a great many indulgences which easily become engrossing; any amusement, yes, even any legitimate occupation that absorbs us too much and becomes necessary to our happiness, is dangerous. Any social friendship, which possesses us and takes away our perfect liberty of conscience and will, is wrong, especially if you find yourself under another's undue influence and power. There is a social hypnotism which has perverted many a true life, and to which you have no right ever to expose your freedom in the Lord.

Another principle and one of far-reaching application is,

> Be careful, however, that the exercise of your freedom does not become a stumbling block to the weak. . . . Therefore, if what I eat causes my brother to fall into sin, I will never eat meat again, so that I will not cause him to fall. (8:9, 13)

This principle ought to settle most of the question relating to our indulgences in things which we believe to be for us harmless and lawful.

Take, for example, the question of the use of stimulants. We are frank to say that we believe alcohol, like leaven, to be forbidden in the Scriptures as a beverage because it involves the principle of fermentation, but we know many excellent men and women who do not believe this. Many biblical expositors contend that the Scriptures do not condemn fermented wine in itself. Assuming, for the sake of argument, that this may be so; still the greater question arises, what is the effect of this indulgence on innumerable lives, and what may the effect of our example be upon others? There can be but one answer to this question, and on the ground of love the sensitive conscience will be prohibited from the use of that which may become a stumbling block to a brother.

The same principle may be applied to the horse race, the theater and the dance. We know of many painful instances where young men that have been saved from the world have been led back to the horse race and the intoxicating cup by the example of their Sunday school teacher or some Christian friend.

A man who loved horses with what he believed to be an innocent affection and a good conscience, and who had no sympathy with the abuses of the track, was the occasion of the ruin of some of the noblest members of his own Bible class who would never have thought of going had they not seen him on his way.

This also includes the Sunday newspaper, the doubtful novel, the society ball, the cigar and pipe of the smoker, and the whole range of doubtful things which may be decided without any difficulty or doubt, by the higher law of what is the best for others, for the glory of God, and what is the most Christian thing for me to do.

Finally, there is one great principle eloquently and impressively brought out in the close of his discussion of these questions which should lift the whole subject to a higher plane, and that is, that all earthly things are but mere passing stage scenes in the drama of human life, and that none of them are important enough in themselves to become the objects of our attention. They are only the drapery of the stage or the scenes of the passing hour, and life must take hold of something far beyond them.

In that company of actors on the stage some of them are laughing, but their laughter is not real; some of them are crying, but their tears are not sincere; some of them are being wedded, but the marriage is not real; some of them are buying great estates, but nothing is owned; some of them are posing as kings, but they will be uncrowned in an hour. It is an unreal world, and so he says the stage scenes of this world pass away, and nothing temporal is worthy of being directly the object of our life; it is merely a means to something better and more enduring. And so, the tears of life are not to be made too important; the smiles of joy are not to fascinate us too long; the joys of home are but the entertainment of a night at a wayside inn; the business of life is but a steppingstone to a higher gain. All these things are transitory and purely incidental. We are to live beyond them. We are to use the world, but not abuse it. Our life below is to be lived under the powers of the world to come.

CHAPTER 6

THE CHRISTIAN MINISTRY: ITS AUTHORITY AND SUPPORT

In the same way, the Lord has commanded that those who preach the gospel should receive their living from the gospel.

But I have not used any of these rights. And I am not writing this in the hope that you will do such things for me. I would rather die than have anyone deprive me of this boast. . . . No, I beat my body and make it my slave so that after I have preached to others, I myself will not be disqualified for the prize. (1 Corinthians 9:14– 15, 27)

This chapter expounds the principles underlying the authority and support of the gospel ministry, and also its true spirit and aim. It is a good thing for the pew sometimes to hear the pulpit preach to itself; and it is a very good thing for the pulpit to preach to itself, and to be thoroughly imbued with the apostolic spirit so finely exemplified in Paul.

SECTION I—*The Authority of the Ministry*

Paul asks,

> Am I not an apostle? . . . Are you not the result of my work in the Lord? . . . For you are the seal of my apostleship in the Lord. . . . I am compelled to preach. Woe to me if I do not preach the gospel! . . . I am simply discharging the trust committed to me. (1 Corinthians 9:1–2, 16–17)

This is surely a sufficient basis for the authority and obligation of the Christian ministry.

A TRUST

First, he tells us that a dispensation (KJV, NIV has "trust") of the gospel has been committed unto him. The word "dispensation" means stewardship or trusteeship. He has been appointed a steward of the treasures of his Lord and of the supplies of his Lord's household. Such a dispensation is committed to every true minister, and it is a very solemn thing to be invested with an office so responsible and standing under an accountability so tremendous.

Next, he tells us not only has this trust been committed to him, but he has accepted it with such a profound sense of obligation that it has become an imperative necessity to his conscience and his life. It has put the woe on him, and the go in him, that he must preach. This is the true secret of successful service, not to take a text, but to have the text take us, and to be so baptized with our message that we can honestly say, like the apostles after Pentecost, "We cannot help speaking about what we have seen and heard" (Acts 4:20). It is this "cannot help" that tells. It is the bursting fountain coming from the depths and drenching the heights. Like the old astronomer who was forced for a time by the thumb screws to recant his heresy of the earth going around the sun, but the moment the pressure was removed, almost unconsciously to himself, the honest expression burst from his lips, "It moves all the same."

THE SEALS

Further, he can point to the seals of his apostleship and his work in the Lord. He has more than a prefix to his name; he has a lot of glorious suffixes—the souls that have been added to him and into whose faces he can look and say, "In Christ Jesus I became your father through the gospel" (1 Corinthians 4:15). Every true servant of Christ ought to be successful, and to be able to point to the actual fruits of a faithful ministry. The Bible has no sympathy with the idea that it is all right to go on for a quarter of a century doing our best and seeing no results. The anomaly of 1,000 churches in one of our great denominations that have not had a single addition during the past year by profession of faith, has no recognition of the New Testament. Such churches do not deserve to die, for they are dead already.

Only today a gentleman told us of the conversion of a girl who served in his kitchen, through a few loving acts of personal kindness in helping her to pump the water and getting her through the hard places. She told him with innocent frankness she had never been used that way before, and it quite broke her down; in the first test that came to her she yielded her heart to God. Your workshop, your store, your office, can each become a sacred pulpit and a birthplace of souls if you have the "cannot but" running over from your own heart.

SECTION II—*The Rights of the Ministry*

THE NECESSITIES OF LIFE

The minister has a right to the necessities and comforts of life. "Don't we have the right to food and drink?" (9:4). The minister of Christ has a right to have a living. Some good people scarcely concede this. It is said that once a committee waited upon Lyman Beecher to ask him to secure for them a pastor for their church in one of the New England towns. They wanted a man of great ability, good in the pulpit and good out of it, with attractive gifts and deep piety. The doctor asked them about how much they expected to give this extraordinary minister. They said if he was all right they could probably raise $300 a year for him. The keen witted doctor suppressed a rippling smile, and cooly suggested to the brethren that the only man he could think of that met their standard was the late Dr. Dwight; and he would suggest that they send a message to the angel Gabriel to send him back to take charge of this church, and, especially as he had been in heaven so long and had obtained a spiritual body, he would probably be able to live on $300 a year. The time was when his sarcasm was more deserved than it is today, but there are not wanting many sections of the country where the faithful ministry is still starved.

Paul claims the right of support. "Is it only I and Barnabas who must work for a living?" (9:6). He claims for himself and his brother the right of their appropriate support. There is no reason why he should be compelled to toil with his own hands for the livelihood of himself and his brother. And yet the fact was that he went through his ministry not merely living a life of trust, but living a life of toil. His entrance to a Roman town found him among the day laborers at the loom earning his wages like a common workman, and at the end of the week paying his board and supplying the wants of his brother from his hard-earned wages. But this he had no right to do.

He then proceeds to establish the right of the ministry to a proper support from a most cogent and conclusive argument.

First, he says even nature ought to teach us this. "Who serves as a soldier at his own expense? Who plants a vineyard and does not eat of its grapes? Who tends a flock and does not drink of the milk?" (9:7). Even under the ancient law the ox that trampled out the grain must not be muzzled. "Is it about oxen that God is concerned? Surely he says this for us, doesn't he?" (9:9–10).

Next, he shows that under the old dispensation God made ample provision for the support of His ministers. "Those who serve at the altar share in what is offered on the altar" (9:13). One whole tithe of the income of the Hebrew people went to the support of the Levites, and surely God is not estimating at a lower value the lives of His servants in the larger blessing of the New Testament dispensation.

But, further, he tells us that this is an ordinance of the New Testament distinctly appointed and commanded. "In the same way, the Lord has commanded that those who preach the gospel should receive their living from the gospel" (9:14). It is as much a divine ordinance as any of the sacred appointments of the Holy Scriptures. It is well that God's people should fully understand this, and it is well that some of us are able to stand in a position of such freedom in this matter that we can speak frankly to our brethren without being misunderstood or supposed to be seeking our own advantage. The church or the Christian that does not definitely and systematically contribute, not merely for general missionary objects, but for the support of those who minister to them in the Lord, will lose spiritually. This rests upon the law of equity, and there is no answer to his invincible argument, "If we have sown spiritual seed among you, is it too much if we reap a material harvest from you?" (9:11).

A HOME LIFE

Paul claims the right to home life and to his ties of affection. "Don't we have the right to take a believing wife along with us, as do the other apostles?" (9:5). The ministry is not improved by celibacy. It needs the gentle touch of human kindness, loving sympathy, and to be able to speak from every avenue of human life to every variety of human experience.

SECTION III—*The Voluntary Sacrifice of Rights*

Now he rises to higher ground. Having claimed the right both for himself and his brother, he voluntarily renounces it on his own behalf, and takes the place of surrender, of sacrifice, of manual toil and of all the hardships incident to the great renunciation he has so gladly made. He does this with great deliberation. He is not by any means deceived about it. He has the glorious future in view, and the compensation which he feels will well repay him for all of the sacrifices involved. And it is this—he has no glory and no reward for preaching the gospel. That is simply a matter of duty and the honest discharge of a sacred trust. The only way, therefore, that he can add the element of recompense and bring into his ministry a higher quality of heroism and love is by the spirit of sacrifice. And so he adds,

> But I have not used any of these rights. And I am not writing this in the hope that you will do such things for me. I would

rather die than have anyone deprive me of this boast. . . . What then is my reward? Just this: that in preaching the gospel I may offer it free of charge. (9:15, 18)

The teaching of the apostle in this matter is exceedingly clear and most important to understand. No man has a right to leave the ministry of Christ without support; but if a minister of Christ chooses himself to stand in a place of personal independence, to trust the Lord alone for his needs, or to toil with honest hands for his own support, he has the right. And he should be accredited the consideration which Paul asked for himself. In some respects he will have a freedom and a claim to disinterested service which may give his testimony a greater effectiveness for God and the cause of truth.

SECTION IV—*The Principle of Accommodation*

Next there is the principle of accommodation to the prejudices and infirmities of others in order to do them greater good. This is a fine touch of Christian love.

> Though I am free and belong to no man, I make myself a slave to everyone, to win as many as possible. To the Jews I became like a Jew, to win the Jews. To those under the law I became like one under the law (though I myself am not under the law), so as to win those under the law. To those not having the law I became like one not having the law (though I am not free from God's law but am under Christ's law), so as to win those not having the law. To the weak I became weak, to win the weak. I have become all things to all men so that by all possible means I might save some. (9:19–22)

Now, let us carefully observe that while Paul yields much to the prejudices, weaknesses and sensibilities of those whom he seeks to win, yet he never compromises principle; he never stoops to their level. He says, "To those not having the law I became like one not having the law," but he adds immediately, "though I am not free from God's law but am under Christ's law" (9:21). What he means is simply this—that he does not contend for petty theories, forms of speech, phases of doctrine, nonessential questions, but he does not once surrender his purity. He will meet the man of the world on his own ground, but he will not do what the man of the world does. Standing on a higher plane and reaching to him, he will lift him by his love and strength. This does not mean we are to marry ungodly people to save them; that we are to go to the theater in order to influence our husbands, wives or friends who go; that we are to play cards in order to get to the hearts of some of the players; that we are to get people in love with us that we may lead them to Christ; but it means that we are to approach men with the love of the gospel. We are not to come to them with our crotchets and our technicalities and our sharp angles; but we are to recognize in them what is good, and touch everything that can be made a point to contact with Christianity and in the right sense be all things to them that we may gain them for Christ and their own selves.

SECTION V—*The High and Glorious Ambition*

WINNING THE PRIZE

Next comes his high and glorious ambition to win the prize of the high calling of God in Christ Jesus. Every noble life must have an uplift, an attraction, an inspiration, a hope, a vision, a goal of attraction and expectation. Paul had a glowing heart alive with divine enthusiasm. He had caught the light of the Eternal Hills. He had seen afar the vision of the coming glory. He had anticipated the rapture of that hour when he should receive a crown from the glorified Lord. For this all else was counted loss, and "forgetting what is behind," sacrificing the things that were secondary, he pressed "on toward the goal to win the prize" to which God had called him from on high (Philippians 3:13–14).

DISQUALIFICATION

So he speaks to us, in the closing paragraph of this chapter, of the incorruptible crown which he himself set out to win. He reminds us that it is only for a few. "All the runners run, but only one gets the prize" (1 Corinthians 9:24), and he is deeply sensible that this prize may be lost. Very solemnly does he speak of the possibility of his preaching the gospel to others and yet being "disqualified" (9:27); not lost, for Paul never contemplated such a prospect or doubted his final salvation, but rejected in the day of award and recompense. The word literally means "disapproved." Therefore he pressed forward and trampled under foot everything that could hinder his holy ambition. "I beat my body," he says, "and make it my slave" (9:27). The Greek word is, "I buffet my body." It is the training of the athlete for the arena. It is the self-denial and abstinence from soft indulgences, and everything that could soften or emasculate the strength of manhood. This is what he means.

We may have the easy place, if we will. We may take the rose-strewn path, if we want to. We may evade the cross. We may shun the trying ordeal. We may be popular and have things pleasant for a little while. Or we may endure hardness as good soldiers of Jesus Christ, and beat our body for the incorruptible crown. Some day we will not regret a single tear or sacrifice when the heart's blood will have congealed into rubies, and the teardrops will have become crystal jewels in an unfading crown. Oh, then we shall be so glad that we were not afraid to sacrifice or suffer for His sake, and be partakers of the sufferings of Christ and the glory that will be revealed!

CHAPTER 7

LIVING IN THE END OF THE AGE

These things happened to them as examples and were written down as warnings for us, on whom the fulfillment of the ages has come. (1 Corinthians 10:11)

This chapter describes the relation of the Church of the New Testament to the saints of the Old. It places us in the end of the age, standing the heirs of the past, the sentinels of the solemn future, at the very gates of the coming kingdom. And it points out the peculiar responsibilities and privileges which devolve upon us all in view of these things as the men and women upon whom "the fulfillment of the ages has come" (10:11).

SECTION I—*The Types and Examples of the Past*

Four great types are held forth here, drawn from the history of ancient Israel and embodying the great truths of redemption, and we are shown how really identical the gospel preached to the ancient fathers was with that which is today the ground of our salvation. "They all ate the same spiritual food and drank the same spiritual drink; for they drank from the spiritual rock that accompanied them, and that rock was Christ" (10:3–4).

THE CLOUD
1. The first great type held forth is the Cloud, which led them through the wilderness and covered them as a pavilion from their enemies. It is here spoken of as a divine baptism which came upon them as they passed through the sea. The account of that cloud is very striking and beautiful. First, it preceded and guided them as they went forth out of the land of bondage. So the Holy Spirit leads us out of the world and sin into Christ, going before us at first, while we follow somewhat at a distance. But when at last they came to the deep, dark flood and went down into the death of

199

which it was a symbol, then that cloud that had gone before them gently turned backward. And passing through the camp it baptized them into its very substance, covered them over as a pavilion, wrapped itself around them as a garment, penetrated their very being as the element of their living and breathing. Then it passed behind and stood above them as a wall of majestic protection from their enemies and a glorious light to shine upon their pathway as they marched on before.

So, after we have followed the Holy Spirit in His earlier leadings, and have come to the place of surrender and death to self and sin, then He comes nearer, passes through our very being, baptizes us into Himself and then passes through all our life and becomes our reward, gathering up our past, protecting us as a mighty Providence from all evil, and guarding and guiding all our future way. Beautiful, majestic symbol of the presence of God with His people and the baptism of the Holy Spirit!

THE SEA

2. The next type was the sea. "They were all baptized into Moses . . . in the sea" (10:2). There is no doubt that primarily the sea represented our baptism by water. We know the Red Sea represented the idea of their death to the old life of Egypt, and we know that baptism is the symbol of death, for "all of us who were baptized into Christ Jesus were baptized into his death" (Romans 6:3).

But it represents much more than the ceremony of baptism. It is a vivid figure of that real death to self and sin in which all true life must begin. This is the first goal to which the Holy Spirit is ever leading us—the grave. It was of this the Master said, "I have a baptism to undergo, and how distressed I am until it is completed!" (Luke 12:50). Every true servant must follow Him by the same steps, by the same death. Is it not our deepest need? Is it not the secret of all our failures, all our sorrows, all our defeats? Is it not our deepest desire that we may be dead indeed unto self and sin? Oh, let us go forth with Him to the cross. Let us follow the pillar of cloud and fire down into the very bottom of the sea, and when we reach its depths and all seems lost, then the heavenly cloud will meet us and will enfold us in the bosom of God and baptize us into all His glorious fullness.

THE MANNA

3. The third symbol is manna, the heavenly bread provided for the people in the wilderness. This was the type of Christ as the sustenance of our spiritual life. The most remarkable thing about this bread was that it was supernatural food. There was no support to be found for them in the natural world, nor is there any supply for the needs of the new man to be found in any earthly thing. It may try to feed on human love, or human sympathy, or

human success, but it will wither and die. It must have Jesus Christ to nourish it, and live on His very life. Spirit, soul and body must draw their subsistence from the very mouth of God.

> I am the living bread that came down from heaven. If anyone eats of this bread, he will live forever. . . . Just as the living Father sent me and I live because of the Father, so the one who feeds on me will live because of me. (John 6:51, 57)

It was daily bread. It was not an accumulation stored up for a year, but every morning it must be received fresh; so as we enter upon the year before us the watchword must be, "Give us each day our daily bread" (Luke 11:3).

THE ROCK AND THE LIVING WATER

4. Next comes the Rock of Horeb and the Living Water, representing the Holy Spirit as the supply of our spiritual life through Jesus Christ. The rock represents Christ, but the Water represents the Holy Spirit, who flows from His riven side.

There were three stages in the history of this rock and its lessons. The first was when the rock was smitten at Horeb and the water gushed forth, representing Christ's crucifixion and the coming of the Holy Spirit. But there was another stage 40 years later, when they came to Kadesh and again were without water. Then God commanded Moses not to strike the rock, for it was already smitten and open, but to "speak to that rock" (Numbers 20:8), and the water would flow forth at the bidding of faith and satisfy their need. Moses despised this gentle command, and rashly struck the rock two times with the tender rod of the high priest. The result was that God was angry at his unbelief and rashness of spirit, and debarred him in consequence from the Promised Land. At the same time the water came all the same. The promise of God was fulfilled and the full tides overflowed, satisfying man and beast from the living fountain.

This represents the second or deeper outflow of the Holy Spirit when we come to Him in full consecration and simple trust, not to open the fountain which is already there through Christ's finished work, but to take, at the bidding of simple faith, the fullness that is waiting to satisfy all our need. This represents the Holy Spirit in His deeper work in the consecrated heart. It is the water of Kadesh, which means holiness. It is the baptism of sanctification and of power from on high.

But there was a third manifestation of that flowing rock. It is referred to here in the 10th chapter of First Corinthians by the phrase, "the spiritual rock that accompanied them" (1 Corinthians 10:4). How could the rock follow them? Why, in a very simple way. The rock itself did not move, but the waters that poured from it followed them like a stream through the desert. Sometimes the stream was out of sight, and they seemed to be in a desolate and barren wilderness with nothing but mounds of arid sand without a drop of moisture. But even then the water was following them, and the stream was flowing as a subterranean river far down beneath their feet. They had but to stop and dig a well in the desert and the waters burst forth and flowed again until they covered all the land.

This is beautifully described in one of the chapters of Numbers, where the people are represented as gathering in a circle in the sand and lifting up their voices in song, crying, "Spring up, O well!" (Numbers 21:17). The princes with their staves dug, and soon the gurgling waters burst through their barriers and the fountain poured out its living stream to satisfy the thirsty multitude and their panting flocks and herds.

So, along life's desert way we, too, may strike down in the barren sands with the staff of promise and the song of faith. And we shall find the deep tides of His blessed fullness, and the Holy Spirit will overflow in blessing and satisfaction to our hearts and lives.

Such, then, were the ancient types and their precious meaning even to them. How much richer and sweeter the deeper fullness of truth and reality which the ends of the age have brought to us. Oh, let us prize that glorious fulfillment! God is expecting better men today than even Abraham and Moses, Joshua and Caleb, and the saints, patriarchs and prophets of that morning twilight of the distant past.

SECTION II—*Warnings of the Past*

While they had their examples they also had their beacons. Five distinct incidents are referred to with their lessons of solemn admonition for our times, for human nature is still just the same and as liable as then to sink into idolatry, licentiousness, worldliness, presumption and unbelief.

IDOLATRY

1. The first warning is against idolatry. "Do not be idolaters, as some of them were; as it is written: 'The people sat down to eat and drink and got up to indulge in pagan revelry' " (1 Corinthians 10:7). Under the very shadow of Sinai, and with the noise of God's awful voice still ringing in their ears, they were ready at the slightest provocation to forget their sacred voices and join in a carnival of idolatrous revelry around the golden calf that their own hands had fashioned for a god.

Perhaps we may not worship idols so tangible, but our hearts are just as truly centered on idols of human flesh, idols of worldly ambition, idols of selfish desire and willfulness. When John wrote his first epistle the danger of literal idolatry had long passed away. After the days of the Babylonian captivity we never hear any more of Israel worshiping the gods of the heathen, and yet he says to these very disciples, "Dear children, keep yourselves from idols" (1 John 5:21). Surely he must mean the idol whose throne is in the heart and whose sway is an invisible kingdom of affection, desire and strong self-will.

SEXUAL IMMORALITY

2. The second warning is against licentiousness or sexual immorality. "We should not commit sexual immorality, as some of them did—and in one day twenty-three thousand of them died" (1 Corinthians 10:8). He refers to the experience of the Israelites with the daughters of Midian. After Balaam had failed to curse Israel he persuaded them to meet with beautiful women of the neighboring tribe of the Midianites. As they mingled in the dance and in the song they were seduced by the wiles and attractions of the ungodly Midianites. And in reckless abandonment they plunged into all the excesses of sin until the fearful judgment of God alone awoke them from their foolish madness. If God were to deal today as He dealt with Israel, how many would be left on our church rolls? And yet, how much baser the sin of uncleanness is in the light of Christianity and the spotless life of Jesus Christ and the ineffable purity of the Holy Spirit than in the rude, semi-barbarous days of ancient Israel. There is no sin against which God has flashed out His fierce detestation and anger as against the sin of licentiousness, in which no true child of God can allow himself willfully to indulge. If for a moment any one who names the name of Christ has been tempted from the path of purity, the only hope for salvation is to fly from the very appearance of evil as you would fly from the yawning mouth of hell.

WORLDLY DESIRE

3. Next appears worldly desire, the lusting after evil things (10:6). This would seem to imply that the real source of all sin is in the spirit of our own desires. The last of the Ten Commandments strikes down to the very taproot of all evil: "You shall not covet" (Exodus 20:17). All sin commences with the kindling of forbidden desire. The Apostle James gives us the pedigree:

> Each one is tempted when, by his own evil desire, he is dragged away and enticed. Then, after desire has conceived, it gives birth to sin; and sin, when it is full-grown, gives birth to death. (James 1:14–15)

The secret of victory, therefore, is not to allow the mind and heart to dwell for a moment upon any forbidden thing. Therefore it is true that "the thought of foolishness is sin" (Proverbs 24:9, KJV). It is the germ of sin. It breeds actual sin. The whole life of modern Christians is terribly fitted to stimulate unholy desire. The little child is taught from infancy to covet the vain and glittering attractions of the world—dress, equipage, pleasure, praise, fashion, display and a thousand worldly allurements. These are things that are absorbing the hearts of men and women, and they leave no room for God. It is all summed up in one great word, "Mammon," which stands for everything which antagonizes God, and especially for this great, godless and absorbing world with all its countless snares, attractions and vanities. They began by lusting after the leeks and onions of Egypt, and they ended by lusting after the pomp and glory of earthly kings and courts until they got what they wanted. The issue of it all was the loss of Canaan first, and the loss of God afterward, and the bitter bondage of subjection and captivity at the hand of the very kings whose dazzling glories had beguiled them.

THE SIN OF PRESUMPTION

4. The next sin against which He warns us by their example is the sin of presumption. "We should not test the Lord, as some of them did" (1 Corinthians 10:9). They seem to have tempted God in various ways. One of them was by limiting His power saying, "Can God spread a table in the wilderness?" Another was questioning His love. They might all be summed up in the word unbelief. There is nothing that so tempts God as doubt, and it was their unbelief that lost them the Land of Promise, and it will lose us the pardon of our sins, the baptism of the Spirit, the blessing of sanctification, the healing of our bodies, the answer of our prayers and even part in the coming of our Lord.

THE SPIRIT OF MURMURING

5. The last of their dangers which He holds up as a warning to us is the spirit of murmuring. "Do not grumble, as some of them did—and were killed by the destroying angel" (10:10). Their entire declension, which culminated in God's awful oath that they should not enter into His rest, all began with the one little sentence, "So the people grumbled against Moses" (Exodus 15:24). It was just the faintest kind of murmuring. It was one fly in the ointment, one speck on the spotless linen, one worm in the fruit, one blot of leprosy on the healthy face. We cannot afford for an instant to lose our joy. The spirit of depression and discontent leaves us open to every temptation and danger. We must trust in the Lord forever, rejoice evermore, in everything give thanks and always triumph in Christ Jesus.

SECTION III—*Our Responsibility*

These are the incitements and the admonitions of the sacred past calling us at once both to hope and fear. And in view of all, the great apostle finally in the third place, impresses upon us with great solemnity the responsibilities and privileges of our solemn place as those who are living in the end of the age. As you have seen the child trundling its little hoop by touching it on both sides alternately to keep it from either extreme, so God teaches us both with warning and with promise as our spiritual condition requires. Sometimes it is warning we need, and He shouts in our ear the solemn admonition, as a mother would cry to her babe in wild alarm if she were, too, in danger of falling over the precipice. But, again, when we are in danger of being too much depressed He speaks to us with notes of encouragement and promise. He tells us there is no real danger of our failing utterly, and that He will never allow us to be tempted above what we are able to bear. And so we hear Him saying on one hand, "If you think you are standing firm, be careful that you don't fall!" (1 Corinthians 10:12); but immediately after, adding on the other side, "God is faithful; he will not let you be tempted beyond what you can bear. But when you are tempted, he will also provide a way out so that you can stand up under it" (10:13).

On the one hand then, let us go forth with deep and holy seriousness; on the other, with divine encouragement and confidence. He assures us of His restraining and sustaining grace. He will keep back the flood from going too far. There is nothing that can come to us but what He allows and can prevent and will arrest before it goes too far. On the other hand, He will sustain us. He will give us a way to escape. He will deliver us from evil.

What is the way of escape? It is not always our way of fighting our own battles. It is rather the way of flying into the open arms of Jesus, letting Him fight the battle for us and rest us on His peaceful breast. Then armed both with hope and fear let us go forth into the days before us. Days of blessing they will doubtless be; days of trial they are sure to be. The ends of the age are upon us. The hosts of hell and earth are massing for the final conflict. Let us not expect easy circumstances or dress parades, but set our faces as a flint to endure hardness as good soldiers of Christ, and, "when the day of evil comes, you may be able to stand your ground" (Ephesians 6:13), at last, having done all, stand approved, triumphant, crowned at the coming of our blessed Lord. God has honored us by letting us stand as those "on whom the fulfillment of the ages has come" (1 Corinthians 10:11), guarding, as it were, the very bridal chamber of our coming Lord, and opening the gates for the marriage of the Lamb. Surely He expects of us more than He expected of Abraham, Moses, Joshua, Elijah or Paul! Will He be disappointed? Will He find us wholly true?

CHAPTER 8

THE ORDINANCES OF THE CHURCH

For I received from the Lord what I also passed on to you: The Lord Jesus, on the night he was betrayed, took bread, and when he had given thanks, he broke it and said, "This is my body, which is for you; do this in remembrance of me." In the same way, after supper he took the cup, saying, "This cup is the new covenant in my blood; do this, whenever you drink it, in remembrance of me." For whenever you eat this bread and drink this cup, you proclaim the Lord's death until he comes. (1 Corinthians 11:23–26)

In his comprehensive manual of the Christian Church, the apostle next takes up the ordinances of the Church, more especially the sacred ordinance of the Lord's Supper. He calls attention first to the prevalent abuses among them with respect to this ordinance; next, he unfolds with deep tenderness and fullness the nature and design of this beautiful rite, the true spirit of its observance.

SECTION I—*Abuses in Connection with the Lord's Supper*

THE SPIRIT OF DIVISION

The first of these was the spirit of division in the Church.

In the first place, I hear that when you come together as a church, there are divisions among you, and to some extent I believe it. No doubt there have to be differences among you to show which of you have God's approval. (1 Corinthians 11:18–19)

The Lord's Supper is a beautiful type of the unity of the Church of Christ. Speaking of it in the 10th chapter, he says,

Is not the cup of thanksgiving for which we give thanks a participation in the blood of Christ? And is not the bread that we break a participation in the body of Christ? Because there is one loaf, we, who are many, are one body, for we all partake of the one loaf. (10:16–17)

We are to discern the Lord's body in this ordinance; and that does not mean merely His personal body, but His mystical body, the Church, which is one in Him. It is therefore a sin against the Head, and an abuse of this symbolical ordinance, to come to the communion table with divisions, strifes or alienations. We are to sit here as brethren, and every wrong should be righted, and every grievance healed, before we partake of the same bread and the same cup. To this, more than to any other spiritual service, does the command of the Savior apply:

Therefore, if you are offering your gift at the altar and there remember that your brother has something against you, leave your gift there in front of the altar. First go and be reconciled to your brother; then come and offer your gift. (Matthew 5:23–24)

THE INDULGENCE OF APPETITES

2. The next abuse was the coarse and sensual indulgence of their appetites by turning this sacred rite into a common feast, eating and drinking in gross and shameful sensuality. The apostle condemns this in unmeasured terms, and it is scarcely necessary that we should emphasize or dwell upon this part of the subject. It is utterly removed from the very idea of the worldly feast or heathen banquet; the elements in it are purely symbolic of higher spiritual things and the earthly and physical are only meant to be a steppingstone to the spiritual and divine.

DISCERNING THE LORD'S BODY

3. The next abuse is one in which we are more likely to share. He defines it as not discerning the Lord's body. It is a failure to understand and enter into the deep spiritual meaning of this holy ordinance, or spiritual apathy and indifference. We are to engage in this service with mind and heart intent upon its great central object, the Lord Jesus Christ Himself. We are to meet with Him, and recognize Him in His personal presence, His suffering love, and especially the great fact here commemorated, His atoning death for us upon the cross.

Our abuse of the Lord's Supper is a very serious matter, and we are here taught that it is certain to bring upon us God's marked and severe chastenings. "That is why," he tells them, "many among you are weak and sick, and a number of you have fallen asleep" (1 Corinthians 11:30). Disease comes in consequence of such irreverent and sacrilegious conduct, and even life is prematurely shortened, and untimely death is often the penalty of such sin.

There is no doubt, on the one hand, that the Lord's Supper is very intimately connected with our physical life, and it brings to us the actual bodily strength of the Lord Jesus Christ if we rightly partake. And so, on the other hand, it brings to us sickness and death if we abuse it. The two-edged sword cuts both ways, either in blessing or in judgment as we meet it. There is no doubt that many Christians are suffering from sickness, and perhaps their very lives have been shortened because they have sat down at this holy table cherishing willfully unholy resentments and knowingly indulging in the forbidden things.

These judgments are not penal and permanent. The word "damnation" (KJV), used in the 29th verse, is most unfortunate. Its proper translation is simply judgment, and these judgments are explained in a later verse as the gracious chastenings of the Lord to bring us to repentance so that we will not "be condemned with the world" (11:32). The way to avert such judgments is by the self-examination here prescribed: "But if we judged ourselves, we would not come under judgment" (11:31). The moment we see our fault, and penitently and obediently turn from it, the judgment is immediately turned away. "A man ought to examine himself before he eats of the bread and drinks of the cup" (11:28).

SECTION II—*The True Nature and Right Observance of the Lord's Supper*

ITS INSTITUTION

1. Attention is first called to its institution. This is very marked and definite. "For I received from the Lord what I also passed on to you" (11:23). This seems to have been a special revelation given to Paul for the Gentile churches, lest they should be tempted to think that it was merely a Jewish rite. Thinking of us all through the coming ages, our blessed Master gave this special revelation to Paul, the apostle, for the Gentiles, that we might know that down to the end of time He was thinking of us and lovingly assuring us of His personal remembrance.

THE ASSOCIATIONS

2. The associations of this institution are also very touching. "On the night he was betrayed" (11:23) is the dark background. Surely He had enough trouble to absorb His attention to Himself, but He was only thinking of us and providing for our comfort in the future ages. Over against that

dark background of betrayal, it is not hard to read the lines that tell of His faithful love and the thought in His heart that would call for our love and faithfulness in return.

THE EMBLEMS

3. The emblems used are full of beautiful fitness and significance. The bread is a whole parable of suffering love. First, the seed was planted, and had to die before it could spring into life and become the living grain. Then the grain had to be crushed before it could become material for bread. Then the very meal had to be kneaded, beaten and exposed to intense heat in the fiery oven before it could become bread. All this lies back of the heavenly Bread on which we feed today.

Then, the wine is crushed from the grape and flows like the living blood, and tells of life poured out and life poured in. It is the most perfect type of the Savior's very life given for us and given to us.

THE WORDS

4. The words of the institution are a whole theology. "This is my body" (11:24) is a figurative statement of the doctrine of the incarnation. It tells us of Bethlehem and the manger, of the Son of God becoming the Son of man, of the oneness of our Kinsman-redeemer with our very nature. He who meets us today is our Brother forevermore, flesh of our flesh, heart of our heart, life of our life, very Man as well as very God.

Next, "broken" (11:24, KJV). How it tells of the nails, and the spear, the drooping head and the dying agony, the atoning death, the shameful cross, the doctrine of the great Sacrifice. The theologies may go wrong, and the standards of the Church may change, but the Lord's Supper forever will bear witness of the true cross and the blood-marked way of life.

"For you" (11:24). This is the great truth of substitution. It was a vicarious sacrifice. It was for others that He died. It was for us. It was for *me*.

Next, the appeal, "Take, eat" (11:24, KJV), expresses the whole truth of appropriating faith. "Take" is the first act of faith which claims our salvation. "Eat" is the deeper experience which enters into, realizes and enjoys the blessing which we claim, the Christ whom we receive.

Next, we have the life of consecration and obedience in the sweet verse, "Do this in remembrance of me" (11:24). It becomes a watchword for every day and every act, a loving reminder saying to us every moment, "This do, and this, and this for My sake, for love of Me."

And finally, the blessed hope of His coming shines out clearly and gloriously in the last words, "until he comes" (11:26). Out across the gulf of sorrow, the cross, the grave, the changes that lie between time's rolling flood, our lives with their changes and their sorrows, away across time He was looking; and we are to look this day and from this place, to the sunlit heights of glory, to the blessed morning of His return, to the unspeakable meaning of those three little monosyllables, "Till he come" (11:26, KJV). What a theology! What a Christology! What an alphabet of truth stands out in vivid characters of light and love from this memorial table with its elemental signs and suggestive words of redeeming love!

THE NAMES

5. The names that have been given to this sacred ordinance are also suggestive of precious and profitable things. One of its latest names is the Eucharist. This means a service of thanksgiving and praise. It is an expression of our gratitude for the unspeakable blessings of redemption, and it is suggested by the first act of the Lord Jesus Christ in the ordinance, "When he had given thanks, he broke it" (11:24). It ought to be a season of deep thankfulness and holy joy.

Another traditional name is the Sacrament. This is derived from an old Latin word, *sacramentum,* meaning an oath. It was the oath of enlistment which the Roman soldier took when he entered the services of the state. It expresses, therefore, the idea of our dedication to God, and engagement in His service to be loyal and true to our Master. It is thus connected with the idea of a profession of faith and consecration of life. It is not a scriptural expression, but it represents a scriptural idea.

The word communion is very frequently applied to this service. This is a scriptural word, and it denotes our fellowship with the Lord Jesus and with one another at this sacred table.

The Lord's Supper is the more scriptural and comprehensive term for this ordinance. This expression denotes spiritual nourishment and heavenly sustenance.

Briefly summing up the purpose of the Lord's Supper we may say:

a. That it is a service of *commemoration,* not only recalling to our minds, but signalizing and publicly honoring the memory of the Lord Jesus Christ, and especially of His death for us—the supreme act of His life and love.

b. It is a service of *communion,* not only bringing the remembrance of the Lord, but bringing His own personal presence in living communion with us and loving fellowship with one another.

c. It is the means not only for communion, but of *communication* of His life and grace to us. It is thus a means of grace and channel of actual spiritual impartation from Him to those who are in living fellowship with Him. We strike here the great Roman Catholic heresy of transubstantiation. This is an honest and sincere attempt of the human heart to find something true after which it is feeling. That something is the real presence and the physical presence of Christ in the Lord's Supper. The Romanist has tried to explain this as the literal flesh of the Lord Jesus in the wafer of which he partakes; but it would be of little use to us to partake of the flesh of Christ even if it were present. Back of this error lies the real truth that has been overlooked by the Church of God, that is, the truth expressed in the sixth chapter of John,

> I am the bread of life. . . . I am the living bread. . . . If anyone eats of this bread, he will live forever. This bread is my flesh, which I will give for the life of the world. . . . Whoever eats my flesh and drinks my blood has eternal life, and I will raise him up at the last day. (John 6:35, 51, 54)

Here He promises us not only spiritual life, but physical life from His own body. This is the blessed truth which our faith has learned to apprehend in the Lord's Supper. It is the truth commonly known as divine healing. It is deeper than mere healing; it is the actual participation in the physical strength, vitality and energy of our risen Lord. It is again and again referred to in the writings of Paul as the Lord's Supper, and is especially to us glorious and vivid, simple and expressive.

d. One more truth in connection with this ordinance is expressed in the word, covenant. It is the milestone on life's way. It is a time and a place to take blessings for days to come, and looking back to where we have failed, and forward to all we may meet, renew afresh our covenant with Him for His all-sufficient grace for spirit, soul and body, home and business, circumstances and service, time and eternity, and go forth with His blessed assurance, "I will be with you; I will never leave you nor forsake you" (Joshua 1:5b). "Your strength will equal your days" (Deuteronomy 33:25).

SECTION III—*Conclusion*

And now, in conclusion, it remains only to sum up in practical application the precious lessons of this subject. How shall we prepare for the Lord's table? How shall we partake of this holy feast?

First, let us do so with honest self-examination, not to know if we are Christians—that ought to have been settled long ago— but to know that we are in actual and habitual exercise of all that belongs to a true Christian life, and to know the needs that we are to bring and the grace that we are to claim at His blessed feet.

Next, we are to exercise our minds and memories in intelligent recollection and realization of His love to us in His life and death of sacrifice, and in the personal story of our own salvation and all the providences of our life. We are to think of the way that He has led us, and remember all His love until our hearts shall bring Him an oblation of grateful praise.

Next, we are to meet with Him to touch Him, to listen to His voice, to rest upon His bosom and to take His loving promises as we go forth as they went from the mountains in Galilee and the upper chamber in Jerusalem.

Then we are to reach out to a larger love and a closer fellowship with our brethren. We are to enter into the communion of saints, and take His blessing for the whole family in heaven and on the earth, for the gathering and preparation of the Bride and for the completing of the whole body of Christ. It is to be a radiating as well as a rallying point from which we shall go forth with a love as large as His to bless the whole world.

Finally, we are to look out from this watch tower to the morning star, to the rising day, to the advent glory, to the millennial age, and go forth looking for and hastening forward the coming of our precious Lord.

CHAPTER 9

THE SUPERNATURAL GIFTS AND THE MINISTRIES OF THE CHURCH

*Now about spiritual gifts, brothers, I do not want you to be
ignorant. (1 Corinthians 12:1)*

If there was danger of ignorance concerning the spiritual gifts of the
Church in the apostle's day, how much greater the danger today! The tendency of modern religious thought is to eliminate the supernatural from the
Bible, the Church and the life of the Christian, and reduce religion to a
form of human culture and the Church to a religious club, bound together
by social affinities, entertained by intellectual culture and sacred art, and
moderately exercised and occupied in respectable forms to benevolence and
usefulness. It is scarcely respectable to recognize any such thing as a personal
or present Deity, the supernatural answer to prayer, or any extraordinary occurrence which claims to be miraculous and is not subject to scientific explanation.

Meanwhile the devil is producing and exercising his supernatural gifts, and
so endeavoring, with not a little success, to palm himself off as God, to establish his claims on the credulity of those who will not receive the divine
and holy religion of Christ.

The only way to meet the counterfeit is by the true. The facts of
spiritualism and its kindred errors are undoubtedly real, and they can only
be met by the divine realities which are as much mightier than they as they
are more pure and consistent with the character of God and the well-being
of man.

Closely related to the manifestations of Satanic power are the extravagances, fanaticisms and mistakes of honest and well-meaning Christians who are
in danger of accepting delusions for divine manifestations, and thus throwing doubt upon the real facts of God's supernatural power which do exist.
On the one hand there is danger of utter naturalism, rejecting all that is su-

pernatural; and, on the other, there is danger of a false supernaturalism, counterfeiting the workings of God's power or substituting for them the workings of demon power, which are to be the most marked features of the last days.

The only security for the balance of truth between these two extremes lies in our not being ignorant concerning spiritual gifts, but rightly understanding, exercising and exhibiting to the world the real power of God in harmony with the Scriptures and guarded from the extremes and extravagances of human error and Satanic delusion.

CHARISMATA

1. First we must look at the supernatural gifts bestowed upon the Church by her ascended Lord. The Greek word for these gifts is *charismata,* and it is used to denote the gifts of power for service which constituted the Pentecostal enduement of the Church.

It was customary for Roman conquerors, when they entered the city in triumph, or for great potentates, when signalizing their coronation or entrance upon some great office, to distribute largesses and scatter costly gifts of treasure along the avenues through which they passed. So when Christ "ascended on high/ . . . [he] gave gifts to men" (Ephesians 4:8), and abundantly distributed to the waiting disciples the rich and varied gifts of the Holy Spirit. Jewels they were in the costly robes of His glorious Bride, the insignia and tokens of her high honor and fellowship in His kingly glory and mighty power. These *charismata* are specifically described in this chapter.

The first of these gifts is wisdom (1 Corinthians 12:8), that divine quality which discerns the actual situation, and knows how to act under all circumstances. It is distinguished from knowledge, the next gift, in this respect, that knowledge has to do with truth and wisdom with conduct. Knowledge is intellectual; wisdom is practical. Knowledge enables us to understand God's Word, wisdom, to apply it to the case in hand. The two together constitute our perfect investiture for intelligent and effective service.

The next of these gifts is faith. This does not mean faith for our personal salvation, for that is the privilege and duty of all believers and, in fact, is essential to salvation. This is the special faith given by the Holy Spirit to enable us to exercise our Christian ministries, to claim the answers to our prayers and to take the power of God which is awaiting our appropriation.

Then come the gifts of healing. They are spoken of in the plural. There are various forms and ministries of healing. They are distinguished from miracles in the next clause. These also are gifts of the Spirit. They are undoubtedly recognized here as included in the Church's enduement of power. There is no hint here, or indeed anywhere in the New Testament, that the age of miracles is past. That is one of the axioms of modern theology, but it has no countenance from the Scriptures. God always intended His Church to be as supernatural and as divine as the host that marched through the wilderness of old behind the pillar of cloud and fire, and left the footprints of the Deity all along their unearthly way.

But miracles and gifts of healing are not necessarily the same. There are many cases of healing that are not miracles, and there are some that are. There is a quiet, normal receiving of divine life for our physical frame which becomes as natural as breathing, and almost as spontaneous. It is not mere constitutional strength. It comes from God, but it comes through the operation of the spiritual law into which we may rise, and through which we can appropriate supernatural strength from our living Lord just as freely as we take the oxygen from the air and absorb the sunshine from the sky.

A miracle is somewhat different. It is more bold and startling, involving a suspension of natural law and an effect so impressive as to become to all observers a distinct manifestation of the presence and power of God. These meteor flashes of supernatural power would lose their very emphasis if they were to become so frequent as to cease to be extraordinary. Both have a place in the economy of the Church and among the gifts of the Spirit.

Then we have the gift of prophecy specially denoting the ministry which gives to men the direct messages of God. It is not always the power to foretell future events. A prophet is rather a divine messenger, the man who catches the mind of his Master, and gives it out to his fellowmen at the divine direction. He is not so much a teacher of the written Word as a messenger of the very thing that God would say at the time to the generation to which he speaks or the community to whom he bears witness. The definition of a prophet given by the apostle in the 14th chapter of First Corinthians is very satisfactory. "But everyone who prophesies speaks to men for their strengthening, encouragement and comfort" (14:3). The prophet, therefore, while including the office of teacher in this chapter, more especially carries with it, we believe, the idea of specially witnessing, in the immediate power and unction of the Holy Spirit, the messages of God to men.

Then come the gifts of distinguishing between spirits and speaking in different kinds of tongues with the associated gift of interpretation of tongues, which was the power to translate and understand the message given by another in an unknown tongue. This makes it very certain that the language in which the ministry of tongues was exercised was not always the language of the people who were addressed. It could not, therefore, be a vehicle for missionary work. In that case no interpretation would be needed, and the necessity for an interpreter would obviate its very intention. It was not for this purpose that it was given, but rather as an expression of lofty spiritual feeling and the intense moving of the heart, the subject of this gift, by the divine Spirit leading him to express the state of spiritual elevation by which he was moved in some utterance, which, while not always intelligible, yet always left the impression of divine presence and power.

This gift seems to have been abused from an early period and turned rather to the display of spiritual pride than to the edification of the Church, and appears to have been withdrawn, in a great measure, at least, at an early day. Its apparent revival in modern times has been associated with much confusion, and created grave doubts respecting its preeminent value as compared, at least, with other gifts of the Spirit. In the classification of the *charismata* at the end of this chapter it is quite significant that it is mentioned last, and we find the apostle himself declaring in another place, "I would rather speak five intelligible words to instruct others than ten thousand words in a tongue" (1 Corinthians 14:19).

THE SOURCE

2. The Holy Spirit is the source of all these gifts, and is the divine Agent who exercises them in the Church and through its members. We are deeply thankful to the Holy Spirit for a single verse in this chapter which shuts out all possibility of spiritual pride and human glory in connection with the gifts and the ministries of the Spirit. It is the 11th verse, in which we are told that all these gifts "are the work of one and the same Spirit" (12:11). Literally this means all these gifts the Spirit Himself works. The man is but an instrument. Even the gift is not a permanent quality in man, but the divine Presence uses him for the time in the exercise of the ministry in which God holds the power, and the subject is but His humble instrument. No man, therefore, can call these works his works, or these gifts his gifts, or this power his own. Very wisely the Master has said in anticipation of this very danger, "All authority in heaven and on earth has been given to me. . . . I am with you always, to the very end of the age" (Matthew 28:18, 20). He is the power and we have Him.

Whenever, therefore, we see the spirit of self-display, human exaltation and adulation, the advertising of men and the disposition to glory in even the most honored servants of God, we may know that we are on forbidden ground and in danger of sacrilegiously abusing the very grace of God and worshiping the creature more than the Creator. Every gift and ministry is dependent upon our contact with the Holy Spirit every moment. We have no strength apart from Him, and if we had, our power would become our curse and our own weight would sink us where once the archangels fell through their own self-conscious brilliancy and self-centered pride.

RECEIVE AND USE

3. The Holy Spirit in His supernatural powers is given to every disciple who will receive and use His supernatural powers for the purpose intended.

"Now to each one the manifestation of the Spirit is given for the common good" (12:7). This supernatural enduement is not an exclusive privilege of favor to the few. The Holy Spirit is poured today upon all flesh. You cannot have a private wire to your office or the use of a telephone without some expense, but every disciple can have the ear of heaven at any moment and draw from the infinite resources of the skies all needed strength for all emergencies and ministries.

The mina in the parable of Luke 19, was given to all the servants equally; yet the time came when the single mina had, in the case of one of these servants, been multiplied to 10 minas. They all started on equal footing, but they did not so end their service or stand before their judge. What was the secret of the difference? The faithful and profitable servants invested their mina and added interest by trading.

Is not this the meaning of the apostle in this chapter when he speaks of the manifestation of the Spirit being given to every man "for the common good" (1 Corinthians 12:7)? Does it not mean that we may use or neglect this great investment, and that it may become a spiritual fortune or a spiritual default as we improve it or neglect it? To each of us is given, not part of the Holy Spirit, not a touch of His finger, but the Holy Spirit Himself in His personal and undivided fullness. We may have just as much of this power as we will utilize and expend for His glory and the service committed to our hands. Those who wisely use it will find at last that their efficiency has multiplied tenfold, while those who simply hoard it will stand condemned before their Lord and lose even that which they for a little seemed to have.

What a responsibility this truth throws upon us! Are we using all the possibilities of grace? Are we improving the investments of the Master committed to our hands? Are we growing in spiritual usefulness and efficiency? Are we going to meet our Master to hear Him say, "Well done, good and faithful servant! You have been faithful with a few things; I will put you in charge of many things" (Matthew 25:21)?

DIVERSITIES AND MINISTRIES

4. The diversity of spiritual gifts and ministries is very clearly pointed out in this passage. The apostle speaks of three different things—gifts, ministries and works or operations. He says there are different gifts. There are also different ministries or spheres providentially assigned to us; consequently there are different works performed by us. There seems to be a distinct allusion to the three persons of the Trinity in these three classifications of gifts, spheres and services. Some persons are specially fitted by their gifts for one line of ministry. Then, their providential environments are different and call them to various duties. Consequently their work will be different.

One is called and fitted to be a businessman. To him is given wisdom, faith and service in the large field of usefulness, and it is not necessary for him to leave his sphere in order to exercise a Holy Spirit ministry. There is no need today so great in the Church as the need of men full of the Holy Spirit and wisdom, like Stephen of old, and fitted to represent Christ in the place where business experience, wise counsels, wide influence, are of peculiar value. In our great missionary operations and in the magnificent work committed to the Church of Christ, God has likewise His chosen ambassadors to mankind.

Another is called and fitted for the ministries of the home or school, or for the work of faithful helping and serving, or perhaps for superintending and the exercise of executive talent. There are no people so scarce as wise, well-balanced and sweet-tempered workers for the many departments of any great movement which requires capacity, and at the same time holy, loving character and unselfish fidelity and loyalty.

Again, another is called to the special ministry of understanding and teaching the Word of God. Another is more gifted for evangelistic work. Another is fitted to minister to the sick, and lead them to trust in God and take His healing power. Others again are called to the ministry of evangelization, to the bold, aggressive work of the foreign field, to the rescue home or mission, to the patient pastoral oversight of the flock of Christ, to the cry of the little ones, to the uplifting of the fallen. Each of these is legitimate, and for each of these the Holy Spirit supplies the necessary qualifications, and will accept and bless the works that follow. Let us, therefore, not lose our life in wishing we had some one else's work; but let us find the sphere to which we belong, let us take the gifts that will fit us for it, and let us present the works to God as a sacrifice of a sweet smelling savor. Be yourself, and be your best, and God will use you much more than if you try to be somebody else.

THE PRINCIPLE OF UNITY

5. The principle of unity in all this diversity is essential. We are to recognize the work of others as part of our own. The most truly spiritual people are the people who can get on best with others, and very often God places us in the most uncongenial and difficult associations for the very purpose of teaching us to adjust ourselves to everything. We cannot afford to meet with anyone along life's pathway and fail to get along with them. He will probably keep us where we are until we have so learned His Spirit, and been rounded and mellowed by His grace, that we can keep rank in the host of God and walk in step with the most unsteady and uncongenial of our brethren.

Long ago God taught David to rejoice in a work which he was to plan and another was to perform, and in one of his first lessons on service the Lord

Jesus taught His disciples that "one sows and another reaps" (John 4:37), and he that sows and he that reaps must learn to rejoice together.

THE ORDER OF THE GIFTS

6. The order of spiritual gifts is very instructive, encouraging and also humbling. The first-mentioned gifts are those of the apostles, prophets and teachers, the spiritual ministries of the Church. Next come the miraculous gifts of healing subordinate to spiritual ministry—important but not preeminent. Thirdly comes helps, people that just fit in, and by love, fellowship, prayer and often subordinate service, fill up the innumerable places and become the countless links without which all else would be in vain. After these, in a lower order, come the governments, the rulers, the people with authority, wisely placed near the bottom to keep them from falling over with the weight of their importance. No one can rule another until he has walked in the ranks and learned to keep his head low.

The last in procession are the gifts of tongues, the showy gifts that sometimes turn the heads of ambitious disciples, and have been least honored of all the supernatural enduements of the Christian Church.

A RIGHT AMBITION

7. A right ambition for the widest and highest usefulness is encouraged. "But eagerly desire the greater gifts" (1 Corinthians 12:31). God wants us to be ambitious for service, and not only for one kind of service, but for as many kinds as we can faithfully add to the record of a useful life. If we fulfill one ministry well He will add another if we can be trusted with it, and the one mina may at last grow to 10. It is right that we should recognize this life as full of unspeakable prospects and possibilities for the higher ministries and the eternal honors of the age to come. We are candidates for the great government appointments in the mighty empire of the future. Let us be ambitious to show ourselves fitted for the highest place. Our lot is cast in times of most intense interest and importance. We are on the threshold of the coming kingdom. We are in the midst of a mighty competition. Prophets and martyrs are already waiting for their appointments. Busy and earnest lives today are sweeping on in the power of the Holy Spirit. Don't be left behind!

May God arouse us from lethargy, apathy and trifling. We have a glorious crown to win. We have a living age in which to win it. We have one short life to accomplish. We have the mighty Holy Spirit to enable us to win the conflict and gain the prize. Let us eagerly desire the best gifts, and let all our being be invested in the one stupendous opportunity of a life for God, for humanity and for an eternal prize.

CHAPTER 10

LOVE, THE CROWNING GRACE OF THE CHURCH AND THE CHRISTIAN

But eagerly desire the greater gifts.
And now I will show you the most excellent way. (1 Corinthians 12:31)

And now these three remain: faith, hope and love. But the greatest of these is love. (13:13)

The apostle, having spoken of the various other gifts of the Holy Spirit, next turns to the highest of all gifts, the crowning grace of love. The gifts of power are the jewels upon the robes of the Bride. Love is the robe itself, the very texture and tissue of the spiritual life. Those are things which we may have, but this is something which we must be. For love is not an accompaniment, an adornment, or even an attribute of character, it is character itself. As God is love so love is the substance of the believer's life. This sublime chapter is a portrait of the divine love and a delineation of the features of the Christ life.

We owe it, as we owe many other precious things, to the very faults which it was intended to correct. The chief fault of the Corinthian Christians was the lack of love and the spirit of disunion, division and strife. Just as Christ's most gracious words were often called forth by the very aggravations of human unworthiness and sin, so this most perfect picture of the ideal life has for its frame and its background a state of things as unlike the ideal here presented as it is possible to conceive, a situation which had its prototype in the Corinthian church, and its parallel, in too many instances, in the Church today.

It is delineation marked by the most acute analysis and the most skilled art. It is at once a portrait, a poem and a panegyric of love. It is always difficult to analyze a living organism without destroying life in the process of dissection. It is like pulling a flower to pieces, or dissecting a face to find its charm, and losing your flower and the general impression of your portrait in the analysis. And yet it is well for the purposes of practical application, and as a touchstone by which to search our own hearts, to follow the keen analysis of this picture into all the depths and ramifications of our own soul until we stand convicted and exposed in the light of divine love and the humiliating view of our own likeness.

SECTION I—*The Negative Qualities of Love*

It is very impressive to notice how much of character consists in what we are not and do not say or do. The Ten Commandments consist chiefly of "Thou shalt not." The first requirement that the Lord Jesus Christ laid down in connection with discipleship was self-denial. Now, to deny self is not to torment, lacerate and inflict penance on yourself. It simply means to say "No" to yourself, to suppress yourself, to refuse to obey yourself, your own will, impulse and preference. It is just a great *not* laid across human nature's path.

Now, love consists largely in nots. If you do nothing more than simply keep still, hold back and suppress yourself you will have lived the larger half of the life of love. You may think this very tedious, trifling and unnecessary trouble, but you will find that it is the little foxes that destroy the vines, and the little negligences of Christian watchfulness which perforate the organism of a holy life, and let your love and joy leak out as from broken vessels.

DOES NOT ENVY

1. "Love . . . does not envy" (1 Corinthians 13:4). She has no jealousy of others; she is not unhappy over their successes or happiness. She is not watching for their defeat or failure, nor criticizing their achievements and victories. She looks on with calm and artless simplicity and frankness when they are successful, appreciated, praised and honored. She is incapable of a mean or unworthy suspicion or treacherous blow at the character or happiness of any human being. It simply is not in her to feel and do such things. First in the brood of hell is the low, groveling serpent of envy, jealousy and suspicion.

DOES NOT BOAST

2. The next negative quality is conceit, vanity and braggart vainglory. Love "does not boast" (13:4). She is modest. She never boasts. Love never wants people to advertise her, appreciate and praise her. This is the mildest form of the demon of pride. It is more concerned about what people think of us than about what we are, and it is satisfied with a name and a transient fame whether it deserves it or not. Love despises and disdains this spirit of

vainglory, and shrinks instinctively from the glory of the public gaze and the arena of the world's empty fame.

NOT PUFFED UP

3. Deeper and more dangerous is the quality of pride expressed by the next clause, "is not puffed up" (13:4, KJV). This describes an exaggerated idea of ourselves, an undue estimate of our abilities and worth. It is associated frequently with indifference to public applause or criticism. Satisfied with its own good opinion, it scorns either the blame or the praise of men; but it has an egregious estimate of itself, and it grows into an intolerable egotism. It is interested in everything chiefly as it concerns the mighty "I," which stands in the center of all its conversation, thought and plans. But love is removed from this false realm of exaggeration and pride. She estimates herself truly as nothing and less than nothing. Love has found out that human nature is a failure. She has sentenced herself to death. And she has buried herself forever out of sight, and taken her life and reputation on borrowed capital through the merits and righteousness of the Lord Jesus Christ alone. You must reach the place where you have forever renounced your own rights and your own righteousness, and stand henceforth in humility and confidence in the name of Christ and righteousness alone.

IS NOT RUDE

4. The next antagonism of love is rudeness. She "is not rude" (13:5). She does not do things that hurt, offend or wound others. Her manners are gentle and considerate. She does not cut people on the street or allow herself to freeze with studied chill the victims of her resentment. A soul baptized with love will always be gentle. The spirit of Jesus makes us gentlemen and ladies, and the grace of God transforms the manners of the barroom into the culture and even courtliness of the society of heaven.

IS NOT SELF-SEEKING

5. The spirit of selfishness is the deep root from which all these things come, and against which love is a living protest. She "is not self-seeking" (13:5). She has no place for self-seeking. Her one business is to seek the interest of others and the glory of her Master, and let Him care for all that concerns her rights and happiness. Human nature looks first at our end of things and asks, "How does this affect me?" Love inverts this order and thinks first, "How will this please Him? How will this help others?"

IS NOT EASILY ANGERED

6. Temper, irritation, exasperation and angry passion are utterly excluded

from the life of love. She "is not easily angered" (13:5). It is scarcely necessary to say that the word "easily" is not in the original. The Holy Spirit gives no place for paroxysms of anger. It is true that a Christian may fall into them, but if he does it is because he has fallen back into the flesh, and is not walking in the Spirit. It is not he that is doing and saying these things, but his old carnal heart and nature, and it is just as real a case of backsliding as if he had fallen into open immorality.

NO RECORD OF WRONGS

7. Love affects the memory. It has no malignant recollection. It "keeps no record of wrongs" (13:5), or rather, "makes no account of evil." It does not cover over the fault today and carefully put it away in reserve for use tomorrow if something should provoke a reference to it. It ingeniously and cordially drops the past, forgets the fault, and acts as if it had not been.

DOES NOT DELIGHT IN EVIL

8. Love "does not delight in evil" (13:6). This seems to refer to the case of those who have done us wrong, and afterwards meet the retribution that their wrong deserved by coming into wrong themselves. God often punishes people for an injustice by allowing them to fall into sin, and to meet the consequences of that for which they have already blamed someone else with harsh and unjust severity. Now, we are not to take advantage of this and take pleasure in the misfortunes of our enemies, even when God may have brought that upon them as a retribution for their wrongs to others. True, God avenges His people's wrongs, but we must let Him do this without our interference. Indeed, when we know it we must meet their calamities with the spirit of compassion, and pray for them who have despitefully used us and abused us. There is no time when you are in so much danger as when you find that God has been dealing with someone because of their injustice to you, and you are tempted to say, "They are getting what they deserved because of their treatment of me." Grace alone will enable you to rise above those things and meet God's test of your love with the love that would save them from the judgments which they have brought upon themselves.

SECTION II—*The Positive Qualities of Love*

KINDNESS

1. She "is kind" (13:4). This is a word that describes the benignity of love in the simplest, sweetest and most human way. The root of the word is "kin," and it literally denotes the kindness with which we would treat one who is our relative and belongs to our own family. It describes that spirit

that instinctively loves to do others good. It is just goodness, beneficence and benevolence.

REJOICES WITH THE TRUTH

2. "Love . . . rejoices with the truth" (13:6). This lifts its spirit and sphere above mere personality and partisanship. It isn't just a preference for one or two individuals because they please us; but it is a high and holy sympathy with the truth, with the cause of Christ, with the things that He loves and approves, and it gives a tone or rightness and loftiness to all our attachments. It keeps love back from entanglements with faults and wrongs. It is a loyalty that is always on God's side and loves our friends in Him, for Him and as part of His great cause.

TRUSTS

3. It "believeth [trusts, NIV] all things" (13:7, KJV). That is, when things seem all contrary to love, love still believes in spite of the seeming, and by believing lifts its object up to that for which we believe. Thus God treated His ancient people. He said, "Surely they are my people,/ sons who will not be false to me" (Isaiah 63:8). They did not deserve His confidence, but He gave them His confidence, and by confidence and grace lifted them up to deserve it and loved them into it. So He takes the sinner who is unworthy of confidence, and, blotting out his sin, He takes him into the place of a child, and treats him as a sinner no longer, but as a child of His love. So He takes the earthborn soul, the fallen child of Adam's race, and He speaks of him as in the heavenly realms, and counts him as if already glorified and seated with Christ upon the throne. God believes for us and treats us as He believes. So let us believe for others, and love by faith where we cannot love by sight.

ALWAYS HOPES

4. Love "always hopes" (1 Corinthians 13:7). When faith fails and seems long to wait in vain for the realization, then hope comes to her aid and says, "It is not, but it shall be." "Let us not become weary in doing good, for at the proper time we will reap a harvest if we do not give up" (Galatians 6:9). Some day this soul will be brighter than an angel and whiter than the snow. So love hopes forever and clothes her object with the glory of her expectation.

What a blessed uplift this is to our own discouraged hearts! God give us the love that believes all things and hopes all things.

SECTION III—*The Passive Qualities of Love*

The sublime picture of this heavenly grace is as the suffering one. She steps upon the stage, "suffering long" (1 Corinthians 13:4) and she passes off of it, "bearing all things, enduring all things" (see 13:7, KJV). The long suffering has reference to her capacity for continued forbearance. The bearing has reference to the faults of others, and is translated sometimes, "covers all things"; and the enduring has reference to the trials that come to us from the hand of God. Now let us remember that this is not stoical endurance, because we cannot help it, but loving enduring, because we do not look upon the dark side. We see it in the light of love.

This is the analysis of love; but how beautiful and divine it seems when we rise from the delineation, and see it full-orbed and shining in the face of Jesus Christ Himself. He is the impersonation of love. It was He who suffered long and was kind, who sought not His own, never was provoked, who made no account of evil, who believed all things, hoped all things, endured all things, and whose love never failed.

It is necessary for us to dwell on the preeminence of such a grace above tongues, above prophecy, above knowledge, above faith, above even hope itself. The chief reason of love's preeminence is that love is the very essence and inherent quality of the heavenly life. It is not said anywhere that God is faith, or power, or wisdom, or even holiness. God has these attributes, but it *is* said that "God is love" (1 John 4:16). And so Christian character is love. When you abstract love you abstract the very tissue and essence of life itself. Without love, the apostle says, "I am nothing" (see 1 Corinthians 13:2). There isn't anybody there to wear the quality or use the gift. Love, therefore, is essential because intrinsic, the life of our life, and the substance of our spiritual being, for God is our life and "God is love."

But it is necessary for us to ask, "How can we have this superlative gift?" And the answer is very plain. It is not a growth or development of human nature. It is wholly divine. It must come to us from above, and the only way to have it is by having Him. You cannot live in the 13th chapter of First Corinthians without having the experience of entire sanctification, and entire sanctification simply means the death of self and the union of the soul with God through the baptism of the Holy Spirit. It is not possible for human nature to live this chapter out. It is not possible for a converted Christian to do it unless he has received the very gift of gifts, the Spirit of Jesus to dwell within him. Its first use is to search your heart and utterly discourage you from attempting it in your own strength, and so throw you at His feet that you will accept Him and let Him live His life in you. Let us do this here and now, and expiring at the feet of love take love to be our resurrection life and Christ to relive in us His own life once more.

But further, having done this, He will teach you, step by step, day by day, moment by moment, to watch against the things that militate against the life of love. And you will find that you must guard the crossroads, you must watch against the "nots," you must go down into the minutiae of life, and live out with Him in detail all the delineations of this chapter over which we have passed. This is where many fail. They want to have it come like some favoring gale, and bear them without a thought into the heavenly harbor. It is not so. Love must stand upon the bridge, and watch against the shoals and currents, and steer her course with ceaseless, patient toil untiring to the goal.

There are two other thoughts suggested in the closing verses of this chapter that are very helpful in the experiences of the life of love. One is the childishness from which our strifes come. He seems to think of them as infantile follies which should be put away with the maturity of spiritual manhood.

The other thought is the imperfect knowledge by reason of which most of our misunderstandings come. We see, he says, as in an enigma and through a mirror. Now, the mirror distorts everything you see. When you look at another through a mirror you see him inverted; the right hand is where the left hand should be, and the whole figure is misplaced, and you must correct your impression by your knowledge of this fact. Now, you frequently see people and things as through a mirror, and you will find some day in the clear light of heaven that you saw everything wrong, and that you often formed your prejudices and your likes and your dislikes in blind and stupid ignorance through your distorted vision. True love is blind to the lights of earth and the vision of sense, and sees everything in the light of God; and if we live in the light of His love it will give a heavenly glory to all else around us.

I remember a glorious sunset once in which the clouds of the golden west were tinted like the chariots of some sublime procession. As I gazed I saw that everything around me had taken on the heavenly hue, and I looked at the faces of my friends until they glowed in the purple and gold of the heavens above.

And if we live in the vision of God and in the love of Jesus, we will cover all around us with His beauty and His glory. And the things that otherwise would be dark and sad and strange will be lighted with the reflection of those skies, where the sun no more goes down and where evil will never come again.

CHAPTER 11

THE WORSHIP AND FELLOWSHIP
OF THE CHURCH

Follow the way of love and eagerly desire spiritual gifts, especially the gift of prophecy. . . . But everyone who prophesies speaks to men for their strengthening, encouragement and comfort. (1 Corinthians 14:1, 3)

When you come together, everyone has a hymn, or a word of instruction, a revelation, a tongue or an interpretation. All of these must be done for the strengthening of the church. (14:26)

Therefore, my brothers, be eager to prophesy, and do not forbid speaking in tongues. But everything should be done in a fitting and orderly way. (14:39–40)

W e find in this chapter and in some paragraphs of the 11th chapter the apostle unfolding some important and practical principles relating to the exercise of the gifts of the Spirit in the worship and fellowship of the Church.

PREEMINENCE OF LOVE

1. He emphasizes afresh the preeminence of love. "Follow the way of love" (14:1), he says. The verb is an intense one. Literally it means "pursue love" as the hunter pursues his game, as the miser pursues his gold. It is the most valuable of all attainments, therefore pursue it. It is the most difficult of all attainments, therefore pursue it. It is the crowning perfection of Christian life. It may sometimes seem very tedious that we should, after long experience in the school of Christ, have to be held down to little tests and conflicts from day to day, when it would be much more delightful to sweep out into the larger scope of some great achievement, or even to bear some tremendous trial and be done with it. And yet the artist spends much more time in finishing the details of his picture than in drawing the outline. A few

freehand touches will easily sketch the foreground and the perspective, but days and weeks and even months are spent in little touches, faint tints and deepening shades. And it is just these little touches that constitute the difference between the work of genius and the superficial attempt of an amateur. So, too, in the Christian life the finishing touches are the most important and often come very near the end. Let us not be weary in the school or easily give up the lesson, but let us follow after love, and so run that we may obtain. Let us always realize that more than all our works and words, our seemingly great achievements, our most heroic sufferings, it is patience that perfects love. And it is love that constitutes the essential quality and the crowning glory of all true character.

PROPHECY

2. The place of prophecy is next discussed. While we are to pursue love we are also to desire spiritual gifts, and chief among them the gift of prophecy. Now this gift is very clearly defined in the next verse. It is not merely or mainly the power which foretells future events, nor is it at all the mission of receiving inspired revelations and adding to the already finished Word of God, but it is a simple and practical ministry of help to men. He defines it by three terms: "But everyone who prophesies speaks to men for their strengthening, encouragement and comfort" (14:3). In a word, the prophet's business is to build up men, to stir up men and to cheer up sorrowing and troubled hearts.

To strengthen (edify, KJV) includes the ministry of instruction. To encourage (exhort, KJV) belongs the important work of rousing, stimulating and awakening the consciences and hearts of men. This is quite different from unfolding the teachings of the Scriptures. This is the ministry which convicts men of sin and startles the slumbering conscience into action. This is the ministry which forces the heart and conscience to a sense of its shortcomings and failures. This is the ministry that arouses the will to decision and action for God and for duty. This is the ministry that inspires enthusiasm, stirs up high purposes and calls to noble sacrifice and service. It stands as the living mouthpiece of God, and kindles and sets on fire the truth that has been already unfolded.

Then the third element in prophecy is the ministry of comfort. It binds up the broken heart; it dries the falling tear; it cheers the mourner; it lifts up the depressed and discouraged; it quickens faith, hope and patience; it sends us forth like Barnabas as sons of consolation; it takes healing to the sick, hope to the mourner and opens the gates of heaven to the dying believer. What an attractive ministry is the prophetic office, following in the steps of Him who said,

> The Spirit of the Lord is on me,
>   because he has anointed me
>   to preach good news to the poor.
> He has sent me to proclaim freedom for the prisoners
>   and recovery of sight for the blind,
> to release the oppressed,
>   to proclaim the year of the Lord's favor. (Luke 4:18–19)

TONGUES

3. Next is presented the place of tongues. The gift of tongues represents the less practical and more brilliant enduements of the Spirit in the early Church. It was a divine influence which elevated the soul to a state of ecstasy and found expression in utterance of an elevated character, impressing the hearer with the manifest presence and power of the Holy Spirit in the subject of this influence. But the utterances were not always articulate or intelligible either to the speaker or hearer, and in many cases had to be translated by an interpreter. This gift of interpreting tongues was just as distinct as the tongues themselves, and, where it was lacking, the tongues were not understood, and the message was not immediately helpful to the hearers. Indeed, without a proper regard to edification and decorum it might become a stumbling block and even a cause of confusion and disgrace.

It is quite evident from some of the quotations in this passage that the gift of tongues was not primarily intended to be a vehicle for preaching the gospel to foreign nations: "For anyone who speaks in a tongue does not speak to men but to God. Indeed, no one understands him; he utters mysteries with his spirit" (1 Corinthians 14:2). Surely that is sufficient without any further argument to show that this was not usually a vehicle of intelligent instruction to a foreigner. Again, "He who speaks in a tongue edifies himself, but he who prophesies edifies the church" (14:4). Again, "He who prophesies is greater than one who speaks in tongues, unless he interprets, so that the church may be edified" (14:5). Here it is evident that there had to be another person to interpret the tongue, or else the man himself might, if he understood his own tongue.

Again, in verse 13 we read, "For this reason anyone who speaks in a tongue should pray that he may interpret what he says," i.e., let him ask God for a second gift, namely, the gift of translating the tongue in which he has spoken into the tongue understood by the hearers. Again we read,

> For if I pray in a tongue, my spirit prays, but my mind is unfruitful. . . . how can one who finds himself among those who do not

understand say "Amen" to your thanksgiving, since he does not
know what you are saying? (14:14, 16)

The apostle himself had the gift of tongues, but he says with great emphasis, "But in the church I would rather speak five intelligible words to instruct others than ten thousand words in a tongue" (14:19). Let us notice
carefully, by the way, that the word "unknown" used in the King James Version is not in the original, being printed in italics, and that the apostle is not
here drawing a distinction between known and unknown tongues, but
speaking generally of all tongues as unknown. The whole argument is con-
firmed and summed up by the statement in the 22nd verse, "Tongues, then,
are a sign, not for believers but for unbelievers." They are a sign of a definite
influence present upon the speaker. But for that very reason they ought to be
used with great caution. He illustrates this by a picture of an unbeliever
coming into one of their meetings, when they were speaking with tongues,
and concluding that they were mad. But, on the contrary, if he should come
in and find them prophesying in intelligent speech he would fall down on
his face and worship God, and report that God was in them of a truth. He
adds, "If anyone speaks in a tongue, two—or at the most three—should
speak, one at a time, and someone must interpret. If there is no interpreter,
the speaker should keep quiet in the church and speak to himself and God"
(14:27–28).

This surely settles the question. If more is needed to be said it would be
sufficient to add that the apostle preached the gospel to the people among
whom he moved through the Greek, Latin and Hebrew languages which he
had himself acquired, and on one or two occasions his audiences were
surprised to find that he could speak their language through the large and
liberal culture which he had received.

This gift of tongues being chiefly of the character of a sign, was liable to
great abuse and seems to have been early withdrawn from the primitive
Church. In modern times it has been revived, but with some liability of
abuse.

The story of Edward Irving is well known. After a career of extraordinary
brilliancy and power, in his last days he adopted the theory that the supernatural gifts of the early church should be claimed in our own day, and there
were undoubted instances, not only of miraculous power, but especially in
the exercise of the gift of tongues. But through exaggeration of this gift and
the strong temptation to use it sensationally, it became a source of much
confusion and even ridicule, and a work that had in it undoubted elements
of truth and power was discredited and hindered.

In our own day there is the same strained and extravagant attempt to unduly exaggerate the gift of tongues, and some have even proposed that we

should send our missionaries to the foreign field under a sort of moral obligation to claim this gift, and to despise the ordinary methods of acquiring a language. Such a movement would end in wild fanaticism and bring discredit upon the truth itself. We know of more than one instance where our beloved missionaries have been saved from this error and led to prosecute their studies in foreign languages with fidelity and diligence; and their efforts have been rewarded by supernatural help in acquiring foreign tongues in a remarkably short time, but not in despising proper industry and the use of their own faculties under God's direction in acquiring these languages.

THE PLACE OF EDIFICATION

4. Paul goes on to discuss the place of edification in the worship of the Church. "All of these must be done for the strengthening (edifying, KJV) of the church" (14:26). God's object in everything He does is the practical help and real benefit of His people. God never works a miracle for the sake of showing He can work a miracle. He is a wise economist of force. He has no machinery simply for the purpose of displaying it. When we use any gift in order to show that we have the gift, we are desecrating God's sacred trusts. The temptation of today is to the display of brilliancy, and easily runs into self-consciousness, vainglory and the worship of the creature more than the Creator. The true principle that should regulate all our words and acts is the glory of God and the good of our fellowmen. This will give attractiveness and sobriety to our words and acts in the Church of our Lord Jesus Christ. The highest ambition that any minister can cherish is to supply plain, wholesome bread to the household of Christ. Let others go in for confectionery and pyrotechnic displays; let ours be the ambition to supply food to the children of God. There is nothing so popular and so sure to succeed as the simple gospel and the Word of the living God. Let us aim to reach the average man and leave it to others to attract the intellectual and the brilliant. Christ was a teacher for the common people, and we will find that His people in every age are still very simple, average people. The Church of Christ today is in danger of becoming a poor rival to the sensational journal and the extravagant modern stage. They can outdo us every time in this unequal competition, and we shall have not only the humiliation of defeat in bidding for the popular ear, but we shall have the displeasure and the curse of heaven for the sacrilegious abuse of an awful trust committed to us for the salvation and help of dying men.

THE PLACE OF TESTIMONY

5. Another practical principle Paul discusses is the place of testimony in the worship of God. Have we scriptural warrant for the testimony meeting,

for the freedom of a service thrown open to the people and allowing every-one to have some part in the chorus of praises and witness bearing? Certainly we have. That is the very meaning of the remarkable verse which we have quoted above. "Everyone has a hymn, or a word of instruction, a revelation" (14:26). Let everyone come to contribute some part to the service. Break in with your chorus of grateful song, if the Spirit so impresses you, and let no one stare or sneer at the irregularity. Come out with your simple testimony of some truth that has helped you, and that you have been told to pass on for the help of others. Fear not to speak the message which the Holy Spirit has burned into your soul for the quickening and the rousing of your brethren. It will be a word in season for some weary soul. And if you have, in some simple form, even the old gift of tongues welling up in your heart, some Hallelujah which you could not put into articulate speech, some unut-terable cry of love or joy, out with it.

I remember a dear old black saint, now in heaven, who used to accentuate the most important periods and passages in the sermon, or the meeting, by sometimes springing to her feet with a burst of ecstatic overflow that no lan-guage could express. It was a sort of inarticulate cry, while her face literally blazed in its ebony blackness with the light of glory. She was simply beating time to one of God's great strains, and while the ear of exquisite taste was sometimes offended, I believe the Holy Spirit was pleased, and the true heart of His Church ought always make room for the artless freedom of the Spirit's voice. There are no monopolies in the Church of Jesus Christ, and reverent faith will always say, "Let the Lord speak by whom He will."

THE PLACE OF ORDER

6. Following the practice of freedom in testimony Paul points out the place of order in the worship of the Church. But along with all this we must never forget the reverence and decorum due to the house of God and the services of His sanctuary. "But everything should be done in a fitting and or-derly way" (14:40) is the apostle's mandate. There is no need that devotion should run riot or that emotional excitement should carry us off our feet or lead us into extravagance and excesses of mere natural feeling. Let one wait for another. Let there be thoughtful deference and loving consideration. Even if the Spirit does impress you to speak, He can wait for the fitting op-portunity. If you are controlled by Him you will wait, too. "The spirits of prophets are subject to the control of prophets" (14:32).

The Holy Spirit does not ride roughshod over a sanctified judgment and a sensitive courtesy. He always recognizes the rights of others and your own sense of propriety. Some people are afraid to yield themselves to the Spirit for fear He will make them do some crazy thing. He does not act in this way. He has given us an instance of delicacy, modesty, order, self-respect, and He never outrages it in His children. He is a gentle Spirit. He suggests, directs and even commands; but He wants our whole being to work in harmony with Him. A true regard to this would prevent many rude exhibitions of fanaticism or wild fire which are justified too often by the pretence of divine inspiration. "Everything should be done in a fitting and orderly way" (14:40).

THE PLACE OF WOMEN

7. Finally, Paul deals with the place of women in the work and worship of the Church. What right has a woman to minister in the Church of Christ, and how far is she restricted by the apostle's guarded regulation?

a. Let it be remembered that in previous passages (11:5) he has already recognized woman's right to prophesy and pray in public, simply requiring her to do it modestly and with simplicity, which was then recognized as her subordinate place as a woman. If, then, he recognized the right of ministry certainly it would be inconsistent to suppose that he withdraws it.

b. Women did exercise many vocations of Christian ministry in the apostolic Church without question. We read of those women that "labored with him in the gospel" (see Philippians 4:3), and we know that Phoebe was a deaconess in the church at Cenchrea (Romans 16:1).

c. Prophesying, which was recognized in First Corinthians 11:5 as a woman's legitimate ministry, included speaking unto men "for their strengthening, encouragement and comfort" (1 Corinthians 14:3). Therefore, a woman's right to speak to men as well as to women for their instruction, quickening and comfort is clearly recognized.

d. What then are the restrictions? Well, it is very certain that she is to so exercise her ministry as not to transcend the limits of modesty and womanly propriety. The wearing of the covering upon her head was the recognition of this in that day, and it simply means today that she is to act with such reserve that she will never unsex herself or try to take the place of a man.

The apostle distinctly recognizes not her inferiority to man, but her subordination to man. She is man's equal in ability and honor, but she is subordinate to his authority. Just as two judges who sit on the same bench are equal in ability and dignity, but one is the head of the court and the other is a member of it. "The head of every man is Christ, and the head of the woman is man" (11:3). The head of Christ is God, and yet Christ is equal to God.

Every modest and sensible woman will clearly recognize the scriptural principle and save herself the loss of power that always comes from getting out of place.

Further, this was more marked in the case of the wives than of other women. In the relationship of home the woman voluntarily placed herself under the authority of her husband. Rotherham solves the difficulty in this passage by translating the word wife for woman. "Let the wives keep silence in the churches, and if they will learn anything let them ask their husbands at home, for it is a shame for the wives to speak in Church" (14:34–35). This translation throws much light upon the passage, which is increased by the word "disgraceful," which seems to refer to the social customs of that day, especially the discredit that would attach to a woman by bursting through the etiquette of their time. Were a woman in the East today to throw off her veil and appear with uncovered face to the public it would be a shame, and yet it would not be a sin. It would at once, however, brand her as a woman of bad character.

There is yet one more consideration which throws light on this passage. It is the technical sense of the word Church. It does not mean a church building, which they did not then possess, but it meant the ecclesiastical order, formal assembly of the congregation. In this view the passage might mean that woman was not to take an official place in the ecclesiastical organization, was not to be one of its elders, its rulers, its ecclesiastical leaders.

But within these modest and reasonable restraints, a woman has no restriction placed upon her highest usefulness. He who allowed a woman of old to be His preeminent instrument of witness and blessing to the world, has put no unreasonable barrier in the way of her testimony and service now. She was first to herald the Savior's resurrection, let her be the first to welcome Him at His advent and to strike the note that will announce His coming. In a day when a woman is not ashamed to expose herself on the indecent stage, and in the wild and riotous revel of modern society, let her not be ashamed to stand for Christ as His loving and faithful witness, and be found when He comes not only with Mary at His feet, but with Anna of Jerusalem, and with the Magdalene of the resurrection morn going forth with flying feet to tell to men the glad story of His resurrection, ascension and coming again.

CHAPTER 12

THE HOPE OF THE CHURCH

But Christ has indeed been raised from the dead, the firstfruits of those who have fallen asleep. . . . For as in Adam all die, so in Christ all will be made alive. . . .

Therefore, my dear brothers, stand firm. Let nothing move you. Always give yourselves fully to the work of the Lord, because you know that your labor in the Lord is not in vain. (1 Corinthians 15:20, 22, 58)

The 15th chapter of First Corinthians presents to us one of the sublimest arguments of the inspired Word for the blessed hope and final destiny of the Church of Christ.

There never was a time when the reality and certainty of this hope needed more to be emphasized than today. While human thought is growing more materialistic, the theology of the Church itself is less and less positive in its testimony to the great doctrine of the resurrection and the personal return of the Lord Jesus Christ. One of the leading pulpits of the country has publicly declared within a short time that the resurrection is purely spiritual. Along with the tendency to eliminate the supernatural in every way from Christianity, the doctrine of the resurrection is being shaded off into a mere figurative conception.

One of the most deeply spiritual volumes of the century, a book that has been blessed to great multitudes of seekers after God, and which, perhaps, more than any other volume except the Bible has enabled tens of thousands to understand and accept the Lord Jesus in His fullness, is written by one who unhesitatingly denies the doctrine of the literal resurrection, and whose influence in this direction renders it exceedingly difficult to encourage the circulation of her other volumes even where they are without just cause for criticism.

There is no other influence so fitted to counteract the spirit of worldliness abroad today as the power of the blessed hope of the Lord's return and all that it is to bring. Our present course of action is greatly determined by our future outlook. An earthly minded Church will always seek her portion here; and it is only when the people of God are deeply imbued with the conviction and expectation of their Master's imminent return that they will be saved from the dangers of this present evil world.

This chapter gives us a most comprehensive view of the whole subject of the resurrection as connected with the gospel of Christ.

SECTION I—*A Distinct Definition*

We have no clearer statement anywhere by which we may distinguish between the gospel and its counterfeits. "I want to remind you of the gospel I preached to you" (15:1), is the apostle's language, and he immediately proceeds to tell us what the gospel is.

ITS FUNDAMENTAL DOCTRINE

First, its fundamental doctrine is that "Christ died for our sins according to the Scriptures," and, secondly, that "he was raised on the third day according to the Scriptures" and was seen by competent witnesses (15:3–4ff). These two truths, the death and the resurrection of the Lord Jesus Christ, constitute the essence of the gospel, and anything short of this is not the gospel. There may be much eloquent preaching, much devotional spirit, much deep earnestness, much profound religious experience, but if it is not identified by the print of the nails and the mark of the cross it is not the gospel of Jesus Christ. Many of the most popular preachers and writers of our time, according to this definition, are not preachers of the gospel.

I was once offered a very large sum if I could produce a single sentence from the published works of the most popular preacher of this country 20 [1870s–1880s] years ago, which, according to Paul's definition, could be called gospel preaching. After searching through many volumes I was unable to find a single sentence that would meet the test. These teachings are full of devout passages; they speak freely of Christ; they talk much about His Presence and Spirit—indeed, they are the teachers of the larger Christ and the Christ of today, and all that sort of thing. But somehow they all get on to the way without entering by the door. They have climbed up a little beyond the cross. They have much of the rest of it except the beginning; and while it may seem uncharitable and severe, yet the apostle has himself said that they are preaching another gospel; and he has also said, "If anybody is preaching to you a gospel other than what you accepted, let him be eternally condemned!" (Galatians 1:9).

THE CROSS

The gospel of Jesus Christ recognizes the deep fact of sin, the divine fact of the atonement and the supernatural fact of the resurrection and the risen life of the Lord Jesus Christ. It is not merely the cross, but it is the cross from which the Crucified has been taken, and beyond which we see the open grave and the ascension throne. It is the cross as beautifully set forth in Thorwaldsen's dream in marble where he has carved the white cross, and then has covered it over with the tracery of a beautiful and luxuriant vine, almost hiding the cross with its hanging cluster. It is the cross with its glorious fruition, the risen Lord and the fruits that have come from His life and death. It is His own sublime description of Himself, "I am the Living One; I was dead, and behold I am alive for ever and ever!" (Revelation 1:18).

SECTION II—*A Great Evidence*

Next we have the cornerstone of the gospel, the great evidence and proof of Christianity—the resurrection of the Lord Jesus Christ. This is the one foundation on which Paul rests the whole fabric of Christianity. "If Christ has not been raised, our preaching is useless. . . . your faith is futile; you are still in your sins" (1 Corinthians 15:14, 17). This was the one test to which the Savior always appealed when asked for a sign of His Messiahship and divinity. It was the sign of the temple destroyed and raised in three days; the sign of the prophet Jonah, which was a symbol of the resurrection; the sign of the buried kernel dying and living through death. He publicly appealed to His Father and the world on the ground of His resurrection. Had He not risen from the dead His claims would have utterly failed; but when we see Him come forth in defiance of every natural and designed obstruction and impossibility, how can we doubt the truth of His claims and His teachings?

OF CONCLUSIVE CHARACTER

God ordered it so that the evidence should be of the most conclusive and unassailable character. His death was public and official. The highest officials of the Roman government were its executioners and witnesses. It was made doubly sure by the thrust of the soldier's spear. The very idea of the resurrection had been anticipated by His enemies and guarded against, and the most stringent precautions were taken to prevent His body from being stolen and a story of His resurrection circulated. It was sealed with the official stamp of the Roman government, and the tomb was guarded by their own soldiers under the eagle eye of the Jewish authorities, who were determined that there should be no possible recovery of the body. And when, notwithstanding all these precautions and provisions, He came forth on the appointed day, and was seen and identified by the multitudes who were alive when Paul's letter was written, and to whom he appealed for confirmation, and when we find no record anywhere of the denial of these statements at the time, or any attempt to question this weighty testimony, every candid mind is forced to admit that the argument for the resurrection is the strongest possible kind. And if the resurrection be true, then all His teachings and miracles must also be true. The supreme miracle of Christianity carries with it the conviction of all the rest, and so the whole edifice hangs on this great truth, the cornerstone.

I was once called upon by a well-informed skeptic, who was a lawyer, accustomed to weigh evidence, and quite doubtful of the truth of Christianity, and was asked to give to him the most convincing proofs of the truth of the religion of Christ. Instead of attempting a long and discursive discussion of apologetics, I simply told him that there was a single argument by which the whole question might be settled, and if that were true all the others were unnecessary. He offered to rest the entire case upon the one fact of the resurrection of Jesus Christ. And then I submitted to cross-examination on that subject, giving the data furnished by the New Testament and other contemporary literature, and I permitted this skilled legal mind to ask whatever questions he wished in the course of cross-examination that would satisfy him as fully as he would be before a judge or jury.

After two hours spent in this way the gentleman took his leave, promising to investigate the argument in detail, and return in a fortnight and give his decision. He returned according to appointment, and immediately acknowledged that the argument was convincing; that he had no doubt whatever of the truth of Christianity, and that the resurrection of the Lord Jesus Christ was established as fully as the laws of evidence could reasonably require. But he immediately added that he was not yet a Christian, and he felt that he was no more willing to become one even though he had accepted the truth of Christianity. He found the objection was moral as well as intellectual, and he realized he was not willing to accept the sacrifices required by a true Christian life. Years afterward he repeated the same statement, still believing in Christianity, but personally an unbeliever in Christ as His own Savior.

This is the high place the apostle gives the doctrine of the resurrection. It would be wise if, instead of endeavoring to meet unbelief with our speculations and reasonings, we would stand more simply and securely on the old apostolic testimony, "God has raised this Jesus to life, and we are all witnesses of the fact" (Acts 2:32).

SECTION III—*A Great Theme*

All this is preliminary, however, to the great theme of the chapter, namely, the hope of our resurrection. For Christ's resurrection is the pledge of ours, and our resurrection is the precious hope that dispels the darkness of the grave, and illuminates the future with all the glory that shines from His exaltation. And while He is the pledge of our resurrection, He is its pattern, too; and as He is so shall we be when He shall appear.

In his long and majestic argument for the resurrection he covers a wide field, and it can only be briefly summarized within these limits.

THE ANALOGY OF NATURE

1. He tells us that it is hinted at even in the analogy of nature. The seed that we plant in our garden and that springs out of the grave and develops its life out of death is a parable of the resurrection. The great Faraday, standing before an immense audience and dissolving a jewel of gold in a powerful acid, and then by another acid precipitating it and bringing it back, and then molding it into a more beautiful form and presenting it to the audience, was but giving them a little analogy of the resurrection as set forth in the processes of science. If man can do this much with an inert metal, how much more can God do with the human body formed for His glory and destined to immortality?

NOT OUR NATURAL BIRTHRIGHT

2. The resurrection is not our natural birthright, but it comes to us through our union with the Lord Jesus Christ, the second Head of humanity. There are two human races passing along the course of time. One is the race of Adam; the other the race of Jesus Christ. One was born from our fallen father; the other has been begotten out of the heart of the Son of God. From one we inherit death; from the other, life.

> As was the earthly man, so are those who are of the earth; and as is the man from heaven, so also are those who are of heaven. And just as we have borne the likeness of the earthly man, so shall we bear the likeness of the man from heaven. . . . For as in Adam all die, so in Christ all will be made alive. (1 Corinthians 15:48–49, 22)

Receiving from Him a new spiritual life and a new physical life in embryo, it becomes the deathless seed of a more glorious life, which will burst from the tomb as the blossoms of the spring burst forth from the ground and unfold amid the imperishable glories of the summerland on high.

Which race do you belong to? Which nature have you received? Which life are you developing, the Adam or the Christ?

THE FIGURE OF BAPTISM

3. The figure of baptism is introduced in the 29th verse. "Those . . . who are baptized for the dead," no doubt, simply means those that were baptized as a symbol of death. Baptism is the especial sign of death and resurrection, and this very ordinance of Christianity has no significance and is but a delusive mockery if the dead rise not.

THE RESURRECTION ORDER

4. The order of the resurrection is very clearly unfolded in verses 23–28. "Christ, the firstfruits; then, when he comes, those who belong to him" (15:23).

There are three stages of the resurrection. The first is personal. It is the resurrection of Jesus Christ Himself, the lone Conqueror of the grave, as He stands at the open tomb, the Firstborn from the dead.

The second stage is coming when those that sleep in Jesus will be raised and the living translated into His glorious image. Not before are we to expect our resurrection. The departed dead are waiting the simultaneous hour when they will all alike be lifted from their long sleep in the dust, and will put on their robes of resurrection life and gather with Him in the air.

Then there is a third stage at the end when His millennial reign will be over, when He will have accomplished His victorious plan and put all enemies under His feet; then will the wicked dead come forth, death itself will be destroyed and cast into the lake of fire to slay no more the children of our race.

THE GLORY OF THE RESURRECTION

5. The glory of the resurrection is very clearly set forth in the natural analogy. He draws a splendid contrast between the bare seed that you put in the soil and the glorious harvest that crowns it on the golden field. As that harvest is much greater than the little seed that died, or as that splendid tree with its luxuriant foliage, its rich bloom and its abundant fruit is immeasurably more than the little dry seed from which it sprang, so shall our resurrection body surpass the earthly form that was laid down in corruption, dishonor and weakness. It shall come forth in all the glory of His resurrection, and share all His mental endowments and His perfect physical powers, and enter into the lordship of creation which was the inheritance of man at the first, and is given back in the Son of man and in the new creation.

SECTION IV—*The Practical Application*

"Therefore, my dear brothers, stand firm. Let nothing move you. Always give yourselves fully to the work of the Lord, because you know that your labor in the Lord is not in vain" (15:58).

Three things will follow a realizing faith and hope of the Lord's coming.

First, we will be steadfast in the faith. We will stand firm in these days of doubt and disbelief, and take heed that we may be able to say at last, "I have kept the faith" (2 Timothy 4:7).

Next, we shall be immovable from the right. We will walk the narrow path. We will keep our garments spotless. We will watch and pray lest we enter into temptation. We will be firm amid the seductions of the world, the flesh and the devil. We will stand with girded loins, spotless robes and shining lamps, awaiting His coming.

Thirdly, we will be busy in His service and occupied in holy activities to prepare the world for His coming. We will be working to finish what He has given us to do, to lead others to the partnership of this blessed hope, and especially to carry forth the invitations to the wedding, send out the gospel to the world, proclaim the witness to all the nations, gather out a people for His name from every country and tribe and tongue, and thus hasten His coming and prepare His way. This will be our joy and crown of rejoicing in the presence of Christ at His coming. Thus we are laying up our treasures yonder, and life is being invested in the glorious possibilities and prospects of the ages to come and the kingdom which shall never pass away. Let us then "stand firm. Let nothing move you. Always give yourselves fully to the work of the Lord," for "you know that your labor in the Lord is not in vain" (1 Corinthians 15:58).

CHAPTER 13

THE LORD'S DAY

On the first day of every week, each one of you should set aside a sum of money in keeping with his income. (1 Corinthians 16:2)

On the Lord's Day I was in the Spirit. (Revelation 1:10)

Mention of this unique epistle of the Church would not be complete without an authoritative reference to the sacred and important institution of the Christian Sabbath so inseparably associated with the worship and fellowship of the Church of Christ. As we have seen in the case of several other themes discussed in this epistle, there are two extremes between which the truth is to be found; the extreme on the one side of unlimited license and the utter secularizing of the Sabbath day; on the other a return to the spirit of legalism and disposition to Judaize the Christian Sabbath, and insist upon the observance of the seventh day as essential to its true meaning and divine character. There is a widespread propagandism abroad among the churches which would throw around this sweet and holy Christian institution the shadows of Mount Sinai, and which would make the mere question of the seventh day a principle of cardinal importance and, indeed, the very central point of our faith and testimony. It is most unwholesome to elevate any subordinate question to so supreme a place of importance. And it is very necessary that God's people should be guarded against misrepresentations and misconceptions which otherwise would bring their consciences into bondage and detach them from the true center of faith and testimony to what may easily become a mere side issue. Let us, therefore, endeavor to trace the true Scriptural doctrine of the Sabbath through the various dispensations.

SECTION I—*An Ancient Institution*

The Sabbath is a primeval institution as old as creation. Its supreme authority does not rest upon Mosaic law, but it has come down itself from Eden and is as old as the human race, the institution of marriage and the first promise of redemption. It was given for man, and not for any single race of men. It was given for rest and refreshment, and not for bondage and ceremonial observances merely. It was given because it recognizes an essential need in human nature. Even races that have not known the beneficent teachings of the Bible have been led to institute appropriate times of rest and relaxation as a necessity of the constitution of man.

It is essential in considering this subject that we always recognize the earlier institution of the Sabbath, because this at once lifts the character and claims of the day above all questions connected with Jewish law. Even the fourth commandment, which reinstated the Sabbath, distinctly recognizes its prior existence by using the words, "Remember the Sabbath day" (Exodus 20:8). Speaking of another matter, the covenant made with Abraham for his seed, the Apostle Paul in the Epistle to the Galatians brings out an important principle, that the law, which came centuries later, could not annul the previous covenant or make it of non-effect. The primary institution stands, notwithstanding any later and more legal and special commands which may have been added to it. So the Sabbath of creation stands, notwithstanding all that may have been supplemented for the Jewish people and the Mosaic dispensation at Sinai. This lifts this sacred day to a lofty height and a universal scope that cannot be claimed for any of the older institutions of the Mosaic system. This blessed memorial of the crowning of creation comes down to us with sweetness, the beneficence, the liberty and love of unfallen Eden, and heaven's first smile over a newborn world.

SECTION II—*A Mosaic Institution*

It was taken up by the great Lawgiver, and reenacted for God's peculiar people with all the lawful sanctions of that fiery law. Its observance was most rigidly specified and enforced. Its desecration was punished with death. It became as much a law of fear as a law of love, and while still retaining its ancient purpose, yet it suffered inevitably the peculiar touches and tints of that dark dispensation. "(For the law made nothing perfect), and a better hope is introduced, by which we draw near to God" (Hebrews 7:19). "So the law was put in charge to lead us to Christ that we might be justified by faith" (Galatians 3:24). The law was essentially educational, temporary and a ministry of condemnation. It was designed to impress the human conscience with the supreme authority of God, and the awful nature and effects of sin. It was fitted to reveal man's depravity and disobedience, to produce conviction of sin and to drive a guilty conscience to the Lord Jesus Christ and the grace of the gospel for relief. It was not intended or fitted to be permanent.

While it contains the elements of the highest and purest morality, while its essential principles are holy and divine, yet its modus and its spirit are essentially legal and engendering to bondage, and God never meant the sweet and holy Sabbath to come down to us in New Testament times associated only with restrictions, severities and shadows of Mount Sinai. For a time they gathered round it, but they have passed away, and it stands out in the clear sunlight of its ancient institution and its yet higher Christian significance.

THE LESSON OF SINAI

As has been beautifully expressed in metaphorical language, it is like that same Mount Sinai, where it was reenacted 3,000 years ago. For days that lofty mountain had stood on the Arabian plain, with its clear summit piercing the sky and crowned with the cloudless sunlight of the heavens. Suddenly there gathered around it a dark and dreadful stormy cloud, lurid with awful lightnings, and rending the earth and air with its thunders of threatening judgment. For a time the Mount was lost to view in the enshrouding clouds of smoke and flame. So the Sabbath rose through the Patriarchal age like that sunlit mountain until at length it became enwrapped in the shadows and the awful threatenings of Mount Sinai. But after a while Sinai's shadows passed away. The fearful cloud, with its smoke and flame, ceased to hang around its awful brow. The camp of Israel moved forward, and the sunshine again bathed the mountain's crown; so Judaism, too, has passed away, and left the Sabbath in the clear and beautiful light of its first beautiful dawning upon the new created world. Nay, there has come a new and brighter light, for now there is shining around it the glory of the resurrection. And it is not merely the memorial of creation, but it is the sign and seal of a new creation. Jesus canceled for us the curse through the cross, opened the grave of doomed humanity, gave to us life and immortality through the gospel, and made the Sabbath for us the hallowed type of the rest of faith into which we enter now and the still sweeter, everlasting rest which remains for the people of God.

Beloved, don't let us go back to Judaism; don't let us get bound by the entanglements of the law; don't let us take the Sabbath back 3,000 years, and blot out the light of the open grave and the new creation. It is not necessary in order to honor it that we should bind ourselves with the yoke of bondage which our fathers were not able to bear. Let us move on with the dispensation, let us live in the light of the gospel, and let us take the Sabbath from the hands of our risen Lord and our reconciled Father.

SECTION III—*Reenacted under the New Testament Dispensation*

Now it is well to notice that God had already been preparing the minds and hearts of His people for a very radical change with the incoming of the new covenant. He told them He was not going to deal with them according to the covenant that He had made with their fathers, but He was to enter upon the covenant of grace in which love, forgiveness and liberty were to take the place of constraint, bondage and selfish effort. Very distinctly and repeatedly the old prophets intimated that there was to be such a change in the new creation, that the old heavens and the old earth should come no more into mind, and that all old things should pass away and all things be made new (see Isaiah 65:17).

THE ATTITUDE OF JESUS

When the Lord Jesus appeared we find Him at once facing the Sabbath question, and we notice two distinct attitudes which He takes from the beginning. The first is a positive recognition of the Sabbath as one of the institutions which He assumed and incorporated into His kingdom and took under His direction and authority. "So the Son of Man," He says, "is Lord even of the Sabbath" (Mark 2:28). In the parallel passage in Matthew 12:1–8, He assumes still more authoritative direction of this day; and, after citing several Old Testament precedents for a proper freedom in the observance of the day, as, for example, in the case of David and the priests themselves, who were obliged to minister in the many manual services, He then adds the strong expression of His authority to deal with the Sabbath supremely: "I tell you that one greater than the temple is here. . . . For the Son of Man is Lord of the Sabbath" (Matthew 12:6, 8). The Lord Jesus thus distinctly recognizes the Sabbath; but, on the other hand, He has distinctly set His face against the severe Jewish conception of it, and from the very beginning insisted upon the new construction of its meaning and a new charter of liberty and beneficence in its observance.

He openly defied the prejudices of the people by walking through the grainfields on the Sabbath day and allowing His disciples to pluck the heads of grain. He healed the man with the withered hand when He knew they were waiting to watch Him and condemn Him for it.

He met their prejudices with the keenest sense of showing the inhumanity and cruelty of straining their conventional ideas to the extent of allowing a poor brute to lie in a ditch rather than break the Sabbath (see Matthew 12:11), and He most distinctly laid down the law that true Sabbath observance always carries along with it a spirit of thoughtful love which would not hesitate to perform any work of real necessity or mercy. While He recognized the Sabbath as an institution of Christianity, He also recognized His right to change it and set it free from all that was peculiar to the transitory system of Judaism that had encrusted around it. Not in any sudden or formal propaganda of a new Sabbath law did He startle and shock even His disciples, but gently He allowed a new character and significance of the day to grow up out of incidents and events, as He allowed almost all the important acts and ordinances of His kingdom to develop out of the circumstances that gave them birth.

THE FIRST DAY

The gospel did not start out as a rigid system of theology laying down cardinal principles and enacting written laws like the Mosaic economy, but it grew out of living facts so that every institution and ordinance of Christianity has behind it an incident rather than a proclamation. Even the Lord's Supper grew out of the farewell meeting of Christ with His disciples. The very assemblies of Christianity evolved themselves out of the simple gatherings of the apostles. The government of the Christian Church was not laid down in any textbook or manual of laws, but evolved gradually out of the history of the early Church. So it was with the Sabbath and its important changes. He wanted it to spring spontaneously in their hearts as the new memorial of something dearer than even the deliverance from Egypt, or the first creation. So keeping ever before their minds the great fact of His coming resurrection as the central point of the Christian faith and hope, He ordered that glorious event to come, not on the Jewish Sabbath, which was not fitted to signalize it, for it marked rather the end of things than the beginning of a new series of glorious events which ran through eternal ages.

Having thus struck the new keynote, He prolonged it by arranging His meetings with them after His resurrection on the same day. Again and again He marked it by coming back to them on the first day until they quickly took the hint and in a far sweeter way than if it had been a rigid commandment, and as often as it returned it found them waiting for His coming until it came to be to them the memorial day of faith and love. Doubtless it was then that the name was attached to it, which we find afterwards repeated by John from the lonely isle of Patmos, "the Lord's Day" (Revelation 1:10).

So identified was the hallowed day with the resurrection of Christ that in the early Church the customary salutation on the first day morning always was, "The Lord has risen indeed."

Thus two beautiful ordinances were linked together as comparison pictures: the Lord's Supper, representing Calvary, and the Lord's Day, representing the resurrection. Established thus by such beautiful and repeated precedents, it is not strange that we find the early Church after His ascension still coming together on the same day. For a time their continuous Pentecostal blessing swept all days into one great tidal wave of blessing, but when things settled down to their normal condition, they began to assemble on this day for religious worship, fellowship and especially the observance of the Lord's Supper. And so we find in the 20th chapter of Acts, verse seven, like a glint of sunshine on a stormy sea, the picture of one of these meetings. In a chain of evidence one fact is as good as a thousand. It shows what the habit of the disciples was. The sea captain often traverses the whole Atlantic with just one observation from the heavens, and this single beam of light is enough to illumine the whole practice of the early Church. Here they had come together, not by special summons, because Paul was there, but to break bread according to their usual custom to keep the Lord's Supper. It was their stated time of worship, and Paul himself had waited through the week for this very day to come; and when it came it was so precious that he just spent the whole day and half the whole night with them in teaching and preaching; and before the time was over God had honored that wondrous New Testament Sabbath with the opening of the gates of death and the bringing back of a soul from the world of spirits.

So likewise our present text is just such another glimpse of the light revealing the usual practice of the Church. The apostle tells us here (1 Corinthians 16:1–2) that it was not an accidental thing that they should thus observe the first day, but he had given order to this effect to the churches of Galatia and he repeated the order to them. It had now become a New Testament institution, and as he founded the first churches and established their order this was the order that was settled. They were to come together on this day and mark it by their offerings for the work of the gospel.

One other glimpse of the light shines through the dimness (Revelation 1:10), where we find the Apostle John going apart on this same day and the Holy Spirit recognizing it, and the Lord Jesus making a personal visit from the heavens and giving to his aged servant the apocalyptic vision of the coming ages and the kingdom of glory.

Do we want more light? Does not love know how to take a hint? Is not the Sabbath sweeter to Christ as the quick response of our spontaneous love than as a mere matter of rigid ordinance? It would seem as if Jesus wanted it to spring up with this sort of freedom from all the associations fitted to make it so dear. And if His sweet example and the example of the early Church and all the sacred associations of the day are not enough for this spontaneous observance, the heart of love must be cold and dull indeed.

But, further, we know that our Lord gave to His disciples a great many commandments which have not come to us in categorical form. The Apostle John and other apostles tell us that during the 40 days He spoke to them in detail all things concerning the kingdom of God, and commanded them to teach the Church to observe these things. John also tells us that if all the things which Jesus said and did were written, the world could not contain the books that should be written. Doubtless, therefore, in these intervening days He gave them specific directions about the Sabbath, as well as the government of the Church, and many other things respecting which we have no specific word from His lips. But we have the example of the apostles, we have the pattern they set, we have the things they did, and we know they must have had the authority of His Word for all these things, so that their acts come to us with the authority of His commands.

OTHER CONSIDERATIONS

It is interesting to add one or two supplementary considerations in connection with the change of the day, which is, at the present time, being made the subject of much needless discussion and distraction among simple-minded Christians.

The first day of the week was really the day most signally honored in the Old Testament. Circumcision occurred on the eighth day, which was the first day of the second week. It was intended thus to be a special type of the new creation, and the new life which Christ was to bring. The great day of the Jewish feasts was usually the eighth day, which, of course, was the first day of the second series. The Jubilee happened on the year after the series of sevens, after seven Sabbatic periods of years, making 49; then came the 50th year which was the first of the new series, which was the gladdest, grandest day in all their cycles, typifying thus the new beginning which Christ was to bring in the coming ages.

Furthermore, it is a fact that the first day Adam ever spent on earth was really the Sabbath. He was created on earth just at the end of the sixth day, and as the days began at six in the evening he must have been immediately ushered into the Sabbath. The first sun that ever rose upon him was a Sabbath sun; and really the first day was the Sabbath day.

It may not be important to observe that according to the laws of longitude there is a difference of an entire day in the circuit of the globe. Were you to travel from here by way of England to China and back to San Francisco you have gained an entire day, and when you got back to San Francisco it would be Sunday for you while the people in the United States would still be keeping Saturday. What are you going to do in such a case? Suppose you have a Sabbath law compelling the keeping of the Sabbath day, here is one section of the world keeping the first day and another the seventh. This alone is sufficient to show that the whole question of numerical days is impossible. It is the principle of one day in seven that God requires, and it is the association of that day now, not with the law of Moses, nor even the creation of the universe, but the glorious new creation and resurrection of our Savior from the dead.

One other consideration will suffice. The very idea of the Old Testament was work first, and then rest as its recompense. It was therefore proper that their Sabbath should come at the end of the week. But the very idea of Christianity is rest first and then work. We work not for life, but from life.

We have entered into His rest and ceased from our works, and then we go to work with a new zeal, liberty and power. To go back to the old principle would be the reversing of the wheels of the dispensations and the denying of the very essential principles of the gospel of grace.

THREE THOUGHTS

In connection there are three thoughts that may well be fastened on our hearts as we leave this subject.

1. Let the Sabbath be to us, more than it has been, the memorial of the resurrection, and let it ever lift us to a high and heavenly plane of our life in the risen and ascended One.

2. Let it be to us God's memorial and message of the rest of faith. Let it remind us that the true Sabbath is one of the heart, the everlasting rest of the Christ who is within us through the ceasing from our own works and entering into His, and thus finding the rest that remains for the people of God.

3. Let the Sabbath claim our loving observance and our watchful regard, not merely through the sanctions of a law, but from the impulse of the deepest love. There are some things God asks of us, not merely because they are commanded, but because they are our instinctive delight. He did not tell Mary to pour out the treasures of her alabaster vase. He would not have praised her so much if He had been obliged to tell her. What He loved in her was that she had instinct enough to think for herself of this graceful expression of her faith and love. The very spontaneousness of it was its charm. So He wants us to keep the Sabbath sacred and holy, not because we would be stoned if we do not do so, but because it is like a wife's honor, a mother's name, a thing too sacred to be dragged on earth's common places. It is like the best room in the family. You don't use it to put your workbench in it and your kitchen pots. You don't wash the dishes there, and put away the ash barrels and garbage cans; but you keep it for the family reunion, for the visit of cherished friends, for the sanctuary of the household and the heart. This is the place of the Sabbath. Let us keep it clean. Let us keep it sacred. Let us keep it sweet. Not because we have to, but because we love to and it brings to us the memorial of a cloudless evening and the remembrance of an Easter dawn, and the blessed hope of that sweet morn whose dawn shall break on a deathless, sinless, tearless world.

CHAPTER 14

THE SUPPORT OF THE CHURCH: THE PRINCIPLE OF TRUE SPIRITUAL GIVING

> *Now about the collection for God's people: Do what I told the Galatian churches to do. On the first day of every week, each one of you should set aside a sum of money in keeping with his income, saving it up, so that when I come no collections will have to be made. Then, when I arrive, I will give letters of introduction to the men you approve and send them with your gift to Jerusalem. (1 Corinthians 16:1–3)*

This manual of Church principles and polity would not be complete without a statement of the scriptural method of finance and God's plan for supporting His Church. The ancient tabernacle was borne by the Levites on their shoulders, and God has provided that His Church should be sustained by the offerings of His people. Many false methods are abroad, and Christ is often dishonored by the appeals of His Church to an ungodly world, and the compromises that her rulers often make for the sake of securing the mercenary gifts of unholy men.

This subject is discussed by the apostle at still greater length in the eighth and ninth chapters of the Second Epistle to the Corinthians, and in the following discussions we shall first briefly outline the points brought out in the present passage, and then more fully unfold the comprehensive and exhaustive treatment of the whole subject in the longer passage in the second epistle.

SECTION I—*The Divine Law of Giving*

He speaks of the matter here as an order which he has given to the churches of Galatia, and which he now reenacts in the church at Corinth. The subject of giving formed part of an elaborate system under the Mosaic law. It was not a mere matter of caprice, but it was regulated by the most positive and binding ordinances. God's ancient people were required to give what practically amounted to almost 30 percent of their income for the support of the priesthood and the service of the tabernacle, and for the great national feasts. And so long as they were faithful to these ordinances and claims of their covenant God, they were never found to be a burden, but increasing prosperity rewarded their liberality and obedience.

THE LARGER FREEDOM

It is generally supposed that giving in the New Testament is left entirely to the impulse and good will of the individual Christian. This is excused under the plea of the larger freedom of the gospel. Now, surely, if the grace of God has advanced with the advent of the Christian age, and we are living in a larger dispensation of privilege and blessing, surely the Christian liberty on the new dispensation should lead to a larger beneficence and a nobler liberality than the bondage of the law. It would be a shame, surely, if we should content ourselves with giving one-tenth of our income, or even three-tenths as they did. More fitting is it that our love and liberty should give all. And yet, the fact is, that the average gifts of the people of God today do not begin to amount to a single tenth of their actual revenues. Three-tenths of the income of the people of God in this country alone would give us sufficient revenue to evangelize the whole world in a few years.

The New Testament Church, however, is not left without a definite law on the subject of giving. The "order" (1 Corinthians 16:1, KJV) which Paul gave to the churches of Galatia and Corinth is still binding upon us, and no Christian can expect God's blessing to rest on the spirit of stinginess and selfishness. It is still as true as ever, that "God loves a cheerful giver" (2 Corinthians 9:7), and "he who refreshes others will himself be refreshed" (Proverbs 11:25).

SECTION II—*The Divine Method of Giving*

"On the first day of every week, each one of you should set aside a sum of money in keeping with his income" (1 Corinthians 16:2). This clearly suggests systematic beneficence. It is not to be a matter of caprice or random impulse, but it is to be done regularly and periodically. It is to be done even when there is no urgent need appealing for help and no cause in distress addressing its claims to our sympathy. We are to have a fund always available for the Lord's claims and the Lord's cause. While we are to recognize all we spend even upon ourselves and our families as spent for Him, we are to take a proper proportion of it, and set it aside to be available whenever needed for the special needs of the Lord's work.

The advantages of this system are obvious. It prevents mere giving through excitement or haste. It makes our beneficence deliberate and conscientious, and it provides a fund which is always available, and which only makes it necessary for us to determine where the greatest need is. It is delightful to receive letters, as we often do, with such statements as this: "I have some of the Lord's money, and I believe He wants it to go for China," or "for Africa," as the case may be. This makes us stewards and trustees of what the Lord commits to our keeping, and "God's fellow workers" (2 Corinthians 6:1).

The fact that it was to be offered on the Lord's day gives the transaction a distinctly sacred character, and makes it an act of worship quite as much as our praises and our prayers. How different this from some of the ordinary methods of so-called Christian societies to extort their needed financial supplies through the devices of the auction mart, the produce exchange or the theater, or, still lower, the cheap restaurant.

SECTION III— *The Standard of Christian Giving*

The standard is to be "in keeping with his income" (1 Corinthians 16:2). This is intended as a definite recognition of the fact that everything we have belongs to God, and our offering is just the tribute of glad acknowledgment of His proprietary right to us and all we call our own.

The expression, "so that when I come no collections will have to be made" (16:2), is a very suggestive hint that Christian giving should be so conscientious and deliberate that it would not need to be stimulated by special appeals or public excitement. Indeed, the apostle seemed desirous of having no appearance of his seeking their gifts. He wished rather the whole impression of his visit to be spiritual, and their offering to be so entirely spontaneous that it would be complete before his arrival.

SECTION IV— *The Administration of the Gifts of God's People*

Careful provision is here made for the financial administration of Christ's Church. The donors are to have the privilege of selecting the one that will administer their gifts. "I will give letters of introduction to the men you approve and send them with your gift to Jerusalem" (16:3). He recognized the importance of the utmost care in the administration of the business of Christ's cause and the avoidance of all possible blame. It is most important that those who are entrusted with the gifts of Christ's people should see to it that they are administered economically, honestly and with the most conscientious regard to their accomplishing in the most effective way the purpose of the donors and the benefit of the cause of Christ.

Passing now to the larger discussion of this subject in the second epistle we are gratified to find the whole subject is developed with the utmost completeness and attractiveness, reducing almost to a science the principles of Christian beneficence.

THE HIGH PLACE

1. The high place of giving is first recognized. It is called "a grace" (2 Corinthians 8:7), and is classed with "faith . . . speech . . . knowledge . . . complete earnestness and . . . love" (8:7). It is pressed upon them as one of the fruits of the Spirit and the essential graces of the Christian character. We may be fervid in our religious emotions, and ardent in our expressions of consecration, but if we are stingy and selfish it will detract from everything. The lack of the grace of giving is a fatal blemish upon our Christian character.

THE DIVINE MOTIVE

2. Next Paul points to the divine motive of giving. "For you know the grace of our Lord Jesus Christ, that though he was rich, yet for your sakes he became poor, so that you through his poverty might become rich" (8:9). This is the supreme motive, the sacrifice and love of Jesus Christ. "Thanks be to God for his indescribable gift!" (9:15). This is the watchword of all true beneficence. After Calvary nothing is too costly for Him. The very figure by which the sacrifice of Christ is here expressed as an impoverishing of Himself is unspeakably tender and appropriate. And after such a spectacle, we may well say of any sacrifice, as a dying Christian woman once said to us of the sacrifice of her life and her dearest ones, "It is little to give for Him."

OUR PERSONAL CONSECRATION

3. The deep source of Christian giving should be our own personal consecration. "And they did not do as we expected, but they gave themselves first to the Lord and then to us in keeping with God's will" (8:5). The gifts of these saints began in self-giving. Nothing is of value to God that does not bear the marks of divine ownership, and it is vain to look for the support of Christ's cause to halfhearted Christians. Let there be an entire surrender to Him, and the offerings of a few consecrated Christians will outweigh all that the wealth of millions could do. Our Christian efforts must not begin at the pockets of people, but at their hearts. Slay the idol of self, and the treasures of our beneficence will be sufficient to save the world.

Once in India a British officer gave orders that a heathen idol should be smashed to pieces. The priests resisted long and obstinately, but at last the order was fulfilled, and, as the idol fell in shattered fragments, a great flood of golden coins poured out amid the ruins! Slay the idol of self, we again repeat, and the treasures will be enough to evangelize all the earth.

THE CROWNING GLORY

4. The crowning glory of Christian giving is sacrifice. "Out of the most severe trial, their overflowing joy and their extreme poverty welled up in rich generosity. For I testify that they gave as much as they were able, and even beyond their ability" (8:2–3). So strongly does the apostle express this overflow of love that he ruins his grammar to give utterance to his thought, and uses the hyperbole, "the superabundance of their joy, and their deep destitution, superabounded unto the riches of their liberality." Giving reaches its climax in sacrifice, and sacrifice reaches its fullness in a joy that does not feel the sacrifice, for we read of superabounding joy side by side with superabounding giving. Sacrifice is worth nothing until it ceases to be a sacrifice, and giving never reaches its blossom until it runs over into the sacrifice of joy. "Giving," as has been well said, "until it hurts and then giving until it doesn't hurt."

PERFECT VOLUNTARINESS

5. The true spirit of Christian giving is perfect voluntariness. "Entirely on their own" (8:3), and again, "For if the willingness is there, the gift is acceptable according to what one has, not according to what he does not have" (8:12). What God looks at is the intention of the heart. He sees the throbbing love that prompts the gift, and He often sees the still deeper love that weeps because it has nothing to give; and He counts the will for the deed, and says, as He did of old of another of His servants, "You did well to have this in your heart" (1 Kings 8:18).

These Corinthians Christians had so longed to give that they had even ventured to pledge their offerings before they had the power to give them, and God had accepted the pledge and had now enabled them to make it good in actual performance. Therefore, He reminds them in the next place of the necessity of conscientiousness.

NECESSITY OF CONSCIENTIOUSNESS

6. Paul next points out the necessity of conscientiousness in the performance of our purposes and the fulfillment of our pledges. "Now finish the work," he says, "so that your eager willingness to do it may be matched by your completion of it, according to your means" (2 Corinthians 8:11). It is most important that our giving be conscientious and honest, and that we be careful not to let our purposes and promises be easily forgotten or lightly excused, for God does not forget them; and He takes great delight in our conscientious fidelity to these things, and our keeping faith with Him as strictly

as we would with a fellow being in any matter of a common and business interest.

PROPORTIONATE GIVING

7. The principle of proportionate giving is presented.

> Our desire is not that others might be relieved while you are hard pressed, but that there might be equality. At the present time your plenty will supply what they need, so that in turn their plenty will supply what you need. Then there will be equality, as it is written: "He who gathered much did not have too much, and he who gathered little did not have too little." (8:13–15)

This is the principle of true Christian communism. God does not always require you to hand your money over absolutely to some other man to be the trustee and agent of your beneficence, but He may want you to retain your money, and still act as His steward and trustee; but in so doing be very sure that you are not transgressing this divine law of proportion. Your abundance is to be the supply for the want of some other, and if you can hold that abundance and see the cause of Christ in distress and extremity, your heart is not responsive to the life and touch of your living Head. For "If one part suffers, every part suffers with it; if one part is honored, every part rejoices with it" (1 Corinthians 12:26).

We believe this lesson is yet to be learned by the wealthy members of Christ's Church. We most fully believe that if there were more business men and women today who would accept the trust of becoming the dispensers of God's money, absolutely at God's bidding, that He would surely place in the hands of some of these individuals the millions which now are consumed wholly in selfishness and greed, and give them the divine joy of seeing the world evangelized and the Lord's immediate coming brought nigh.

THE ADMINISTRATION OF THE GIFTS

8. The administration of the gifts of God's people is again presented in this passage. The apostle shows with delicate tact how careful he was to have it, "to avoid any criticism of the way we administer this liberal gift. For we are taking pains to do what is right, not only in the eyes of the Lord but also in the eyes of men" (2 Corinthians 8:20–21).

He tells them about Titus and another brother who are to administer this fund, reminding them that his "praise is in the gospel throughout all the churches" (8:18, KJV), and he informs them of the appointment of the other officers also who have been chosen by the various churches to travel with him and carry these offerings. Nothing can be finer than the thoughtful

consideration here given to every question affecting the confidence of the
people of God in all things.

THE BEAUTIFUL FRUITION

9. The beautiful fruition of Christian giving is next presented. First, it
bears fruit in blessing to the giver:

> Whoever sows sparingly will also reap sparingly, and whoever
> sows generously will also reap generously. . . . And God is able to
> make all grace abound to you, so that in all things at all times,
> having all that you need, you will abound in every good work.
> (9:6, 8)

This undoubtedly refers to temporal prosperity. Some people think that all
the promises of this kind belong to the Old Testament. That is not so. God's
promise to reward the liberal giver is just as true as it ever was. Still the man
that "withholds unduly" will find that he "comes to poverty" (Proverbs
11:24), and "A generous man will prosper" (11:25). If we use God's gifts
honestly and generously for God's glory, He will prosper us and enlarge our
power to give more.

Again, not only will it bring prosperity to the giver, but it will bring him
abundant usefulness, or, as the apostle expresses it so forcibly in the 10th
verse, as happily translated by Rotherham, "He who supplies seed to him
who is sowing and bread for eating, will supply and multiply your seed and
cause to grow the products of your righteousness" (see 2 Corinthians 9:10).
Thus you will have a partnership in the work with him whom you sustain.
You will be a sharer in his joy, in his fruit, in the work he does and the souls
he saves. Thus, although you may never set your feet on foreign shores,
some day there will come trooping to your side the children of distant continents, who will hail you as the instrument that led them into the blessed
hopes and privileges of the gospel.

One other blessed effect of your giving will be the prayers that will ascend
to God for you from those you help. It is a blessed thing to have the prayers
of God's children follow us, and this is peculiarly the privilege of those who
help others. They come surrounded with the intercession that holds them
ever to the heart of God, and becomes a channel of unspeakable blessing to
their lives.

GLORY TO GOD

10. Finally, Paul points out the glory that rebounds to God from our
giving. The apostle speaks here of the thanksgivings that go up to God on
account of the gifts of His people, and the glory that rebounds to His name

through the multiplied fruits of our beneficence. As God Himself is the great Giver, so He has made it the law of the universe that we can only reach the highest blessing through the love that gives.

Abraham could not enter into the fullness of his covenant until he had laid his all upon the altar of Moriah. Moses could not become the leader of Israel until his mother had given him unreservedly away in the floating ark of sacrifice amid the weeds of the Nile. Samuel, the great reformer, was a mother's sacrificial gift. The temple of Solomon was reared on a site that had already been the scene of Isaac's sacrifice, and which David insisted on buying and paying for; for, he said, "I will not sacrifice to the LORD my God burnt offerings that cost me nothing" (2 Samuel 24:24). The first Old Testament miracle of resurrection from the dead came to one who had already given her last morsel of meal and her last drop of oil at the prophet's bidding. The great miracle of the feeding of the 5,000 started in the gift of a little lad, who gave up his lunch in the lone wilderness that others might be fed. Among the last and sweetest words ever spoken by our Savior was His commendation of the woman that gave the alabaster box with its precious ointment for love of Him; and the other woman who poured her all into the treasury, and received a crown of recognition greater than all the magnificent largesses of the rich and proud could ever have claimed.

The most solemn judgment upon the Pentecostal Day was upon two people who did not give honestly to God. And the most distinguished example of apostolic ministry was the noble Barnabas, who laid down his all at the apostle's feet and became the son of consolation and the princely pattern of consecrated businessmen for all time.

In the closing days of the Restoration period the poor captives in Babylon sent an offering to their brethren in Jerusalem, who were laboring to rebuild the temple. As soon as it came God commanded that the gold should be fashioned into crowns, bearing perhaps the names of the donors, and that these should be hung up in the temple of the Lord as memorials of the gift and perhaps worn some day by the givers as the acknowledgment of their noble sacrifice and glorious recompense. So our gifts are taken by our blessed Master, and melted into crowns to be placed first upon the head of our Lord Himself, who alone is worthy of all the glory, and perhaps to be worn on the coronation day by those who loved and sacrificed for Him below.

Oh, that we may be saved from the blight of selfishness! Oh, for the blessedness and glory of self-renouncing love and sacrifice!

> God Himself is always giving,
> Loving is the truest living,
> Letting go is twice possessing;
> Would you double every blessing?

SECOND CORINTHIANS

CHAPTER 1

VICTORIOUS SUFFERING

Praise be to the God and Father of our Lord Jesus Christ, the Father of compassion and the God of all comfort, who comforts us in all our troubles, so that we can comfort those in any trouble with the comfort we ourselves have received from God. For just as the sufferings of Christ flow over into our lives, so also through Christ our comfort overflows. (2 Corinthians 1:3–5)

Paul's first letter to the Corinthians gives us a picture of the apostolic church, the second gives us the testimony of the apostle himself. It is intensely personal, and introduces us to the deepest experience of this man who stood nearest of all to the heart of the Lord Jesus Christ. His testimony in the present passage has reference to suffering—victorious suffering—suffering so borne as to bring out of it not only triumph but boundless blessing to other lives as well as his own. This passage contains several important points.

TRIAL

The word used for trial in this passage and repeated several times is the same Greek word in every instance, although it is variously translated in the King James by the several terms "tribulation," "trouble" and "suffering." The word "tribulation" first used is derived from a Latin root which literally means a flail, and it describes the crushing and humiliating blows which would be caused by such a fearful club as a flail applied to a bound and helpless human victim. The figure is not too strong to describe such sufferings as the Apostle Paul tells us were his frequent, indeed, his almost constant lot. We need not go farther than his Epistle to the Corinthians to find a picture of suffering most tragic and unprecedented in human life. If we turn to First Corinthians 4:9–13 we have an extraordinary array of dramatic and tragic afflictions:

For it seems to me that God has put us apostles on display at the
end of the procession, like men condemned to die in the arena.
We have been made a spectacle to the whole universe, to angels
as well as to men. We are fools for Christ, but you are so wise in
Christ! We are weak, but you are strong! You are honored, we are
dishonored! To this very hour we go hungry and thirsty, we are
in rags, we are brutally treated, we are homeless. We work hard
with our own hands. When we are cursed, we bless; when we are
persecuted, we endure it; when we are slandered, we answer
kindly. Up to this moment we have become the scum of the
earth, the refuse of the world.

1. A Spectacle

The figure is exceedingly strong. The Roman emperors were accustomed
at the close of the day, in the bloody amphitheater, to bring on as the last
performance of the circus a battle unto the death. So Paul says that on the
stage of Christian suffering, "God has put us apostles on display at the end
of the procession, like men condemned to die in the arena. We have been
made a spectacle to the whole universe, to angels as well as to men" (4:9).
The Greek word for spectacle means a theater. Then he describes the various
humiliations and afflictions appointed to him, ending with the vivid expression, "Up to this moment we have become the scum of the earth, the refuse
of the world" (4:13).

If we turn to our present epistle we read, "For I wrote you out of great distress and anguish of heart and with many tears" (2 Corinthians 2:4). Again
in the fourth chapter we find him thus describing his trials, even in the
midst of victory: "We are hard pressed on every side, but not crushed;
perplexed, but not in despair; persecuted, but not abandoned; struck down,
but not destroyed. We always carry around in our body the death of Jesus"
(4:8–10). We read on a little farther and we come to the sixth chapter, and
read such phrases as these: "in troubles" (6:4), "hardships" (6:4), "distresses"
(6:4), "in beatings" (6:5), "imprisonments" (6:5), "riots" (6:5), "in hard
work" (6:5), "sleepless nights" (6:5), "hunger" (6:5), "through glory and
dishonor" (6:8), "bad report and good report" (6:8), "genuine, yet regarded
as impostors" (6:8), "known, yet regarded as unknown" (6:9), "dying, and
yet we live on" (6:9), "beaten, and yet not killed" (6:9), "sorrowful, yet always rejoicing" (6:10), "poor, yet making many rich" (6:10), "having nothing, and yet possessing everything" (6:10).

2. Unrest

Again in the seventh chapter we find this great apostle confesses to a state of unusual unrest that many of us, no doubt, had supposed he was exempt from, and that such hours of weakness only belonged to Christians like us: "This body of ours had no rest, but we were harassed at every turn—conflicts on the outside, fears within" (7:5).

3. Sufferings

Once more we turn to Second Corinthians 11:23–30, and the picture reaches its deepest coloring:

> I have worked much harder, been in prison more frequently, been flogged more severely, and been exposed to death again and again. Five times I received from the Jews the forty lashes minus one. Three times I was beaten with rods, once I was stoned, three times I was shipwrecked, I spent a night and a day in the open sea, I have been constantly on the move. I have been in danger from rivers, in danger from bandits, in danger from my own countrymen, in danger from Gentiles; in danger in the city, in danger in the country, in danger at sea; and in danger from false brothers. I have labored and toiled and have often gone without sleep; I have known hunger and thirst and have often gone without food; I have been cold and naked. Besides everything else, I face daily the pressure of my concern for all the churches. Who is weak, and I do not feel weak? Who is led into sin, and I do not inwardly burn? If I must boast, I will boast of the things that show my weakness.

It would seem as if this heroic soul possessed the sublime ambition to surpass all other men in his sufferings for his Master, and that the only glory he sought was to have the heaviest share of the cross of Jesus and the sorrows of His church.

4. Our Lot

"As water reflects a face,/ so a man's heart reflects the man" (Proverbs 27:19). While his sufferings may have been preeminent, yet he was also the forerunner in that path of affliction which all the saints have walked. One of his earliest messages to the churches of Asia was, "We must go through many hardships to enter the kingdom of God" (Acts 14:22). Still it is indeed sadly true, as so finely expressed in the world's oldest poem, "Man born of woman/ is of few days and full of trouble" (Job 14:1). "For hardship does not spring from the soil,/ nor does trouble sprout from the ground./ Yet man is born to trouble/ as surely as sparks fly upward" (5:6–7).

And yet how light our sorrows seem compared with his. After the catalog we have just read, some of us must feel ashamed that we have ever murmured or complained. But trial is always hard, and sometimes the lesser afflictions are more difficult to bear than the greater ones. Let us recognize this fact at the very outset and go forth expecting trial, and we will not be disappointed when it comes. If, on the contrary, we go forth expecting sunny skies and paths of roses, we will indeed be ill-fitted to meet the realities of life, and defeat and disappointment will face us at every turn. God has woven the strands of sorrow into the web of human life, and they are as necessary for our discipline and our usefulness as the golden threads of gladness.

COMFORT

How beautiful and cheering is the picture here given of God as "the Father of compassion and the God of all comfort" (2 Corinthians 1:3). We cannot know Him in this blessed and benignant capacity if we do not have suffering and trial. We would never see the stars without the darkness, and we never know our Father's heart until our heart aches with sorrow. Nothing is more beautiful than some of the inspired pictures of the tenderness of God. Is an earthly father compassionate? "As a father has compassion on his children,/ so the LORD has compassion on those who fear him" (Psalm 103:13). Is an earthly mother quick to feel the anguish of her children, and the best healer of a broken heart? "As a mother comforts her child,/ so will I comfort you;/ and you will be comforted over Jerusalem" (Isaiah 66:13). Do father and mother sometimes fail us? "Though my father and mother forsake me,/ the LORD will receive me" (Psalm 27:10). "Can a mother forget the baby at her breast/ and have no compassion on the child she has borne?/ Though she may forget,/ I will not forget you!" (Isaiah 49:15).

1. Human Comforters

God comforts us sometimes by human instruments: "But God, who comforts the downcast, comforted us by the coming of Titus" (2 Corinthians 7:6). There is a sweet ministry of human sympathy, and none of us can be indifferent to the love and fellowship of our friends in the hour of sorrow, nor should we be slow to "carry each other's burdens, and in this way [we] will fulfill the law of Christ" (Galatians 6:2).

2. God Our Comforter

But the best of all consolations is the "comfort of the Holy Ghost" (Acts 9:31, KJV). God has His own way of healing the broken heart and filling the soul with joy and peace when it is sinking with sorrow.

There are moments when the heavens seem to open and the heart of God touches our hearts with strange, supernal rest, and even ecstatic exultation, and we wonder why we are thus visited and loved. Frequently it is in preparation for some severe blow that is about to strike us. God is forearming us by a special touch of His love. Sometimes again, when everything around us is fitted to depress and crush us, the heart is lifted up with strange joy and strength which surpass all human explanation, and our first thought, perhaps, is: "Surely someone is praying for me just now, I feel so strengthened and comforted." And so it comes to pass, as we have already said, that in the severest trials we are often carried most triumphantly, while in those of less weight we sometimes become irritable and lose our victory.

But the special teaching of this passage is that the comfort is always commensurate with the tribulation. "For just as the sufferings of Christ flow over into our lives, so also through Christ our comfort overflows" (2 Corinthians 1:5). As far as the pendulum swings downward in the stroke of agony, it rises in the rebound of consolation.

Our sufferings are the sufferings of Christ; our comfort is also His. We have a little glimpse of the source of His peace and joy in the picture of His earthly life. In that hour when His heart was crushed with the foreboding of the coming cross, we are told that He was "full of joy through the Holy Spirit" (Luke 10:21), and again, "who for the joy set before him endured the cross, scorning its shame" (Hebrews 12:2).

It is your privilege to claim His joy in proportion to your weight of trial. If He is pleased to test you with unusual afflictions, just turn around and test Him with unusual behests upon His grace and sympathy; for the promise is, "Just as you share in our sufferings, so also you share in our comfort" (2 Corinthians 1:7).

SERVICE

"If we are distressed, it is for your comfort and salvation; if we are comforted, it is for your comfort" (1:6). The apostle tells us here that the very object of our peculiar experiences of suffering and trial is "so that we can comfort those in any trouble with the comfort we ourselves have received from God" (1:4). His sorrow is the school of Christ that disciplines him and equips him for the ministry of consolation.

Indeed, we will often find that after we have passed through some special experience of trial, God will send to us someone who has been similarly afflicted and use us to lift them up and bear them through even as He has carried us. Sorrow, therefore, is not accidental, but part of the divine plan of love and education for us.

A SPECIAL EMERGENCY

He has spoken generally of trial and affliction, but now he comes to a particular experience. "We do not want you to be uninformed," he says, "about the hardships we suffered in the province of Asia" (1:8). And then he proceeds to describe in detail that great and mysterious blow that crushed him sometime during his evangelistic campaign either in Ephesus or Asia Minor. What that trial was Bible expositors are far from agreed upon. Some regard it as a physical attack of sickness which almost took his life. Others, and the larger number, connect it with his grief on account of the sad condition of the church in Corinth, which had in great measure repudiated his apostolic authority, and even gone into the grossest and most shameless immorality. His heart was quite broken about it, and it would appear as if he had even been hindered from visiting them lest he should bring sorrow to them instead of gladness.

1. What It Was

It is very touching that this great and good man should have been so sensitive to the sins of men and the glory of his Master that it made him ill to hear of their wrongdoing. Certainly it became a physical stroke which nearly took his life; but it is delightful to think of it as having originated in a spiritual cause and having sprung from the noble unselfishness of his heart.

2. Physical

Whatever its cause, a few things are very certain about it. In the first place, it was "far beyond our ability to endure" (1:8). It was beyond what seemed possible for him to bear, and, indeed, his strength gave way under it and he was ready to sink in physical prostration and really die. "We despaired," he says, "even of life" (1:8). Not only so, "indeed, in our hearts we felt the sentence of death. But this happened that we might not rely on ourselves" (1:9). Literally it might be translated, "We had the answer of death in ourselves." His very prayers seemed ineffectual, his faith failed to grasp deliverance, and death was written on every part of the firmament and horizon.

What a trial, dear child of God! What a comfort to you to know that if such a trial should ever come to you, a trial in which outward pressure and inward depression combine to plunge you in utmost despair, still you may hope and trust and overcome.

A GREAT DELIVERANCE

He overcame. "He has delivered us from such a deadly peril" (1:10). It would indeed have been a great death; for had it come to that, Paul would have failed, his enemies would have triumphed, the great adversary would have been pleased and God's cause would have seemed to go down in a dark and humiliating defeat. It was something like that hour in Gethsemane when the Master felt that He could not die, and yet it seemed as if He must. "With loud cries and tears" He pleaded with His Father, "the one who could save him from death, and he was heard because of his reverent submission" (Hebrews 5:7). He did not die, but overcame and lived to offer up His life later without defeat, a voluntary sacrifice of victorious love. And so there are times when we cannot afford to sink and God will give us victory.

Not only so but he adds, "He will deliver us" (2 Corinthians 1:10). The deliverance continues, the experience of God's help in the past has established a habit of trusting and triumphing in the present. And still farther it reaches on to the future and faith rises to triumphant hope as he adds, "On him we have set our hope that he will continue to deliver us" (1:10).

In this conflict, he tells us his confidence was not in himself, for all human light had failed, but "on God, who raises the dead" (1:9). He looked for a deliverance that required nothing less than the Almighty Power which raised Jesus Christ from the dead and set Him in the heavens. This is the divine pattern of the power that we may still claim. Ours is the God of Resurrection and we may still sing,

> Nothing is too hard for Jesus,
> No man can work like Him.

Finally, he tells us that in this great conflict, he was upheld and helped by the faith of his friends. "You help us by your prayers. Then many will give thanks on our behalf for the gracious favor granted us in answer to the prayers of many" (1:11).

And so we come back again to the ministry of mutual help and helpful prayer. This is the special province of the Holy Spirit: to lay upon our hearts the needs of friends and lead us out in intercession for them, sometimes when we do not even know the circumstances of their need. Enough for us to respond to the burden of the Spirit and hold ourselves ready to bear the sufferings of others and share in the priesthood of our blessed Master as He continually makes intercession for us.

CONCLUSION

In conclusion, our first duty in trial is to accept it, whether we understand it or not, as a dispensation of divine wisdom and love. God has two hands, and the first presses us down, the second lifts us up. In a very fine metaphor, the Apostle Peter bids us first "Humble yourselves, therefore, under God's mighty hand," and then adds "that he may lift you up in due time" (1 Peter 5:6).

1. Submission

In a school for the deaf a distinguished visitor was listening to the silent examination of the little ones. Not a word was spoken, but as each question was presented in the language of signs, a little one would write the answer on the blackboard. Finally the visitor was asked if he did not wish to submit some questions himself. Noticing a little shriveled, pinched face in front of him that seemed a living embodiment of pain, he asked, "How do you explain the fact that a God of infinite power and wisdom has allowed you to be such a sufferer?" The question was translated into the language of signs and the little fellow was called to the platform. For a moment, the pinched face took on a shade of deeper pain, and then it lighted up as he stepped to the blackboard and wrote the words, "Even so, Father, for so it seemed good in Thy sight." The hush of silence that had rested upon that audience was broken by murmurs and sobs of deep response. Surely, that is quite as glorious as the faith that overcomes disease and pain.

2. Deliverance

But having learned the first lesson, let us not forget the second. There is a time for resignation and there is a time for aggressive faith and victorious deliverance. It came to Paul, it came to Jesus, it comes to every trusting soul. "I will be with him in trouble," is only one-half the promise. After we have learned that lesson well, there comes the rest, "I will deliver him" (Psalm 91:15). God has made complete provision for our victory over suffering as well as over sin. Let us not miss our sorrows or lose our battles, but take the comfort He has so dearly bought and pass it on to a brokenhearted world.

CHAPTER 2

THE DEPENDABLENESS OF GOD

For no matter how many promises God has made, they are "Yes" in Christ. And so through him the "Amen" is spoken by us to the glory of God. Now it is God who makes both us and you stand firm in Christ. He anointed us, set his seal of ownership on us, and put his Spirit in our hearts as a deposit, guaranteeing what is to come. (2 Corinthians 1:20–22)

There is no quality more valuable in people than dependableness. The late Dean Stanley once said, "Show me a young man who is utterly trustworthy, whose word is as good as his affidavit, who keeps his engagements and who can always be found at his post and depended upon to do his best, and I will show you a fragment from the Rock of Ages."

There is nothing more rare in officers of public trust and positions of responsibility and in private business than this quality of dependableness and trustworthiness, and it is counted of greater value than the most brilliant gifts and the most impulsive enthusiasm.

Now this is the aspect of the divine character the apostle brings out in the striking words of our text. His enemies at Corinth had just challenged his own trustworthiness. He had promised to visit them some time before and failed to keep his appointment, and they were saying that "in the same breath [he] say[s], 'Yes, yes' and 'No, no'" (2 Corinthians 1:17). What tried him much more was that they were also ascribing the same uncertainty to the message which he had brought them and criticizing the Word of God and the gospel of Christ as if quite as unreliable as the apostle's own promises.

He earnestly repudiates the reflection, and explains that his failure to keep his appointment to visit them was prompted solely by their own interests. He had learned that they were in such a sad spiritual condition that a visit from him would have meant the severest censure and the deepest distress and pain for them and him. "I call God as my witness," he says, "that it was in order to spare you that I did not return to Corinth" (1:23); and then he adds in the next chapter, "So I made up my mind that I would not make another painful visit to you" (2:1).

So far therefore from a spirit of vacillation he was animated by the highest honor and affection. Then he proceeds to vindicate the Word of God from the more serious criticism which they had made against it. "For the Son of God, Jesus Christ, who was preached among you by me and Silas and Timothy, was not 'Yes' and 'No,' but in him it has always been 'Yes' " (1:19).

Not only so, but the work of His grace in fulfillment of His word is just as sure and steadfast as His promises; and so Paul goes on to say, "Now it is God who makes both us and you stand firm in Christ. He anointed us, set his seal of ownership on us, and put his Spirit in our hearts as a deposit" (1:21–22).

God, therefore, is not a changeable and uncertain Being, but One whose word is sure and whose work is enduring, even as His everlasting throne. We have a God on whom we can utterly depend. We have a Savior who is truly "the Rock of Ages."

> There is One amid all changes who standeth ever fast;
> One who covers all the future, the present and the past;
> It is Christ, the Rock of Ages, the First and the Last.

God's dependableness is unfolded in this verse in two respects, with reference to His promises and His grace.

THE PROMISES OF GOD

"For no matter how many promises God has made, they are 'Yes' in Christ" (1:20). God never forgets His word. Long ago He promised a Redeemer, and although He waited 4,000 years, the promise was at last most surely fulfilled. He promised Abraham a son, and although a quarter of a century of testing intervened, that promise at last came literally true. He promised Abraham the land of promise as his inheritance, and although 400 years of trial intervened, at last the land was possessed. He promised Jeremiah that after 70 years the captives should return from Babylon, and on the very hour the action answered to the word. He promised Daniel that after 69 prophetic weeks, that is 483 years, Messiah should appear, and at the very day the promise was fulfilled, and the most extraordinary evidence which we have to offer to the doubting Hebrew today that Jesus is his Messiah is the literal fulfillment of the prophecy of Daniel at the exact date. The Lord Jesus promised the coming of the Holy Spirit, and when the day of

Pentecost was fully come, the heavens were opened and the Spirit descended. Just as true are all His individual promises to the believer. Not the smallest letter or the least stroke of a pen shall fail until all shall be fulfilled (see Matthew 5:18). "Heaven and earth will pass away, but my words will never pass away" (24:35).

Some very beautiful and striking things are taught us in this passage about the promises of God.

1. Their Variety

The literal translation of the pronoun "all" here is not only universal but particular, and has been rendered "all the promises of God, how many soever they be." It carries the idea of a great number and variety, and yet notwithstanding their number and variety, every one is pure gold. When men talk much, the intrinsic value of their words depreciates. People of brief speech are usually people of surer performance; but God, although He has spoken to us more than 40,000 words of promise, never wearies of making good each one.

How many and varied they are. There are promises of salvation, and they are more than can be numbered. There are promises of cleansing and sanctifying and keeping, and they cover every possible spiritual condition. There are promises of healing, and they meet every physical need. There are promises of comfort for the sorrowing as tender as the breathing of a mother's love. There are promises of deliverance for the tried and tempted that cover every danger of life's pathway. There are promises for our homes, our friends, our work, our financial and temporal needs, and all possible conditions of life. They are repeated in every variety of phrase and fitted to encourage our timidity and inspire our faith and lead us out in confidence and prayer, and every one of them can be depended upon. Some of them take hold of us at one time and some at another. God has a thousand hands, but the touch of a single finger will bring us into the embrace of His everlasting arms.

2. The Surety

"They are 'Yes' in Christ" (2 Corinthians 1:20). He has guaranteed them. The promises of God form a great checkbook and every one is endorsed by the Mediator, the Lord Jesus Christ, and His word and honor are pledged to their fulfillment. Indeed, they are all given to Him primarily as our federal Head and Representative. In the everlasting covenant, He undertook to fulfill the conditions of redemption and received in return all the promises of God. He has met those conditions, He has earned those promises, He has fulfilled that covenant; and now, for His sake, we can claim every one of them just as fully as if we had fulfilled the conditions ourselves.

3. The Reassurance

"Yes." Why is this added? "For no matter how many promises God has made, they are 'Yes' in Christ" (1:20). Does it perhaps mean that God not only assures, but reassures? Not only does He give His promise in the Word, but He sends His Holy Spirit to whisper it personally in our hearts and awake within us the spirit of confidence and trust.

As a man passed with his little child through a dark tunnel, the little one kept turning anxiously to the father and asking again and again, "Will we soon be through? Is it all right? Is there any danger?" And the father kept reassuring the anxious child and repeating his comforting "Yes." It is thus that the Father of mercies speaks in our troubled hearts. "Yes," he says, "I have loved you with an everlasting love;/ I have drawn you with lovingkindness" (Jeremiah 31:36). When the apostle was troubled about his mysterious "thorn in the flesh" he asked the Lord again and again about it, and the beautiful record he has given us of the answer is, "He said to me, 'My grace is sufficient for you' " (2 Corinthians 12:9).

It is thus that the Father repeats His loving words and breathes renewed consolations into the anxious and troubled heart until like the soothing of a mother with a sobbing child, we sink to rest in our Father's arms.

Perhaps, also, the "Yes" means the Lord Jesus Christ is God's answer to all other promises. Everything that God has told us is fulfilled in Him. He is the substance of all blessing and the answer to all our need, and therefore "no matter how many promises God has made, they are 'Yes' in Christ" (1:20).

4. The Response

"Amen" (1:20). The "amen" is our answer to God's "yes." It is an act of faith by which we make the promises our own. When you receive a check from the bank, it is of no value until you first write your own name upon the back of it, and thus personally appropriate it to yourself. Then it becomes payable. So every promise of God must be subscribed by you and receive your "amen." It is our privilege to put our name in the promise. The pronouns "my" and "me" have a high place in the experience of faith and deeper Christian life.

This "amen" is also through Jesus Christ: "through him the 'Amen' is spoken" (1:20). It is He who prompts and sustains and inspires our faith. We can never appropriate the promises ourselves, but must take Him to work in us the effectual prayer and the faith which takes all that He is waiting to give. Not only does He give us His precious blood and His perfect righteousness, but His own faith too, and in Him we are able to claim all the fullness of His grace.

5. The Glory of God

Our appropriating the promises redounds to the glory of God, and we honor Him most, not by showing Him how much we can do, but by showing how much He can do in us and for us. Every time we claim one of His promises, we illustrate to the heavenly powers as well as the world around us the resources and sufficiency of our God, and we shed more glory upon His name and the victorious work of His dear Son, the Lord Jesus Christ.

God wants us to be living witnesses, proving to the world not only His almightiness but His dependableness, so that as others see what He has become to us, they will learn to trust Him too.

GOD'S GRACE

The apostle next proceeds to show the stability of God's grace and gracious work in the hearts of His people.

1. Its Stability

"Now it is God who makes both us and you stand firm in Christ" (1:21). The salvation He offers us is not a state of probation, but an everlasting insurance. "I give them eternal life, and they shall never perish; no one can snatch them out of my hand" (John 10:28). "He who began a good work in you will carry it on to completion until the day of Christ Jesus" (Philippians 1:6). Therefore He purposes not only to forgive our past transgressions, but to establish us by working out in our inmost being all the fullness of His grace.

The process of establishing includes all the provisions of His Holy Spirit and all the deep experiences of trial, temptation and victory through which He calls us to pass and which He has planned for each one of us according to our special conditions and needs for the purpose of strengthening, establishing and settling us.

2. Spiritual Power

"He anointed us" (2 Corinthians 1:21). This includes the baptism of the Holy Spirit. This is the first step in establishing us: to put into us His own Spirit and thus supply us with the resources of His power and grace in spite of all our weaknesses, temptation and failures. Not only does He save us from the curse of sin, but He commits all the resources of His infinite grace to see us through to the glorious end.

Some years ago, a millionaire bought a large tract of land in the neighborhood of a village. For some years the land remained unimproved and the value of the real estate in the neighborhood hung in the balance. Was he simply speculating and holding it for the future, or was he going to make great improvements, or would he someday sell it again? Nothing was certain. But one summer gangs of workmen moved upon the place; engineers, masons, carpenters, painters and landscape gardeners began the process of transformation. A splendid mansion rose from the highest point of land; roads were laid out, trees and flowers crowned every picturesque approach, and at last his own family moved into the splendid villa, and it was known that he had made it his home. Then, indeed, was its value assured, and all the property in the vicinity rose in sympathy to the highest point. He had committed his fortunes and family to this transaction.

Something like this happens when God moves into a human heart and the Holy Spirit anoints us and brings the living Christ to dwell within us and make our heart His home. Henceforth we are no longer the victims of every wind that blows nor at the mercy of our own capricious and feeble purposes, but we are established, strengthened and divinely enabled and we know that "he who began a good work in you will carry it on to completion until the day of Christ Jesus" (Philippians 1:6).

3. Security

"He . . . set his seal of ownership on us" (2 Corinthians 1:21–22). The seal is the mark of authenticity and authority. And so when the Holy Spirit seals us, He makes it certain that we belong to God, and He also makes it certain to us that God's grace in all its fullness belongs to us. Not only so, the seal brings the mark of reality. You can feel its sharp imprint; you can see the image which it cuts into the sensitive wax. It is something tangible and real. It speaks to every sense.

So the Holy Spirit makes divine things real. He puts an edge on our spiritual consciousness. He makes vivid to us words that had been before but sounds. He wakes up in us spiritual senses that take hold of God just as truly as the ear takes hold of music and the sense of smell of sweet perfume. Divine things become intensely actual, and Christ a living, bright Reality.

Once more, the seal reproduces the image and brings actual resemblance. So the Holy Spirit gives to the heart into which He comes the very likeness of Jesus Christ, conforms us to the image of God and reflects in us the very spirit and qualities of our blessed Savior, reliving His own life in the disciple and gradually forming us to His will and character in everything.

All this is intensely real. The salvation which brings such results is not a dream, a fiction, an uncertainty. The God who does such things is a God on whom we can depend, and the salvation that fulfills such expectations is indeed a blessing that satisfies.

4. Continuance and Permanence

There is one thing more required to complete this picture of security, and that is the future. How long will it last? The answer is, "He . . . put his Spirit in our hearts" (1:21–22). This word "earnest" (1:22, KJV) means a pledge of the future; nay, more, the very germ and embryo of that future already planted in our hearts. The Holy Spirit in the believer is to his future inheritance what the bulb you planted last autumn is to the glorious blossoms of the Easter lily or the little dry seed to the golden harvests of the summer. The "earnest" is the sample, as well as the guarantee, of the full harvest; the handful of soil, telling us that all the broad acres are yet to be ours.

This has both a spiritual and a physical side. Our spiritual life now is the "earnest" and pledge of all that heaven will be to our soul. But there is another touch of grace which the Spirit brings to our body when He heals and quickens our suffering frame. This is the pledge of that physical resurrection which by and by is to come to all our mortal frame and lead us into the glorious life of the age to come. All this we anticipate here and now, and by the earnest we know that we shall not be disappointed in the larger unfolding.

What has the world to offer in comparison with such a glorious assurance? Robert Burns wrote of earthly pleasures which he had tasted in all their sweetness:

> Our pleasures are like poppies spread;
> We snatch the flower, the bloom has fled;
> Or like the snowflake on the river
> A moment seen, then gone forever;
> Or like the Borealis' blaze,
> Which mocks our vision as we gaze;
> Or like the rainbow's glorious form
> Evanishing amid the storm.

In contrast with this, how inspiring the hope expressed in Dean Alford's beautiful hymn:

> My bark is wafted to the strand
>   By breath divine;
> And on the helm there rests a hand
>   Mightier than mine;
> One who has known in storms to sail
>   I have on board;
> Above the raging of the gale
>   I hear my Lord;
> Safe to the land, safe to the land
>   The end is this,
> And then with Him go hand in hand
>   Far into bliss.

Was it ever better told than when the little child described the story of Enoch? "Enoch used to walk with God every day. One day they took a longer walk than usual, and at the end God said to Enoch, 'You are far from home; just come in and stay,' and Enoch went in and stayed."

Is not such a God dependable? Is not such a salvation worth more than all this world can offer? Is not such a hope like an anchor, sure and steadfast? God help us to receive it, to prove it to the uttermost, and then to commend it to all around us.

CHAPTER 3

VICTORY

But thanks be to God, who always leads us in triumphal procession in Christ and through us spreads everywhere the fragrance of the knowledge of him. For we are to God the aroma of Christ among those who are being saved and those who are perishing. To the one we are the smell of death; to the other, the fragrance of life. (2 Corinthians 2:14–16)

This is Paul's testimony concerning his victory in the conflicts of life and especially in the severe ordeal through which he was then passing. In the pronoun "us" he takes us into partnership with his victory and reminds us that we may go forth into every battle with the prestige of assured triumph and the victorious battle cry, "Thanks be to God, who always leads us in triumphal procession in Christ" (2:14).

VICTORY OVER SORROW

He had a great sorrow. It was so severe that it unfitted him for his work. "When I went to Troas," he says, "to preach the gospel of Christ and found that the Lord had opened a door for me, I still had no peace of mind" (2:12–13). Speaking of the same experience again, in chapter 7:5, he tells us that even after he left Troas and came into Macedonia, he was still utterly discouraged and distracted: "This body of ours had no rest, but we were harassed at every turn—conflicts on the outside, fears within."

His trouble was caused by others and most of it by the sins of others. How many of our troubles come from the same source. How many fathers, mothers and wives are brokenhearted because of the wrongdoing of loved ones. But there is victory even for this. The Apostle could say, "Thanks be to God, who always leads us in triumphal procession" (2:14). We must not give way to discouragement even when everything and every person may seem to fail us. How often we hear people say, "I am utterly discouraged, I do not care to live, I do not feel like trying any more." Someone has died, or someone has failed you, and all the light and hope have gone from life. This is cowardly and wrong; God still lives and reigns. Take heart and trust in Him, and out of this dark cloud will come, by and by, perhaps the brightest blessings of your life. Let us never give way to circumstances. The most unfavorable conditions often are God's very way of developing some higher quality in us.

It is said that a gentleman stood watching a lot of young athletes at a game of baseball. He himself was crippled and almost helpless, and as he watched their free and agile movements his face mantled with a look of grim and bitter agony. A friend tapped him on the shoulder and quietly said, "I suppose you were thinking just now that you would like to be as those young fellows, free and strong, and that you were realizing how different it all was." "Yes," said he, "that was just what I was thinking." "Well," said his friend, "my brother, I was just thinking that God had let all this trouble come to you to do you good and make a man out of you." It was a new thought, and as he went away, it clung to him. Was there, then, some higher purpose in this terrible disappointment? And as he thought, he began to cultivate and develop the other qualities of mind and character, until his life began to develop in new directions and new purposes and plans were formed. Soon the man, whose life had seemed to be a failure, became not only successful but wonderfully useful in inventing and developing new methods for the relief of the suffering, and for the restoration of the crippled and infirm. It did indeed become true that the trouble which seemed at one time to crush him really became in the hands of God the means of lifting him to a new manhood and usefulness.

Christ has redeemed us from sorrow as well as sin and we must not let our trials conquer us; rather let them challenge us to higher manhood and more victorious faith.

VICTORY OVER HIS OWN HEART

Before we can have victory over circumstances we must be ourselves subdued. The verb employed here is susceptible of two translations. It means either in a passive sense, "Thanks be unto God who always leads us in triumph," or in an active sense, "Thanks be unto God who always causes us to triumph."

The first sense is supported by very high authority and undoubtedly is included with the other. There seems no good reason why we should not take both. God first leads us in triumph Himself and then "He causes us to triumph." But no man can be victor over others until he has been a self-conqueror. "Better . . . a man who controls his temper than one who takes a city" (Proverbs 16:32).

The apostle tells us in this chapter of his glorious victory over himself. He had been wronged and grieved by the conduct of the Corinthians; some of them had grossly sinned and even gloried in it and defied his authority and discipline, and others had supported them in it. But instead of the least resentment we find nothing in the apostle's spirit but the sweetest gentleness, self-restraint and forgiveness. He tells them about his grief and his tears; there is no resentment but only sorrow. There is no weakness in condoning evil; he has dealt with the sin with utmost faithfulness and now he is ready to deal with the sinner with equal tenderness. It is most touching to see his anxiety lest the erring one should be unduly discouraged and "overwhelmed by excessive sorrow" (2 Corinthians 2:7). And so he begs them to confirm their love unto him and offer him the forgiveness of Paul as well as the Savior's.

It is a great blessing to be able to forgive and forget. Unforgiveness is one of the unpardonable sins, and when the enemy succeeds in causing someone to do you wrong, the sting which he inserts in your heart—in your hate and vindictiveness—is far more poisonous than the outward blow by which he sought to do you wrong.

There is no heart battle harder than a battle with our sensitiveness and our sense of wrong. Many of us have found it the very turning point of life. Some cruel wrong, some injury that the natural heart could never forgive, has rankled there until we felt we should lose our souls if we did not gain the victory. But mere human effort is unavailing here, and the heart gives up the struggle with a sense of utter helplessness and despair. But this is just where His grace overcomes and where the love of Jesus in us can accomplish what our love and our self-control never could. God has sometimes to let such tests come to us to show us our helplessness and bring us to His feet.

There is no picture more sublime than that of a strong nature breaking down and acknowledging its fault and rising superior to its sensitiveness and pride in the spirit of true forgiveness and love. It is said of Professor Blackie of Edinburgh, that on one occasion he ordered his students to put up their right hands with their exercise books. One young man put up his left hand; the professor repeated the order in a stern voice, addressing him, but still he held up his left hand. Then, calling him by name, he once more repeated his demand in tones of anger. Then the lad slowly lifted up the stump of an amputated arm and meekly said, "Sir, I have no right hand." A storm of hisses burst from the students which even the authority of the professor could not restrain. But suddenly they all beheld his dignified form swiftly passing down the aisle and bending over the Scotch lad, and then his arm was around his neck and in tender tones he said, "Forgive me, lad, I was over rough; forgive me, I did not know," and then there burst from those students a storm of cheers just as emphatic as the former expression of their displeasure. Never was their teacher more noble than in that attitude of humility and self-abnegation.

VICTORY OVER HIS ENEMIES

"When a man's ways are pleasing to the LORD,/ he makes even his enemies live at peace with him" (Proverbs 16:7). God's providence in external things keeps pace with the provisions of His Holy Spirit in our interior life. The apostle having himself taken the right position toward his enemies, the Lord now undertakes for him and makes all things right respecting his own interests and authority. The offending one is brought to repentance and the church to harmony and loyalty. The best way to reach our adversaries is by way of the throne. Vainly we may struggle to make things right; let us but be right ourselves, and then the hand of God will move upon all others and subdue all things unto Himself.

I once knew a brother minister who had been unkindly treated by some members of his flock and had fallen into a spirit of deep resentment. His own heart became clouded and separated from God, and he fell into a spirit of bitterness that almost threatened the salvation of his soul. Much prayer was offered for him. At length the answer came in a most remarkable way. First, there fell upon him a spirit of prayer for his bitter enemies, and he found himself irresistibly pouring out his heart to God for them. Then he was prompted by a deep desire to return to his people, whom he had left for a time under a sense of injury. As he finished his morning service, the first persons to greet him were the two brethren that had so grievously wronged him. To his surprise they hastened forward with the most cordial welcome, and the reconciliation that followed was deep and lasting and evident to all concerned as the work of the Holy Spirit. The moment his own heart had gotten right, God had made all other things right.

It is ever so. As it is the Lamb in the midst of the throne that is victorious over all His enemies, so it is the Spirit of the Lamb in us that conquers Satan and all his emissaries. Let us be less concerned about people and things, and only seek to be right ourselves, and then we can safely trust our interests, our reputation, our enemies with Him who has said, "I will give men in exchange for you,/ and people in exchange for your life" (Isaiah 43:4).

VICTORY OVER THE ERRING ONE

The most beautiful thing about the apostle's spirit had been his deep concern for the offender. Now his joy was complete in his repentance and restoration, and he hastened in the most tender spirit to beseech them to restore him and confirm their love to him lest in the reaction his distress of mind might become extreme and Satan take advantage of his depression to drive him to despair.

There is no finer triumph over those that wrong us than to be made a blessing to them. There is no more touching picture in the apostolic story than that suggested by the opening verse of the first Epistle of Paul to the Corinthians compared with the story of his visit to Corinth, as given in the Acts of the Apostles. A wicked Jewish mob had brought accusations against him and dragged him before the Roman magistrate, Gallio. The leader of this mob was Sosthenes, described as "the synagogue ruler" (Acts 18:17). The attack failed because Gallio refused to entertain the charges and dismissed them as a petty case of Jewish spite. Then the crowd waiting outside fell upon Sosthenes and his people and abused and beat them. No doubt Paul looked on with deep sympathy and sorrow, but the striking part of it is that in the first verse of the first epistle to the Corinthians Paul associated Sosthenes with him as a fellow worker, speaking of him in somewhat emphatic terms as "our brother" (1 Corinthians 1:1). It looks as if Sosthenes had been meanwhile converted and become one of the apostle's fellow laborers. And now Paul had the glorious revenge of blessing and saving the man that had been his bitterest foe and uniting him himself in his first message to this very church in Corinth.

If we could only see over the heads of our enemies and accusers the wicked one urging them on and controlling their actions, our resentment would give place to deep compassion and earnest prayer that God would save them from his power and from the sad and fearful fate awaiting them when they wake to find that they have been led captive by him at his will.

VICTORY OVER SATAN

"In order that Satan might not outwit us. For we are not unaware of his schemes" (2 Corinthians 2:11). The apostle only saw two forces, the power of the devil on the one hand and the person and honor of the Lord Jesus on the other; and, in comparison with these two opposing forces, the injustice of his enemies and his own personal wrongs all sank into insignificance.

It is Satan that inspires every case of spiritual declension, every separation of friends and flocks, every ecclesiastical controversy, every mutual injury and resentment, and when we yield to vindictiveness or impatience, we are but pleasing him and playing into his hands. His deep design was to destroy the soul that he had led astray, and his most powerful weapon was discouragement and despair. If he could only lead this man to give up hope and to consider himself rejected and lost, then his point would have been gained. The apostle therefore was deeply concerned lest "he . . . be overwhelmed by excessive sorrow" (2:7), and thus Satan gain the advantage over him.

The great adversary loves to hide his hand and work in disguise. He tries to make people prominent in our thoughts and judgments, so that in their misconduct we shall overlook the greater plotter who simply uses them as pawns on the great chessboard. Let us recognize him and we shall always find that he cannot bear the light of exposure, and the moment we see his hand our victory is assured.

VICTORY FOR GOD

This triumph was not a selfish one. He was representing his Lord, and the spirit that he was manifesting to others was just an exhibition and revelation to the world of the Spirit of Jesus Christ. Therefore he says, "We are . . . the aroma of Christ" (2:15). His love, His patience, His gentleness, His forgiveness were just making the Spirit of his Master more real to men. That is why God has placed us here to represent our Lord. And just as Christ's gentleness and sweetness were revealed by the anguish of the garden and the cross, so God has to bruise us in order to bring forth from our lives the holy fragrance of divine love and patience. It has been forcibly said that all things must be crushed before they can give out their highest qualities. The most exquisite violins are not whole violins but instruments that have been broken and then repaired, and the fracture has left a fine touch of sweetness and sadness in the tone that could not otherwise have been brought out. This has been finely suggested by these exquisite lines:

> They tell us we must bruise
>   The rose's leaf,
> Ere we can keep and use
>   Its fragrance brief.
>
> They tell us we must break
>   The skylark's heart,
> Ere her caged song will make
>   The silence start.
>
> And it is always so
>   With precious things;
> They must be bruised and go
>   With broken wings.

This, then, dear Christian reader, is the explanation of the trials of your life. Are you getting out of them the sweetness and fragrance which God meant them to breathe for Him to men?

VICTORY EVEN WHEN MEN PERISH

"We are . . . the aroma of Christ among those who are being saved and those who are perishing" (2:15).

A good deed is not lost even when it fails to benefit the person intended. Its sweet fragrance comes back to God, and its memory will linger with the erring one even though it failed to save. God wants us to leave upon the minds of men the sweet eternal recollection of divine love. Not in fiery anger will He at last condemn them, but doubtless with a look of pity and a word of compassion will He bid them depart and feel, as they do, that the fault was all their own; that God was never anything but love to them, and that their sin and fault were without excuse. Therefore, God would have us represent Him in the spirit of sweetness and tenderness even to those whom we fail to save.

THE PRESTIGE OF VICTORY

The apostle's advantage implies not merely that he has won a triumph in his present trial, but that God is always causing him to triumph, and that he is going into every conflict with the confidence of victory. There is a strange power in prestige. There are armies that never look for defeat; there are trumpeters that never learn to sound a retreat; there are soldiers that always expect to overcome. Such soldiers, Christians should ever be. Our blessed Lord has overcome for us, and He has promised us that we shall be more than conquerors, too. His victory assures ours, and He bids us to go into every trial expecting to come off victorious. Are we doing so? Is our life one of victory, or are we letting circumstances, discouragements, people and things bear us down and rob us of our immortal crown? This is very foolish and very sinful.

If anyone who reads these lines has been yielding to discouragement, may God bid you rise and put on the garments of praise and take up the shout of victory.

It is said that Norman McLeod when a lad was greatly discouraged one day, and said to his mother that he wished he had never been born. He had the good fortune to have a Scotch mother, who had little sympathy to spare for such people, and she quietly turned to him and said, "Why, Norman, you are born, and it seems to me the thing for you to do is to find out why you were born and get to work as soon as you can to accomplish the purpose for which God brought you into existence." The rebuke went home, and the discouraged boy rose up and went forth to live a life of glorious manhood and worldwide blessing to his fellow men.

Will we do likewise? Christ has purchased our triumph at great cost. Let us go forth in His strength to meet every adversary as a conquered foe, and to shout our watchword all the way to the gates of glory, "Thanks be to God, who always leads us in triumphal procession in Christ" (2:14).

CHAPTER 4

PAUL'S TESTIMONY ABOUT HIS MINISTRY

Therefore, since through God's mercy we have this ministry, we do not lose heart. Rather, we have renounced secret and shameful ways; we do not use deception, nor do we distort the word of God. On the contrary, by setting forth the truth plainly we commend ourselves to every man's conscience in the sight of God. And even if our gospel is veiled, it is veiled to those who are perishing. (2 Corinthians 4:1–3)

There is nothing more delicate and difficult, even for the most sensitive and sanctified Christian, than to speak of his own work. The writer has never forgotten the impression produced upon him when first listening to George Muller as he told the story of the Lord's dealings with him. There was no reserve; there was no false modesty; there was no withholding of any important fact or testimony; but there was absolutely no self-consciousness, no shadow of vainglory, no trace of his own shadow. One would think in listening to him that he was telling of the work of some other servant of the Lord. He had that perfect humility that does not think meanly of itself, but simply does not think of itself at all.

We have a fine example of the apostle's spirit in his testimony in the present chapter about his ministry.

HIS CREDENTIALS

"Are we beginning to commend ourselves again?" he asks. "Or do we need, like some people, letters of recommendation to you or from you? You yourselves are our letter, written on our hearts, known and read by everybody. You show that you are a letter from Christ, the result of our ministry, written not with ink but with the Spirit of the living God, not on tablets of stone but on tablets of human hearts" (3:1–3).

His credentials are the lives that have been transformed through his ministry by the power of the Holy Spirit. What better monument can any Christian worker desire? It is said of the famous Sir Christopher Wren that he was rescued as a foundling child on the very site of that glorious St. Paul's cathedral that he afterwards built in the city of London. At the close of an honored life his dust was buried beneath its foundations, and by his own directions a plain slab covered his tomb with the simple inscription on it, "If you seek my monument, look around you." That splendid building was his sufficient monument. His work was the memorial of his life. Are we transcribing ourselves, or, better, our Master's image on the hearts and lives of men? Paul did not mean that he despised letters of introduction. They possess a certain value, and we all need to be prudent in guarding against impostors. But he had something better. His work was his highest witness. Can we say it is ours? True character will always discover itself to the world, like a spice ship sailing into the harbor, by the fragrance it diffuses all around it.

It is said that a missionary was sent to an obscure Hindu village to receive a score of new converts into the mission, of whom the report had come that they had all become true Christians. As one by one they were examined, the missionary was delighted with their knowledge and experience, and they were all accepted. At last there came a poor, deformed and stammering fellow, who seemed to have little knowledge or character, and the missionary was about to reject him when the natives all exclaimed, "Why that is the man from whom we learned all we know of Jesus. It is he who brought us to Christ, and how can you accept us and reject him?" Truly he needed no letters of commendation after that. They were living epistles witnessing to his work and his worth. It is impossible that we can possess true spiritual qualities without impressing our own influence upon other lives. "By their fruit you will recognize them" (Matthew 7:20). "Others . . . produce a crop—thirty, sixty or even a hundred times what was sown" (Mark 4:20). Let us apply the lesson faithfully and searchingly to our influence in our families, in our Sunday school classes, in our social relations, in our work for God.

> There needs not for such the love-written record,
>   The name and the monument graven on stone;
> The things we have lived for—let these be our glory,
>   And we be remembered by what we have done.

THE SOURCE OF HIS POWER

"Not that we are competent in ourselves to claim anything for ourselves, but our competence comes from God. He has made us competent as ministers of a new covenant" (2 Corinthians 3:5–6). The use of "competence" used in this passage expresses the whole volume of testimony and experience—insufficiency, all sufficiency and efficiency. First he had to realize his own insufficiency. This is where every Christian worker must begin, and this is where he must stay, realizing to the end of the chapter that his strength is all imparted and divine.

But the mere sense of insufficiency will discourage and crush. And so we must move on and learn to say, "Our competence comes from God" (3:5). We must see in the Lord Jesus our infinite divine resources in the gifts and graces of the Holy Spirit, and all the equipment we need in every kind of ministry. Then it is false modesty to say we are no good; we have but one talent, and therefore it is not worth trying to use it. True humility and faith will finish the apostle's climax. "He has made us competent as ministers of a new covenant" (3:6).

But, even then, we must still remember that our efficiency is not our own, but must be continually drawn from the ever-present Christ by a life of dependence and faith. How exquisitely true are the superb lines:

> My hands were strong in fancied strength,
>   But not in power divine;
> And bold to take up tasks at length,
>   That were not His but mine.
> The Master came and touched my hands;
>   And might was in His own;
> But mine, since then, have powerless been,
>   Save His are laid thereon.
> And it is only thus, said He,
> That I can work My works in thee.

THE GLORY OF HIS MINISTRY

In the remaining verses of this chapter he contrasts the gospel with the old dispensation and shows its incomparable superiority.

1. The one is the letter; the other is the Spirit.

The law is a mere set of tasks and penances which affect only the outward forms of life. The gospel reaches the inner heart of things and purifies the spirit, the heart and all the fountains of life.

2. The one is a ministry of death; the other of life.

The law can only condemn; the gospel can quicken. The law can tell us what we are not to do; but the gospel imparts the power to do things.

3. The one is the ministry of condemnation; the other of righteousness.

The law shows us where we are wrong, but cannot make us right. It is the mirror that reveals to us the defilement upon our face, but as has been well said, no man would think of trying to wash his face in a mirror.

4. The law was transient; the gospel is permanent and abiding.

It was but a parenthesis in the revelation of God's plan, like the clouds that gathered round the brow of Sinai and then passed away and left the sunshine of heaven to gather upon its head. When we accept the gospel we feel by a deep intuition that we have reached our true resting place and we need seek no further for God and truth and heaven.

5. The law is a mere mechanical and external attempt to reform conduct and cultivate character.

The gospel is a vital process by which we are transformed through the vision of Jesus Christ into His own image by the Holy Spirit. This is brought out in a most beautiful figure in the last verse of the chapter. "And we, who with unveiled faces all reflect the Lord's glory, are being transformed into his likeness with ever-increasing glory, which comes from the Lord, who is the Spirit" (3:18).

The figure reminds us of the difference between the old and the new process of engraving. Our cuts used to be slowly carved by hand on blocks of wood, and were tedious and expensive. A few years ago the process of photo-engraving was discovered by which, in a moment, the image was transferred to a metal plate, and then in a few minutes a penetrating acid cut away the metal and left only the lines of the picture, thus literally engraving in the solid metal by light and chemical action. It is thus that God paints His pictures; not by a clumsy process of our poor striving, but by the flashlight of the Holy Spirit and a vision of the face of Jesus Christ, transferring the picture instantly, like the photograph on the film, to our heart and conforming us to His likeness. No wonder Paul gloried in such a gospel. He felt that a great secret had been revealed to him for lifting human lives into glorious transformations. "The mystery," he said, "that has been kept hidden for ages and generations, but is now disclosed to the saints. . . . which is Christ in you, the hope of glory" (Colossians 1:26–27).

When that mystery was first revealed to some of us we felt we must go and tell everybody we had ever known, and we expected them at once to bow to its glorious light and accept its message. Dear reader, have you looked upon that Face until its light has shone back into your own, and you have been "transformed into his likeness with ever-increasing glory, which comes from the Lord, who is the Spirit" (2 Corinthians 3:18)?

Two very fine figures begin and end this chapter. The first is the figure of the epistle, and the second the figure of the photograph. The Christian is described first as a book, and secondly, as an illustrated book. Each of us is a volume telling forth the story of Jesus, and on every page His face should shine so that the world shall not see us, but Him, and shall so see Him in us that each shall want to make the experience his own.

THE SIMPLICITY OF HIS MINISTRY

"Seeing, then, that we have such hope, we use great plainness of speech" (3:12, KJV). The law was dim and men saw "a poor reflection as in a mirror" (1 Corinthians 13:12). The gospel is so plain that "a herald may run with it" (Habakkuk 2:2). The true minister will always be characterized by great simplicity, and make it his object so to preach that every message shall reach the lowest understanding among his hearers and be plain enough to make Christ real and Christ possible to every man.

How solemn the reproof in the story of the famous painter, who had invited a friend to see the unveiling of one of his canvases containing a painting of the First Communion Service. The eyes of the visitor were fastened on the brilliant colors, and his first exclamation was, "What beautiful cups!" But the countenance of the artist fell. He saw that his work had been a failure. He had failed to make Christ the center of the picture, and he drew his brush across the canvas and covered it up, and then started anew and painted it over again. How much of our preaching is just like these beautiful cups—everything in it but the Savior.

THE FAITHFULNESS OF HIS MINISTRY

"Rather, we have renounced secret and shameful ways; we do not use deception, nor do we distort the word of God. On the contrary, by setting forth the truth plainly we commend ourselves to every man's conscience in the sight of God" (2 Corinthians 4:2.) What a picture of an earnest, conscientious, heart-searching ministry that deals with human souls, as one which realizes that God is standing at our shoulder and eternity is just before us. All true soul-winners are characterized by this direct and holy earnestness. The writer recalls one fearful night when he had been so pressed by the Holy Spirit to call upon a certain ungodly man, of wide influence and great indifference, and speak to him about his soul. He tried to shake off the impression, but could not, and, late at night, in a howling blizzard, he rang the bell and asked to see him. The man was surprised at such a call at that hour, and still more surprised when he heard the message that brought him. He quite broke down and yielded to God, and ere they parted said, "To think that you should come this wild and stormy night to seek my soul, while I have lived in this world for nearly 70 years and never thought of it myself." The very directness of the appeal seemed to reach his conscience as no ordinary method perhaps would have done.

The story is told of Mr. Moody that he was requested by a Christian wife to go and talk with her husband, who was a vaunting infidel. Mr. Moody hesitated because the man had gloried in the fact that he had silenced many such messengers before. But he prayed over it and in his own blunt way made up his mind to go. As he passed into the inner office the clerks smiled to think of the humiliation with which he would soon come out. He took the hand of the gentleman, which was offered with a cynical smile, and said, "Mr. Blank, I have been asked to come and talk with you about your soul. Now there is no use of my talking about the Bible to a man who knows a hundred times as much as I do, but I just want to say this, that when you get converted to God please let me know it. Good morning." The man was thunderstruck, and Mr. Moody walked out without being greeted with the usual contemptuous smiles from the long row of desks. Sure enough, the day came when through the power of prayer that proud heart broke down. Two nights in succession the rich man sneaked off to a prayer meeting and slipped back into his home and went to bed without telling his wife where he had been. But the third night he confessed to her that he had given his heart to God, and the very first thing that he did was to send a telegram to Moody.

Let us bring men face to face with God. Let us remember that we speak with the authority of divine ambassadors. Let us not use our worthless intellects trying to gild the sunshine, but let us bring them into immediate dealing with their Maker, their Judge and their Savior, and leave them there, commending ourselves to every man's conscience in the sight of God.

There is implied here the idea of great faithfulness and deep concern for the souls of men. Paul was always seeking for souls. Even before King Agrippa he could not help but plead, "I pray God that not only you but all who are listening to me today may become what I am, except for these chains" (Acts 26:29). Who can measure the deep significance of that solemn appeal, "I could wish that I myself were cursed and cut off from Christ for the sake of . . . those of my own race" (Romans 9:3)?

Do you know any such earnest travailing for the souls of men? Perhaps that is why some very dear to you are yet unsaved.

The incident was related recently in New England of a young lady that had somewhat suddenly died, and a Christian friend who was deeply attached to her was unspeakably concerned about her soul. On the day of her funeral he sought out her minister and asked him if he could tell him whether she was saved. The minister confessed with a good deal of pain that just three weeks before he had been very strongly impressed to speak to her about her soul, but he had allowed something to deter his mind from the purpose and now he could not tell. He then sought out her Sunday school teacher and asked her the same question. The young lady said with deep emotion, "Just two weeks ago I felt strangely and strongly impressed to talk to her about her personal salvation, and I allowed myself to be diverted from it, and, alas, I cannot tell whether she is saved or not." At last he sought her mother and asked her. The mother quite broke down as she confessed that just one week previous she, too, had felt some strong impression to talk to her daughter about deciding for God, but shame and sensitiveness had kept her silent; "and now, alas," she said, "it is too late, and I know not whether she is lost or saved."

Such solemn lessons need no application. Let them speak to each of our hearts and arouse us to holier earnestness and more conscientious faithfulness in dealing with the souls of men.

HINDRANCES TO HIS MINISTRY

"But if our gospel be hid, it is hid to them that are lost" (2 Corinthians 4:3, KJV). A better translation of this remarkable passage is, "it is hid by the things that perish." The word "lost" means perish, and the preposition "to" in the Greek has also the force of "by." The sentence, therefore, would read, "If our gospel be hid it is hid by the perishing things of earth." The idea is that Satan weaves a beautiful blindfold and holds it before our eyes to keep us from seeing "the light of the gospel of the glory of Christ" (4:4).

I will never forget the first impression given to me in my boyhood of an execution. I did not witness it, but the description was repeated to me by one who had. He said the unfortunate man was blindfolded and then led along the scaffold, not seeing where he went, until suddenly the fearful drop fell, and, without a moment's warning, the man was hurled into eternity. What a picture of the way the devil is blindfolding men and then taking from beneath their feet the sands of time, and plunging them into ruin and despair. Oh, will we learn the lesson which our message brings not only for the minister of the gospel, but for the hearer of the gospel, too, and come "with unveiled faces" (3:18) to the light of His love and the grace that will so gladly save us if we will only allow it.

CHAPTER 5

PAUL'S TESTIMONY CONCERNING SUPERNATURAL LIFE FOR THE BODY

For we who are alive are always being given over to death for Jesus' sake, so that his life may be revealed in our mortal body. (2 Corinthians 4:11)

Unlike many false religions, Christianity does not depreciate or degrade the human body. The very paragon of the first creation, God has no less dignified it in the new creation. His own Son did not deem it beneath Him to become incarnate in our mortal frame, and in that body He has been resurrected and glorified as the Head and Pattern of our future life. The provisions of Christ's redemption include the body as well as the soul and spirit.

While it is only the steed that carries the traveler across the desert journey of life, yet the steed is most necessary to the traveler, and the failure of the one may involve the destruction of the other. Christ and His apostles, therefore, recognized most distinctly the place of our physical life in the scheme of redemption, and both by their teaching and example they leave us in no doubt about God's provision for our physical healing and the strength that we need in these earthen vessels to uphold us until our work is done.

Man has always been seeking some Fountain of Youth, some Elixir of Life from which he might draw supernatural supplies of strength for his decaying powers. But all these have failed, and from age to age still

> Our hearts, like muffled drums, are beating
> Funeral marches to the grave.

But Paul must have discovered some new and divine secret of superior strength or he never could have told that story that we have already read in chapter 1:8, of the deliverance that came to him in Asia when he was "under great pressure, far beyond our ability to endure, so that we despaired even of life." The story of his life is full of hardship, privation, exposure and suffering sufficient to have worn out a dozen lives.

The man who could give this catalogue, "I have . . . been in prison more frequently, been flogged more severely, and been exposed to death again and again. Five times I received . . . the forty lashes minus one. Three times I was beaten with rods, once I was stoned, three times I was shipwrecked, I spent a night and a day in the open sea" (11:23–25), and yet live to a good old age in the full vigor of unwearied work and still have strength enough to have gone on indefinitely had not his noble life been suddenly closed by martyrdom. Such a man must have had unwonted sources of physical strength and endurance, and his physical life was as much a miracle as his spiritual victories and missionary achievements. In this fourth chapter of Second Corinthians he tells us the secret of his strength. Unlike Samson of old, from whom this secret had to be wrung by treachery, Paul glories in the telling of it, for it is an open secret for every brother of his suffering race.

THE PRINCIPLE

"But we have this treasure in jars of clay to show that this all-surpassing power is from God and not from us" (4:7). He means that the strength imparted to him is not in the form of bone and brawn or any material conditions which could appeal to our outward senses. It is not that his body was exceptionally robust, for, indeed, it remained frail to the end; but rather that a principle of vitality was imparted to it, so that the paradox was literally true, "when I am weak, then I am strong" (12:10).

We know that even in the natural world many elements that are extremely common and simple become the channels of tremendous forces. Radium comes from one of the commonest material elements, pitchblende, which might perhaps be called a kind of tar. The magnet which lifts the heaviest bodies, does not derive its strength from its material weight or form, but from a hidden force that pulsates within the cold clay and lifts the most massive weights as though by celestial fingers. In the arsenal at Woolwich, you can see these magnets lifting vast projectiles and pieces of ordnance as though they were toys.

The electric current which carries our trains and our cars and moves our factories does not need massive iron girders to convey it, but runs along a little wire which a child might bend. The power is not in the material, but in the invisible current behind it. The human body itself does not derive its strength from mere structural form. A giant seven feet high, weighing 300 pounds, falls like a mass of stone if life becomes extinct and requires several men to carry him; but animated by the principle of life, he can not only carry his own weight, but as much more besides.

Now, in the spiritual realm there are forces far stronger than electricity, magnetism or the vital force, and what the apostle means is that such a force has been brought into touch with his weak body; and while he still remains weak in himself, he has found back of him and within him a new source of strength which makes him equal to every pressure. It is the "treasure" in "jars of clay," and it proves to the world that the "all-surpassing power is from God and not from us."

THE SECRET OF HIS PHYSICAL LIFE

He tells us in plain terms just what this power is. It is not an electric current; it is not the power of mind or will as Christian Science would teach us; but it is the power of a divine Person, the life of another added to his own, "Jesus' . . . life . . . in our mortal body" (4:11). Truly, this is a mystery, how one life can be added to another, and doubtless none will comprehend it unless they have in some measure experienced it. But a moment's reflection will show us how reasonable it is. The Lord Jesus Christ is a living Being in human form. They saw Him rise from earth to heaven with all the organs and members of a literal body, and yet with such supernal power in that body that He could spurn the fetters of earth and the forces of gravitation and rise without an effort into space. Now, He is still living in that glorified humanity somewhere in the center of this universe, and from that exalted place He is still in touch with His people here. The Holy Spirit is the mighty Medium who conveys to us His power and life, the divine Engineer, if we may use the figure without irreverence, who makes and maintains the contact between the mighty Dynamo yonder and our weak natures here on earth.

It is not thought strange in our modern scientific progress when men convey the power of Niagara Falls hundreds of miles along electric wires to run machines in distant places. It is not thought strange that the sun, 93,000,000 miles away, can send down its radiating life to quicken the forces of nature and create the verdure, the bloom and the manifold fruitfulness of earth. Why should it be thought strange that Jesus Christ, from the center of the universe, should be able to impart to souls and bodies that are in vital touch with Him, His own overflowing life and make His promise true both in our bodily and spiritual experience, "Because I live, you also will live" (John 14:19)?

If we look at a single scene in the apostle's life, we shall see the operation of this secret. At the gates of Lystra a cruel mob has hurled him beneath a heap of stones and left him for dead after they have done their worst on his mutilated body. But we read in the simple narrative, "But after the disciples had gathered around him, he got up and went back into the city. The next day he and Barnabas left for Derbe" (Acts 14:20). What was the strange power that raised him up from seeming martyrdom? The answer is the simple, striking expression of our text: "Jesus' . . . life" (2 Corinthians 4:11). Paul's life had been beaten out but there was just enough left, a single spark, to form the point of contact with that other life that could not be beaten out, the life of his indwelling Lord; and as that life thrilled through his paralyzed powers, he rose up in new divine strength and quietly went forward in his work.

George Whitefield has left us a similar testimony of a day when he was supposed to be dying some miles from Newburyport while the congregation there was praying in tearful intercession that God would restore his life. Suddenly, he tells us, a strange new life began to breathe through him and pass through his frame, gradually rising from his extremities until it reached his heart and lungs and brain, imparting a quiet, peaceful glow of conscious strength and rest. Dispelling all pain and weakness it prompted him to rise and dress, to call his carriage and drive many miles to Newburyport where the church was waiting to hear each moment of his end.

His coming seemed at first almost like an apparition, but when they saw that God had really raised him up and listened to his testimony, the power of God came down once more and multitudes were saved, and for many years the good evangelist continued in the strength of God to preach the gospel and to finish his work.

THE PRESSURE AND TEST THAT FOLLOWED

There is a prevalent idea that the power of God in a human life should lift us above all trials, conflicts and struggles. The fact is, the power of God always brings a conflict and a struggle. One would have thought that on his great missionary journey to Rome, Paul would have been carried by some mighty providence above the power of storms and tempests and enemies. But, on the contrary, it was one long, hard fight with persecuting Jews, with wild tempests, with venomous vipers and all the powers of earth and hell; and at last he was saved, as it seemed, by the narrowest margin and had to swim ashore at Malta on a piece of wreckage and barely escape a watery grave.

Was that like a God of infinite power? Yes, just like Him. And so Paul tells us that when he took the Lord Jesus Christ as the life of his body, a severe conflict immediately came; indeed, a conflict that never ended, a pressure that was persistent, but out of which he always emerged victorious through the strength of Jesus Christ.

The language in which he describes this is most graphic. "We are hard pressed on every side, but not crushed; perplexed, but not in despair; persecuted, but not abandoned; struck down, but not destroyed. We always carry around in our body the death of Jesus, so that the life of Jesus may also be revealed in our body" (4:8–10).

What a ceaseless, strenuous struggle! It is impossible to express in English the forcible language of the original. There are five pictures in succession. In the first, the idea is crowding enemies pressing in from every side, and yet not crushing him because the police of heaven cleared the way just wide enough for him to get through. The literal translation would be, "We are crowded on every side, but not crushed."

The second picture is that of one whose way seems utterly closed and yet he has pressed through; there is light enough to show him the next step. The Revised Version translates it, "perplexed but not unto despair." Rotherham still more literally renders it, "without a way but not without a byway."

The third figure is that of an enemy in hot pursuit while the divine Defender still stands by, and he is not left alone. Again we adopt the fine rendering of Rotherham, "Pursued but not abandoned."

The fourth figure is still more vivid and dramatic. The enemy has overtaken him, has struck him, has knocked him down. But it is not a fatal blow; he is able to rise again. It might be translated, "overthrown but not overcome."

Once more the figure advances, and now it seems to be even death itself: "We always carry around in our body the death of Jesus." But he does not die, for "the life of Jesus" now comes to his aid and he lives in the life of Another until his work is done.

The reason so many fail in the experience of divine healing is because they expect to have it all without a struggle, and when the conflict comes and the battle wages long, they become discouraged and surrender. God has nothing worth having that is easy. There are no cheap goods in the heavenly market. Our redemption cost all that God had to give, and everything worth having is expensive. Hard places are the very school of faith and character, and if we are to rise over mere human strength and prove the power of life living in these mortal bodies, it must be through a process of conflict that may well be called the birth travail of a new life. It is the old figure of the bush that burned but was not consumed, or of the Vision in the house of the Interpreter of the flame that would not expire—notwithstanding the fact that the demon ceaselessly poured water on it—because in the background stood an angel ever pouring oil and keeping the flame aglow.

No, dear suffering child of God, you cannot fail if only you dare to believe, to stand fast and refuse to be overcome.

THE PROCESS OF RECEIVING THIS SUPERNATURAL LIFE

1. It is by faith. " 'I believed; therefore I have spoken.' With that same spirit of faith we also believe and therefore speak" (4:13). We can only retain

the life of Christ while we trust Him.

2. It must be moment by moment and day by day. "Therefore we do not lose heart. Though outwardly we are wasting away, yet inwardly we are being renewed day by day" (4:16). It must be a habit of receiving, a constant dependence. It is not one or two remarkable experiences of healing, but a lifelong drinking in of strength from Christ even as the plant continually draws its nourishment from the soil by 10,000 rootlets. It is here that we must learn to maintain the habit of physical union with Christ and vital dependence upon His strength, breath by breath and step by step.

THE PLEDGE OF FUTURE GLORY

All this is but the earnest of something better by and by. Therefore the apostle adds, "Now we know that if the earthly tent we live in is destroyed, we have a building from God, an eternal house in heaven, not built by human hands" (5:1). And then he adds a little later, "Now it is God who has made us for this very purpose and has given us the Spirit as a deposit, guaranteeing what is to come" (5:5). The apostle means that the life of Jesus in our bodies now is but the beginning and the pledge of that glorious life which is to come to us at the resurrection and the kingdom above. Just as the bulb you plant in autumn has in it the promise of the Easter lily and the acorn is but an oak in miniature, and the seed carries in its bosom the embryo of the golden harvest, so the touch of Christ upon our bodies now carries with it the pledge and the very substance of all the glorious immortality which is to be ours in the age to come.

What a sad morning that was when our first parents went forth weeping and ashamed from the gates of Eden and knew that the Tree of Life was henceforth closed to them as the source of physical immortality. What a glad moment that would be if a glorious angel should come down from heaven and plant it in our gardens once more.

Something better, we are permitted to bring in this glorious message of the supernatural life of Christ. Not only are we permitted to transplant from the soil of heaven the Tree of Life, but He, who is the source of life itself, has come down, not only to walk among us for a little while as an example of the life divine, but to dwell within us as the perennial foundation in our entire being of that life which, although exposed to conflict and testing and suffering now, is pressing on through storm and wind and tide to that glorious hour when:

> His gracious hand shall wipe the tears
>   From every weeping eye;
> And pains and groans and griefs and fears
>   And Death itself shall die.

CHAPTER 6

PAUL'S TESTIMONY ABOUT SALVATION

We are therefore Christ's ambassadors, as though God were making his appeal through us. We implore you on Christ's behalf: Be reconciled to God. (2 Corinthians 5:20)

The apostle has given us his testimony about trial and victory, about his ministry and his own physical life. He now comes to the theme he loves best of all, the gospel of our reconciliation, the great salvation for which God had made him an ambassador to men.

A NEW CREATION

"Therefore, if anyone is in Christ, he is a new creation; the old has gone, the new has come! All this is from God" (5:17–18). Paul's remedy for the world's need was no mere scheme of social reform, educational progress, ethical culture or fine arts. He had seen the failure of mere culture in Greece and Rome, and had turned away from the world's noblest monuments of art with disgust and horror as he saw the city of Athens wholly given to idolatry. The Augustinian age of Roman literature was only just closing, but it had failed to lift man higher than the earthly plane of cultivated selfishness and moral degradation. No higher school of ethics was ever known than the teaching of Moses and the Jewish law. But Paul had found the utter worthlessness of the righteousness of the law and the powerlessness of the highest ideals to lift man above his fallen nature. And so he came to his fellow men to tell them that our fallen race must have, not an evolution, but a revolution. Humanity is too far gone for self-improvement or any principle of recuperation. There must be a new creation. "No one can see the kingdom of God unless he is born again" (John 3:3).

This was the first principle of his great message of salvation. Dear friend, have you seen its utter and imperative necessity? You are trying to be good with a bad heart. You are trying to serve God with a nature utterly depraved

303

and fallen. You are trying to bring a clean thing out of an unclean. As well might you try to develop a dove out of a hawk, or a fawn out of the groveling swine. The best gift that Christ has brought to fallen man is a new heart and an automatic salvation that works spontaneously from a living principle that loves the good and hates the evil because of the law of the fitness of things as strong as the law of gravitation and the will of God. We all know how in our modern industrial life the old clumsy methods of doing things have been superseded by automatic machinery that simply needs to be started and then it works out all the complicated processes of our manifold manufacturing enterprises by a law inherent in itself. This is God's great secret of the new life. He puts in us a vital principle and sets in operation an automatic process that makes it as easy to be humble and holy as once it was easy to be wicked and vile. Have you come to Christ for this great gift, a heaven-born heart, a new nature, a spirit born from above? You cannot develop it by education. You cannot create it by willpower. It is the gift of God. It is eternal life begun on earth and made perfect in the skies. And it comes to every yielded soul that recognizes its absolute necessity and accepts it from Jesus Christ as the gift of His Grace. "If anyone is in Christ, he is a new creation; the old has gone, the new has come!" (2 Corinthians 5:17).

A DIVINE RECONCILIATION

All this is from God, who reconciled us to himself through Christ and gave us the ministry of reconciliation: that God was reconciling the world to himself in Christ, not counting men's sins against them. And he has committed to us the message of reconciliation. We are therefore Christ's ambassadors, as though God were making his appeal through us. We implore you on Christ's behalf: Be reconciled to God. God made him who had no sin to be sin for us, so that in him we might become the righteousness of God. (5:18–21)

The new creation which we have just described cannot begin until a previous process of reconciliation has been effected. There were barriers in the way which had to be removed before the life and love of God could become operative upon the hearts of men. It was like the week of creation. The sun was made in the beginning, but it was the fourth day before its radiance reached the earth and established the beautiful order of day and night, light and heat, vegetable and animal life. Vast obstacles in the earth's atmosphere intervened and made the surface of our globe and the earth a seething chaos. All this had to be cleared away and a firmament and atmosphere created before the sun could pour its beams upon the earth and create a world of beauty and of bloom. So, before God could reach the human heart with the renewing influence of His Holy Spirit, it was necessary that the great work of preparation should be accomplished. This is described by the apostle as "reconciliation." It includes three stages.

1. Revelation

God had to be revealed to man in His true character and beneficence. Our sinful hearts and the lies of our adversary, the devil, had so distorted our conception of the Father that it was impossible for us to love and trust Him. To the natural man, God is an object of terror and not of love. This is because they do not know Him, for to know Him is to love Him. It was necessary, therefore, for God to reveal Himself as a Father, a Friend and a Restorer. He did this through the person and work of the Lord Jesus Christ. "God was reconciling the world to himself in Christ" (5:19). That life of gentleness, unselfishness, sacrifice and ceaseless service was just an object lesson of God. "Anyone who has seen me has seen the Father" (John 14:9). And when at last He hung upon that cross, "He himself bore . . . in his body" (1 Peter 2:24) the sins and the curse of men, a spectacle was presented of the Father's heart toward the sinner, which, when rightly understood and accepted by simple faith, is fitted to put to shame our unworthy thoughts of our loving Father and inspire our hearts with confidence and love. Instead of an avenging fury, waiting to destroy us, we see Him taking our sins upon Himself, and by a plan of mercy as marvelous in its wisdom as in its grace, satisfying every claim against the righteousness of the law and opening the way for our forgiveness and salvation. This was the first object of Christ's coming, to bring God to us. The second is to bring us to God. But He must first come down and show us the Father and then go back and take us with Him to the Father.

So sublimely beautiful is this conception of Christ's work that in many minds it has crowded out altogether the other and equally important aspect of His work as a sacrifice for sin. Many can only see the benevolence and heroic aspect of His life and death as a sublime example of love, and they leave out the deeper meaning of the precious blood. Both are true; and let us not in our zeal for the doctrine of the atonement forget the other aspect of Christ's work as a revelation of a Father's heart toward His rebellious children.

The apostle's conception reminds us of the familiar story of the Scottish maiden who had left her mother and her home and had fallen into the depths of sin, partly through severe Scottish discipline which had shown her the harder side of that mother's justice, rather than the gentler side of her love. When she found her child was gone, her whole nature changed, and her love sought far and wide for the wandering daughter. At last she devised the ingenious idea of hanging up her photograph in many of the dance halls of the great city, with a loving message and her own autograph at the foot of the picture. One night the eyes of the lost one suddenly fell upon the picture and the message inviting her home, and a new vision of her mother came to her heart. She saw her now, not as the severe parent, restraining, disciplining, punishing her rebellious child, but with a heart of love, breaking with sorrow and waiting to forgive. As she recovered from her swoon, she cried, "Take me home," and the rest of the story can better be imagined than told.

Jesus Christ came down to this world of sin to hold up before God's rebellious children the picture of the Father's face and the vision of the Father's love. We love to think of all this in connection with Jesus, but let us not forget that other Face behind the Savior, "God was reconciling the world to himself in Christ" (5:19).

2. Propitiation

More was needed, however, than the revelation of God's love. There were real barriers to overcome. There were tremendous facts of sin, righteousness and law; and only infinite wisdom could have devised a way to meet all these contradictions of the problem and enable God to be at once "a just God and a Savior" (Isaiah 45:21, KJV).

This is where propitiation comes in, and the apostle has not left it out of his gospel. "God was reconciling the world to himself in Christ, not counting men's sins against them" (2 Corinthians 5:19). But this was not a whitewashing of humanity; this was not an erasure of the records in God's eternal books; but it was a mighty settlement in which every claim was met, and every attribute of God was satisfied. Here is the solution of the problem, "God made him who had no sin to be sin for us" (5:21). There in the most explicit terms is the doctrine of the atonement, God's great settlement for the sins of men. Jesus Christ, a Man, the Head of our race, and thus fitted to be our Representative, takes our place, assumes our liabilities, meets our penalties, satisfies all the demands of infinite justice and law and then passes this all over to every man who is willing to accept it as the ground of a settlement with God and to choose Jesus Christ his Attorney for this settlement. This last is indispensable. While His atonement is sufficient for the race, it only becomes efficient for every one who personally commits himself to it by an act of appropriating faith.

3. Justification

The result of all this is the justification of the sinner. "God made him who had no sin to be sin for us, so that in him we might become the righteousness of God" (5:21). The position in which all this places us is "righteousness." We are not merely forgiven and our guilt overlooked, but we are "justified." We are put in the same position as if we had never sinned, or, as if having sinned, we had made the full settlement for our sin which Christ has made for us. If you have ever been in the position of a debtor and know the humiliation of being repeatedly dunned for the claim, you know something of the difference between offering your creditor an apology or a check, asking from him either his forbearance or his receipt. There is nothing that more fully establishes your sense of manhood than to be able to meet your creditor and look in his face without embarrassment as you hand him a settlement of his account and ask him to please write out a receipt in full. This is the happy situation which God has prepared for every saved soul who accepts the atonement of Jesus Christ. Your sin is so completely settled by Christ Jesus and His righteousness so effectually imputed to you that you become "the righteousness of God" (5:21). Looking in the face of earth and heaven and hell, you can say with humble heart and yet triumphant faith, "Who will bring any charge against those whom God has chosen? It is God who justifies. Who is he that condemns? Christ Jesus, who died . . . is at the right hand of God and is also interceding for us" (Romans 8:33–34).

THE HUMAN AGENCY

In this great salvation, God has provided for the ministry of men. "We are therefore Christ's ambassadors, as though God were making his appeal through us. We implore you on Christ's behalf: Be reconciled to God" (2 Corinthians 5:20).

Later, in the first verse of the next chapter, he adds, "As God's fellow workers we urge you not to receive God's grace in vain" (6:1).

1. First Be Reconciled

The messenger of the divine mercy must first be himself reconciled. "God . . . reconciled us to himself through Christ and gave us the ministry of reconciliation" (5:18). We cannot lead others until we first have found the way ourselves; and the first duty and instinct of the saved soul is to save others. God takes us from the depths of sin that we may be able to reach the people that are in the very same place where we once were. Your salvation is a trust as well as a privilege.

2. The Spirit of Soul-winning

The messenger must be specially baptized with the spirit of soul-winning. The word "gave" here in verse 18 has been more literally translated, "has put into us." It suggests the idea of a new instinct and passion for soul saving, being given to the Christian worker, so that it becomes the very impulse of his or her nature to seek and save the lost. Just as certain animals have an instinct that fits them for the hunt and with the power of an absorbing passion for pursuing a special game which they are fitted to hunt, so the love of souls becomes the master-passion of those who give themselves wholly up to it, and they can say as the apostles said, "We cannot help speaking about what we have seen and heard" (Acts 4:20). Has God given to you this intense love of souls, and this divine instinct to seek and to win them for Christ?

3. Human Sympathy and Tact

There is a place in all this for human sympathy and tact. God will use the things that are strongest in your nature to reach men and women. He will especially use you with the class that you are best fitted to reach and attract. If you are to be made a blessing to the unsaved, He will take from you the stiffness, selfishness and exclusiveness which would naturally indispose you to put yourself to the trouble of reaching others. And He will give you the tact, the wisdom and the personal magnetism which will make it easy for you to attract men to Christ. What a wonderful object lesson we have of this gift in the ministry of our Lord! How marvelously He found His way to the heart and conscience of that woman at Jacob's well; how promptly He brought Zacchaeus from the sycamore tree like a skillful hunter by a single shot, and how effectually He won the very policemen that went to arrest Him, but came back confounded, crying, "No one ever spoke the way this man does!" (John 7:46).

4. Power from God

But above all this, the real power of the ministry of soul-winning must come from God. "We are therefore Christ's ambassadors, as though God were making his appeal through us. We implore you on Christ's behalf" (2 Corinthians 5:20). We must come to men not with our love, but with Christ's. We must attract them not to ourselves, but to the Savior. We must make them realize that our message is one of authority and that they are dealing not with us, but with their God. This is what Paul meant when he said, "We commend ourselves to every man's conscience in the sight of God" (4:2).

The story is told of a little child that was once brought into contact with a brutal criminal in a railway station, where the man was waiting between two policemen to be taken to a state's prison. He looked so sad that the little child crept up to him and looking into his face, said, "Poor man, I'm so sorry for you." The sudden revelation to him of that little touch of love seemed for a moment to wake up in him all his worst nature and bring back to him the memory of what he himself had lost, and for a moment he became so excited that it seemed as if he would strike her. Her father drew her away; but as the train waited for some time, the little thing managed once more to steal unobserved to where he sat, and once more looking up in his face, she said, "Poor man, Jesus is so sorry for you." It was a child's gospel, but it broke his heart. He burst into tears, and just then the train came up and he was hurried away. But years afterwards, as a reclaimed convict and a Christian evangelist, he told the story himself, how that revelation of the Savior and His love had brought him to repentance and salvation. Let us give to men the vision of the message of the Savior and ever hide behind our Master and His cross.

THE SINNER'S RESPONSE AND RESPONSIBILITY

There is something for the sinner to do.

1. It is possible for him "to receive God's grace in vain" (6:1). All the kind provision of God's reconciling love, all the precious blood of Christ's atonement may be lost. God will force salvation on no one. He has left the human will free to choose or to refuse, and the blood of every lost sinner shall be upon his own head.

2. God commands the sinner to be reconciled. It is in the imperative mood, "Be reconciled to God" (5:20). God is reconciled and offers His mercy through Jesus Christ to every man and commands him to accept it. There is a moment in every life when that great decision must be definitely made, and nobody can make it but you. It is the crisis hour and a solemn responsibility. Oh, that someone who is reading these lines might this moment accept that responsibility and meet that simple, everlasting responsibility which settles the question for his immortal soul, and say: "God helping me, I will, I do, I now believe."

3. And it must be done now. The first two verses of the next chapter belong to this paragraph. "For he says, 'In the time of my favor I heard you,/ and in the day of salvation I helped you.' I tell you, now is the time of God's favor, now is the day of salvation" (6:2). When God has entered the human heart, convicted it of sin and brought it face to face with the Savior, then it is now or never. Perhaps it is now or never with some one to whom this message has just come.

How easy it is to be saved, but, oh, how easy it is to be lost. The story is told by a distinguished minister, and has been published in tract form, that just after the war of the Union, he was summoned to the front to see his son, who was believed to be dying of a mortal wound. Arriving at the hospital, the doctors told him that his boy would live only about an hour, and that his seeing him might even lessen that time. But the father, after earnest prayer, resolved that he must see him. Coming into the ward, the lad looked up into his face with deep earnestness and said, "Papa, they tell me I cannot live, and I am not ready to die. Could you tell me in just two minutes how I can be saved, for I haven't time or strength for more." And the father said "Yes." Taking the clammy hand of his boy, he added, "Do you remember the time when you disobeyed me and for hours I punished you by refusing to speak to you or even let you kiss me or come upon my knee? And how at last you could stand it no longer and came with trembling feet and voice and said, 'Father, I'm sorry; forgive me'? Do you remember how quickly I opened my arms and took you to my heart and sealed that forgiveness by the kiss of love and how happy you felt as you lay there? My dear boy, that is just the way to come back to God, and that is all."

The boy looked up with wonder. "Is that all?" he said, "then I will try," and closing his eyes and covering his face with the sheet, he prayed for a few moments, and the bed shook with his emotions, while the father silently waited and prayed. Then there was a little cry and that face looked up smiling through its tears as he said: "Papa, I have done it and I feel it's all right."

That was all, but that was enough. Enough to save him and enough to heal him, for the uplift of that new joy gave him the strength that carried him through the crisis and he recovered, and was for many years the honored official in one of the departments of the United States Government.

Dear Reader, that is all. God help you also to say, "I have done it and it is all settled." "Be reconciled to God" (5:20).

CHAPTER 7

PAUL'S TESTIMONY ABOUT HOLINESS

W e have had Paul's testimony about salvation, the supernatural life of the body, victory over trial and other important experiences. In the sixth chapter of Second Corinthians we have his testimony about holy living. There were special reasons why this should be emphasized in Corinth, because some of the members of that church had been guilty of flagrant offenses against purity, and their conduct had been condoned by many in the church. It was therefore necessary that a most emphatic protest should be made by him for practical righteousness and holy living. But this is just as important in every other age and place, and the apostle's message is of permanent application. Let us gather out of this paragraph the principal elements that constitute the life of practical holiness.

SEPARATION FROM EVIL ASSOCIATION

The life of practical holiness means separation from evil association.

> Do not be yoked together with unbelievers. For what do righteousness and wickedness have in common? Or what fellowship can light have with darkness? What harmony is there between Christ and Belial? What does a believer have in common with an unbeliever? What agreement is there between the temple of God and idols? For we are the temple of the living God. As God has said: "I will live with them and walk among them, and I will be their God, and they will be my people."

> "Therefore come out from them
>   and be separate,
>   says the Lord.
> Touch no unclean thing,
>   and I will receive you." (2 Corinthians 6:14–17)

The idea of separation is fundamental to the Church of Christ. The very word for church in the Greek language means called out. From the first God has always kept His people separate from the ungodly world. The principle of contagion through association needs no proof. No sensible man or woman would continue to live in the same house with a smallpox patient, and no wise Christian will presume on fellowship and intimacy beyond the absolute necessities of life with those who are necessarily the fountains of moral and spiritual defilement. When Balaam could not curse Israel, he succeeded in destroying them by drawing them into unholy intimacy with their enemies.

The prohibition of this chapter applies to our whole practical life. It takes in our personal friendships and affections which we should not allow to become bound up with the ungodly, for it is in the heart that all the evil first begins. "Above all else, guard your heart,/ for it is the wellspring of life" (Proverbs 4:23).

It embraces the family and prohibits intermarriage between God's children and the ungodly world. One reason why the Hebrew race has been preserved distinct among the nations for thousands of years, and is steadily today recovering its place of supremacy, is that the true children of this race refuse to allow intermarriages beyond their own people. No Christian man has a right to marry an ungodly wife; no Christian woman has a right to marry an ungodly man; and no Christian minister has the right to solemnize the marriage ceremony between such parties.

Further, this applies to the business of life and forbids partnerships between children of God and ungodly men. Such combinations are almost sure to involve you in compromises and make you a consenting party to wrongs that you yourself would never think of doing in your private business. God was much displeased with one of His servants of old, who was faultless in every other respect, but it is said of him that "he allied himself with Ahab . . . Jehu the seer . . . went out to meet him and said to the king, 'Should you help the wicked and love those who hate the LORD? Because of this, the wrath of the LORD is upon you' " (2 Chronicles 18:1, 19:2).

Little wonder that Jehoshaphat's partnerships failed, that his ships were lost, his investments a failure and his very life narrowly saved.

The Church is equally forbidden to allow herself to be compromised with the world either by admitting an ungodly member, by adopting worldly methods of finance, or by allowing secular control, social ambition, worldly amusements or fashionable extravagances to mar her sacred purity and compromise her testimony against this present evil world.

The apostle tells us that such yokes are always unequal. The adversary will get the advantage of you if you allow yourself to be drawn into any sort of partnership with him. He can afford to do things that you cannot, and at the end of the partnership you will find yourself in the situation of the too confiding foreigner who was persuaded by a sharp American speculator to invest his money with him in an enterprise where the American had all the necessary experience and the foreigner's money was considered an equivalent in the partnership. At the end of the year our friend was very glad to get out, and in referring to the affair he said: "When we started he had the experience and I had the money, but when we ended he had the money and I had the experience." The enemy is too keen to fail to get advantage of you at every point. You may think that you can influence your ungodly husband by marrying him, but you will find it all the other way. You can lift people up only by keeping on a higher level. If you sink to theirs, they will surely drag you still further down. God help us to be true to our separation.

CLEANSING

To live a life of holiness there must be cleansing. "Since we have these promises, dear friends, let us purify ourselves from everything that contaminates body and spirit, perfecting holiness out of reverence for God" (2 Corinthians 7:1).

Sanctification includes a good deal more than mere outward separation from evil persons. The worst evil is in our own hearts, and that must be removed by the deeper work of the Holy Spirit. But in this we must ourselves cooperate. There is a step for us to take first, and then there is the work of God. We must consent to the work of cleansing. We must pass sentence upon our sinful heart and give God the right to cleanse it. Then His grace will come in and accomplish the work, but not until we first of all have given Him the right of way. God will not take one step till we have handed ourselves over to Him unreservedly and pronounced the sentence of death upon our carnal nature and our sinful heart. Therefore we read constantly in the Old Testament of God's command to the people, "consecrate yourselves and be holy" (see Leviticus 11:44; 20:7–8), and at the same time of God's promise that He will sanctify them. Both are true. We must cleanse ourselves by putting away all known evil, renouncing every sin and yielding ourselves unreservedly to God to cleanse every sin and fill us with the Holy Spirit.

All kinds of defilement are mentioned. The first is of filthiness of the flesh. This includes not only the indulgences of the body in disobedience to the divine law, but it also means those passions and desires which have their seat in the soul and find in the body the instrument of their unhallowed indulgences. The word for flesh here is not the usual word for the body, which is *soma,* but it is the word *sarx,* which always carries with it the idea of the carnal nature and the fleshly heart.

Then the apostle speaks of the filthiness of the spirit as well as the flesh. We may be outwardly free from immorality, but our minds and hearts may be filled with vile imaginations and unholy desires, and this God counts sinful and unholy. True holiness includes the thoughts, the emotions, the sensibilities and tastes and all the faculties and powers of our being. You may not yourself be guilty of immorality, but you may feed your eyes upon it on the stage in some prurient play. You may follow its sensuousness in the modern novel, and grovel in all the unrestrained depths of insinuating vice. You may have your spirit softly fanned by its fetid breath in the insidious poetry of romance. So saturated is much of this with the very spirit of darkness that Lord Byron gave express commands that his most famous poetical romance should never be allowed in the hands of his own daughter. Too well he knew the fatal blight which it would bring to her modesty and purity. Many of the new philosophies are permeated with an unhallowed spirit. Theosophy, Christian Science and most of occult teachings current with a certain class, who have caught the craze for higher culture, are of this nature. A sensitive spiritual conscience will find itself barred at the gateway of all this class of literature and be conscious of the very breath of hell the moment it comes under its influence. May God give us a quickened conscience and an obedient will to detect every form of defilement and cleanse ourselves from all filthiness of the flesh and spirit.

THE PERFECTING OF HOLINESS

Next comes the perfecting of holiness. "Perfecting holiness out of reverence for God" (2 Corinthians 7:1). This has reference to the progressive side of sanctification. There are two experiences in holiness. The first is the act by which God definitely accepts our entire surrender, cleanses us by the blood of Christ from sin, and puts within us His Holy Spirit and the life of Jesus to constitute the very source and principle of our new life. But after this there comes a gradual growth. There is a place for the growth as well as for the more instant transformation. In the first chapter of Second Peter, the apostle describes both. He tells of a moment when "you may . . . escape the corruption in the world caused by evil desires" (2 Peter 1:4). Then he proceeds to lead them forward to the life of progress. "For this very reason," he says, "Make every effort to add to your faith goodness; and to goodness, knowledge; and to knowledge, self-control" (1:5–6). And then a little later he adds, "For if you possess these qualities in increasing measure, they will keep you from being ineffective and unproductive in your knowledge of our Lord Jesus Christ" (1:8). Here we have the addition of many graces to our Christian character and in each of them a still higher degree of progress and grace.

The word "perfecting" (2 Corinthians 7:1) here does not at all imply our sinless perfection. The sense of the word is completing, finishing, carrying forward to maturity that work that has already been begun. The idea is that of the garden which has been cleansed from weeds and planted with seeds, and now it is being carried forward to the fullness of the blossom and the fruit. Do not, therefore, let us settle down in self-complacency because we have received the baptism of the Holy Spirit and entered upon a deeper life, but let us go deeper and press farther on until we reach "the whole measure of the fullness of Christ" (Ephesians 4:13).

THE INDWELLING OF GOD

Next we look at the indwelling of God. "For we are the temple of the living God. As God has said: 'I will live with them and walk among them, and I will be their God, and they will be my people' " (2 Corinthians 6:16). This is the deepest truth in connection with sanctification. This is the climax of all other experiences and preparation. This is variously described in the New Testament as "baptized by one Spirit" (1 Corinthians 12:13), "remain in me [Jesus], and I will remain in you" (John 15:4), and such promises as John 14:23, "My Father will love him, and we will come to him and make our home with him." They are not essentially distinct, but phases of the same great fact. It is the Holy Spirit that first comes, and when He comes He brings Jesus and reveals Him, for He never works apart from Him; but Jesus always comes to reveal to us the Father. And where Jesus dwells, there the Father dwells in Him, so that the consecrated believer is the home and the temple of the Father, Son and Holy Spirit. This is the very principle of divine holiness. Paul expresses it in First Corinthians 1:30, in the clearest terms, "It is because of him that you are in Christ Jesus, who has become for us wisdom from God—that is, our righteousness, holiness and redemption." The yielded heart becomes the home of God and all our holiness and righteousness is but the reliving by the Lord of His own life once more in an earthly temple.

But not only does He dwell in us; He walks in us. All the activities of our Christian life are prompted by Him. He goes forth with us not only to our sacred duties, but to our secular calling. And so it is said, "Brothers, each man, as responsible to God, should remain in the situation God called him to" (1 Corinthians 7:24). We ought to be willing to go nowhere where He would not also be willing to go, and when our divine Companion calls a halt, it is always safe for you to tarry and dangerous for you to go. So let us walk with Him, and some day He will lead us so far that we shall never come back to this sinful earth again, but go in like Enoch, and "walk with [Him], dressed in white" (Revelation 3:4).

LIVING AS CHILDREN OF GOD

To live in holiness we must live as the children of God. The apostle presents a very high ideal of the holy life in this passage, "I will be a Father to you,/ and you will be my sons and daughters, says the Lord Almighty" (2 Corinthians 6:18). The idea is that we are to walk as the children of God with that holy dignity and consistency which will do honor to our royal dignity and our divine Father. A true child will cherish his father's wants and interest and avoid everything that would throw a shadow of reproach upon his name. Our loving Father is always watching over us for our highest good, and seeking to give us His best things, but He does this only as we ourselves meet the conditions and rise to the essential qualifications.

Someone tells of a wealthy businessman who had two of his sons in his business, one in a position of high responsibility, and the other in a much lower position, but the visitor noticed that in the family circle both sons were treated with equal affection. He asked the gentleman if he was really doing as well by the second son as he could, and he replied that he was doing as well as he could, but not as well as he would if he could. "I have longed," he said, "to be able to advance my boy to a much higher place, but I cannot do so until he qualifies, and I am doing all for him at present that I really can, but not all that I would love to do." This is the heart of our Father. Let us make it possible for Him to do for each of us His best.

> God has His best things for the few
>   Who dare to stand the test;
> God has His second choice for those
>   Who will not have His best.

ENLARGEMENT

The final principle of living a life of holiness is the idea of enlargement. It is possible to be free from sin, utterly sanctified and walking with God as His children, and yet be living a very narrow, circumscribed life.

There is one more message in this passage which may well form the climax of this subject. "We are not withholding our affection from you, but you are withholding yours from us. As a fair exchange—I speak as to my children—open wide your hearts also" (6:12–13). God wants us not only pure but glorious, not only robed in the spotless garments of the priest, but in the beautiful array of the Bride.

The story is told of a Hindu girl, who, walking on the shore, picked up a silver spangle. As she held it in her hand, she saw attached to it a golden thread coming out of the sea. Drawing this to her she found spangle after spangle upon its apparently endless length. She began to wrap it about her neck and form, and as she did so it grew more beautiful and glorious, until at last she was decked in a garment of shining silver and resplendent gold.

The parable is true of our spiritual life. As we put on each new grace of the

Holy Spirit, we find that it but leads the way to something still higher, and thus God would have us go on and "add to your faith goodness; and to goodness, knowledge; and to knowledge, self-control; and to self-control, perseverance; and to perseverance, godliness; and to godliness, brotherly kindness; and to brotherly kindness, love" (2 Peter 1:5–7). And then He would have these things so increase and abound that "you will receive a rich welcome into the eternal kingdom of our Lord and Savior Jesus Christ" (1:11).

May God increase our capacity for growth, and give us the blessing He gave to Solomon, "a breadth of understanding as measureless as the sand on the seashore" (1 Kings 4:29).

CHAPTER 8

TWO KINDS OF SORROW

Godly sorrow brings repentance that leads to salvation and leaves no regret, but worldly sorrow brings death. (2 Corinthians 7:10)

The world is full of sorrow. It comes both to the sinner and to the saint, but oh, how different it comes to each.

THE SORROW OF THE WORLD

There is no comfort for the sinner's sorrow. There is no profit in his pain. Like the fire which consumes the dross, so the flames of suffering burn his heart to ashes and leave nothing but the bitter dregs and the burning lye.

1. Comfortless Trials

What can we say to comfort the heart that has no God, no Christ, no hope beyond and no faith in an overruling Providence here? Is there any task so trying as to stand at the funeral of one who has died without the Savior and speak to a sorrowing household, who are equally destitute of His love and to whom that parting is forever? One can understand the terrible force and meaning of the apostle's words, "grieve like the rest of men, who have no hope" (1 Thessalonians 4:13).

2. Wasted Sorrow

The Christian's trials are a wholesome discipline intended to teach him precious lessons in the school of holy character. Our trials are but "the Lord's discipline" (Hebrews 12:5) as the apostle beautifully calls it, but the sufferings of the ungodly have no such issue. True, they are intended to arouse the conscience and transform the life, but they are unheeded and unblessed. Then God at last gets tired of inflicting pain that does no good, and we hear Him crying in the pathetic language of the prophet, "Why should you be beaten anymore?/ Why do you persist in rebellion?/ Your

319

whole head is injured,/ your whole heart afflicted" (Isaiah 1:5). How sad that so many have to suffer bereavement, disappointment, loss and failure and after all be like the one of whom Jehovah says in Isaiah, "I was enraged by his sinful greed;/ I punished him, and hid my face in anger,/ yet he kept on in his willful ways" (57:17). If our trials only taught us any good, they would not seem so hard, but to suffer in vain and find it has only embittered and hardened the heart, this indeed is the very sharpness of grief.

3. Vain Regrets

One of the sources of the worldling's sorrow is the painful reflection upon his past and the stinging memory of opportunities lost, of loved ones wronged, of sin and suffering that never can be repaired again. There is no more bitter drop in the cup of retribution than to have God say to a soul, "Son, remember" (Luke 16:25). To go alone with our own heart and retrace our wretched steps through all the chambers of memory, and see in the full light of experience the consequences of our sin and folly and know that it is irremediable, this indeed is the "worldly sorrow [that] brings death" (2 Corinthians 7:10).

4. Futile Fears and Griefs

One of the sweetest comforts of the Christian is the thought that he is saved both from his past and future. The promise of the Lord is, "The LORD will go before you,/ the God of Israel will be your rear guard" (Isaiah 52:12). That is, God will take care of your future and your past. But the ungodly have no such overshadowing Presence. The past remains in all its grim reality and fraught with all its future fruition, and, before, there is foreboding, fear and the thousand anxieties that all the world's philosophy is unable to still.

5. Self-Judging

Conscience is the dread accuser of the wrongdoer, and conscience, without the restraint of divine mercy, is a terrible tyrant. There is no punishment more severe than that which we have power to inflict upon ourselves. To see your worthlessness, to know that you are wholly bad and helpless to make yourself better, to condemn yourself in utter disgust and self-despair has no healing virtue in it, no help for you and no balm to alleviate the pain. It is but the beginning of the eternal fire. People sometimes think because they call themselves hard names and inflict severe penances they have somehow made atonement for their evils. There is nothing in this. It is but the scorpion which spends its life in stinging others and then ends its life in stinging itself to death.

6. Chagrin and Humiliation

Chagrin and humiliation because of the deserved punishment of sin is another form of the vain suffering of the world. Many people are quite comfortable about their wrongdoing until it is found out. Then it looms up in lurid colors and the keenest suffering comes from wounded pride and the sense of humiliation before others. But there is no uplifting power in this. It does not reform the criminal to degrade him and expose him. It only destroys the last lingering spark of manhood and drives him into deeper despair. God does not thus try to reform and save, but rather blots out the very remembrance of the evil and lifts us up again into confidence and hope.

7. Despair

The climax of the world's sorrow is despair. One of the illustrious statesmen of this land a century ago is said to have ended his life by repeating in tones of deepest anguish over and over again the one word, "remorse, remorse, remorse." But that remorse did not bring true repentance or take away one particle of the deep depravity of his soul. It is but the beginning of the worm that never dies and the fire that never shall be quenched.

We have several instances in the Bible of people who said, "I have sinned," and yet it did not save them. Pharaoh cried out, "I have sinned" (Exodus 9:27), but it was only because he wanted to escape the judgments of God which his sin had brought upon him. Saul said more than once, "I sinned" (see 1 Samuel 15:24), but it did not save him from going back and repeating his sin until at last he perished in his infatuation. Judas brought back the price of the Savior's blood and threw it at the feet of the Pharisees, crying, "I have sinned . . . for I have betrayed innocent blood" (Matthew 27:4), but Judas went headlong immediately afterwards to self-destruction.

We have many instances also of people that were sorry, but it did not make them better. Herod was very sorry that he had to behead his much respected friend, John the Baptist, to please an infamous woman and a bold, heartless girl, but he did it all the same, and brought upon himself the curse of innocent blood. The young ruler that came to Christ was very sorry that he could not accede to Christ's terms and part with all his earthly treasures and follow the Master. "He went away sad, because he had great wealth" (19:22). But his sorrow did not bring him back or lead him to true decision for God. He is sorry still, no doubt, for his fearful mistake, but his sorrow is that of the lost.

Sentiment will not save you; tears will not wash away your sin. The question asked of one who was bewailing his evil course may well apply to every one who reads these lines: "Sorry, are you, for what you have done? Well, are you sorry enough to stop?"

True repentance means more than a gush of emotion. It is a change of will, an altered attitude toward sin and God. Is that your attitude?

GODLY SORROW

There are many kinds of godly sorrow besides true repentance.

1. There is the sorrow that God comforts, the trials that bring Him closer to us and reveal Him to us as "the God of all comfort" (2 Corinthians 1:3). That is a beautiful promise in the Psalms, "He will be like rain falling on a mown field" (72:6). The grass has just been cut down by the gardener to prevent it going to seed and drying up at the root, but it is bleeding at every pore and the gardener pours water on it or the rain falls in healing showers and the wounds are assuaged and the roots refreshed, and, lo, it springs up again. So God loves to visit the wounded heart, and it is never until we have suffered that we really know Him in all the tenderness of His love and understand such promises as this, "As a mother comforts her child,/ so will I comfort you" (Isaiah 66:13).

2. There is trial sanctified. The gardener mows that grass for its good and the Father chastens us "for our good" (Hebrews 12:10). That richly laden vine would have no fruit if it had not been cut back by the pruning knife, and so we shall some time thank God for our hours of deepest trial and the radiant memories of life's retrospect.

3. There is also suffering with Christ. The highest form of human suffering is fellowship with Jesus Christ in His burdens. "For it has been granted to you on behalf of Christ not only to believe on him, but also to suffer for him" (Philippians 1:29).

4. Then there is the sorrow for the sins of others. This is one of the sublimest heights of Christian love, to take on ourselves the load of another's wrongdoing and make intercession like Him who "had no sin [was made] to be sin for us" (2 Corinthians 5:21), and still bears upon His bleeding hands the names of sinful men in intercession before His Father.

This is why God sometimes has to let us know the bitterness of having some loved one go astray that we may know the Father's sorrow over His wandering child and the shepherd's grief for the poor lost sheep.

5. There is sorrow for our own sins. There is a place for repentance in every Christian experience. There must be a definite conviction of sin, a calling of things by their right names and a turning away from all evil and giving God the right to cleanse and destroy it. Then God not only forgives but cleanses and takes away from us its memory and power.

But this is not the terrible and hopeless sorrow of the world. It comes through a different process and from a different source. It is born of faith and love and not of doubt and fear. The truly contrite heart is sorrier for its sins after it knows that they are forever forgiven.

How beautiful are the Bible's pictures of repentance. Look at that woman weeping at the Savior's feet and bathing them with her tears of love, while the Master says "Her many sins have been forgiven—for she loved much. But he who has been forgiven little loves little" (Luke 7:47).

Listen to Zacchaeus standing among his acquaintances and declaring, "I give half of my possessions to the poor, and if I have cheated anybody out of anything, I will pay back four times the amount" (19:8). What could be more beautiful, more inspiring, more encouraging than that kind of sorrow for sin?

Look at Peter turning his face toward his Master in the moment of his profane denial. He catches, not a withering look of anger, but a pleading glance of sorrow and love, and breaking away from the multitude he hurries out to hide his tears of uncontrollable anguish and sorrow for the wrong he has done his Savior.

Listen to the prodigal hastening home and crying upon his father's chest, "Father, I have sinned against heaven and against you. I am no longer worthy to be called your son" (15:21).

This is repentance, and it is almost the most beautiful thing in the world. No wonder that God says, "The sacrifices of God are a broken spirit" (Psalm 51:17). "This is the one I esteem:/ he who is humble and contrite in spirit,/ and trembles at my word" (Isaiah 66:2).

6. There is the sorrow that comes from a deeper sense, not merely of our actual sins, but of our sinfulness and lack of entire conformity to the will of God. As the light of self-revelation comes to the heart and we see ourselves as God sees us, there comes a deep, intense longing for purity and entire conformity to God. How finely this comes out in the 51st Psalm, which was David's cry when he saw his own heart in the light of his terrible fall. It was not that he was afraid of punishment, but it was the sense of having grieved God and lost spiritual purity and blessing.

How keenly Job felt this when the searchlight of God was let in upon his soul and he cried, "My ears had heard of you/ but now my eyes have seen you./ Therefore I despise myself/ and repent in dust and ashes" (Job 42:5–6).

How beautifully the Lord Jesus describes this in the fifth chapter of Matthew in the opening paragraphs of the Sermon on the Mount, where He pronounces the blessing first on those that are poor in spirit, that is, the souls that have seen their spiritual shortcomings, and then adds a similar benediction on those that mourn, that is, that mourn because of their spiritual poverty and are deeply affected by their shortcomings and failures. On such, the Lord says, there rests a great blessing, and to such surely comes the divine consolation.

7. Finally there are the fruits of godly sorrow. In the following verse the apostle describes the fruits of true sorrow for sin. "See what this godly sor-

row has produced in you: what earnestness, what eagerness to clear your-selves, what indignation, what alarm, what longing, what concern, what readiness to see justice done. At every point you have proved yourselves to be innocent in this matter" (2 Corinthians 7:11).

"What earnestness [this godly sorrow has produced in you]," that is, what watching against the recurrence of a similar fall. "What eagerness to clear yourselves," that is, what honest, earnest efforts to undo any ill effects of our wrongdoing upon others. "What indignation," not against others, but against ourselves. "What alarm," that is, what godly fear and vigilance lest we should be again entangled. "What longing, what concern, what readiness to see justice done," that is, what earnest resolve, by the grace of God, to retrace our steps over the same ground and recover all that we have lost.

God lets us do this in infinite longsuffering, and like Samson, whose dying joy it was to win the victory even by the sacrifice of his life that he had thrown away through his sinful folly, God permits us to retrieve our failures.

The story is told of a regiment, which by cowardice had lost its colors, and the Colonel had refused to give them a new flag. At length, in a bloody cam-paign, the opportunity came to recover their lost honors. The enemy was posted upon a hill and the Colonel, pointing to it, said, "Boys, there are your colors. You can win them back." And up that hill they charged, cap-tured the enemy's flags and guns, and got back the colors they had forfeited.

So God brings into each of our lives some hard place, some strong tempta-tion, which is just another name for a new opportunity to recover what we have lost, and it is then that our true sincerity and godly sorrow are fully vin-dicated. God has deliverance for His tempted children. God has victory for us over every failure and every defeat. Let us take heart and allow Him to make us more than conquerors through His love.

A jeweler was once engaged in cutting a beautiful cameo figure. Suddenly he discovered a dark streak in the stone. It was a flaw. At first he thought he should have to throw it away, but after thinking hard over it, there came to him the fine conception of working that stain into the drapery of the figure. This he succeeded in doing, so that it became an actual ornament and ap-peared like a flowing robe upon the spotless figure of the design and added immeasurably to its beauty and effect.

So God permits us take our hard places and failures and shape them into robes of transfiguration to show to wondering angels through all eternity the marvelous power of that grace for which nothing is too hard, so that "where sin increased, grace increased all the more" (Romans 5:20).

CHAPTER 9

OUR SPIRITUAL WARFARE

For though we live in the world, we do not wage war as the world does. The weapons we fight with are not the weapons of the world. On the contrary, they have divine power to demolish strongholds. We demolish arguments and every pretension that sets itself up against the knowledge of God, and we take captive every thought to make it obedient to Christ. And we will be ready to punish every act of disobedience, once your obedience is complete. (2 Corinthians 10:3–6)

The world is fond of the pomp and circumstance of war, and conflict and victory constitute the largest part of human history.

The Bible is full of military metaphors and the Christian's life is one long battlefield, but the forces engaged and the weapons employed are very different from man's campaigns. The greatest victories of the Bible all foreshadow these higher forces and hidden foes. The capture of Jericho by a shout of faith, the defeat of Goliath by a shepherd boy, and the victory of Jehoshaphat over his myriad foes by the music of a sacred choir; these are suggestions of those unseen powers which are waging the battle of eternity and fighting the good fight of faith.

It is of this warfare that our text speaks. "Though we live in the world, we do not wage war as the world does" (10:3). There are conflicts in the name of Christianity which are not able to make this claim. When we try to serve God with an unsaved and unsanctified heart; when we endeavor to develop character by culture; when we try to build up the kingdom of God through social influence, intellectual power, skillful organization and financial methods without the Holy Spirit and the supernatural power of God, we are attempting to fight the battles of the Lord by the arm of flesh. And we will find it true, " 'Not by might nor by power, but by my Spirit,' says the LORD Almighty" (Zechariah 4:6).

The warfare in which we are engaged is the fight against sin, Satan and the world. The battlefield is very often within our own heart; the foe is invisible and the conflict is secret and all unseen by mortal eyes; but nonetheless is it intense and decisive for the issues of heaven and hell.

Indeed, it requires far higher qualities to stand true in the spiritual conflict than even upon the bloody battlefield, and "better . . . a man who controls his temper than one who takes a city" (Proverbs 16:32).

SPIRITUAL WEAPONS

The weapons of our warfare are spiritual.

The first is the name of Jesus. We cannot fight under our own flag. Satan has little fear of us. The battle is not ours, but God's, and as we go forth making Christ responsible and meeting every temptation in His name, we shall be conquerors.

The Holy Spirit is our strength in this warfare. It was He that led Jesus Christ into the wilderness to be tempted of the devil and brought Him forth crowned with victory, and the Christian's most essential weapon is the "sword of the Spirit, which is the word of God" (Ephesians 6:17).

Archimedes dreamed of a scientific process by which he could, through a burning glass, set fire to the ships of the enemy; and it is a question whether some day our marvelous scientific progress will not evolve, through electricity, a power so subtle and far-reaching that by a flash it can annihilate a battleship and explode a powder magazine, and thus, by its destructiveness, render war practically impossible.

But this we know: That in the Holy Spirit we have a "consuming fire" (Deuteronomy 4:24; Hebrews 12:29) which we can turn upon every enemy, every temptation, every thought, every lingering trace of evil in ourselves, and triumph "not by might nor by power" (Zechariah 4:6), but by the Spirit of the Lord of hosts.

The armor of righteousness is described as the Christian's breastplate, and indeed, it is a very panoply of victory. When Joseph was assailed by the subtle temptress, he was sin-proof through one single principle: "How then could I do such a wicked thing and sin against God?" (Genesis 39:9). When the men of Babylon were threatened with the burning, fiery furnace, they had but one answer: "We do not need to defend ourselves before you in this matter. If we are thrown into the blazing furnace, the God we serve is able to save us from it, and he will rescue us from your hand, O king. But even if he does not, we want you to know, O king, that we will not serve your gods or worship the image of gold you have set up" (Daniel 3:16–18). Such a spirit is invincible. The devil never attacked the power of Jesus, but he did assail His righteousness. If he could only have gotten Him to turn aside for a moment from the will of God, he knew that human redemption was defeated and God dethroned. The spirit of implicit, uncompromising obedience to

God, an everlasting "No" to everything that is contrary to His will, will carry us through every conflict and crown us with eternal victory.

FAITH

Faith is a great weapon in our spiritual warfare. "This is the victory that has overcome the world, even our faith" (1 John 5:4). "By faith the walls of Jericho fell" (Hebrews 11:30). Through faith they "conquered kingdoms, administered justice, . . . became powerful in battle and routed foreign armies" (11:33–34).

LOVE

Love is a still more certain weapon. When Satan assails us with wrong and injustice, his chief object is to provoke us to irritation and destroy the sweetness of our spirit. When we meet his fiery darts with a panoply of love, they are quenched and neutralized. Nothing can harm us if our love only remains unconquered. There is no sublimer heroism than to stand in silence amid misrepresentation and wrong, returning good for evil, and like Jesus on the cruel cross simply saying, "Father, forgive them, for they do not know what they are doing" (Luke 23:34).

The story is told of a poor African who was caught on the premises of a foreigner in South Africa and suspected of stealing some valuable articles that had been missed. He earnestly denied the crime, but the cruel white man bound him, and forcing him to lay his hand upon the block, with one blow severed it from the arm, and sent him away bleeding and mutilated into the bush. A few months later, in the fortunes of the Boer war, this white man found himself in the bush and one night he was compelled to seek refuge in a native hut. He was kindly entertained, and in the morning his host met him, and holding up the stump of his arm asked him if he recognized him. The man was horror stricken; it was the victim of his former cruelty and he was in his power. But the native smiled and said, "Yes, I could kill you, and you perhaps deserve it, but I am a Christian and I have learned that love is sweeter than revenge, and so I forgive you. You can go." These are battles of the heart that cost something and mean everything.

PATIENCE

Patience is the twin sister of love and is also one of our effective weapons in the spiritual conflict. Among the typical characters of the book of Genesis, much place is given to the story of Isaac. This is not without reason, for Isaac represents especially the victories of Patience. He was always giving place to others. Truly this is the story of love: "Love is patient, love is kind. . . . It always protects, always trusts, always hopes, always perseveres" (1 Corinthians 13:4, 7).

PRAYER AND PRAISE

Prayer also is, perhaps, our mightiest weapon. Our best victories are won by its influence.

Praise is a still higher form of prayer and prayer never reaches its victory until it becomes praise. Dr. Miller tells of a party visiting the Lakes of Killarney who were attracted one day by some beautiful singing in a cabin. They asked a girl who had just come out who the singer was. "Oh," she said, "it's Uncle Tim singing away the pain. He's just had a bad spell and it's the only thing that helps him when he is in great pain." Humble sufferer! He was indeed a "hero in the strife," and many of us would find his remedy for pain much better than our groans and grumblings.

THE STRONGHOLDS

Our text speaks of the "strongholds" (2 Corinthians 10:4), which we may "demolish" (10:4) in this great warfare. The figure suggests the story of Canaan and the great strongholds captured by Joshua and his armies from the enemy. There were three especially that seem to be types of our spiritual conflicts. One at the commencement of their campaign, one at its next critical stage, and one at the end. Each of these involved a great advance movement.

The first of these was Jericho, and it had to be captured before they could enter the land at all. And so there is in every Christian life a stronghold at the very gateway of salvation, some besetting sin, some inveterate habit, some insuperable barrier. The second was Hebron, captured by Caleb after the land had been subdued. This represented the new advance movement to the choice possession of the land and may well stand for the strongholds that face us as we enter upon the deeper life.

There is always some crisis to be passed, some Hebron to be captured, some idol to be slain, some fight of faith to be won before we come into our inheritance of perfect love.

The third was far down in their national history long after Canaan had been won and when David had at length established his throne in Hebron. It was the stronghold of Jebus, afterwards known as Zion, and its heroic capture by Joab won for him the place of commander in chief of David's armies.

In like manner, there often remains late in our spiritual history some remaining stronghold which has not been captured from the foe. Perhaps it is a sick body; perhaps it is some victory over our circumstances; perhaps it is the salvation of some soul that has long remained obdurate, and when this is won our kingdom is complete.

Is God calling you, beloved friends, to some of these decisive battles, and waiting to cast down before you these strongholds of the adversary?

THE CAPTIVES

Once more our text tells us of the captives of this conflict. "We take captive every thought to make it obedient to Christ" (2 Corinthians 10:5). Here the conflict seems to be confined to the battlefield of our minds and hearts. The foes to be subdued are our wandering, wayward and sinful thoughts. Surely everyone who has known much of the fight of faith has found that there is nothing more necessary or more difficult than the subjection of our thoughts and imaginations. All evil begins in some mental conception or some impulse of the heart. Impure thoughts, vain thoughts, wandering thoughts, anxious thoughts, remorseful memories of the past or corroding cares for the future: how great a part these things play in the tragedy of human life! God has victory for us over our thoughts. He is able to keep our minds stayed on Him (Isaiah 26:3, KJV). He is able to give "the mind of Christ" (1 Corinthians 2:16), and "the peace of God, which transcends all understanding, will guard your hearts and your minds in Christ Jesus" (Philippians 4:7).

AGGRESSIVE WARFARE

Finally, there is the aggressive warfare against evil in others. "And we will be ready to punish every act of disobedience" (2 Corinthians 10:6). But there is a limitation to this, "once your obedience is complete" (10:6). We cannot attack the sins of others till we have taken the plank out of our own eye. Our own spiritual and mental victory are essential for our influence over others. Therefore God has to keep back many a life from its highest calling until it has slowly achieved self-conquest.

The power that runs our factories and trains today was made millions of years ago in the bowels of the earth, when the sun burnt up the forests of primeval ages and turned them into mountains of coal. That coal is lying there on deposit now, and the miner brings it forth and simply converts it into steam and sets it to work moving our modern industries and even fighting our battles. But it had to be slowly deposited there first as a hidden source of undiscovered power.

So God is burning up things in our lives today and turning them into spiritual forces, and some time He will bring them forth for the battles of His kingdom. Let us not be impatient while the spiritual processes are going on. What we are is more than what we do. This is true, alas, of evil as well as good. There are lives slowly preparing to be an eternal curse. There are others getting ready to be a worldwide blessing.

May God help us to be willing to stand on the silent battlefield of our own hearts and win our victory, and then go forth "strong in the Lord and in his mighty power" (Ephesians 6:10), to fight the battles of the Lord and the world.

CHAPTER 10

THE GRACE OF GIVING

But just as you excel in everything—in faith, in speech, in knowledge, in complete earnestness and in your love for us—see that you also excel in this grace of giving. . . . For you know the grace of our Lord Jesus Christ, that though he was rich, yet for your sakes he became poor, so that you through his poverty might become rich. (2 Corinthians 8:7, 9)

T he eighth and ninth chapters of this epistle unfold the scriptural principles of Christian giving with a fullness and clearness nowhere else to be found.

THE PLACE AND GRACE OF GIVING

The subject of giving to God is here placed on the very highest plane, not as a secondary and merely incidental quality and exercise of religious sentiment, but as one of the cardinal graces of the Christian life. He commences his argument by referring to the grace of God bestowed upon the churches of Macedonia as evidenced in their giving to God and their suffering brethren, and he places giving on the very same exalted level as faith, knowledge and love, so that one cannot be deficient in this grace without lacking the very essential qualities of the Christian character and life.

THE JOY OF GIVING

But while it is one of the graces of the Spirit, it is as free and spontaneous as every true fruit of the Spirit must be. It is not to be a mere matter of duty but of glad and heartfelt choice and even delight. "Their overflowing joy," he says, "and their extreme poverty welled up in rich generosity. . . . Entirely on their own, they urgently pleaded with us for the privilege of sharing in this service to the saints" (2 Corinthians 8:2–4). Ordinarily we expect to see a solicitor begging the people to give, but here we see the people begging with much entreaty that the apostle will accept their gifts and help them to distribute them to their needy brethren. Again in the next chapter we have a fine passage, "Each man should give what he has decided in his heart to give, not reluctantly or under compulsion, for God loves a cheerful giver" (9:7).

It is a joy so great that it runs over in divine enthusiasm and hallelujahs of praise. Here we are distinctly taught that our giving is to be prompted not by our calculations of how little we can spare but by the impulses of our heart. Hence it is according to the purpose of the heart that our giving is to be gauged. The old proverbial exhortation that we should "give till it hurts" falls far short of the divine philosophy. Here we are taught that we should give till it doesn't hurt; and if we give enough to really reach and kill the core of our selfishness, it will slay the thing that hurts and make it a divine and eternal joy. The old farmer who gave five dollars, and after he had left the altar felt so bad and was so strongly tempted to go back and get his five dollars and give one for it, took the right course when he grasped his old selfish nature by the throat and marching boldly back said to the collector, "Here, give me that five dollars," and handed out a 10 dollar bill instead, then turned on himself with a look of infinite scorn and triumph and exclaimed, "Now, old nature, squirm." He gave till it hurt and gave till it ceased to hurt. The people who give so grandly in these days for missions do it because of the overflowing joy that fills their hearts. It has ceased to be a sacrifice, for even sacrifice is swallowed up in love.

THE TRUE SECRET OF GIVING

"They gave themselves first to the Lord and then to us in keeping with God's will" (8:5). Personal consecration must ever be the spring both of beneficence and service. When we cease to own ourselves, then all the selfish bonds that hold us to our belongings are sweetly broken, and we rise into the glorious liberty of a life of unselfish love. It seems to be clearly taught in the Scriptures that God does not want either our gifts or our services until He has us. The Greek word for servant is a slave, and the idea suggested by it is that God wants to own us wholly before He uses us. Just as in royal palaces and princely mansions every bit of table service and plate bears the monogram of the owner, so God wants His name stamped on every vessel that He employs in the heavenly household. Beloved, have you given yourself away to Jesus so completely that the gift carries with it all you call your own? Then you have entered into the riches of His infinite resources and it is easy to give anything to Him.

Therefore, it is that in our Christian convocations we do not begin by asking people for their gifts but by leading them to an entire and joyful consecration of all to God; and then it is that these magnificent offerings follow, because they have first given themselves to the Lord and then their means follow as a matter of course. Oh, that the church of Christ would learn the true secret both of service and of beneficence. Then should it be true, "Thy people shall be willing in the day of thy power" (Psalm 110:3, KJV). The day of His power would indeed come, and the world be speedily brought to Christ. No power less than love of Christ can lift a selfish church to the heights of sacrifice. The iceberg floating in the Atlantic could not be lifted half an inch by all the hydraulic engines of the world, but the sun can lift it among the clouds in a little while by the power of evaporation until it floats amid the blue depths of space in many-tinted glory. The only magnet that can lift our hearts to God is the love of Christ, and therefore He is the great motive and example of Christian giving.

THE GREAT MOTIVE AND EXAMPLE OF CHRISTIAN GIVING

"For you know the grace of our Lord Jesus Christ, that though he was rich, yet for your sakes he became poor, so that you through his poverty might become rich" (2 Corinthians 8:9). Here the Lord appears among His people as a great and infinite Giver. He gives not a part but the whole. He gives till He has exhausted all His riches and absolutely impoverished Himself, for we are told that "though he was rich, yet for your sakes he became poor" (8:9). He emptied Himself, He kept nothing back. He has nothing left but the heritage of His people. "For the LORD'S portion is his people" (Deuteronomy 32:9). All else He has given away. There is no standard by which we can measure His infinite sacrifice and surrender. If a king should stoop to become a worm it would still be one creature becoming another, a lower gradation of the same class of being. But when Christ became a man and took upon Him the form of a created being, He stepped out of His class completely and plunged to a depth of condescension which is absolutely without any standard of comparison. And He did this that we might be made rich and clothed with all the glory and blessing which He gave up that we might have it. With such an example and such an inheritance, how shameful and how foolish that we should ever hesitate to let go the tinsel toys of earth for the infinite treasures of our inheritance in Him. It is only when we realize Christ's love for us that we truly learn and love to give.

Let us reflect upon that love. What has He done for you? What has He not done? Has He redeemed you by His blood? Has He blotted out your guilt and sin? Has He brought peace to your troubled heart? Has He cleansed your soul from its pollutions and its passions? Has He given you His Holy Spirit without measure? Has He surrounded you with the blessings of His providence? Has He blessed your home and filled your life with love and sweetness? Has He given you a thousand gifts of His providence and a thousand tokens of His care? Has He answered your prayers and filled your heart with joy and praise? Then beloved, you can say of the greatest and the most precious sacrifice that He asks from your love, as once a dear, dying woman whispered to us as we asked her if she could give up her husband, if she could give up her children, if she could give up even her life for Jesus, with a face lighted up with the glory of an opening heaven she stretched out her hands and cried over and over again, "It's little to give to Him, it's little to give to Him."

THE PRIVILEGE OF THE POOR

We are beautifully taught in this passage that giving is not the prerogative of the rich alone but the joyful privilege of God's poor. There is a deep pathos in the second verse of this chapter, "Out of the most severe trial, their overflowing joy and their extreme poverty welled up in rich generosity" (2 Corinthians 8:2). They were not excused from giving because they were in circumstances not only of poverty but of indigence. On the contrary, this only enhanced the love, the sacrifice and the acceptability of their gifts. When God has some great work to do He generally calls for some noble act of sacrifice and for some gift that costs. And so when He would nourish and preserve the great prophet of fire, Elijah, during the days of famine, He sent him not to the court of Ahab, or even the friendly hospitality of Obadiah, his noble friend at court; but He sent him to a poor widow at Zarephath. God allowed her to give her last morsel of meal and her last drop of oil for Elijah's support, and then He multiplied the gift and made it sufficient to keep them both through all the days of famine.

So again, a little before His Passion, the blessed Master during His last visit to the temple sat down for a little over against the treasury to watch the gifts of the people as they passed by. He paid no attention while the rich and noble cast in their splendid offerings, but when a poor widow came up and put in all her living, His heart was so deeply stirred that He called His disciples and marked the act as an everlasting memorial and example. It was because it was her all and because she was so poor. Christ did not forbid the gift. He did not bid her to take it back, but He let it go, and He placed upon it a valuation which all the millions of earth could not outweigh.

Once, it is said, a splendid temple was built in Constantinople by the Emperor Theodosius. Millions of dollars and years of skill and toil were spent upon the cherished enterprise until at last it was ready for dedication. The architect had emblazoned upon its front the inscription, "This church Theodosius built for God," but when the curtain was removed that covered the facade, to the astonishment of the Emperor, the architect and the crowd of attendant princes and generals, the inscription read, "This church the widow Eudoxia built for God." The ceremonies were instantly stopped and search was made for the presuming widow, but it was days before she could be found, and then it was discovered that she was a poor widow living far out in the suburbs who had done nothing for the splendid sanctuary but simply pull up the long grass from the roadside and spread it over the rough track to keep the beautiful stones as they were drawn to the temple from being scratched and effaced by the rocky road. The Emperor and his advisors, when they found out all about her, wisely concluded that she had not intruded, but that perhaps some angel unseen had changed that record in the night and put upon the front of the splendid temple a little example of the records that God is writing every day in the books of eternity, when the gifts of the poor will be found to have outranked and outweighed the most splendid endowments of wealth and luxury whose gifts have cost them nothing.

Let us not forget that it is possible for the poorest to try to hide themselves behind their poverty. It was the man with the one talent that missed his crown. Because he had so little he did nothing. And it was the widow with the one farthing that won the Savior's love and the everlasting memorial of His approval.

THE PRINCIPLE OF MISSIONARY PLEDGES

Is it right for Christians to make pledges in advance for their gifts to the cause of Christ, or should they only give of that which they actually have? Have we scriptural authority for missionary pledges? It seems very clear from this passage that these believers at Corinth had arranged and planned for their giving a year in advance, and that the apostle had taken special pains in preparing their offering beforehand. We read,

> And here is my advice about what is best for you in this matter: Last year you were the first not only to give but also to have the desire to do so. Now finish the work, so that your eager willingness to do it may be matched by your completion of it, according to your means. For if the willingness is there, the gift is acceptable according to what one has, not according to what he does not have. (8:10–12)

So again in the ninth chapter and the fifth verse he tells us that he "thought it necessary to urge the brothers to visit you in advance and finish the arrangements for the generous gift you had promised." It is very manifest from these passages that there had been much consideration, much preparation, much planning for this offering, and some of the most eminent brethren had even gone before to lay the matter fully upon the hearts of these disciples and make full preparation for their offering. For a whole year they had purposed to give these contributions, and now he appeals to them to make good their purpose and fulfill the performance of that which had been so heartily purposed. This surely is the very method which God has led us to adopt in these great offerings: namely, to lay upon the hearts and consciences of God's children the claims of Christ, the needs of the world and the obligation of giving liberally to send the gospel everywhere, and also encourage them to form the largest purposes and plans of giving and even sacrificing in the spirit of a generous love and a lofty faith, and then deliberately to go to work by labor, prayer and sacrifice to gather the means thus pledged day by day until the purpose shall have become an actual performance. There is something in such a principle and system fitted to give an inspiring motive and a glorious incentive to our whole business and life and to put into even our secular pursuits and daily callings a sacredness and sweetness that no language can express. As we go back to our homes and occupations we are carrying on our business for Christ and the world's evangelization, and we are encouraged to ask tenfold blessing on all our investments and enterprises and to throw our hearts into our work with a gladness and an energy inspired by the high purpose for which we are laboring. Our business becomes not a selfish struggle for existence but a noble partnership with God for the advance of His kingdom and the spread of His glorious gospel.

At the same time we are faithfully reminded in these passages that the obligation of paying these pledges is as sacred as that of making them. "Now finish the work, so that your eager willingness to do it may be matched by your completion of it, according to your means" (8:11). But even here there is the utmost tenderness and consideration for those who have failed to fulfill their well-meaning pledges. They are not to be discouraged and humiliated if they have really done it in uprightness of spirit, for God does not press us for more than we are able to do. If we have really done our best He will take the will for the deed, "For if the willingness is there, the gift is acceptable according to what one has, not according to what he does not have" (8:12).

PROPORTIONATE GIVING

Our desire is not that others might be relieved while you are hard pressed, but that there might be equality. At the present time your plenty will supply what they need, so that in turn their plenty will supply what you need. Then there will be equality, as it is written: "He who gathered much did not have too much, and he who gathered little did not have too little." (8:13–15)

Here we have God's message to the rich just as we had it a little while ago to the poor. How often it happens that when our means are limited our hearts are large, and when our resources increase our desire shrinks. "How is it, madame," said the minister to a lady who had come into the possession of a great fortune, "that you used to give so much when you were poor, and now that you are so rich you give so little?" "Ah," she answered, "when I had the penny purse, I had a guinea heart. Now that I have the guinea purse, I find that I have the penny heart."

Beloved, have your gifts to the Lord been increasing with your income? Has He shared proportionately the fruits of His blessing upon your business? "Will a man rob God? Yet you rob me. . . . In tithes and offerings" (Malachi 3:8).

The Bible has much to say of God's estimate of the gifts of the wealthy. When Moses received the offerings of the nobles of Israel they brought their wealth munificently, and the longest chapter in the Bible is devoted to the account of their gifts (Numbers 7), and at the close of that day of noble giving God was pleased to manifest Himself in a marvelous way in the tabernacle, "Moses . . . heard the voice speaking to him from between the two cherubim above the atonement cover on the ark of the Testimony" (7:89). Again, in the 29th chapter of First Chronicles, we have an account of the splendid offerings of David and his princes for the building of the temple. David's personal contributions amounted to over 80 million dollars on that one day, and the gifts of his nobles were over 120 million, and this was 3,000 years ago, in what we are pleased to call the age of semibarbarism.

When Jesus Christ was crucified it was a rich man who gave Him a tomb; and when the infant church was organized, the wealth of Barnabas was exchanged for the commission of an evangelist and the glorious work of planting Christianity throughout the world. The rich men of our day think nothing of investing millions in a new railway or a great trust. When will the day come that will show us the spectacle of a consecrated capitalist taking up a whole nation and providing for its evangelization? What a sublime sight it will be for the Christian men whom God has so splendidly enriched to come to the leaders of our great evangelistic movements and say, one by one, "I will give the gospel to Vietnam," "I will evangelize Cuba," "I will send 100 missionaries to the Philippines," until the whole world shall be parceled out for God as the commercial and political ambitions of our age are parceling it out for their own selfish aggrandizement.

ADMINISTRATION OF GIFTS

The administration of the gifts of God's people is a matter that should receive the most careful consideration from those entrusted with the executive work of the Church and her missionary plans. The apostle was most careful about this. "We want to avoid," he says, "any criticism of the way we administer this liberal gift. For we are taking pains to do what is right, not only in the eyes of the Lord but also in the eyes of men" (2 Corinthians 8:20–21). Therefore, it is most important that the business of our missionary societies and Christian churches should be carefully and faithfully performed.

1. It stirs up others to give. "Your enthusiasm has stirred most of them to action" (9:2). There is no doubt that the noble gifts at a great convention stimulate a vast increase of missionary liberality on the part of other churches and religious societies.

2. The blessing of God upon our temporal affairs is the certain fruit of our giving. "Whoever sows sparingly will also reap sparingly, and whoever sows generously will also reap generously. . . . And God is able to make all grace abound to you, so that in all things at all times, having all that you need, you will abound in every good work" (9:6, 8). There is no doubt that this passage refers directly to temporal blessing and God's promise to prosper us when we give liberally that we may be able to give more.

3. Our giving enables us to have a partnership in the work of others and to sow the seed of the gospel in fields which we personally could never visit. The men whom we support are simply the bearers of our own precious seed and "increase your store of seed and . . . enlarge the harvest of your righteousness" (9:10). The businessman who never can visit China or Africa may be able to preach the gospel around the world through the lips and hands and feet that he sends around the world. Some day groups of souls will meet him in the great harvest and be counted the fruit of his own direct ministry. If men could only realize in life what they will realize so fully after death, the joy of greeting in the heavenly world the souls whom they have brought home through their loving gifts, or on the other hand the anguish of seeing the means they might have left for God wasted by selfish heirs and turned into an eternal curse through their unfaithfulness in the disposition of the means which God had entrusted to them.

4. A great tribute of thanksgiving will be brought to God and a great cloud of prayer will ascend to the throne for you through the love that your generosity inspires and the blessing that your help shall bring. And it may be that in the coming years the blessing will flow back to you, and God will lay upon these very hearts a prayer for you in some hour when your heart is sinking and your life is in need and peril, and by and by in the heavenly world Christ will show you how you mutually ministered the one to the other, while the glory redounded to Jesus' name!

CHAPTER 11

THE THINGS PAUL GLORIED IN

I will boast about a man like that, but I will not boast about myself, except about my weaknesses. (2 Corinthians 12:5)

It is sometimes necessary even for a Christian to assert his manhood and self-respect. Most of the time Solomon's first prescription is best: "Do not answer a fool according to his folly,/ or you will be like him yourself" (Proverbs 26:4). But there are times when his second prescription is necessary: "Answer a fool according to his folly,/ or he will be wise in his own eyes" (26:5).

The apostle shrank from vindicating himself, but for the sake of the truth and the church in Corinth it became necessary for him to say something in answer to his enemies in that city, who were undermining his influence, ignoring his authority, ridiculing his claims and destroying his work.

In the course of this vindication, which occupies the last part of the epistle, there is a marked change in the general tone of the epistle and a deep sense on his part of being engaged in very uncongenial work. "I have made a fool of myself" (2 Corinthians 12:11), he says, and yet he adds: "For even if I boast somewhat freely about the authority the Lord gave us for building you up rather than pulling you down, I will not be ashamed of it" (10:8). In the course of his vindication he tells us of several things in which he feels he may well glory.

HIS MISSIONARY SERVICE

Paul felt that he had reason to glory in the privilege of preaching the gospel in foreign lands. He speaks of this in Second Corinthians 10:14–16:

> We are not going too far in our boasting, as would be the case if we had not come to you, for we did get as far as you with the gospel of Christ. Neither do we go beyond our limits by boasting

of work done by others. Our hope is that, as your faith continues
to grow, our area of activity among you will greatly expand, so
that we can preach the gospel in the regions beyond you. For we
do not want to boast about work already done in another man's
territory.

It was his supreme ambition and his great privilege to be permitted to
reach beyond the line of other men's labors and be the first to carry the
message of salvation to a large portion of the heathen world. This was an
honor of which his enemies did not even pretend to boast. Your teacher of
error, your higher critic, Christian Scientist and hydra-headed fanatic does
not run the risk of carrying his doctrines to the heathen world. He very
much prefers to work under the cover and shelter of a respectable pulpit, a
professor's chair and a comfortable salary at home, and to propagate his
theories among the easily accessible multitudes who have already been
brought, through someone else's labors, into the fold of Christ. False
doctrine seldom has much missionary zeal behind it; but as the wolf in
sheep's clothing, it prowls about the shepherd's tent and preys upon the
stragglers from the fold.

What a sublime ambition it is to be the first to tell the story of salvation to
some poor benighted soul, and perhaps become the father or the mother of
whole generations and new tribes and tongues! All honor to the heroic men
and women of our own day who have been the pioneers of the gospel in
Uganda, Congo, the Philippines, Hunan, Kwangsi, Tibet and other unevan-
gelized lands.

God speak to some who are wasting their lives in the narrow competitions
of business or Christian work at home and call them to the regions beyond.

NOT SELLING THE GOSPEL

Paul could glory in the privilege of preaching the gospel without charge.
Again he boasts thus in Second Corinthians 11:7–10:

Was it a sin for me to lower myself in order to elevate you by
preaching the gospel of God to you free of charge? I robbed other
churches by receiving support from them so as to serve you. And
when I was with you and needed something, I was not a burden
to anyone, for the brothers who came from Macedonia supplied
what I needed. I have kept myself from being a burden to you in
any way, and will continue to do so. As surely as the truth of
Christ is in me, nobody in the regions of Achaia will stop this
boasting of mine.

He almost apologizes to them for having deprived them of the privilege of his support, but he tells them that he is unwilling to relinquish the glory of preaching the gospel without a touch of heroic sacrifice and holy independence. In the parallel passage—First Corinthians 9:14–18—he explains more fully his attitude on this question:

> In the same way, the Lord has commanded that those who preach the gospel should receive their living from the gospel.
>
> But I have not used any of these rights. And I am not writing this in the hope that you will do such things for me. I would rather die than have anyone deprive me of this boast. Yet when I preach the gospel, I cannot boast, for I am compelled to preach. Woe to me if I do not preach the gospel! If I preach voluntarily, I have a reward; if not voluntarily, I am simply discharging the trust committed to me. What then is my reward? Just this: that in preaching the gospel I may offer it free of charge, and so not make use of my rights in preaching it.

He explains in these words that the support of the gospel ministry is one of God's ordinances, and there would be nothing wrong in his receiving a salary from his people if it were given in a scriptural way. But he says: "But I have not used any of these rights. . . . I would rather die than have anyone deprive me of this boast" (9:15). The preaching of the gospel brings him no reward, for this is simply his duty, but the preaching of the gospel without charge and the encountering of the trials and sacrifices it brings is one of the ways in which he is winning his crown. This act on his part was entirely voluntary and God accepted it, and accepts it still from some of His servants, and makes up to them in other ways Himself.

Paul gloried in this not only because it was an opportunity of sacrificing something for his Master, but also because it added a new force to his ministry, and met the reproaches of his enemies that he was preaching for personal aggrandizement or gain. Every missionary in China knows how hard it is to persuade the people that we are influenced by purely benevolent motives in seeking their salvation. They find it difficult to understand anybody giving something for nothing, and when they really discover that the object of the missionaries is purely disinterested, the impression is most profound and is one of the most powerful assets of the missionaries in winning their confidence. There is nothing more important in our Christian work than that we should be free from all men, and that the spirit of self-sacrifice and independence should inspire every servant of the Lord Jesus. We have no business to be any man's echo or hired preacher. Our authority comes to us directly from the High Court of Heaven, and the gifts of God's people lay us under no human obligations, but are simply their own duty to Him whose representatives and ministers we are.

A LIFE OF SUFFERING, TOIL AND DANGER

Paul gloried in a life of suffering, toil and danger in the service of His Master. What a catalog of his labors and privations he has left us:

> I have worked much harder, been in prison more frequently, been flogged more severely, and been exposed to death again and again. Five times I received from the Jews the forty lashes minus one. Three times I was beaten with rods, once I was stoned, three times I was shipwrecked, I spent a night and a day in the open sea, I have been constantly on the move. I have been in danger from rivers, in danger from bandits, in danger from my own countrymen, in danger from Gentiles; in danger in the city, in danger in the country, in danger at sea; and in danger from false brothers. I have labored and toiled and have often gone without sleep; I have known hunger and thirst and have often gone without food; I have been cold and naked. Besides everything else, I face daily the pressure of my concern for all the churches. Who is weak, and I do not feel weak? Who is led into sin, and I do not inwardly burn?
>
> If I must boast, I will boast of the things that show my weakness. (2 Corinthians 11:23–30)

What a life, filled up with such a catalog of privation and pain! And yet there is no shade of complaint, there is no pleading for sympathy, but on the contrary these are prized by him as a soldier glories in his scars and counts it his highest honor even to die for his country.

Even in human affairs the strength of a nation's spirit is largely dependent upon the heroic sacrifices of its sons. The Greek soul was kindled to higher valor by the remembrances of Leonidas and the Spartan heroes. Rome cherished the early memories of the accomplishments of her people. England and America count these their richest heritages. And probably the secret of the extraordinary success of Japan arises from the fact that every Japanese soldier is trained from his infancy to count it his highest glory to die for his Emperor.

The story of the Bible is strung upon the same crimson thread of heroic sacrifice. Abraham had to give up his Isaac, Moses his earthly ambition, and Hannah her beloved son, before God could give His highest blessing.

David could not sit upon his throne until he had won it by heroic courage and suffering. The very life-blood of Christianity is the spirit of sacrifice.

The root of decay begins with self-indulgence and ease. The curse of lukewarmness is destroying the vital power of religion. The greatest need of modern missions is a heroic spirit both in the workers abroad and the supporters at home. Oh, for a revival of the spirit of Moriah and Calvary's cross!

> Oh Love that gave Thy life for me,
> Help me to live and love like Thee
> And kindle in this heart of mine
> The passion fire of love divine.

> Make duty joy and suffering sweet
> As both are laid at Jesus' feet,
> And kindle in this heart of mine
> The passion fire of love divine.

HIS DIVINE REVELATIONS

He gloried in His divine revelations. What a disclosure he gives us of the high honor confided to him by the Lord!

> I know a man in Christ who fourteen years ago was caught up to the third heaven. Whether it was in the body or out of the body I do not know—God knows. And I know that this man—whether in the body or apart from the body I do not know, but God knows—was caught up to paradise. He heard inexpressible things, things that man is not permitted to tell. (12:2–4)

And this was no isolated instance, for he lived in the society of heaven. Again and again the Master's presence was vouchsafed for him in the critical moments of his life, and the Lord stood by him with words of encouragement and promise and with His mighty interposing providences.

What an honor men and women count it to be presented to an earthly king, perhaps once in a lifetime, and it is handed down to many generations as a family record! How the ambitious literary aspirants of the day covet the honor of telling of the friendship of a Gladstone, a Tennyson or some distinguished name; but Paul had the privilege of many an audience with the very Court of Heaven and with the Sovereign of the universe. Indeed, he could always claim such an audience, and by the telephone of prayer connect without limitation with the heart of God. This is the highest honor that God can give to mortals, and "This is the glory of all his saints" (Psalm 149:9).

The apostle refers here to some special revelations from the Lord. God has already spoken to us through His Word, and we are not to wait for private revelations to know His will. And yet He does speak to the individual heart, making the things of God intensely real, for " 'No eye has seen,/ no ear has heard,/ no mind has conceived/ what God has prepared for those who love him'—/ but God has revealed it to us by his Spirit. The Spirit searches all things, even the deep things of God" (1 Corinthians 2:9–10). Such revelations as God sometimes makes to the waiting hearts of His children are not intended for other ears. The apostle distinctly says that what he heard was not lawful for a man to utter.

Let us not make the mistake of exposing the secrets of the Lord and confusing the hearts of His humble people with things which perhaps God only meant for you.

TEMPTATIONS AND COMPENSATIONS

Paul gloried in his temptations and their compensations.

> To keep me from becoming conceited because of these surpassingly great revelations, there was given me a thorn in my flesh, a messenger of Satan, to torment me. Three times I pleaded with the Lord to take it away from me. But he said to me, "My grace is sufficient for you, for my power is made perfect in weakness." Therefore I will boast all the more gladly about my weaknesses, so that Christ's power may rest on me. That is why, for Christ's sake, I delight in weaknesses, in insults, in hardships, in persecutions, in difficulties. For when I am weak, then I am strong. (2 Corinthians 12:7–10)

The revelations which came to Paul were so extraordinary that there was danger of his mind becoming unbalanced, and therefore God gave, as a balance wheel to him, severe temptations. One particular test was permitted which is somewhat obscure in its exact character. It was "a thorn in my flesh, a messenger of Satan, to torment me" (12:7). It may have been physical, it certainly was partly spiritual, and the effect of it was much humiliation. He asked the Lord for its removal, and he continued to ask again and yet again. But at length the answer came. God would not take away the trial, but would send additional strength through it and would be more to him than if the trial had been removed. Thereupon the apostle accepted it as a blessing in disguise and began to praise God for it, and even to glory in the very infirmities, reproaches and distress which seemed to hinder, but which became the occasion rather "so that Christ's power may rest on [him]" (12:9).

The transformation of trial into blessing is one of the deepest mysteries of God's providence and grace. In the realm of nature we have many illustrations of bringing good out of evil. They say that the song bird will not learn its notes in the sunlight, but its cage has to be darkened; and then, separated from the distracting sights and sounds of the world, it listens to its lesson and it learns its beautiful melody. So God has to put us into the place of silence and gloom to teach us the everlasting song.

It is a well-known secret that electric power is produced by friction. Go to a great power house and there you will see the cylinders revolving against strong pressure, and out of the pressure comes the electric fire. So God develops spiritual power in our lives through the pressure of hard places.

Trial reveals us to ourselves and shows us our weakness and nothingness. Then it reveals Christ to us and shows us His infinite resources until we hear Him saying, "My grace is sufficient for you, for my power is made perfect in weakness" (12:9).

Trial develops and brings to perfection the fruits of the Spirit, deepening the soil and cultivating the garden of the great Gardener and bringing forth the sweetness and the strength of His grace. And trial brings to us the power of God and presents to the world the amazing spectacle of a soul elevated above all surrounding circumstances and conditions, in the hardest places and yet able to say, "sorrowful, yet always rejoicing; poor, yet making many rich; having nothing, and yet possessing everything" (6:10).

> It is easy enough to be pleasant
>   When life goes by with a song,
> But the man worthwhile is the man who can smile
>   When everything goes dead wrong.
>
> For the heart is tested by trouble
>   And it grows with the passing years;
> And the smile that is worth all the treasures of earth
>   Is the smile that shines through our tears.

GALATIANS

CHAPTER 1

FREE GRACE, OR CHRIST IN GALATIANS

I am astonished that you are so quickly deserting the one who called you by the grace of Christ and are turning to a different gospel. (Galatians 1:6)

It is for freedom that Christ has set us free. Stand firm, then, and do not let yourselves be burdened again by a yoke of slavery. (5:1)

The Galatians were the Celts of western Asia. Like the French, the Irish and the Scottish Highlanders of our day, they were a high-spirited, impulsive people, as quick to be perverted as they had been to be converted at the preaching of Paul. They had received him on his first visit with intense enthusiasm, "as if I were an angel of God, as if I were Christ Jesus himself" (4:14b), and "if you could have done so, you would have torn out your eyes and given them to me" (4:15b). But now they have turned back at the bidding of false teachers and just as promptly gone after "those weak and miserable principles. Do you wish to be enslaved by them all over again? You are observing special days and months and seasons and years! . . . You were running a good race. Who cut in on you and kept you from obeying the truth?" (4:9b–10; 5:7).

They had already fallen into the hands of the high church or ritualistic party of that day. It is the old and favorite counterfeit of the enemy which again today is sweeping so many by a resistless current on to the inevitable shores of Romanism—a desire for ceremony and outward form instead of spirituality and holiness. This was the delusion which had drawn away the once fervid and evangelical churches of Galatia. These false teachers were trying to draw them back to Judaism, the ceremonial law, the rite of circumcision, and the bondage of the past. And in order to fortify their position, they had persuaded the Galatians that Paul had no authority to preach the gospel to them; that he was inferior to the other apostles, and that James and

349

Peter were the true leaders of the Church, and the supreme authorities on matters of Church law and practice.

Paul therefore is compelled to vindicate his apostleship, and so he rehearses the story of his call and ministry. He reminds them that his authority is not of man, nor by man, but directly from God the Father and the Lord Jesus Christ. He reminds them of his independent stand with the other apostles, and of his direct commission to the Gentiles, which even the apostles themselves freely admitted. He tells them also of his firm attitude when the Judaizing party demanded that Titus the Gentile should be circumcised, to whom he "did not give in to them for a moment, so that the truth of the gospel might remain with you" (2:5). Nay, further, when Peter became inconsistent, and, after having received the Gentiles through the deeper teaching of the Spirit, went back through fear of the Jews and resumed his old conservative and exclusive attitude, drawing away even Barnabas with him, he reminds them: "When I saw that they were not acting in line with the truth of the gospel" (2:14a), "I opposed [Peter] to his face, because he was clearly in the wrong" (2:11).

Having thus vindicated his own apostleship and proved his consistent attitude in relation to the gospel, he proceeds to unfold his great argument for free grace, and against the false teachers and Judaizing elements of the day. The result is one of the most precious of the New Testament epistles of which the keynote throughout is the term "free grace," especially as we trace it in our salvation, our sanctification, and our spirit toward others.

THE MEANING OF FREE GRACE

1. Divine Goodness

Grace is the divine goodness with special reference to the unworthy and the helpless. It is not love to the good, but to the bad. There is something in God which can love the unlovely, and can take hold of wrong, and by the power of His grace lift it to the right and even turn the curse into a blessing. "How wonderful!" said one, after speaking of the grace of God to poor sinners. "No," said a poor slave, who had lately been saved; "It is not wonderful at all; it is just like Him." And yet it is so unlike us that the natural heart cannot understand it.

On the Cornish coast there were once two fishermen who were on unfriendly terms. One was a rude and most ungodly man who took every opportunity to injure and insult the other who was a Christian, even destroying his fishing nets on the pretext that he had trespassed on his grounds. One stormy day the fishing boat of the former was drifting out to sea and would certainly have been lost had not the other leaped into the surf and by desperate exertions rescued it. As he slowly drew it to its moorings and came ashore, the owner had come out of an ale house and was standing with sulky mien on the shore.

Too rude to thank him, he looked up with a sullen glance and said, "Why did you do that?"

"Because," said the other, "I couldn't help it."

"But how could you do it after the way I have treated you?"

"Why," said the other, "I couldn't help it."

"What are you?" said the first.

"I am a Christian," he answered.

"Well," said the other, "you are the first I have met."

That is grace, the sort of love that cannot help blessing those who curse us, and doing good to the unthankful and undeserving. The apostle has defined it in another of his epistles thus: "But because of his great love for us, God, who is rich in mercy, made us alive with Christ even when we were dead in transgressions" (Ephesians 2:4–5a). "But God demonstrates his own love for us in this: While we were still sinners, Christ died for us" (Romans 5:8).

2. Salvation

Salvation is the gift of God's free grace. It is not deserved or earned by works, but it is the bestowment of God's sovereign grace. "The gift of God is eternal life in Christ Jesus our Lord" (6:23b). "For it is by grace you have been saved, through faith—and this not from yourselves, it is the gift of God—not by works, so that no one can boast" (Ephesians 2:8–9). The only terms on which we can have salvation at all is by taking the place of the sinner and accepting the mercy of God, for Christ's sake.

3. Ransom

This grace is purchased through the ransom of Christ's blood. While free to us, it was most costly to Him, and the price paid was His own life. "Who gave himself for our sins to rescue us from the present evil age, according to the will of our God and Father" (Galatians 1:4). "Christ redeemed us from the curse of the law by becoming a curse for us" (3:13a).

4. Justification

The grace of God for Christ's sake justifies us and puts us in the same position as if we had never sinned. It is not mere scant deliverance from condemnation, but it is complete and honorable justification. It is not our discharge because the jury has failed to agree upon a conviction, or the executive has determined upon a pardon; but it is a decree of the supreme court of the universe, proclaiming us faultless and blameless and putting us in as good a position as the Lord Jesus Christ Himself, our Surety and Substitute.

5. Calling

But grace has yet another direction in the sinner's salvation. "God . . . called me by his grace" (1:15). It was the grace of God that brought Paul even to know and receive God's grace. Vainly for him had the gift been offered and the ransom paid, unless grace had also stooped so low as to reach him in his unbelief and win him in his alienation and sin. For Paul had been a bitter enemy of the grace of God; he had rejected the Savior and was doing all in his power to oppose the gospel and destroy its followers, and at the very moment of his conversion was in the high tide of his rebellion and unbelief. But the grace of God struck him down in the blossom of his sin, and compelled him to accept its proffered love. And so Paul became a captive of grace and never tired of celebrating the love that when he was still an enemy, reconciled him to God.

We may think that we have had a very different history and that we were quite as earnest in seeking God as He was in seeking us; but when the whole story is told, it will be found at last that there is not much difference between the best of us and the blunt Scotchman, who, when asked how his conversion came about, said that it took two to do it, one was God and the other was himself. When his good Calvinistic pastor asked him how he could claim any part in it, he answered him, "God drew me, and I resisted all I could." That is about the most we can say for our part. "By the grace of God I am what I am," was the testimony of Paul, and the epitaph on the monument of William Carey may well take us all in:

> A worthless, weak, and helpless worm,
>   On Thy kind arms I fall,
> Be Thou my perfect righteousness,
>   My Saviour and my All.

HIS ARGUMENT FOR FREE GRACE

1. The Covenant with Abraham

He proves it from the covenant with Abraham. "Consider Abraham: 'He believed God, and it was credited to him as righteousness.' . . . The Scripture foresaw that God would justify the Gentiles by faith, and announced the gospel in advance to Abraham: 'All nations will be blessed through you.' So those who have faith are blessed along with Abraham, the man of faith" (3:6, 8–9).

The authority of Abraham, their father, was supreme with every Jew, and therefore Paul appeals to it and reminds them that the covenant of salvation made with Abraham for himself and his seed was purely one of faith and grace. For even in Genesis we are told that Abraham's faith was counted to him for righteousness (Genesis 15:6). Then later in the chapter Paul reminds them that the covenant with Abraham was made 430 years before the law on Sinai, and, therefore, that later law could not disannul or make the promise of none effect (Galatians 3:17).

The covenant with Abraham was an everlasting covenant, and its very principle was free grace and not works, faith and not personal merit. And so all believers still are recognized as the children of Abraham and coinheritors with him of the grace of God.

2. The Law of Moses

His next argument for free grace is founded on the law of Moses. For even the law, he tells us, had in it the principle of grace. The very object of the law was to convict men of sin and so throw them upon the mercy of God. "Is the law, therefore, opposed to the promises of God? Absolutely not! . . . But the Scripture declares that the whole world is a prisoner of sin, so that what was promised, being given through faith in Jesus Christ, might be given to those who believe" (3:21a–22).

"So," he adds, introducing a fine figure, "the law was put in charge [was our schoolmaster, KJV] to lead us to Christ that we might be justified by faith" (3:24). The Greek word translated "schoolmaster" is *pedagogue*. Now the pedagogue was not a schoolmaster exactly, but the manservant who took the children to school and delivered them over to the schoolmaster who took charge of their studies. Christ is the real Teacher, and the law was just the servant to conduct us to Christ; and when Christ comes, the work of the law is accomplished: "Now that faith has come, we are no longer under the supervision of the law. You are all sons of God through faith in Christ Jesus" (3:25–26). The law never was intended to save men, but to convince them of their need of a Savior and point forward to Him who was to be the Redeemer of men.

In the next paragraph the apostle uses still another figure to explain the place of the law. It is the figure of the minor, the child under age, who is under tutors and governors until he reaches his maturity. "So also," he says, "when we were children, we were in slavery under the basic principles of the world. But when the time had fully come, God sent his Son, born of a woman, born under law, to redeem those under law, that we might receive the full rights of sons. Because you are sons, God sent the Spirit of his Son into our hearts, the Spirit who calls out, 'Abba, Father.' So you are no longer a slave, but a son; and since you are a son, God has made you also an heir" (4:3–7). And so the law leads on to the gospel, and the gospel is liberty, the freedom of the Father's house, the filial spirit, the privileges of a happy child; and if we return to the law, we must set back the hands of the clock of time more than 3,000 years, and go back to Sinai and the infancy and minority of the children of God.

3. Ishmael and Isaac

His next argument is the allegory of Ishmael and Isaac (4:22–31).

Hagar, the bondwoman, represents the law, and Ishmael, her son, the flesh. For the law can only produce the flesh. Our best efforts even in the direction of righteousness end only in self-righteousness, and we must die to our goodness, quite as much as to our badness, before we can enter the kingdom of heaven.

On the other hand, Sarah represents the gospel and the covenant of grace, while Isaac, her son, is the type of the life of the Spirit which is the offspring of grace. Just as Ishmael persecuted Isaac, so the flesh lusts against the Spirit. Ishmael cannot be improved; he must be cast out with his mother. But you cannot get rid of Ishmael alone—you must cast out both the bondwoman and her son. The spirit of legality must go with the flesh.

Free grace alone can bring forth the new life, and under its nourishing influence alone can the spiritual life be educated and matured. The law in every form, whether it be the ceremonial law, the moral law, or the penances, tortures and struggles of conscience and self-effort of the natural man, can only end in failure and in some other form of fleshly life. "For sin shall not be your master, because you are not under law, but under grace" (Romans 6:14).

THE REASONS WHY THE APOSTLE CONTENDS SO EARNESTLY FOR FREE GRACE

Are the doctrines of evangelical religion so supremely important? Are we justified in contending so earnestly for the faith once delivered unto the saints? Have the spiritual leaders of our time cause to fear the downgrade movement which is carrying so large a part of the Church of today into ethical culture, rationalism and Christian socialism, through the preaching of Christ without a cross? Have we reason to dread the subtle influence of such teaching, beautiful in its theories of an ideal Christ-life, but like cut flowers that have no root?

Certainly Paul had no sentimental weakness about the matter. The language he uses is uncompromising and unmistakable. "But even if we or an angel from heaven should preach a gospel other than the one we preached to you," he says, "let him be eternally condemned!" (Galatians 1:8). It is not merely a matter of difference of opinion. It is a matter of life and death to preach the pure gospel of Jesus Christ and nothing else and nothing less.

1. Free Grace Is Sovereign

Nothing else is worthy of God. The glory of Christianity is the sovereign grace from which it sprang, and no loyal Christian heart will hold back any of the glory due to the Father's love and the Savior's cross.

2. Free Grace Meets Our Need

It is the only salvation that is adapted to fallen man. Nothing but mercy can meet the needs of the worthless and the helpless. Because God expects nothing of us, therefore the worst and weakest of us may hope and trust. "It took me half a lifetime," says a distinguished writer, "to find out three things: namely, first, that I could not do anything to save myself; second, that God did not expect me to do anything; and third, that Christ has done all for me, and I have only to accept Him and thank Him for the free gift of eternal life."

3. Free Grace Makes Us Holy

Free grace is the only thing that can make men holy. Instead of encouraging men to sin, it inspires them to love and serve God.

In the Peninsular War a deserter was brought before the Duke of Wellington and condemned by the court-martial over which he presided, to be shot. Before passing sentence, the Duke remarked, "We have tried everything with this man. We have punished him again and again, but he seems hopeless. I am afraid we shall have to sentence him to the extreme penalty."

At that moment a comrade touched his cap and asked permission to speak.

"Your Grace," he said, "may I venture to suggest that there is one thing you have not tried?"

"What is that?" asked the Duke.

"I think," said the man, "you have never tried forgiving him."

"Well," said the Duke, "we'll try that."

The effect upon the man was extraordinary. He seemed quite overcome with gratitude, and he went from that court-martial to prove himself the bravest and truest of the soldiers of the Peninsula, rising to rank and distinction by brave service and fully proving the wisdom of his comrade's suggestion.

To a true nature love is always a higher inspiration than slavish fear. God trusts us, thinks His best thoughts of us, refuses to think evil of us, and encourages us to think of ourselves accordingly. It is His love that constrains us to goodness and lifts us to love and grateful obedience. Even when we abuse God's liberty by falling into sin, His grace overrules it to teach us, by the discipline, the bitterness of sin and the better way of loving obedience.

John Ruskin tells us that his earliest recollection of youthful liberty is of sitting on his mother's knee as she was preparing tea in the glowing urn which stood on the table steaming with boiling water, while the nurse stood by. Little John gazed a while at the burnished brass and the pretty clouds of steam, and insisted on reaching out his little hand and touching the urn. His mother tried to keep him back, but he grew rebellious.

"Let him touch it," said the nurse, "it will do him good."

And so the mother gave him the coveted liberty. There was a sudden cry, and speaking of it afterwards, John says, "That was the last time for many years that I remember asking to have my own way."

So God can sanctify to us even our own abuse of free grace. He will let you disobey Him if you will. He will let you sin if you want to. But as you think of His love and find by experience the bitterness of sin and the sweetness of obedience, you do not want to sin; you do not want to abuse so kind a Friend. His gentleness makes you good and gentle, too.

John Wesley and John Bradford had a severe quarrel which separated them for some days. Meeting shortly afterwards, John Wesley asked John Bradford, "Don't you want to ask my forgiveness, John?"

"No," said Bradford.

"Well," said Wesley, "I want to ask yours."

And the two friends fell into each other's arms. Humility and grace had conquered as they ever will. It is thus that God treats the rebel and the sinner. Shall we be worthy of His grace? Shall we accept His generous love and let it lift us to higher things? Shall we stop thinking hard of ourselves lest we end by thinking hard of Him? Shall we take the place the Father gives the prodigal—not the kitchen and the servant's place, but the best robe, the ring, the feast, the Father's heart—and go forth to live as we often sing:

Oh, the love that sought me!
Oh, the blood that bought me!
Oh, the grace that brought me to the fold!
Wondrous grace that brought me to the fold!

CHAPTER 2

FREE GRACE IN OUR SANCTIFICATION

So I say, live by the Spirit, and you will not gratify the desires of the sinful nature. (Galatians 5:16)

Are you so foolish? After beginning with the Spirit, are you now trying to attain your goal by human effort? (3:3)

I have been crucified with Christ and I no longer live, but Christ lives in me. The life I live in the body, I live by faith in the Son of God, who loved me and gave himself for me. (2:20)

Most of us have been taught that, while our salvation and justification are given us through the free grace of God and received by simple faith alone, yet our sanctification must be worked out by ourselves, and the struggle between evil and good in our own hearts and lives must be a long and painful one.

This was the error into which the Galatians had been led by false teachers. Having begun in the Spirit, they were seeking to be made perfect in the flesh. Having taught them, as we have already seen, the doctrine of free grace in their salvation, the apostle now proceeds to show them that their sanctification is just as much a gift as their justification, and that the deeper work of the Holy Spirit and the indwelling Christ in their hearts is also a work of grace as free and as complete as the first chapter in their religious experience.

In the course of this discussion he brings out a number of most important principles respecting the spiritual life which may be best stated as distinct propositions.

1. A Gift of Grace

Our sanctification is part of Christ's redemption and therefore must be a gift of grace.

"Grace and peace to you," he says, "from God our Father and the Lord Jesus Christ, who gave himself for our sins to rescue us from the present evil age, according to the will of our God and Father" (Galatians 1:3–4). Here we are taught that Christ died to deliver us not only from the future evil that threatens every sinner, but from this present evil age, that is, from evil of the present in all its forms, and, of course, from the evil of our own sinful hearts. Sanctification, therefore, is the purchase of Christ's blood and part of our great redemption. "Because by one sacrifice he has made perfect forever those who are being made holy" (Hebrews 10:14).

2. By Faith

Sanctification is by faith and not by works.

"But by faith we eagerly await through the Spirit the righteousness for which we hope. For in Christ Jesus neither circumcision nor uncircumcision has any value. The only thing that counts is faith expressing itself through love" (Galatians 5:5–6). Things which come to us by faith must come without works, for faith is but the hand to receive what God bestows, and we cannot believe for a thing if we have yet to work it out. Faith recognizes the blessing as an accomplished fact and "we who have believed enter that rest" (Hebrews 4:3). Sanctification by faith, therefore, is the rest of faith.

3. A Positive Experience

Sanctification is a positive and not a negative experience.

That is, it comes not through the act of struggling against evil, but rather through the receiving of the good and letting this displace the evil. This is a very profound and practical principle. The old familiar illustration of letting in the light instead of sweeping out the darkness, tells the whole story. Dr. Chalmers found his great sermon on the expulsive power of a new affection in the simple incident of hearing the coachman tell that, when his shying horse came near a certain turn in the road where he usually became frightened, he gave him a sharp cut with his whip just beforehand, which so preoccupied him that he dashed by the critical point without noticing it. As the driver put it, he "gave him something to think about." When God would save us from the consciousness and pressure of temptation and sin, He preoccupies our mind and fills our heart with something stronger and higher, and thus by the expulsive power of a stronger influence, the evil is banished, and the soul is purified and preserved in the abiding life of Christ.

Playing with a dangerous pair of scissors, a little child could not be per-suaded by his anxious mother to give them up. Fearing that violence might provoke him to hurt himself with his perilous weapon, the mother called her little daughter to her aid. Sending her to a closet for a beautiful orange, the game of strategy began.

The little girl commenced by gentle approaches to attract Willie's attention to the big yellow orange. As it came nearer, eyes, mouth and hands were all stretched out wide open for it, and before the little fellow realized it, the scissors were dropped and quickly snatched and put out of harm's way by the watchful mother, and heart and hands were filled with the more attractive fruit. That is God's way of saving and sanctifying men. He gives us something better. He overcomes evil with good, and the heart filled with Christ and satisfied with His love drops the baubles of sin as worthless things and scorns to call it even a sacrifice to "consider everything a loss compared to the surpassing greatness of knowing Christ Jesus" (Philippians 3:8), and even as refuse in comparison with His attractions. This is the meaning of Galatians 5:16: "So I say, live by the Spirit, and you will not gratify the desires of the sinful nature." The secret of holiness is to receive the Holy Spirit and to be ever filled with His presence, His love, His joy, and His power, and to let Him deal with sin.

4. Through the Spirit

Sanctification is through the supernatural power of the Spirit and not through our struggles and our strength.

"For the sinful nature desires what is contrary to the Spirit, and the Spirit what is contrary to the sinful nature. They are in conflict with each other, so that you do not do [or better, may not do] what you want. But if you are led by the Spirit, you are not under law" (Galatians 5:17–18).

Many of us have been taught that the normal Christian life is a ceaseless struggle between two natures in the human soul, the evil and the good within us, and that a Christian is a sort of menagerie of wild beasts, with the keeper and the savage brutes continually at war. We find such a struggle in the seventh chapter of Romans. This is not the normal condition of the Christian, but the preparatory stage to a true experience of peace, rest and victory described in the following chapter, the life of the Spirit. This misunderstanding is partly due to the verse quoted above, which in our old Bibles used to be printed with a small "s" in the word Spirit, giving the impression that the conflict was between the man's flesh and the man's spirit, and that the issue was interminable war and a hopeless struggle in which it became true that "you do not do [cannot do, KJV] what you want" (5:17). This would be very sad indeed and would quench all the springs of hope in the Christian heart. Thank God our Bibles are now better printed, and the capital "S" leaves no doubt who the second Party in the conflict is—the Holy Spirit. It is the Holy Spirit that lusts against the flesh, and not our human spirit, and the word "cannot" should be "may not." Because the Holy Spirit is fighting the battle with the flesh, we must take sides with Him by refusing to do the bidding of the flesh and walking in obedience to the

Spirit. If we do this, He will fight the battle of the flesh, and it will be true as of old, "The battle is not yours, but God's" (2 Chronicles 20:15b).

The writer will be pardoned for recalling a moment in his own experience which tells the whole story, at least of his Christian life. It was the moment after he had yielded himself to Christ and received Him as the all-sufficiency of his future life, handing over in one supreme transaction all his sin, self-life, strength and weakness, all his conflicts, cares, temptations, needs, to the keeping of the indwelling Christ who henceforth became the Sponsor for all his future. He rose from that prayer with a quiet sense of rest. There was no special emotional feeling, no marvelous experience, but a deep sense of a great transaction done and a question settled.

Then came the first test. It was a deep, subtle suggestion of the adversary, almost as if he had said, "You fool. You think you have been sanctified. But you are just the same as you were 10 minutes ago. You have simply humbugged yourself and imagined that something has come to you, but you feel nothing, you have nothing. You have just fooled yourself."

For an instant the effect was utterly bewildering, and the first impulse was to fly into the old battle and begin to fight the tempter with my own reasonings against his suggestion. But instantly there came, as though from a heavenly suggestion, the quiet thought, "This is not your battle, but Christ's. Don't answer him. Hand it over to your great Deliverer. Roll the burden on the Lord. Tell the devil that you have nothing to do with him now, that you have just taken Christ to manage all your temptations, answer all your questions, and meet all your enemies."

It was such a strange and new conception, so easy and yet so effectual. In a moment the silent prayer had been offered, the question referred to Christ, the burden dropped, and lo, the cloud had gone, I knew not where! But this I knew, something real was there. Something actual had come to pass. A victory was won and with it the secret of victory for all time to come. This, beloved, is the secret of the new life. It is the power of the Holy Spirit, not of your wrestlings and strivings.

Through the skill of Mr. Edison, a method was devised enabling manufacturers to utilize the cheap iron ore which formerly was not worth the labor of working. It is now taken and crushed by simple machinery; then a magnet is passed through the dust, and instantly all the metal crystallizes around the magnet and leaves the sand and rock to be washed away. By a perfectly simple and self-acting principle, the precious is separated from the vile and fused into one mass of unalloyed metal. So the Holy Spirit has a magic touchstone by which He drops out of our life the evil, gathers about His own Person the good, the true, the pure, breathes into it His own Spirit, and keeps it by His own living power. Happy are they who learn to let the Spirit lust against the flesh and leave the burdens even of their sanctification and their temptations restfully and victoriously with Him.

5. Through the Indwelling Christ

Sanctification is through the personal indwelling of the Lord Jesus.

This is the end to which the Spirit is always working, not to develop in us a character, a set of human virtues and high qualities that we can call our own, but to form Christ in us and teach us to live in constant dependence upon Him. It is not a state, but a relation, a union with a Person, a living Presence who carries in Himself all the forces and resources of our new life.

In the city of Naples there stood for many months a splendid marble figure gradually assuming finer proportions and more perfect finish as the sculptors chiseled and polished from day to day. But there was no name upon the marble block and no sign to indicate for whom the monument was being reared. At last, when all was done, six letters were cut in the base in bold capitals, "CRISPI," and every Italian knew that it was the monument of the greatest statesman of their country, who had lately passed away. So we have been taught character grows slowly through the years as education, association, example, patient effort, constant self-culture, and all the ethical influences which are supposed to make character, are brought to bear upon a life, until at last the ideal is complete, and the man stands before an admiring universe a finished character.

This may be human ethics, but it is not divine holiness. True, there is a figure, perfect and complete, and over it you can read the name, not "CRISPI," but "CHRIST." But it is not cut in stone; it is not a splendid example for us to imitate. It is a *Living Presence*. It is a Man like ourselves who has traversed every phase of human experience, and yet, so glorified, so spiritualized, and so divine, that he can now come back and enter into living union with us, and relive His life once more in every Christ-filled man.

This is the apostle's ideal of sanctification in Galatians. He expresses it in that incomparable passage which is the very essence of the gospel of the deeper Christian life. "I have been crucified with Christ and I no longer live, but Christ lives in me. The life I live in the body, I live by faith in [the faith of, KJV] the Son of God, who loved me and gave himself for me" (Galatians 2:20). Here the substitution is so complete that not only is the old "I" of the natural self left out and crucified with Christ, but even the new "I" that has risen with Him is suppressed, and Christ, as a personal Presence, takes its place.

Even the very faith by which this life is maintained in union with Jesus is not our faith, but the faith of the Son of God actively manifested in us by virtue of that substitution through which He gave Himself to be instead of us. This is a wonderful, though mystical, truth. It is indeed "the mystery that has been kept hidden for ages and generations, but is now disclosed to the saints" (Colossians 1:26), and it is "Christ in you, the hope of glory" (1:27). Remember, beloved, it is not a figure, but a fact. It is not a feeling, but a Person. It is not an improved self, but it is the Lord Himself.

> Once it was the blessing,
> Now it is the Lord.

Do you know this blessed life hid with Christ in God? Have you learned to take His yoke on you and find it easy just because He bears the load Himself?

A farmer's boy, once listening to an exposition of this beautiful promise, "My yoke is easy and my burden is light" (Matthew 11:30), said that his father always fixed the ring in their yoke close to one end, and he put the short end of the yoke on the big ox, and the long end on the weak one. The result was that the big one drew nearly all the load, and the little one just walked along and sort of felt as if he were helping. That is the sort of yoke Jesus puts on us. He takes the heavy end and lets us have just enough to feel that we are in the partnership. But the burden rests on Him. Blessed partnership! Blessed Yokefellow! Blessed rest to sing:

> Not I, but Christ, my every need supplying,
>   Not I, but Christ, my Strength and Health to be;
> Christ, only Christ, for body, soul and spirit,
>   Christ, only Christ, live Thou Thy life in me.

6. Through Love

Sanctification is not through the necessity of law, but through the power of love.

"The entire law is summed up in a single command: 'Love your neighbor as yourself' " (Galatians 5:14). And "the fruit of the Spirit is love, joy, peace, patience, kindness, goodness, faithfulness, gentleness and self-control. Against such things there is no law" (5:22–23). It is a principle of human nature that the things which we would not do under necessity we would often gladly do from love.

The story is told of two young people who had been predestined to marry because their fathers' estates adjoined. They had never met as they were absent at distant schools. But on their way home to be presented to society and each other; they accidentally met incognito on the train and became attracted to each other; and the young man before he realized it found himself telling his impromptu friend of the distasteful plan that had been made for him, and his determination not to be forced into a marriage of convenience for the sake of uniting two estates.

Soon afterwards they met, and to their mutual astonishment found out that they were already in love. That which law and necessity never could have brought about, but only made the more distasteful, took care of itself when left to the influence of love. So God has seized upon that principle which is the key to every human heart and life, and made it the motive power of holiness and obedience. He gives us liberty to sin if we want to, but He adds, "If you love me, you will obey what I command" (John 14:15). What a mighty teacher love is! What a perfect disciplinarian love is!

The poet Chatterton, when he first went to school, was pronounced a dunce by his stern old despot of a teacher because he was so frightened of the old pedagogue that his senses forsook him and he could remember nothing. But when he went home to his mother that night and she gently taught him his lessons, he became the brightest boy in the school because love was his teacher now, and he grew to be one of the illustrious literary men of England. It is thus that the Holy Spirit teaches us in the school of love.

In a New England parish the people determined by a great majority to abolish the old method of corporeal punishment, and a new teacher was employed who was to control the school by the principle of love instead of rawhides. It was not long till the leader of the war party found occasion for a breach of discipline and a state of war became all the more welcome because the hands of the teacher were now tied. The gentle and tactful teacher called him into her room and said to him, "If I cannot rule this school by love, I will resign. I am not going to punish you in any way, but I want you boys to understand that if my authority is not strictly supported by the school, I will immediately leave."

The boys really liked her, and this was an alternative that they were quite unprepared for and a responsibility that they were not willing to assume. Then throwing herself upon the honor of the lad who had already shown signs of weakening, she asked him to help her in ruling by love. From that day she had no stauncher friend, and the school became a model at once of discipline and kindness.

But the love which the Holy Spirit brings is no earthly passion or emotion, for in the life of Christ we are called evermore to face things that no natural love can meet. And it is here that the love of the Spirit comes to our aid, nothing less, in short, than the life of Christ Himself, which He lived once on earth and now relives in us. It is the love that could stand in the judgment hour amid the spitting and the smiting, an untiring love on to the end that could only seek to bless and save the men who wronged Him. We, too, must stand with Him in such places here, and then it is we find a strength which human virtue cannot reach, a love which earthly affection cannot approach.

It is beautiful to notice that all the graces mentioned in Galatians 5:22–23, are so many forms of love: joy is love exulting; peace is love reposing; patience is love in action; faith is love confiding; gentleness is love with bowed head; self-control is true self-love. These are not so many fruits, but like the lobes of an orange they form together one fruit which is only love.

7. Fruit Not Work

Sanctification is fruit, not work. It is a spontaneous development of life, not the result of effort and labor. It is just as natural and easy as the growth of the cluster on the vine, or the bursting of the bud into fragrance and beauty on the branch. The works of the flesh cost many a strain, for the way of transgressors is hard, but the fruit of the Spirit is a living joy. Of the life of the sanctified it is true indeed, "Her ways are pleasant ways,/ and all her paths are peace" (Proverbs 3:17).

Finally, the sanctified life is a habit and not an event. "Since we live by the Spirit, let us keep in step with the Spirit" (Galatians 5:25). Step by step, moment by moment, little by little we dwell in Him and walk in Him. The grace that can keep us for a moment can keep us for a lifetime. The strength that is sufficient for today is pledged for all the days. So let us live in the Spirit; so let us walk in the Spirit; so let us abide in Him who has said, "If a man remains in me and I in him, he will bear much fruit; apart from me you can do nothing" (John 15:5b).

CHAPTER 3

BURDEN BEARING

Brothers, if someone is caught in a sin, you who are spiritual should restore him gently. But watch yourself, or you also may be tempted. Carry each other's burdens, and in this way you will fulfill the law of Christ. (Galatians 6:1–2)

We have been studying the epistle of Paul to the Galatians, and have found the keynote to be the free grace of God as opposed to the law and the works of the flesh. We have seen the grace of God in our salvation and sanctification—the gift of God equally for our justification and our deeper life.

We shall now look at the work of free grace in our own spirit toward others, the outworking of grace in a gracious life, a life marked by the fullness and large-heartedness of that grace from which our own salvation came. For according to the measure of our salvation will be our influence over others and the tone and temper of our own Christian life. If you have a small salvation, you will be a small Christian; but if you have a large salvation, it will be an overflowing life and a luxury to do good, also a luxury for people to meet and know you. You will not only be blessed, but a blessing. It all depends on how much grace you have. You cannot pay more interest than your investment calls for, and if you are a small soul, God does not expect you to be big; but if you want to be big, God will fulfill this desire.

You have heard of the captive of Toulon who bought from a vendor a little bird at a high price and then set it free. The man asked, "How could you be so foolish as to set it free? You must be a rich man."

He answered, "No, I am not rich. I gave you all I had for the bird; but I have been a prisoner and have just gained my liberty, and I know what freedom means, and my business is to give to others what is so sweet to me."

So, if you have tasted that the Lord is gracious, you will be a gracious Christian; not a reflection on the Lord, but a reflection of the beauty and grace of the Lord Jesus. We have four manifestations of the grace of God in the Christian's life pointed out here in these verses.

RESTORATION

The first is the restoring of those who have been overtaken by temptation and have fallen.

"Brothers, if someone is caught in a sin [fault, KJV], you who are spiritual should restore him gently. But watch yourself, or you also may be tempted" (6:1). Now, if you have received the free grace of God, you will be very tender to those who have sinned and fallen. It is the immature Christian who is harsh and fond of judging. A ripe, mellow, and mature Christian is like his Master, ready to forgive, able to help and lift up the fallen. How beautifully every word used here speaks of gentleness and tenderness!

1. The mildest term is used. It is a "fault"; not a crime, but a fault; something less than he ought to have been or done. And who is without a fault?

2. He was overtaken by it. He was overtaken by a ruthless pursuer, stronger and swifter than he. He has fallen; lift him up. Burns has said:

> They know a little of what is done,
> But not of what's resisted.

His failure led him to you that you may lift him up and establish his goings. Look at it as God looks at it. He may have to let you get caught to make you merciful.

3. You are to restore him. You are not to punish him and make him feel how mean he is. God's purposes are remedial, restorative and gracious. He wants you to be workers together with Him. Even if you have to resort to discipline, let the end always be restoration. Let everything tend to the uplifting of that within him which alone can save him, the spirit of confidence and hope, that which will see the bright side rather than the dark, not the accuser, but the Restorer.

4. You who are spiritual are to do this. You cannot do this unless you have the Holy Spirit, unless you have been sanctified from your self-confidence and received the broken spirit which is the surest mark of a deeply spiritual life. I remember a woman coming to me one day and saying she was going to give someone a piece of her mind. "But," I said, "my dear friend, you are too angry for it now." I believe it would have been a positive luxury for her to have met the person she spoke of just then. "Wait," I said, "till it breaks your heart, and you can speak with tenderness, tears and the compassion of Jesus to restore him." This is how Christ wants the spiritual to restore the one who has fallen.

5. But it is to be done in a "spirit of meekness," not in harshness and

superiority, "or you also may be tempted." John Newton used to say when he saw a reeling drunkard, "There goes John Newton, but for the grace of God." If you remember that, it will make you humble and helpful; you might have fallen too, but for the grace of God. You never know what you owe to restraining grace.

The difference between the fallen and the victor is that the Lord in His mercy knew "how to rescue godly men from trials [temptations, KJV]" (2 Peter 2:9). The most terrible punishment of one who has rejected light is that he is allowed to be tempted, and handed over to Satan and his fierce assaults. The reason you have not been blasted by him is because God has held him back. "You also may be tempted" (Galatians 6:2). You may have to be humbled and broken like Peter to make you of more use to the lost. God's free grace is given to you now. Give a little away to others.

Yet, do not let us forget that all weakness, softness and sentimentalism is wrong. We must be firm and true to them. God's love makes no compromise with wrong, neither must ours. God has no indulgence for people who have erred and who fight against the right. If anyone reading these lines has erred and stumbled, God expects you to meet that spirit of love just as it meets you, to take the lowest place, not fighting for recognition, but letting God lift you up. So shall the Valley of Achor become "a door of hope" (Hosea 2:15) and "instead of their shame/ my people will receive a double portion" (Isaiah 61:7) in God's time, but not by your contention.

LIFTED BURDENS

The second manifestation of the grace of God at work in our lives is our ministering to the burdened lives around us.

"Carry each other's burdens, and in this way you will fulfill the law of Christ" (Galatians 6:2). If you receive the spirit of the Master and have been the beneficiary of His free grace, you will learn that the law of Christ is the law of burden bearing, the law of sacrifice and the law of loving helpfulness. You will recognize the fact that God has adjusted your life so as to bring into it the opportunities and occasions for the ministry of unselfishness, love and helpfulness to others.

And so it comes to pass that when the poor, the destitute, the helpless and the suffering are brought into contact with your life and meet you with their need, it is not an accident or a misfortune. It is the providence of God, the school of love and the law of Christ. He puts them there for your training and for an opportunity for you to dispense the grace that He has given to you. Freely you have received, as freely you must give.

Thus the rich and the poor meet together for the sake of the rich as much as for the sake of the poor, because the rich need the opportunity of learning unselfishness and bearing the burdens of the less fortunate. The happy and the wretched are brought into contact that the happy may bear the other's sorrow and distress. The weak Christian is linked with the strong. God links with you the people who need you to manifest to them the same gentleness, consideration and helpfulness that the Master has shown to you. Thus these ministries grow up around us and become part of the law of our Christian life. God therefore overrules even the evil and makes it ultimately an occasion for good and for the uplifting of our spiritual nature.

God has called every one of us to some of these ministries, and He expects us to be practical. It is not a matter of sentiment or feeling, but of real giving and doing. There is not a day but someone comes to you who needs sympathy and relief of some kind, and it takes the wisdom and help of Christ to know how to do this without encouraging dependence and indolence.

John Wesley used to spend a large amount of money in helping those less fortunate than himself. On one occasion a poor minister received a very loving letter from him containing the words, "Trust in the LORD, and do good; . . . and verily thou shalt be fed" (Psalm 37:3, KJV). The good founder of Methodism said, "I felt impressed to write and call your attention to this great promise," etc. He enclosed a five-pound note, but said nothing of this in his letter.

The answer from this minister has happily been preserved. "My dear Mr. Wesley, how can I sufficiently thank you for your letter and gift. I have often read that verse and many expositions of it, but this is the best expository note I have ever seen."

Do not forget the practical side of it. Many a time He may call you to sacrifice. Do not shrink from it. These sacrifices are little tests of your love for Christ. How much little things count, as the gift of a flower in a sick room. How often our missionaries have been cheered on the field by an unexpected letter or a little remembrance, simply an indication that they were remembered. I saw a letter yesterday from India, from a dear toiling missionary who has gone through the famine, and he told how above everything else a little remembrance sent to him in the shape of a book of little intrinsic value, carried by one of the outgoing missionaries, had cheered his heart and made him feel he was not forgotten.

Somebody sent her love to a poor little cripple in a hospital, and the messenger brought it, saying, "Mrs. So-and-So sends her love to you." The little fellow said, "Thank you, but dear me, I think I would like to *see* a little of her love." The messenger went back unknown to him, and the next day there came in the shape of a box of chocolate caramels, "a little of her love."

It would do many of us good to write three letters a year to some missionary who is not likely to get many letters, say at Easter, Thanksgiving and Christmas. It would cheer them in their service. Will you not try it?

Then again in the home life God puts us in these family ties just to train us to exercise His beneficence, His graciousness, and learn His love. Every affection is but a letter in the alphabet that teaches us about God. Our fatherhood teaches us His Fatherhood; our filial relations make us understand the Father's heart. And so in the home there is much need for practical consecration. Someone asked a woman if her husband were not a beautiful Christian. She answered, "When I see him in the prayer meeting, I think he is, but at home I have my doubts sometimes."

Somebody asked Wendell Phillips one night after giving a lecture, to stay all night and go back in the morning, as it was very stormy and he had to drive 12 miles. He answered, "Ann Phillips is at the other end, and therefore nothing can keep me here." He thought of the lonely companion at the other end, and that outweighed his personal convenience and comfort.

I am so glad that the 12th chapter of Romans, telling about the living sacrifice and the highest Christian life, is just filled with simple home touches and social qualities: "Be devoted to one another in brotherly love. Honor one another above yourselves. Never be lacking in zeal, but keep your spiritual fervor, . . . Share with God's people who are in need. Practice hospitality. . . . Rejoice with those who rejoice; mourn with those who mourn" (12:10–11, 13, 15). That is what Christ expects of us. If we have the free grace of God in our hearts, it will flow out in all our lives and touch all with whom we come in contact. We can at least be courteous and smile and give the pressure of the hand and show "How great is the love the Father has lavished on us" (1 John 3:1).

Meeting a wretched, hideous beggar, a devoted Christian tells us that every natural instinct recoiled from his touch and presence. His face was covered with ulcers and his body and dress were unclean. Everything about him froze his natural sympathy, but the poor man stretched out his helpless hands for aid. Instinctively the Christian put his hand in his pocket to give him help, but he had nothing. He looked at him, reached out his hand, and pressed the hand of the poor diseased mass of humanity, saying, "My dear brother, I am sorry I have left my purse at home, and I have nothing to give you but my love."

The poor man burst out weeping and replied, "My friend, that is the richest gift you could bestow. I have had money from many, but love from none but you."

Nothing but the touch of grace that had started from the throne and found its fountain at the cross could have done this. That is the richest gift. How it lifts our burdens! How the testimony comes back in later years of some forgotten service, and how sweet it is to have them tell you of the help and sympathy you have given them.

In the great revival in London many noble men and women were doing special Christian work. One of these high-born men was standing in front of the great evangelistic hall and spoke to a cabman, saying, "Can you not go to the meetings?"

"No," he replied, "I have to sit on the box and can't go."

"Will you go if I sit on the box till you come back?"

"Why, yes, I would be a thousand times obliged, but I would not ask you to."

But the man took the horses and the reins, and sending the cabman in, he remained until the man came out with a shining face bedewed with tears. He had found the Lord. The nobleman had been bearing another's burden and so fulfilled the law of Christ.

Then, if you are willing, He will give you the burden of prayer, the best way of helping. I was retiring one night when there came over my heart the consciousness of some poor toiling fellow working all night, who had told me about the lonely office. It came to me to pray for a long time for that desolate heart, that it might be strengthened and blessed.

These are but little ministries, but there is no ministry so delightful and none so fruitful as carrying the burdens of God's children. That is what the Lord is doing now. His business in heaven is to carry them. His priesthood is just sympathy and love. On His heart and shoulders, in the place of love and strength, are engraved their names. It is there He is bearing you and me, and we can help by bearing others.

Our help in this direction does accomplish results mightier than our words or even our gifts. So may we learn the second lesson of free grace, "Carry each other's burdens, and in this way you will fulfill the law of Christ" (Galatians 6:2). It was the law of His life, and so it should be of ours—the law of sacrificial love, cooperation and mutual fellowship. For no man is independent of his brother, and our blessing and burdens must be shared.

OUTFLOWINGS OF GRACE

The third manifestation is exercising the spirit of liberality. This is one of the outflowings of the free grace of God in our lives.

> Anyone who receives instruction in the word must share all good things with his instructor.
>
> Do not be deceived: God cannot be mocked. A man reaps what he sows. The one who sows to please his sinful nature, from that nature will reap destruction; the one who sows to please the Spirit, from the Spirit will reap eternal life. Let us not become weary in doing good, for at the proper time we will reap a harvest if we do not give up. (6:6–9)

There is no doubt that this refers to liberality. If you have the free grace of God in your heart, it will even affect your pocketbook and you will give money for God's work. If you do not love to do this, you will be but a poor and small-hearted Christian; you have not known "the grace of our Lord Jesus Christ, that though he was rich, yet for your sakes he became poor" (2 Corinthians 8:9). God does not especially want your money, but He will let you use it for Him. You can have just what you desire. "A man reaps what he sows" (Galatians 6:7).

Money has a large place in the great world we are living in, and there is a great place for it in God's work. If you want to sow your money in earthly gain and selfishness, God will let you do it. He will give you the chance of a lifetime to be petty, selfish and mean. Or you can sow it to "life everlasting" in unselfish blessing. It will all depend on how rich the grace of God has been to you.

It is so solemn to know that God lets us have our way, and the spirit of Christian ethics is not compulsion but free grace. There is no law to make you do it, but there is a mighty responsibility. Daniel Webster said that the most awful thing he knew was "accountability to God." Yes, Pilate, you can crucify Him, smite Him, let them spit in His face and do Him hideous wrong, and no one will stop you. Go on, high priest, Scribes and Pharisees, you have your day. But oh, there is another day coming.

> The mills of God grind slowly,
>   But they grind exceeding small;
> Though with patience He stands waiting,
>   With exactness grinds He all.

It has all come back, and Christ is on the judgment seat now, and what would not Pilate give for a chance to make his choice anew? So you can have your choice. The money, the strength, the youth, the manhood, home, friends and love are all your own, but only for a little while are you on trial. The reaping day will come. You are free now, but it is an awful liberty. God help us to use it as Jesus did His. He did not need to come to earth. He did not need to die, that is, it was not compulsion. But He came, "a sacrifice for our fallen world"; and if we know His grace, we will be like Him now and we shall be like Him by and by.

LIFE OF SERVICE

The fourth manifestation is leading a life of service, usefulness and beneficence in every way.

"Therefore, as we have opportunity, let us do good to all people, especially to those who belong to the family of believers" (6:10). It will reach out to your whole life, and if you are large-hearted in your relation to God, you will be just as magnanimous in your service for men. You will watch for opportunities, and they will come. God brings them to the hearts that watch, and He hides them from those who are not willing.

It is not necessary that you should go and make some field. "If you want a field of service, you can find it anywhere." A dozen times a day the opportunities will come in your business, in your home, among your friends, upon the street, and you will be always in uniform, a light will be in your face, a touch in your hand, a message in your eye—not much, but oh, so gracious. Free grace has filled you with Christ's love, and it is a joy to pour it out in blessing.

Your life, like your Master's, will be made up of little incidents. It was not much to meet a woman drawing water out of a well; not much to forget His lunch for a poor, forsaken soul. But these are the things that make our crowns. So the best work of Christ was just incidental, all along the way; and even as He hung on Calvary, God brought Him His audience there, the poor dying malefactor. Yes, you will find work to the very close. You cannot live to yourself or die to yourself. "As [you] have opportunity" (6:10), your whole life will speak for God.

It was Mrs. Bartle Frere who said of her husband a simple thing that will stand repeating. She had hired a new coachman and sent him to the station to meet her husband who had been away.

The coachman said, "Madam, how shall I know your husband? I have never seen him."

"Oh," she replied, "you will have no difficulty in finding him. Just look for a great big man helping someone."

The train came in and he saw a massive form half carrying a poor, crippled lady out of the car and taking her to the carriage—a big manly fellow helping somebody. So let us live and give the grace that has saved and sanctified us.

EPHESIANS

CHAPTER 1

CHOSEN IN HIM

For he chose us in him before the creation of the world to be holy and blameless in his sight. In love he predestined us to be adopted as his sons through Jesus Christ, in accordance with his pleasure and will— to the praise of his glorious grace. (Ephesians 1:4–6)

P aul's epistle to the Ephesians is the most deeply spiritual of all his letters. It reaches a higher plane of spiritual experience than any of his lofty writings. It has been compared to the book of Joshua in the Old Testament as a manual of the higher Christian life and the saints' inheritance in the Land of Promise. Some of the fathers have compared it to the place of the heart in the human body, the most vital and important organ, and therefore not in the extremities, but in the very core of our physical organism. So this epistle is in the very heart of the New Testament, and constitutes the very core of spiritual teaching and experience.

The keynote is the third verse of the first chapter, "Praise be to the God and Father of our Lord Jesus Christ, who has blessed us in the heavenly realms [places, KJV] with every spiritual blessing in Christ."

ALL THE BLESSINGS OF THE SPIRIT IN THE HEAVENLIES

This verse, unhappily translated "in heavenly places," describes not so much a local situation as a spiritual region—that sphere of resurrection life, that realm of divine things, that higher, holier element of the supernatural where we know God and dwell with Jesus Christ in the atmosphere of the Holy Spirit, and find ourselves in a real world of unseen, yet glorious verities which the deeper senses of the spiritual nature alone can perceive and realize. We have been translated into this celestial realm through our resurrection life in Christ. It is illuminated and vivified by the Holy Spirit. It is the very element of our new life, and in it we have been introduced to the enjoyment of unspeakable blessings which are here called "spiritual blessings."

These blessings are unfolded in detail throughout the epistle. The first is the blessing of our divine election in the eternal purpose of God. Next is the blessing of redemption, followed by the blessing of our personal salvation and calling. Then comes the blessing of our sealing by the Holy Spirit. This is followed by the blessing of our divine illumination, to know "the hope to which he has called you, the riches of his glorious inheritance in the saints" (1:18). These fill up the first chapter.

The second chapter leads us into the unspeakable blessing of our quickening with Christ through death and resurrection, and our exaltation in Him to share His ascension life in the heavenlies. Next comes the blessing of our collective life as the Body, the Bride and the Building of God, the blessing which we share with the household of faith and the Church of Jesus Christ.

This leads us into a still deeper personal experience of blessing as, "with all the saints," we come to know in the third chapter, "how wide and long and high and deep is the love of Christ, and to know this love . . . that you may be filled to the measure of all the fullness of God" (3:18–19).

Having led us onward and upward to this infinite height of blessing, the apostle next brings us back to earth, and takes us to the practical sphere of our common life in our homes, our business and our social relationships; and he unfolds to us the blessing of practical holiness in all the minutiae of our daily experience as husbands and wives, parents and children, masters and servants, brethren and citizens—representing Christ, living out His life amid the secularities, temptations and trials of common life.

Finally, the crowning blessing is the supreme conflict and the complete victory of the risen life unfolded in the closing paragraph, where we meet at the very gates of heaven and in the very heavenlies, the principalities and powers of hell, and become "more than conquerors through him who loved us" (Romans 8:37).

Such is the scope of this great epistle. Altogether it contains as many words as an ordinary sermon, it outweighs in richness, beauty and spiritual power all the sermons that have ever been written and all the combined libraries of earth. Let us reverently follow our heavenly Guide through all the blessings of the Spirit in the heavenlies, and, as each new vision unfolds, may faith hear Him say, "All this is yours," for "we have . . . received . . . the Spirit who is from God, that we may understand what God has freely given us" (1 Corinthians 2:12).

CHOSEN IN HIM

We are approaching a theme which introduces us at once to the very highest region of thought. Let earthly reason grow dumb, and let faith listen with hushed veneration and submission to the voice of revelation and learn to believe even where she cannot see. We are exploring a realm of truth, which, notwithstanding all the difficulties which confront man's poor intellect, is undoubtedly one of the teachings of divine revelation, and which we believe will be found one of the most comforting, encouraging and uplifting truths which the Holy Spirit has given to the disciples of Christ.

Two great truths run with unbroken clearness through the Word of God. One is the purpose of God, and the other is the freedom of man. We may not always be able to harmonize them, but we know that both are true.

When Joseph's brethren cruelly and wickedly sold him into Egypt, we know that it was their voluntary sin, and years afterwards the finger of conscience pointed it out even to them in the lurid light of their own sorrows until they cried, "Surely we are being punished because of our brother. We saw how distressed he was . . . but we would not listen" (Genesis 42:21). But years afterwards Joseph also revealed the other side of this strange story when he said by inspiration, "God sent me ahead of you to . . . save your lives by a great deliverance. . . . You intended to harm me, but God intended it for good" (45:7, 50:20). There is the fact of the freedom and responsibility of these wicked men, but there is the other fact that God's purpose through it all is to accomplish His grand design for the world.

So again, Peter, speaking to the men who crucified the Lord, declared with indignation and divine inspiration, "You, with the help of wicked men, put him to death by nailing him to the cross" (Acts 2:23b) "though [Pilate] had decided to let him go" (3:13b). But at the same time Peter says that "This man was handed over to you by God's set purpose and foreknowledge" (Acts 2:23a). There are the two facts. Reject them if you can. They are both true, and yet reason's feet are too limited to span the gulf between; but, thank God, as Dr. Cairns has said with graphic eloquence, "We can take the wings of faith and fly across the gulf from peak to peak, and believe them both, though we may not always be able to perfectly comprehend them."

1. The Time of Our Election

"He chose us in him before the creation of the world" (Ephesians 1:4). At a bound we are carried back into the remotest ages of the past eternity, and we are taught that God was thinking about us, loving us and planning to bless us long ago. Redemption is then no afterthought, no hasty provision to remedy the catastrophe of the fall, but a great original and eternal thought of God's heart of love. We seem to hear Him saying to us in the words of Jeremiah, "The LORD appeared to us in the past, saying: 'I have loved you with an everlasting love' " (Jeremiah 31:3), eternal in its beginning and in its duration. God chose us and purposed to save and bless us before He ever made us. Therefore He must have made us on purpose that He might save us. Our very creation must be designed for some higher destiny than human nature alone would indicate. We were always intended for the high dignity of the sons of God.

Moreover, if this be true, God's purpose for our salvation and blessing was anterior to the creation of the world itself. Therefore the very world must have been made with a view to man's eternal future. The whole creation must have been designed to illustrate and set forth the greater work of the new creation. The light that shines in heaven must have been shot from the quiver of His hand in order that it might set forth the light of life. The beauty and glory of nature were constituted just as an alphabet, to spell out the story of redemption.

Further, this implies that the thought of our salvation was prior to the fact of our fall. We were chosen in Him before Satan ever appeared upon the scene and sin ever entered earth's spotless Eden to wreck man's innocence and happiness. Therefore God began long before the devil did. Redemption is no second thought, no mere remedial scheme to undo the work of the fall, but God's great primary plan for which all nature was formed, all existence brought into being and all other things created.

What a wonderful sweep this gives to the wings of faith! What a wonderful horizon is extended before the vision of the heaven-taught soul! What a grandeur and a majesty it adds to existence and to the standpoint and outlook of the child of God and heir to glory!

2. The Christo-centric Standpoint of Our Election

"He chose us in him" (Ephesians 1:4). God's purpose of blessing toward us is related to the Lord Jesus Christ, and to Him alone. He has been from all eternity the central Object of the Father's thought and Agent of all His purposes and plans. Away back of the story of salvation is the ancient covenant of redemption between the Father and the Son—that sublime transaction in which the Father promised all the blessings of His grace, and the Son undertook to fulfill all the conditions through which He now claims the mighty reward, not only of man's salvation, but of that inheritance of glory which was given Him for us in the remotest ages of the past. Christ, therefore, as the Son of God, the Son of man, the great Head of the covenant of redemption, stands above all things as the archetype for whom and by whom are all things.

It was for Him as well as by Him that the first creation sprang into being. "He is before all things, and in him all things hold together" (Colossians 1:17). So the apostle expresses this sublime truth in the sister epistle to the Colossians, which he wrote about the same time that he wrote this one to the Ephesians. He is called in the book of Revelation, "the Lamb that was slain from the creation of the world" (13:8). In God's thought He was always the Christ who was to live and to die, and rise and reign for the redemption of men. So we find Him in the remarkable vision of the eighth chapter of Proverbs speaking of the time when there were no depths, no fountains of water, before the mountains were brought forth, before the earth was spread abroad, before the firmament was stretched on high: "Then," He says, "I was the craftsman at his side./ I was filled with delight day after day,/ rejoicing always in his presence" (8:30). Then, with unutterable tenderness he adds, "Rejoicing in his whole world/ and delighting in mankind" (8:31).

It was then that we were chosen in Him, and that God perfected the mighty plan of bringing many sons unto glory through the Captain of their salvation, and creating in the ages to come a new order of beings who should bridge the infinite chasm between the Creator and the creation.

3. Nature of the Election

1. "Chosen" (Ephesians 1:4, KJV)—this denotes our particular selection. "You did not choose me, but I chose you" (John 15:16), He says to His disciples. "You are a chosen people" (1 Peter 2:9), the Apostle Peter declares to the saints to whom he wrote.

2. "Predestined" (Ephesians 1:5)—this carries the thought a step further, and expresses the idea of a particular purpose and destiny planned for the object of His choice. There is no doubt that God has such a plan, not only for the universe, but for every man, and the greatest thing that any of us can wish or obtain is to meet His thought and plan.

3. "In accordance with his pleasure and will" (1:5)—this denotes the sovereignty of His choice, the independence of His will, His right to choose, to plan, to own, to govern our life and being. In this age of license it is well to remember that there is one throne that is fixed of old; one scepter that is universal and supreme; one will that has the right to choose and to dispose; one Being who "does as he pleases/ with the powers of heaven/ and the people of the earth./ No one can hold back his hand/ or say to Him: 'What have you done?' " (Daniel 4:35). It is well that earthly monarchs are limited because they are imperfect, but there is one monarchy that is not limited because it cannot err. Resist, rebel, refuse as we may, we are all inexorably tending to the footstool of that throne where every knee shall bow and every tongue confess that He is Lord (Philippians 2:10–11), and the universe shall proclaim, "Our Lord God Almighty reigns" (Revelation 19:6b). There is a place for the sovereignty of God, and that place is at the foundation of every true character and every spiritual blessing.

4. "To the praise of his glorious grace" (Ephesians 1:6)—that covers all the splendors of His throne with the halo of love, with the gentle light of grace. It is not arbitrary. It is not despotic, though it be so mighty and supreme; but it is always kind, and all its degrees are prompted by infinite

love and the purpose to bless the subjects of His sway. Such is the doctrine of divine election.

4. Purpose of His Election

1. That we should be His sons (see 1:5). His eternal object was that a new order of creation might be developed. The mightiest archangel in the glory was not a son—only a servant. But His Father-heart longed for the fellowship of children, and purposed that marvelous design which should bring into being a whole race of His own very offspring, representing on the one side the lower sphere of creation itself, and on the other the sublime height of His throne.

This is the race to which it is our privilege to belong; not the creatures of God merely, not the servants of God only, but His very sons. Sons, not only by the new creation, but sons by our very union with the Lord Jesus Christ and the participation of His own nature, so that He can say of us, "my Father and your Father, . . . my God and your God" (John 20:17b). "How great is the love the Father has lavished on us, that we should be called children of God" (1 John 3:1).

2. "To be holy and blameless in his sight" (Ephesians 1:4)—His purpose for us is that we should resemble Him, that we should wear His perfect image, that we should be beyond question of criticism, and that this holiness should consist in the perfection of love which is the glory and the essence of His own nature. It is very evident, therefore, that anyone who talks about being elected to salvation and being saved in consequence, no matter what they may do, is talking in the blindest ignorance. We are not elected to salvation and heaven; we are elected to holiness and faith, and if we are not receiving and exhibiting these qualities, it is an idle dream and a shocking mockery to rest in any such delusion, which is simply fatalism of the grossest kind.

3. We are elected "to the praise of his glorious grace" (1:6). We are to show in the ages to come, to the universe, how God can love and save a sinful race, and lift a being from the lowest to the highest condition, "in order that in the coming ages he might show the incomparable riches of his grace, expressed in his kindness to us in Christ Jesus" (2:7).

5. Practical Value and Comfort

1. It heightens and intensifies our conception of the love of God. Time is an element in human affection. Old friends are especially dear. Love accumulates with the lapse of years, but the oldest friendship is but as yesterday compared with God's ancient and eternal love. How long He has loved us! How long ago He thought of us! How infinitely touching to think that He made everything in this universe with special reference to our happiness and future

destiny! He loved us before we were born. He wants us to know the length and strength of that eternal love, and He is ever saying to us, "I have loved you with an everlasting love;/ I have drawn you with loving-kindness" (Jeremiah 31:3b). Let us not think that even our choice of Him was the first choice.

> Why was I made to hear His voice
>   And enter while there's room,
> While others make a wretched choice,
>   And rather starve than come?
> His was the love that spread the feast
>   And sweetly drew me in,
> Lest I had still refused to taste,
>   And perished in my sin.

2. It guarantees security to the trusting soul. Our salvation becomes primarily God's interest and part of God's plan. The old Scotch woman had a sound theology when someone asked her, "Suppose God should some day let you go?" And she answered, "Well, if He did, He would lose much more than I." God has staked His character and His glory upon our future, and we may humbly and yet triumphantly say, "I am convinced that neither death nor life, neither angels nor demons, neither the present nor the future, nor any powers, neither height nor depth, nor anything else in all creation, will be able to separate us from the love of God that is in Christ Jesus our Lord" (Romans 8:38–39).

3. It gives grandeur to our spiritual outlook and our heavenly dignity. It makes us partakers of God's two eternities. Not only can we look down through the ages that will never end and think of all that it means to be forever saved, but we can look back to the most distant past and know that we are partakers of His eternal years in the retrospect, as well as the prospect.

There is a truth lying here half hidden which seems at least suggested, if not distinctly revealed. The life that we have received from God is not our old Adam-born life. That has been laid down, surrendered, crucified and buried, and we have received a new life in Jesus Christ and count ourselves alive in Him forevermore. But what is that new life? It is Christ's life; and when we receive it from Him, we receive eternity with it. That life is not of yesterday. That life was in Him when He rose for us from the dead, and was born in us from His very heart, and is part of Him. Nay, that life was in Him in the ages long ago when He became our living Head first, and so we can look back to the time when we were in Him yet unborn.

Have you ever had a strange consciousness through your being at the sight of some beautiful scene or the occurrence of some striking circumstance, that made you almost feel that you had been there before? The Buddhist would explain this by the doctrine of transmigration, but the child of God recognizes the loftier fact that he is sharing the thoughts of Him from whom his nature sprang, and whose goings forth have been of old, even from everlasting. The Psalmist has the true conception: "LORD, you have been our dwelling place/ throughout all generations" (Psalm 90:1). Let us realize our high calling and our heavenly dignity and live up to it.

4. What infinite comfort this truth brings to us in view of Satan's assaults and life's temptations! Our salvation was planned before Satan appeared upon the scene and his coming cannot change it. God knew all that was coming, and in the light of all the perils and pleasures that were to meet us He chose us. He looked down into the future, and He anticipated and provided against all that might ever come; and now, when trial and temptation meet us, let us just place over against it the eternal God and the purpose of His grace, which neither earth nor hell can turn aside if we only be true.

5. Let us not hinder His purpose. Cooperate with it, and by our implicit obedience enable Him to accomplish all that He has ever had in His heart for our life and destiny. There is a solemn and awful possibility lying somewhere here that we cannot ignore. There is such a thing as failing of the grace of God, and there is such a thing as being workers together with Him. Therefore one apostle prays that we may "not lose what you have worked for, but that you may be rewarded fully" (2 John 8), and another pleads that "God may count you worthy of his calling, and that by his power he may fulfill every good purpose of yours and every act prompted by your faith" (2 Thessalonians 1:11).

There is a very solemn parable in the book of Jeremiah (18:1–6) telling of a potter who wrought upon a wheel a plastic piece of clay, but through some failure of the clay to yield to his touch perhaps, the vessel was marred in the hands of the potter and he had to throw it aside for a time. Then he took it up again and wrought another vessel as it pleased him to make it. May it be that we, by failing to yield to His gentle touch may fall short of His first purpose for us, and that He will have to make some other use of our life, and give us His second best. Oh, let us watch and pray, and press hard up to His blessed will that we may not miss God's best.

6. Let us make sure of being inside God's purpose by choosing Christ ourselves, and making sure that we are in Him; for it is in Him we are chosen, and out of Him we have nothing. Talk as you will about all things ending well, it is only true that "in all things God works for the good of those who love him, who have been called according to his purpose" (Romans 8:28).

Outside of Christ you are "excluded from citizenship in Israel and foreigners to the covenants of the promise, without hope and without God in the world" (Ephesians 2:12). Outside of Christ you are treading on crumbling ground; beneath you are a yawning grave and an eternal fire, and above you is a cloud all lurid with judgment and despair. In Him alone do you meet God and enter into His plan of love. That plan you can never understand till you get inside.

As someone has finely illustrated it, it is like a splendid temple on whose front you will see these lines in golden letters, "Whoever is thirsty, let him come" (Revelation 22:17b). But when you get inside you find another inscription, "he chose us in him before the creation of the world" (Ephesians 1:4); but you cannot understand this until you have first accepted the other. God has given you the freedom of choice or refusal; and when you have made that happy choice, you have made your "election sure" (2 Peter 1:10b). Oh, make it now.

CHAPTER 2

REDEMPTION THROUGH HIS BLOOD

He has freely given us in the One he loves. In him we have redemption through his blood, the forgiveness of sins, in accordance with the riches of God's grace that he lavished on us with all wisdom and understanding. . . .

In him we were also chosen, having been predestined according to the plan of him who works out everything in conformity with the purpose of his will, in order that we, who were the first to hope in Christ, might be for the praise of his glory. (Ephesians 1:6b–8, 11–12)

In the clear, logical order of thought in this great epistle the writer punctuates the different paragraphs, and marks the sequence of his lofty argument by closing each section by a kind of doxology. This is expressed by the phrase which appears so often in this chapter, "to the praise of his glorious grace," or, "for the praise of his glory."

Following this suggestion, the second great section of his review of the blessing of the Spirit commences in the middle of the sixth verse, and leads to the discussion of the glorious blessing of our redemption through the blood of Christ, and our acceptance, forgiveness and final and full salvation in Him.

The first step in pursuance of the divine purpose with which the epistle opens is redemption. This is described with great completeness and spiritual fervor.

THE REDEEMER

"He has freely given us in the One he loves" (1:6). Literally this reads, "in the Son of his love." The whole story of redemption is personal. It brings us at every step into direct contact with the Redeemer Himself. At the very outset He is presented to us in the most attractive, majestic and tender aspect as the "Son of his love." The Father did not commit this mighty undertaking to any ordinary agent. He chose heaven's noblest, brightest, mightiest Being. The verse implies that He is the Son of God in the most exclusive and special sense. Elsewhere He is represented as His "only Begotten" (John 1:14, margin) and His "wellbeloved" Son (Mark 12:6, KJV).

His high and divine character gives the first assurance of His ability to carry out the supreme task with which He was entrusted. All the infinite resources of Deity were at His command. He had right of access to the Father under all circumstances, and His divine dignity gave to His personal work the value which no created being could have claimed. One drop of His precious blood would have been sufficient to atone for the sins of a world.

But the special aspect under which He is presented here is that of nearness and dearness to the Father. He is the Son of His love. This assures us of the Father's intense and affectionate interest in the great work of redemption, and the subjects who are to be benefited by that work. He puts their case in the hands of the One who is dearest to Him. It becomes bound up with the very life of His Beloved, and it is impossible therefore that it could in any way be neglected or allowed to fail.

It is said that once an Egyptian king was so concerned in the successful raising of a valuable obelisk that he fastened his only son, the heir to the throne, to the highest point of the obelisk, and then said to his engineers: "The life of my son is bound up with the success of your work—be careful what you do. The failure of your task means death to my child and profound responsibility for you." So God bound up the redemption of this world with His well-beloved Son, and all that is dear to Him is responsible for the successful accomplishment of this plan of infinite grace and love.

But, again, this beautiful description of the Redeemer implies also a nearness and dearness of the place into which we are brought through our connection with Him. Accepted in the Son of His love, we become like Him, the children of His love, as dear as He. Identified with His person and with His name, clothed with His righteousness, covered with His blood, we can sing:

> Dear, so very dear to God,
>   Dearer I cannot be;
> For in the person of His Son,
>   I am as dear as He.

THE REDEMPTION

"In him we have redemption through his blood" (Ephesians 1:7a). Redemption means deliverance through a ransom, release from a claim and the judgment through a settlement of the claim. It is not mere good will and clemency overlooking a fault and blotting out a record, but it is strict justice recognizing the claim to its fullest extent, meeting every liability, and giving the receipt in full through the substitution of another's worth and kindness.

There is a milk-and-water type of sentimental theology widely prevalent and wandering from the truth, perhaps through a morbid straining after originality and philosophical speculation, which would make us believe that the cross of Jesus Christ was just an object lesson on the part of God to show to the world the beauty of patience, submission, self-sacrifice and the passive virtues so sublimely exhibited in the character of Jesus. Many are willing to admit also that it was a striking exhibition of God's love fitted to attract and melt the hearts of men; but it was for stage effect, and back of it there was no essential necessity for any vicarious suffering. There was no question of law or expiation or the substitution of an innocent for a guilty person. In a word, there was no real atonement by blood, but it was all designed for moral impression and spiritual persuasion.

This is not the Bible doctrine of redemption. This is another gospel, of which the Apostle Paul has said, whosoever preaches it, "let him be eternally condemned" (Galatians 1:8).

Redemption by the blood recognizes, in the first place, the real fact of sin, and the inexorable necessity of satisfying the claims of justice, equity and law. There is something in the instincts of humanity which is part of the fitness of things, and a direct intuition from the Creator Himself, which tells us that to lightly overlook wrong is in itself the grossest wrong. The man who can think with cold blood and unmoved spirit of the shameful abuse of innocence, helplessness and virtue is himself destitute of a true moral sense and capable, perhaps, of doing these very things.

The old heroic Roman but gave voice to this sentiment when his own son was brought before him charged with treasonable crime, and the law and the testimony both demanded his instant death. A thousand voices—from family, from state, from the father's own heart—pleaded for his life; but he sternly said: "I am a father, and have my human feelings as truly as you; but I am a judge, and I must be just."

This is part of the constitution of the nature and very character of God, and therefore He could not overlook sin without ceasing to be God. His father-heart prompted the love that would save the guilty, but His perfect attributes demanded the settlement of the question of eternal righteousness. It was then that His wisdom devised the wondrous plan that the Son of His love should come and take upon Himself the nature and the responsibility of the sinful race, and should be punished in their stead, and settle in their behalf every question and every claim; and then, that they, on His account, should be dealt with on the ground of His settlement and released through the ransom that He paid.

Blood, which is here described as the ransom, just means life. "The life . . . is in the blood, and I have given it to you to make atonement" (Leviticus 17:11). Our life had been forfeited. He gave His life instead; and then, through His divine power, He received back a new life, and He gives us this resurrection life as ours. Thus His life was given *for us* first, and now it is given *to us*.

This is the scriptural doctrine of the atonement. It runs like a crimson thread through every ancient sacrifice and type. We see it in the scapegoat upon the head of which the priest laid his hands and confessed the sins of the people, and then sent it out in the lone wilderness to die in agony as an accursed thing. We see it in the sin offering, the spotless lamb, on whose head the sinner lay his hand and confessed his sin. That innocent victim became in the eye of the law a mass of horrid wickedness, and was carried outside the camp, flayed, laid open in ghastly gore and held upon the consuming flame as a spectacle of judgment. So "God made him who had no sin to be sin for us, so that in him we might become the righteousness of God" (2 Corinthians 5:21).

Now we do not come cringing and begging for mercy as a capricious favor, but our blessed Advocate stands with us at court. He presents the full atonement for every claim, offers a receipt in full written in His own blood, and demands from the Judge a verdict in our favor and full victory—nay, a public justification—and sends us forth without a spot or stain upon our record, able to look in the face of Satan and the universe, crying, "Who is he that condemns? Christ Jesus, who died . . . is also interceding for us" (Romans 8:34). "Who will bring any charge against those whom God has chosen?" (8:33).

This, we believe, was the meaning of that sublime scene described in the Apocalypse. Jesus Christ returned after His triumphant resurrection, presented the settlement in full of all demands for His redeemed people, and the order went forth that Satan, the accuser of the brethren, should be expelled from the court of heaven and never allowed to lift his voice against us again. As the angels drove him forth with their fiery swords, the shout went up, "The accuser of our brothers,/ who accuses them before our God day and night,/ has been hurled down. . . . Therefore rejoice, you heavens/ and you who dwell in them!" (Revelation 12:10, 12).

Beloved, this is redemption. Can you say with humble and yet triumphant faith, "In him we have redemption through his blood" (Ephesians 1:7a)?

FORGIVENESS

We have "the forgiveness of sins, in accordance with the riches of God's grace" (1:7b). Forgiveness is not the same as redemption. It is the effect of redemption. Redemption is the settlement of the claim. Forgiveness is the receipt handed to us and a shaking of hands over the adjustment. Redemption is the paying off of the mortgage. Forgiveness is the "satisfaction peace," which is handed over after the release.

Forgiveness is not a mere feeling of peace or effort. It is the simple fact accepted by faith on the ground of completed redemption. It does not depend upon your good feelings or even the promise of your good behavior; it rests entirely upon the finished atonement of Jesus and is claimed according to His Word by simple trust. Therefore, we read, "If we confess our sins, he is faithful and just and will forgive us our sins" (1 John 1:9). His mercy and love are not even appealed to here; it is His faithfulness and justice that are represented as demanding our forgiveness. His faithfulness simply means that He keeps His Word, and His justice means that He does that which is right. Now, if God did not forgive us when we came claiming it on the ground of Christ's redemption, He would be a liar, and "anyone who does not believe God has made him out to be a liar" (5:10).

If it were possible for you to go down to the depths of hell and proclaim throughout eternity, "I came to Christ as He invited me, and He cast me out," your testimony would do God more harm than all that the devil ever said or did. God can never afford to have a soul say, "He refused to forgive me when I came and took Him at His word." He is faithful to forgive and He is just to forgive.

There is not a man or woman in the world who makes the faintest claim to honesty who would dare to take two prices for the same article. If your customer shows you a receipt proving that he has paid you for it once, you would be a scoundrel if you demanded he should pay for it again. Now, if Christ has paid for our salvation, and the price has been accepted by God, it would be simple dishonesty for God to make us pay the debt again. It is, therefore, a simple matter of justice for God to forgive us our sins. So He says to us, "I have swept away your offenses like a cloud,/ your sins like the morning mist" (Isaiah 44:22).

"Review the past for me,/ let us argue the matter together;/ state the case for your innocence" (43:26). He wants you to bring your arguments, to plead His promises, to claim your redemption rights, to take your place by faith as a sinner, and then to claim the sinner's Savior. Oh, how strong a consolation He has given us, "who have fled to take hold of the hope offered to us" (Hebrews 6:18)!

Beloved, have you received forgiveness through the blood of redemption, and are you rejoicing in the glad testimony, "I will praise you, O LORD./ Although you were angry with me,/ your anger has turned away and you have comforted me" (Isaiah 12:1)?

THE RICHES OF HIS GRACE

Not only is it forgiveness, but abundant forgiveness "according to the riches of his grace; wherein he made to superabound toward us in all wisdom and prudence" (Ephesians 1:7b–8, Rotherham). How abundant His forgiving love! Listen to the description of His mercy. He says He will cast our sins into the depths of the sea. He will cast them behind His back. He will remember them no more. As a thick cloud He has blotted them out. "As far as the east is from the west, [and they never meet]/ so far has he removed our transgressions from us" (Psalm 103:12).

He tells us in this passage that He has superabounded to us in all wisdom and prudence. This might be translated *foresight*. He has looked forward to our failures and our faults. He has foreseen every one of them. When He took us first, He knew all that we would do and fail to do. Nay, when He chose us in the eternal ages, He fortified Himself even against our unworthiness. He is ready for every emergency. This should not make us presume to sin; for if we continue to do this willfully, we do not belong to Him. But it should give us encouragement and comfort. At the same time the language here throws a fine light on God's disciplinary dealings with us even when He forgives us. He does it with all wisdom and prudence. He sometimes keeps back from us for a time the comfort and joy for which we are seeking, and makes us feel the keen pain of sin, not because He is angry, but because He is lovingly making us understand how exceedingly bitter and evil a thing sin is; and He is putting the bitter herbs of a heavenly discipline along with the blood of the Passover and the assurance of His mercy and His grace. Let us take His mercy under all circumstances, and let us, at the same time, trust His wisdom and His heavenly love.

THE RICHES OF HIS GLORY

The lofty flight of the apostle's argument does not end until it reaches a still higher region. In the last theme he began way back in the eternal past. He carries us in a series of bold and transcendent flights to a lofty vision of the ages to come, and reveals to us how much redemption cost and how much it brought us.

First, He tells us that in the fullness of time Christ is to gather together into one all things in heaven and on earth. He is not merely undoing the calamity of the Fall, but He is working out a sublime consummation for which the worlds were made. He is preparing an empire of unutterable glory in which He and His redeemed Bride will share the throne, and will be the center of the whole economy of God. What that gathering into one will be, imagination's highest thought in wonder dies away. It will be a consummation in which everything glorious in heaven and everything dear and beautiful on earth will have a part. It will be the combination of all history and all creation in a glorious new creation. It will be all that is best and brightest and sweetest and gladdest from every part of the universe of God brought together in one eternal paragon of beauty and of blessing. Everything will be in harmony. There will be no discords. He is to gather everything into one. We will have no uncongenial surroundings. We will be in harmony with our surroundings, and Christ will be the center and the crown, the joy and the All in all.

He tells us that we have obtained an inheritance in this glorious consummation. It was for that He chose us ages ago. It was for that He redeemed us. It is for that He saves us. It is for that we have let go all other heritages of selfishness, earthliness and the forbidden world of sense and sin. O beloved, have you made your eternal inheritance secure?

But there is a fine term in this verse. Rotherham translates it "In whom we also were taken as an inheritance." Not only have we an inheritance, but we are His inheritance. For us He has let go all other honors, glories and joys, and taken us to be His portion. "For the LORD'S portion is his people,/ Jacob his allotted inheritance" (Deuteronomy 32:9). What is He going to get out of us? Will we let Him refine, educate and glorify us until we will meet His own ideal and reach His glorious likeness, and He will have the ineffable joy of presenting us to Himself a "radiant church, without stain or wrinkle or any other blemish" (Ephesians 5:27)? In this consummation "He shall see of the travail of his soul, and shall be satisfied" (Isaiah 53:11, KJV), and "when [we] awake, [we] will be satisfied with seeing your likeness" (Psalm 17:15).

We are standing between two mighty eternities. We have just looked back to the ages past and seen in the dim distance the moment when we were chosen in Him, and we have attempted to look into the radiant glory in the remote future and catch a glimpse of what it will be when in the ages to come His mighty purpose will be fulfilled. Oh, let these two infinite outlooks inspire us, enlarge us and lift us up into the high and holy dignity of the sons of God and heirs of glory, and send us forth to walk henceforth worthy of the vocation wherewith we are called!

CHAPTER 3

SAVED AND SEALED

In order that we, who were the first to hope in Christ, might be for the praise of his glory. And you also were included in Christ when you heard the word of truth, the gospel of your salvation. Having believed, you were marked in him with a seal, the promised Holy Spirit, who is a deposit guaranteeing our inheritance until the redemption of those who are God's possession—to the praise of his glory. (Ephesians 1:12–14)

This is the third of the blessings of the Spirit in the heavenlies which the apostle is unfolding in this sublime treatise. First, we were chosen in Him; next, we were redeemed by His blood; now we are saved through His Word and sealed by His Spirit.

THE RELATION OF THE WORD OF GOD TO OUR SALVATION

It is here called "the word of truth, the gospel of your salvation" (1:13). This is important. Salvation is not a mere emotional feeling or subjective experience, but a transaction resting upon a definite word from God. We are saved by the truth and the gospel of our salvation. "You will know the truth, and the truth will set you free" (John 8:32).

If I am indebted to a man for a large amount, and know that I have not the means to pay him, I cannot be relieved of my difficulty by my friends trying to cheer me with kind speeches and good feelings. I must know by definite and authoritative documents that my debt is paid and my obligation canceled; a check for the amount or a receipt from my creditor alone can bring relief to my anxious mind. And so our salvation rests upon a word of God, an authoritative statement from the Judge Himself, by whom we have been condemned, that the debt is paid and we are released from condemnation.

This is the word which the gospel brings us, which states a definite and stupendous fact, namely, that Christ has redeemed us, that God has provided for our salvation long ago, that in fact we were saved in Christ's work before we were born; and all we have to do now is to know it, to claim it, and to enter into its enjoyment and the rest it brings.

This word is called "the gospel of your salvation" (Ephesians 1:13); that is, the good news, that you may be saved by simply accepting it. It is not a mere statement of abstract truth; it is a personal message for you. Christianity differs from all other religions in this. They are speculations and ethical theories. This is a personal message of love and mercy from God to every man, offering him eternal life.

Two men stood before an audience of 1,000 prisoners in a state penitentiary. One delivered a moral address, and was listened to with moderate interest. The other simply stood up and said: "Will John Smith please to stand up; I have a pardon for him." Instantly 12 men sprang to their feet, and so intense was the excitement that some of them fainted. They were all named John Smith. It was a question of their personal salvation. That is the gospel Christ sends to sinful men. It is intensely personal and profoundly important.

Beloved, have you accepted it for yourself as the gospel of "your salvation"?

THE RELATION OF FAITH TO OUR SALVATION

Not only are we saved through the word of the gospel, but this word must become a matter of personal faith. And so we read, "Who were the first to hope in Christ . . . And you also were included in Christ when you heard the word of truth, the gospel of your salvation. Having believed, you were marked in him with a seal" (1:12–13). Here faith is described under three terms, namely: trust or fore-trust, verse 12; trust, verse 13 (KJV); and believe, verse 13. They had fore-trust in Christ, that was previous to His coming. They had looked forward in hope and expectation to Him as their promised Messiah. Next, after they heard that He had come and received the gospel of salvation through Him, they trusted Him for themselves. Then this grew into a stronger faith so that they fully believed in Him, and entered into the actual reception of all the blessing of His salvation.

Trusting, while not essentially different from believing, expresses a slightly different phase of faith. Believing is the more mature experience. Trusting is the heart word; believing, the intellectual act. Trusting is the soul feeling after God and reaching out its tendrils toward Christ; believing is the deep and full assurance which has found Him, accepted Him, and entered into rest and confidence in Him. Our trust may be weak, timid and lacking in full assurance, and yet it is trusting all it can. But we must come to the place where we believe, rest and receive.

What is it to believe for salvation? It is not enough to believe that God is able to save us, to hope that someday He will take us to heaven. It is more definite, robust and committed than this. It is to believe that He does save us as He said He would, if we sincerely take Him at His word. His command is, "Whatever you ask for in prayer, believe that you have received it, and it will be yours" (Mark 11:24). The secret, therefore, of finding salvation is first to understand that it is offered to us in the Word of truth, the gospel of our salvation, and then frankly and fully to accept it and believe that it is ours for the taking.

In the same way we must believe for every other experience of the Christian life, and especially for the sealing of the Spirit, which is next mentioned here as coming to us after we believe.

Let there be no mistake here; faith is the only door of mercy, the only way of receiving what God has given. It is part of the very nature of things that we can take things from God only by believing. God gives to all men, of course, but of the unbeliever and waverer He says, "That man should not think he will receive anything from the Lord" (James 1:7). Doubt, distrust and fear hinder the heart from trusting, and shut all the receptive organs of our spiritual being, so that we cannot even take what our Father longs to give.

THE RELATION OF THE HOLY SPIRIT TO OUR SALVATION

While the Word of God is the ground of our faith, and faith is the receptive act by which we take salvation through the Word, yet, back of all that there is a personal and divine Agent, the Holy Spirit, through whom we are able to believe the Word, and by whom we are sealed after we have believed the Word and are led on into all the fullness to which this great salvation introduces us. Undoubtedly the Holy Spirit is actively engaged in leading us on, even in the earlier steps of faith; but after we have taken these steps, the Spirit comes into entirely new relations with us, and becomes the personal and indwelling presence and power of our Christian life. This is here described by the strong figure, "You were marked in him with a seal, the promised Holy Spirit" (Ephesians 1:13), or, as it might be translated, "with that Spirit of promise, the Holy One."

Now it is important to notice at the outset of this part of the subject the force of the preposition *with*. He does not use the word *by* but *with*. If *by* had been used, the meaning would be that it was the Holy Spirit who did the sealing, and that the seal was something different from the one sealing; but the *with* conveys the idea than it was God the Father who sealed us, and that the seal was nothing less that the Holy Spirit Himself. Sealing therefore is not some experience or feeling that the Holy Spirit brings us, but it is the actual reception of the Holy Spirit Himself, and He comes personally to live within us and to become the power of our new life.

This is a most important truth. It had already been taught in the life of our Lord Himself, and the fact that He received the Holy Spirit as a Person to dwell in Him long after his birth and childhood, in the 30th year of His age, and just before beginning His public ministry. It is also certain that the apostles received the Holy Spirit as a Person long after their conversion. In like manner, the believer, after he has accepted salvation through faith in the Word, comes into a new relation with the Holy Spirit who enters into personal union with him and thus seals him, stamps him, sets him apart for God, and becomes the Guarantee and Keeper of his life against all the power of Satan, self and sin.

Let us pause here and ask, Have we received the Holy Spirit since we believed? Have we first received Christ as our Savior, and then received the Spirit as our Keeper and our Power for life and service?

At the same time let us not make the mistake of supposing that there need be a long interval between our receiving Christ and our being sealed with the Spirit. Here we are told it was after they believed, probably just after that they received the Holy Spirit. This should immediately follow the experience of conversion. Indeed, there is no assurance that we can keep our conversion without the sealing of the Holy Spirit. That is the great lack in the religious teaching of today. Men and women are hurried into a profession of religion under a superficial excitement, and it is little wonder if they fall away. Every disciple ought to be led on to a baptism of the Spirit, which is as essential for our own Christian life and walk as it is for our work for others.

This sealing of the Spirit is presented to us under two very striking figures. The first is that of the *seal*, the second a *deposit*.

The seal is a familiar figure, both in ancient and modern life. It is used in connection with public documents and commercial contracts. As applied to the Holy Spirit, it expresses three things: reality, security and resemblance.

1. Reality

The mark of the seal is unmistakable. It cuts a deep impression into the wax or paper, so that it is patent to every sense. This figure means that when we receive the Holy Spirit something very real occurs; there is no mistake about it, you know it and others know it. Your Christian life is not a vague "perhaps," but your convictions, impressions, hopes and purposes are clearcut, definite and unequivocal. Your Christian experience becomes real and thorough; people know where to find you, and you have no doubt about your own bearings. Christ is very real to you; the things of eternity are intensely vivid; you are alive to God in all the powers of your being; your life is a life in earnest; your soul is a soul on fire.

2. Security

The Holy Spirit brings certainty. You know that you belong to God; you know that you have passed from death unto life; God has marked you for His own, and you know that you will be kept from Satan, self and sin, and your heart learns to say, "I know whom I have believed, and am convinced that he is able to guard what I have entrusted to him for that day" (2 Timothy 1:12b). "We know that in all things God works for the good of those who love him" (Romans 8:28).

3. Resemblance

It impresses the object sealed; the very mark on the seal itself stamps its own likeness on the soft wax. So the Holy Spirit stamps upon us the image of Christ and makes us Christlike. Nay, more, He stamps upon us identity with Christ. Not only are we like Christ, but we have Christ Himself to live within us, and to reproduce His own character, life and loveliness within us. The Holy Spirit brings us not only His own personality but also the personality of the Lord Jesus, and thus we come into closer personal union with our dear Lord and our living Head.

Such then is the blessed privilege of being sealed with the Holy Spirit of promise. So important is it that in the literal translation of the verse it is often spoken of as the "Holy Spirit of promise." It is emphasized as if there were no other promise as important as this one.

How may this unspeakable blessing be received? It is made very plain in this passage, "Having believed, you were marked in him with a seal" (Ephesians 1:13). You take Him by believing; that is, you believe that you receive Him, and you begin to act immediately as if you had Him. This is the secret of every advance in the Christian life. You must take what He gives by simple faith, and then reckon upon His word and act your reckoning out, and God will make it real. Oh, that some who read these lines would thus receive Him now!

But there is another figure in this fine passage describing the work of the Holy Spirit in the believer's life. It is the word *earnest* (KJV) or *deposit*. "Who is a deposit guaranteeing our inheritance until the redemption of those who are God's possession" (1:14). Now an *earnest* in ancient times was a legal pledge of a commercial transaction. When a man bought a piece of land, he received from the seller, not only a covenant to deliver the land to him in due time, but also a little handful of soil as a guarantee that the whole property would be transferred to him. Now the Holy Spirit is such a guarantee and pledge, and is also a sample of the inheritance of glory which Christ has purchased for us, and is in due time to convey in all its fullness.

We have been looking, in this sublime epistle, into two eternities. The first is that past eternity when we were chosen in Him before the foundation of the world for our great salvation and heavenly calling. The second is that eternity to come, for which He has been preparing us; and when He will gather together into one, all things in Himself, and we will sit with Him in the center of a universe of harmony, righteousness, beauty, glory and ineffable happiness, as the sharers of His throne and the very bride of His heart.

But how will we understand that distant vision? How will we foretaste that coming glory? What telescope, what eagle eye can disclose the passing glories of that heavenly vision? Listen! The Holy Spirit is the "deposit guaranteeing our inheritance" (1:14). He comes to be the revealer of the ages to come, to be the celestial telescope that pierces the distant firmament and brings nearer the vision of the coming glory. Nay more, He comes to be the beginning, the foretaste of what heaven will be, and to give us in our present experience some little taste of the fruits of paradise and the river of the water of life. Best of all, He comes to be to us the guarantee and pledge that all this will yet be ours in full fruition.

That is the meaning of the earnest of our inheritance. Like Eliezer, Abraham's servant, who went to bring a bride home for Isaac, and who showed her, as they traveled homeward, some of the glories of her future lord; so the Holy Spirit is trying to make us understand what our future home and hope will be.

Sometimes our hearts grow too big for our bodies. Sometimes it seems to us as if we would burst these frail shells and break forth into some vaster realm. Sometimes we almost catch the foregleam of the light that never shone on land or sea. Sometimes we almost hear the music of harpists playing their harps (Revelation 14:2). Sometimes when loved ones pass through and leave the gates ajar, we can feel for days our hearts throbbing with their rapturous joy, and we are almost conscious of their ascension through those heights of glory.

Ah, beloved, these are the throbbings of the Spirit, the Deposit of our inheritance. These are the buds of faith's springtime bursting into millennial blossoms. These are the throes and birthpangs of a greater life to come; and He has said of such foretastes and sweet hopes, "If it were not so, I would have told you" (John 14:2).

Will we know each other there? Will we meet our loved ones again on that bright shore? Ah, beloved, the old Scotchman answered this well when he said to his weeping wife, when she asked him this question on his deathbed, "Janet, do you think we will be bigger fools than we are now? But," he added, "I may be a thousand years in heaven before I shall be able to take my eyes off Jesus even to look at you."

Oh! if we could but lie closer on His breast and listen more carefully to His whisperings, He would often speak to us of things to come, and we would dwell with Him in the soft, sweet light of the land of Beulah, living under the powers of the world to come, and seeing "the king in his beauty" and "a land that stretches afar" (Isaiah 33:17); for "No eye has seen,/ no ear has heard,/ no mind has conceived/ what God has prepared for those who love him—but God has revealed it to us by his Spirit. The Spirit searches all things, even the deep things of God" (1 Corinthians 2:9–10).

CHAPTER 4

THE SPIRIT OF ILLUMINATION AND REVELATION

I keep asking that the God of our Lord Jesus Christ, the glorious Father, may give you the Spirit of wisdom and revelation, so that you may know him better. I pray also that the eyes of your heart may be enlightened in order that you may know the hope to which he has called you, the riches of his glorious inheritance in the saints, and his incomparably great power for us who believe. That power is like the working of his mighty strength, which he exerted in Christ when he raised him from the dead and seated him at his right hand in the heavenly realms, far above all rule and authority, power and dominion, and every title that can be given, not only in the present age but also in the one to come. And God placed all things under his feet and appointed him to be head over everything for the church, which is his body, the fullness of him who fills everything in every way. (Ephesians 1:17–23)

In the previous context the apostle referred to the Holy Spirit as the Deposit of our inheritance, the foretaste and pledge of the glory yet to be revealed. In connection with this Paul now unfolds more fully the way in which the Holy Spirit makes known to us the riches of our great inheritance, and opens our eyes to see and realize all that is laid up for us in Christ in the heavenlies.

The first step in any spiritual experience must necessarily be to apprehend and understand it; then we shall be able to appropriate and enjoy it. The Spirit's first work, therefore, is to make known to us all the fullness of the blessings of the Spirit in the heavenlies. The little mouse that enters the splendid cathedral has no eyes for the beauties of the architecture, no ears for the harmonies of the music, and no soul for the inspiration of the message given. All it sees is the crumb which is to satisfy its hunger, and all the rest is lost upon it. To the quickened mind and the spiritual heart there are higher things to perceive and receive. But we must have eyes to see them and hearts to understand them. "Where there is no vision, the people perish" (Proverbs 29:18a, KJV).

Poor Hagar, weeping yonder in the desert because her boy is dying of thirst, knows not that the fountain is flowing just at her side. All she needs is the voice of the angel to tell her to lift up her eyes, and, lo, there is deliverance and supply. The tears of sorrow are exchanged for smiles of thankfulness (see Genesis 21:14–19).

Moses standing beside Marah's bitter well did not need any new creation to remedy the misery. All he had to do was to lift up his eyes and behold the branch which was growing in the thicket by his side, and to cut it and cast it into the springs of Marah, and, lo, the waters were healed (see Exodus 15:23–25)!

Elisha's servant standing by his side on yonder mountain, trembling and quaking as he saw the Syrian squadrons closing round them, needed only to have his eyes opened to behold the angel battalions of horses and chariots all around the mountain, protecting them. Then his fears were changed to confidence and peace (see 2 Kings 6:15–17).

So many a heart, like Hagar, is famishing for the waters of life, and needs only to see the fountains of grace to be saved and satisfied. Many a suffering body is standing at Marah's bitter fountain, needing only to behold the branch of healing to be set free. Many a troubled life would change its groans and wails of doubt and fear, for shouts of praise if God would but open the eyes of spiritual vision and enable them to see that the angel of the Lord is encamping round about them to deliver and preserve (see Psalm 34:7). Oh, that the Holy Spirit would open our eyes, and that we would let Him! What God said to Abraham He is still saying to us: "All the land that you see I will give to you" (Genesis 13:15). We must see it first, and then we can take it. The vision comes before the victory.

So in this great epistle, before we can enter into all the blessing of the Spirit in the heavenlies, the apostle puts to our eye the telescope of celestial vision and touches our sight with the eye salve of divine anointing. Then He bids us look, and look, and look until we see and fully understand all the meaning of the hope of our calling and the riches of the glory of our inheritance.

THE AGENT OF THIS NEW VISION

"The Spirit of wisdom and revelation" (Ephesians 1:17). The Holy Spirit is the source of this new light, and He gives it in two ways: first, by giving us knowledge of the truth; and, secondly, by giving us a direct touch of revelation, a distinct flash of celestial light that makes it all vivid and real to our spiritual senses. It is not enough merely to know the truth, but we must have the quickening of God to make it real to us and to cause it to live within our spiritual consciousness.

There is a place of revelation in the spiritual life; not the revelation of new doctrines and truths, but the revelation to us of the principles and doctrines already given. It was by such a revelation that we saw our sins and were convicted of our guilt. It was by such a revelation that we saw our Savior and accepted Him. It is by such a revelation that we behold the deeper life He has for us through the indwelling of the Holy Spirit. The apostle speaks of this when he says, "It pleased God . . . to reveal his Son in me" (Galatians 1:15–16, KJV). There is a living Holy Spirit, and there is a light He gives which the eyes of the earthly mind or the most cultured scholar never see. Let us ask Him for it. Let us not rest short of it.

THE ORGAN OF THE VISION

"The eyes of your heart may be enlightened" (Ephesians 1:17). This is very different from the eyes of the intellect. A cultivated mind may see the truth while the heart is cold and still untouched. Men see very much what they look for. The mere scholar looks for literary beauties or defects in the Bible. The saint looks for the face of Jesus. Each finds what he is able to perceive.

An English traveler was telling a missionary that all the time he was in India he never saw a convert. He did not believe there were any there. The missionary asked him what he saw. He said he saw tigers, lots of them.

"What did you go for?" said the missionary.

"Well," he said, "I went to hunt tigers."

"Then you got what you were looking for. I never saw a tiger all the years I was in India, but I saw thousands of converts. You went for tigers and you found them. I looked for converts and I found them."

The mere powers of the human intellect cannot find God. There is a deeper spiritual nature which must be awakened, educated and divinely quickened. It is the heart. It is something like the intuition of the bird which, knowing when winter is coming on, sets its bosom toward southern skies, and detects by inward instinct the poison berry which the botanist may fail by all his senses to discover.

There is an inner life born of the Holy Spirit to which He can speak, and through which He can show a world of living realities which "No eye has seen,/ no ear has heard,/ no mind has conceived/ what God has prepared for those who love him—/ but God has revealed it to us by his Spirit" (1 Corinthians 2:9–10a).

THE OBJECT OF THE SPIRITUAL VISION

"That . . . God . . . may give you the Spirit of wisdom and revelation, so that you may know him better" (Ephesians 1:17). He is the object of this vision. It reveals to us the person and love of the Lord Jesus Christ. It is not mere ideas, truths or even blessings that form the center of vital Christianity, but it is the personal presence and love of Jesus Christ Himself. This is something which the cold intellect cannot understand, and which a correct aesthetic taste may even despise. You may call it sentiment or mysticism if you please, but it is something which the saints of every age have had in common, that deep, intense personal affection which led Mary to sit at Jesus' feet and pour out upon Him her precious gift; which led Paul to say, "for Christ's love compels us" (2 Corinthians 5:14); which led Faber to sing:

> O Jesus, Jesus, dearest Lord,
>   Forgive me if I say
> For very love Thy sacred name,
>   A thousand times a day.

And which finds its simple heartfelt fervor in the response that often bursts from your lips unconsciously with a hallelujah of praise. It is the secret of the saint. It is the mystery of love. It is in an infinitely higher form than that vast, wondrous thing which fastens the eye of the babe upon its mother, and the mother's glance of absorbing love upon her babe; which explains the soft endearments and the tender interchanges of personal affection in private friendships and sacred home affections of life. These things would be ridiculous if others looked at them. They could not stand exposure or repetition, but they have a deep reality for loving hearts that will never cease as long as life and love will last.

So in the higher realm of spiritual things there is a place for tender, affectionate fellowship between the soul and the Savior. There is a revelation of Him, an intimacy with Him, a personal knowledge of Him of which we can only say,

> The love of Jesus what it is,
>   None but His loved ones know.

The Greek word here translated "know" is an intensive word, and denotes the intimate and full knowledge of Him. It is derived from the Greek word "know" (*gnosis*) prefixed by the preposition *epi*. The difference between the two words may be seen in First Corinthians 13:12, where the word *gnosis* is used in the first clause, "Now I know in part." But in the second clause a form of the word *epignosis* is used in both places: "Then I shall know fully, even as I am fully known." In this sense the Holy Spirit would have us "fully know" the Lord in that deep intimacy and fellowship divine which constitutes the highest happiness of a Christ-filled soul.

Dearly beloved, have you not often longed to have Christ real to you, and to be conscious of His presence in a sense as deep, at least, as you are conscious of other objects and other friends? Have you not often prayed,

> Lord Jesus, make Thyself to me
> A living bright Reality.

This is the prayer of our text. This is one of the blessings of the Spirit in the heavenlies. This is the very business of the Comforter, to reveal Christ and make Him actual in your life. Claim it. Follow on until you know Him in all His fullness and you shall not seek His face in vain.

THE OUTLOOK OF THE VISION

"That you may know the hope to which he has called you, the riches of his glorious inheritance in the saints" (Ephesians 1:18). The life of every human being is largely bound up in the future. Hope is an instinctive aspiration of the human breast. Men are constantly investing large sums from which they expect no immediate return, but they see in the distance immense results, and with farseeing enterprise they plant the seeds for future fortunes.

Now God wants us to catch the foregleam of the coming glory and to realize the fortune laid up for us beyond, and let it become the incentive to faith, sacrifice and undiscouraged toil, knowing that in due season we will reap if we faint not. Most people are living under the power of the present. The things immediately around them color their thought and feeling so strongly that a present trifle outweighs the future crown.

God wants to break the power of the present. Christ died for us that we might be redeemed from this present evil world and learn to live under the power of the age to come. The Holy Spirit alone can make this real. He can paint upon the chambers of imagination the picture of the celestial city, the inviting crown, the unending day, the life where death and sin and sorrow shall come no more, the thrones and principalities that we have conquered, and the realization of all the hopes, longings and outreachings which the things of time have only mocked and which must often find their satisfaction there. The heart needs the inspiration of hope, the uplift and attraction of the heavenly vision. Bunyan's pilgrim was wisely taken at intervals along his way to the house of vision, where he was permitted to see from the Delectable Mountains the towers of the Celestial City and the glorified beings who had reached their great reward. Even Christ Himself, midway to the cross, turned aside that from the Mount of Transfiguration so He and His disciples might have a glimpse of the glory yet to be revealed. In the strength and inspiration of this vision He went forward to the cross scorning its shame for the joy set before Him (see Hebrews 12:2). Oh, when we see it, realize it, claim it as our own, the world has lost its power to draw our hearts aside and our triumphant soul can sing:

> Should earth against my soul engage
>   And hellish darts be hurled;
> Then I can smile at Satan's rage,
>   And face a frowning world.
> Let cares like a wild deluge come,
>   And storms of sorrow fall;
> May I but safely reach my home,
>   My God, my heaven, my all.

THE POWER REVEALED BY THIS VISION

"His incomparably great power for us who believe" (Ephesians 1:19). After all, the greatest need of our life lies in the present, and for this real conflict we need actual resources and practical power. And so the last vision revealed in this divine illumination is, "His incomparably great power for us who believe." This vision of power is so immense that our strength fails, through the vastness of the vision, adequately to take it in.

1. It is described by a combination of nouns, adjectives and adverbs quite unexampled even in the intense style of Paul himself. First, we have the three words for power: one denoting strength, another authority and another extraordinary power, which is our word dynamite. Then we have supporting it this qualifying phrase, "His incomparably great power."

He piles mountain upon mountain in order to reach the height of this transcendent vision. We know something of these words from what we see around us. The power of dynamite, the strength of man's explosive may be seen in the fearful effects of modern military and naval warfare. A shell of heavy weight can be hurled miles, and in its very explosion shatter the most powerful armorplate in the world to pieces. A torpedo has but to touch that massive ship with steel plates more than a foot thick, and it is twisted and torn into fragments, its living freight hurled into an awful death. Mightier than these are the forces that work the spring and swing the planet around its solar center. These are but lessons of that surpassing might which quietly and constantly is going forth from the hand of Him who sits upon the throne as our Savior and our living Head, and that each of us may claim for every need of life.

2. Next, he illustrates this power by the resurrection of Jesus Christ. It raised Him from the dead. That is more than man's might can do. Man can kill his millions, but he cannot give back life to a fluttering insect. Look at that sealed stone and guarded tomb, that lifeless clay with the marks of the

nails and the spear. Look again! The guard has fled! The seal is broken! The stone is rolled away! The Lord is standing in the Easter morning with the light and glory of the resurrection on His countenance, saying to His wondering disciples: "All hail!" That is the power we may claim, stronger than the grave.

3. It is next illustrated in His ascension. He "seated him at his right hand in the heavenly realms" (1:20). Man has found no power as strong as gravitation. He has tried to build a tower to scale the heavens, but he has not yet reached the height even of earth's shallow atmosphere. But look at yonder form gently rising from the hills of Bethany, His hands stretched out in blessing, His face shining with love, His tender parting words still falling upon their ears. Gradually, majestically He rises into space without an effort. The law of gravitation has lost its power, for He is the center of gravitation now. Higher and higher He ascends, while they gaze with rapt wonder until a little cloud intervenes, and then He pauses! He waits long enough to send one more parting message down, and then He sails away through the ether ocean to some distant world, which God has made the metropolis of His empire. There He sits down calmly, triumphantly, at the right hand of the eternal throne. It is the attitude of repose, of dignity, of absolute resistless power.

Beloved, that is the power that He would reveal to you, and that He is waiting to share with you for the smallest need and the greatest extremity of your life.

4. Still further is this power emphasized by comparison with the objects that it has surmounted. He has ascended "far above all rule and authority, power and dominion, and every title that can be given, not only in the present age but also in the one to come" (1:21). Here every kind of superior being is named. There are high names and mighty dominions even of this earth, but He is far above them all. Nebuchadnezzar, Herod—all are but subjects of His will, and at His bidding must sink into abasement or corruption.

There are greater names in the spiritual realm, wicked spirits, swift and terrible as the lightning which Christ saw fall from heaven; great principalities of evil rising in successive ranks until they reach that mighty personality himself, the god of this world and the sovereign of an empire of innumerable spirits far mightier than the loftiest human mind. In modern times spiritualism is beginning to uncover some of the mysteries of this underworld which can almost imitate the miracles of God Himself. But there is one Power who is far above them all, Jesus Christ, the King of kings and Lord of lords, the glorious and only potentate.

Even the laws of nature themselves are subject to His will. Even the forces of life and death and the things which seem so uniform and unchangeable are liable to His intervention and suspension whenever our needs may require. His ascension is a protest against every other force, and it is according to the power of His ascension that we may now claim His help.

5. The vision of His power is further strengthened by the relation which He sustains at once to the universe and to us. This is the crowning picture: "Head over everything for the church, which is his body" (1:22–23). He is not only Head over all things, but He is Head for the one purpose of blessing us. He holds His high throne wholly on our behalf. He has entered heaven as our Representative. He has left the other half of Himself behind on earth. He is but a Head. We are His body, and He reigns yonder and here for the sake of that body. The wheels of the universe are moving entirely for the sake of His Church. The forces of nature and providence are subject to the need and help and blessing and glory of His little flock, His glorious bride. This gives us the right to claim His fullness. Not as gratuity, but as a primary claim, and the very object for which He has ascended to His mediatorial throne.

Beloved, will we rise to this celestial vision? Will we gaze upon it until it blinds our eyes to every other object, and burns into our consciousness the realization of our boundless resources? Then will we come back in the light of that vision to set it over against the things that have been too hard for us? As we look at temptation, sin, Satan, the world, sickness, sorrow, guilt, enemies, earth's attractions or Satan's hate, the inveterate weakness of souls we love, or even the helplessness of our own poor, weak hearts will we henceforth say, "Christ, my living and ascended Lord, is far above all these things, and what is Christ's is mine, for I am part of His body, and He is my living Head, my other self, my all in all?"

Lord, show us the vision, then help us to claim it, to prove it, to bring it down into every moment of a victorious life in Jesus' name. Amen.

CHAPTER 5

RESURRECTED AND SEATED IN THE HEAVENLIES

But because of his great love for us, God, who is rich in mercy, made us alive with Christ even when we were dead in transgressions—it is by grace you have been saved. And God raised us up with Christ and seated us with him in the heavenly realms in Christ Jesus, in order that in the coming ages he might show the incomparable riches of his grace, expressed in his kindness to us in Christ Jesus. (Ephesians 2:4–7)

In perfecting any great product of human invention, the first thing is to secure a perfect pattern, a model, a sample, an actual specimen, after which all other copies may be made. The inventor often spends nearly a lifetime in revising, remodeling or modifying his pattern; and when at last it is complete, and the model is placed in the patent office, it is a comparatively easy matter to reproduce that pattern in millions of copies.

This illustration is scarcely worthy of its transcendent object; but if we may rise from the earthly to the heavenly by such an imperfect steppingstone, it is true in a much higher sense that God has been spending the eternal ages in preparing and revealing His divine pattern for redeemed humanity. Pathetically the ancient prophet represents Him as saying, "I looked for a man among them . . . but I found none" (Ezekiel 22:30). Vainly did God scan the highest types of mere humanity only to have an Adam, a Noah, an Abraham, a Moses, a David, a Solomon, an Elijah completely break down under the final test, and often prove weak in the strongest place.

At last, however, there stood on the banks of the Jordan a Man on whom the Father looked with complacent gaze, and exclaimed: "This is my Son, whom I love; with him I am well pleased" (Matthew 3:17). At last He found a Man who met His expectation and fulfilled the standard of true humanity. Since that time God's one business with the human race has been to make men after that heavenly pattern. Christ is the one great Type, and every saint is but a copy of the divine Original.

But it was not merely in His earthly life that Christ was the ideal Man. Much more it was in His death, resurrection, ascension and heavenly life that He was designed to be our Prototype and Head for He represents humanity after it has passed through the crisis of death and come into a resurrection, an ascension, a supernatural, incorruptible and eternal life. It is not the Man of Nazareth or of Bethany merely that is our Pattern and our Head. It is the Man upon the throne, seated at the Father's side, "head over everything for the church, which is his body" (Ephesians 1:22–23), and bringing redeemed humanity up to His own level.

This is the sublime conception of the passage before us in connection with the former context. There we were taught that the power, the grace and the glory which God has for us are according to what "he exerted in Christ when he raised him from the dead and seated him at his right hand in the heavenly realms" (1:20). This passage goes a step further, reaching down to us on our low plane of helpless ruin, and lifting us up to share all the glory of that transcendent vision. As He is so are we to be. You have seen Him on the throne, now ascend and sit with Him there. For "God . . . made us alive with Christ even when we were dead in transgressions" (2:5).

And this is not nearly all. It is not as a hope, an ambition, an ideal, a pursuit that this high object is presented, but it is recognized as something that is already ours. The tenses are all perfect. He "made us alive with Christ" (2:5). He "raised us up" (2:6) with Him. He has "seated us with him in the heavenly realms in Christ Jesus" (2:6). It is all counted as something already ours as certainly as the purpose of God, as certainly as the reckoning of faith.

Here we come face to face with that extraordinary principle which underlies all God's operations, the principle of faith—a faith that counts the things that are not as though they already were; that reckons upon the future as though it were already past; and that feels and acts in the light of God's promises as if they had already become accomplished performances. This is God's principle of action, and in accordance with it Jesus Christ was counted "the Lamb that was slain from the creation of the world" (Revelations 13:8). We are recognized and dealt with by God as though all His eternal purposes for us had already been fulfilled. God discounts His own notes, and turns into actual currency the facts which to human reason would seem to be only probabilities and promises. And so He requires us to meet Him and take Him at His Word, and to reckon upon things as real long before they come to pass. Hence we take our forgiveness and salvation in the exercise of immediate faith. We take the answers to our prayers by believing that we receive the things we ask, and then we have them. And here we are called to take the place which is to be ours after centuries have passed, and to look upon things as though we were already seated upon our millennial thrones and enjoying the glories and felicities of the ages to come.

Let us examine this extraordinary picture a little more in detail.

OUR FORMER STATE

We were not born into these high dignities, but have been translated out of darkness into light, out of death into life, out of degradation and misery into glory and blessing, out of the power of darkness into the kingdom of God's dear Son.

1. Of the World

Our former state is first described as "when you followed the ways of this world" (2:2). We belonged to the present age. We were under the influence of natural things. We followed the trend of the age, the opinions, tendencies, ideas of the world. That is where the worldling is today. He belongs to the realm of pure naturalism; and he has no part, and can have none, in the kingdom of God and the destinies and glories of the coming age.

2. Of the Devil

We were under the power of "the prince of this world" (John 16:11), here described as the "ruler of the kingdom of the air, the spirit who is now at work in those who are disobedient" (Ephesians 2:2b). We were born of Satan, his offspring spiritually, and his willing, helpless subjects. Many do not like to hear this, but it is the plain teaching of the Scriptures that the natural man is at once the offspring and slave of Satan.

The regions around us and above us are teeming with innumerable beings, spiritual creatures, once perhaps clothed in material forms, making countless ranks of hierarchies and principalities, and all under the absolute dominion of one mighty mind who is only less than God, and who is even called in the Scriptures "the god of this world" (2 Corinthians 4:4, KJV).

We never know the power of this spiritual tyranny until we resist it and attempt to overthrow it. The natural man is absolutely led by demon powers. It is their policy to make their control as agreeable as possible, and make us feel the terror of their might only when they are in danger of losing us as their prey. There is no doubt that in these last days especially, the forces of the demon world are concentrating their strength for the last terrific conflict of the ages, and that just before the Lord's return we shall know more fully the meaning of the last picture of this epistle, the conflict with the principalities and powers.

3. Socially Corrupted

We were living like the people around us, the children of disobedience, among whom we all had our own conduct in times past. We were going with the great crowd that tread the broad way. We were under the influence of sinful associations, unholy companionships, entangling affections, and a thousand social cords were pulling us downward to the dark abyss.

4. Slaves to Our Nature

We were the slaves of ourselves, following the bend of our evil natures, "gratifying the cravings of our sinful nature and following its desires and thoughts" (Ephesians 2:3b).

The two classes of lust are here described: the one more coarse and sensual, the desires of the flesh; the other more refined and aesthetic, the desires of the mind. But they are both equally selfish and ungodly, and they both belong to the natural life. For this realm of the present age is not all a cesspool of nauseous corruption; it is a beautiful realm, bright with color and action, and includes in its brilliant attraction all that is most beautiful, illustrious and delightful in human history and life.

5. Dead in Sin

Back of all the glamour and glitter is the hideous spectacle of a reeking corpse and a moldering grave. "Dead in your transgressions and sins" (2:1) is the fearful word that calls up all that is darkest, saddest and most terrible in human thought and speech, and turns the vision of beauty, pleasure and fame into a charnel house and a putrefying corpse. Human nature is as help-less and as offensive as an open sepulcher and a reeking tomb. Decorate it as you please with the fairest flowers, the most splendid monuments; under all are corruption and the worm—death in all its terrors and all its helplessness. Man is dead, and the transgressions and sins which are added to the picture are but the ghastly ulcers that mark the fatal wound.

6. Objects of Wrath

One more verse completes the picture and gives the climax of horrors. It is the relation of our fallen nature to God, "like the rest, we were by nature ob-jects of wrath" (2:3). It is a fearful word. It tells us we are naturally born into a state of wrath. There is something in God's nature and holiness which in-evitably must consume and destroy the sinful soul as naturally as the flame of a lamp scorches and destroys the fluttering moth that falls into its fiery beam.

That flaming wrath is suspended for a season through the mediation of Christ. But when at last the day of grace is ended, and God appears in His true relation to sin and sinful men, so awful will be the sight, that earth's in-habitants, even her kings, her captains and her great ones will cry in despair-ing anguish for the rocks to fall on them to hide them from the very face of Him who sits upon the throne and the wrath of the Lamb. This is the natural state of human nature. This is the pit from whence we were dug and the rock from whence we were hewn. In this age of maudlin sentiment and milk-and-water moral conceptions, it is well to understand what God thinks of sin and sinful men.

RESURRECTED AND RAISED

But from this state the infinite grace of God has lifted us, and the process is here described by three great words:

1. Regeneration

We were "quickened" (2:5, KJV)—that is, made alive. It is a touch of the new creation in the human soul. It is the experience of regeneration. It is the beginning not of reformation or outward improvement, but of that strange and mighty experience that we call life. What a difference between a dead man and a live one. It takes half a dozen pallbearers to carry a dead man, but a live man can carry himself and somebody else besides. God wants to put life in us, and thus we rise in divine strength, and stand and move in the divine order by the principle within. Let a touch of life pass over nature, and in one day it accomplishes more than all the gardeners in the country could do in a year in decorating and enrobing the landscape with beauty and bloom. The first step in the new life is the quickening of the Holy Spirit and the new creation which it brings in the soul. "If anyone is in Christ, he is a new creation; the old has gone, the new has come!" (2 Corinthians 5:17).

2. Resurrection

This is more than regeneration. Regeneration imparts life, but resurrection lifts us quite out of the realm of death and sets us free from all the shackles of the tomb. There seems to be no doubt that the Lord Jesus Christ was "quickened" into life before He rose from the grave, and silently in the sealed tomb He had time to roll up and put away the napkin that was wrapped around His brow, and the body shroud of His brief entombment. After this He came forth by power of the resurrection, passing through the sealed stone, even before it was removed, and standing in all the beauty and buoyancy of that Easter morning in the garden where He met the first witnesses of His triumph. And so we are not only to receive a touch of the new life, but we are to break from the fetters of the old life and rise to all the freedom and fullness of the very life of Christ, our risen Lord.

3. Ascension

He "raised us up with Christ and seated us" (Ephesians 2:6) with Him in the heavenlies. This is much more than resurrection. It is ascension. It is taking the place of accomplished victory and conceded right, and sitting down in an attitude of complete repose, from henceforth expecting with Him until all our enemies be made our footstool. It is not even the effect of struggling to rise, but it is the rest of one who has ascended and is living in the realization of accomplished victory.

It is a beautiful sight to see the morning lark beating its wings and pinioning its way up through the air, until far out of sight it warbles out its little song, and then drops down again to its resting place in the meadow. But it is a much more beautiful sight to see that summer bird with outstretched wing lying like a stately ship on the bosom of the air, every fiber of its being in full activity, and yet, in perfect repose, a spectacle of majestic rest and strength. It is not trying to ascend; it has ascended, and it is calmly reposing on the bosom of the element where it dwells at home among the chariot clouds and blue firmament. The first is the picture of the soul that is beating heavenward, the other, of the soul that has entered into rest. It is throne life. It is dwelling with Christ on high, your head in the heavens even while your feet still walk the paths of the lower world of sense and time. This is our high privilege, to live as if time were past, as if the millennial morning had come, and we were sitting upon our throne and realizing the felicities and glories of the ages to come.

THE SOURCE OF THIS WONDROUS GRACE

What is the secret of this mighty transformation? The answer is given in a wondrous climax of praise to divine love.

1. "But God"

The first touch of the light upon the picture is a bold and brief one. Two little words describe it, "But . . . God" (2:4a). He is the one and the only explanation of it. The former picture is a very dark one. It tells of the tremendous force of the present age, the prince of the powers of the air, the example of innumerable wicked men, the dreadful trend of our own heart, the ghastly picture of even death itself, and the more terrific vision of God's holy wrath for sin. The situation would seem to be an impossible one, the problem too hard for solution, and yet, over against this dark and awful cloud, like a spanning rainbow, these two little words explain and solve it all: "but God." The problem was not too hard for Him. His infinite resources spanned the cleft and wrought a remedy.

So, beloved, you may take those same two words, and write them over against every dark cloud, every difficult problem, every impossible situation of your life. It may be too hard for you. It may be too hard for others. It may be too hard to bear, "but God" is equal to it. He is the remedy for it. He is waiting now to turn it into a background on which He will write the eternal records of His grace.

2. His Mercy

The next touch is the word "mercy." It is one of the attributes of God and one of the phases of God's love. It is the phase of love which deals with the unworthy, the wicked, the most undeserving. It tells of a love that can pardon, welcome and bless where no other could tolerate or endure. Oh, if there is one who is reading these lines who is past all human hope and even your own self-respect, who feels that you deserve nothing but judgment and ruin, look up, beloved, to Him who is "rich in mercy" (2:4b); and act like Manasseh, of whom it is said that when he "humbled himself . . . and . . . prayed," God was "moved by his entreaty" (2 Chronicles 33:12–13); or, like Paul, to say, "I am the worst [of sinners]. But . . . I was shown mercy" (1 Timothy 1:15b–16a).

3. His Grace

Next we have the word "grace," but it is strengthened by two attributes, "the *incomparable riches* of his grace" (Ephesians 2:7, italics added). Grace, like mercy, is a special phase of divine love. It is love to the helpless, to those who can make no return, and to those who cannot even help themselves. It is the priest going outside the camp to the leper who has not strength enough to go in. It is mercy meeting man not halfway, but all the way. It is the father seeing the son a great way off and running to welcome him home. Are you wicked? Have you lost power even to choose the right? Do you feel unable to believe or trust or lift a finger to save yourself? Beloved, you are the very one whom the grace of God is waiting to lift from the depths of helplessness to the heights of heaven.

4. His Love

Next, we have the word "love," the sweetest word of human language or heavenly speech. It is a hard word to define. If you would ask what it means, look at the mother's sacrifice; look at the prophet's blood; look at the hero's sufferings; look at the dying Redeemer; look at John 3:16: "God so loved the world." It is an outstretching impulse which has no explanation, no reason but its own deep fountain of fullness. It is something that you or I will never fully understand, even though we may know it and receive it.

> Could I with ink the ocean fill,
>   Were the whole sky of parchment made,
> Were every blade of grass a quill,
>   And every man a scribe by trade;
>
> To write the love of God above
>   Would drain that ocean dry;

> Nor could the scroll contain the whole,
>   Though spread from sky to sky.

Here it is heightened by the adjective, "his *great* love," and the additional statement, "because of his great love for us . . . even when we were dead in transgressions" (Ephesians 2:4–5a). He did not wait until we were deserving, nor even until we wanted to be loved or saved, but when we were worthless, indifferent, ungrateful, there was something in His heart that loved us with a love that was great enough to give heaven's richest gift, and take a race of guilty rebels to His bosom and His throne.

5. His Kindness

One more word remains, "his kindness to us in Christ Jesus" (2:7). This is a very sweet expression. It is founded on the word *kin*, and it suggests the idea that God treats us as His kindred. In order to do this, He makes us His kindred first by giving us His own nature, making us His children; then by taking human nature into His own person through the incarnate Son of God; and then by wedding us to the Lord Jesus Christ and making us the Bride of the Lamb. Every tie of kinship that God can create, He has used to bind our sinful race to His heart. He treats us as His children, as His beloved, as His friends. This covers all the 10,000 bounties and blessings of His Fatherly care, the things that fill the overflowing cup of daily mercies and leads us oft to say:

> When all Thy mercies, O my God,
>   My rising soul surveys—
> Transported with the view, I'm lost
>   In wonder, love, and praise.

6. His Gift

All this inheritance of grace and glory comes to us as a gift; for "it is by grace you have been saved, through faith—and this not from yourselves, it is the gift of God" (2:8). It is thus that we have received it. This is the priceless, immeasurable gift that the infinite mercy, grace, love and kindness of God is offering now to some heart who reads these lines. Beloved, will you accept the gift of God, and give Him in return your gratitude, your love, yourself? All the wealth of the universe could not buy it, but you can have it freely.

A poor woman came up one day to the gardener of Windsor Castle, and tried to buy a cluster of splendid grapes from the royal greenhouse for her dying child. The gardener rudely refused her, and asked her if she did not know better than to think that the queen would sell her grapes. At that moment the gentle queen who had overheard the request and the answer, stepped forward, and, turning to the poor woman, said: "John is right, my good woman; the queen never sells her grapes, but just take your apron and hold it out. And now, John, give her as much as she can take away; for the queen freely gives what she could not sell." Today a kinder heart and a nobler Sovereign is saying to us, "You cannot buy My mercy, but you can have as much as you will take away."

THE PURPOSE OF GOD'S GRACE

Two purposes are here unfolded, an ultimate and an immediate purpose.

1. To Show His Grace

The ultimate purpose is this: "That in the coming ages he might show the incomparable riches of his grace, expressed in his kindness to us in Christ Jesus" (2:7). God's object is some day to make us patterns to the future generations of the universe even as now He has made Jesus Christ the Pattern to us. God is preparing a mighty rehearsal for the inhabitants of this great universe, and some day each of us will have a little part in that mighty chorus and that glorious scene, as innumerable angels and created beings from many a distant star, perhaps, will gather to learn the history of redemption. Then you and I will tell them of the exceeding riches of His grace in the story of our life, and His kindness toward us in Christ Jesus. Let us begin to tell it now, and let us take so much that we will have more to tell.

2. To Do Good Works

The immediate purpose of His grace is, "For we are God's workmanship, created in Christ Jesus to do good works, which God prepared in advance for us to do" (2:10). The object of all this marvelous grace is that we should exhibit here the fruits of it as well as in the ages to come.

The outcome of such a salvation must be intensely practical and lead to works of righteousness and lives of heavenly beauty. But even this is not our working but His grace; for while we are "created in Christ Jesus to do good works," these works are "prepared . . . for us to do." They are not our works, but His in us. They are supplied to us through the Holy Spirit's energy and the indwelling life of Christ. "From the fullness of his grace we have all received one blessing after another" (John 1:16), and we go forth and live out what He lives in us. This is the climax of grace, that it not only bestows upon us God's part, but it enables us in return to perform our part also. Our very faith and love, our sacrifice and service are only richer gifts of His own grace of which we can but say, as David of old in the hour of his highest consecration, "But who am I, and who are my people, that we should be able to give as generously as this? Everything comes from you, and we have given you only what comes from your hand" (1 Chronicles 29:14). "Therefore, since we are receiving a kingdom that cannot be shaken, let us be thankful, and so worship God acceptably with reverence and awe" (Hebrews 12:28).

CHAPTER 6

BROUGHT NEAR

But now in Christ Jesus you who once were far away have been brought near through the blood of Christ. (Ephesians 2:13)

Famous painters often heighten the effect of some beautiful landscape or portrait by putting in the foreground some hideous contrasted object. Over against a face of loveliness you may notice in the corner of the foreground a hideous reptile. The artist's design is to emphasize the picture of loveliness by the repulsive contrast from which the mind instinctively turns to gaze with fonder complacency on the attractive contrast.

So God in the present passage heightens the picture of our glorious place with Christ in the heavenlies by contrasting it with our former state of alienation and separation from His presence and favor. It was with some such thought as this that the ancient Hebrews mingled with their Paschal feast to celebrate their deliverance from Egypt the bitter herbs which reminded them of the years of bondage from which they had escaped. It is well for us to remember the rock from whence we were hewn and the pit from whence we were dug. A wholesome humility will intensify our thankfulness and help us to prize the blessings which have saved us from so dark and sad a fate. There are two sides to the picture: "far away" and "brought near."

"FAR AWAY"

There are four touches of strong color in this dark picture—Christless, godless, homeless and hopeless.

1. Christless

"At that time you were separate from Christ" (2:12). To be without Christ is to be ignorant of God's plan of salvation through the Mediator. You may know Him as the deist knows Him; you may know Him as the Creator, the

Sovereign of the universe, as the ultimate fountain of all power and wisdom; but without Christ this God is nothing to you. The gospel is emphatically a revelation of Christ. God was in Christ, and until you receive Christ as God's Messenger and Channel of all blessing, you have not met the God of redemption—you are without Christ. The very first step in the Christian life is to come to Christ, to receive Christ, to become united to Christ, and to find Christ the Channel, Condition and Source of every blessing and all intercourse with God. The question for every man is the Christ question. It is not: Have you informed your mind? Have you reformed your morals? Are you engaged in benevolent works? But, Have you received Christ? Do you know God in Christ? The saddest fact about the heathen world is that they are without Christ. The turning point of every life is its direct relationship to the Lord Jesus Christ.

Some years ago I knew a man of culture and most attractive qualities, in whose salvation I became intensely interested, and for which I labored many years. This man was an inebriate and a Unitarian. Many and many a time have I labored with him, not to induce him to give up drinking, but to induce him to accept Christ as His Savior, for I knew that the other would soon follow this last act. But he politely, persistently, and at last defiantly refused to have anything to do with Jesus Christ. "I can be a gentleman, and I will be a moral man and master my appetite, but I will have nothing to do with your Christ." From that hour my hopes died, and I saw him steadily go down in spite of every loving restraint that was thrown around him. My prayers seemed to strike an unbreakable wall, a voice whispered, "There is no hope, for 'there is no other name under heaven given to men by which we must be saved' (Acts 4:12)," and at last one day tidings came that he had died suddenly in a saloon.

Beloved, God has decreed that you can have nothing without Christ, and that apart from Him, Satan has the right to control you and will inevitably destroy you.

2. Godless

To be without Christ is to be without God. No man comes to the Father but by Him (John 14:6). "Go to Joseph" (Genesis 41:55), was Pharaoh's decree as the famine stricken land turned to the throne for help. "Go to Joseph. All help must come through him."

"Go to Jesus," is the Father's message to sinful men. There is mercy, there is grace to help in every time of need. There is all-sufficient power, but it is all centered in the Lord Jesus Christ. Apart from Him we cannot understand or know God; we cannot approach God, and we could not stand one flash of the light of His holiness. It would consume us to ashes. But "God was reconciling the world to himself in Christ" (2 Corinthians 5:19), and "now in Christ Jesus you who once were far away have been brought near" (Ephesians 2:13).

Christless one, you have no God. There is no almighty love to shield you. Everything in the universe, everything in God is bound to be against you because you are not only separated from Him, but contrary to Him. You are "without God in the world" (2:12b).

3. Homeless

"Excluded from citizenship in Israel and foreigners to the covenants of the promise" (2:12). You have no right to the promises of this Book. You have no fellowship with a single immunity, right or privilege of the children of God. There are gracious words here, but they are not for you. "In all things God works for the good" (Romans 8:28a), is true, but it is for "those who love him, who have been called according to his purpose" (8:28b). You may kneel down and say, "Our Father in heaven, . . . forgive us our debts" (Matthew 6:9–12); but He is not your Father, and without Christ that forgiveness is not for you.

4. Hopeless

The future is all dark. A thousand dangers beset your path on earth. Danger and death lurk on every side. The gloomy grave lies before you. The dark mystery of eternity frowns with inconceivable dread. The depths of despair yawn before you. There is no hand that can hold you back. You are without Christ and without God in the world. Like the lonely orphan that lays its head down at night on the pavement and cries itself to sleep—homeless, hungry, fatherless and friendless—so you some night shall lay your head down upon the cold pavement of the tomb, and sink into the terrible sleep of a sorrow that will have no glad awakening, and a night that will have no bright dawning, Christless, godless, homeless, hopeless, "far away." How sad! How dark the picture of what we were and how pitiful to think of the multitudes that are there!

"BROUGHT NEAR"

1. By the Blood of Christ

An atonement was necessary. A settlement was demanded. A wrong had to be righted. A debt had to be satisfied. A penalty had to be paid. Somebody must take the place of the guilty; somebody that had a right to represent them; somebody that had worth and weight sufficient to meet their every obligation. This Jesus Christ has done. This is the meaning of His blood. His life was offered as a ransom for the forfeited lives of sinful men, and now, through His atonement, God and the sinner can meet with perfect understanding on both sides, for every claim has been settled, every difficulty adjusted, every obligation met; and the soul that has put its trust in that precious blood has a right to stand, not in a place of toleration but of vindication and say, "Who is he that condemns? Christ Jesus, who died—more than that, who was raised to life—is at the right hand of God and is also interceding for us" (Romans 8:34).

2. By the Person of Christ

"For he himself is our peace, who has . . . destroyed the barrier . . . to create in himself one new man out of the two, thus making peace" (Ephesians 2:14–15). This applies not only to the settlement of the long-standing alienation between Jew and Gentile, but to the settlement of the breach between man and God. Not only has Christ made a settlement for us on God's side, meeting all claims of His law, but He comes to the sinner and meets his need by reconciling him to God and taking away the old natural heart of enmity and alienation, and giving him the Spirit of Christ as a Spirit of trust and love. He lifts us into the new creation. He puts His own nature within us, and He puts us into the very relation with the Father that He Himself sustains. Thus He becomes in our heart the Spirit of peace as well as the Mediator who brings us to God. Like the dying mother who called her husband and boy to meet by her bedside after long years of alienation, and joining their hands in the clasp of her own, bade them to be reconciled for her sake, so Jesus Christ stretching out one hand to God pleads, "Father, forgive them, for they do not know what they are doing" (Luke 23:34), and extending the other to sinful men, He cries, "Be reconciled to God" (2 Corinthians 5:20).

3. By the Gospel

There is the word of peace which forms the basis of reconciliation. So we read, "He came and preached peace to you who were far away and peace to those who were near" (Ephesians 2:17). This is the gospel of reconciliation which God proclaims to every sinful man. It is not enough that there should be peace between God and man definitely arranged, waiting for acceptance, but it is necessary that we should know it and accept it. So we read, "We are therefore Christ's ambassadors" (2 Corinthians 5:20), and "God . . . reconciled us to himself through Christ and gave us the ministry of reconciliation" (5:18); wherefore "we implore you on Christ's behalf: Be reconciled to God" (5:20).

In the last war between America and England, peace was made in Great Britain between the ambassadors of the powers several weeks before it was known on this side of the Atlantic. Meanwhile the conflict went on, and one of the greatest battles of the war was fought and won several days after peace was made. But they did not know it, and therefore it was null and void. Many a soul is separated from God simply through ignorance of the divine message of mercy, and therefore God bids us to announce to every soul separated from His love that peace is made.

You do not have to make your peace with God. Christ has made it. He offers it to you, and He comes to undertake your part of the agreement as well as to guarantee God's promise to be your peace. If you will this moment accept His terms and be reconciled to God, you may enter into the eternal friendship of the Lord of heaven and earth, and rise to all that is meant by being "brought near through the blood of Christ."

4. To the Father

This includes much more than mere reconciliation. It brings us into the most intimate relations with God. The first of these is the relation of sonship; for He says, "You are no longer foreigners and aliens, but fellow citizens with God's people and members of God's household" (Ephesians 2:19). We come into His household. We become members of His family. We are treated as His sons and daughters. We call Him Father. We stand nearer to Him than the highest angels in glory. We are "heirs of God and coheirs with Christ" (Romans 8:17). We are firstborn sons in the firstborn One. We are born into His very nature and received into the bosom of His love. "How great is the love the Father has lavished on us, that we should be called children of God! . . . now we are children of God" (1 John 3:1–2).

5. By the Spirit

Not only are we brought into the relation of children, but we enjoy the fellowship of children, "For through him we both have access to the Father by one Spirit" (Ephesians 2:18).

We draw near to Him in the fellowship of prayer. We commune with Him about what is within our hearts. We roll over on Him all our cares, fears, griefs, and sins. We "approach the throne of grace with confidence" (Hebrews 4:16), and may ask largely not only the greatest but the least thing that our life can need. We are invited to abide continually in His presence, to dwell in His communion, and to know the fellowship more perfect, unclouded, and eternal than it is possible to know with the fondest human friend.

6. To the Family

Not only are we "brought near" to the Father, but we are introduced to the fellowship of the family. We become related to an illustrious circle of the glorious company of apostles and prophets. The glorious company of the apostles, the noble army of the martyrs, the goodly fellowship of the prophets, the saints of all ages—these are our brethren, our associates in the high and glorious employ in the ages and principalities yet to come.

7. To the Kingdom

We are introduced to lofty and noble citizenship, for we are "fellow citizens with God's people" (Ephesians 2:19). We come into another kingdom. We become subjects of the divine commonwealth, and while we still retain our human relationships, and our aspirations of earthly patriotism, yet we have "a better country—a heavenly one" (Hebrews 11:16); and we are waiting for the "kingdom that cannot be shaken" (12:28), and a King who will be worthy of our highest loyalty and our eternal devotion.

We are being trained to be the rulers of that kingdom. Some day that kingdom is to embrace not only all the things of this world, but all the realms of the heavenly world, and its vast colonies will extend from star to star, and we shall be rulers over many cities and principalities.

8. To Be the Habitation of God

But there is still a higher honor and place involved in His bringing us "near." It is brought out in the last verses of the chapter. It is a great thing that we should be brought into His family and that we should find our home in God; but it is a much greater thing that God should find His home in us, and that He, whom the heavens cannot contain, should condescend to seek and find His dwelling in these houses of clay, in these hearts of human sympathy and love.

But so it is, for we read, "In him the whole building is joined together and rises to become a holy temple in the Lord. And in him you too are being built together to become a dwelling [habitation, KJV] in which God lives by his Spirit" (Ephesians 2:21–22). The heart of God looks out in vain to the mighty worlds that roll in space for a response to His affection. Vainly He turns for fellowship to the glowing seraphs that sing and shine around His throne. They can worship and adore; they can fly and obey Him, but they cannot meet the longing of His heart of love.

Have you not seen some human heart, surrounded with splendor, wealth and troops of admiring friends, turn wearily away from all the magnificence of a palace, longing only for the touch of a vanished hand and the sound of a voice that is still? All these things cannot satisfy love nor fill the void of a human soul. So we can think of God alone amid the majesty of the universe, reaching out for love and forming the heart of man to meet His own, and to give him that understanding, fellowship, sympathy and devotion which are worth more than shining constellations or treasures untold.

God wants our love and wants to find in our hearts a home. This is the mysterious promise of Christ: "If anyone loves me . . . My Father will love him, and we will come to him and make our home with him" (John 14:23). So He stands knocking at the door of His lukewarm Church, and crying, "Here I am! I stand at the door and knock. If anyone hears my voice and opens the door, I will go in and eat with him, and he with me" (Revelation 3:20).

Two phrases are used here to denote two aspects of His indwelling. The one is the word "temple" and the other "habitation." The temple is the place of worship. A habitation is a place for residence. God wants to find both in the human heart. He comes as our Lord and King to claim our submission, our homage, the adoration of all our being. But He comes also, as of old when He came to Bethany, to dwell at home with us, to find rest for His heart in our communion, to rest in His love, to joy over us with singing (Zephaniah 3:17b, KJV), to enter into all the minutiae of our lives, to take care of the household, to look after the body and keep it in repair, to meet the little trials of every day and every moment, to rejoice with us when we rejoice, to weep with us when we weep, to be our Brother, our Bridegroom, our Friend, our Mother God, the God of our life and the Guest of our heart. This is what it means to be "brought near" by the blood of Christ.

In conclusion, there are two lessons:

1. Come home, prodigal child, come home to God.

2. Draw near and dwell in the shelter of the Most High (Psalm 91:1), and give Him a dwelling place in every chamber of your heart. Will we not meet His love and say: "He is my God, and I will prepare him an habitation" (Exodus 15:2, KJV)?

CHAPTER 7

THE MYSTERY OF THE NEW LIFE: THE INDWELLING CHRIST

That Christ may dwell in your hearts through faith. . . . that you may be filled to the measure of all the fullness of God. (Ephesians 3:17a, 19b)

In our last chapter we found ourselves carried forward to the great thought of Christ's indwelling in the believer's heart, "a holy temple in the Lord" (2:21b), and "a dwelling in which God lives by his Spirit" (2:22b). These were the two figures under which this heavenly relationship was described. In the present passage Paul takes up this transcendent thought and works it out to its fullest development.

This was the great secret which God had specially revealed to the Apostle Paul, and which was the glory of his ministry. A secret it was which had been "kept hidden for ages and generations, but now," at last, was "disclosed to the saints. . . . Christ in you, the hope of glory" (Colossians 1:26–27).

Look back for a moment and mark the superb sweep of the apostle's thought. At the close of the first chapter the scene was laid in the "heavenly realms" (Ephesians 1:20), and there we beheld the ascended Christ in His risen glory as the great "head over everything for the church" (1:22), and the Type and Pattern of the exalted life to which his own people were to be raised. In the following chapter we see the believer exalted to the place his living Head has already reached, and we are represented as resurrected from the dead and raised up conjointly with Him to sit with Him in the heavenlies.

But now the scene is suddenly changed from heaven to earth, and that glorious throne on which we have been gazing in the heavenlies is transferred to the believer's heart, the dwelling place of Him whom the heavens cannot contain.

First, he takes us up to heaven and makes us sit with Him on the throne;

then He takes heaven down to us and brings God down to sit upon the throne of the consecrated heart to make that heart a heaven within.

Let us dwell for a little upon the inspired unfolding of this great theme, and may a living experience lend a new touch of reality to the vision of truth and faith.

THE INDWELLING CHRIST

There is nothing in human experience to interpret this extraordinary relationship. It transcends all other bonds, and is the very mystery of life and love.

Human Figures

There is a sense in which the father lives in his child, and the mother and her babe are, in a measure, one. There is a sense in which the memory and the name of a Washington or a Garibaldi are enshrined in the nation's heart. But these are all figurative. This is a literal and real fact that God does dwell in the heart of the believer. It does not mean that the doctrine of Christ, the influence of Christ, the example of Christ, the memory of Christ, but the very person of Christ is united to the person of the believer so that there are two persons in living touch and conscious fellowship.

The strange phenomenon of hypnotism by which one mind can control another and seem to possess it; the still stranger fact of demon possession by which one wicked spirit becomes personal and controls the mind of a human being—these are mere vivid and literal approximations to the truth of the union of God with the human soul. Certainly if an evil spirit can possess a human being, there is no reason why a Holy Spirit cannot control the will and the affections.

That Christ does really do so is the most precious promise of the New Testament:

> If anyone loves me, he will obey my teaching. (John 14:23a)

> I too will love him and show myself to him. (14:21c)

> He who loves me will be loved by my Father. (14:21b)

> We will come to him and make our home with him. (14:23b)

> I will put my dwelling place among you, and . . . walk among you, and be your God, and you will be my people. (Leviticus 26:11–12)

And I will put my Spirit in you and move you to follow my
decrees and be careful to keep my laws. (Ezekiel 36:27)

These are some of the promises that very distinctly express this sublime
fact of the indwelling Christ.

I remember an incident in my early ministry when my own heart was very
full of this new-found joy of the Lord's indwelling. God had given me the
precious soul of a young businessman. For some time after his conversion he
used to call on me every day at noon, taking half of his lunch hour for con-
ference and prayer with his pastor, and saying, as he went away, "I feel
stronger now for another day of Christian life."

One day I said to him, "Will, suppose that I should be able to enter into
your mind and heart, and go home with you to your office and your house
and live in you for the rest of your life, what would you think of that?"

"Why," said he, "that would be splendid, for I would think just as you
think, feel as you feel, do as you do, and it would be so easy to live a Christian life. But, of course, this is impossible."

I had got the thought I wanted into his mind, and so I turned the figure
around and said, "Will, what is it that makes me a help to you? It is not my
natural mind or even my personal love to you, but it is the fact that there is
Somebody in me more than myself who enables me to bless and help you.
Now, Will, the same Christ that lives in me and makes me what I am, is
waiting and willing to enter into your mind and heart to relive His own life
in you. I cannot enter into your brain and go home with you in your soul,
but my Christ can."

He saw it in a moment, and we knelt together for a little season of tender,
consecrated prayer; and when he arose, a new light was in his eye, a new
glory was upon his brow, and the tears that were moistening his eyes were
the softening tears of love. He pressed my hand, left me, saying quietly,
"God bless you. I shan't need you so much now."

Beloved, have you received Him? Do you know the greatest secret, "Christ
in you, the hope of glory" (Colossians 1:27)?

THE AGENCY OF THE HOLY SPIRIT IN THIS UNION

That "he may strengthen you . . . through his Spirit in your inner being,
so that Christ may dwell in your hearts through faith" (Ephesians 3:16–
17a). It is the special mission of the Holy Spirit to bring about this union
with Christ. The Spirit's work does not terminate directly upon Himself,
but always leads up to the personality of Jesus. Therefore, Christ in His parting discourses in the 14th chapter of John explained to His disciples that it
was necessary for Him to go away, that the Counselor might come and bring
Him back to them in another form as a spiritual Presence. Then He added,

"On that day you will realize that I am in my Father, and you are in me, and I am in you" (John 14:20).

Now, the Spirit has come to bring about the relationship. Part of His work is to make Jesus real to us, to give us a conception of Him, and the witness of His personal union with us. The Holy Spirit is the Spirit that once dwelt in Christ, and He brings to us a spiritual Christ with a new touch and a higher form of manifestation than when He walked the earth of old and touched the bodies of men with His living hands.

Part of His ministry is to prepare us on our side to receive the indwelling Christ. Our coarse and fleshly natures cannot understand, much less enter into this high mystery of the heavenly life. Therefore we are told here that we need to be "strengthen[ed] . . . through his Spirit in [our] inner being" (Ephesians 3:16). First, our "inner being" must be quickened. This is not the intellect of the scholar, nor even the sensibilities of the emotional nature, but it is a new spiritual self, created in Christ Jesus, with senses and organs that know God directly, and that can enter into the realities of the heavenly world.

But even this new life must be strengthened by the Spirit in order to be able to stand the power of this divine addition to its experience. Many people are crying for the baptism of the Holy Spirit, who would not be able to stand it if they received it. It would be like putting a great charge of dynamite or powder into a sheet-iron pipe. It would burst into a thousand fragments. When the naval department attempts to fire a large shell a number of miles, it takes a ponderous mass of steel, and for months it forges and twists it until a mighty mass of metal comes forth, many tons in weight. Then, through this mass of tested steel a shell of half a ton in weight is hurled many a mile, and falls in destroying havoc upon the foe.

So God prepares us to receive His power. He deepens us to hold His fullness. Slowly often the Holy Spirit leads us through the depths of testing experiences, awakening spiritual desire, slaying the strength of our own self-conscious life, separating us from our self-confidence and all earthly help, burning out the emotional and ephemeral life of the fleshly mind, and settling us down into God where we can let all go but Him, and step out in naked faith to trust and obey Him.

So, perhaps, He is testing and preparing some of us today. Let us trust Him in the dark. Let us lie yielded in His hands. Let our one cry be, "Take me, break me, make me what Thou wilt; empty me and fill me, crucify and quicken, prepare me for Thy perfect will, and fit me to receive the indwelling Christ, and to be filled with all the fullness of God."

THE INSTRUMENTALITY OF FAITH IN THIS RELATIONSHIP

"That Christ may dwell in your hearts through faith" (3:17a). This does not mean that the relationship of Christ's indwelling is mere make-believe, as some would teach us; that He only dwells there by faith, but that He is not there in reality. There is nothing so real as the things we believe; for "faith is being sure of what we hope for and certain of what we do not see" (Hebrews 11:1). It simply means that faith is the organ by which we receive Him, the new sense of the soul which reaches out to apprehend and appropriate Him and then to communicate with Him. Christ does not come to us through our feelings, but through our convictions. His union with us is not a sensation, but a fact.

I once asked a young lady after I had married her to her husband, "Do you feel married?" She looked at me in surprise, and said, "Why, no; I don't feel anything; I am married." The fact existed, and she had never thought of the feeling. So we take Christ by an act of faith, believing He does come to take up His abode within us, looking to Him in all our need, recognizing Him as an actual Presence, bringing to Him all our difficulties and trials, and living in actual habitual dependence upon Him as our All in all.

Thus the act becomes a habit as natural as breathing, as spontaneous as the circulation of the blood. And then, in due time, the habit develops the senses of the new life. A whole group of spiritual organs and senses grows up as a channel of communion between us and Him. They are like the rootlets of a little plant after it has become imbedded in the soil. If you look at them through the microscope, you will find a thousand spongy pores open to receive the moisture and nourishment of the soil, and drinking in at every pore the sustenance which nature so richly supplies. So the Spirit grows into an organic life, and every fiber of our being becomes a channel of communion with Him. We know Him by an inner sense that we could not explain. Just as the sailor is conscious that the land is near, just as the dog scents his master's presence, and just as the bird of passage knows where southern breezes blow, so we become intensely sensitive to the presence and voice of Christ. Like faithful sheep, we "know his voice" and "follow him" (John 10:4). We are "of quick understanding in the fear of the LORD" (Isaiah 11:3a, KJV). Our ear is open to hear His faintest whisper. We know the touch of His presence, and the breathings of His quickening love and faith have become a heavenly organism of a thousand sensibilities through which we "live and move and have our being" (Acts 17:28) in Him.

THE ELEMENT OF LOVE INTO WHICH FAITH AT LENGTH DEVELOPS AND MATURES

"That you, being rooted and established in love, may have power, together with all the saints, to grasp how wide and long and high and deep is the love of Christ, and to know this love that surpasses knowledge" (Ephesians 3:17–19). After faith has reached a certain point, it changes its character and becomes love. This is not a new fact. The natural world is full of it. Heat that water in a steam boiler up to a certain temperature, and you lose your water, for it has all become steam and has changed into a new and mighty force that propels your machinery and revolutionizes your industrial life. That little seed that you plant in the ground after a while becomes a stem, and the stem becomes a flower, and the flower breathes out its life in fragrance. The little dry seed has become a vial of richest perfume.

So faith when it has reached its fruition grows into a heavenly life of love. For faith perfected is just the confidence of love, and the best trust comes from a loving heart. When I get completely united to Christ, I do not have to reason out my faith. I do not have to ask, Does He love me? Do I love Him? It is so deep and spontaneous that I never think of asking. It is like the action of my joints. When they are healthy, I have no feeling in them, and I do not realize that I have any joints. To feel your joints is rheumatism. To be unconscious of physical conditions is health.

So faith reaches that stage at last where the intellectual element is lost in love, and the heart so fitly falls into Christ that its attitude is that of the disciple who leaned on Jesus' breast and who artlessly told us, without thinking there was any self-consciousness in the statement, that he was the disciple whom Jesus loved. Love feeds upon the love of Christ. At first we reach our apprehension of this love by some sort of intellectual process. We try to take its measure, its breadth, its depth, its height, but soon we get lost in the fullness that no fathoming line nor geometric measure can express, and we just sink back into the immensity of this boundless and fathomless flood and say, "It surpasses knowledge."

When a soul has reached this blessed experience, it dwells in a summer land of peculiar sweetness and rich maturity. There is a point in our Christian life where the tone of our character is legal, moral and marked by conviction of sin and the struggle of right against wrong. Farther on comes the element of surrender, of choice, of submission of the will, of singleness of purpose with which we cleave to God. Then comes the intellectual side of faith that believes on the testimony of the Word, that holds its ground against the assaults of temptation. All this has in it the element of struggle and effort. But as we go farther on, we enter into the spirit of rest, of trust, of gladness and of confidence. The winter gives place to spring; and still farther on we come to the summer land of love, where the soul is lost in God, where even experiences are forgotten in the consciousness of Himself, and "rooted and established in love," we begin to fully "know this love that surpasses knowledge" (3:17, 19).

NEXT COMES THE FULLNESS OF GOD

It is one thing to have Christ; it is another thing to be filled with Christ. It is one thing to receive the Holy Spirit; it is another thing to be filled with the Spirit. It is one thing to come to Christ, and to have Christ come to us; but it is another and a greater thing to have Christ bring us to God. When the disciples were filled with the Spirit, then something came to pass. There was power, and there was an overflow from their hearts and lives till the world wondered and believed. Oh, for Spirit-filled men and women! Oh, for a Spirit-filled life!

FINALLY, THE OUTCOME OF ALL THIS IS POWER

"Now to him who is able to do immeasurably more than all we ask or imagine" (3:20a). This is no mere self-centered, self-complacent experience of blessing. It is something that leads to practical results and accomplishes definite things. There is power in it. It takes hold of God until something is done. If God is reigning in us, He will rule over everything around us. If we have the Holy Spirit within us, we will see the providence of God in His marvels of answered prayer and accomplished results. The limits are all on our side. We must ask. But He "is able to do immeasurably more than all we ask." We must think and intelligently ask. But He "is able to do immeasurably more than all we . . . imagine."

There is one limitation: "according to his power that is at work within us" (3:20b). He will do as much *for* us as we let Him do *in* us. "On the day I cleanse you from all your sins, I will resettle your towns . . . This land that was laid waste" will be "like the garden of Eden" (Ezekiel 36:33, 35). This was His ancient promise, and it means that as fully as we receive Him as our Guest and Friend, so mightily will we know Him in the wonder-working providences of life, and the power that can meet every emergency, overcome every adversary, every circumstance, and "meet all your needs according to his glorious riches in Christ Jesus" (Philippians 4:19).

CHAPTER 8

THE CHURCH IN THE HEAVENLIES

Built on the foundation of the apostles and prophets, with Christ Jesus himself as the chief cornerstone. In him the whole building is joined together and rises to become a holy temple in the Lord. (Ephesians 2:20–21)

There is one body and one Spirit—just as you were called to one hope when you were called. . . . From him the whole body, joined and held together by every supporting ligament, grows and builds itself up in love, as each part does its work. (4:4, 16)

For the husband is the head of the wife as Christ is the head of the church. . . . Christ loved the church and gave himself up for her to make her holy, cleansing her by the washing with water through the word, and to present her to himself as a radiant church, without stain or wrinkle or any other blemish, but holy and blameless . . . This is a profound mystery—but I am talking about Christ and the church. (5:23, 25–27, 32)

We have been looking at the believer in the heavenlies. Now we are to see the Church in the heavenlies. We have seen the blessings of the Spirit in the individual saint. Now we are to behold them consummated in the collective body of the saints, the glorious Church of the Lord Jesus Christ.

The parable of the treasure hid in the field, representing the people of God in their separate capacities, reaches its climax in the parable of the pearl of great price, where we behold them in their united capacity. That which is true of the disciples of Christ one by one is more completely and gloriously true of the whole company of disciples when they will be gathered into one in their living Head and glorious Lord.

This vision of the Church was given to Paul as one of the peculiar revelations of his ministry along with the kindred mystery of the indwelling of Christ in the individual heart. "The mystery made known to me by revelation," we read in chapter 3:3, "which was not made known to men in other generations . . . that through the gospel the Gentiles are heirs together with Israel, members together of one body, and sharers together in the promise of Christ Jesus" (3:5–6).

Already in the theme of the preceding chapter he had given us a hint of this great truth when, after speaking of the indwelling of Christ in the believer's heart and the marvelous revelation that it was fitted to bring of the unfathomable love of Christ, he added that we "may have power, together with all the saints, to grasp" (3:18) the knowledge of the surpassing love of Christ.

Not singly can we grasp this mighty vision. It is only when we enter into the perfect fellowship of the body of Christ that we can know the fullness of our great salvation. If it is true in the natural world,

> God never made an independent man;
>   'Twould mar the general concord of His plan,

much more is it true in the spiritual world, where the whole progression of redemption is toward one grand consummation, the reconciling and uniting of all in one, and the crystallizing of God's wisdom, power and love in the story of creation and redemption into a single ideal, the paragon of the universe, the glory of the ages to come, the new Jerusalem, the Bride of the Lamb, the Church of Jesus Christ.

In this great epistle the Church is presented under three striking figures: the Building, the Body and the Bride.

THE BUILDING

Architecture, one of the most attractive arts and sciences, has conceived and executed many wonderful buildings. Its crowning triumph is to embody in the lifeless stone a living idea. This has been successfully accomplished in such creations as the triumphs of Gothic art, of Moorish architecture, the Greek column, the Roman arch, the Byzantine porch, the Gothic spire, the Italian dome or the Moorish Alhambra. Each conveys some distinct and impressive conception of grace or majesty or awe. Gazing at the splendid dome of the Capitol at Washington, the forest of pinnacles that rise from the towers of Milan Cathedral or the strange ethereal charm of that "Dream in Marble," the Taj Mahal, at Agra, one is conscious that mind has triumphed over matter, and that the stone is speaking unutterable thoughts and feelings to the cultivated mind.

The supreme charm of the architect's pile is unity. His conception is to produce a single building and a unique effect.

God is building a spiritual house on a similar principle, but far transcending man's highest thought. He is rearing an invisible temple for the exhibition of His greatest thought and the manifestation of His own infinite presence and glory. The only two structures ever built on earth by divine architecture are entirely controlled by this idea. They were expressive of the highest truths.

Look at the little tabernacle in the wilderness, the first church God ever built. Everything about it was eloquent of redemption and significant of Christ. You looked at the exterior, so plain and unattractive, and then at the interior, so glorious and resplendent, and you saw at once an image of the Church of Christ and her glorious Head and Lord, despised and rejected of men, yet "all glorious . . . within her chamber" (Psalm 45:13a).

You entered the court, and the sacrificial altar and cleansing laver at once proclaimed the truths of salvation and sanctification. You entered the holy place, and the golden lamps revealed not their own beauty, but the table of shewbread and the rich provision of that sacred chamber for the privileged worshipers. You became immediately conscious that the air was laden with richest perfume; and you found that the frankincense from the golden altar, breathing throughout the chamber, was speaking to you through your finest senses of the very presence of God—the breath of heaven and the wafted odors from the fields of the Paradise of God.

Still further you venture through the torn veil, and lo! the winged cherubim, the blood-sprinkled mercy seat, the ark of the covenant, and the awful Shekinah were speaking to you of the innermost presence of God Himself, and the highest truths of divine union and heavenly glory. The whole building was just an object lesson of redemption and an exhibition of Jesus Christ.

The same thing was true of the Temple which afterwards rose on Mount Moriah on a grander scale, but with equal spiritual significance. So God intended His Church to be an exhibition of His glorious gospel, His heavenly character and the riches of His grace. Its business here is to exhibit Christ, to manifest God and to afford a channel for His revelation and indwelling among men. Its message to the world is, "The church of the living God [is] the pillar and foundation of the truth" (1 Timothy 3:15). "The dwelling of God is with men, and he will live with them" (Revelation 21:3).

Whenever the Church becomes self-conscious and self-centered, she fails to accomplish her real divine calling. Her highest glory is to be seen only in the revealing of her Lord.

Deep and true is the lesson taught by the ancient legend of the three architects who brought to the Oriental king their models for a temple of the sun. The first was of stone, finely chiseled and richly polished; and as the king beheld it, he could only admire and praise the splendid work. The second was of gold, and well did the architect descant on the burnished walls as they reflected in every angle and facet the image of the sun itself. But the third presented a temple of glass so transparent that at first it was invisible, and it did not take long to show, as the sunlight poured unhindered through the transparent walls, that this was the true temple of the sun, reflecting not its own glory, but revealing and receiving in every part the glorious object to whose honor it was dedicated.

This is the supreme object of the Church of Jesus Christ, and only in so far as we are revealing and reflecting Him who is our Head are we accomplishing the object for which the Church was founded.

Of this glorious building Christ is the cornerstone. He is at once the foundation and the center. From that stone every vertical line is drawn. From that stone every horizontal line is projected. It unites the two walls, decides the true angle, and in relation to it every particle of the wall is located and erected.

As there is but one cornerstone, there is but one building. Alas, if we look at the Church today, we will behold, not so much a building as a block of buildings, scores of fragmentary structures, the foundations of human names and humanly constructed constitutions. Need we wonder that the walls are often off the plumb line and the square, that through the unguarded gates the moneychangers have right of way, and that from within there often comes, not the Shekinah glory of the Master's presence, but the sad cry, "Look, your house is left to you desolate" (Matthew 23:38)?

The unity of the Church is the point most strongly emphasized by the apostle in this passage. "There is one body and one Spirit" (Ephesians 4:4). There are not two ages of the Church, the apostolic and the modern, but we are the same Church which Christ founded, and in which the apostles laid the first tier of masonry. We have the same promises, the same enduement of power, and should have the same manifestations of the presence and power of God.

Not only are we one chronologically, but we are one in diversity. Notwithstanding all the peculiarities of the individual character, the heart, the spirit, the life of the Church is ever one. In the tabernacle there were hundreds of parts, but there was one building. There was no need that one should displace another. Each had its place. They were "joined and held together" (4:16), and placed in position they formed a unique and complete whole. So should the Church of Jesus Christ be "joined and held together," and stand in the beauty of a unity the more perfect because of its diversity. Each of us is but a single part in the whole structure. If we shrink from our neighboring board, or if we swell beyond our place so as to displace another, it is because we are not properly seasoned and we are not in the divine order and plan.

It is a great thing for every child of God to learn and fully understand what it means to be one of many; not *the one*, but only one. When we come to understand that God has millions of lives just as necessary and just as precious as ours, then we will learn to give place to our brethren and keep rank in the host of God.

God's two ancient buildings, the tabernacle and the temple, were intended to set forth the two stages of the Church's history, the earthly and the heavenly. That moving tabernacle represented the earthly Church, with no continuing city and no inheritance below the skies. The glorious structure on Mount Moriah's height represented the heavenly Church, when all the materials will have been gathered home and the universe will come to gaze upon the jeweled walls of the new Jerusalem and behold the Bride, the Lamb's wife.

THE BODY

The difference between a building and a body is immense. The building is mechanical, the body is organic. The first is put together by forces outside itself; the second grows up a force within itself. The building is a lifeless mass; the body is a living organism. And so the apostle's thought advances to higher ground, for the Church of Jesus Christ is not merely constructed, it is created; it is born; it is formed out of the very life of Christ, its living Head, and it grows in Him up to "the whole measure of the fullness of Christ" (4:13). The science of anatomy is therefore much higher in the sphere of its investigations than that of architecture, and the study of the human body is fitted to afford a thousand illustrations of the beauty and significance of this striking figure. On these we cannot dwell in detail in this brief space. It is enough that we individually realize the heart of the conception, that in the body of Christ our life comes directly from Him, and our relationship with each other is dependent upon our relationship with the Head. Three points will suffice to bring out these truths.

1. We derive our life from the Head.

As Eve was made out of Adam's substance, so the Church was born out of Christ, and every individual is part of the life of his Lord. And as we sprang from Him, so we must live by Him in intimate organic communion. His life is imparted to our threefold being—spirit, soul and body—and "in him we live and move and have our being" (Acts 17:28). No one really belongs to the Church of Christ who is not personally united to Christ in regeneration and communion.

2. He is the Head of authority and control as well as of life.

The head directs the members of the body, and so the Church of Jesus

Christ should be subject in everything to the will of her Lord. Instinctively every member should move obediently to the touch of the Head, and by a thousand connecting cords of holy intuition we may learn to catch the faintest intimation of His will, and become responsive to His every thought and inspiration.

3. Our relationships to each other are in and through the Head, and only as we meet in Him can we be rightly adjusted to one another.

The members of the body are related to each other only through the Head. Your fingers work together simply because they are both in direct connection with the brain. Let one be separated from its source of power, and it will be at once separated from its associate member. A simple illustration will show how all true unity in the human body depends upon the brain.

Sitting at an organ, a singer is using four members of her body in unison. First, her feet are pressing the pedals and supplying air to the pump organ. Secondly, her fingers are sweeping the keyboard and striking the several keys. Thirdly, her eyes are watching the page and studying the appropriate keys to strike. Fourthly, her voice is keeping tune and time with the notes on the page and the keys of the organ. There are four members acting in concert. How are they to keep up the concert? Are the eyes to watch the fingers? Then how are they to watch the page? Is the voice to be thinking about the organ keys? No. Each member is acting independently under direct orders from the brain, and through the one head they all produce the one tune, the one song, the one harmonious result.

There is the secret of Christian harmony. If you and I come together with our separate minds and feelings, we will never harmonize. But if we suspend our personal life and take Christ's instead, we will always agree. "He himself is our peace" (Ephesians 2:14), and in Him we can have harmony, unity and power. We should never touch people apart from Jesus. A heavenly halo of divine presence should ever encompass us. And as we meet each other in this holy encompassment of divine life and love, we will be one in Him, and we will fulfill the glorious ideal so finely described in this figure: "In love may grow into him in all things who is the head, Christ; out of whom all the body fitly framing itself together and connecting itself through means of every joint of supply, according to an inward working in measure of each single part, is securing the growth of the body unto an upbuilding of itself in love" (4:15–16, Rotherham).

THE BRIDE

This is a still higher conception of the Church. The building is an architectural figure. The body is a physiological figure. The Bridegroom and the Bride take us into the deeper life of love. This is the figure which runs like a golden thread of divine romance through the whole story of revelation and redemption. It is as old as Eden. It reaches its consummation in the Marriage of the Lamb. How beautiful the picture that comes back to us from Paradise! First, the bride was formed out of the body of Adam, and then she was given to Adam as his bride. So, recurring in the last figure, the Church is born out of Christ and then wedded to Him.

In the 16th chapter of Ezekiel there is a beautiful parable of this mystery of love. The prophet describes the foundling child lying in her blood, repulsive and utterly wretched; but as the Lord passed by, He saw her in her blood. It was the time of love, and so He spread His skirt over her and gently took her, washed her, robed her, educated her, trained her, crowned her and made her all His own. So He has loved us, saved us, quickened us together with Him, and now He takes us into this intimate and unspeakable relationship which all earthly figures fail fully to express—the marriage of the Lamb.

First of all, let us ask the Holy Spirit to purify our minds from every earthly conception, and every shade of mere human passion or affection. A breath may cloud the face of a mirror, and so it is possible to obscure this exquisite figure of a real divine relationship by investing it with something of the coarseness of earthly passion. It is as holy as the Shekinah light. Flesh and blood cannot inherit this kingdom of heaven. It is only the death-born life that can enter here. There is a union between Christ and His beloved which meets our entire being, and which satisfies our whole nature, which thrills with holy joy the heart of love, and quickens the mortal frame into heavenly life. But it is possible for us to enter into this divine relationship and fellowship only as we die to the earthly, the sensuous, and the human, and receive the cleansing, sanctifying and quickening power of the Holy Spirit.

Therefore it will be noticed that as we rise to this third figure, the purifying work of Christ is peculiarly emphasized. It is possible to enter into it only as we meet Him in the heart-searching processes of His grace, and remember that He gave Himself for the Church "to make her holy, cleansing her by the washing with water through the word" (Ephesians 5:26). And still more intensely does the description press to the very depths of purity "to present her to himself as a radiant church, without stain or wrinkle or any other blemish" (5:27), but she should be "holy and blameless."

How the very soul quivers under the white light of this searching sentence! Not a spot must remain. Your garment may be white and clean except a single speck, but that is fatal. Will we bring to Him today the single stains, the flaws in the fabric, the specks on the cambric?

No, there must not be a wrinkle. A wrinkle may be the result not of defilement, but of neglect, carelessness, imperfect work, or advancing age and infirmity. A wrinkle in the linen results from careless ironing. A wrinkle in the countenance comes by feebleness. We must not only be pure, but we must be vigorous. We must be in full spiritual strength, and we must have no marks of negligence, but be up to the standard of His holy will.

Still finer is the last phrase, "any other blemish." There may be clouds upon the finished surface, dinginess, shades, faint suggestions of a fault or a flaw. His love demands that these must go, and so He touches and retouches, tests and touches again, and in His faithfulness works out the inward processes of His inexorable grace until someday with a pride and joy far greater than our own He shall present us to Himself, a glorious Bride, "without stain or wrinkle or any other blemish" (5:27), while the wondering universe shall cry: Come and let us see the "bride, the wife of the Lamb" (Revelation 21:9).

It is said that once a young man of noble birth married a country girl to whom he had been engaged since childhood, but forgetting that in the interval he had grown beyond her, through the influence of higher education and worldwide travel, he never realized till their lives were linked indissolubly together that it was impossible for her to understand him or enter into the higher meaning of his life. He loved her dearly, treated her chivalrously, but pined and died of a broken heart because there could never be companionship.

Beloved, Christ has betrothed you to Him. You are to spend eternity in His palaces and on His throne. You are to be the companion and partner of His mightiest enterprises in the ages to come. Perhaps with Him you are to colonize a constellation of space and govern the boundless universe of God. Do you know that He is educating you now to be a fit companion for such a kingdom? Will you let Him love you all He wants to, and fit you for such a destiny as will some day fill you with everlasting wonder and adoring love? Or will you—will you disappoint Him?

CHAPTER 9

THE SPIRITUAL AND PRACTICAL

As a prisoner for the Lord, then, I urge you to live a life worthy of the calling you have received. (Ephesians 4:1)

There is an epigrammatic sentence whose authorship we have not been able to trace, but which expresses a whole world of profound truth. It is this: "The highest life consists not in doing magnificent things, but rather in doing common things in a magnificent way." That expresses in a single sentence the principle underlying the fourth and fifth chapters of Ephesians.

Paul has been looking at the very sublimities of Christian truth and life. He has shown us Christ seated on the heavenly throne far above all principalities and powers. He has raised us up and seated us by His side, and then He has brought Him down to enter the sanctuary of the individual heart and bring a heaven to dwell within. Next he has enlarged this conception of God dwelling with man until, from the individual heart, it has grown to include the whole collective body of believers and the glorious Church and Bride of Jesus Christ.

But now we behold another transition and transformation: the commonplace and everyday world of secular affairs—domestic and social life and ordinary things—becomes the theater where these lofty principles and spiritual forces are brought into practical operation. This heavenly life is not a theory for the speculator and the dreamer. It is designed for the severest tests and the most commonplace needs of human experience; and while it is at home amid the sanctities of the closet and the sublimities of the heavenly throne, it is not less at home in the marketplace of toil, the drudgery of the kitchen, the avenues of commerce, the din of battle and the hurry and worry of everyday life. Indeed, there is no grander triumph for the gospel of Christ than this very fact that it does not require us to become hermits and recluses and hide our religion in a cloister or a closet, but it is God's all-sufficient provision for life's practical needs, and its congenial home is among common people and the ordinary affairs of our human life. It comes to bring heaven down to the home circle and counting-room, and to bring earth up to the plane of heaven.

Two great thoughts are unfolded in these practical paragraphs; namely, the earthly side of heavenly things, and the heavenly side of earthly things. Let us look at them in detail.

THE EARTHLY SIDE OF HEAVENLY THINGS

One might almost think it too sudden a transition to come from the lofty outlook of his glowing vision down to the question of common morality and honesty, and that it is almost an insult to Christians who have been living in the higher life in the heavenlies to talk to them about stealing, lying and personal purity. But such is not the mind of the Spirit of God. He knows that extremes must quickly meet, and that in the very highest realms of spiritual truth and life lie the most subtle temptations and the most serious perils. Therefore the gospel of Jesus Christ has a distinctly moral side to it, and emphasizes with the strongest definiteness the necessity of guarding our walk and conversations as carefully as we guard our inward experience.

1. Our Walk

Our walk is to be carefully guarded. "Live a life worthy of the calling you have received" (4:1). This includes our whole deportment and conduct.

2. Our Talk

Our talk is to be guarded as carefully as our walk. Physical disease indicates itself by a foul tongue, and there is no quicker test of spiritual healthfulness than the conversation of a disciple. We are to be strictly truthful. "Therefore each of you must put off falsehood and speak truthfully to his neighbor" (4:25). We are to renounce evil speaking, slander, calumny and harsh criticism. We are to "not let any unwholesome talk come out" of our mouths, "but only what is helpful for building others up according to their needs, that it may benefit those who listen" (4:29). We are to be free from filthiness, foolish talking and jesting, and to substitute for them the language of thanksgiving and praise (see 5:4). All idle words, all irreverent speech, all obscene conversation, all talk flavored with frivolousness or gossip passes under the severe censorship of the Holy Spirit, and distinguishes the character of the Christian or the counterfeit.

3. Our Temper

Our temper must be guarded. Sinful anger is to be put away. Bitterness, wrath, anger and all malice are to be eschewed, and we are to be "kind and compassionate to one another," and forgiving (4:26, 31, 32).

Disposition has a supremely important place in the truly spiritual life. We cannot dwell in the heavenlies with Christ and be harsh, snappish, quarrelsome, sensitive, vindictive, sarcastic, cutting and unforgiving. The fruit of the Spirit must ever be "love, joy, peace, patience, kindness, goodness, faithfulness, gentleness and self-control" (Galatians 5:22–23).

4. Our Integrity

Honesty and industry will ever characterize the truly spiritual man. "He who has been stealing must steal no longer, but must work, doing something useful with his own hands, that he may have something to share with those in need" (Ephesians 4:28). A holy heart will always make a man honest and take the indolence out of him. It is impossible to live a sanctified life in idleness. A man who is full of the Holy Spirit will always be about his Father's business; and even if he is independent of the necessity of toil for his own support, will regard life as a sacred trust, and will provide not only for his own needs but for the needs of others. There is no greater auxiliary to a happy, useful and holy life than constant congenial activity in the service of God and man.

5. Our Purity

Personal purity is indispensable in the heavenly life, and all approaches to immorality, whether in manner, speech, thought or action, are absolutely inconsistent with the very name of holiness. The apostle regards such things as not fit to be named among them, and yet he is very definite and specific in his delineation of Christian character and its counterfeits. He calls things by their right names, and he puts the awful ban of the Holy Spirit upon filthiness of language, fornication, which covers all acts of impurity; uncleanness, which includes all forms of approach to it in spirit, thought, reading, imagination, language, dress or manner. He tells them in inexorable speech that "no immoral, impure . . . person . . . has any inheritance in the kingdom of Christ and of God . . . for because of such things God's wrath comes on those who are disobedient" (5:5–6).

6. Unworldliness

He includes covetousness in the same class with uncleanness. The greed of money is as gross as the lusts of sensuality. Both belong to the same swine herd, and both are excluded from "any inheritance in the kingdom of Christ and of God" (5:5).

7. Gravity

Foolishness, frivolousness and folly are condemned, and the necessity of sense and discretion is impressed upon the disciples of Christ. "Be very careful, then," he says, "how you live—not as unwise but as wise" (5:15). He had already condemned foolish talking and jesting. There are people who at first sight seem to be almost immoral to judge from their loud dress and loose manners, and yet, on closer investigation, we often find that these young people are simply silly. They are playing with temptation, but they have not yet been corrupted. They are sailing on the edge of the pit, and they wear the livery of hell. Little wonder if they sail too close to the fiery gulf to get back safely.

Christ forbids such manners and dispositions on the part of His children. Discretion, prudence and practical sense are jewels of the highest spiritual value, especially in the young. Let us remember that our bearing, our expression, our dress, our mien, must distinguish us from the world, and mark us as the meek and lowly followers of the Lamb.

8. Our Time

The improvement of time is included among the graces of the spiritual life. "Making the most of every opportunity, because the days are evil" (5:16). This includes more than the mere employment of time. Literally it should be translated, "Buying up the opportunity." It means alertness and quickness in making the most of time and opportunity, and meeting the providence of God and the emergencies of life with that fitness of wisdom and that timeliness of action which characterized our Master, and which will keep us always in the time and order of God's highest will. No sanctified Christian can play with time or throw away the golden moments which are worth more than treasure. Our familiar phrase, "pastime," is an outrage on the sacredness of human life and its vast responsibilities. The consecrated life will always recognize our moments as sacred trusts to be given back to God with holy improvement and compound interest.

9. Sobriety

Temperance and sobriety are included in the practical exercises and habits of a sanctified life. "Do not get drunk on wine, which leads to debauchery. Instead, be filled with the Spirit" (5:18). The indwelling of the Holy Spirit will give the child of God a holy carefulness in restricting the indulgence of our animal nature which must be held under holy restraint, if we would be vessels for the occupation and use of the sensitive Spirit of the Holy One.

10. Our Homes

The highest Christian life will manifest its practical influence immediately in the home and in the relationship of husbands and wives. It will make the husband loving and gentle and the wife yielded, affectionate and faithful.

Domestic fidelity will not be a matter of romantic attachment, but of holy watchfulness, self-restraint, constant regard to the will of God and the highest good of each other. Domestic brawls, jealousies and strife have no place in a Christian family circle, and there is no place where our example and testimony speak more for God than in the practical and sacred sphere of the Christian family (5:22–33).

11. Our Children

The relations of parents and children will be equally affected by the indwelling of the Holy Spirit and the power of a sanctified life. No child can consistently claim to be filled with the Spirit and be disrespectful, willful and disobedient. True, there is a place where the parent's authority ceases over the conscience of a Christian child; but even when we must assert our independence and obey God rather than man in things that relate to God, there will be the utmost respect and gentleness of spirit and manner; and in matters where we owe earthly duties to our parents, we will be more careful because we have to differ in heavenly things. And the Christian parent who would walk worthy of his high vocation must be free from passion, harshness or even indulgence, and carefully stand as representing the high authority of God Himself in the Christian home (6:1–4).

12. Our Employees

Masters and servants complete the list of earthly relationships affected by our heavenly calling. These relationships have changed since the days of Paul when the servant was a slave, but the obligations which they entail remain the same. Many of us are servants. We occupy positions of trust and responsibility. We are under the authority of some superintendent. God has created ranks and orders of responsibility all through His universe, and he that would resist them resists God. A wise and rightly constituted Christian will always recognize superior authority, yielding to it in fidelity and obedience. An unfaithful servant will become an unholy Christian. He that is unjust in that which is least is unjust also in that which is most. The Spirit of Christ requires that the employee should conscientiously regard his master's interests in everything, and should seek to promote them just as faithfully when not under severe inspection as when watched and guarded by the strictest scrutiny. The spirit of considerateness and conscientiousness in our secular callings, in promptness, faithfulness and energy, will always indicate high character, and ultimately lead to lasting and great reward. It is by these little things that quality is determined, and in the end the noblest recompenses are won and the highest possibilities of influence determined.

Let us remember in our business situations that we are witnesses of God, and He wants us to show to an ungodly world that a Christian employee is better than a worldling.

And so, on the other hand, the Spirit of Christ should show itself in the spirit of the master. How often it is sadly true that employers take advantage of their power to be harsh, despotic, cruel and unjust, and sometimes to place temptation in the way of those dependent upon them which almost constrain the weak and dependent one to yield to evil rather than face the risks that may be entailed. Let us remember that in positions of authority we represent God, and let us seek to be to those dependent upon us like Joseph instead of God.

THE HEAVENLY SIDE OF EARTHLY THINGS

How will we measure up to this high standard? How will we be inspired and enabled to walk according to these practical and beautiful precepts? Thank God we are not left without heavenly armor. Before we are sent out on these paths of practical righteousness and service, we are supplied with an incentive and an inspiration which are fitted to lift us to the highest plane of duty and faithfulness. By one bold and heavenly touch the whole sphere of earthly duty is lifted up to a lofty and glorious plane, and all these human relationships are at once represented under the bright and glowing touch of their divine significance. They cease to be mere places of earthly toil, and they become occupations in direct relation to God and heaven. The servant ceases to be the servile drudge of his master, and becomes at once the servant of Jesus Christ and the candidate for a heavenly reward, and every earthly relationship and duty become attached to some higher connection and some heavenly calling. For example:

1. Our Walk

Our walk is connected with our calling. We are shown a picture of our high vocation and glorious destiny, and then we are told to live up to it. As the children of a King, the heirs of a throne, we are to walk in a kingly fashion and royal dignity: "Live a life worthy of the calling you have received" (4:1).

2. Our Talk

We are called to be truthful. But this is not based on the fear of an inspection, but because we are members one of another; and untruthfulness and deceit would be a wrong to the body of Christ (4:25).

3. Our Temper

We are summoned to righteousness and holiness of life, but not until we have put on the new man, and are reminded that with our new and heavenly nature it would be unbecoming for us to wear the old rags of sin (4:22–24).

4. Our Integrity

We are bidden to be gentle and forgiving, but it is because Christ has thus forgiven us (5:32).

5. Our Purity

We are warned against the filthy lusts of the flesh, but we are at once reminded that such things are not becoming to saints. Our honor is appealed to, and the very nature and fitness of things given as a sufficient reason why such gross and unbecoming habits should not be even once named among us (5:3).

6. Unworldliness

We are counseled against frivolousness and foolish talking, but we are immediately reminded, as an incentive and inspiration to a higher and holier conversation, that such things are "not convenient," "do not comport," or as Rotherham translates it, are "beneath us." The consciousness of our heavenly dignity will lift us above such unbecoming and degrading habits (5:4).

7. Gravity

We are admonished to walk in love, but we are immediately reminded as our example and motive that Christ also has loved us, and given Himself for us an offering and sacrifice unto God for a sweet-smelling savor; and we, like Him, are to spend our lives giving ourselves for others, and become a sweet savor as fragrant as He (5:2).

8. Our Time

We are told to be followers of God, "imitators," literally, of God. But it is at once added, "as dearly loved children." It is a very much easier thing to imitate God when we know that He loves us more tenderly than any human parent (5:1).

9. Sobriety

We are warned against intemperance and excess, but immediately we have the antidote, "be filled with the Spirit" (5:18). There is a fine antithesis, and the suggestion undoubtedly is that the true stimulant and intoxicant is the Holy Spirit.

10. Our Homes

Coming next to our domestic relations, the husband and wife are reminded that their union is not a mere matter of earthly fondness, but is a sacred emblem of the marriage of Christ and His Church, and therefore they are to elevate it to its heavenly dignity and walk worthy of its high and holy significance. The husband is to represent Christ to his wife, and the wife is to represent the holy Bride of Jesus in her spirit and conduct to her husband (5:24–25).

11. Our Children

Even the relation of parents and of children has a higher character than a mere domestic tie. The child is to obey his parents in the Lord and as to the Lord. The parent is to bring up his child "in the training and instruction of the Lord," that is, as the Lord nurtures and deals with us, remembering that it will be done to us as we have done. If we neglect or ill-treat our children, so the Lord may make us feel the weight of His own severe and faithful discipline (6:1–4).

12. Our Employees

Even the servant and the master are elevated to a higher sphere, and reminded that they are serving a supreme Master and hastening to a greater tribunal where each will receive of the Lord "whatever good" he does, "whether he is slave or free" (6:8). Therefore they are to do their work "not only to win their favor when their eye is on you, but like slaves of Christ, doing the will of God from your heart. Serve wholeheartedly, as if you were serving the Lord, not men" (6:6–7).

Thus we see that a holy, heavenly sanction attaches to each earthly command. The human is lifted to the divine, the earthly to the heavenly, and God is brought down to mingle with every part of our personal existence. What a sacredness it gives to common things! What a witness for God if all our life might thus be stamped with His seal and consecrated to His service! Thus life, while it may not consist of magnificent things, may be made up from myriads of common things, all done in a magnificent way. The old plan, which Sir William Jones is said to have made out for every 24 hours of his life, may become the diary of every saint: "Eight hours for sleep, eight hours for labor, eight hours for prayer, the study of the Scriptures, meals and recreation, but all for heaven."

CHAPTER 10

THE CONFLICT IN THE HEAVENLIES

Finally, be strong in the Lord and in his mighty power. Put on the full armor of God so that you can take your stand against the devil's schemes. For our struggle is not against flesh and blood, but against the rulers, against the authorities [principalities, KJV], against the powers of this dark world and against the spiritual forces of evil in the heavenly realms. Therefore put on the full armor of God, so that when the day of evil comes, you may be able to stand your ground, and after you have done everything, to stand. (Ephesians 6:10–13)

We have been looking in a series of successive visions at the exceeding riches of the heavenly places which form the sphere of our spiritual life. We have seen in the distant past the eternal purpose of divine love, and in the distant future the consummation of that purpose in glory. We have seen that purpose of grace successively wrought out in all the stages of the plan of redemption. We have seen it in the exalted place to which our Redeemer has been raised at the Father's right hand, above all principality and power. We have seen it in the exaltation of the people of God to share the resurrection and the ascension glory of their Head. We have seen it in the calling and destiny of the Church, His Body and His Bride. We have that glory brought down and revealed through the indwelling of Christ in the heart of the believer. We have seen it carried forth into all the stations and situations of our practical human life. We are now to see it finally displayed in conflict with the superior powers of evil, and triumphant over even Satan's hate and rage. Higher than the heights of heaven, sufficient for all the needs of earth, we are now to behold it stronger and deeper than the gates of hell.

In this vivid picture of the greatest war of the ages let us look at the Adversary, the Onset and the Defense.

THE ADVERSARY

It is foolish to underestimate the power of an enemy. The Bible nowhere deprecates the tremendous resources of our spiritual foes. Satan is not omnipotent; but he is the highest created intelligence, strong through the mighty nature with which the Creator endowed him, and wise through the experience of 10,000 ages.

We have a vivid picture here of that fearful underworld of which Satan is the sovereign lord. Rank by rank the authorities and powers of the kingdom of darkness are brought before us.

1. Principalities

This term denotes spheres of government, authority and influence. It denotes not so much their power as their rank and authority. The spiritual world is really after the order of earthly governments. The prototype of all government is the heavenly state and the kingdom of God. Satan has copied and counterfeited this, and set up his thrones and hierarchies, and played the part of a god since his fearful fall. The kingdoms of this world and their governments have been set up largely by him.

In the vision of the Apocalypse we see the seven-headed and crowned dragon with the seven-headed and crowned beast, exact copies of each other. The dragon represents the devil and his kingdom, and the beast represents the world powers, of which it is said he gives them their "power," their "seat and great authority" (Revelation 13:2). We may therefore expect that the gradations of rank and power that we have seen in human government from the beginning of man's imperial ambition are all reproduced from the government of Satan.

These principalities represent the rulers of the great departments of state under Satan's control. We get a little glimpse of one of these in the vision of Daniel, in the 10th chapter of his prophecy, where we find that the angel Michael, on his way to Daniel, was detained for 21 days in conflict with the demon prince that was appointed as the patron spirit of the kingdom of Persia. Now if Persia had a principality so mighty as that, we may suppose that Babylon, Egypt, Greece and Rome had each their territorial demon, supported by innumerable hosts of darkness, and that Satan has not yet changed his plans, but the selfish and cruel governments of earth today are under the protection of similar powers.

Satan is the god of the world, and no doubt his diplomacy and skill are as astute as ever, and as earnestly pursued as the age hastens to its close. Indeed, it is distinctly predicted that in the last days, under the sixth vial which seems to mark our own age, three unclean spirits like frogs are to come out from the pit and take possession of the kings of the earth, to gather them to battle for the great day of the Lord God Almighty.

Besides these principalities that rule the kings of the earth there are, doubtless, in the kingdom of nature and providence, spirits in charge of the elements; principalities in control of the lightning, the tempest, the ocean, the fire, the passions of men, the powers of disease and death, the earthquake, and the solar and stellar realms in their influence upon this earth. These principalities are arrayed against us.

2. Powers

This word denotes not so much authority as force. We know something of the great forces of nature, but we are only beginning to know what marvelous advances science has made in the revelation of the powers of dynamite, electricity, magnetism and even the mind. But Satan has known far more about them than we, and is doubtless able to control these forces with strong and skillful hand. We know that it was his hand that stirred up the tempest and the fire that destroyed the property and family of Job. We know that Christ saw him once, like lightning, fall from heaven. We know something of the revelations of spiritualism, and its occult and unquestioned power to make real to our senses the very faces and forms of those long dead, so that the eye can behold, and the very fingers touch, that speaks to our hearing some message that it seems, at least, as if no one else could ever know except the very one that is presented. There seems to be no doubt that this awful mystery of darkness can apparently create the very objects of nature, and present to the spectator out of the empty air bouquets of flowers that to the sense of touch and smell are real flowers, and then melt away even as you gaze. It can even clothe the forms that claim to be the bodies of our dead with dress and drapery that the observer can handle and examine in its every fiber until it dissolves in his touch.

We know that there is some subtle power behind these manifestations which neither science nor jugglery can sufficiently explain. It is the power of Satan's kingdom.

Then there is a strange force of mind over mind, and mind over matter. It is looming up in forms in our day as Christian Science, mental healing, mind cure, hypnotism, animal magnetism and mesmerism. There is some unquestioned force behind it all. Creditable witnesses have told us how they have seen two medicine men among the Indian tribes of the great West meet in severe combat, not with hands or daggers, but with flaming eyes and defiant minds, exercising their strange spell of witchcraft over each other, until at last the dominant mind, fixing his eyes upon the other with resistless spell, and with a gesture of demoniac hate and emphasis, shrieked out the one word, "Die!" and his adversary fell lifeless at his feet, stricken to death by some invisible electric flash from mind to mind or mind to matter.

These are all the cropping out of forces of which we have as yet but the dim approximation, but which the king of darkness doubtless has under his complete control. We know something of the forces of disease, subtle poisons that are felt in the air, the bacteria and animalcule, to whose swiftly breeding germs medical science today attributes almost all forms of disease. These, we know from Scripture testimony, are under the direct control of Satan. These are the powers against which we contend. How helpless our vainglorious strength! How defenseless our weakness against these super-human foes! How essential it is that we should hide under the panoply of God, and be "strong in the Lord and in his mighty power" (Ephesians 6:10).

3. Rulers

"The world rulers of this darkness" is the literal translation of the next phrase. Satan is the god of this world, and he rules it with a spell of resistless control and dark, unwholesome influence. One is especially conscious of this evil atmosphere in heathen lands. There the darkness can be felt. Your spirit is conscious of a weight of evil crushing out the presence and consciousness of God, and injecting a thousand stings that remind you that you are in Satan's realm. The lone missionary feels it at his isolated post. William Burns, of China, used to write to his family of the awful reality of the fearful satanic presence that constantly oppressed him.

The course of this world is directed by this influence. Public opinion is a kind of spell. The current of society, the trend of human thought and feeling, the power of minds thinking and feeling alike—all these form the drift and trend of the age, and only the mighty force of a heavenly impulse can lift and hold us above it. The great mass of men walk following "the ways of this world . . . the spirit who is now at work in those who are disobedient" (2:2). All this we have to contend with, and only divine strength can lift us above it.

4. Spiritual Forces

"Spiritual forces of evil in the heavenly realms" (6:12), represents another class of spiritual foes, a very numerous one. Literally, it means "hosts of wicked spirits." But their sphere is distinctly marked. They are in the heavenlies. They are not the spirits of the slums. They are not the demons that incite to lust, drunkenness, cruelty, bloodshed and the grosser forms of crime. They are not the demon powers that rule in the sense of heathen barbarism. They are higher spirits. You find them in the cultured Brahmins of India, the reformers of Buddhism, the high thinkers of philosophy, the apostles of science, the professors in our colleges and seminaries, the popular preachers of the modern pulpits, the clever editors of our religious press, the leaders of free thought and liberal theology. They come as angels of light.

They edit and issue the popular magazine, the journals of higher criticism. They tell you about the Christ of today; and while exalting His social and moral influence in practical life, they take away His cross and eliminate His sacrificial blood. They publish the polychrome Bible, and with many skillfully blended tints they try to teach the common people that portions of this holy Book are not authentic and inspired, and the larger part is but an accumulation of fragments and editorial editions that have been gathered through the ages until it simply ranks among the literary remnants of the past, a little better perhaps than the Vedas of India or the hieroglyphics of Egypt.

These heavenly spirits invade the very realm of sanctity, and lead their votaries to claim a perfection so high that they cannot sin, an infallibility so extreme that they defy temptation; and so from the pinnacle of spiritual pride they fall to the abyss of fanaticism, and find a way to hell from the gates of heaven.

5. Satan

The leader of all these hosts is Satan himself, that mighty angel who fell from heaven in his pride and impious plan to usurp the throne of God. Of how great he was before his fall we have a picture in Ezekiel 28:12–15,

> You were the model of perfection,
>   full of wisdom and perfect in beauty.
> You were in Eden,
>   the garden of God;
> every precious stone adorned you:
>   ruby, topaz and emerald,
>   chrysolite, onyx and jasper,
>   sapphire, turquoise and beryl.
> Your settings and mountings were made of gold;
>   on the day you were created they were prepared.
> You were anointed as a guardian cherub . . .
> You were on the holy mount of God;
>   you walked among the fiery stones.
> You were blameless in your ways
>   from the day you were created
>   till wickedness was found in you.

This terrific foe is not omnipresent, and perhaps he seldom meets the individual saint; but he directs all the forces of his dark and malign empire, and he strikes individually wherever the blow is most needed. He has the power of death, and the graves of earth's 200 generations are the saddest evidence that he is still living. He has the dominion of hell, and he has not yet been confined within its fiery dungeons. He is the adversary, the embodiment of malignity and hate, and all who know his power will be wise to hide under the shadows of the Almighty.

THE ONSET

This is described in a series of impressive figures.

1. Schemes

"Take your stand against the devil's schemes" (6:11b). He does not come openly. He is the master of strategy. He disguises his approaches. He does not expect us to walk deliberately into his snares. He aims to make the wrong appear right, and to deceive us and destroy us through our good intentions and our thoughtless, unwatchful innocence. His last ruse is to try to persuade men that he is not the devil at all; that this is all a mistake; and when he gets them to believe it, his triumph is secure.

2. Flaming Arrows

"You can extinguish all the flaming arrows of the evil one" (6:16b). As soon as he has deceived us and has us in the position of his choice, then he opens his guns on us, and we become the targets of his flaming arrows. No modern military ordnance can approximate the fierceness of their assaults. He can inject them into the spirit until it is as dark as the very abysses of despair. He can hurl them into the mind until our thoughts are clouded and reason reels upon the throne. He can strike down a body until nerves and brain and physical organism are a furnace of fiery pain. And when he strikes us at a disadvantage, when he gets the soul under condemnation, when he springs upon you after some unwary act of sin, and adds to spiritual darkness mental confusion, nights of sleeplessness, nervous distraction and physical disease—then, indeed, life can be made a very hell of horror and agony. Many of us have good cause to remember some of these fiery darts. Alas for those who become exposed to them without the sheltering shadow of God's wing!

3. Wrestling

Then comes the closer contact described by the figure of wrestling (6:12, KJV). This is as when in naval warfare the two hostile ships come together and grapple with each other, and hand to hand and man to man they fight for mastery, until the decks are slippery with human blood. Satan can come so close to us that his very thoughts seem to be our own, and we almost lose our own consciousness, and the demon spirit wraps itself around us and tries to make us responsible for its vilest suggestions and most impious thoughts.

4. The Evil Day

Then comes that startling expression that calls up a picture that is sometimes so terrible, "the day of evil" (6:13). It describes some crisis hour when the hosts of hell have concentrated their fire upon us; when mind, body and spirit all seem to be involved in the heat of battle, and every circumstance of life conspires to crush us; when even God seems to have withdrawn, and the soul cries out like Christ in His agony, "My God, my God, why have you forsaken me?" (Mark 15:34). Every strong and tested life has its Gethsemane, its "day of evil," its crisis hour; and he who has passed through it knows how helpless is all our strength unless we understand the power and panoply of God.

THE DEFENSE

1. Be Strong

The very first thing in this battle scene is the command "Be strong in the Lord and in his mighty power" (Ephesians 6:10). The original is much more emphatic. Translated by Rotherham it reads, "Be getting empowered in the Lord, and in the strength of his might." That does not mean that you are to cultivate your own strength, but you are to discount it altogether, and take the power of God Himself at the very outset of the conflict.

2. The Armor of God

The panoply of God is next provided. This is like the armor of the battleship which comes between the soldier and the foe. God has provided for hiding us in the strife and covering us with a heavenly armor, without which we should be crushed.

In naval war we have seen a whole fleet of old-fashioned battleships annihilated by a smaller number of armored vessels without the loss of a single man on the part of the assailing fleet. They were armored. They were panoplied. They were protected. Rash is the man who attempts to fight the devil with his own resolutions, purposes or strength.

3. Put on

We have a part to do in putting on this armor. The Greek word is, "take up" the complete armor of God, and all through the vivid figurative language the command is in the active and imperative form. "With the belt of truth buckled around your waist, with the breastplate of righteousness in place, and with your feet fitted with the readiness that comes from the gospel of peace. In addition to all this, take up the shield of faith" (6:14–16a). We are to be active in this war, not in fighting, but in covering ourselves with Christ by His divine provision for strength and victory.

4. The Girdle

The panoply itself is described in detail. First is the girdle (belt) of the loins, which is truth. Doubtless this means a deep sincerity of purpose, a single heart, a choice that has no equivocation, hesitation, or compromise; a surrender that is complete; a consecration that is wholehearted, irrevocable and utterly sincere. Any compromise here will be sure to ruin us in the battle of the heavenly places. You cannot possibly stand in two places here. If there is a least possible deviation of your aim, the least wavering of your footing, you slip and fall. Therefore, beloved, gird your loins with truth, sincerity, singleness of purpose and truth in the inward part. Be true.

5. The Breastplate

The breastplate of righteousness is to cover your heart, and shield your bosom from the assaults of the foe. This means the righteousness of Christ. Of course, it is His imputed righteousness through which we are justified and which answers every charge against you. But it is more than this. It is the imparted righteousness of Christ. It is Jesus made unto you sanctification (1 Corinthians 1:30, KJV). It is the heart that has received Him to dwell within as its purity, its sanctity. Its answer to Satan's every question is "Jesus cleanses," "Jesus enables," "Jesus keeps." "I can do everything through him who gives me strength" (Philippians 4:13).

6. The Feet

The feet are to be shod with the preparation (readiness) of the gospel of peace. This denotes our spiritual activity in living and working for others. There is no greater safeguard against temptation than to give up the defensive attitude, and go forth against the devil by seeking and saving others. In recent naval battles the attacking fleet always kept moving, thus becoming a target that was difficult to hit. An active Christian is a very difficult target for Satan. Your feet are to keep moving, carrying the gospel of peace to men, and God will fence you in from Satan's fiercest blows.

7. The Shield

We are to take up the shield of faith. The Romans had two kinds of shields: the one, a small buckler, held on the arm; the other, an immense shield, covered the whole person. This is the one here described. Christ is our shield; and as we hold Him up by faith, the devil's blows do not reach us at all, but are all buried and quenched before they strike us. Counting them unreal makes them so.

8. The Helmet

The helmet of salvation covers our head. Most of Satan's wounds are made at our brain. He wants to lodge a thought in our mind, and this becomes either a doubt, a fear, an imagination, a desire or purpose; then comes the word, an act and sin. Therefore we need to have our head well covered. The only thing seen on this warrior's head is salvation. This is all he knows, and it is enough for us to know. If our thoughts are all absorbed in salvation and the Savior, we will be delivered from all the devil's darts.

9. The Sword

"The sword of the Spirit, which is the word of God" (Ephesians 6:17), describes the use which the Holy Spirit makes of the Scriptures in the battle of temptation. This is partly a defensive and partly an offensive weapon. To a mind well stored with Scripture promises, the Holy Spirit will instantly suggest the word in season to meet the enemy's assaults—a promise, the direction, the correction appropriate—bringing all things to our remembrance whatsoever He has said unto us, and quickly disarming every attack of the adversary.

But the sword of the Spirit is meant for offensive warfare. We are to go forth to save others and guard them from the adversary, and the only weapon that Satan fears or the Spirit of God ever owns is the truth of the Holy Scriptures. All the speculations of modern thought, the theories and finely woven fancies of intellectual brains will dissolve before the fiery breath of hell; but against the steel armor of God's Word his shafts fall powerless, and he knows that he is defeated. If you will stand in the awful ordeals of these closing ages, be familiar with your Bible. Have your mind and memory crowded with Scripture promises. Meditate upon His law day and night. Be mighty in the Scriptures, and your life will be strong and your work will remain.

10. Prayer

The artillery of prayer is important. "And pray in the Spirit on all occasions with all kinds of prayers and requests. With this in mind, be alert and always keep on praying for all the saints. Pray also for me" (Ephesians 6:18–19). This brings into play all the armor already described, and, best of all, brings God into the action and covers us with His presence and almighty power.

It will be noticed that the moment He gets us to pray, the devil disappears from the scene. The battle seems to be over, and we even stop praying about ourselves and our conflict. But the whole scene ends in prayer for others, and a high and holy unselfishness that loses itself in the cause of God and the needs of others. This is literally true. Satan runs away from a saint upon his knees; and when we become occupied with God in prayer, we are lifted to a sphere where the dragon cannot reach us. This is not so much the act of occasional prayer under some great emergency, but it is the habit of prayer that is here described, a life encased in prayer, the spirit armored in God's overshadowing presence, so that it is impenetrable and unapproachable by the devil's wiles or wicked assaults.

This should be the normal attitude of the believer's life, and in this heavenly place we can smile at Satan's rage even as God sits in heaven and laughs at the futile fury of His foes.

It is probably true that many of the most terrible temptations that come to Christians come because they have gotten out of communion with God, and away from the true place of abiding. "The Lord knows how to rescue godly men from trials" (1 Peter 2:9), and the Lord lets the devil scourge the disobedient child to frighten him back to the fold.

Oh, beloved, if you are suffering this most fearful of earthly agonies, a season of spiritual conflict, a dark and dreadful struggle with the powers of hell, remember your only remedy is to fly to Christ, and in sincerity of heart surrender, and return to God. Throwing yourself wholly upon His grace and power, you will have cause to say: "Thanks be to God! He gives us the victory through our Lord Jesus Christ" (1 Corinthians 15:57).

Finally, is there any sinful soul struggling helplessly against temptation? Remember, the devil is mightier than you, and you will never gain the victory over the power of drink or any earthly lust by your own striving and resolving. You are "taken captive [by Satan] to do his will" (2 Timothy 2:26), and your only hope of deliverance and salvation is in a complete and immediate surrender to Christ, and

> He breaks the power of canceled sin
>   He sets the prisoner free;
> His blood can make the foulest clean;
>   His blood availed for me.

PHILIPPIANS

INTRODUCTION

T he epistle to the Philippians is an inspired delineation of the Christian temper. While Ephesians describes the highest Christian life, Philippians portrays the sweetest Christian life. It deals not so much with the essential elements of holy character as the finer quality of these elements.

The difference between that exquisite hairspring in a costly watch, more valuable than the same weight in gold, and the rough bar of pig iron, is wholly in the temper. They are both iron, but the one is exquisitely refined and the other is coarse and crude. The difference between that flashing diamond that blazes like a coal of celestial fire and the common lump of coal that you throw into your furnace, is merely a question of temper. They are both carbon, but the one is refined carbon polished and cut into flashing facets of light and beauty, while the other is common, rough coal. The difference between the ordinary tombstone that you can buy for a few dollars in the marble shop, and the classic bust by Michelangelo worth hundreds of thousands of dollars, lies not in the material but in the finer touches of genius and art. It is all a matter of quality. The difference between the crabapple that falls from the apple tree by the roadside and the perfectly developed and exquisitely flavored pippin, is of the same character.

And these are all but feeble illustrations of the infinite difference in the religious character and the divine workmanship of the Holy Spirit in molding human hearts and lives. There are infinite degrees of progress in the refining and sanctifying work of the Holy Spirit, and this epistle leads us out into the less ordinary lines of holy character and spiritual culture. Let us not be surprised if we find many of these qualities lacking in us, because they are not ordinary qualities, but let us press on to their attainment and realization by the grace of Jesus Christ, as we learn in all its length and breadth and depth and height, to have in us the same mind which was also in Christ Jesus (Philippians 2:5).

It was peculiarly fitting that this exquisite epistle should have been written to the church in Philippi. This was the first of the European churches planted by the early missionaries. This was the pioneer of that glorious chain of Christian congregations which form part of the ecclesiastical succession. Looking down through the coming ages, the Holy Spirit called the apostles to leave the continent of Asia and plant the gospel in Europe which was to be the seat of the history of the coming centuries. And so we have a peculiar interest in this mother church of the European nations. It was always very true to Paul, and out of these close and affectionate ties, as a sort of exquisite environment, there grew ideals and conceptions of truth and life which could not have been developed in colder or less tender associations. It is in the genial climate and the tropical atmosphere of love that we get our highest thoughts of God and godliness. And it was to the people who loved so tenderly that the greatest heart that ever throbbed since Christ's ascension brought out these tender messages of heavenly truth and love.

CHAPTER 1

THE CHRISTIAN TEMPER AS EXEMPLIFIED
AND ILLUSTRATED IN PAUL

I have you in my heart. (Philippians 1:7)

For to me, to live is Christ and to die is gain. (1:21)

The first chapter of Philippians gives us a portrait of the apostle's own heart and character. It is drawn by his own hand. Yet he is free from egotism, and even unconscious of himself while so fully unfolding his inmost heart. It is possible for us to reveal ourselves in perfect transparency, and yet have no thought of ourselves at all, even as a little child most completely reveals itself and yet most completely forgets itself. A letter has this advantage over a sermon, in that it lets out the heart of the writer, and the teachings of the New Testament are not sermons or homilies, but letters of affection.

PAUL'S SPIRIT

1. The first trait that strikes us in this sketch is the affectionateness of Paul's spirit. Sanctification does not take out of our hearts the spirit of tenderness and love. It purifies and intensifies every heartstring. "I have you in my heart" (1:7), he says, and "God can testify how I long for all of you with the affection of Christ Jesus" (1:8).

The very cords of his sensitive being were alive with tender yearning; for these beloved friends are children in the Lord. The nearer we get to Christ the nearer we get to Christian people, and the tenderer is every holy tie. And so in that exquisite picture of consecration that he has given us in the 12th chapter of Romans we find such passages as this, "Be kindly affectioned one to another with brotherly love" (12:10, KJV). And here we find him saying a little later, "If you have any encouragement from being united with Christ, if any comfort from his love, if any fellowship with the Spirit, if any tenderness and compassion, then make my joy complete by being like-minded, having the same love, being one in spirit and purpose" (Philippians 2:1–2).

CHRISTIAN FELLOWSHIP

2. Christian fellowship is next recognized, especially in connection with his relations to his beloved Philippian brethren. There are some natures that are coldly isolated and independent. They naturally and instinctively stand apart in their joys and sorrows, refusing to open their petals to the sunshine of love, and dwelling in a little world of their own. This is not the genius of Christianity, nor was it the spirit of Paul. His heart was open as the full-blown rose, giving and receiving the sweetness and fragrance of love in relation to all. And so he speaks with the deepest thankfulness of their "partnership in the gospel from the first day until now" (1:5), and adds with deep appreciation of their sympathy and help, "Whether I am in chains or defending and confirming the gospel, all of you share in God's grace with me" (1:7). He recognizes their help to him and he rejoices in his power to be a blessing to them. God has thus linked us one to the other even as the members of the human body are linked by joints and ligaments, and made us members one of another so that we can share each other's blessings, we can feel each other's sufferings, we can enrich each other's experience. Christian fellowship is God's ordinance, and every true heart should be able to join in the ancient creed with true wholehearted fullness, "I believe in the communion of saints."

THE SPIRIT OF CHEER, HOPE AND THANKS

3. The next quality we note in this portraiture is the spirit of cheerfulness, hopefulness and thankfulness. There is no depression about it. There is no reproachfulness about it. There is no shadow of discontent, criticism or gloom, but it is all appreciation, thankfulness and confidence. "I thank my God every time I remember you" (1:3). The very recollection of them brings pleasure to him; and as he looks forward to their future he has no premonitions, doubts or fears, but he can say, "Being confident of this, that he who began a good work in you will carry it on to completion until the day of Christ Jesus" (1:6).

This is a beautiful quality in Christian character. There are some people who make us tired by their concern for us, their fears for our future, their criticisms of our faults. If Paul had any suggestion to make to his brethren he always first bathed them in an ocean of love and then they hardly knew that he was even criticizing. In one of his most beautiful passages he bids us to "admonish one another with all wisdom, and as you sing psalms, hymns and spiritual songs" (Colossians 3:16). Sing to our friends our counsels and admonitions rather than scold them.

We find this in a very marked way in the epistles of our Lord to the seven churches in Asia. His first word is always commendation, and after He has recognized at their full value the things that are excellent, He then tells them of the things that should be changed. God give us the love that "always trusts, always hopes," as well as "always perseveres" (1 Corinthians 13:7).

UNSELFISH PRAYER

4. We next note the spirit of unselfish prayer for his brethren. In all this epistle we do not find Paul offering a single prayer for himself. In fact, he tells them a little later that he has no needs, "I have received full payment and even more; I am amply supplied" (Philippians 4:18). He has enough to give away, and his one thought is to bless others. We find him praying for them with every breath and every remembrance, "In all my prayers for all of you, I always pray with joy" (1:4).

And yet his prayer is not a mere redundancy of words or emotions. It is an intelligent, discriminating, positive and most helpful petition for real things, things that they actually need. "And this is my prayer," he says, "that your love may abound more and more in knowledge and depth of insight, so that you may be able to discern what is best and may be pure and blameless until the day of Christ" (1:9–10). He wants them to have real and very definite blessings, to be clear-cut in their character and experience, and to reach the highest possibilities of Christian perfection, so that in the day of Christ he may be able to present them blameless and harmless, and may rejoice that he has not run in vain, neither labored in vain.

VICTORIOUS FAITH

5. Then there is the spirit of victorious faith over difficulties and trials. His was no soft, effeminate character languidly developed by easy, sentimental associations, but it was disciplined in the sturdy conflict of adversity and suffering. As he wrote these exquisite lines of courage, thankfulness and love, he was himself a prisoner in the Roman barracks, sleeping every night between two soldiers, and waiting to be brought before a cruel and wicked judge to be tried for his life. Yet he is so afraid that they may be discouraged by his difficulties that he hastens to have them understand that "what has happened to me has really served to advance the gospel" (1:12), and that his very bonds and afflictions have really led to more glorious results for the Master's cause. The soldiers that have been chained to him have been converted through his influence, and the brethren that were timid before have been encouraged by his brave example to give a bolder testimony for Christ. None of his trials move him or even depress him for a moment, but he rises supreme above them all in the singleness of his desire to glorify his Master. Brave, glorious spirit, undaunted, unintimidated, not discouraged by the persecutions of earth or the hate of hell, shining like a glowing star the

brighter for the darkness around him, blooming like a sweet rose amid the glaciers of the Alps, "sorrowful, yet always rejoicing; poor, yet making many rich; having nothing, and yet possessing everything" (2 Corinthians 6:10).

VICTORY OVER PEOPLE

6. Next there is victory over people. More trying even than circumstances, are human hearts, natures out of sympathy with us, souls that seem especially adjusted to irritate, lacerate and rasp our most sensitive feelings.

Paul speaks of some who "preach Christ out of envy and rivalry" (Philippians 1:15), and, under the very guise of goodness and service, aim only to humiliate and injure him. It is very hard to rise superior to people who misrepresent our best endeavors, oppose us in our holiest efforts and in the very name of religion are but emissaries of hate and evil. But Paul could stand even this so long as they preached Christ. Though it were for "contention," and in "pretense," he could say, "The important thing is that in every way, whether from false motives or true, Christ is preached. And because of this I rejoice" (1:18). If the Master was glorified, if the truth was spread, if the gospel was made known, that was his one concern and his supreme satisfaction. Surely this is a nature larger, nobler than all the petty jealousies and rivalries of sects and parties. The thought may well cover with a blush of shame many who have used even their Christian work as a means of self-glorification or the gratification of bigotry, prejudice and controversy.

DEVOTION TO CHRIST

7. Next, Paul's devotion to Christ stands out. The secret of all this was his single-hearted devotion to Jesus Christ. The one thing he cared for, lived for, and was willing to die for, was that "Christ shall be magnified in my body whether it be by life, or by death" (1:20, KJV), and the one illustrious sentence in which he emblazons it forth like a passion sign of love is this immortal epigram, "For to me, to live is Christ and to die is gain" (1:21). This is the secret of every glorious soul and every earnest life: intense, fervid devotion to the Lord Jesus Christ. It was the one ambition of Paul's life, and like a great volcanic torrent it swept away everything in its current, transfused everything into its own burning flame, and made him the bond slave of Jesus Christ. "For Christ's love compels us" (2 Corinthians 5:14). It was not living for Christ, but it was living for Christ alone.

HOLY INDIFFERENCE

8. Paul displayed a holy indifference. His supreme motive of love to Christ raised him above every selfish preference and enabled him to care little for gain or loss, life or death for their own sakes. When he stopped to think whether he preferred to live or die, he was at a loss to determine. Per-

sonally he preferred to go and be with Christ, and yet when he thought of his work and his brethren he longed to remain with them. He was in that state of mind where the world could neither attract him nor distract him. Like General Gordon, when the Mahdi threatened him with death, he smiled in his face and said, "You could not do me a greater favor than thus quickly to introduce me into the presence of my best Friend, and the enjoyment of highest reward." Such men have nothing to lose, nothing to gain, nothing to fear. Life has found a perfect equilibrium by being poised from the center and fixed forever on its true axis in devotion to Christ alone.

SUBLIME CONFIDENCE

9. Paul had a sublime confidence. His very indifference gave him faith. Because he did not care for life for its own sake, he knew that he should live, and was able to claim it, not for himself, but for Christ and for others; and so he could add, "Convinced of this, I know that I will remain, and I will continue with all of you for your progress and joy in the faith" (Philippians 1:25).

The way to have faith for healing is to give up your life for Christ, and then take it back from Christ for Christ. While we want even life for its own sake, we shall not be able to believe for it; but when it ceases to be our own and becomes a consecrated trust for Him, then we can say with him, "I know that I will remain, and I will continue" (1:25) until our life work is done.

Thus we have glanced all too briefly at the unconscious portrait which this simple-hearted yet glorious saint has given of his own heart and life. His qualities as we have already said are not ordinary qualities. They represent a very high plane of Christian experience. We shall find the secret of them in the next chapter, "Your attitude should be the same as that of Christ Jesus" (2:5).

It is a comfort to know that not only has this life once been lived by Christ, but it has also been lived by Paul. It is not only a divine pattern but it has been a human experience. Not only has the Son of man walked through the path of time in these beautiful habits of loveliness and grace, but another man, animated with His Spirit, united to His life and exposed to all the trials and hindrances which could beset a human existence, has trod the same path and has passed on to a triumph unsullied by failure and a glory unalloyed and everlasting. Let us not be slothful, "But . . . imitate those who through faith and patience inherit what has been promised" (Hebrews 6:12). Let us look at our shortcomings and failures in the light of these sublime examples, and then sinking into the nothingness of our insufficiency, let us claim His all-sufficiency and let Him live out in us His own victorious life, even as He lived it in this blessed pattern man who speaks to

CHAPTER 2

THE CHRISTIAN TEMPER AS EXEMPLIFIED IN CHRIST

Your attitude [mind, KJV] should be the same as that of Christ Jesus. (Philippians 2:5)

Every great creation must have an archetype and pattern. Many a waiting year and many a patient effort are spent in perfecting the model of some marvelous invention which is to revolutionize modern mechanics or industrial art. After the model is made it is not hard to reproduce it in millions of copies. It is the first machine that counts. The others are but copies.

God spent 4,000 years showing the inadequacy of all human types of character. Then, after an Adam, an Abraham, a Moses, a David and even an Elijah had failed, He revealed the Man for whom the ages had been waiting, the perfect Pattern and Type of human character, by which all others were to be molded and fashioned. As He looked upon Him on the banks of the Jordan He exclaimed in approving love, "You are my Son, whom I love; with you I am well pleased" (Luke 3:22). Henceforth all redeemed men are to be conformed to that divine Pattern, the image of His Son, the Firstborn among many brethren.

CHRIST'S CHARACTER AND EXAMPLE

Even Paul is a secondary example, and we are to follow him only as he followed Christ. All other lights are but reflected lights receiving their illumination from Him, and shedding it in return on others. With glowing love and admiration the apostle proceeds to delineate His heavenly character and example.

1. Conscious Dignity

The conscious dignity of Christ is the starting point of the description. While it is a picture of humility and voluntary humiliation, yet it begins with a height of glory transcendently beyond any human character. He was "in very nature God" (Philippians 2:6). The language has the force and bears the construction that He was equal with God, that He was a possessor of the very nature of God, was Himself a divine Person. It was because of His high dignity and His consciousness of it that He was able to stoop so low. It is the lofty character that is able to condescend, while the person ambitious of vain display and earthly honor is always trying to hold up the little reputation he has. One of true rank is easily indifferent to outward appearances because he knows that his dignity cannot be questioned, and mere adventitious circumstances cannot take it away.

This is very strikingly illustrated in the 13th chapter of John in the account of the washing of the disciples' feet. It was because Jesus knew that He came from God and went to God, that without any thought of His own honor or dignity, He rose from supper and immediately began to wash the disciples' feet and to wipe them with the towel with which He was girded.

And so, before we can imitate Christ's example of humility, we must know our high calling and heavenly dignity as the sons of God. Then it will not be hard to stoop to the lowest depths of self-abasement and self-sacrifice.

2. Voluntary Surrender

The translation of the next clause is a little unfortunate. He "thought it not robbery to be equal with God" (Philippians 2:6, KJV), has been rendered by the common consent of scholars, "did not consider equality with God something to be grasped." He did not hold on to His rights and honors, but willingly yielded them. It was His rights that He yielded, the things that He might have retained, and no one ever questioned or gainsaid His holding to His high prerogative. But He suspended His deity for a time and took the place of a servant and a man.

3. Complete Surrender

Not only did He give up something but He gave up all. "But made himself nothing" (2:7) is better rendered, "He emptied himself." He let all go like Boaz, who sacrificed his own inheritance and family name and became merged into the family of Ruth because he loved her. So Jesus Christ became a part of humanity and is forever known in heaven as a man.

4. Surrendered Will

Jesus surrendered His own will. This is the last thing we let go. Man would rather be a king in a cottage than a servant in a palace. But Jesus, who had created all things and ruled the whole creation, stooped to be a servant in His own world—to be controlled by His Father's will and the will of others; to hold Himself in constant subjection to the people around Him; to comfort the disciples who leaned upon Him and claimed Him as a brood of children would a fond mother; even to submit to the very enemies that at last deprived Him of His liberty and His life. And He yielded all, step by step, sacrifice by sacrifice, until at last He was "led like a lamb to the slaughter,/ and as a sheep before her shearers is silent,/ so he did not open his mouth" (Isaiah 53:7). Like Him, the Christian temper enables us to yield our personal will, to be subject one to another in the fear of God and to count ourselves the servants of God, waiting on His bidding, listening to His word and surrendering all to His supreme command.

5. His Earthly Position

Lower still He descended, to be found not only in fashion like a man but the lowest of men, the humblest of the race. He was not a child of wealth or royalty or honor, but was born among the poor and lowly, and of a maiden mother, whose peculiar situation even threw upon His birth a shadow of suspicion and dishonor.

6. Obedient to Death

And even this lowly and humble lot was at last surrendered, when He "became obedient to death" (Philippians 2:8), and gave up His very life in complete sacrifice for the world's redemption.

7. His Final Sacrifice

His final sacrifice was rendered as humbling, as painful and as full of reproach and shame as it was possible. It was no heroic death. It was no illustrious tragedy. It was no such passing out of existence as the military hero whose fame is chronicled to latest ages; but it was as a criminal, as the scum of the world that Jesus died. Carried outside the city gate as one vile enough to defile the whole precincts of Jerusalem by His execution, crucified between two thieves as if He were a common convict, and buried at last in a stranger's grave, the death of Christ was as humbling as His life had been, and His sacrifice was made complete from beginning to end.

There are thousands of people who are willing to make a sacrifice and to do some heroic things if it brings them distinction. Men are dying today by hundreds on the battlefield, and proud and glad to have the honor of winning an illustrious name. If there can be something dramatic in our trials, some heroic luster, some halo of earthly fame, human nature will stoop to the very depths of sacrifice.

> Man for man will boldly brave
> The terrors of the yawning grave;
> And friend for friend, and child for sire

Undaunted and unmoved expire
For love or piety or pride;
But who can die as Jesus died?

And yet this was the character of ancient martyrdom. The men and women who suffered in the Roman Colosseum were not slain as heroes of the faith, but as pests of society. Gentle women were charged with the basest crimes, treated with the foulest outrage, and cast to the wild beasts as monsters of iniquity; they knew that they had no glory in the minds of men for heroism or even decency.

And so, beloved, if you step out with your Master to humiliation and sacrifice, do not be surprised if the world misunderstands you, and if even the very people that call themselves Christians often misjudge your motives and character. The cross was not only painful but shameful, and the tests of Christian character which God gives will lead us all the way to Calvary. But if we have learned our high and heavenly dignity, we shall be so possessed with "the joy set before" us (Hebrews 12:2), and the vision of His glory, that "scorning its shame" (12:2), we shall not fear the reproach, we shall not shrink from humiliation; but we shall rather rejoice that we are "counted worthy of suffering disgrace for the Name" (Acts 5:41).

MORE THAN A PATTERN

Such is the picture of the divine Pattern. But it is much more than a pattern, more than an example, more than a standard for our imitation. One of the greatest books written is *The Imitation of Christ*. It is indeed a sublime theme, the work of a master spirit, and worthy of its circulation as the most widely published book in the world except the Holy Scriptures themselves. But the human heart unaided cannot imitate Christ any more than the canary can imitate Patti [an Italian operatic soprano] or the babe can imitate a giant.

Christ is more than a Pattern to us, more than a bright and glorious Example. He becomes the Power to reproduce that pattern and to transfer to our lives that example. Our text does not bid us to imitate Christ or have a mind like Him, but to have the *same* mind in us which was also in Christ Jesus. This is the deepest truth of all Christian experience. It is Christ Himself who comes to imitate Himself in us and reproduce His own life in the lives of His followers. This is the mystery of the gospel. This is the secret of the Lord. This is the power that sanctifies, that fills, that keeps the consecrated heart. This is the only way that we can be like Christ. And so we change the little song:

Give me a heart like Thine;
By Thy wonderful power,

> By Thy grace every hour
> Give me a heart like Thine.

to:

> Give me Thy heart in mine;
>   By Thy wonderful power,
>   By Thy grace every hour
> Give me Thy heart in mine.

The word "let" expresses the whole idea of the divine life. It is not our doing but His. We do not accomplish it, but we let Him live out His life within us. It is the "expulsive power of a new affection." It is the divine transcending the human. It is the "I no longer live, but Christ lives in me" (Galatians 2:20). Even the teachers of holiness are in danger of substituting holiness for Him, a clean heart for the divine nature. The mystery of godliness is "Christ in you, the hope of glory" (Colossians 1:27).

The end of all experience is union with God. God has made everything for Himself, and the heart never rests till it receives Him and draws all its life from Him. Just as the flower needs the sunshine, and all its exquisite tints are but the outshining of the light that has first shone in, so the graces of the Christian life are but the reflection of the Christ who dwells within. Redemption is not the restoration of fallen man, but the new creation of a redeemed family under the headship of the second Adam on an infinitely higher plane than even unfallen humanity could ever have reached alone. "As was the earthly man, so are those who are of the earth; and as is the man from heaven, so also are those who are of heaven" (1 Corinthians 15:48). We are first born of the Christ, then united to Him, just as Eve was formed out of her husband, and then wedded to Him. The redeemed soul is formed out of the Savior, and then united to Him in an everlasting bond of love and unity, more intimate than any human relationship can ever express.

It is not by a figure that Christ lives in us, in the sense of His truth, the ideas which He has inculcated in the gospel, or the influences which He brings to bear upon us. The message of godliness is nothing less than this: that the very person of Jesus is revealed to and formed in the sanctified soul, and our whole Christian life henceforth is a putting on of Christ and taking from Him moment by moment each grace that we need to live it out, so that it is literally true that "in him we live and move and have our being" (Acts 17:28).

Do we want humility? We receive the spirit of humility from Him, and let the same mind be in us which was also in Him. Do we want love? We open our hearts for a baptism of His love and it flows into us and lives through us.

Do we want patience, courage, wisdom, anything? We simply put on the Lord Jesus, and "Your attitude should be the same as that of Christ Jesus" (Philippians 2:5).

Does this destroy our individuality and make each of us simply an automation without will or responsibility? Certainly not. So perfect is the divine adjustment to our human nature, so delicately does God recognize in us the power of choice and the right of personal liberty, that He will not come until we invite Him, and He will not act except as we cooperate by constant yielding and receiving. The slightest hesitation on our part to follow will check His grace. He will not force Himself into our life, but He will meet the surrendered will and fill the heart that opens all its being to receive Him. Just as the flower is made to receive the sun and only reaches its individuality when filled with sunshine; just as the soil needs the rain and the seed, and only accomplishes the purpose of its being when it receives the seed and absorbs the rain; so the human heart is made for Christ and it is incomplete until it receives Him. He is the complement of its being, and it unfolds and blossoms into all its predestined powers when quickened by His life, and inspired by His presence, and planted and watered by His indwelling life and love.

The 15th chapter of the Gospel of John is perhaps the most perfect unfolding of this message of the abiding life. The three keynotes are "in him," "in us," and "abide." We are not to struggle. We are not to try. We are not to do. We are not to be. We are simply to let Him be and so abide that His life shall flow through us as the sap flows through the branches of the vine, and the rich clusters hang without an effort through the spontaneous life which flows through all the beautiful organism of the plant.

The word "mind" (Philippians 2:5, KJV) here employed suggests that this is not only a spiritual experience but that it is also designed for our intellectual life, for our mental being, for our thoughts, affections, emotions and all the sensibilities of the soul as well as the spirit. Indeed, we have learned that it includes the body too, and there is no power of our redeemed humanity which this blessed Christ cannot fill, and of which He is not fitted to be the fountain of life, and the source of all our power, and the supply of all our need.

What an exquisite simplicity this gives to Christian life. It takes all the complications out of it. It is not a thousand things we have to do, but one. We are occupied with Him, and He takes care of us. We are not watching ourselves and keeping ourselves in constant strain, but we are sweetly abiding in Him. And just as the water flows from the fountain into all the pipes, just as the law of gravitation goes out from the sun to the smallest world that circles in its orbit around that central sun, so while we are attached to Him and in touch with Him it is true every moment, "Because I live, you also will live" (John 14:19). Thus we find such expressions as this, especially in the writings of Paul and John: "I can do everything through him who gives me strength" (Philippians 4:13). "No one who lives in him keeps on sinning" (1 John 3:6). "From the fullness of his grace we have all received one blessing after another" (John 1:16). "The life I live in the body, I live by faith in the Son of God, who loved me and gave himself for me" (Galatians 2:20).

In conclusion let us behold the divine Pattern in all its beauty and completeness, until it humbles us in the dust with the sense of our own failure. Then let us turn to the divine Original, and opening our hearts, receive Him with loving surrender and constant dependence. Thus shall this "mind be in [us] which was also in Christ Jesus" (Philippians 2:5, KJV).

CHAPTER 3

THE CHRISTIAN TEMPER AS ILLUSTRATED
IN THE FRIENDS OF PAUL

I have no one else like him, who takes a genuine interest in your welfare. For everyone looks out for his own interests, not those of Jesus Christ. But you know that Timothy has proved himself, because as a son with his father he has served with me in the work of the gospel. (Philippians 2:20–22)

But I think it is necessary to send back to you Epaphroditus, my brother, fellow worker and fellow soldier, who is also your messenger, whom you sent to take care of my needs. For he longs for all of you and is distressed because you heard he was ill. Indeed he was ill, and almost died. But God had mercy on him, and not on him only but also on me, to spare me sorrow upon sorrow. Therefore I am all the more eager to send him, so that when you see him again you may be glad and I may have less anxiety. Welcome him in the Lord with great joy, and honor men like him. (2:25–29)

There is no brighter galaxy of beautiful lives than the cluster of friends that circled around the Apostle Paul. Their personality stands out in bold relief in his various epistles. The figures of Aquila and Priscilla, Silas and Barnabas, Tychicus and Trophimus, Onesiphorus and Epaphroditus, Timothy and Titus, Luke and even Mark, stand out as familiar friends. Their relations with the great apostle were most intimate, affectionate and helpful. With a heart peculiarly sensitive and loving, his whole being was open to every tie of holy friendship, and the glimpses his letters give us of these sacred friendships are full of the rarest touches of lofty character and nobility.

Two special pictures are given in the texts we have quoted.

479

TIMOTHY, OR THE LOYAL HELPER

The relation of Timothy to Paul was filial. "To Timothy, my true son in the faith" (1 Timothy 1:2) was Paul's usual salutation to his beloved disciple. Converted to God through the ministry of Paul, adopted by him from the beginning of his Christian life as his disciple, companion and helper, and associated with him till the very close of the apostle's career in the most intimate and confidential relations, he could say of him, "I have no one else like him, who takes a genuine interest in your welfare. For everyone looks out for his own interests, not those of Jesus Christ. But you know that Timothy has proved himself, because as a son with his father he has served with me in the work of the gospel" (Philippians 2:20–22).

1. Timothy was a helper.

It is not easy to take the second place. It needs more grace to be a good helper than a good principal. There are plenty of people who are willing to take a subordinate place for a time to serve some ultimate ambition, but it takes a rare quality of humility and devotion to fit into second place and live to carry out the plans and objects which another has originated. And yet this is the true spirit of the New Testament. "You know that the rulers of the Gentiles lord it over them . . . Not so with you. Instead, whoever wants to become great among you must be your servant, and whoever wants to be first must be your slave" (Matthew 20:25–27). One of the most successful of modern missionaries went to the field in the first instance as a body-servant of a missionary, and God honored him afterwards equally with his former master and made the name of Marshman immortal among the records of noble lives. "My fellow workers in Christ Jesus" (Romans 16:3). This clause included many of the noblest lives in apostolic times. This is the trust that is given to most of us. May God make us true "helpers in Christ Jesus."

2. Timothy was a truehearted and loyal helper.

In every age truth and honor have been counted sacred, and treachery base. The ethics of Christianity give no lower place to loyalty, and among the signs of the declension and apostasy of the last days, are mentioned "trucebreakers" (2 Timothy 3:3, KJV) and "covenantbreakers" (Romans 1:31, KJV). A man who will be false to his fellow man will also prove recreant to his trust and to his God, if the temptation and inducement are only sufficiently strong. Let us ask God to make us true to every trust.

3. Timothy was an unselfish and disinterested helper and fellow-worker.

Paul had found few such helpers. Even in apostolic days men used the Christian ministry to further selfish ends. "For everyone looks out for his own interests, not those of Jesus Christ" (Philippians 2:21). "I have no one else like him, who takes a genuine interest in your welfare" (2:20). But here was one truehearted shepherd who only desired the good of the flock and the things that would please the Chief Shepherd. It was more than human friendship; it was more than loyalty to a leader; it was more than zeal for a cause—it was a love for souls that "takes a genuine interest in your welfare" (2:20). It was the heart of the Master in the minister, pitying, sympathizing, entering into the very needs and conditions of the flock and caring for them even as Christ would care. Without this there can be no true service. "What I want is not your possessions but you" (2 Corinthians 12:14), the true-hearted apostle could say. And so every true minister of Christ should be filled with the unselfish love, the disinterested aim, the shepherd heart—the very affection of Jesus Christ—toward the people for whom we stand in the Master's name. All others are but hirelings. These only are the true under-shepherds of the sheep.

EPAPHRODITUS, OR THE CONSIDERATE FRIEND

The story of Epaphroditus is unique. He belonged to the church in Philippi, and was sent to Rome by the Philippian church while Paul was there in prison. He was probably one of the elders or pastors of the Philippian church. Hearing of the apostle's sufferings, he made strenuous exertions to find him out and minister to him, and through his violent over-exertions, he became ill himself, dangerously ill. But so unselfish was he that he took special pains to conceal the knowledge of his sickness from his friends in Philippi lest they should be anxious about him. And when at length he found that they had heard the tidings he was "distressed" (Philippians 2:26) because they had heard that he had been sick. At length, however, God graciously restored him to health and spared the apostle the bitter sorrow which his death would have caused him, and Paul now sends him back to the Philippians as the bearer of this epistle and commends him to their confidence and love as one who "for the work of Christ, risking his life to make up for the help you could not give me" (2:30).

There are some exquisitely fine touches of character in this picture:

1. Epaphroditus had the spirit of service.

Epaphroditus had gone from Philippi to Rome to carry to Paul the gifts of the Philippian Christians and to assist the apostle in his work. And Paul speaks of him as "My brother, fellow worker and fellow soldier, who is also your messenger, whom you sent to take care of my needs" (2:25).

He was undoubtedly a spiritual worker, and able to minister Christ to the souls of men. But he was not above the humblest ministration of help to the bodies of men. He carried with his own hands the gifts of his brethren to the lone apostle at Rome, and doubtless ministered personally with lowly service to his physical necessities. Are we ministering to Christ's suffering ones? Are we seeking out His poor, His sick, His prisoners, and doing it as unto Him?

2. Epaphroditus had the spirit of sacrifice.

Such was Epaphroditus' spirit of sacrifice that he risked his very life to minister to Paul. He toiled and traveled till he became exhausted and ill. He went beyond his strength. He lingered in the cold barracks or the damp dungeon until he contracted malignant disease and "almost died" (2:30). He did it willingly, "risking his life" (2:30). He was glad to sacrifice as well as serve for the sake of his Master and his friend.

Beloved, how much have you sacrificed for Christ? How often have you risked your health and life in the unwholesome garret, the damp prison, the pestilential hospital, the long vigil of some sick saint's bedside, who perhaps could not afford a nurse to watch her? How often have you given up a pleasant evening with your family to carry comfort or salvation to some other soul? How often have you denied yourself some gratification or necessity that you might have something to give to Christ to send the gospel to the perishing? These are the only badges of honor and reward in the kingdom of God. Service is only duty. When we have done all "we are unworthy servants; we have only done our duty" (Luke 17:10). It is only the crimson blood of sacrifice that can make us partakers of the sufferings and glory of our Lord.

3. Epaphroditus possessed the spirit of silence and self-forgetfulness in service and suffering.

Most people want their sacrifices known and the story of their service told in the glowing records of human praise. Their chief sorrow is the sense of the world's neglect and want of sympathy. But here is a man whose only desire is to keep his friends from knowing of his troubles, and whose only heaviness was because they "heard he was ill" (Philippians 2:26). So unselfish and considerate was he that he only desired to spare them the news that might bring anxiety and concern. This is very fine. It touches the deepest lines of love and Christlikeness. It is the veil of humility and the covering of unselfishness which adds to sacrifice and service a divine touch and claims for it a heavenly reward. The things we do to be seen by men—the things that others appreciate, pity, praise—of these the Master says: "They have received their reward" (Matthew 6:16). But the things done only unto Him, and forgotten perhaps by us as soon as done, or esteemed as of small account because it was merely second nature for us to do them, of these He says, "Your Father, who sees what is done in secret, will reward you" (6:18).

The happy souls who are to sit at the right hand of the King when He comes in the glory of His Father, and hear Him say, "Come, you who are blessed by my Father; take your inheritance, the kingdom prepared for you since the creation of the world. For I was hungry and you gave me something to eat, I was thirsty and you gave me something to drink" (25:34–35), will have forgotten all about their service and will answer, "Lord, when did we see you hungry and feed you, or thirsty and give you something to drink" (25:37)? But their very self-unconsciousness will but add to the value of their service, and the greatness of their reward in the day when He shall "bring to light what is hidden in darkness and will expose the motives of men's hearts. At that time each will receive his praise from God" (1 Corinthians 4:5).

LESSONS FOR US

Now the qualities we have been describing are among the finest touches of character. One may be a sincere Christian, and an irreproachable and righteous man, and not possess them. Yes, but it is these fine qualities that constitute the difference between the boor and the gentleman, between the piece of charcoal and the diamond, between the sunflower and the rose, between the soul saved "as one escaping through the flames" (1 Corinthians 3:15), and the glorified saint sweeping through the gates with an abundant entrance "into the eternal kingdom of our Lord and Savior Jesus Christ" (2 Peter 1:11).

And it is not infrequently that a great issue is decided by what seems a trifling incident, but what really indicates some high quality beneath. The fact that 300 of Gideon's 10,000 men lapped up the water when they drank, showed that they alone possessed the qualities that could be depended upon in the crisis hour. The fact that the widow of Zarephath was willing to give up her last handful of meal and her last drop of oil, marked in her spirit a quality which prepared her in later years to receive back her boy as the first to rise from the dead. The readiness of Abraham to give up his only son at God's command was but a straw on the tide of his life, but it showed the bent and purpose of his being, and God could say, "Now I know that you fear God" (Genesis 22:12). The simple incident in Daniel's history when he refused the royal dainties and stuck to his simple fare, was an index to his entire character and demonstrated the fixed purpose, the inflexible principle, and the self-denying simplicity of the man whom God could depend upon in any test.

These may seem trifles, "but trifles make perfection, and perfection is no trifle." These may not be among "whatever is true and whatever is pure" (Philippians 4:8), but they are among "whatever is lovely" (4:8). And God wants us to be arrayed "in the splendor of his holiness" (Psalms 96:9), as well as "a robe of righteousness" (Isaiah 61:10). It is this that constitutes the difference between the justified and the sanctified, the clean robe and the marriage robe, the mere forgiveness of our sins and the great reward of him who overcomes.

God is giving us all along the way the opportunity of winning these victories, of putting on these wedding robes, of gaining these great rewards. Let us not miss the opportunity; let us not despise the proffered prize.

The soldiers of England and America have counted it the chance of a lifetime to be called to the post of danger and the opportunity of swift promotion. This is the way the heroes of Santiago, Manila, Dhargai and Glencoe, have looked upon their hardships and their dangers. And the verdict of history has already been pronounced, that, so far as earthly fame is worth contending for, they have not counted amiss or suffered in vain. And shall we who strive for a better crown think less of the promised prize, or complain when the trials come, through which we are permitted to win it? Shall we not rather meet every situation with holy and jealous care? Forge our future crowns out of our fiery trials? Turn opposition, temptation and suffering into occasions for putting on more fully all the graces of the Spirit and all the strength of Christ? So that at last we shall stand perfect and complete in all the will of God, with that happy company of whom it shall be said: "For the wedding of the Lamb has come,/ and his bride has made herself ready/ Fine linen, bright and clean,/ was given her to wear. (Fine linen stands for the righteous acts of the saints.)" (Revelation 19:7). "They follow the Lamb wherever he goes . . . No lie was found in their mouths; they are blameless" (14:4–5).

CHAPTER 4

THE CHRISTIAN TEMPER, SUPERNATURAL AND DIVINE

I want to know Christ and the power of his resurrection and the fellowship of sharing in his sufferings, becoming like him in his death, and so, somehow, to attain to the resurrection from the dead. (Philippians 3:10–11)

The temper of which we have been speaking is not natural but supernatural. This delicate plant is not indigenous to the soil of time, but must be transplanted from heavenly soil and grow from a supernatural seed. We talk about innocent babies, angelic maidens and lovely dispositions, but these things all disappear when the real test comes, and we find ourselves like one sitting down on a beautiful mossy bank covered with verdure and bloom, and suddenly seeing the poisonous asp glide from beneath our seat. The life described in this heavenly picture must come from a heavenly source, and is possible only after the natural has died out and the resurrection life of Christ has taken its place.

In our text the apostle describes by a reference to his own experience the evolution of the Christian temper.

1. A Natural Virtue

There is such a thing as natural virtue. There are moral differences in human nature, and God does not disparage or deprecate whatever goodness still remains after the wreck of the fall. Paul acknowledges that even he had been possessed of many qualities of virtue and morality. If any man had cause to have confidence in himself, surely he had. He gives a list of his virtues, and moral and religious advantages. He was strictly orthodox, born of Hebrew blood, circumcised according to the rigid ritual of Judaism, a "Hebrew of the Hebrews," a Pharisee of the Pharisees, blameless so far as outward righteousness was concerned, and intensely earnest so far as religious zeal could go. Yet all this he renounces and disclaims with one emphatic sentence, "But whatever was to my profit I now consider loss for the sake of Christ" (Philippians 3:7).

2. Renounce Our Own Righteousness

In order to receive the righteousness of Christ we must renounce all our own righteousness. The surrender which Christianity demands is not the abandoning of evil, but the renouncing of even that which is good for the sake of God's better and best. All his own righteousness and all his own rights Paul gladly surrendered. He had counted them loss. He had suffered their loss and then he had not allowed one lingering regret, one reluctant thought, but counted them all refuse, not worthy to speak about in comparison with the excellence of the knowledge and the glory of the righteousness of his precious Lord. He had accepted a new righteousness by faith from Christ, and it was all divine. He does not mean by this merely his justification from past sin through the imputed righteousness of Christ; but he means that he had accepted from his Lord an interior, intrinsic and personal righteousness, that his inward character and whole nature henceforth were not the result of self-culture but the infusion of the very life and spirit of his blessed Master.

3. A Deeper Place of Surrender

There is a deeper place of surrender than the renunciation of our righteousness. "I want to know Christ . . . and the fellowship of sharing in his sufferings" (3:10). Merely to die to our sinfulness or our righteousness is but a preliminary of holy character. The essence of it is to enter into the most profound and perfect union with the Lord Jesus even to the extent of longing to be made partakers of His very sufferings.

I once knew a Christian friend who offered this singular prayer for a loved one, and I know nothing that ever impressed me more. "Lord," she said, "I ask Thee that Thou wilt lay on me all the burdens, sufferings, trials and needs of my friend. I do not ask to share the joys, but I do ask if there be pain, pressure, danger, that I can bear, to lay it upon me in sympathy, fellowship, prayer, and the power to lift and help so that the life for which I suffer may be the more free to serve and work for Thee."

Love always longs to bear another's pain, and so the heart of the apostle intensely longed to share the sufferings of Christ. There is a sense in which this may be done if we live near enough to His heart.

There are some sufferings which we cannot call the sufferings of Christ. They are our own. The sufferings which we bring upon ourselves by sin or folly we have no right to call His sufferings. The sufferings that come to us even through sickness we may lay on Him, for He has already borne them, and He does not ask us to bear them again if we are walking in His will and trusting in His Word. The reproaches and persecutions, as we call them, which we bring upon ourselves by indiscretion or wrongdoing, these are not the sufferings of Christ, although He lovingly helps us in the trials which we needlessly endure.

Then He had sufferings which we cannot share. His vicarious suffering as our Substitute and Sacrifice for sin, we can never endure and never need to. Once for all He has appeared to "do away with sin by the sacrifice of himself" (Hebrews 9:26), and "no sacrifice for sins is left" (10:26).

But there are sufferings which we may share with Him. There was His voluntary self-sacrifice for the world's salvation into which we may enter as we give ourselves for others and sacrifice the pleasures of the world that we may walk with Him. There is again the misunderstanding and loneliness, persecution and distress which will come to all who live godly in Christ Jesus in every age, and which we may joyfully accept, counting it a privilege that we are esteemed worthy to suffer for the name of Jesus. And deeper than all, there is the spirit of sympathy with the suffering around us, the tempted and tried, the sorrows and even the sins of a lost world. This is the deepest element in the priesthood of Christ which His disciples may share. "For we do not have a high priest who is unable to sympathize with our weaknesses" (4:15). The Christlike life will enter with Him into His deep sense of the needs of others, into the ministry of prayer and agony for the sins and sorrows of men and into His deepest thoughts and tenderest solicitude for the lost world. Paul tells us in his epistles of the burdens, care and griefs that came upon him constantly for the cause of His Master and the condition of his brethren.

Now in his letter to the Colossians he tells us, "Now I rejoice in what was suffered for you, and I fill up in my flesh what is still lacking in regard to Christ's afflictions, for the sake of his body, which is the church" (1:24). That is to say, Christ has left certain sufferings for His body, the Church, to finish, and Paul rejoiced in being partaker of these sufferings. Writing to the Philippians he says of this very thing, "But even if I am being poured out like a drink offering on the sacrifice and service coming from your faith, I am glad and rejoice with all of you. So you too should be glad and rejoice with me" (2:17). It was his joy and glory to be a living sacrifice for his beloved brethren, and he expected them to respond in the same spirit, "Carry each other's burdens, and in this way you will fulfill the law of Christ" (Galatians 6:2). And accordingly in one of his letters to the Corinthians, he exclaims, "Who is weak, and I do not feel weak? Who is led into sin, and I do not inwardly burn? Besides everything else, I face daily the pressure of my concern for all the churches" (2 Corinthians 11:29, 28).

4. Becoming Like Him in His Death

There is one step more. "Becoming like him in his death" (Philippians 3:10). The difference between suffering and death is that there is no suffering after death. The dead man is one whom the suffering has ceased to hurt, and when we are truly conformable unto Christ's death, we are in that happy place where the promise of Jeremiah is true, "It does not fear when heat comes,/ . . . It has no worries in a year of drought/ and never fails to bear fruit" (Jeremiah 17:8). The people that are always talking about their deadness are not yet dead. The people who are fond of dwelling on their sufferings have not yet become like him in His death. To be dead with Christ is to be as if we were not, and to so recognize ourselves in Him that we shall not know our old selves, and shall even think and speak of ourselves as Paul when he said, "I [knew] a man in Christ . . . fourteen years ago" (2 Corinthians 12:2). It was as if it were another, and not himself. It is not to die with Christ that the apostle is speaking of, but it is to *be dead* with Christ. This everlasting dying is not deadness, but it is aliveness. Many are like the cowardly Nero, who when pursued by his enemies, stabbed himself in a score of places, but was careful every time to avoid a fatal part. The place of victory and rest is where we are really dead, and so dead that we have even ceased to be conscious of it, and are conscious only of Christ and the resurrection life which has come to us through Him.

5. Spiritual Resurrection

But now we come to something far more important than this, namely, the spiritual resurrection by which we are able to enter into the sufferings and death of our Lord. Now this whole passage is a perfect paradox, and runs directly contrary to the natural order of logical thought. In such an order we would expect the death to come first and the resurrection afterwards, but here it is quite different. It is "the power of his resurrection" first, then the "fellowship of his sufferings" and the conformity to His death. The explanation of this leads us to the deepest spiritual truths. We can never truly suffer or die with Christ by mere willpower or in stern, cold, dead surrender. We can never do it truly until we have first entered into His life, and are enabled for it by the power of life, hope and love. The reason the Lord Jesus was able to stoop to the very grave and lay down all His rights and honors was because He had so much above and beyond all this in His Father's love and His own eternal glory, that the sacrifice and surrender could not really harm or impoverish Him. His life was not in the things He laid down, but in the things He could not lose; and it was for the joy set before Him that He endured the cross, scorning the shame (Hebrews 12:2). The power of an endless life was filling all His being and gave Him strength to make the mighty sacrifice and go down among the dead, because just before Him He saw the brightness of the resurrection, the glory of the ascension and the kingdom of the coming age. And so His people must know the power of His resurrection and the fellowship of His glory, before they can in any true spirit enter into the fellowship of His sufferings and the partnership of His death.

How was it that the patriarch Abraham was able to sacrifice on the altar of Moriah, him in whom all his hopes, as well as affections, were bound up, and with whom all the promises of God's covenant were inseparably connected? It was only because of the power of His resurrection which Abraham had already felt and seen. In commenting on this scene the apostle explains to the Hebrews that he esteemed that "Abraham reasoned that God could raise the dead, and figuratively speaking, he did receive Isaac back from death" (11:19). This makes it certain that Abraham confidently expected Isaac's resurrection before he offered him up to death.

We can see this plainly even in the Old Testament narrative, when he said to the attendant, "Stay here with the donkey while I and the boy go over there. We will worship and then we will come back to you" (Genesis 22:5). He certainly expected to return with Isaac, and it was this blessed hope and this triumphant faith that took the sting from his sorrow and gave life and victory to his awful sacrifice.

And so we must have the spring of divine joy and victorious faith before we can stoop to a true surrender. It is not yielding to blind fate; it is not giving up in dark despair. It is simply entering the dark tunnel, knowing that the light of home is on the farther side, and that we have a hope and a certainty which even death itself cannot destroy.

Indeed, beloved friends, we cannot yield in anything acceptably to God, unless we have the life and strength of God within us to make it possible and real. We are not even able to consecrate ourselves in our own strength. We must take His life for all, even for the surrender, and through the power of His resurrection enter into His death and share the fellowship of His sufferings. This takes the spirit of asceticism out of Christian life, and crowns our very sacrifice with all the joy and the glory of victorious faith. It is faith that works by love and overcomes the world and even the grave.

Be assured, beloved brethren, that this is the deepest secret of spiritual life. There is no merit in enforced suffering or unwilling sacrifice. God asks no sacrifice from you until it is such joy that it has ceased to be a sacrifice. He wants no tears of reluctance on His altar; but He wants our hearts to come with willing, joyful yieldedness, and count it a privilege and honor that He will condescend to take us, own us, and make the best of our worthless lives. The spirit of the New Testament is this, radiant and bright with the light of love and promise.

Therefore, I urge you, brothers, in view of God's mercy, to

offer your bodies as living sacrifices, holy and pleasing to God—
this is your spiritual act of worship. Do not conform any longer
to the pattern of this world, but be transformed by the renewing
of your mind. Then you will be able to test and approve what
God's will is—his good, pleasing, and perfect will. (Romans
12:1–2)

6. The Light of Hope

Once more, we have not only the light of faith, but the still more radiant
light of hope, as the inspiration of this glad surrender: "and so, somehow, to
attain to the resurrection from the dead" (Philippians 3:11). There can be
no doubt about the application of this passage to the resurrection of God's
prepared people, who are to rise and meet the Bridegroom at His glorious
coming. It is not a general resurrection of all the dead, but it is a select resurrection and an elect company who are taken from among the rest of the
dead. It is the resurrection described in the 20th chapter of Revelation where
the crowned ones come forth to sit on the millennial throne with their
regent Lord,

> (The rest of the dead did not come to life until the thousand
> years were ended.) This is the first resurrection. Blessed and holy
> are those who have part in the first resurrection. The second
> death has no power over them, but they will be priests of God
> and of Christ and will reign with him for a thousand years.
> (Revelation 20:5–6)

This was the hope which inspired the apostle to let all else go, and rise in
the present life to the highest and holiest possibilities of Christian experience
and communion with his Lord. For this he counted all but loss, and said he
was still striving for something unto which he had not yet fully attained. It is
very solemn to hear this extraordinary man, even at this ripe stage of his life,
speaking of the blessed hope of the first resurrection as something to which
he had not yet surely attained. Later, in his second letter to Timothy, it is
different. He speaks of it there as a crown that is laid up for him, a fight that
is fought, a race that is run, a course that is finished, and a prize that is sure.
But in this chapter he is still pressing on to gain it, and it is the inspiration
of his glorious career. Shall it be the inspiration of our lives?

Is it not true even in the nature of things that our inward character takes
on its appropriate outward form? It is part of the law of the fitness of things
that the coarse and grovelling nature of the swine should be embodied in the
gross form of the hog; that the deep and subtle, cunning serpent should take
shape in the slimy, crawling reptile; and that the gentleness of the dove

should be expressed in its downy bosom and its gentle, lovely form. Do we not see this in human character? Do we not find character expressing itself in the personal appearance? Does not the criminal become stereotyped with the lines of cruelty, hardness and coarseness in his very visage? Does not purity, gentleness and nobility stamp its effect on the brow of the good and cover the sweet face of some aged saint with a beauty and glory that shine from the sacred Holy of holies within? Have we not all looked upon faces that were an absolute reflection of the transparent life that we knew was there behind the lovely countenance, and have we not looked upon countenances that were but the outward photograph of the dark, deep, dreadful hell that was raging in the heart beneath? And if this be in so great a measure true in this imperfect state, how much more will it be realized in that world where the law of the fitness of things shall be absolute and eternal. There Judas shall not only find his own place, but be clothed with his own form. There the wicked shall come creeping forth from their dark tombs with all the meanness, malignity and terror of their past lives and their future doom expressed in their terrific personality. And there the holy and the good shall rise with every feature beaming, and every movement telling of the gladness within and the glory that is to come.

Yes, we are forging our crowns day by day. We are weaving our triumphal robes. We are making our eternal destiny. We are settling into our final place. And the glory which the Master is preparing for each of us, He is working into us now in the firstfruits of the Spirit, who is "a deposit guaranteeing our inheritance until the redemption of those who are God's possession" (Ephesians 1:14).

"Grant," cried the mother of two disciples, "that one of these two sons of mine may sit at your right and the other at your left in your kingdom" (Matthew 20:21). The Master did not refuse her behest, but He told them very solemnly that it was largely in their own hands, and that these places of honor were to be given by the Father to those for whom they were prepared. He also showed very plainly what this preparation meant by the question: "Can you drink the cup I am going to drink" (20:22)? Thus alone could they enter into His glory, "If we died with him,/ we will also live with him;/ if we endure,/ we will also reign with him" (2 Timothy 2:11–12).

CHAPTER 5

THE CHRISTIAN TEMPER, AGGRESSIVE
AND PROGRESSIVE

*Not that I have already obtained all this, or have already been
made perfect, but I press on to take hold of that for which Christ
Jesus took hold of me. Brothers, I do not consider myself yet to have
taken hold of it. But one thing I do: Forgetting what is behind and
straining toward what is ahead, I press on toward the goal to win
the prize for which God has called me heavenward in Christ Jesus.
(Philippians 3:12–14)*

It might be supposed that a spirit of sweetness would necessarily be a spirit
of weakness, and that a yielded and gentle disposition is lacking in the spirit
of forceful aggressiveness and manly energy. This is not always true. The
bravest soldier is often the gentlest man. The quiet forces of nature are the
most irresistible and overwhelming, and the strength of God is often hidden
behind His gentleness.

And so this passage proves that the man who could be most yielding,
tender and affectionate, could stand adamant or sweep like the cyclone. This
fine passage has about it something that reminds us of the clarion call of the
trumpet summoning to arms and to victory, something that suggests the atmosphere of the arena where men struggle for the mastery and where crowns
are dearly won.

The spirit of our age is marked by physical culture. Our young people are
taught in schools, universities and colleges to train for athletic skill and
physical strength. This is perhaps carried to an extreme degree as it was in
the luxurious days of ancient Rome which preceded the final catastrophe. At
least, it expresses a longing in the soul for manly energy, and may well
stimulate us to the higher pursuit of spiritual manhood and aggressive force-
fulness. If the flower of our manhood is contending in the athletic arena or
on the field of battle for the prizes of victory, how much more should we

strive for a crown that is incorruptible and a glory which does not fade?

This is the picture of our text. It is the spectacle of a man pressing forward in the racecourse with muscles strained to their utmost tension, with nerves alert and senses all alive to every advantage of the fray, and with his whole being intensely absorbed in the struggle for a prize which is flashing before his kindling eye from the open heavens where the great Umpire stands beckoning him on and holding out the glorious diadem.

There are three important features in the picture, full of precious lessons for us who with him are also in the race.

A SPIRIT OF SELF-DISSATISFACTION

"Not that I have already obtained all this, or have already been made perfect, . . . I do not consider myself yet to have taken hold of it" (3:12–13). There is nothing that so deadens the spiritual activities and aspirations as an overwhelming self-complacency. If we look at mere human standards, or even our own ideals, we shall easily be satisfied. The story of the artist who turned away from his perfect and finished workmanship with a cry of despair, "I have surpassed myself; henceforth there is nothing left for my ambition," is a true glimpse of the paralyzing power of a too-easy self-content. It needs the sense of our own shortcomings to incite us to nobler endeavors. There is a discouraging way of looking at your faults and failures which takes all the heart out of you. But there is a wholesome mean between conceit and self-condemnation which is the fruitful soil of new endeavor and loftier aspiration.

In two respects Paul felt that he had up to this time failed to reach the full ideal. First, he had not yet obtained the prize or made sure of it. This word translated *attained* (KJV) ought to be rendered *obtained* [which the modern NIV uses]. He is not referring to character but to reward. A little later he felt he had secured it, and in writing to Timothy he could say, "I have fought the good fight, I have finished the race, I have kept the faith. Now there is in store for me the crown of righteousness" (2 Timothy 4:7).

Next, however, he adds, "or have already been made perfect" (Philippians 3:12). This should be translated "perfected," and it refers to personal character and attainment. What then does the apostle mean when later in the paragraph he adds, "All of us who are mature [perfect, KJV] should take such a view of things" (3:15)? How can he be perfect if he is not yet perfect? The answer will be plain if we paraphrase his statement in a very simple form. We are perfect but not perfected. We are complete but not completed. "And you have been given fullness [are complete, KJV] in Christ" (Colossians 2:10), says the apostle to the Colossians, and yet in the same epistle he adds, "that you may stand firm in all the will of God, mature and fully assured [perfect and complete, KJV]" (4:12). There is a sense, a true sense in which we may accept the righteousness and grace of the Lord Jesus Christ and count it real and sufficient, and dare to say, "He is made unto me sanctification," and "I am complete in Him." As far as our faith goes, as far as our light goes, we are fully saved. We are all there in Christ just as fully as the newborn baby is complete in all its parts. But it is not yet full-grown. It has all the organs its father has, but they are yet immature. It is complete but not completed. It is perfect but not perfected. And so the consecrated soul that has taken Christ in His fullness has Him in His fullness, but yet there is to be a deeper revelation and larger fullness step by step and day by day, until at last he shall reach the "whole measure of the fullness of Christ" (Ephesians 4:13).

Do not let us, therefore, depreciate ourselves too much or fail to recognize our glorious standing and our heavenly place in Christ Jesus our Lord. But do not let us, at the same time, forget how much there still remains to be possessed, and standing midway between the confidence of faith and the aspiration of hope, let us press on from strength to strength, from faith to faith, from grace to glory.

A SPIRIT OF HEAVENLY ASPIRATION AND HOLY AGGRESSIVENESS

Along with this sense of shortcoming there comes to the apostle the deep, intense desire to press on to all that yet remains in his inheritance of grace. The picture is an intense one. It flashes with the light of the arena; it rings with the bugle notes of battle and triumph. It sweeps on with the celerity of the cavalry charge and the triumphal march. There is something about its phrases that stirs our very hearts, and makes every drop of blood to throb with strange intensity. It is a soul in earnest. It is a heart aflame. It is a life all aglow with divine enthusiasm and superhuman strength. It is no soft sentimentalism, but it is spiritual manhood in the glory of its mightiest strength. It is the athlete in the arena. It is the conqueror on the field of victory.

1. Forgetting the Past

"Forgetting what is behind" (Philippians 3:13). There is much behind and it is not to be despised, but it is not to be a pillow of soft and indolent repose to stifle and satisfy our higher ambition. Compared with all that is yet before us it is only a foundation. And the larger that foundation is the mightier must be the superstructure that is to crown it. Suppose that you were to point me to a massive pile of brick and stone on some splendid site no higher than the foundation walls of some great building, and tell me with exultant pride of the deep excavations, the costly carvings and the splendid building you had erected. I would laugh in your face as I looked at the cel-

lars flooded with the storm, the walls crumbling under the destroying elements, the rubbish accumulating on the terraces, and the very creatures of
the wilderness finding a lair and hiding place amid the rubbish. I would say
to you, "The very grandeur of your foundation calls for a still grander superstructure. It is ridiculous for you to boast of what you have already done
until these walls have been reared at least a dozen stories higher, and the roof
has enclosed these spaces and the chambers are divided and adorned in a
manner worthy of your costly beginnings." And so the more God has done
for you already, the more need there is that you should look well to it, "that
you do not lose what you have worked for, but that you may be rewarded
fully" (2 John 8).

2. A Right Concept of the Future

"Straining toward what is ahead" (Philippians 3:13). Man differs from the
lower orders of creation in this, that while like them his past is limited by
the little space of time since his existence, unlike them his future is unlimited; his lifetime is eternity. He is endowed with the divine gift of an immortal future. He has the ages upon ages yet to come in which to expand
and develop forevermore.

When Alexander the Great divided his old dominion among his faithful
followers, he kept nothing for himself. They asked him in surprise about his
portion. "What have you kept for yourself?" they said, and he pointed into
the distance and simply said, "Hope." The future was his inheritance, and
before many months had passed that future had brought him an empire
vaster than all he had given away, and mightier than the world ever knew.

And so God is teaching us to live in the imperial realm of hope. There are
souls who have no eyes for the future. They cannot see over the heads of the
things that immediately surround them. They live in the present, and they
are baffled by their immediate difficulties, toils and troubles. Life for them is
enclosed by the boundaries of the setting sun. But there are other souls who
see into life's tomorrow, and over the head of difficulty, disaster and even
death itself. They see evermore the eternal morning, and they sing, "it is better farther on." The things that are not are to them more real than the things
that are. Faith and hope create a world yet unrevealed and yet most real,
which satisfies and stimulates their triumphant spirits as they press on to the
things that are before.

Beloved, ask God to give you a sanctified imagination, a quickened vision
of the unseen, a power to see what others cannot see, and to hear what
others do not hear. May He put eternity in your heart and make your life as
large as the immeasurable years on which God has projected the orbit of
your being.

3. Following After

Having turned from the past and caught the vision of the future he now presses on to meet it. The figure is that of the hunter pursuing the coveted game. There is a strange fascination in this. Men will follow a trail for days and weeks to get a single moose up in the woods of Maine, and after exposure, toil and suffering will feel amply repaid by a single specimen of the splendid quarry. Mile after mile the snow-covered forest is traversed over windfalls, morasses, pitfalls and perils which they would not think of encountering in the sober business of life. But it is nothing to them as they pursue their prey with a fascination that takes away all sense of toil or computation of time. So, when God has given the glowing vision of His highest will, nothing is hard or long in its attainment. Step by step through toil and trial the soul presses on for the crown incorruptible and the heavenly goal.

Beloved, are you as much in earnest about the best things as you are for your pleasures, recreations or your earthly gain? Let this lofty standard measure our individual lives.

4. Pressing Toward the Goal

"I press on toward the goal" (Philippians 3:14). The language is intense. It is the expression of the most profound earnestness of which a human soul is capable. It is no child's play. It is no sentimental dream. It is no incidental mood. It is no mere occasional fit of transient enthusiasm. It is the habit of the life. It is the sweep of the volcano down the mountain side which carries everything in its course and transforms everything into its fiery torrent. Beloved, it is a life in earnest. Is it yours?

5. Singleness of Purpose

Singleness of purpose is the secret of this successful and intensely earnest life. "But one thing I do" (3:13). The grandeur of his great purpose eclipses all other aims and excludes all competing interests. Our life is too short and too small to be scattered in a dozen directions. We can be our best only as we let God compact us and press us with all His power and all the strenuousness of our strength in one direction, and that, of course, the highest and the best. Beloved, is this the single purpose of your life? You have but one life. God help you to give it all to Him and gain it all from Him in its glorious outcome.

THE DIVINE COOPERATION

There is more than the figure of the spiritual athlete pressing on for the prize. There is another Form in this picture that is standing behind him and helping him on. Or, to change the metaphor, the glorious Umpire at the heavenly goal is not an indifferent spectator, coolly waiting to give the crowns to the conquering ones without any personal interest as to who shall overcome. No, He is an interested partner in the race. He is bending from His throne and beckoning to the racer as he runs, and with encouraging smile and gesture of inspiration is calling to him: "Be of good cheer, press on. You will overcome. I am holding your hand as well as holding out your crown. I have overcome for you and you will overcome through Me." This is the finest part of the picture. Paul is not alone with his struggle; his Master is with him, and he is only apprehending that for which he has been also apprehended of Christ Jesus (3:12, KJV).

In three respects Christ cooperates with His people's heavenly aspirations.

1. He reveals the vision and the prize.

It is He who reveals the vision of the glory and the prize. A little later in the passage we read, "All of us who are mature should take such a view of things. And if on some point you think differently, that too God will make clear to you" (3:15). Perhaps this glowing picture has not appealed to all your hearts. Perhaps there are some simple commonplace lives who have said, "I have no imagination, I have no opportunity for these glorious things. My task is one of lowly toil and ceaseless drudgery. I try to do my duty as best I can, but I don't understand the exalted feelings of which you have been telling me. This is not for me."

Beloved, "And if on some point you think differently, that too God will make clear to you" (3:15).

There was a time when it was nothing to Paul but a light in his heart above the brightness of the sunshine. Then God revealed to him another world of reality, and gave him the spiritual senses to discern it and dwell in it. The same revelation will come to you if you humbly ask and wait for it.

A lady in London once called upon Dr. Boardman and complained to him that she had no spiritual feeling. The good doctor turned to Ephesians 3:20: "Now to him who is able to do immeasurably more than all we ask or imagine." He told her to go home and pray over that one verse until God made it fully real to her, and then come back and tell him when her experience measured up to it. She went away and continued for many days to pray that one prayer, not expecting much from it at first. But one day she came back to see the good minister. With eyes moist with tears and lips trembling with holy gladness, she told him that no language could describe, no prayer could express, no thought could compass, the unutterable fullness of joy which the Holy Spirit had poured into her heart. God had revealed even this to her.

I had a brother once on earth, now in heaven, who was very rigid and conservative in his ideas of religious experience. He looked upon all demonstrations of feeling as sentimental and unscriptural. He was much disgusted with many of the manifestations of spiritual power and earnestness connected with the early days of our own work. At length his health broke down, and he was manifestly drawing near to a great crisis. I endeavored in vain to bring him to that place of tender spiritual feeling where he could take Christ as his Healer or even as his Comforter. But it only met with recoil. Then the case was committed to God in believing prayer; and he waited. One day several months later, a letter came from that brother telling of a marvelous change. The day before while reading a verse in his Bible, a flood of light had burst in to his soul, and for hours he could only praise and pray and wonder. Yes, he, too, had become a fanatic, if this were fanaticism, and God had done exceeding abundantly above all that he could ask or think. His cold intellectual nature was submerged in a baptism of love which never ceased to pour its fullness through his being, until a few weeks later he swept through the gates of glory shouting the praises of his Redeemer.

Beloved, would you have the vision? "And if on some point you think differently, that too God will make clear to you" (Philippians 3:15).

2. He calls us to the prize.

"Of the high calling of God in Christ Jesus" (3:14, KJV), is translated better in the revised version, "the upward calling," or, better still in another version, "the prize to which he has called us from on high." God called Abraham in Mesopotamia, and he left all and followed. He called Moses in the desert, and he gave up everything to obey. He called Elisha from his plow, and he quickly responded. He called the disciples from their fishing nets, and they went with the Master. He called Paul, and he was "not disobedient unto the heavenly vision" (Acts 26:19, KJV). Beloved, He is calling you. Do not miss the call and the crown.

3. He holds our hand.

He is holding the hand of the competitor for the prize, and upholding him in the conflict. This expression, "obtained," literally means "grasped," and the apostle says that he is grasping that for which Christ has grasped him. There is a hand underneath. There is a power behind. There is a loving pressure that will not let him go. God loves us better than we love ourselves. In spite of ourselves, He is saving us to the uttermost and carrying us through to the fullness of His uttermost salvation. We are not alone. He will not let us fail.

CHAPTER 6

A SPIRIT OF LOVE, JOY AND PEACE

I plead with Euodia and I plead with Syntyche to agree with each other in the Lord. . . .

Rejoice in the Lord always. I will say it again: Rejoice! Let your gentleness be evident to all. The Lord is near. Do not be anxious about anything, but in everything, by prayer and petition, with thanksgiving, present your requests to God. (Philippians 4:2, 4–6)

This passage reaches the very heart of the sweetest Christian life. It combines the four choicest ingredients of the fruit of the Spirit namely, love, joy, peace and sweetness.

LOVE

The first is love. There are three kinds of love unfolded in these verses. The first is Paul's love to his friends and flock. How tenderly he addresses them: "My brothers" (3:1), he says, associating himself with them in the heavenly ties of the divine family. "You whom I love" (4:1), he adds, mingling with this holy relationship all the tenderness of human affection. And "long for" (4:1). This is more than tenderness. This is the affection that dwells continually on the beloved object, wearies of his absence and longs for fellowship and reunion. "My joy" (4:1), a still stronger expression of the dependence of his very happiness upon their fellowship and love. "And crown"(4:1), this carries forward the bonds of love and friendship to the eternal sphere, and links all his eternal hopes and rewards with his dearly beloved friends at Philippi. It was thus that the early Christians loved one another, and it is still true that "everyone who loves the father loves his child as well" (1 John 5:1).

Next, we have a reference to their mutual love of one another. Among the saints at Philippi were two sisters whose names signify "success" and "fame." They were evidently valued workers in the church, but, like many good women, they were not able to agree with each other in the same mind and judgment. Each was a woman of such strong character and individuality and such excellent common sense and judgment that she could not see how she could be wrong in her view of the matter, and her sister be right; and so they were frequently at variance, and their misunderstandings were evidently hurting the little flock. Paul does not reprove them or even enjoin them, but he gets down on his knees to one of them and asks his friend Epaphroditus to do the same with the other, and they just beseech them to "agree with each other in the Lord" (Philippians 4:2). This is very touching and humbling to us in our misunderstandings and strifes. Thus the Master is beseeching us to be of one mind and one spirit in the Lord.

But the best of all is that the apostle gives us here the secret of attaining to oneness of spirit, a thing not so easily done with strong and independent minds, especially when each is sure she is right. The secret is this, "in the Lord." Don't try to bring your sister to your mind. Don't try to come to her mind, but let each of you drop her own opinion and preference and move out of yourselves into the Lord, and agree jointly and severally to take His thought about it whatever it may be, and even before you know it. And you will always find that His mind about everything is one that does justice to both parties, and lifts both to a higher plane where they can be fully one.

At the same time the apostle entreats his friend to help them both, and he very distinctly tells him of their value and importance; for it is of them he speaks when he says they "contended at my side in the cause of the gospel" (4:3), and "Whose names are in the book of life" (4:3).

Then there is a third expression of love in the little phrase which he addresses to his own fellow laborer, "loyal yokefellow" (4:3). This tells not only of Paul's love to his friends but of their love to him. It is a beautiful figure and speaks of perfect fellowship and mutual service and suffering. The Lord Himself uses the same figure respecting His fellowship with us when He says: "Take my yoke upon you and learn from me, for I am gentle and humble in heart" (Matthew 11:29). How beautiful and blessed if we might be to each other as true yokefellows as our blessed and heavenly Friend has been to us!

JOY

Here again we have the same little talisman which tells the secret of the heavenly life, "in the Lord." We may not be able to rejoice in circumstances, feelings or even friends, but we can still rejoice in the Lord. This is the heavenly element of our joy. It comes entirely from sources beyond our own nature or surroundings, and it often contradicts every rational consideration and makes us wonder even at our own joy. It is the joy of Christ throbbing in the heart where He dwells. It was of this He spoke when He said, "I have told you this so that my joy may be in you and that your joy may be complete" (John 15:11).

Again, it is a constant, uninterrupted and unlimited joy. "Rejoice in the Lord always" (Philippians 4:4). There is positively no situation where we should cease to rejoice; no reason that could justify us in discouragement or depression. It is the normal, uniform and unvarying temper of the Christian life. "Your sun will never set again,/ and your moon will wane no more;/ the LORD will be your everlasting light,/ and your days of sorrow will end" (Isaiah 60:20). If the fig tree does not blossom, and the fruit is not upon the vine, we must still "rejoice in the LORD,/ . . . [and] be joyful in God my Savior" (Habakkuk 3:18).

If the dearest friends disappoint us or leave us, the Lord remains, and we must not cease our singing. If our own feelings even betray us, and our hearts seem dead and cold, still we must "Consider it pure joy" (James 1:2), though we do not feel it, and take by faith the gladness that we do not find in our own consciousness. And if trials roll over us like surging waves and raging billows, we must raise the keynote higher, and exchanging joy for triumph, we must "glory in tribulation also" (Romans 5:3, KJV).

Once more, this joy is persistent and refuses to be defeated or discouraged, for he repeats the command with strange insistence, and as though he were speaking against some barrier of difficulty, some cloud of discouragement, some weight of deep depression; "again," he adds, "I say rejoice" (Philippians 4:4). It is a redoubled command. It has a twofold significance, and whatever else we fail to do we must rejoice.

Now, dear friends, we do not say this is the uniform experience of the children of God. We are simply pointing out in this epistle the rarer and choicer qualities of the Christian temper. It is the ideal character if it is not always the real, and as we pursue the ideal and refuse to take lower ground, God will make it real. Do not, therefore, be discouraged if you have sometimes failed to reach this lofty and settled standard, and to dwell on high in this lofty poise of victorious gladness; but take it as your ideal, pursue it as your goal, claim it as your privilege. Remember that sadness, discouragement, depression, are always of the enemy and must surely weaken your faith, your love, your holiness, your usefulness, your healing, your prayers, your whole Christian life. Therefore, "Rejoice in the Lord always. I will say it again: Rejoice!" (4:4).

SWEETNESS OF SPIRIT

"Let your gentleness be evident to all" (4:5). The Greek word translated "gentleness" is difficult to turn into English, but the various meanings that have been given to it are all suggestive and helpful, and each has certain degrees of truth in it. The first of these is the Authorized Version, "moderation." This is the temperate spirit, the disciplined heart, the self-control which comes to a well-ordered mind, the quietness, sense and moderation which keep us from all extremes, and hold us in the golden mean of a sound mind.

Again, it has been translated "yieldedness." This is also a valuable trait of character. It marks the chastened spirit, the soul that has surrendered, the will that has been subdued, the heart that has learned to wait and sacrifice. This is one of the most valuable qualities of the highest Christian life.

Again it is translated "gentleness," the spirit of Christian refinement, free from harshness, rudeness, coarseness, unkindness, the spirit that is harmless as the dove and gentle as the soft breath of evening. This is always characteristic of the heart that is possessed by the heavenly Dove. It is also translated "humility," and there is no rarer or richer element in Christian loveliness than the lowly spirit, which has learned not so much to think less of itself as not to think at all of self; which takes its true place and never intrudes into another's; which never gets in the way of others, or asserts its self-importance, but leans, like John the beloved, on Jesus' breast, his face hidden on the Savior's bosom while the Master's alone is seen.

But the Syriac version has probably given us the most striking translation of this word. It is the word "sweetness." "Let your sweetness be known unto all men." It is that quality that probably blends all the qualities already named, and clothes us with the divine attractiveness that makes us a blessing to all we meet, a balm to the suffering, a rest to the weary, an inspiration to the depressed and a rebuke to the unkind. It is the quality which can "suffer long and be kind"; which can endure all with "great endurance and patience" (Colossians 1:11), and come through the flame without the smell of fire. We have seen it in some of His dear saints, and it was always manifest in Him. Let it be known unto all men. Do not hide it in your closet. Do not keep it for select occasions, but wear it as a beautiful garment. Shed it around you as a holy radiance. Take it into the bustling street until it breathes its fragrance on the agitated and excited ones around you. Carry it into the place where others wrong you or despise you, until it shall reprove them as your resentment never could. Show it to your enemies, and don't forget to show it to your friends. Pour it out in the home circle to husband, wife, child and friend, until all you meet shall feel as if a breath of summer and a gleam of sunshine had passed by. "Let your sweetness be known to all men."

Don't wait till people die to plant your flowers on their grave, but while they live shed the fragrance of love on their tired and tempted hearts. For all this the incentive and encouragement is given in the next brief sentence: "The Lord is near" (Philippians 4:5). Perhaps it means that the Lord is nearby watching you, testing you, ready to help and sustain you; and perhaps it means the Lord is coming soon, and all these trials will seem but little things in the light of that blessed hope and surpassing glory. "Let your sweetness therefore, be known to all men, for the Lord is at hand."

PEACE

"And the peace of God, which transcends all understanding, will guard your hearts and your minds in Christ Jesus" (4:7). Peace is the most precious of all the gifts and graces of the Spirit; so precious indeed is peace that it was the one legacy left us by our departing Lord. "Peace I leave with you; my peace I give you. I do not give to you as the world gives. Do not let your hearts be troubled and do not be afraid" (John 14:27). Joy may be more exciting, but peace is more sustaining. Joy may be the wine of life, but peace is its refreshing water and its daily bread.

Let us look a little more closely at this precious gift.

1. It is God's peace.

It is the "peace of God." It is not peace with God, which comes to us with forgiveness and salvation, but is the very peace of God Himself—His own calm, restful heart possessing ours, and filling us with His divine stillness.

2. It transcends understanding.

It is a "peace of God, which transcends all understanding" (Philippians 4:7). There is no rational explanation of it. It does not come to us by reasoning things out, and seeing our way clear, but it is often most profound when all the circumstances of our life are perplexing and distressing. It contradicts all conditions and constantly proves its heavenly origin and its supernatural birth. It is indeed the peace of God, and as wonderful as was His own calm, tranquil spirit when standing on the threshold of the garden and the cross.

I remember a Christian woman, for a long time a member of my church, on whom there suddenly fell the greatest sorrow that can come to a loving heart. It was the death of her husband, the companion of half a century of happy wedded life. She was a quiet, practical woman, with no natural emotion or sentiment in her temperament. But she had received the Holy Spirit years before and, in a very calm, consistent way, had been living a very devoted life. Hastening to her home I expected to find her plunged in deep distress, but she met me at the door with radiant face and overflowing joy. "My dear pastor," she cried, "my family all think that I am wrong to feel as I do, for I cannot shed a tear, and my heart is so happy that I cannot understand it. God has filled me with such a peace as passes all understanding, and I really cannot help rejoicing and praising Him all the time. What shall I do?" Of course I told her to rejoice with all her heart, and thank God that she could rejoice in such an hour. It was indeed the peace that passed all understanding. There was no human cause for it. It was the deep artesian well flowing from the heart of God.

3. It saves us from care.

It is the peace that saves us from anxious care. Its watchword is "Do not be anxious about anything" (4:6). It simply crowds out all our corroding anxieties and fills us with such satisfaction that there is really nothing that we can fear. No, nothing. The command is unconditional and unlimited. "Do not be anxious about anything." Not even for your spiritual life. Not even for your friends. Not even for the answers to your prayers. Not even for the highest and holiest things. Cast every burden on the Lord and trust everything with Him.

4. It leads to prayer.

It is a peace that leads to constant prayer and is sustained by a life of prayer. "But in everything, by prayer and petition, with thanksgiving, present your requests to God" (4:6). This does not mean that we are to be indifferent to the things that concern us or others, but that we are to be free from worry about them by handing them over to One who can attend to them better than we can, and who is already carrying the responsibility and the care. This is really the truest self-interest, to hand over our interest to a wisdom and a love superior to our own, and then we know that all must be well.

The word "supplication" is derived from a root that signifies "many ply." It refers to the minutiae of life and the innumerable details of life's cares and burdens, all of which we may bring, and bring again and again, to Him who cares for us, and then leave them at His feet and know that they are safe in His keeping.

5. It fills the heart with thankfulness.

It is a peace that fills the heart with constant thankfulness and the lips with praise. Our prayers are turned to praise, and as we thank Him for what we have, we have new cause for more thanksgiving. The surest way to receive answers to our prayers is to praise for what we have received, and then to praise for what we have not yet received. A life of peace leads to a life of praise, and a life of praise in turn leads to a life of peace. There are some natures that always see the dark side first. There are some that can see only the sunshine, the silver lining and the coming morning.

6. It guards our heart.

This peace is the guardian and the garrison of our heart. It keeps us, or, in the meaning of the Greek word, "garrisons" us, shutting out unhappy and unholy thoughts, and creating an atmosphere out of which only righteousness and blessing can spring.

7. It keeps our heart and mind.

It keeps our heart and mind—the heart first, and then the mind in consequence. It is not the mind first and then the heart, but it is heart foremost,
that the sweetest Christian life always moves. Would you know the remedy
for anxious, distracting and ill-regulated thoughts? It is a heart kept by the
peace of God, and still as ocean's depths where the surging billows that toss
the surface into angry foam never come. This is the very element and atmosphere where faith and love may dwell deep in the heart of God. This is "the
peace of God, which transcends all understanding."

CHAPTER 7

WHATEVER IS LOVELY

Finally, brothers, whatever is true, whatever is noble, whatever is right, whatever is pure, whatever is lovely, whatever is admirable— if anything is excellent or praiseworthy—think about such things. (Philippians 4:8)

This passage expresses the very point of the apostle's subject in this letter, and by one discriminating flash of light points out the difference between the essentials of holy character and the lighter touches of grace and loveliness which may be added to these.

Two classes of virtues are here specified, and each class is designated by a special word: "If anything is excellent" called fundamental and essential to holy character; "or praiseworthy," denotes those qualities, which, while not essential, are ornamental.

The first class includes three specifications, namely, "whatever is true, . . . whatever is right, whatever is pure." Without these there can be no morality and no religion. These are the cardinal virtues of life, the solid texture out of which the web is woven, the warp and woof on which the other qualities are embroidered as decorations and adornings.

The second class includes also three specifications. "Whatever is noble." This ought to be translated honorable, venerable, lofty, for it denotes not so much practical righteousness as rather the qualities that demand admiration and veneration. Next, "whatever is lovely," those qualities that are inherently beautiful and attractive, and make the possessor to be esteemed and beloved. The third specification is "whatever is admirable," or those things that constitute influence, reputation and public esteem and respect. These are objects of praise and are to be added to the others. The qualities of virtue are like the solid granite rock; the qualities of praise resemble the luxuriant forest, the verdant grass, the mossy banks, the blooming shrubs and flowers, the sparkling waterfalls that cover those substantial rocks and turn the desert into a garden of beauty and delight. Let us look at these two classes of moral qualities, but especially the second.

MORAL QUALITIES

1. The essentials of character.

There are three essentials of character. The first is truth. Our religious character must be founded upon right principles, and having adopted them we must be true to them. Truth must be at once objective and subjective. We must have the truth, and we must be true to it. Sound doctrine must be held by a sound and sincere heart.

Next, "whatever is right," covers the whole range of our relationships to our fellowmen, our practical righteousness, our rightness of life in the family, in the social world, and in our business fellowships with others.

Finally, "whatever is pure," has reference to our own personal life. It describes a heart cleansed by the blood of Christ, filled with holy motives, thoughts and affections and leading to right relations toward all men and toward God. These are the essential qualities of the Christian life. Without them there can be no morality and no religion.

2. The graces of Christian character.

But next are the graces of Christian character, "the beauties of holiness" (Psalm 110:3, KJV), as the Old Testament expresses it. One may be a Christian without these, but not without those mentioned before. They are the refinements of holy character—the lesser touches by which perfection is attained. Even as the marble is polished by a thousand little touches. The difference between an ordinary copy and a work of genius lies in minute details which the coarse, uncultivated eye might never be able to detect.

Now, some of these graces are connected with the cardinal virtues already described. That is to say, there are people who may be said to be truthful, and who would not deliberately misrepresent, yet they will exaggerate, they will shade the truth by little touches and faint colorings which practically do misrepresent and mislead. Then, again, there are some who are, in the main, honest, just and righteous, and would not willfully or knowingly do another a wrong. Yet perhaps they are too careless or too keen, and by little touches of unrighteousness mar the testimony of their lives. Then there are others who are pure in their purpose and intent, but it may be in their dress, manners, deportment or conversation, compromise their influence enough to miss the full effectiveness of a holy life. Thus it becomes important to give heed to the message: "Do not allow what you consider good to be spoken of as evil" (Romans 14:16), and even in the things that are just and pure and true, to be careful to add the "things that are lovely" and "admirable."

ANOTHER CLASS OF QUALITIES

But there is a distinct field, represented by another class of qualities altogether, which constitute the graces and refinements of the holy life, and of which it is true "You should have practiced the latter without leaving the former undone" (Luke 11:42).

1. Dignity and Self-respect

Dignity and self-respect are the things that add to the weight of our character and influence and may be covered by the first phase, "whatever is true," or rather, "venerable." The estimate which others place upon us will always be proportioned to our true estimate of ourselves. There is a great difference between conceit and self-respect. "Don't let anyone look down on you" (1 Timothy 4:12), is the dictate at once of true instinct and Holy Scripture. The Lord Jesus always bore Himself with true dignity, and allowed no person to be too familiar. Even the disciple that leaned upon His breast looked up to Him with sacred awe. We can be simple, unaffected and humble, and yet carry ourselves with the holy dignity of the sons and daughters of God. Paul was a fine example of true manliness. When unjustly imprisoned, he refused to sneak out and run away, but manfully answered, "They beat us publicly without a trial, even though we are Roman citizens, and threw us into prison. And now do they want to get rid of us quietly? No! Let them come themselves and escort us out" (Acts 16:37). The soul in which the Holy Spirit dwells will always carry itself with sacred loftiness, as well as sweet humility. This is the safeguard of woman, and the glory of man.

2. Necessary Modesty

Modesty is as necessary as dignity, and at once corrects it and adorns it. It does not lower our self-respect, but it simply veils us with the beautiful covering of self-unconsciousness. You may always know John, the beloved, by the fact that he never mentions himself, but speaks of the "disciple whom Jesus loved" (John 13:23). When Moses' face shone with the brightest glow, he did not know that it shone at all. When beauty is conscious of itself it becomes disgusting. When talent and genius begin to show off, then they sink below contempt. When spiritual gifts and holy services are used to glorify the possessor or the worker, then they become objects of derision and lose their merit.

The seraphim not only covered their faces but their feet with their wings, and tried to hide not only their beauty but their work. God gives us the sweetly chastened spirit that bows its head and stands veiled with heavenly modesty.

3. Personal Habits

Personal habits have much to do with the loveliness of our character and our lives. While we do not believe with that old lady that "cleanliness is next to godliness," yet we certainly believe that cleanliness stands near to godliness. While we do not go so far as to denounce chewing, smoking and snuffing as the basest of crimes, yet it is enough to say that they are not among the things that are lovely, venerable or of good report. And there are a thousand other things which a sanctified soul will learn, by holy intuition and watchfulness, to lay aside as defects if not defilements.

4. Refinement and Courtesy

Good manners, refinement, and courtesy are among the things that are lovely and attractive in our Christian example. There is an affectation of refinement that is but the gloss and the counterfeit, but the true follower of Jesus Christ will always be gentle and gentlemanly, considerate of others and careful to avoid offense, and will act toward all with whom he comes in contact with that thoughtful consideration and courteous politeness which speak so strongly for Christ. After the greatest gentleman in Europe, Lord Chesterfield, had spent a few days with Archbishop Fénelon, who was as sweet as he was saintly, he remarked, "If I had stayed much longer I should have been charmed into accepting his religion." "Be courteous" is one of the commands of the Holy Spirit. The Christian lady and the Christian gentleman will carry their good manners into the kitchen and the factory, as well as into the social circle; the wife will be as polite to her husband and her cook as she is to the fashionable caller in the afternoon. The parent will be as gentle and considerate in speaking to his child, as when called to receive some distinguished visitor, or in wearing some courtly air on a great public occasion. Let us adorn the little things and the commonplaces of life with that "great . . . love," which "the Father has lavished on us" (1 John 3:1), and which He would have us reflect.

5. Propriety

Propriety, good sense, and the instinct of knowing the fitness of things, and always acting with good taste are among the most charming features of a well-balanced character. It is what the apostle calls, "the spirit . . . of a sound mind" (2 Timothy 1:7, KJV). The Lord Jesus was always on time and in order. We never find Him making a mistake or doing an unbecoming thing. And so of divine love it is said, "It is not rude, it is not self-seeking, it is not easily angered, it keeps no record of wrongs" (1 Corinthians 13:5). A very simple remark, if appropriate to the occasion, is more effective then the most eloquent speech which is out of place. The Holy Spirit will give the heavenly quality of doing the right thing at the right time and in the right manner.

6. Fitting Speech

A well-balanced character will display wise and fitting speech, a well-governed tongue and a discreet pen. Briefly, fitness in the use of words. This has much to do with the effectiveness of our lives and the attractiveness of our example. To be able to state in a few brief words the matter about which you wish to confer, to come quickly to the point and stop when you get there—what a rare gift! To be able to put on the first page of your letter the exact idea that you mean to express, and to get to the point of your subject before you exhaust the patience and interest of your correspondent, these are things that do not require so much education as consideration. The conversational bore not only wearies his listener, but must often weary the Lord Himself.

Such errors largely arise either from selfishness, self-consciousness or lack of consideration for others. These are little things, but they are the flies that spoil the ointment or the touches that polish the workmanship and glorify the grace of God. Reserve in conversation is just as necessary as frankness. "A fool gives full vent to his anger,/ but a wise man keeps himself under control" (Proverbs 29:11). There is a silence that is golden, and a quiet dignity that belongs to all spiritual force and that speaks for God in our very manner.

7. Cheerfulness of Disposition

Cheerfulness of disposition and manner have much to do with our influence and example. There are people who clasp your hand with a clammy touch that makes you think of a corpse. There are other touches that stir you, and looks that inspire you, and faces that lift you to heavenly things.

It is told of a Christian minister who was in deep depression, that while attending certain religious meetings in England he was attracted by the face of a lady who attended the services from day to day. Her calm and peaceful expression of countenance impressed him with a sense of the Lord's presence, and encouraged him to seek and obtain the baptism of the Holy Spirit and the same source of light and gladness which he saw reflected in her. Long afterwards he met her and told her how her silent look had been the benediction of his life. Our faces can speak for God; and, if the heart is illuminated within, we ought to show it in every feature, in every tone, in every gesture. Our whole expression and bearing should be such as to make men say of us, as they said of some of old, "Each one with the bearing of a prince" (Judges 8:18).

8. Cordiality and Heartiness

Cordiality and heartiness of spirit and manner are desirable. There are people that chill us and repel us, and there are others that draw us and encourage us. There is a stiffness that is sometimes born of diffidence, sometimes of selfishness, sometimes of natural coldness. But it can be overcome by a true spirit and by a watchful discipline.

Just as a graceful carriage can be acquired by thoughtful attention, and a careless, clumsy and clownish walk can grow upon one through carelessness and neglect, so we can accustom ourselves to such thoughtful and loving consideration of others as will transform our very manner, and make us, as the divine picture so beautifully characterizes it, "Be devoted to one another in brotherly love. Honor one another above yourselves" (Romans 12:10). "Finally, all of you, live in harmony with one another" (1 Peter 3:8). A very large part of our Christian life consists of our social and domestic relations and communication. It is in the little touches of love, kindness and mutual consideration that the spirit of Christ shines out most constantly; and the lack of it is often most painfully manifest.

9. Sensitivity to Others

Sensitiveness to the feelings of others is a beautiful quality often found wanting in good people. If they meet a poor consumptive, they will be very likely to tell him how dreadful he looks, throwing over him the shadow of the grave, until he feels as if he had been at his own funeral. If there is a sore place anywhere they are sure to step on it. If you have some peculiar and deep affliction, they are very likely to refer to it in some coarse and thoughtless manner, until you find relief in silent tears and hasten to shorten the painful interview.

True Christian sweetness adjusts itself to others. It rejoices with them that do rejoice, and weeps with them that weep. The law of love is its great impulse, and it is ever watching with kind consideration to avoid offenses on the one hand, and on the other to contribute to the happiness of all with whom we come in contact.

10. Tact

Tact is an indefinable quality, but we are very distinctly conscious of it when we see it, and we are often painfully sensible of its absence. Its possessor has a charmed life, and a golden secret that melts away difficulties, misunderstandings and angry countenances, as the gentle sunshine. A good-natured remark, a playful witticism, a happy change in the subject of conversation, a word that provokes a smile, how often these things have prevented the gravest misunderstandings and solved the hardest problems.

In dealing with souls it is essential to study our cases and adapt ourselves to conditions. "He who wins souls is wise" (Proverbs 11:30). A brusque address, an intrusive remark, an offensive question or a lot of tiresome talk, will do far more harm than good to the soul that you seek to benefit, and often retard for years the work of conviction that may have already begun. How delicately Christ dealt with the woman of Samaria, the publican of Jericho, and the dying thief upon the cross! If His Spirit dwells in us we shall have His wisdom and skill.

11. Others' Faults

In dealing with the faults of others there is room for the graces of Christian character. On the one hand there should be divine tenderness and gentleness. We are never fit to speak to others of their faults until our hearts are overflowing with love and free from resentment. Divine tact will always find some good thing to commend before we blame or criticize. On the other hand, there is a holy firmness and a righteous indignation which are just as becoming and necessary under certain circumstances, and which only the grace of the Holy Spirit can keep from becoming natural temper or unholy excess.

12. Loyalty to Truth

Loyalty to truth, to God, to the cause to which we are committed and to the friends that God has given us—these are qualities essential to the highest Christian character. They are rare, and their price is above rubies; they are the elements that constitute heroism and lead to the noblest sacrifices and the brightest examples of human friendship or public patriotism.

13. Self-sacrifice

Self-sacrifice is among the things that are lofty, and this alone can lift us to the noblest heights of character and conduct. The mountaintops of sacred biography all reach their summits on some Moriah height where something has been sacrificed for principle or for God: where Abraham gave up his Isaac; or Mary poured out her costly ointment; or David's heroes dashed through the ranks of their foes, and gladly risked their lives to bring back to their king their helmets filled with the water of Bethlehem's well for which he longed. This was the glory of the great apostle, and the only way in which he could expect to earn a prize. For preaching the gospel he tells us there was no glory. That was simply duty. But for preaching the gospel without charge there was a chance of winning a crown, and this was the glory of his life. God will give to every true life such opportunities for sacrifice and reward if we only desire to meet them. Thus alone can the jewels of the eternal crown be won.

14. Devoutness

This is the spirit of prayer, communion, devotion to God and seraphic love. It was the spirit of John the Divine; of Fénelon, the medieval saint; of

Madame Guyon; the loving heart of Samuel Rutherford; the holiness of Edward Payson; the spiritual zeal of Robert Murray McCheyne— all were lives that lived in the light of an open heaven and breathed the sweet fragrance of the land of Beulah. Devoutness is one of the things that are venerable, the things that are lovely, the things that are of good report which the humblest saint may emulate.

15. Enthusiasm

Enthusiasm is important. No soul can greatly influence others unless it is itself on fire. Personal magnetism is borne of intense feeling and profound interest in the object that we have chosen. It is a shining quality, and a resistless force in Christian character. It gives impulse to our work, and wings our thoughts and words with heavenly power.

16. A Holy Ambition

A holy ambition, a heavenly aspiration, a life of hope and lofty endeavor will lift us above earthly and common things and make our lives sublime. We are the children of eternity. We are the heirs of glory. We have in prospect a crown that does not fade away, and an existence transcendently grander than the highest possibilities of earthly hope. How noble, how glorious, how aspiring we should be! What a grandeur it should add to our thoughts, conceptions, imaginations, to our very faces and bearing, as we press on to the glorious prize with the Spirit of the Master reflected in our countenances, and the light of the opening heaven shining on our transfigured brow. So "May the favor of the Lord our God rest upon us" (Psalm 90:17), even "the splendor of his holiness" (96:9), with the dew of His youth.

So let us prove not only the things that are true and right and pure, but whatever things are honest, whatever things are lovely, whatever are admirable, let us think about these things. And let us put on not only the clean robes of holiness, but the wedding robes of beauty and glory for the Marriage of the Lamb.

CHAPTER 8

THE GREAT SECRET

For I have learned to be content whatever the circumstances. I know what it is to be in need, and I know what it is to have plenty. I have learned the secret of being content in any and every situation, whether well fed or hungry, whether living in plenty or in want. I can do everything through him who gives me strength. (Philippians 4:11–13)

There is a secret in everything. Back of the discoveries of genius, the inventions of art and the marvelous transformations of our modern commercial and industrial life, there is always hidden away in some gifted brain a mighty secret whose potential value may be estimated by millions and billions of dollars. The very process by which this sentence will be turned into type, by the simple touch on a keyboard, is one of the most marvelous secrets of modern machinery, the linotype. The wizard of electrical science, from his laboratory in New Jersey, is working out new secrets every year in the practical applications of the electric current. The patent office in Washington protects innumerable little secrets of inventions of all the processes of modern business and machinery.

In the higher realm of the spiritual world everything depends on knowing how to do it. Human morals have failed because they had not learned God's secret. The ancient philosophers had their outer and inner circles, their mysteries into which the few were initiated and their occult science and philosophy. But it was all a labyrinth of useless speculation, and had no power to lift humanity out of its helplessness and sinfulness. Only by divine revelation could the problem be solved and the mystery revealed.

The great apostle tells us that the secret has at last been made known. The Revised Version furnishes a striking and beautiful translation of the last part of our text. "I have learned the secret, . . . I can do all things through Christ who strengtheneth me" (4:12–13). It is not the first time that Paul speaks of this secret. In his Epistle to the Colossians, there is a striking passage in which he refers to the "mystery," literally the secret "that has been kept hidden for ages and generations, but is now disclosed to the saints. To them God has chosen to make known among the Gentiles the glorious riches of this mystery" (Colossians 1:26–27). And then he tells us what it is: "Christ in you, the hope of glory" (1:27).

This was the great trust committed to him to deliver to the world. It is an open secret, and yet it is only comprehended by those who enter into the "shelter of the Most High [and] rest in the shadow of the Almighty" (Psalms 91:1). It is to these that he whispers it in our beautiful text, as he tells them how, by a power beyond themselves, they can live out the beautiful ideal which he has been presenting to them in this exquisite epistle.

THE NATURE OF THE SECRET

He does not leave us one moment in doubt about it. It is thus, "I can do everything through him who gives me strength" (Philippians 4:13). The literal translation of this verse adds much force to it. "I am strong for everything in *the endynamiting Christ.*" The Greek root of this last phrase has acquired a peculiar significance. Dynamite denotes the most powerful of material forces. The apostle means that he has found a power outside of himself and beyond his own power, the infinite power of Christ, and that he has come into connection with this power in such a way that it has become available for his every need, and while in touch with it, he is strong for everything and for all things.

Let us carefully note that this power is all centered in a Person, namely, the living Christ. And it is only while one is in this Christ, abiding in Him, depending upon Him, drawing his life from Him, that he has the command of this all-sufficient strength. It is not merely through the Christ, but it is in the Christ; that is, in actual union with Him, that the strength comes. It is not that so much power is communicated to him to be at his own control and disposal as a dynamo or battery might be, but that the power remains in the person of Christ, and is shared by the believer only while he is in direct union and communion with the Lord Himself.

This, then, was Paul's mighty secret, that God had united him with the Lord Jesus as the living source of all possible blessing, strength and sufficiency, and that it was his privilege to draw from Him moment by moment the supply for all his needs, just as the human system derives life from the oxygen we breathe through the inhalation of air into our lungs.

The human mind has always been straining after some closer union with the divine powers, and ancient art is just an attempt to bring the gods down in the likeness of men through the sculpture, paintings and mythologies of ancient Greece. But all this was cold and unsatisfying, the out-reaching of an arm too short to reach the heavenly help for which human hearts are faint-ing. Paul, however, had found the secret. Not a god in marble, in poetry or in the legendary stories of ancient mythology, but a God in human flesh, a God who had lived our life with all its trials and experiences, and who, now exalted to a spiritual and heavenly manhood, still comes to dwell in human hearts and relive His life in our actual experiences from day to day. It is not merely occasional help, but His constant life and presence. There is no part of our existence which He cannot touch. There is no place in our varied ex-perience where He cannot meet us. His humanity is as broad as ours, and His presence and touch as real and tender as in the old Galilean days. This is the secret of all-sufficiency—the friendship of Jesus, the indwelling life of Christ, our union heart to heart with One who, as no other friend could possibly do, lives out His very life in ours.

Beloved, have you learned this secret? To distrust yourself and fully trust Him? To cease from your own works and let Him work in you to will and to do of His good pleasure?

THE APPLICATION OF THIS SECRET

1. It is universal.

It applies to all things. It is a universal secret, and covers the whole range of our life and need. It extends to our spirit, our soul and our body, to our temporal as well as to our religious interest, to our families and friends as well as to ourselves, to our business, our circumstances, our health, our life, our death, our whole eternity. It is a universal secret.

2. It is particular.

It applies to everything, as well as to all things. It is particular, as well as general. It must be applied moment by moment to all the details of life. It is not something to think about in church, at communion seasons, on birthdays and anniversaries, at morning and evening prayer and on the great occasions of trial and need. But it is something that comes afresh with every breath, and that in order to be effectual must be constantly employed and applied in every separate link in the whole chain of human life, 60 seconds in the minute, and 24 hours in the day. This is where we often fail. We try to live wholesale lives. God's method is moment by moment, breath by breath, line upon line, here a little and there a little. We find, alas, too often that the chain is no stronger than its weakest link, and that the stitches we have dropped, the links we have lost, have destroyed the effectiveness of life as a whole.

3. It is self-contained.

It is a self-contained secret. There is a fine expression in the original translation of the word rendered "content" in our Revised Version. It is not exactly content, but rather self-sufficient or self-contained. "I have learned in all circumstances to be sufficient in myself." The idea is for the Christian to be independent of circumstances, and to have a source of satisfaction and comfort in his own soul that lifts him above the things outside of him. "My mind to me a kingdom is," is the human way of expressing independence of character and sufficiency of source. Much higher is the inspired statement of the greater truth, "The kingdom of God is within you" (Luke 17:21), and "The kingdom of God is not a matter of eating and drinking, but of righteousness, peace and joy in the Holy Spirit" (Romans 14:17).

One of our wisest Christian workers, recently addressing a party of missionary candidates, advised them not to go to the foreign field unless they had sufficient spiritual resources to make them happy within their own hearts even in loneliness and isolation. If you are going to be fretting in six months on account of homesickness or lonesomeness don't go to China. But if you have a Christ and a joy that make you happy in the loneliest place, quite independently of the things around you, then you can be happy anywhere and at leisure from your own cares to work effectively for God.

Now this was what Paul meant when he talked about being self-sufficient in every condition. He had within himself a kingdom of peace and joy that mere outward things could not disturb.

This expression was a technical term with the ancient Stoics. They were fond of talking about their independence of circumstances and things. Their philosophy taught them to despise circumstances and material gratifications, and they were able to maintain the form of outward stoicism, even as the Indian could stand at the stake with countenance unblanched amid all the terrors of a violent death. But this was only apparent. The heart was clinging to a shadow and really holding on to itself. The apostle meant something different from this; not merely the resolution of a firm, determined will, but the restful satisfaction of a heart filled with the peace and joy of the Lord, and finding its heaven within. This Christ can give, and in His perfect peace the heart can sing:

> Everything in Jesus,
> And Jesus everything.

4. It is sufficient.

This secret is sufficient for the severest trials and the deepest depression. "I know what it is to be in need" (Philippians 4:12), he exclaims, "I have learned how to be hungry. I know how to suffer need." All this he had proved by the severest experiences through which a human life has ever passed. There was no sort of trial that he had not proved, and yet his secret had stood the test. Look at him on the tossing deck of the vessel in the Mediterranean, the only bright and fearless spirit in all that company. Look at him chained to the soldier in the Roman barracks, rejoicing that he is permitted to bear testimony for Christ to the rude men around him. Listen to him as he bids farewell to his weeping friends at Ephesus, expressing the one ambition to finish his course with joy. Sometimes we see his spirit sinking just enough to put him in touch with his suffering brethren and have them know that he understands their trials and afflictions. The only time his spirit seems to break is when he is thinking of others and suffering for their sakes. For himself his spirit is always victorious, and he did indeed finish his course with joy, and prove to the end that Christ was all-sufficient for the most tried and suffering life.

How often people succeed under favorable circumstances and break down when trial comes. Tropical plants cannot stand the breath of frost. God has to expose every life to the fire, and only that which stands the fire of trial can have a part in the final reward.

5. It is equal to the test.

His secret was equal to the severer test of prosperity. More difficult to stand even than trial, is happiness and success. Many a soul that has stood with fortitude amid the storms of adversity has sunk into soft and languid weakness under the enervating of prosperity and the world's approval. The wealth for which you longed has come, but the liberal heart has gone. The opportunities for usefulness for which you craved have been bestowed upon you, but the unselfish and obedient spirit which would have once improved them has disappeared. The holy courage that stood for God when others quailed, cannot now afford to sacrifice the good opinion of a world whose smile has proven too sweet for your once high purpose and principle. The world has become so necessary for your happiness that you cannot sacrifice it, and the work that once was strong in God in the day of small things is now, alas, like Laodicea, "rich; [having] acquired wealth and [not needing] a thing" (Revelation 3:17). But alas, the Master is standing at the door and saying, "You do not realize that you are wretched, pitiful, poor, blind and naked" (3:17).

This is not necessary. The grace of Christ is able to sustain the heart in the highest as well as the lowest place, to fill you with humble thankfulness for the prosperity that is but a trust for God, and to make you a faithful steward of the means and resources which He has bestowed upon you only that you might use them for Him. And so there are gifts without pride, of spiritual blessings that have not separated us from the Giver, of five talents that have been multiplied into ten, and of trusts so used for God that they have been increased a hundredfold.

You will notice in this classification the great variety of extremes covered by this experience. It is a secret that is equally applicable to the most opposite conditions of life.

The Brooklyn Bridge, it is said, contracts and expands with winter cold and summer heat nearly two feet in its entire length. But the great iron strands are adjusted so as to slip past each other on the mighty towers and allow for these extremes. More perfect is God's adjustment for the vicissitudes of His people. There is an inward life that is unmoved alike by heat and cold, a fixed and steadfast principle that presses on through the darkness and the light, through Him who is its source, "the same yesterday and today and forever" (Hebrews 13:8).

THE LEARNING OF THIS SECRET

Three times the apostle refers to his spiritual education. First he says, "I have learned" (Philippians 4:11). Then he adds later, "I know" (4:12). And finally he tells us, "I am instructed" (4:12, KJV). This last expression is translated in the new version, "I have learned the secret"; and in one of the best versions it is, "I have been initiated."

There are really two stages in learning this great secret. The first is the acquiring of the principle. The second is the practice of its application, until we become perfectly familiar with its use and thoroughly proficient in its application.

To take a familiar illustration: in the art of phonography the principle is soon acquired. In a few days you can learn the characters and the general principles. But it takes months and sometimes years of patient application to be able to use them quickly and efficiently. And so we can soon comprehend the great principle of the spiritual life, the indwelling Christ and the Holy Spirit. We can very soon, if our hearts are true and sincere, begin the deeper life and receive the Holy Spirit.

But it is a very different thing to take this deep secret and apply it moment by moment to all the details of holy living. It is here that we constantly fail. At some consecration meeting, at some sacred altar, you gave yourself to Christ and received Him as your life and strength. But that was but the start. It is the abiding that tells. It is walking with Him step by step that makes Him real and proves His all-sufficiency. Alas, many of us are satisfied with a mere smattering of the holy art of walking with God. What we need is what an old writer calls "The practice of the presence of God"—the constant, patient, ceaseless dependence upon Him for everything; the applying of our secret to every test that comes in life, to every moment of every day until we can say with the great apostle, "I have been initiated, I have been instructed, I can do all things through him who gives me strength."

Beloved, shall we take this mighty secret, and go out to live it step by step and day by day, until we have walked through "the length and breadth of the land" (Genesis 13:17); and until, in the all things and the everything, the always and the everywhere, we shall have proved "what God's will is—his good, pleasing and perfect will" (Romans 12:2).

CHAPTER 9

THE BOUNDLESS SUFFICIENCY

And my God will meet all your needs according to his glorious riches in Christ Jesus. (Philippians 4:19)

There are some souls that always seem to be kept on scant measure. Their spiritual garments are threadbare, their faces pinched and their whole bearing is that of people who are poverty stricken and kept on short allowance. They are always "hard up," and on "the ragged edge" of want and bankruptcy. To use the vivid figure of Job they come through by "the skin of [their] teeth" (Job 19:20). or as Paul expresses it in a stronger figure, they are "saved . . . as by fire" (1 Corinthians 3:15, KJV). They are represented in Bunyan's glorious dream, not by sturdy Christian, buoyant Hopeful, and heroic Faithful, but by poor old Ready to Halt, with his crutches, Mr. Much Afraid, with his downcast look, and Miss Despondency, with her long and miserable face.

They sing sometimes, but it is generally this:

> Tis a point I long to know,
> Oft it causes anxious thought,
> Do I love the Lord or no,
> Am I His or am I not?

And when they go to the prayer meeting their usual cry is, "Pray for me." They are always begging, always hungry, always waiting for somebody to help them, and seldom looking for a chance to help. Like Pharaoh's lean cows, they eat everything in sight, but still they are always half starved.

Loved? Yes, they are loved and cared for by the dear Lord, loved as the crippled child, as the invalid member of the family. Saved? Yes, they are saved through the exceeding grace of Jesus Christ, "He is able to deal gently with those who are ignorant and are going astray" (Hebrews 5:2). But they never can be samples of the King's household, representatives of His grace or attractions to draw men to His fold. They are poor, half-starved sheep that cast reflection on the goodness and the care of the Shepherd, and not happy, well-fed lambs that "lie down in green pastures" (Psalm 23:2) for very satiety, and make others feel like saying, "The LORD is my shepherd, I shall not be in want" (23:1). On the contrary many who look at them will say, "If that is Christianity, save me from it."

In contrast with such as these, there is another type of Christian character that we might call the "life more abundant." It is a life which overflows in thankful joy and unselfish blessing to others. Its faith is full assurance. Its love "always protects, always trusts, always hopes, always perseveres" (1 Corinthians 13:7), and "never fails" (13:8). Its patience has "longsuffering with joyfulness" (Colossians 1:11, KJV). Its peace "transcends all understanding" (Philippians 4:7). Its joy is "an inexpressible and glorious joy" (1 Peter 1:8). Its service is so free and glad that duty is delight and work a luxury of love. Its giving is not only cheerful but "hilarious." Its sacrifice is so willing that even pain is joy, if borne for others and for God. It has enough and to spare, and its love and joy find their outlet in giving the overflow to others and finding that "it is more blessed to give than to receive" (Acts 20:35).

In a word it has got out into the infinite as well as the eternal, and sails on the shoreless and fathomless sea of God and His infinite grace.

What a difference! It is the difference between the barren desert and the luxuriant oasis with waving palms and glorious verdure. It is the difference between the gaunt and hungry flock and the herds that lie down in green pastures and beside the still waters. It is the difference between the poor burdened horse that is trying to drag you up the hill, and the flying locomotive that carries you without an effort. It is the difference between the old pump by the roadside, out of which you could force a few pailfuls of water after you had poured one in, and the deep artesian well that pours its gushing torrent forth in floods. It is the difference between the viewless plain and the mountain landscape looking far out to the regions beyond, and the "land of far distance." It is the difference between the shallow stream, where your boat every moment touches sand or strikes some hidden rock, and the deep unfathomable sea, where your keel never strikes bottom and you ride in safety amid the ocean's wildest swells.

Oh, the difference of these two lives.

> Once 'twas painful trying,
>   Now 'tis perfect trust;
> Once a half salvation,
>   Now the uttermost.

Once I hoped in Jesus,
  Now I know He's mine;
Once my lamps were dying,
  Now they brightly shine.

Let us look at Paul's testimony of this overflowing life.

IN HIS OWN EXPERIENCE, IT WAS HIS LIFE

"I have received full payment," he cries, "I am amply supplied" (Philippians 4:18). Was there ever such a paradox?

A prisoner chained between two soldiers in a cheerless Roman barracks! A man who says, "I have suffered the loss of all things!" A hated, persecuted outcast, even now awaiting a trial in which his very life hung by a thread on the capricious will of the Roman tyrant! A man who bore in his body the scars of beatings, scourgings, shipwrecks and privations of every kind, and who, only a few days before, had received some scanty offering of clothing, food and perhaps a little money from his congregation in Philippi. It is this man who cries, "I have received full payment and even more" (4:18).

Was it a dream of a diseased imagination? Or was it true in some higher sense than the world could understand?

Yes, he had a life whose sources were not in circumstances or things. And that life was full and satisfying. He had a salvation proportioned to the depth of his sin and need and he could say of it, "The grace of our Lord was poured out on me abundantly, along with the faith and love that are in Christ Jesus" (1 Timothy 1:14). He had a hope of which he could boast, "For I am convinced that neither death nor life, neither angels nor demons, neither the present nor the future, nor any powers, neither height nor depth, nor anything else in all creation, will be able to separate us from the love of God that is in Christ Jesus our Lord" (Romans 8:38). He had a love that could say, "So I will very gladly spend for you everything I have and expend myself as well. If I love you more, will you love me less?" (2 Corinthians 12:15). He had a victory of which he could boast, "No, in all these things we are more than conquerors through him who loved us" (Romans 8:37). His sacrifices were so gladly made that he could say, "But even if I am being poured out like a drink offering on the sacrifice and service coming from your faith, I am glad and rejoice with all of you" (Philippians 2:17). His sufferings so little disturbed him that he could say, "I only know that in every city the Holy Spirit warns me that prison and hardships are facing me. However, I consider my life worth nothing to me, if only I may finish the race and complete the task the Lord Jesus has given me—the task of testifying to the gospel of God's grace" (Acts 20:23–24).

There was not one small thing about him. His whole character was built on the most colossal mold. He was a great, magnanimous soul, with a spiritual life as large as the heart of God. He could say to the Corinthians, "We are not withholding our affection from you, . . . open wide your hearts also" (2 Corinthians 6:12–13). Into this little, sorrow-beaten frame God compressed the grandest character that ever followed Jesus, and standing on the battlements of his sublime exaltation he tells us we may have all he had, and cries, "My God will meet all your needs according to his glorious riches in Christ Jesus" (Philippians 4:19).

FOR OTHERS

Paul's life was an overflow life, and that always means a life that reaches out to bless others. It has enough and to spare for a suffering world and "grows rich in giving." Paul lived in the hearts of others. "I long to see you" (Romans 1:11), he wrote in anticipation of his visit to Rome. Not that he might see the splendid capital of the Caesars, nor even that he might enjoy the fellowship of his cherished friends, but "that I may impart to you some spiritual gift" (1:11). "We loved you so much," he writes to the Thessalonians, "that we were delighted to share with you not only the gospel of God but our lives as well" (1 Thessalonians 2:8).

The sufferings of the children of God were his. "Who is led into sin" (2 Corinthians 11:29), he writes to the Corinthians, "and I do not inwardly burn" (11:29)? His prayers are all for others. Rarely do we find him asking anything for himself. His life was all given away in ministry for others. And it was Christ he ministered. He had a Christ he could give away and yet retain. He was so filled with the Spirit of the Master that he could just pour out His life into every empty and open heart.

How blessed to find, how blessed to live such lives. How delightful it is to come in contact with hearts that are not preoccupied with their own needs, but are at leisure to lift the burdens of other hearts and help men to touch His garment.

Beloved, have you this glorious fullness? Have you gotten beyond your own self-consciousness, your own prayers, your own little circle of friends and family ties, until your heart is in touch with the Savior's and the world's? This is the crowning glory of the sweetest Christian life.

> A heart at leisure from itself
> To soothe and sympathize.

THE SOURCE OF THIS SUPERABUNDANT LIFE

It all came from the revelation and conception he had of God. He was but drinking at a higher fountain, and pouring out the fullness he received. He had found a heavenly spring, and he was but leading others to the same fountain.

The scantiness or the fullness of your life all depends upon how large a God you have! The God of most Christians is not much larger than the dumb idol of wood or stone the heathen worships and then takes down from its pedestal and scolds if it does not answer his prayers or meet his expectations. The God of Paul was a very glorious and mighty Being, and it was the greatness of his God that gave greatness to his character and life. He was but a vessel to receive and reflect the glory of God.

"The people that do know their God shall be strong and do exploits" (Daniel 11:32, KJV). The souls that have learned to clothe themselves with His Almightiness are the people of enlarged vision and victorious faith. Human heroes are honored for what they have become or achieved. God's heroes are honored for the measure in which they have dropped out of sight and simply magnified Him. It is not Elijah but Elijah's God that we remember. It is not Paul, but Paul's Christ that we want.

What then does Paul mean when he says, "My God"?

1. The God of Nature

He means the God of nature. The God who shall fully supply all our need is the God who made the heavens and earth and upholds the whole system of the universe by the hand that once hung from the nails of Calvary. Look at the glory of the heavens and the elements of nature. Multiply every star you see in yonder heavens by 100 and you have not begun to count the worlds of space, but He made them all. They are poised by His power and moved by His omnipotence. In perfect order and awful might they sweep along their orbits through immensity. Yonder in the cluster of the Pleiades that little star is 12,000 times the size of our sun. And there are millions of such suns all along the heavenly fields, each surrounded by systems and satellites. Cannot He who holds them in His hand supply all your need?

2. The God of the Old Testament

He is the God of the Old Testament. He is the El Shaddai of Abraham, the great I AM of Moses, the Captain of Joshua's vision, the Jehovah God of Elijah's miracles, the mighty Providence of Esther and Nehemiah, the God who divided the sea, marched through the wilderness, shattered the walls of Jericho, halted the sun at Joshua's command, raised the dead at Elijah's word, stilled the lions for Daniel's protection, walked through the fire with the Hebrew children and proved equal to all His people's needs through 4,000 years of Old Testament history—history of patriarchs, prophets and saints. Is not the God of Abraham, of Esther, of Daniel, of Elijah, able to supply all your need?

3. The Father of Jesus Christ

He is the God and Father of our Lord and Savior Jesus Christ. The life of Jesus is just the expression of His power and love. He stood among men healing the sick, pardoning sinners, comforting the sad—doing it all in the Father's name and by His authority and will. "My Father is always at his work to this very day, and I, too, am working" (John 5:17), was His constant testimony. "My miracles of power, My words of grace, are just My Father's will, My Father's love." The God who so loved the world as to give His one and only Son (3:16), this is the God who "will meet all your needs according to his glorious riches in Christ Jesus" (Philippians 4:19).

4. The God of the Risen Christ

He is the God of the risen Christ. He is the God for whom even death has no barrier that can hinder His purpose or defy His will. He who burst asunder the bars of the grave, and without an effort passed through that sealed stone and met His sorrowing disciples with the glad "All Hail" of the first Easter morning, He it is who will supply all our need according to "his incomparably great power . . . which he exerted in Christ when he raised him from the dead" (Ephesians 1:19–20).

5. The God of the Ascension

He is the God of the ascension. Not only did He raise Him from the dead, but He "seated him at his right hand in the heavenly realms, far above all rule and authority, power and dominion, and every title that can be given, . . . and appointed him to be head over everything for the church" (1:20–22). He is enthroned above all other power. He controls every force in the universe. And He is yours. Can He not supply your need?

6. The Great Intercessor

He is the great Intercessor. He is in heaven as our Advocate, Representative and Friend. His one business is to hear our petitions, present them to His Father, and send us the answers. We have a right to His constant intervention and efficient aid. With such a Friend what can we ever need, how can we ever fail?

7. The God of Heaven

He is the God of heaven. What do we know of heaven? How much does that expression mean to us, "his glorious riches" (Philippians 4:19)? Something we may gather from the inspired descriptions of that City that has no need of the sun, whose walls are jewels and its streets are shining gold—that glorious New Jerusalem, whose countless streets shall stretch for 1,500 miles north and south and east and west, and then as high up in mid-heaven, for the length, the breadth and the height of it are equal. And surely He who can build that Golden City is rich enough to supply all your need. Sometimes as the gates have parted to let some loved one in we have caught a glimpse of its surpassing glories; and we have felt, oh, if He has all this for us by and by can He not supply all our present needs, and anticipate a little our coming heritage of glory? O beloved, how ashamed we shall be some day that we did not better understand our heavenly calling and walk more truly "with the bearing of a prince" (Judges 8:18).

Yes, this is some feeble measure of "his glorious riches" (Philippians 4:19), and it is according to this that He will supply all our need. Let us trust Him. And let us clothe ourselves with His all-sufficiency and rise to the grandeur of His glorious fullness.

Finally, how shall all this be ours?

First, we must learn to say *my* God.

And secondly, we must learn to understand that "our every need" is just the vessel He is ever sending to hold His fullness. Let us pass down the little buckets of need on the endless chain of faith and prayer, and they will come up brimming with His overflowing fullness, each one saying as it flows: "My God will meet all your needs according to his glorious riches in Christ Jesus" (4:19).

COLOSSIANS

CHAPTER 1

CHRIST IN COLOSSIANS

And he is the head of the body, the church; he is the beginning and the firstborn from among the dead, so that in everything he might have the supremacy. (Colossians 1:18)

Set your minds on things above, not on earthly things. (3:2)

Each of Paul's epistles has an expression peculiar to itself. The Thessalonian epistles are characterized by the advent tinge, and shine with the glory of the second coming. Ephesians is the epistle of the "heavenly realms"; Philippians of the sweetness of the Christian temper; and Colossians is the portrait of Jesus, and its keynote is "Christ is all and in all."

It is said that the celebrated artist, Dannecker, was asked by Napoleon Bonaparte to paint a Venus for the Louvre, and declined. An almost fabulous price was then offered, and he still refused. The insulted emperor, astonished that any one should refuse money, and still more that he should refuse him, demanded why he declined. "I have painted Christ and I can never lower my brush to paint an inferior subject." And it had taken him half a lifetime to paint his picture of Christ. The first time he painted Him, after eight years of labor, he asked his little daughter to look at it. Uncovering the canvas he brought her in. She clapped her hands together with an expression of intense surprise and admiration. "Who do you think it is?" he asked. "Oh," she said, "it is a great man." His countenance fell and he took his brush and daubed the picture into a perfect wreck. "I have failed. It is not Christ." He went to work again and toiled and prayed, and when he took the child in the next time there was not the same expression of wonder, delight and admiration, but the tears came then she stole softly up as though it were the real Christ, whispering, "Let the little children come to me." Ah, it was Christ! The expression was there!

So there are lives that remind you of a great man, and there are others that reveal the vision of a living Savior; and they are messages that are not forgotten. All that remains is the memory of Jesus, and you feel somehow your heart burned within you as you got near the Master, and you are the better for it. Thus the Epistle to the Colossians is the picture of Jesus. It reveals to us the heart of Christ.

THE TRINITY

1. Christ is all and in all in the Trinity. The epistle brings out His relation to the Father, for we read: "For God was pleased to have all his fullness dwell in him" (Colossians 1:19). The Father is pleased to express Himself in the Son, to pour Himself into Christ and stand back while Christ fills the picture and reveals the Father. We do not directly see the Father, but we see the light of the glory of God in the face of Jesus Christ. Again we read, "for in Christ all the fullness of the Deity lives in bodily form" (2:9).

He is the image of the invisible God, for God reveals Himself to us in Christ and He wants us to honor Him. Unitarianism, Deism and all "isms" that make Jesus only an exalted Man, or a superior Being, dishonor the Father as much as the Son; for God has commanded us to render supreme worship to Him even as to the Father; for "anyone who has seen me has seen the Father" (John 14:9), and he that has rejected Him has rejected the Father also. May we keep a high reverential estimate of the Lord Jesus Christ. We are living in an age when people think it is well just to love God, and they talk about the "spirit" of Christ, an ethical Christ, and other human Christs. We have heard recently of the Japanese Christ, a sort of evolution of their own national thought grafted on to Christianity. Then we have the socialistic Christ, and it all sounds very well, but it is direct blasphemy and rebellion against the dignity of Jesus and the authority of the Father. Whatever else we fail in let us be orthodox in our conception of the Person of the Lord Jesus Christ, and honor, worship and glorify Him even as the Father, for "God was pleased to have all his fullness dwell in him" (Colossians 1:19).

THE CREATION

2. Christ is all and in all in creation. "For by him all things were created: things in heaven and on earth, visible and invisible, whether thrones or powers or rulers or authorities; all things were created by him and for him" (1:16). Christ is the Author and the End of creation. All the glory of nature is but the reflection of His own glory. The Father is revealed in the Son. The Son is revealed in the majesty of nature. The shining heavens and verdant earth are but the mirror of His attributes and the work of His hands.

They were made for Him as well as by Him. He is the final cause of creation. The lion with his lordship over the lower creation is but a type of the

Lion of the tribe of Judah. The gentle lamb was made to set forth the sacrifice of the Lamb of God. The ancient rocks and everlasting mountains are but object lessons of the Rock of Ages. The flowers that blossom on the hillside and in the gardens breathe the sweetness of the Rose of Sharon and the Lily of the Valley. The radiant sun is but a figure of the Sun of Righteousness, and the glowing stars proclaim the glory of the Bright and Morning Star. The shepherd and his flock, the bridegroom and the joy, the vine with its hanging clusters, the streamlet with its flowing tide, the very bread we eat, all become an alphabet to spell out the greatness and the grace of Him by whom all earthly things were made and who is the real substance of which they are but the shadow.

"I am the vine" (John 15:5), He says, as though the earthly vine were but a figure created to set forth the true. Even creation will not be complete until the Son of man shall become its recognized Lord and King, and the new creation shall rise as the fair inheritance of Jesus and His saints. And He that sits upon the throne shall say, "I am making everything new!" (Revelation 21:5). In His sublime vision, John pictures every creature that is in heaven and earth and in the sea, the whole universe joining to adore and worship "him who sits on the throne and . . . the Lamb/ . . . for ever" (5:13). Then creation shall have reached its goal and all things shall be for Him as well as through Him.

THE REALM OF PROVIDENCE

3. Christ is all and in all in the realm of providence. "In him all things hold together" (Colossians 1:17). Literally this is translated in the Revised Version, "All things hang together." He is the cohesive center and principle of nature and providence. He is the Lord and Ruler of universal government. He who by one creative act formed the universe, by continuous activity upholds and sustains it.

Not a fluttering bird which sings in the branches, not an insect that floats upon the air, not a bud that bursts in the vernal spring, not a star which shines in the vast empyrean, but is constantly dependent on the activity of His hand. He who bears the universe upon His shoulder carries His loved ones on His heart, and with a more particular providence plans every instant and incident of their life and causes all things to work together for their good.

It is the Lamb who looses the scroll of seven seals and unfolds every destiny for the individual and the universe. The ascended Christ is Head over all things for His Body, the Church. And while the ambitions and passions of man have their full sway in the evolving of human history, yet He rules or overrules in every event and forges every link into a chain of infinite wisdom, power and love, so that even the things that seem to hinder only help at last

His ultimate design. The wrath of man is made to praise (Psalm 76:10, KJV). The dark shadows of seeming calamity are but part of the picture of His life and love, and when all is finished, the saints of earth and the intelligences of heaven shall unite to say, "Great and marvelous are your deeds,/ Lord God Almighty./ Just and true are your ways,/ King of the ages./ Who will not fear you, O Lord,/ and bring glory to your name?/ For you alone are holy" (Revelation 15:3–4a).

THE REALM OF TRUTH

4. Christ is all and in all in the realm of truth. "In [him] are hidden all the treasures of wisdom and knowledge" (Colossians 2:3). The ordinances and ceremonial rites of the old dispensation were but shadows of which He is the substance (2:17). The philosophies and speculations with which false teachers were seeking to dazzle and deceive their minds were but counterfeits of the truth of which Christ is the center and the sun. Instead of pursuing these elusive visions the apostle bids them abide in Him and prays for them "that they may be encouraged in heart and united in love, so that they may have the full riches of complete understanding, in order that they may know the mystery of God, namely, Christ" (2:2).

This is the mystery of mysteries, the fount of wisdom, the sum of knowledge: to know God and Jesus whom He sent. How little our scholarship and learning will avail in the light of the New Jerusalem! How the graduates will go down and the poor illiterate disciples will go up in the heavenly classes, where the test of our standing will be our intimacy with Jesus!

IN REDEMPTION

5. Christ is all and in all in redemption, for the cross is the supreme glory of the gospel and the end to which all revelation has been moving. Indeed, even nature is full of foreshadowings of redemption, some interposition by which wrong should be righted and the lower lifted to a higher life, even as the buried seed grows into the harvest and the chrysalis into the radiant butterfly. And so, early in this epistle we are brought into immediate contact with the great Redeemer:

> For he has rescued us from the dominion of darkness and brought us into the kingdom of the Son he loves, in whom we have redemption [through his blood], the forgiveness of sins. (1:13–14)

> And through him to reconcile to himself all things, whether things on earth or things in heaven, by making peace through his blood, shed on the cross.

> Once you were alienated from God and were enemies in your
> minds because of your evil behavior. But now he has reconciled
> you by Christ's physical body through death to present you holy
> in his sight, without blemish and free from accusation. (1:20–22)

Here we find redemption reaching even farther than sinful men, for Christ
has reconciled all things both in earth and heaven. Perhaps even Gabriel
himself is established more firmly in his high estate because the Son of man
died to reconcile and redeem. At least we know that He has reconciled us
and brought us near to God through His precious blood. And that forevermore He will be the first in the trust, the love and the praise of all the choirs
of ransomed men who shall join to sing, "Worthy is the Lamb, who was
slain,/ to receive power and wealth and wisdom and strength/ and honor
and glory and praise!" (Revelation 5:12).

THE LIFE OF HIS PEOPLE

6. Christ is all and in all in the life of His people. For, in the first place,
our life all begins by receiving Him. "So then, just as you received Christ
Jesus as Lord, continue to live in him" (Colossians 2:6). It is not receiving a
sacrament, a creed, a system of theology, a set of moral precepts, but a living,
personal Savior. That is salvation. "Whoever comes to me I will never drive
away" (John 6:37).

Then further, the continuance and progress of our Christian life is just as
simple and as personal. "Continue to live in him" (Colossians 2:6). It is a life
of dependence and communion, step by step, receiving Him afresh as our
all-sufficiency, our wisdom, strength and holiness.

Still further, we are taught that we are complete in Him (2:10). That is to
say, He fills up every possible need of our life and being. For the deeper life
of sanctification is simply Christ within. This is the mystery, he says,

> that has been kept hidden for ages and generations, but is now
> disclosed to the saints. To them God has chosen to make known
> among the Gentiles the glorious riches of this mystery, which is
> Christ in you, the hope of glory. (1:26–27)

This is so simple that it really cannot be made more plain. It is not a
process of teaching, or even the formation of a character. It is acquaintance
with a Person, an intimate union and fellowship with Him so that He actually comes into our being and becomes the Source and Strength of our
very life, reliving His own life in us; and we falling with perfect naturalness
into His will, His plan, His steps and all His perfect life. So deep and intimate is this union that a great variety of figures are introduced to express

and illustrate its fuller meaning. We are "rooted . . . in him" (2:7). We are "built up in him" (2:7). We are "buried with him" (2:12). When we were "dead in [our] sins" (2:13), we were "raised with Christ" (3:1). Our "life is hidden with Christ in God" (3:3). He Himself is our very life (3:4).

And then when it comes to the question of conduct, our actions are to be determined by our relation to Him. It is because we are in Him that we are to act like Him. And so we read, "Whatever you do, whether in word or deed, do it all in the name of the Lord Jesus" (3:17).

To act in the name of Jesus is to act as if you were Jesus, to sustain His character, His dignity and the life that would be expected from Him if He Himself were here. But it is our relation to Him that inspires our conduct. We need the powerful motive of His life and love, yes, and the actual force of His indwelling Spirit to enable us to live out His life in our daily conduct and conversation.

How many of us are as consistent with our high calling as the simple immigrant servant in an Oakland family who applied for a situation in the family of a professing Christian? Poor John was subject to a pretty thorough examination about his habits, but gave satisfactory and unequivocal answers to all inquiries. "Do you drink?" he was asked. "No, me Christian. Me no drink." "Do you play cards?" "No, me Christian," and so on. He was soon at work in his new home and was found efficient and faithful in everything. But one night the family had a big party and John found himself called upon to wait upon them in the usual attendance at such a function. Faithfully and silently he went through the night without a murmur, and saw them playing cards, dancing and drinking wine. The next morning he presented himself to the mistress with a short and plain announcement, "Me go, me no stay." "Why John, what is the matter?" she asked. "Me no drink, me no play cards, me no stay with heathen who drink and play cards. Me go. Me Christian." To him there was no other logical alternative. If he was a Christian it meant to walk like Christ.

The consciousness of our high calling and our union with such a Master must lift us above the world and all its ways. It is said that the Dauphin of France, the poor orphan child of the murdered Louis XVI and his queen, was committed by his enemies to the care of a very brutal and wicked man who was to teach him only that which was evil. The poor lad had to look and listen to nothing but that which was degrading and wrong, but often he would say when tempted to stoop to the level of his companions, "I cannot say, I cannot do such things. I was born to be a king!" Yes, there was an impulse and a memory of higher things, and it kept him above the low and the base. The love of Christ, the life of Christ, the higher spiritual consciousness which His presence gives must lift us to the place of holiness and lead us to walk worthy of the vocation wherewith we are called.

OUR FUTURE

7. Christ is all and in all in our future hope. "When Christ, who is your life, appears, then you also will appear with him in glory" (3:4). Christ in you is the hope of glory, and when that glory comes it will be all Christ—His presence, His fellowship, His likeness. We shall be like Him. We shall be with Him. The Lamb is all the glory in Emmanuel's land. Such is an imperfect outline of the Christ picture of Colossians. God help us to reproduce it in our lives.

CHAPTER 2

THE CHRISTIAN IN COLOSSIANS

*We always thank God, the Father of our Lord Jesus Christ, when
we pray for you, because we have heard of your faith in Christ Jesus
and of the love you have for all the saints—the faith and love that
spring from the hope that is stored up for you in heaven and that you
have already heard about in the word of truth, the gospel that has
come to you. (Colossians 1:3–6)*

Faith, hope and love, the great trinity of Christian graces, were the foundation of the Christian character of the disciples at Colosse. From these all
the graces of the Spirit unfold in a manifold and beautiful variety and completeness. Nowhere have we a simpler, stronger and more attractive picture
of an ideal Christian life.

THEIR EVOLUTION

It was out of darkness. "For he has rescued us from the dominion of darkness and brought us into the kingdom of the Son he loves" (Colossians 1:13).
It was out of doom. For they had been under condemnation as the enemies of
God. "Once you were alienated from God and were enemies in your minds
because of your evil behavior. But now he has reconciled you" (1:21–22),
"having canceled the written code, with its regulations, that was against us
and that stood opposed to us; he took it away, nailing it to the cross" (2:14).
It was out of death. "When you were dead in your sins and in the uncircumcision of your sinful nature, God made you alive with Christ. He forgave us
all our sins" (2:13). Dead in sin once, they had become dead to sin now
through the cross of Jesus Christ. Crucified with Him they had come forth to
resurrection life. They were risen with Christ, and he could say of them, "For
you died, and your life is now hidden with Christ in God" (3:3).

There is something very definite about their experience. It is all expressed
in the perfect tense. He "has rescued us from the dominion of darkness"

(1:13). He "qualified you to share in the inheritance of the saints in the kingdom of light" (1:12). "He has reconciled you by Christ's physical body through death to present you holy in his sight" (1:22). "In him we have redemption through his blood, the forgiveness of sins" (Ephesians 1:7). We are "raised with [Christ]" (Colossians 2:12). We have "taken off [our] old self with its practices" (3:9). We "have put on the new self" (3:10). We are "complete in him" (2:10, KJV). There is no ambiguity, no place for mere hoping and half believing. We have an accomplished salvation, and the great transaction is done.

THEIR LIFE

It is a redeemed life. It was forfeited and brought back by the ransom of the Savior's blood. Therefore it is not our own, but belongs to Him (1:14). It is a resurrected life. "Since, then, you have been raised"—or better, were resurrected—"with Christ, set your hearts on things above" (3:1). It is not the old natural life improved. It is something of foreign birth, something that has come to us out of heaven, something that is wholly divine. It is Christ Himself living in us. It is a life which is hid. "Your life is now hidden with Christ in God" (3:3). It is hidden from the world which cannot understand us. It is hidden from the devil who cannot steal it. It is hidden often from our own consciousness, and, when we think it gone and mourn our lack of feeling, we find that Christ is still there waiting till the eclipse is over to reveal Himself in unchanging love. The security of our life is not in our experience, but in Him.

John Newton tells us of the singular dream which led to his conversion. Sleeping in his hammock in the Adriatic, he dreamed one night that an angel gave to him a jeweled ring telling him that it was the pledge of his salvation. Soon after a demon form stood by his side and dared him to throw it into the sea. In a moment of reckless madness he yielded to the tempter and the ring was gone. Then the fiend turned to him and told him that he had lost his soul. And at the same moment an awful flame seemed to light up the sea and shore, and a voice whispered that he was lost. Then there appeared another form. It was Jesus. He stood a moment by his side and gave him one look of upbraiding love, and then leaped into the sea. After long struggling with the waves He arose to the surface, and, weary and almost dead, brought back the precious jewel and held it up to his wondering gaze. But He would not let him have it again. "I have rescued your precious soul," He said, "at awful cost, but if I trusted it once more to your keeping, it would be lost again. I will keep it for you, and when you enter the heavenly gates it will be handed back to you as the pledge of your admission." And Newton awoke to seek the Savior, and afterwards to write those precious hymns which tell of His redeeming love.

THEIR DRESS

By a very fine metaphor the apostle describes the Christian life under the figure of disrobing and robing a person. Our garments are frequently used to denote our character. And so the word habit has come to mean both our dress and manner of living. There is first the process of disrobing. It begins with the putting off of our old habits and dispositions, our old clothes. "But now you must rid yourselves of all such things as these: anger, rage, malice, slander, and filthy language from your lips. Do not lie to each other" (3:8–9). All this has reference to sinful acts and dispositions. Next, however, we strip not only to the skin, but to the bone, and to the very heart. For we put off our very selves. "You have taken off your old self with its practices" (3:9). This is the entire renunciation and crucifixion of our old self and our whole natural life.

Next comes the process of robing. This begins inside. There must be a new man first before he can wear his new clothes. You would not put clean and beautiful garments on an unbathed person. And so we read, "And have put on the new self, which is being renewed in knowledge in the image of its Creator. Here there is no Greek or Jew, circumcised or uncircumcised, barbarian, Scythian, slave or free, but Christ is all, and is in all" (3:10–11).

This is not the old man improved, but it is the Christ man, the Lord Jesus Himself becoming our new life so perfectly that even our national, social and ecclesiastical distinctions, peculiarities and characteristics disappear, and Christ is all and in all. Then having put on the new man, we put on the new clothes, "Therefore, as God's chosen people, holy and dearly loved, clothe yourselves with compassion, kindness, humility, gentleness and patience. Bear with each other and forgive whatever grievances you may have against one another. Forgive as the Lord forgave you" (3:12–13). Here we have the fine undergarments of compassion, a sympathetic, tender sensitiveness to the sufferings and feelings of others, a kind and loving manner, a meek and lowly spirit, a longsuffering patience, the beautiful robe of forgiveness full of pockets that are all open at the bottom, where we receive the wrongs of others to drop them behind us.

Then there comes as the last article of our new apparel, the belt, which in Oriental countries binds all the robes compactly around the person, and enables him to move and work without embarrassment. And so love is our belt, compacting all our graces into service and enabling us to use our blessing for the blessing of others. This is the meaning of the 14th verse. "Over all these virtues put on love, which binds them all together." Beloved, here is the fashion plate from the heavenly wardrobe for a well-dressed Christian. Let us see to it that we are in the style of the kingdom and the society above.

THEIR WALK

As soon as we are dressed it is right that we should go forth to our various walks. First we read of their former walk in evil things. "You used to walk in these ways, in the life you once lived" (3:7).

Next we have the companion of their walk. "Just as you received Christ Jesus as Lord, continue to live [walk, KJV] in him" (2:6). This is not a solitary walk, but like Enoch they walk with God. Then we have the posture in which they walk, their pose of lofty dignity as the children of the king. "That you may live a life worthy of the Lord and may please him in every way" (1:10).

And finally, we have their walk before the world. In all carefulness and consistency, so deporting themselves as not to bring reproach upon the name of Christ before the ungodly, and to use every opportunity to bear witness for the Lord and to be a blessing to men. "Be wise in the way you act toward outsiders; make the most of every opportunity" (4:5). Beloved, is this our walk?

THEIR TALK

It is not a silent life. Our conversation forms a large part of our activity and influence, and just as the tongue is the best sign of good or bad health in the physical world, so a wholesome tongue is the symptom of true holiness, and an ungoverned tongue sets on fire the whole course of nature, and it is set on fire by hell. James has said with awful emphasis that "If anyone is never at fault in what he says, he is a perfect man, able to keep his whole body in check" (James 3:2). Our conversation among our Christian associates is vividly described in Colossians 3:16. "Let the word of Christ dwell in you richly as you teach and admonish one another with all wisdom, and as you sing psalms, hymns and spiritual songs with gratitude in your hearts to God." It is to be flavored with the word of Christ. It is to be illuminated by songs and gladness; and even when we have to admonish and reprove our brethren, it is to be with sweetness and love. But especially in our general conversation are we reminded, "Let your conversation be always full of grace, seasoned with salt, so that you may know how to answer everyone" (4:6).

This is a high standard and excludes a good deal of the light and frivolous and inane conversation even of Christians. We should never speak without saying something. The salt suggests wholesomeness, purity and good sense. The word grace suggests enough of religion to lift it above the ordinary plane, yet not too much to make it stilted and set. It is possible to talk to the people of the world in such a way as to commend Christ without preaching at them. "That you may know how to answer everyone," suggests the need of tact and discrimination. "Do not answer a fool according to his folly" (Proverbs 26:4), is just as timely sometimes as the other precept, "Answer a fool according to his folly" (26:5), is at other times.

Christ was the Master of right speech. His noblest victories were in silencing the criticisms and carpings of His enemies by replies which searched their very hearts and exposed them to their own contempt and the ridicule of the people, so that "no one dared to ask him any more questions" (Luke 20:40). God give to us a wholesome tongue.

THEIR EDUCATION

For just as the child must be instructed, so the Christian has to pass through the school of discipline. And so we read "[We] have not stopped praying for you and asking God to fill you with the knowledge of his will through all spiritual wisdom and understanding; . . . growing in the knowledge of God" (Colossians 1:9–10). It is spiritual wisdom and the knowledge of God that formed the subjects of their high study. And the special theme of their deepest inquiry, the philosophy that is more profound than all the wisdom of the ages, is the "mystery that has been kept hidden for ages and generations, but is now disclosed to the saints. To them God has chosen to make known among the Gentiles the glorious riches of this mystery, which is Christ in you, the hope of glory" (1:26–27).

He prays for them in the next chapter that they may "have the full riches of complete understanding, in order that they may know the mystery of God, namely, Christ, in whom are hidden all the treasures of wisdom and knowledge" (2:2–3). This was to be their safeguard against the seductions of false philosophy. This was to save them from going "into great detail about what [they have] seen, and [their] unspiritual mind [puffs them] up with idle notions" (2:18).

Christ is the wisdom of God, and there are depths and heights of truth for those who are taught of the Spirit the deep things of God, truths that satisfy the intellect and feed the heart and bring not only light but life and love.

THEIR TEMPER

The Christian temper has reference especially to the finer qualities of disposition rather than to the cardinal virtues, moralities and proprieties, which, of course, are taken for granted in a life of holiness. Many of these finer traits are touched upon in this beautiful portrait. Here is a finer touch. "Strengthened with all power according to his glorious might so that . . ." not some great achievement, some eloquent address, some outward activity, but to suffer in sweetness, or as is so finely expressed here, "so that you may have great endurance and patience, and joyfully [give] thanks to the Father, who has qualified you to share in the inheritance of the saints in the kingdom of light" (1:11–12). To suffer—to suffer long, to suffer all—not only with patience, but with joyfulness. That, indeed, is a final touch of the refining fire. Here again is a fine touch. "Let the peace of Christ rule in your hearts" (3:15). "Set your hearts on things above" (3:1). "Set your minds on things above, not on earthly things" (3:2). This gives loftiness to the character and lifts the soul above the groveling things of time. Finally, there is the thankful and happy temper which runs as an undertone through many passages in this epistle, "And be thankful . . . sing . . . with gratitude in your hearts to God . . . giving thanks to God the Father through him" (3:15–17). There is nothing more welcome in this world of clouds and tears than a cheerful disposition, a shining face, a thankful heart. Of such a spirit one of our simplest poets has said:

> There's not a cheaper thing on earth,
>   Nor yet one half so dear;
> 'Tis better than distinguished birth,
>   Or thousands gained a year.

THEIR PRINCIPLES AND PRACTICE

Of course, their Christian life was a practical one, reaching through a whole circle of domestic, social and public life, making them better wives, husbands, fathers, children, masters, servants and business men. But it is not their practice so much as their principles that the apostle emphasizes. Christian ethics do not consist so much in a thousand minute directions about the details of duty, as in a few sound, comprehensive principles of action which apply to every question and settle every point. Three such principles are given here.

1. "Live a life worthy of the Lord and . . . please him in every way" (1:10).

2. "Whatever you do, whether in word or deed, do it all in the name of the Lord Jesus" (3:17).

3. "Whatever you do, work at it with all your heart, as working for the Lord, not for men" (3:23).

The first of these principles sets before us a high aim and we are inspired to live up to it. We have been lately told that the reason the late Commissioner Waring [turn of the century commissioner in New York City] required his street cleaning brigade to wear white duck suits at their dirty work was because he felt that it would be an incentive to them to keep the streets so clean that their clothes would not be soiled, and he succeeded. And so God robes us in the garments of kingliness, and then bids us live up to it by keeping them clean.

The second of these principles requires us to identify ourselves so fully with Christ that we really act as if we were He. A great actress lately said that when she was acting the part of some strong character she actually felt all the emotions, affections and sufferings required by the play, and that her tears, her smiles and all her expressions were absolutely natural and spontaneous, and for the time being she was really lost in her character. Beloved, God gives to you and me the honor of acting the title role in the greatest drama of the ages. You are permitted to represent the very character of Christ Himself and exhibit to the world the excellencies and graces of Him who is the glory of heaven and the paragon of all goodness, loveliness and grace. Surely this is an inspiration to live up to the highest things.

Then the third of these principles, a single aim to glorify God, is as far-reaching and uplifting in its power. A distinguished clergyman once told me that he announced a special sermon on popular amusements, and great numbers of young people came to hear it. He did not once mention cards, dancing or the theater, and yet at least two of his auditors went home that night saying to each other, "I will not play cards, I will not go to the theater, I will not indulge in the worldly dance again." He had simply brought home with convincing power to the hearts of his hearers the single verse, "[The Father] has not left me alone, for I always do what pleases him" (John 8:29). This will accomplish more to lift people above the world than all our denunciation of forbidden things.

THEIR HOPE

"Faith and love . . . spring from the hope that is stored up for you in heaven" (Colossians 1:5). This was one of the things for which he thanked God. "To present you holy in his sight, without blemish and free from accusation" (1:22). This was the glorious purpose of Christ's atonement. "That we may present everyone perfect in Christ" (1:28). This was the holy ambition of his own personal ministry, "When Christ, who is your life, appears, then you also will appear with him in glory" (3:4).

This was the glorious transfiguration which the Lord's coming was to bring to them. "Since you know that you will receive an inheritance from the Lord as a reward. It is the Lord Christ you are serving" (3:24). This was the recompense for which they were toiling at their lowly and servile task. "Giving thanks to the Father, who has qualified you to share in the inheritance of the saints in the kingdom of light" (1:12). This was the present preparation for the Lord's coming which His grace had bestowed upon them. And this is the attitude in which we still should be waiting for His coming. Be fit now and ready always that we may be found of Him in peace. Thus would He have us waiting for His appearing.

It has lately been stated that the great Von Moltke, who planned with such signal success the victorious campaign of the German army against France, had been ready for many years for that expected event. And when one night an orderly knocked at his door with a message from the king that war was imminent, he simply directed the orderly to go to a certain pigeonhole in his office where he would find all the directions to the different commanders with all the necessary papers ready for instant delivery. And there they were, the plans of the campaign, plans of fortresses, orders to generals of divisions, all ready; and then he turned over and quietly went to sleep. He had been ready for years.

So should we be diligent that we may be found by Him in peace, and that when He comes we may open to Him immediately. So may we be found fit for the inheritance of the saints of light.

CHAPTER 3

THE CHRISTIAN WORKER IN COLOSSIANS

A faithful minister and fellow servant in the Lord. (Colossians 4:7)

We have had the picture of Christ and of the Christian in Colossians. Now let us study the composite portrait of the Christian worker as presented in the different ideals set forth in this delightful apostolic letter. One of the highest qualities of a great life is to inspire others with its own spirit and aims, and reproduce its work in other workers. The divine Master has done more through the workers that He called and commissioned than through His own personal ministry. And so the great Apostle Paul had the peculiar gift of setting others to work and so communicating to them the principles and objects for which he lived that his life and work were reproduced in them. Paul was the center of a glorious cluster of men and women who finely represent the manifold gifts and ministries of the Spirit. A number of them are brought to the front in the incidental allusions and the personal salutations of this epistle, and as we have said, they together form a composite picture of the ideal Christian worker.

TYCHICUS, OR THE FAITHFUL MINISTER

This is a very simple but a very high picture of a true minister of Christ. First of all he is "a dear brother" (4:7), for it is more important to be than to do. His personal character is the foundation of his public work. Then Paul recognizes him as a servant, "a fellow servant in the Lord" (4:7). For the fundamental idea of service is divine ownership and entire dedication to the Master and His work. But above everything else he is "a faithful minister" (4:7). He may not have been brilliant, but he is true; and this is the highest testimony that can be given to a servant. He can be depended upon. He is thoroughly reliable and he is always ready for whatever message or trust his leader had to commit to his hands.

On the present occasion he was sent from Rome to carry this epistle and to bear the greeting of the apostle to the church at Colosse, and he was just as ready to be an errand boy and a messenger as a teacher or an apostle. He was also a minister of comfort. The apostle sent him that "he may encourage [their] hearts" (4:8).

The true minister must have a heart of sympathy and the power to cheer and comfort the distressed. Beloved, can it be said of us whatever our ministry—pastor, evangelist, elder, Sunday school teacher, parent—that we have been faithful ministers of Jesus Christ?

EPAPHRAS, OR THE PRAYERFUL MINISTRY

This beloved brother was a member of the Colossian church, and in the testimony that Paul bears of him he knows that he is appealing to the people that are acquainted with him and that mere idle words have little weight unless his life bears out the testimony. The ministry of Epaphras was the power of prayer, that silent ministry that the world knows nothing of, but which counts in heaven. It is the work of our great High Priest above, and it is, perhaps, the most potent work that any of us do below. It is no easy dream of sentimental feeling, but a strong and forceful energy "wrestling in prayer for you" (4:12).

This is the power that stands behind every great spiritual movement. The world may see the man who stands upon a platform or leads the advance movement on the field, but mightier than either is the silent heart that wrestles in the closet and brings the power from on high. This was the ministry of Epaphras, and this is the holy priesthood to which God is calling many of His people.

His prayers were very definite and practical. We are accustomed to hear the conventional request for prayer that somebody may be converted or healed, or that deliverance may come in some exigency of life. But here we find a man making it his business to pray for three whole churches, and to hold them up continually to God in intercession that they might "stand firm in all the will of God, mature and fully assured" (4:12).

He was asking for no special emergency, but simply for sustaining grace and sanctifying power, and standing like a great supply pipe in some complicated system of waterworks, whose business it was to convey the water from the reservoir to the various places of distribution. This is exactly the figure used by the prophet Zechariah in his picture of the supernatural supply of the Church of God with heavenly power, where the two anointed ones are compared to the pipes that convey the oil to the various lamps. It is the ministry of believing and habitual prayer. Happy the church that has such ministers of the inner sanctuary, such waiting ones to stand before the Lord with the names of His people upon their hands and upon their hearts in the exercise of an everlasting priesthood. Epaphras had consecrated himself to this work and had a great zeal for it, praying with all his heart for his brethren, not only in Colosse, but for the church in Laodicea of Hierapolis.

Beloved, is there not here a lesson and a pattern for you? Have you been true to your ministry of prayer, and are there souls that are famishing, churches that are barren and fields that are neglected because you have come short in this highest ministry of the children of God?

ARISTARCHUS, OR THE SUFFERING MINISTRY

In "my fellow prisoner Aristarchus" (4:10) we have one engaged in no active service, with silent lips and activity restrained by the fetters of a prison cell. But he can suffer along with his friend. He can bear the reproach and share the loneliness of the apostle's life. He is one of the shut-in ones. His ministry is suffering love. A high and noble ministry indeed it is.

Nanssen, the Norwegian traveler, dedicated his book to his wife in these terms: "To her who christened my boat, and then had the courage and the love to let me go forth alone." Hers was the part of heroic suffering. And while her brave husband went out into the darkness of the frozen North, she waited alone until at last the suspense and suffering became so great that the physicians would not allow his name to be mentioned in her presence, even by her little child, for fear the pressure would snap the last thread of reason and of light. Such is the service of many a mother who waits at home while her boy goes to the mission field or the martyr's grave; many a sister who sacrifices earth's fondest ties to bear the unselfish burden of her home; many a daughter, who gives up affection, wifehood, high Christian work and the ambitions of active life that she may wait as a prisoner of the Lord by some mother's couch or comfort and sustain the old age of some infirm, dependent father. Such is the ministry of those loyal hearts who stand for the sake of principle and some high and holy friendship, sharing the reproaches of some cause which is unpopular, some Christian leader and worker who is misrepresented or maligned, some trust to which the heart has become committed in honor and duty, prisoners of Jesus Christ held back by circumstances which you cannot control, from work which you would love to do, from activities for which every fiber of your being is reaching out, while you can only suffer in silence and find comfort in remembering, "They also serve who only stand and wait."

ONESIMUS, OR THE CONSECRATED SERVANT AND THE HUMBLE HELPER

Onesimus (4:9) was a runaway slave who had been found by Paul in Rome and converted through his ministry, and whom the apostle, with a very tactful letter, was sending back to Philemon, his former master. A happy play is made upon his name, which means "profitable," and which Paul uses as an augury of the future, hoping that he may now prove as profitable as he was unprofitable before. Onesimus is here introduced to them with high honor as one of themselves, and called a faithful and beloved brother. There is no hint of humbler station or his disgraceful fault in escaping from his master. There is a fine tone of Christian ethics about this epistle in dealing with the question of master and servants. There is no encouragement to neglect the servant's duty, but there is a clear recognition of the equality of all men before God, and in the Church of Jesus Christ. In Colossians 3:22–25 those of them who were in menial and servile positions are reminded that they are to consider themselves the servants of Jesus Christ and look over the heads of unjust and unkind masters, and work "not only when their eye is on you and to win their favor, but with sincerity of heart and reverence for the Lord" (3:22). And "work at it with all your heart, as working for the Lord, not for men" (3:23). They are reminded that they shall receive their reward from the heavenly Master, and that there is no respect of persons with Him, but that every wrong done them will be justly punished by Him, and that every service will be recompensed likewise.

Many of us are in similar positions. The curse of slavery is gone, but the law of service is perpetual, and there is high and holy work to be done for Christ in our various positions of dependence and responsibility to human employers. Many a girl in some ungodly household in this city has been used of God in her laundry and her kitchen through her bright and happy face and the sweet temper which the grace of Christ gives, to lead her mistress to seek for higher things. Many a nanny in what might be called the monotony of her life of drudgery and care has exercised an influence upon some child's heart that has given the inspiration of all its future life. In the great world of nature there are millions of blades of grass for one lofty oak or pine, and in the economy of grace there are innumerable little ministries that must be done by someone. It is there that Christian character tells, and that service for Jesus may be made up of many little things. Down in the slums of New York a woman was seen picking up something from the street and hiding it in her apron. A policeman rudely arrested her and demanded to know what she was stealing. She opened her apron and said "Oh, I was just picking up the bits of broken glass that I saw on the pavement for fear that the little barefooted children should step on them and get hurt." It wasn't much to the rough policeman who dismissed her with a coarse laugh, but it was much to the Master.

MARK, OR THE RECLAIMED BACKSLIDER

Mark (4:10) was one of those young enthusiasts who are always stepping out before they are ready, and attempting some great enterprise without counting the cost. Mark had been brought up in luxury in Jerusalem, in the home of Mary, his wealthy mother. Her home was the rendezvous of the early Church, and as he was accustomed to meet the great leaders on familiar terms, he imagined that he was farther on than he was. So when the first great missionary party started, Mark was one of the volunteers and he went along with Paul and his uncle Barnabas. But when they got up into the highlands of Asia Minor and found themselves amid the barren cliffs and savage people of Pisidia and Pamphylia, he became disheartened and, like many other young missionaries, wanted to go home to his mother, and practically deserted his mission. Paul was disgusted, for the time at least, with the new recruit, and would not have him on their next mission. But Barnabas stood by him and took him as his associate, and by and by even Paul was glad to send for him, and say, "bring Mark even to Rome, and the terrors of Nero's presence, 'because he is helpful to me in my ministry' (2 Timothy 4:11)."

There still are Christian workers who have to fail before they can succeed. God has to chasten their young enthusiasm and humble their self-confidence, and in the end, like Peter, they are better for their humbling fall. Do not get discouraged if you have started once and gone back, but start again; and when self has died and you have thoroughly learned that you are utterly insufficient in yourself, then God can use the things that are not, to bring to naught the things that are and make the very Valley of Achor, a door of hope.

DEMAS OR A REAL BACKSLIDER

There is something very sad and hollow in the mention of Demas (Colossians 4:14) in this epistle, when we remember Paul's later announcement, "Demas, because he loved this world, has deserted me" (2 Timothy 4:10). Mark, the deserter, comes back. Demas, the friend, goes back to return no more. The difference in the two men was all in the heart. Mark failed, but still loved the Lord. Demas kept up the appearance of a Christian worker for a while, but he loved the present world.

In the beautiful park in our Grimsby Convention, we saw a striking illustration of the sad story of Demas. A great tree had just fallen across one of the avenues. Its form had been most stately, its branches spreading and symmetrical, its leaves green and verdant; but as it fell we noted that for months and years it had been hanging as by a thread. There was a thin rim of wood fiber around the outside just beneath the bark scarcely an inch thick, and the whole heart was filled with rottenness, the wood decayed and filled with parasites and worms. Its heart was false and had been all the time, and it only needed one touch of the testing storm to overthrow it. Such is the life that is maintaining the semblance of service in profession while the heart is set on earthly things, which can only end like Demas. Awake, dear friend, in time, and ask God to save you from a divided heart and to make you true to Him.

LUKE, THE BELOVED PHYSICIAN

Here we find a man (Colossians 4:14) in professional life rising above and reaching beyond his professional duties, and accomplishing the noblest service for God and man. For Luke became the friend of Paul, the author of one of the most beautiful and valuable of the gospels, and the chronicler of the history of the early Church.

So God loves to use men in unconventional ways. The need of the Church today is not a larger number of ordained clergymen, but a larger number of men and women in social, secular and professional life whose entire influence and talents are at the service of the Master; not a salaried and dependent priesthood who preach the gospel because it is expected of them merely, but a great body of consecrated irregulars, Nehemiahs, Josephs, Esthers, Daniels, who use their earthly station in the providence of God as a standpoint from which to serve and witness for their heavenly Master, and bless their fellowmen.

NYMPHA, OR THE CHURCH IN HER HOUSE

Here (4:15) we have a consecrated home. The early Church had no ecclesiastical edifices. Its sanctuary was the family circle. Mary of Jerusalem, Priscilla of Corinth and Ephesus, Gaius and many an "elect lady" and public-spirited man had the high honor of making his house another Bethany, and entertaining the ascended Lord and the infant Church. Christian families, how are you using your homes for God? In our great and lonely cities there are hundreds of young men who have come from happy home circles, but have little social life except what they find in the club, the theater, the ballroom or the fashionable call. What a blessing it would be to these boys at the crisis of their young manhood to have the advantage of a truly Christian home circle to visit. What a ministry a refined and consecrated woman could exercise! And even the humblest home can be consecrated to the cottage prayer meeting, the parlor meeting, the gathering together in His name of the two or three who often constitute the nucleus of some great spiritual movement, and whose counsels and prayers reach farther frequently than the great ecclesiastical assemblies. There is little doubt that a majority of our best Alliance branches have had their birth in some little home circle of united faith and prayer. May the Holy Spirit give us to see the ministry of many a modern Nympha and the church in her house.

ARCHIPPUS, OR THE FAITHFUL MINISTER

"Tell Archippus: 'See to it that you complete the work you have received in the Lord' " (4:17). This may apply to any ministry whether as pastor, elder, Sunday school teacher, evangelist, mission worker or even parent.

Whatever our service, let us be true to it. Even your little Sunday school class may hold in it all the possibilities of a noble and happy life for some of those young hearts to whom God has given you not only as their teacher, but perhaps the only safe mooring and uplifting influence in all their life. It is not so much the instruction you give them that tells, as the advantage of having in you a friend, a guide, a mature and experienced example and guardian of their undeveloped hearts and lives. Are you doing your best, or have you neglected your trust and allowed some little ship to break to pieces upon the rocks because your light has gone out?

PAUL, OR THE IDEAL MINISTER

But all these patterns meet in the one great life around which they clustered, the great apostle himself, of whose faithful ministry we have so many striking intimations even in this little epistle.

1. A Life of Prayer

We see the deep foundation of it in a life of prayer. "Praying always for you" (1:3, KJV). "I want you to know how much I am struggling for you and for those at Laodicea, and for all who have not met me personally" (2:1). Here we find him praying not only for his acquaintances but for multitudes that he had never met, and holding men to God as "with hooks of steel."

2. Love Was Central

His love was the impulse of his ministry. His heart was with his people. "For though I am absent from you in body, I am present with you in spirit and delight to see how orderly you are and how firm your faith in Christ is" (2:5).

3. His Self-sacrifice

Paul demonstrated the spirit of self-sacrifice. "Now I rejoice in what was suffered for you, and I fill up in my flesh what is still lacking in regard to Christ's afflictions, for the sake of his body, which is the church. I have become its servant by the commission God gave me" (1:24–25). His very life was laid down on the altar of sacrifice, and it was his greatest joy to bear their burdens and share with their great High Priest all their needs and sufferings.

4. A Minister of the Truth

He was a minister of the truth.

I have become its servant by the commission God gave me to

present to you the word of God in its fullness—the mystery that has been kept hidden for ages and generations, but is now disclosed to the saints. To them God has chosen to make known among the Gentiles the glorious riches of this mystery, which is Christ in you, the hope of glory. (1:25–27)

5. His Fidelity

Paul possessed great fidelity. "We proclaim him, admonishing and teaching everyone with all wisdom, so that we may present everyone perfect in Christ" (1:28). He dealt individually with men. He did not try to please them, but to save them. He felt that he must present them one by one at last to his glorious Master and that he stood as one that must give account, and therefore his work must be well done and ready for the testing fire. We cannot always be pleasant with people, but sometimes our faithfulness may seem severe.

I think it is General Booth who tells the story of a little girl who prayed that God would save the little rabbits from being caught in her brother's traps, and after she had prayed quite a while, wound up by saying, "Dear Jesus, I know You will." Her mother asked her why she was so sure that her prayer would be answered. "Why," she said, "Mamma, I smashed the traps." We must not only pray for the souls and point the better way, but uncover and destroy the devil's snares that beset so many heedless lives.

6. The Supernatural Power

There was a supernatural power behind his ministry. "To this end I labor, struggling with all his energy, which so powerfully works in me" (1:29). This is the secret of every effectual ministry: "not I, but Christ" (Galatians 2:20, KJV), the outworking of a life that flows from the inworking of the living One. God is waiting to give such a ministry to every single-hearted servant. He does not ask us for service until He first gives it. He will fill us with His love and clothe us with His power, and when all is done help us to say, "I worked harder than all of them—yet not I, but the grace of God that was with me" (1 Corinthians 15:10). Amen!